An Introduction to the Economic Theory of
Market Behavior

An Introduction to the Economic Theory of Market Behavior

Microeconomics from a Walrasian Perspective

Donald W. Katzner

University of Massachusetts, Amherst, USA

Edward Elgar
Cheltenham, UK • Northampton, MA, USA

Published by
Edward Elgar Publishing Limited
Glensanda House
Montpellier Parade
Cheltenham
Glos GL50 1UA
UK

Edward Elgar Publishing, Inc.
136 West Street
Suite 202
Northampton
Massachusetts 01060
USA

A catalogue record for this book
is available from the British Library

Library of Congress Cataloguing in Publication Data
Katzner, Donald W., 1938
   An introduction to the economic theory of market behavior : microeconomics from a Walrasian perspective/Donald W. Katzner.
      p. cm.
   Rev. ed. of: Walrasian microeconomics. c1988.
   Includes bibliographical references and index.
   1. Microeconomics. 2. Economics, Mathematical. 3. Capitalism. I. Katzner, Donald W., 1938- Walrasian microeconomics. II. Title.

HB 172.K38 2006
338.5—dc22   2006040926

ISBN-13: 978 1 84542 510 4 (cased)
ISBN-10: 1 84542 510 3 (cased)

Printed and bound in Great Britain by MPG Books Ltd, Bodmin, Cornwall.

in memory of
TARA

Contents

CONTENTS

Preface

Since the publication of *Walrasian Microeconomics*: *An Introduction to the Economic Theory of Market Behavior* in 1988, the Walrasian theory of market behavior or, as it is more commonly referred to, general equilibrium theory, has increasingly been abandoned by microeconomists. It has also come under attack for an apparently perceived inadequacy in the ability of its theoretical structure to explain a certain fundamental phenomenon that clearly falls under its purview. These two events are not unrelated. The latter attack stems from the fact that, even with respect to tâtonnement dynamics, an appropriately acceptable analysis of the uniqueness and global stability of Walrasian equilibrium has yet to be found and, hence, a full and completely satisfactory explanation of how prices are determined in a competitive economy cannot yet be given. The persistence of this gap along with the seemingly hopelessness of filling it has, to a considerable extent, led many microeconomists to forsake the general equilibrium conceptualization altogether. As a result, microeconomic theory has, by and large, been reduced to a collection of techniques and tricks for resolving narrow, isolated microeconomic problems and the study of, also narrow and isolated, strategic behaviors.

One of the purposes of this present volume, which is actually a considerably revised version of *Walrasian Microeconomics*, is to suggest that the abandonment of general equilibrium theory by microeconomists is a mistake, and that it is too soon to give up on the possibility of constructing an adequate analysis of uniqueness, global stability, and price determination. Just because something has not yet been demonstrated does not mean that it can never be shown. The issues are taken up and examined in a new chapter — what is now Chapter 10 — and a new direction in which analysis might proceed is proposed.

xi

Of course, there are other reasons for embracing the Walrasian theory of market behavior. First, the general equilibrium construction is a significant component of the theoretical basis of, in its most idealized form, capitalism — that arrangement of economic organization that, for better or worse, presently orders much of the modern economic world. Public discussions in the media, in political arenas, and elsewhere that relate to general equilibrium theory in part or *in toto* are commonplace. For microeconomists to turn their backs on such matters is to dissociate themselves from an important aspect of current affairs to which they have a professional obligation to contribute. Second, most economists are trained in at least the basic conceptualizations of general equilibrium theory, and there is no other widely understood vocabulary for conducting research and communicating among economists (and others) about the microeconomy at large. Abandoning the general equilibrium approach in their work, then, necessarily forces economists to focus their attention on fragments or limited combinations of fragments of the microeconomy rather than on the whole. None of this is to say that there are not, there should not be, and there should not be developed, alternatives to the Walrasian vision, in part or in its entirety, that provide a more realistic picture of what goes on in a modern microeconomy. Indeed, a variety of possibilities is considered in Chapter 15 below.[1] But it does suggest that until there is widespread acceptance of a "better" substitute among economists, the Walrasian system remains the only means for communicative discourse on the microeconomy as a totality.

The original aim of *Walrasian Microeconomics* remains intact in the present version: To set forth, in a highly detailed way, one perception or explanation, as articulated in the investigation of essentially a single model, of how the microeconomy might operate. It focuses primarily on the behavior of individual consumers, firms, and markets under perfectly competitive conditions, and on the simultaneous interactions that occur among them. Its central theme is that all of these elements fit together into a unified whole, and it attempts to construct a complete, consistent, and cohesive picture (*i.e.*, the Walrasian general-equilibrium model) of the perfectly competitive economy.

However, there are still numerous departures from the original. Errors have been corrected and arguments have been rewritten and clarified. In addition to the new chapter on price determination (which also includes a discussion of methodological individualism), I have been able to remove entirely the

---

[1]   An example of those discussed in that chapter, and one that actually furnishes a complete alternative to the fully developed Walrasian system, appears in my *Time, Ignorance, and Uncertainty in Economic Models* (Ann Arbor: University of Michigan Press, 1998). Other examples that may be interpreted as movements in the direction of greater realism and are not mentioned in Chapter 15 include various studies relating to overlapping generations models, the notion of temporary equilibrium, and the dynamics of fixed prices and old Keynesian macroeconomics.

assumption, originally employed to obtain many results in the second half of the book, that the contract set shrinks to a one-dimensional curve in the input space of each industry. An accounting of the so-called constraint qualification now appears in reference to all constrained optimizations (it was ignored in the original), and very limited discussions of uncertainty, game theory, and the core of an exchange economy have been added to Chapter 15, and in the form of exercises at the end of Chapters 7 and 12. On top of the latter, new exercises supplement the old throughout. Notational changes have been kept to a minimum — the most notable being new symbols for individual and social preference orderings.

Finally, I would like to acknowledge and thank all of those who have helped with the preparation of this revised version. Particular thanks go to Pawel Kliber who was instrumental in transferring the manuscript into computer format, and to Adilbek Talkybekuly for providing considerable assistance in the location of errors and opaque passages. Special recognition is also due to Samuel Bowles for his suggestions for Chapter 10, and to Rob Kusner, Frank Sottile, and Theodore Vessey for reviewing several purely mathematical issues and arguments. In addition, Randal Bausor provided abundant commentary on various parts of the manuscript and is also responsible for showing me how to eliminate the assumption, mentioned previously, that the contract set shrinks to a one-dimensional curve in the input space of each industry (Theorem 8.1-12 below). And Douglas Vickers not only read the entire manuscript twice, but also made extensive recommendations for broadening and deepening the analytical significance and reach of many passages.

Preface to
Walrasian Microeconomics

It is difficult to approach the study of microeconomic theory today without some feelings of ambivalence. Certainly, one cannot help but be attracted by the magnetism of success. An uninitiated outsider is unlikely to expect anything but chaos in an economy motivated solely by the self-interest of individuals and firms. That economists are able to assert coherence rather than chaos, at least in theory, is an intellectual achievement of immense proportion. This, by itself, is sufficient justification for taking the subject seriously. But there are additional reasons as well. Current microeconomic theory serves as a basis for the major paradigm within which most present-day economists think and communicate. It provides insight into a variety of isolated collections of empirical data extracted from the real world. Its study yields an understanding of deep and useful analytical tools. Its fundamental notions of simultaneity (both static and dynamic) and general equilibrium apply far beyond the limited boundaries of purely microeconomic, and even economic, phenomena. And the vision from which it springs is intimately intertwined with the historic emphasis on individual imagination and behavior that has formed such an important part of modern Western thought and culture.

Still, doubts remain. Lurking somewhere in the shadows is the suspicion that maybe microeconomic theory is not all that relevant for today's world. The economy is not, after all, exactly what you would call perfectly competitive; it is not clear that actual consumer and firm activity is consistent with behavior based on maximization; and so on. Thus, as one might expect, serious challenges to the main arguments of microeconomic theory have been mounted. Both methodology and assumptions are presently under attack, and alternatives have been proposed. Where all of this will lead is anybody's guess, but none of it can detract from the accomplishments of microeconomic theory described above. The issue is no longer whether coherence in the face of self-interest is theoretically possible, for that has already been established in the affirmative. Rather, the question is, how can we best understand whatever coherence there might be in the actual economic world in which we live? Thus, a final reason for studying microeconomic theory is to determine exactly what various forms of theoretical (microeconomic) coherence entail, so it becomes possible to check which, if any, of these forms has relevance for the real economy.

The present volume (*i.e.*, *Walrasian Microeconomics*) introduces many of the ideas and propositions of the main body of microeconomic theory in a unified way. It focuses on individuals, firms, markets, and their interactions. It looks upon consumer and firm behavior as the outcome of decisions taken for single periods, or instants, of time. And it tries to construct a complete, consistent and cohesive picture of the perfectly competitive economy. This emphasis on unity is the central theme of the book; so much so that a serious effort has been made to avoid anything that detracts from a tightly knit articulation of the single vision it describes. Hopefully, it imparts a whole image, one that stands on its own and that therefore is capable of evaluation.

For lack of a better term, the theory constructed here and the view of economic reality from which it springs are described by the adjective "Walrasian." Although there is still dispute as to whether subsequent development accurately reflects Walras' true vision,[1] such usage is more or less consistent with present practice by economists. The expression "general equilibrium" also is relevant, but because this expression is applied often in other contexts as well, it is not employed below.

The appearance of the word "Introduction" in the title of this book gives license for certain liberties of exposition. Thus attention frequently focuses on the two-commodity, two-person, or two-firm case, while the more general argument is left to the reader. Simplifying assumptions are invoked for expositional ease and convenience. For example, the supposition that all firms within any given industry are identical appears on several occasions; the requirement that factors of production supplied by individuals to firms are fixed is imposed in the discussions of imperfect competition (Chapter 11), welfare (Chapter 12), and the full, economy-wide model with capital included (Chapter 14); and the complicated second-order maximization conditions necessary

---

[1]   See, for example, W. Jaffé, "Walras's Economics as Others See It," *Journal of Economic Literature* 18 (1980), pp. 528-549.

to the traditional analysis of welfare (Chapter 12) are avoided by assuming that they are always satisfied. Lastly, many topics are ignored altogether. The most notable of these include linear programming, joint outputs in production, non-tâtonnement dynamic processes, dated commodities, informational problems, risk, uncertainty, continua of traders, game theory, and the core.

Another aspect of the present work requiring comment is the role of mathematics. The past 50 years have witnessed increasing application of mathematical tools to many areas of economic analysis. There are several explanations for this embrace of mathematics. Jevons[2] and Cournot[3] believed that certain forms of reasoning in economics are mathematical in character. Walras[4] thought that to be scientific was, in part, to be mathematical, and he accurately predicted the explosion of mathematical usage by economists as their science progressed in the 20th century. More recently Debreu[5] cites linguistic convenience and the ability to obtain deeper understanding and analytical extensions that might not otherwise be possible. And Weintraub[6] argues that we comprehend our economic world by organizing what we see and by seeking connections between the things that are observed. In other words, we create mental structure. Because doing mathematics is creating mental structure in its purest form, mathematics has naturally become important in the pursuit of economic inquiry. But regardless of the efficacy of any of these explanations, the fact remains that to understand and communicate ideas today, especially in microeconomic theory, requires the employment of mathematical methods. Succeeding chapters, therefore, must necessarily rely heavily on mathematical deduction. However, an attempt has been made to make "non-mathematical elements," such as the role of assumptions and what happens when they are violated, stand out.

In addition, several pedagogic devices are included to aid the reader. First, the names of concepts that are formally defined in the text are often printed in italics where they are defined. Second, all important mathematical notions employed in the text but not defined therein are rigorously characterized in Appendix A. Third, this appendix provides a self-contained statement,

---

[2] W. S. Jevons, *The Theory of Political Economy*, 5th ed. (New York: Kelley, 1965), pp. xxi-xxv (from the preface to the 2nd edition), and pp. 3-5.

[3] A. Cournot, *Researches into the Mathematical Principles of the Theory of Wealth*, N. T. Bacon trans. (New York: Kelley, 1960), pp. 2-5.

[4] L. Walras, *Elements of Pure Economics*, W. Jaffé trans. (Homewood, Ill.: Irwin, 1954), pp, 47-48.

[5] G. Debreu, "Economic Theory in the Mathematical Mode," *American Economic Review* 74 (1984), p. 275.

[6] E. R. Weintraub, *General Equilibrium Analysis: Studies in Appraisal* (Cambridge: Cambridge University Press, 1985), pp. 178, 179.

occasionally with discussion, of the main mathematical ideas and propositions appearing in the book. No proofs are given, but references to standard treatments are cited throughout both text and appendix. Fourth, as the main argument of the book begins (Chapter 2), formality and rigor of thought are emphasized heavily. Attention is drawn to particularly important lines of reasoning by use of the theorem and proof form of exposition. As the reader comes to understand the disciplined thinking required in microeconomic theory, such properness and rigidity relax gradually into a more fluid and flexible style. By then the reader should be able to supply the formality and rigor on his or her own. Fifth, the mathematical prerequisites are kept to a minimum — namely, a thorough background in calculus and a little familiarity with elementary linear algebra. (Readers should be warned, however, that they will have to develop, if they have not already done so, some sophistication in their ability to reason mathematically.)

For the most part, ensuing discussion is self-contained and builds on itself. Concepts are defined and propositions are usually either proved (at least in the two-dimensional case) or a method of proof is indicated for the interested reader to follow up. (Chapter 1 is an exception. This chapter, in providing background for what is to come, necessarily introduces concepts whose formal definitions have to wait for later development. A second exception appears in Section 2.2 which relies on mathematics somewhat beyond the level of calculus.) Chapter exercises act as foils against which the reader may test her or his understanding, and they provide supplements to and illustrations of textual material. A very broad range of difficulty is represented. The more challenging exercises are marked with an asterisk; the hardest of these are identified by a double asterisk. Many answers and hints may be found in Appendix B. Without any pretense to being complete, references are made in the text to the historical sources of some of the more important economic ideas. Occasional comments in footnotes document the vagaries of several of today's accepted connections between the origins of certain notions and our ancestral economists.

The present work was undertaken in response to the unique demands of the Ph.D. program in economics at the University of Massachusetts at Amherst. Not surprisingly, one purpose of the program's initial graduate-level, two-semester exposure to microeconomic theory is to bring its students to roughly the same level of competence in microeconomics as their counterparts tend to achieve after one year of study of microeconomic theory at other major institutions. The course covers most of the important topics and requires mastery of many standard analytic techniques. But in addition to this, and here is where uniqueness arises, students are expected to develop a concept of microeconomic, "neoclassical" theory as a whole so as to be able to compare the neoclassical construction to alternative paradigms of economic thought. It is my hope that the book will be useful to others with similar needs.

Apart from classroom pedagogy, however, thinking of microeconomic neoclassical theory as a totality naturally becomes important in its own right as the theory is questioned and as it develops in response to criticism. Only from the holistic perspective is one able to speculate and ponder the meaning of it all. Reflections on meaning might include contemplations on the significance of the theory's assumptions, implications, and conclusions; on the merits of the uses to which it might be put; and on its power and limitations as a metaphor for understanding microeconomic activity. Such contemplations involve nothing less than the evaluation of the theory itself. And whether we like it or not, evaluation is inevitable. Indeed, it goes on all the time. Evaluation is both necessary for and an integral part of the evolution of any science.

I owe a considerable debt to those who have contributed to subsequent chapters in their numerous stages of development. Ivor F. Pearce helped to clarify my thinking on many aspects of microeconomic theory during frequent, sometimes long, and always very stimulating conversations over a period of an academic year. His patience and insight were truly inspiring. In addition to teaching me much of what I know about capital theory, Douglas Vickers made more cogent and useful comments on various drafts and supplied more ideas for revision than any author has any right to expect — even from a friend. Randall Bausor, Frederick A. Curtis, Philip E. Mirowski, E. Roy Weintraub, Robert Paul Wolff, and especially John P. Bonin also provided valuable suggestions. Particular thanks are due to all of the graduate students in economics at the University of Massachusetts at Amherst, who painstakingly worked through the manuscript in whatever state they encountered it as one of the main parts of their microeconomic theory course. They are the ones who asked those enormously important questions that only graduate students ask, and who are responsible for keeping my scholarship as honest as possible — right to the end. Finally, I acknowledge with gratitude the support of my wife Ruth, and children Todd and Brett during years past. They surely deserved better but gracefully accepted worse so that I might pursue this task.

Chapter 1

Introduction

Many years ago, Alfred Marshall eloquently characterized economics, in part, as the "study of mankind in the ordinary business of life ..." [10, p. 1]. Today this sweeping idea is strikingly out of style. The present age, with its emphasis on precision of thought, heightened mathematical rigor, and numerical measurement of fact, seems to have settled, at least insofar as Walrasian microeconomics is concerned, for the more confining view of Robbins; namely, that economics "is the science which studies human behavior as a relationship between ends and scarce means which have alternative uses" [15, p. 16]. Although they overlap considerably, the chasm separating various facets of these conceptions runs wide and deep. Whereas Marshall really did attempt to deal "not with an abstract or 'economic' man; but with a man of flesh and blood" [10, p. 27], all that appears to have survived in Walrasian analysis is *homo economicus*. The exorcising of the "flesh and blood," no doubt, is one reason for the frequent complaints that the Walrasian theory of market behavior, the subject-matter of this book, suffers, perhaps fatally, from the unreality of its hypotheses and the uselessness or inapplicability of its conclusions.

Against this background, it is clearly important to know exactly what the Walrasian theory says and what it does not say; what it can do and what it cannot do; and what its assumptions are and the implications that may be drawn from them. A thorough understanding of these matters may then serve as a platform from which the merits and losses of straying from the Marshallian perspective may be surveyed. But before rushing too far ahead, it is well to begin with a description of the thing under investigation.

1.1   A DESCRIPTION OF THE ECONOMY

Every person entering into a scientific inquiry arrives with certain concepts, understandings, beliefs, values, and biases inherited from past experience. This legacy derives from all earlier interactions of social, economic, ideological, psychological, and other forces on the individual, and is taken as given. It is the basis upon which one selects what is important for study and how what is important is to be analyzed.

So, too, with economists. Looking out on any society, the economist sees an innumerable array of economic facts and events. It is impossible to take every one into account. Some must be discarded. Others are organized and grouped into categories according to simplified characteristics commonly shared. As indicated above, criteria for organizing facts in any particular way derive from the economist's acquired knowledge, values, and so on. The process is called abstraction. Its purpose is to enable him to focus on those elements chosen as important.

The following description of the economy is an abstraction that often serves as a foundation for the Walrasian theory of market behavior. It should be regarded as preliminary and subject to subsequent amplification and modification.

The first elements to be discussed are goods. A *good* is a material thing or service that has the capacity of directly satisfying human wants, or can be used to produce something having that capacity, or both. The term *commodity* is synonymous with that of good. *Final goods* are passed immediately into the hands of individuals to satisfy wants. *Resources* are nonproduced goods needed to produce other goods. Occasionally goods produced in the past and productively used in the present, such as machinery, are referred to as resources. *Intermediate goods* are currently produced goods also employed in the productive process. Quantities of goods are measured in appropriate units, and all like goods measured in the same units are treated as homogeneous. Two goods of one general class, but of different qualities or in different geographic locations, appear as distinct goods measured in their own units. No distinction is made between a good at one point in time and the same good at any other point in time.

Goods are bought and sold at prices expressed in terms of, say, dollars per unit of the good in question. Most goods are not available in unlimited quantities. Not every good, however, need be scarce. Some, such as air, may (ignoring the presence of pollution) exist in sufficient amounts so as to satisfy all human wants relating to them. The prices of these goods are zero. A good has a positive price only when, relative to wants, there is not enough of it to go around.

A somewhat old-fashioned but still useful classification of resources is based on the categories of land, labor, capital, and enterprise. In this terminology, land often includes natural resources (like oil) as well as land itself, while labor covers a variety of skilled and unskilled work the population is able to perform. And the term capital may refer to money or to physical objects such as buildings and machinery. In its physical form, capital can contribute directly to production. Money capital, however, participates only indirectly since it is a financial resource that provides command over the physical commodities and labor employable in production. Although it turns out to be irrelevant in the present context (see Section 13.3), enterprise (or entrepreneurship) has historically been defined as the willingness and ability to assume the risk of organizing and operating a business endeavor.[1] The usual names for the rewards accruing to the owners of these resources (with money rather than physical capital in view) are, respectively, rents, wages, interest, and profits.

The terms "rent" and "interest," however, must be employed with care. Clearly the natural resource portion of land is not rented but sold in the usual way. Land itself, as well as physical capital objects, can either be rented or sold. (The relationship between sale and rental prices is described in Section 13.1.) By contrast, money capital is borrowed and then restored, with a fee paid for its use. This fee is the source of the word "interest." To avoid confusion, the following conventions are adopted here: Land is rented and not sold. Physical capital is sold and not rented; that is, as physical capital is exchanged, it warrants a market price, but no rate of return is attributed to it. The fee for borrowing money capital is referred to as the return on money capital rather than as interest. That return is paid on (old) money capital previously borrowed and not yet refunded. No return is paid on current borrowings of money capital since not enough time has elapsed for payment to be due.

The economic activity of human beings in society takes two forms. On one hand, individuals provide land, labor, additions to or new money capital (that is, savings), and enterprise in exchange for income (including returns on money capital previously supplied). On the other hand, they use income to

---

[1]   Walras perceived the reward for entrepreneurial activity as unreliable. Indeed, except for its "normal" component (which, as will be seen in Section 13.3 below, can actually be viewed as a return to money capital) there is no profit at equilibrium. Hence entrepreneurs must make their livings elsewhere as landowners, laborers, or lenders [19, pp. 225, 227].

obtain goods satisfying their wants. (People neither purchase physical capital goods for their own consumption nor sell them to firms for use in production.) In either case, although she may be subject to certain constraints, the individual is free to choose: to work or not, which job, how to spend her income, and so on. The presence of alternatives implies that decisions must be made, and the actual alternative selected usually appears to be in the best interest of the person making the decision. Thus the individual, or *consumer*, as she is often called, is an important decision-making unit in the economy. Households, that is groups of individuals acting as one unit, are counted as single individuals.

A second major type of decision-making unit is the *firm*. A firm is an institution that, using money capital, employs certain goods to produce certain other goods and also operates in its own self-interest.[2] The goods produced are referred to as *outputs*; those employed in production are given the name *inputs*, or *factors*. There are four classes of factors drawn from the four categories of resources described above: land, labor, physical capital, and enterprise. Money capital, although a resource required by the firm for its day-to-day operation, is not used in production and is therefore not a factor. Rather, money capital provides the purchasing power that gives the firm command over factors of production. As part of the process of abstraction, firms are taken to produce only a single output. Each firm must choose the output it produces, the inputs it employs, and the method by which it transforms inputs into output. In so doing, the firm is both aided and confined by existing technology, that is, the pool of all knowledge concerning the methods of obtaining outputs from inputs. Collections of firms with similar outputs are *industries*.

Another important distinction is between flows and stocks. *Flows* are quantities that pass through markets (the concept of a market is characterized momentarily) at definable rates per unit of time. To conceive of flows in this way, of course, is to think in terms of motion over time. However, in much of what follows, the focus of analysis is not on the actual flows that take place across different time units but, rather, on the associated rates of flow that arise at given instants or periods of time. From such a perspective, whatever movement through time that is present can be set aside. Regardless, *stocks* are accumulations of prior flows. Thus the current output of firms, and the current purchases of final goods and the sale of factors (except physical capital) by consumers are all flows per unit of time. Moreover, the machines currently owned by firms constitute stocks, whereas the purchases of new machines rep-

---

[2] In reality, there are persons in the firm who make decisions for the firm and are rewarded for those decisions. But in the present conceptualization, the process by which those decisions are made is ignored.

resent flows. Likewise, the (old) money capital currently tied up in a firm, in the sense that is has been invested in real assets presently held by the firm, is a stock, and any current addition to that money capital, (*i.e.*, new money capital) is a flow.

All goods flowing among individuals and (or) firms, as well as payments for them (expressed in terms of a unit of account) pass through markets. A *market* is nothing more than an institutional arrangement facilitating such exchanges. As there are many different kinds of institutional arrangements, markets may assume a variety of forms. In any event, consumers buy final goods from firms and sell resources to them through markets. Also in markets, firms borrow (new) money capital and buy inputs from consumers (resources), buy inputs including physical capital from firms (intermediate goods), and sell their outputs (final and intermediate goods) to consumers and firms. Observing the pattern of flows through markets it is possible to see what goods are being produced and in what quantities, how and with what quantities of which inputs they are being produced, how much and to which firms consumers are supplying their labor and other resources, the distribution of income across individuals, and the way final commodities are apportioned among consumers. A schematic diagram of these flows, to which the stock of old money capital has been added, is furnished by Figure 1.1. It should be noted that everything supplied by consumers (including past provisions of money capital) that contributes to the production of the top outer flow of goods and services and the production of new physical capital purchased by firms appears in the bottom outer flow of resources; that the purchase and sale of intermediate goods (including physical capital) takes place within the box labeled "firms"; and that in moving around the circles from consumers to firms and back again, no payments or goods are lost or leak out of the system. Thus there is no production for inventories, no government, and no trade with foreign countries or other international relations which would call for the analysis of an "open" economy as distinct from the "closed" economy that is here in view. Of course, Figure 1.1 may be expanded to include such elements, but for the time being there is much to be said for keeping matters as simple as possible.

Moreover, Figure 1.1 is simplified still further when, for pedagogical reasons, money and physical capital are removed from that picture and their economic role ignored in the explanation of the operation of the microeconomy developed in the first 12 chapters of this book. In that case, there are no returns to money capital, firms do not purchase physical capital from other firms, and the inner flow of payments in the diagram exactly offsets the value of the outer flow of goods and non-capital resources.

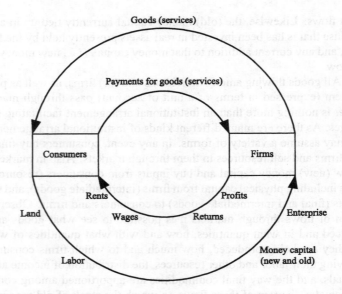

Figure 1.1 Circular flow of goods and payments in the economy

Still further aspects of the economic environment need mention. For example, institutional rules governing property rights and the exchange of commodities emerge from society's political and ideological background. There are also institutional requirements such as the need for decision-making units, especially firms, to record properly all economic operations in accounts expressed in terms of a standard unit of value (such as the dollar), and the need for all decision-making units in general to balance their budgets after appropriate funds have been borrowed.

Finally in all of this is the element of change. Flows of resources and intermediate and final goods respond to price variations. Relative price increases of particular outputs tend to attract an increased flow of money capital and inputs to their production. The flow moderates with relative price declines. Firms and industries thus expand and contract. (Although physical capital tends to accumulate, the process of accumulation is not considered here.)

The foregoing description of an economy has emerged from the same long tradition out of which current economic theory itself has simultaneously been developed. For present purposes, it is regarded as a starting point for an analysis of general market behavior.

1.2 THEORETICAL ANALYSIS

One way to proceed in analyzing the economy described above is to formulate a model. A *model* of something — call the thing T — is a construct having enough in common with the observable facets of T that insight into T can be obtained by studying the construct. To cite an example employed by Einstein and Infeld [2, p. 33], imagine an individual is asked to explain how a particular clock with rotating hands works but is not permitted to remove its cover. After some thought, the person might obtain appropriate springs, gears, and whatever else might be required, and build a physical "model" of the clock whose "observable" behavior duplicates the observed behavior of the original. He could then give an explanation of how his model behaves and say that the original clock works analogously to, or *as if* it were, his model. Clearly, there are many different as-if models, and hence explanations, that could be built. But all explanations operate by identifying something in the model (in the example, the movement of the model's hands) with what is observed (the movement of the hands on the original clock).

In economics, what historically has been taken to be observable is so-called "economic" data consisting of prices, quantities, incomes, and so on. Other elements such as individual preferences and rationality have been regarded as unobservable in the sense of being beyond the limits of the economist's knowledge. (Whether or not these unobservables are actually incapable of observation is a deep philosophical issue that is not explored here.[3] Even if they are not, the terms "observable" and "unobservable" still are employed in their historical usage below.) Hypotheses about these unobservables and their interrelatednesses constitute the inner works of the economist's model, which is intended to reproduce the same observed behavior or data as that generated by the unseeable inner works of the real economy. (In addition to hypotheses on unobservables, sometimes assumptions are introduced with respect to observables. The latter limit the observable domain over which the model may be said to apply.) Economic models, then, do not have the physical qualities of models of clocks. Instead they are usually mental forms or metaphors made up of things such as variables, parameters, relations, and assumptions and propositions derived from them. They also abstract from a multitude of possible forces to concentrate on the minimum number necessary for explanation, and their properties are their own and not properties of that which is the object of explanation. Nevertheless, they frequently function in much the same as-if way as in the clock example.[4]

---

[3] See Ryle [16].

[4] Because of the as-if nature of many economic models, and because of the level of abstraction

Ideally, however, to obtain an understanding of market behavior, a model alone is not enough. The more sweeping and complete structure of a theory is required. A theory contains its own forms of concepts, assumptions, arguments, propositions, and even models. But it is much more than a generalized version of a model. For each of these elements is interconnected in such a way that the propositions and conclusions of the theory derive their purpose and force in relation to each other. The manner in which the elements of a theory are tied together provides its distinctive character.[5] Thus, for example, the development of a theory of market behavior should permit the analysis and comparison of alternative forms of competition (each form explicated in terms of a model) within a unified framework.

One of the principal aims of the Walrasian theory of market behavior, then, is to explain particular observed facts, that is, to impart an understanding of the economy as described in Section 1.1. Why is it that certain commodities are produced in certain quantities? What determines the specific distributions of income and final goods actually realized in the economy? How is it that the economy seems to function smoothly (in the sense that it achieves an allocation of resources) when each of millions of decision-making units operate independently and in their own self-interest? These are a few of the general questions to which the Walrasian theory of market behavior addresses itself.

The theory has other purposes as well. In part, its assumptions define a notion of rational behavior in terms of maximization for decision-making units that leads to outcomes (in the theory) having the properties of efficiency and stability. To many economists these properties seem socially reasonable and morally justifiable despite the fact that none of the decision-making units involved has intended them. Thus the theory provides a standard against which to evaluate the behavior of individuals (and firms). It indicates what an individual's behavior ought to be like if he were rational. And it provides him with behavioral guidelines to follow if he desires to be rational. The theory also serves as a basis for prediction of what will happen in the economy, insofar as people act rationally and other theoretical assumptions are satisfied. It should be noted, however, that prediction requires still additional assumptions beyond

---

they employ, it does not follow that such models are capable of immediate concrete application to specific real-world situations. To confuse a model of a person, a firm, or an economy with, respectively, an actual person, an actual firm, or an actual economy, is to commit what Machlup called the "fallacy of misplaced concreteness." According to Machlup [9, p. 9], the fallacy occurs when theoretical symbols are used "... as though they had a direct, observable, concrete meaning." What a model does do, of course, is to establish principles and modes of causation that can be applied only in very broad and general ways.

[5]   The use of abstract analysis for theory construction in economics dates to Ricardo [14].

those incorporated in the theory of market behavior, and which are surrounded in controversy extending well beyond the confines of economic discourse. The matter is taken up again in Section 15.1. A further intent of the theory is to establish a justification of certain states of affairs as having the characteristics of rationality, efficiency, and so forth. In this regard it furnishes a framework for the analysis of public policy with respect to the economy at large.

Apart from supplying standards, justifications, and the foundation for predictions, the Walrasian theory of market behavior also provides a variety of models. Many of these (for example, models of demand behavior) incorporate well-specified assumptions of rationality, and such models can be made to fit fairly well portions of the mounds of available economic facts. Other models, like the Cobb-Douglas production function, contain no explicit rationality assumptions. Because of their similar confluence with certain types of data, they, too, have gained widespread use in a variety of applications. Models like these can be very useful in providing a basis for investigating diverse practical issues that sometimes have important policy implications. Thus significant insight can be gained into questions such as: What are the costs of environmental pollution, and what (if anything) can be done to control it? What is the economic value of a college education, and how does this value compare with its costs? What are the costs of banning nuclear power plants? And, should a particular road or bridge be built or park be created?

The relationship of the Walrasian theory of market behavior to the abstracted real world as described in Section 1.1 ought to be clarified. Just as the physicist postulates properties of particles too small to be discerned, many of the assumptions of the Walrasian theory are expressed in ways making it difficult to see directly whether, in fact, they are satisfied. By the same token, there are implications and conclusions drawn from them (as in physics) which are, in principle, potentially falsifiable through observation. A substantial portion of these implications and conclusions arises by analyzing the effects on behavior of modulations in certain relevant parameters. For example, consumer reactions to changes in the price of a single (final) commodity can be stated so as to admit the possibility of empirical refutation. If the data derived by watching the behavior of a particular consumer are not consistent with the requirements for that data deduced from the assumptions of the theory, then the theory provides little insight into this person's behavior. In general, any inconsistency between actual observation and those which, according to the theory, ought to obtain, casts doubt on the understanding that the theory imparts to the workings of the economy.

There are some conclusions of the Walrasian theory, however, that even in principle would be formidable to check empirically. The proposition that "if prices are not equal to marginal costs, then it is possible to make at least one person better off and no one else worse off without anyone doing any more work or consuming additional resources," illustrates the point. This is a purely theoretical statement. But if all clearly falsifiable facets of the theory are consistent with observed fact, most people would not wish to accept the lack of ability to verify the proposition empirically as reason to reject it. All the more so if, in addition, the theory were considered plausible or, in other words, if the underlying assumptions were thought to be reasonable in light of whatever data were available.

Furthermore, due to the process of abstraction, any conclusion derived in theory can be regarded only as an approximation of occurrences in the real world. The description of Section 1.1, upon which the Walrasian theory of market behavior is based, and whose underlying reality the theory attempts to explain, omits many details. Clearly, assumptions such as, for example, (i) all consumers and firms make decisions and take actions simultaneously, (ii) all decision-makers have full and identical information concerning all relevant matters, and (iii) all firms within industries are identical or all labor supplied is homogeneous, ignore and hide significant particulars of the actual economic world. To the extent that these excluded details influence those elements of reality in whose direction the conclusions of the theory are addressed, the conclusions of the theory are incomplete. Thus if a single such excluded detail were, in reality, to vary from one observation to the next, and if all remaining data relating to assumptions of the theory stayed constant, then the economy would have changed but the theory would say that it had not. If the disparity between what the theory asserts and what actually happens is too wide, then both the description of the economy and the theory should be enlarged to include the significant omissions. But some discrepancy cannot be avoided.

Another way of saying the same thing is that the Walrasian theory of market behavior describes an idealized but nonexistent economy. It analyzes certain phenomena in their purest of forms, that is, when they are unaffected by numerous and varied elements thought to be of secondary importance and whose influence in the real world may be volatile and not entirely understood. It thus provides insight into the underlying economic forces that seem to arise in reality only as modified by attendant circumstances. In like manner, the physicist determines that all physical objects falling in a vacuum from equal heights must reach the earth in identical times. The fact that the descent of a leaf from a tree actually takes longer than that of an acorn does not violate this proposition. Rather, the discrepancy is explained by the presence of air and its interaction with the falling leaf and acorn.

It might seem from the above that, except for minor differences, the analysis of market behavior is merely a transfer of the idea of a "science" from a physical to a social application. Mill argued the same point: that there is no logical difference between the principles required to explain physical and social phenomena. Just as irregular movement of the tides over the oceans of the world does not mean an absence of regular laws governing them, so too with human behavior [11, pp. 552-555]. The fact that human beings are considerably more complex than tides reflects merely a difference of degree rather than of kind.

But Winch [20] claims that this view is mistaken and that there are significant differences between physical and nonphysical science. His case is based on the notion (due to Wittgenstein) that in order to understand and communicate concepts the researcher must have learned rules that tell her to identify repeatedly specific things with specific words. A camel is called a camel because a rule has been accepted asserting that a creature with certain characteristics shall be called a camel. Similarly, behavior can be meaningful only if it involves the application of a rule. To cast a vote is to follow a rule that identifies a particular action under particular circumstances with the behavior "voting." The learning and application of rules necessarily takes place in a social setting.

Now in any scientific investigation the object of study must be observed, facts about it noticed, and then, as in the case of the analysis of market behavior, theoretical constructions developed. But to be able to notice means the researcher is able to identify certain characteristics; and to do this she must have some concept of what the characteristics are. The Winch argument suggests, however, that the latter is possible only with appropriate rules identifying communicable symbols with the characteristics, and these, in turn, will depend on what has been socially acceptable to others working in the same area.

So far Winch's argument applies to all scientific inquiry. In the case of the physical sciences the phenomena under investigation are controlled by nature; rules are important only insofar as they preside over the investigation itself. But whereas the physical sciences require consideration of only one set of rules, in the behavioral sciences the researcher's objects of study as well as the study of it are human activities and thus are governed according to rules. And it is the rules followed by the objects of study, not those governing behavioral science and the investigation, that must serve as the basis for identifying and communicating symbols. Whether or not two persons uttering dissimilar phrases are both praying depends on the rules they are following, not on those accepted by the researcher. Therefore the relationship between observer and observed is different for inquiry in the behavioral sciences. This, according to Winch, is more than a mere contrast in degree. The physical and nonphysical sciences differ in kind. (It should be noted that a large literature has been directed to this question and has discussed extensively the possibility of epistemological parity between physical and social science.)

In addition to Winch's distinction and the obvious lack of a laboratory for many experimental purposes, there are other contrasts as well. Actual behavior of physical matter and of human beings as observed by scientists differs in that human behavior can be associated with intent or purpose. Although purpose itself cannot be seen in economic data, behavior resulting from it can. Both the investigator and the individual under observation understand and interpret the latter's behavior in terms of rules. As long as the rules employed by both are approximately alike, each will understand the observed behavior in more or less the same way. Thus the researcher is able to infer (approximate) intent through introspection, that is, by determining what her (the researcher's) own purpose would be if she were engaged in what the observed person is seen doing.

To illustrate, suppose the personal economic behavior of an investigator is directed toward the maximization of her own satisfaction. She reasons that if she were someone else with similar cultural background in similar situations, she would probably do the same thing. And she is told by others that they actually attempt to act in this way. There is no reason, then, why her analysis of market behavior should not take these facts into account by inferring satisfaction-maximizing intent on the part of others. To not do so would be to discard potentially useful information. At the same time, of course, the risk of confusing the role of value judgments in her analysis increases.

It is still possible, however, that models employed in physical and social science be formally isomorphic. This would occur if, abstracting from the physical and social spaces in which they are located respectively, two models have identical formal properties (for example, the same assumptions and propositions). The reason such isomorphisms might arise is not surprising: The formal mathematical constructs and logic employed by both physical and social scientists are often quite similar.[6] Thus in the case of the theory of demand (a subtheory of the Walrasian theory of market behavior) there are analogies and isomorphisms to classical mechanics [3, pp. 24-26] and thermodynamics [4, pp. 612-613].[7] If only the formal elements of models were

---

[6] Indeed, Mirowski [13] suggests that mathematical models were imported into economics from physics in the first place.

[7] It is interesting that Marshall [10, p. xiv] thought biological analogies to be more significant

of interest, then the difference between social and physical science would be minimal.

But introspection, that is, the ascription of intent, adds an extra dimension in understanding human behavior beyond formal analysis and the as-if approach to model building.[8] Taking the perspective that, when making purchases, say, individuals actually do intend to maximize utility (that is, in terms of the clock example described earlier, the inner workings of the model are assumed to be identical to the inner workings of the original clock), renders the hypotheses of demand theory meaningful in human terms and permits a deeper comprehension of price determination than could otherwise be achieved. Moreover, certain propositions concerning human welfare (see Section 3.4 and Chapter 12) are senseless without it. Although the possibility of at least partial isomorphism between formal models remains, introspection prevents complete isomorphisms between social and physical theories. The inference of purpose behind behavior is inappropriate in physical science.

It should be pointed out that invoking the assumption that an individual in fact makes decisions on the basis of (constrained) utility maximization transforms the as-if character of the model of his behavior into an *as-being* nature. That is, it presents the model as an accurate description of what generally takes place in reality. As previously indicated, and as will be seen in subsequent chapters, such a transformation plays an important role in certain areas of economic analysis.

Finally, as theories are developed and tested, and hence knowledge in social (behavioral) science expands, the rules governing scientific study could modify. In addition, as this knowledge becomes available to those under observation, the rules upon which their behavior is based may also vary. What under the old set of rules would be considered behavior directed toward a given purpose, might under the new rules be regarded as inappropriate in achieving that end. Hence the acquisition of knowledge could change behavior (and its observation), thus rendering the knowledge obsolete. Alternatively put, if a "correct" explanation of a social system were developed, and if everyone were told what that explanation is, then the system itself (as well as observation of it) might change and the "correct" explanation would no longer apply. In that case, the aim of further theoretical analysis would be to construct a new correct explanation. This could not happen in physical science since the "true" laws of nature do not change with the acquisition of knowledge.

---

for economics than analogies to mechanics. For the most part, however, he was still drawn toward mechanical analogies because of their relative simplicity.

[8]   Keynes [8, p. 297] also believed in the validity of the use of introspection in economics.

1.3 THE APPROACH

The approach adopted by the Walrasian theory of market behavior in viewing
the real world is based on two general characteristics of the economy described
in Section 1.1. The first is that, even with the level of abstraction employed, a
multitude of independent activities seem to be occurring at the same time. Consumers and firms are making decisions and prices are responding accordingly.
Furthermore, each of these activities appears to have some impact, however
small, on the others. A decision by one firm to lower its price reverberates
throughout the economy. Thus any attempt to understand what is going on
must account for the simultaneity and interrelatedness of events.[9] Secondly,
the economy does not stand still. Decisions, distributions, and prices continually vary. Any one change gives the impression of influencing all others
and even feeding back upon itself. Not only are individual events simultaneous and interrelated, but the same can be said of sequences of events moving
across time.

These fundamental observations are incorporated into the Walrasian theory of market behavior by thinking of the workings of the economy in terms of
the operation of a fixed dynamic system unfolding over time.[10] This yields a
model of the economy analogous to the model of the clock of Section 1.2. Depending on whether time is regarded as continuous or discrete, such systems
take the form of, respectively, simultaneous differential or difference equations. In the continuous mode, time consists of sequences of distinct, connected "instants." (For now, an *instant* may be taken to be either an interval of
time of arbitrarily small length, or the limit as lengths descend to zero of a sequence of intervals, each contained in the one before it.) In the discrete mode,
time passes as periods of finite duration. Like instants, these periods do not
overlap. Nor is there "space" between two successive ones. Variables are permitted to take on but one value per instant or period as the case may be. And, of
course, unaccountably many instants may be "combined" sequentially to form
periods, and periods may be concatenated to obtain longer periods. (Some difficulties with these notions of time are examined in Section 15.1.) Formally,
there is little to choose between continuous and discrete time; the mathematics
of differential and difference equations is more or less the same. Subsequent
chapters take time to be continuous.

But regardless of the form time takes on, it is the analysis of the dynamic
system (like the model of the clock) that leads to many of the insights into

---

[9]   Walras [19] notwithstanding, Schumpeter [17, p. 307] suggests that Isnard in 1781 may have
been the first to make the notion of simultaneity explicit in microeconomics.
[10]   Mill takes a similar perspective in his analysis of accumulation [12, pp. 705, 752].

observed phenomena provided by the theory. This means that, in addition to the study of individual behavior both in isolation and in relation to the behavior of others, certain general properties of the system itself must be investigated: Is there an equilibrium or stationary time-path? If so, is it unique? Is the system stable? What other particularities, if any, are attributable to the equilibrium path? Any understanding of market behavior emerging from the system is incomplete until questions such as these have answers.

To be more specific, the dynamic system employed by the Walrasian theory of market behavior is the formal statement of the standard model of the perfectly competitive economy. In the latter, of course, all markets have large numbers of small buyers and sellers, standardized products, free entry and exit, and provide the same price, product, and production information to all market participants. The model itself concerns the simultaneous making of decisions over time by consumers and firms and the consequent impact on markets these decisions have. In this volume most attention centers on the following specific version: Consumer desires (tastes or wants) and an initial collection of resources with which they are endowed are assumed to exist and taken as given. Also fixed are the institutional arrangements with respect to the functioning of markets, and the technology available to firms. Prices indicate relative costs and revenues to decision-makers. The latter use price information to figure out what, in their own best interest, they should buy and sell. Such decisions are made independently at each instant. The possibility of making decisions for more than one moment at a time is ignored. Visualizing what takes place in an actual economy, and starting from an initial allocation of commodities, the activities of producing, buying, and selling cause goods to flow through markets in exchange for payments. As time passes, quantity flows induce price changes which, in turn, alter the flows of quantities. Eventually the system tends to settle on certain prices, on an allocation of resources among firms, and on a distribution of final commodities among consumers. But for purposes of analytical simplicity, neither trading (buying and selling) nor production is permitted to take place in the model until this process is worked out and its end is reached. Providing parameter and initial values are set correctly, the working out of the simultaneous equations of this system (again, like the model of the clock) produces the prices and distribution of goods (up to appropriate approximation) actually seen in the economy. Hence the fundamental issues to which the Walrasian theory of market behavior is addressed, are resolved. Alternatively put, at any selected moment particular values of the system's parameters correspond to the state of the real economy. Using these values and relevant initial conditions, the equilibrium or stationary path of that moment is determined together with the hypothetical path the process follows. The latter is taken to converge to the former. Depending on the particular formulation of the system, stationary paths could be thought of as either "long-run" or "short-run" equilibria. The above interpretation of economic reality is hereafter referred to as the *Walrasian vision*, and the system of equations employed to represent and articulate it is called the *Walrasian system*.

Note in passing that the pursuit of self-interest on the part of consumers and firms is fundamental to the Walrasian vision.[11] It is nothing less than the (hypothetical) driving force behind all behavior. Theoretical representation of it appears in the guise of maximization: Consumer decisions are assumed to be generated from maximizing utility; those of firms from maximizing profits. That the simultaneous pursuit of self-interest by all decision-making units can lead to a coherent result, or in other words that the dynamic system comprising the Walrasian vision has a globally-stable stationary path, cannot be taken for granted. This, rather, is a theoretical proposition that needs to be established with care.

It should be emphasized that in addition to decision making by consumers and firms on the basis of maximization, the Walrasian system contains three other major character-shaping assumptions, the first and third of which have also been previously identified: (i) consumer preferences (which define the ends or goals of the system), resource endowments, and the technology (for producing outputs from inputs) available to firms are given; (ii) markets operate so as to equate market demand with market supply; and (iii) all markets are perfectly competitive. Other highly important qualities include its focus on equilibrium and its individualistic nature. The role that the notion of equilibrium plays will be considered momentarily. Individualism as it relates to the Walrasian system will be taken up in Chapter 10.

There are still further distinctive features in the presentation of the Walrasian theory of market behavior on subsequent pages. First, all markets are understood to clear at equilibrium prices. Second, the theory attempts to determine the relative price of each good or factor in relation to others. Although it may assist comprehension to contemplate each market price as measured in terms of some appropriate counter like, for example, money, such an effort may be regarded simply as a means of establishing and expressing relative price ratios. Third, the levels at which factor markets clear are those for which full employment of factors is maintained in the sense that all units actually

---

[11]   Economists have focused on self-interest ever since Smith wrote, "It is not from the benevolence of the butcher, the brewer, or the baker, that we expect our dinner, but from their regard to their own interest. We address ourselves, not to their humanity but to their self-love, and never talk to them of our own necessities but of their advantages." [18, p. 14].

supplied to the markets will be absorbed by market demands. At these magnitudes there is no unused capacity of available factor resources, and market wages are no less than what is required for human subsistence. Fourth, all markets clear at the same market-clearing velocity. The possibility of variations in velocities from market to market is ignored. Finally, the quantities of resources supplied by consumers, although limited by the amounts of those resources in their possession, are independent of the size of their endowments of them.

According to the definition of the term, along a stationary path variable values do not change over time. All rates of growth are zero. Hence the path, that is, the equilibrium values associated with it, may be studied independently of time. In particular, it may be compared to other stationary paths generated by alternative parameter values. Different parameter values may arise, for example, with modified tastes or technology.[12] The resulting form of analysis is called *comparative statics*. Usually the idea is to compute the rates at which the equilibrium values of specified variables may change with respect to certain parameter modifications that lead to a shift from one stationary path to another. Sometimes only the signs of these rates or derivatives are of interest. Adopting the view that the economy is stable, and hence that all paths on which the economy travels eventually move toward stationary ones, comparative statics and the examination of equilibrium become of paramount importance. Because this is a very common perspective employed by economists, timeless equilibrium is a major concern in the ensuing pages.

Another reason for examining timeless functions and equations is that they are frequently used as a basis for constructing the dynamic model referred to earlier. Thus if the reaction of consumers and firms to all possible price configurations is known, then a dynamic model is obtained simply by specifying the way in which prices adjust over time when out of equilibrium. Economic behavior at each instant is then inferred from the known reactions. Although there are other approaches to the construction of dynamic models, such is the perspective employed below. Timeless reactions to prices are studied first (Chapters 2-8) and integrated into a dynamic model in Chapter 9. At that point, nonstationary time paths and their convergence or stability properties also are considered.

Of course, the view that consumers and firms make decisions for instants rather than for finite intervals (or periods) of time conforms to the convention introduced above that time be continuous. It is worth pointing out, how-

---

[12] Systematic transformation of tastes and technology over time may also be studied in the context of similar dynamic systems in which the notion of stationarity need no longer require the constancy of these elements as time passes. The issue is not considered here.

ever, that the results obtained for either circumstance are quite similar. Certainly there is no difference in the timeless equations and functions relevant to each case. The equilibrium values determined by them are identical regardless of whether the equilibria are appropriate to an instant or period of time. Moreover, variation in dynamical elements of the theory arise only as technical consequences of the distinction between discreteness and continuity. At the substantive level these variations disappear. Thus, although it is clearly an abstraction to think in terms of instantaneous decision-making, no real violence is done to the goal of understanding reality by doing so.

There are also many instances when it is neither necessary nor appropriate to think of equilibrium in terms of the resolution of the entire system. Under these circumstances it is often worthwhile to reduce the number of equations of the system by treating some variables as parameters fixed at particular values.[13] The latter is understood to mean that, for the analytical purpose at hand, the variables in question and any relations among them may be assumed not to exert any determining force. This permits a sharper focus on specific issues. Investigation of the subsystem so obtained proceeds in much the same manner as that of the original system. The "equilibrium" values and results derived from the subsystem often are referred to as "partial-equilibrium" values and results.[14] But in general, there is no presumption that conclusions derived from a partial-equilibrium analysis approximate in any way those produced by the original system. Short-run inquiries in which certain inputs employed by firms are assumed to be fixed in quantity, and analyses in which the quantities of factors supplied by consumers are assumed to be fixed, fall into the partial-equilibrium category.

The domains over which these systems, both original and reduced, range are always taken to be continua. Such a convention implies that all variable values, including quantities of commodities, are perfectly divisible — in spite of the fact that it is impossible to buy, say, $1\frac{1}{2}$ or $2.1417\ldots$ automobiles. But apart from the convenience permitted, it should be pointed out that little is lost by adhering to this tradition. For even though fractional or irrational amounts of variable values may arise in theory, they seldom occur in reality. Thus only theoretical statements concerning whole units of goods can ordinarily be

---

[13]   Actually it is not always necessary to go quite this far in every case. The Hicks and Leontief Composite Commodity Theorems assert that if only the relative prices or quantities of a subset of goods remains fixed, then these goods may be treated as if they were a single good with a single price. (See Katzner [7, pp. 140-145].) Hence the number of equations and variables may be reduced accordingly.

[14]   Marshall, of course, is the grandfather of partial-equilibrium analysis. See, for example, [10, pp. 36, 366].

linked in an exact way to the real world. The remainder, although logically coherent, are either approximations or irrelevant. That outcomes involving fractions of units are possible does not by itself negate the results derived for whole units. It is also convenient to suppose, so that advanced mathematics may be avoided, that all domains are appropriate subsets of Euclidean space of proper dimension.

To illustrate the use of the partial-equilibrium method to focus on specific ideas (including several of those discussed above), consider the elementary demand and supply analysis of a final-good market in isolation. Its purpose is to model the workings of a single market by itself. Let $p \geqslant 0$ vary over market prices and $x \geqslant 0$ over market quantities of the good in question. The market demand function H is a function assigning a market quantity x, demanded by all consumers in the market, to each nonnegative price p. Similarly, the market supply function G identifies for every nonnegative p, a quantity x supplied by all firms in the market. Thus market demand and supply functions summarize, respectively, consumer and firm behavior in response to potential market prices. The variables of the economy-wide dynamic system that are fixed, thereby permitting analytical separation of this market from others, are the prices and quantities of all remaining goods and hence the distribution of income among consumers. The subsystem under consideration therefore consists of the two equations

$$x = H(p),$$
$$x = G(p). \tag{1.3-1}$$

Because these equations are intended to define a stationary path, it is not necessary for time to appear explicitly in them. A typical picture of the situation is provided in Figure 1.2(a). Note that usual practice in economics places the dependent variable, x, on the horizontal axis, and the independent variable, p, on the vertical.[15] Thus, looking at Figure 1.2(a) in isolation, one might tend

---

15   The demand and supply equations of (1.3-1), in which quantity depends on price, along with the equilibrium condition $H(p) = G(p)$ to be discussed momentarily, date to Cournot [1, pp. 47, 91]. Although Cournot [1, p. 53, back insert] provided a graph of his demand function, and although Jevons [6, p. 333] claimed priority, the diagram of intersecting demand and supply curves seems to have made its first appearance in the economics literature in 1870 with Jenkin [5]. However, reflecting Cournot's mathematics and the idea that price determines quantity demanded or supplied, this early geometry, in contrast to Figure 1.2(a), fixes price on the horizontal axis and quantity on the vertical axis. But Marshall [10, pp. 345, 346], of course, thought of demand and supply in terms of quantity determining a "demand price" or a "supply price." Hence, his demand and supply functions [10, p. 853] appear as inversions of Cournot's and in his geometry [10, p. 346n], the price and quantity axes are reversed. Modern practice

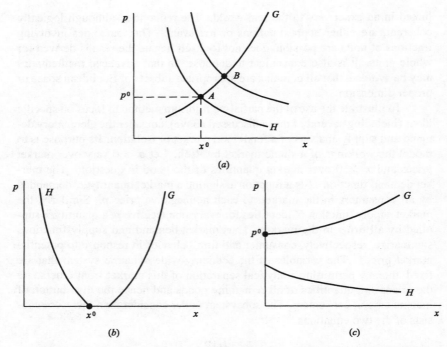

Figure 1.2 Equilibrium in an isolated market: (*a*) equilibrium at positive price and quantity; (*b*) equilibrium at zero price and positive quantity; (*c*) equilibrium at positive price and zero quantity

to interpret the curves labeled H and G, not as the graphs of the respective functions H and G, but rather as graphs of their inverses. Since, however, the diagram is meant only to illustrate a simple case in which inverses normally exist and look something like the curves really intended, problems do not arise by continuing this custom regardless of the interpretation employed. Nevertheless the reversal of mathematical convention should be kept in mind.

In general, *equilibrium* is a circumstance in which there is no tendency to change.[16] With respect to the aforementioned market, then, the point (x^0, p^0)

_____

appears to have combined the mathematics of Cournot and the geometry of Marshall.

[16]   The notion of equilibrium given here is associated implicitly with a stationary state or path of an appropriate dynamic system. This association is made explicit in Section 9.1, where it is assumed that the "economic" is in equilibrium if and only if the economic equilibrium defines the stationary state of the dynamic system modeling the economy described in Section 1.1.

is an equilibrium if at that point no consumer or firm is attempting to alter behavior. Hence for the simultaneous occurrence of the equations of (1.3-1) to describe equilibrium in the model — or in other words, for (1.3-1) to delineate a stationary path — it must be established as a logical proposition that intersection points such as (x^0, p^0) in Figure 1.2(a) and only those points have this equilibrium property. As long as prices and quantities are restricted to be positive, the argument is trivial: At (x^0, p^0) in Figure 1.2(a), firms and consumers buy and sell what they wish. There is no need for anyone to vary behavior. Conversely, at any other price in the diagram, either firms cannot sell all they produce or consumers cannot buy all they want. Said in an alternative way, at any quantity different from x^0, either firms could not receive the price they require for their output or consumers would have to pay more than they will. In either case the result is a change in behavior as consumers and firms successfully compete to modify price and quantity in an effort to reach their goals. With these movements going on, equilibrium cannot prevail.[17] Thus, for positive prices and quantities, there is a logical identification between equilibria and intersection points. But once the possibility of a zero price or quantity is admitted, the proposition breaks down. Figure 1.2(b) shows a market equilibrium at $(x^0, 0)$ with supply unequal to demand. Any forces in the market pushing price toward negative values are exactly offset by the floor of zero below which prices are not permitted to fall. Similarly $(0, p^0)$ is an equilibrium in Figure 1.2(c) but not an intersection point of the demand and supply curves.

It has already been pointed out that the questions of existence, uniqueness, and stability of equilibria are significant in arriving at a complete understanding of such a model and hence of the phenomenon the model is supposed to represent. The argument is made in greater detail for the general model of the economy later on (Section 9.1). Even so, the critical role the notion of equilibrium often plays in the theory of market behavior is worth emphasizing here. To keep matters simple, focus again on an isolated market. Suppose an investigator were to observe the actual market at a given moment in time. All he could see is that at some price, say p^0, so many units of the commodity, say x^0, were sold. His observation would consist of the market flow represented by the single point A in a diagram such as Figure 1.2(a). There would be no empirical evidence to suggest the existence in reality of either the demand function H or supply function G. How is this observation to be understood? What sense can be made of it? One plausible interpretation is to assume that unsee-

---

[17]   Similar characterizations of nonequilibrium situations have been provided by, respectively, Marshall [10, pp. 345, 346] and Walras [19, Lesson 6]. The Marshallian and Walrasian adjustment rules introduced in Chapter 9 formalize these ideas.

able demand and supply curves exist and that they happen to intersect at A. Thus a model explaining the observed flow as a market equilibrium position, that is, as the outcome of the interaction of demand and supply, is obtained in much the same way as the model of the clock explains the clock's behavior. Furthermore, if a subsequent observation produced, say, the point B in Figure 1.2(a), and if there were reason to believe that the original supply curve had remained unchanged and went through B, then the investigator has a ready explanation for the change: There was an increase in demand, which shifted the equilibrium from A to B.

On this view, the concept of equilibrium provides the crucial link between the model and reality. No empirical tests are required. It is a matter of interpretation. Moreover, the question of whether equilibrium exists is vital. If demand and supply curves did not intersect, and if equilibrium did not occur at a zero quantity or price (for an example of this, interchange the labels of the demand and supply curves in Figure 1.2(b)), then the model could have no relevance for the real world. Because equilibrium would not exist in the model, it would be impossible to identify equilibrium with any observed point. The uniqueness problem is also significant. If demand and supply curves intersected more than once, then since the properties of the different equilibria may vary, there would be no way to tell which properties should be identified with the seen point. The model, therefore, would be incomplete. It would admit the possibility of many equilibria as theoretical descriptions of reality without indicating the appropriate one to employ. Lastly, the model must exhibit a certain kind of stability. For if equilibria were not globally stable, then the change in the model that produced the shift in demand, and hence movement away from A, might not result in convergence toward B. Hence the model could not explain the observed passage from A to B.

The above view could be modified by requiring A merely to approximate (be near) an equilibrium rather than to be one itself. Alternative interpretations of observations are also possible, and the role of the equilibrium notion varies accordingly.

1.4   PLAN OF THE BOOK

There are many ways to present the Walrasian theory of market behavior. The plan adopted here is to begin by ignoring money capital and examining the commodity-flow behavior of (perfectly competitive) individual consumers and firms in considerable detail. Because all flows of goods and payments for them pass through markets (Section 1.1), and supposing that all commodity

Table 1.1 Buyers and sellers in various types of markets

Markets	Buyers	Sellers
final commodities	consumers	firms
intermediate commodities	firms	firms
factors	firms	consumers

markets fall into one of the factor, intermediate, or final good categories, this behavior may be classified according to the buyer's or seller's side of the appropriate market with which it is identified. The source of behavior (that is, the decision-maker) in each case is indicated in Table 1.1. Although these classifications occasionally become blurred because some commodities may be sold simultaneously as both final and intermediate goods (Chapters 7 and 9), it is useful to begin by thinking in such terms. Thus, for the time being, consumer behavior (and only consumer behavior) is relevant for the demand sides of final commodities markets and the supply sides of factor markets. All other buyer and seller activity emanates from firms. (A discussion of the market for IOUs, through which money capital flows and in which the buyers [suppliers of money capital] are consumers and sellers [demanders of money capital] are firms, is postponed until money capital is introduced formally in Chapters 13 and 14.)

Upon completion of a fairly extensive discussion of consumer (Chapters 2 and 3) and firm (Chapters 4 and 5) behavior in both buying and selling roles, attention focuses (Chapter 6) on the operation of perfectly competitive markets in isolation. Thereafter all activities of all consumers and all firms in all commodity markets, as well as all interactions among these activities, are considered simultaneously, as models of the entire economy (still without money capital) are studied. First, the equations of such models are written down and the implications of Walras' law explored (Chapter 7). The special situation with factor supplies taken to be fixed also is spelled out (Chapter 8). Next, conditions are investigated under which equilibria (or stationary time-paths) exist, and an inquiry is made into the uniqueness, stability, and welfare properties of them (Sections 8.4 and 10.2, and Chapters 9 and 12). The manner in which market equilibrium prices are determined is also considered (Chapter

10). Lastly, a notion of capital which is faithful to the Walrasian vision of economic reality is introduced (Chapter 13) and integrated with previous analysis (Chapter 14). At this point the market for IOUs is brought into the picture. Along the way (Chapter 11), the problems of permitting the presence of imperfections in competition in output markets are examined. (It should be noted that for pedagogical reasons, the analyses of welfare, capital, and imperfect competition are all set in the context of fixed-factor supplies.) The book concludes (Chapter 15) with a discussion of some assumptions and methods of analysis alternative to those of the Walrasian theory as presented here.

A different presentation of the same material would, at first, dispense with detail and build, in a more skeletal fashion, from individual consumer and firm behavior, through isolated markets, to a grand view of the economic landscape. Such a development would enhance the coherence, connectedness, and elegance of the central argument. Thereafter, the skipped-over detail would be explored, motivated partly by theoretical interest and partly by the usefulness of elaborating theoretical analysis for potential empirical application. There are, of course, a variety of grand views that could be constructed. Attention could center on the long or short run, fixed or variable factor supplies could be assumed, various functions may or may not be taken as differentiable, money capital may or may not be included, and so on. Although this alternative form of organization is not employed below, the general features of most grand views are summarized in Chapter 14. Moreover, the reader should be aware that a line of argument depicting an especially common grand view proceeds through the following sections: consumer behavior, 2.3, 3.3; firm behavior, 4.1, 4.4, 4.5, 5.1 (short-run) and 5.2 (long-run); isolated markets, 6.1 (short-run) and 6.2 (long-run); all markets and individuals interacting simultaneously, 7.2; existence, uniqueness, and stability of equilibria in the general setting, 9.1, 9.2, 9.3, 9.4; price determination 10.2,10.3; optimality of equilibria (fixed-factor-supply context only), 12.2, 12.3; the grand view summarized without capital, 14.1; and if capital is to be accounted for (in the fixed-factor-supply context), add 13.2, 13.3 and 14.3. Note, however, that these sections by themselves are not entirely self-contained. Most readers, at least the first time through, are likely to be more comfortable pursuing the text as written rather than focusing only on them. So that they may keep the unfolding of this particular grand view in mind, frequent reference to it appears in the introductions of subsequent chapters.

Now, a word about notation. In a work such as this, it is very difficult to construct a system of symbolic representation which is at the same time precise, consistent, and readable. Ideally each symbol should have (among other properties) identical meaning in all appearances. Thus, for example, the same notation introduced to elucidate the theory of demand in Chapter 2 should be employed in the proof of existence of equilibrium in Chapter 9 and in the articulation of the grand view of Chapter 14. But compromises have to be made and the repeated use of some symbols in differing senses is unavoidable. Perhaps a reasonable approximation of the ideal has been achieved by standardizing the meaning of the following throughout:

Indices

i or $n = 1, \ldots, I$ \qquad produced and/or consumer goods

j or $n = 1, \ldots J$ \qquad inputs and/or factors

$n = 1, \ldots, I, I+1, \ldots, I+J$

$k = 1, \ldots, K$ \qquad consumers

$\ell = 1, \ldots L$ \qquad firms

Generally, unless otherwise indicated, $I \geqslant 2$, $J \geqslant 2$, $K \geqslant 2$, and $L \geqslant 2$.

Quantities of goods and prices (additional subscripts are sometimes present)

x_i \qquad market or individual quantities of produced good i or consumer good i

p_i \qquad price of produced good i or consumer good i

y_j \qquad market or individual quantities of input or factor j

r_j \qquad price of input or factor j

q_n \qquad excess demand quantities of good n

Q_n \qquad market aggregate excess demand quantities of good n

$$P_n = \begin{cases} p_i, & \text{if } n = i \\ \\ r_j, & \text{if } n = j \end{cases}$$

$$\left. \begin{aligned} x &= (x_1, \ldots, x_I) \\ \\ p &= (p_1, \ldots, p_I) \end{aligned} \right\} \; x \text{ and } p \text{ are scalars when } I = 1$$

$$\left. \begin{aligned} y &= (y_1, \ldots, y_J) \\ \\ r &= (r_1, \ldots, r_J) \end{aligned} \right\} \; y \text{ and } r \text{ are scalars when } J = 1$$

$$Q = (Q_1, \ldots, Q_{I+J})$$
$$P = (P_1, \ldots, P_{I+J})$$

Functions (subscripts and superscripts, asterisks, bars, and such removed)

f	production function
g	firm output supply function or input demand function
g^*	firm expansion-path function
G	industry output supply function or market input demand function
h	consumer (output) demand function or (factor) supply function
h^*	consumer (output) compensated demand function
H	consumer market (output) demand function or (factor) supply function
E	excess demand function for consumers or firms
$\mathcal{E}$	market aggregate excess demand function
u	utility function
v	indirect utility function
t	transformation function

Matrices

F	bordered Hessian of f
$\bar{F}$	Hessian of f
U	bordered Hessian of u
T	Hessian of t

Sets

X	commodity or distribution-of-commodities space
Y	input space
$\mathcal{D}$	set on which $|U| \neq 0$
Ω	set on which consumer demand functions are differentiable
Γ	domain of firm cost function

$C^>_{x^0}$ set of baskets preferred to x^0

$C^{\geq}_{x^0}$ set of baskets preferred or indifferent to x^0

$\mathcal{A}_a$ factor availability set, given vector of factor supplies a

$\mathcal{T}_a$ production possibility set, given vector of factor supplies a

Miscellaneous

TC	total cost
ATC	average total cost
AVC	average variable cost
MC	marginal cost
TR	total revenue
AR	average revenue
MR	marginal revenue
π	profit
m	consumer's income
M	aggregate income
$\lambda;\eta$	Lagrange multipliers
0	zero vector or scalar (according to context)

The following notational rules also are utilized: Subscripts on variable symbols such as x and y denote components of vectors; superscripts, primes, asterisks, and such indicate different vectors. Subscripts on functional symbols such as f and g signify derivatives; superscripts identify components of functional vectors. The symbolic phrase $x' \geqslant x^0$, where $x' = (x'_1, \ldots, x'_I)$ and $x^0 = (x^0_1, \ldots, x^0_I)$ is intended to mean $x'_i \geqslant x^0_i$ for each $i = 1, \ldots, I$. Similarly, $x' > x^0$ is short for $x'_i > x^0_i$, where $i = 1, \ldots, I$. There is no relationship between notation employed in Appendix A (Mathematical Notes) and that appearing in the text.

1.5 ELASTICITY

With the exception of Section 4.3 and several exercises, little attention in subsequent chapters is paid to the concept of elasticity. Because it is convenient, most propositions concerning properties of elasticities are stated in terms of ordinary derivatives instead. Translations of these results into the language of elasticity are quite simple and left to the reader. Nevertheless, elasticity is still sufficiently important in the Walrasian theory of market behavior and its applications to warrant brief consideration here. To expedite matters, attention centers on elasticity in relation to the demand curve introduced in Section 1.3. Elasticities pertaining to alternative curves and surfaces are handled analogously.

Let (x, p) and (x', p') lie on the demand curve described by the demand function H in (1.3-1). Suppose H to be differentiable. The *price elasticity of demand* $\varepsilon(x)$ at x is given by

$$\varepsilon(x) = - \lim_{x' \to x} \frac{\dfrac{x' - x}{x}}{\dfrac{p' - p}{p}}. \tag{1.5-1}$$

Loosely speaking, $\varepsilon(x)$ is the limit (corrected for sign so as not to be negative) of percentage changes in quantity divided by percentage changes in price arising from movement between (x', p') and (x, p) along H. Denoting the inverse of H by H^{-1} and the derivative of the inverse by $H^{-1'}$ (geometrically, the latter is the slope of the demand curve as pictured in Figure 1.2), equation (1.5-1) may be written as

$$\varepsilon(x) = -\frac{1}{H^{-1'}(x)} \frac{H^{-1}(x)}{x}. \tag{1.5-2}$$

In other words, because the reciprocal of $H^{-1'}$ is also the derivative of H, the elasticity $\varepsilon(x)$ is the derivative of the demand function adjusted for both sign and the point on the demand curve at which the elasticity is evaluated. Note that $\varepsilon(x)$ generally varies along the curve. Furthermore, $(x' - x)/x$ is measured in units of x divided by units of x, or no units at all. The same is true of $(p' - p)/p$. Therefore $\varepsilon(x)$ is also a unitless or pure number. It follows that the elasticity of demand for, say, potatoes is identical at x regardless of whether quantities of potatoes are measured in millions of tons and the price of potatoes in pennies per million tons, or whether quantities are reckoned in pounds and price in thousands of dollars per pound. By contrast, the slope of the demand curve for potatoes as identified by $H^{-1'}$ (along with the reciprocal slope obtained from the derivative H') does depend on the units of calibration employed, because in the first instance the demand curve is relatively steep at x (a one-unit fall in price is not likely to increase demand by many millions of tons), and in the second it is relatively flat at x (a one-unit price decline would probably increase demand by a very large number of pounds). This is the reason economists often work with elasticities rather than with unadjusted derivatives.

Total revenue (TR) and marginal revenue (MR) along the demand curve are notions specifically related to elasticity. They are characterized, respectively, as follows:

$$TR(x) = xp = xH^{-1}(x), \tag{1.5-3}$$

$$MR(x) = \frac{dTR(x)}{dx} = H^{-1}(x) + xH^{-1'}(x), \tag{1.5-4}$$

where $p = H^{-1}(x)$. Combining (1.5-2) and (1.5-4),

$$MR(x) = p\left(1 - \frac{1}{\varepsilon(x)}\right). \tag{1.5-5}$$

Five degrees of elasticity are defined in terms of the numerical values of the coefficient of elasticity, as indicated in Table 1.2. The relationships between $\varepsilon(x)$, $H^{-1}(x)$, $TR(x)$ and $MR(x)$ derived from (1.5-1) − (1.5-5) are also summarized there. Moreover, if the demand curve is linear, then it is easy to demonstrate (Exercise 1.2) that the marginal revenue curve is also linear with vertical MR-intercept identical to that of the demand curve and horizontal x-intercept exactly half that of the demand curve. The relationships of Table 1.2 in this case are illustrated in Figure 1.3. Note that the vertical axis in Figure 1.3 really has two scales superimposed upon it: Total revenue is measured in dollars on one, and marginal revenue and price are measured in dollars per unit of the commodity on the other.

EXERCISES

1.1 Suppose demand and supply functions are given, respectively, by the equations

$$H(p) = (p - 1)^3 + 1,$$

$$G(p) = p,$$

for $p \geqslant 0$. Find all equilibria.

1.2 Prove that if the demand curve described by the inverse of $x = H(p)$ is

Table 1.2 Summary of relationships between $\varepsilon(x)$, $H^{-1'}(x)$, $TR(x)$, and $MR(x)$ along a demand curve

	At a point, x, on a demand curve which is				
	Perfectly inelastic	Inelastic	Unitarily elastic	Elastic	Perfectly elastic
Coefficient of elasticity	$\varepsilon(x) = 0$	$0 < \varepsilon(x) < 1$	$\varepsilon(x) = 1$	$1 < \varepsilon(x) < \infty$	$\varepsilon(x) = \infty$ (undefined)
Slope of demand curve $[H^{-1'}(x)]$	vertical	negative	negative	negative	horizontal
Slope of total revenue curve $[MR(x)]$	undefined	less than p at $p = H^{-1'}(x)$ and			p
		negative	0	positive	
As x moves along the demand curve	TR(x) and price move in the same direction		$TR(x)$ is constant	$TR(x)$ and price move in opposite directions	$TR(x)$ and quantity move in the same direction

linear and downward sloping, then the marginal revenue curve is also linear and downward sloping with vertical MR-intercept the same as that of the demand curve, and horizontal x-intercept exactly half that of the demand curve.

1.3 Show that the demand function $H(p) = \alpha/p$, where α is a positive constant, is unitarily elastic everywhere. Compute the total revenue and marginal revenue functions.

1.4 Define the *price elasticity of supply* as in (1.5-1) except, in deference to the supply function G, replace H by G and delete the minus sign. What are the analogues of (1.5-2) – (1.5-5)? Show that the supply function $G(p) = \alpha p$, where α is a positive constant, has unitary elasticity everywhere. Reproduce Table 1.2 and the counterpart to Figure 1.3 in terms of upward-sloping supply curves.

1.5 Let $A = (p', x')$ and $B = (p'', x'')$ denote the coordinates of two points on the demand curve described by the inverse of $x = H(p)$. Assume $H'(p)$

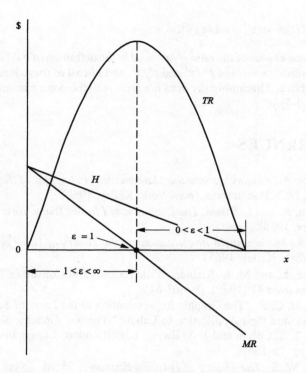

Figure 1.3 Total revenue, marginal revenue, and elasticity
for a linear demand curve

exists continuously and is negative for all $p > 0$. Define the *arc price elasticity of demand* between A and B by

$$\varepsilon_{AB} = -\frac{x' - x''}{p' - p''}\frac{p'}{x''}.$$

Write the marginal revenue between these points as

$$MR_{AB} = \frac{TR(x') - TR(x'')}{x' - x''}.$$

If $p' > p''$ (and hence $x' < x''$), show that

    i) In the limit ε_{AB} approaches $\varepsilon(x')$ as x'' approaches x'.

    ii) $\varepsilon_{AB} \lesseqqgtr 1$ according as $TR(x') \gtreqqless TR(x'')$.

iii) $MR_{AB} = p'[1 - 1/\varepsilon_{AB}]$.

(Note that the choice of the ratio p'/x'' used in the definition of ε_{AB} is arbitrary. Other possibilities include p''/x' and p'/x', and not all of these lead to results (i) – (iii) above. This ambiguity does not arise with the point elasticity concept $\varepsilon(x)$ of (1.5-1).)

REFERENCES

1. Cournot, A., *Researches into the Mathematical Principles of the Theory of Wealth*, N. T. Bacon trans, (New York: Kelley, 1960).
2. Einstein, A. and L. Infeld, *The Evolution of Physics* (New York: Simon & Schuster, 1938).
3. Fisher, I., *Mathematical Investigations in the Theory of Value and Prices* (New York: Kelley, 1965).
4. Hurwicz, L. and M. K. Richter, "Ville Axioms and Consumer Theory," *Econometrica* 47 (1979), pp. 603-619.
5. Jenkin, H. C. F., "The Graphic Representation of the Laws of Supply and Demand, and their Application to Labour," *Papers: Literary, Scientific, etc.*, v. 2, S. Colvin and J. A. Ewing, eds. (London: Longmans Green, 1887), pp. 76-106.
6. Jevons, W. S., *The Theory of Political Economy*, 5th ed. (New York: Kelley, 1965).
7. Katzner, D. W., *Static Demand Theory* (New York: Macmillan, 1970).
8. Keynes, J. M., "Letter to R.F. Harrod on July 4, 1938," *Collected Writings*, v. 14, D. Moggridge, ed. (London: Macmillan, 1973), pp. 295-297.
9. Machlup, F., "Theories of the Firm: Marginalist, Behavioral, Managerial," *American Economic Review* 57 (1967), pp. 1-33.
10. Marshall, A., *Principles of Economics*, 8th ed. (New York: Macmillan, 1948).
11. Mill, J. S., *A System of Logic* (London: Longmans, 1970).
12. ——, *Principles of Political Economy with some of Their Applications to Social Philosophy*, V. W. Bladen and J. M. Robson, eds. (Toronto: University of Toronto Press, 1965).
13. Mirowski, P., *More Heat than Light* (Cambridge: Cambridge University Press, 1989).
14. Ricardo, D., *On the Principles of Political Economy and Taxation*, P. Sraffa and M. H. Dobb, eds. (London: Cambridge University Press, 1951).

15. Robbins, L., *An Essay on the Nature and Significance of Economic Science*, 2nd ed. (London: Macmillan, 1952).
16. Ryle, G., *The Concept of Mind* (London: Hutchinson, 1949).
17. Schumpeter, J. A., *History of Economic Analysis* (New York: Oxford University Press, 1954).
18. Smith, A., *An Inquiry into the Nature and Causes of the Wealth of Nations* (New York: Random House, 1937).
19. Walras, L., *Elements of Pure Economics*, W. Jaffé trans. (Homewood: Irwin, 1954).
20. Winch, P., *The Idea of a Social Science* (London: Routledge and Kegan Paul, 1958).

Chapter 2

The Theory of Demand:
Utility Maximization

The theory of demand may be regarded either as a theory in its own right or as a subtheory of the Walrasian theory of market behavior.[1] As the former, its intent is to explain observed[2] behavior of individual consumers in markets. In so doing it provides the basis for estimating and predicting actual demand.[3]

---

[1] A similar assertion holds for the theory of the firm and the theory of the operation of an isolated market.

[2] Recall the distinction between observables and unobservables introduced in Section 1.2. Observables show up as economic data (namely, prices and quantities). Unobservables are taken as unknown to the economist.

[3] Tests of the empirical viability of demand theory to date are inconclusive. One of the more appropriate and remarkable tests was proposed (but never executed) by Lloyd. In his words, "the project was to be a controlled experiment conducted in a permanent real village that is isolated from the rest of the world through much of the year. The village has a single store which is government owned. In early fall a shipload of commodities is received by the store and shortly thereafter winter sets in isolating the village from commercial traffic. Because the store practices cost-plus pricing all the prices in the community are fixed through the winter months. We were granted permission to control and alter prices within the store. We were also granted permission to station observers in the store in order to observe consumer's reactions to such alterations in price. We planned to compensate consumers for price changes and by observing their reactions, to directly test ... [the weak axiom of revealed preference] ... as an implication of the theory of consumer demand." [8, pp. 1, 2]. Deaton and Muellbauer [2] survey much of

As the latter, it furnishes a source for the demand equations employed in the Walrasian theory of market behavior. By relating consumer activity to human wants and desires, it contributes to a deeper understanding of economic activity than would be available if the demand equations were assumed merely to be given. In either context demand theory also acts as a guide for comparing the welfare of consumers under alternative circumstances when the term "welfare" is construed narrowly to arise solely from the consumption of material goods and services.

This chapter and the one succeeding it treat the theory of demand as an independent theory.[4] Such an approach permits the introduction of a wider variety of ideas and makes certain topics discussed later on easier to expound. Furthermore, everything required for the Walrasian theory of market behavior is obtained in the process. In both cases the models presented are timeless. Of course they may be interpreted as describing the stationary path of an appropriate, though unspecified, dynamic system (Section 1.3). Appropriate conclusions, then, would be of the comparative statics variety.

The observed behavior the theory of demand seeks to explain is summarized in the concept of individual demand function. Although such functions often are defined with respect to constrained utility maximization, it is worth considering a preliminary, more general characterization first. Thus let x_i vary over quantities of commodity i, chosen, consumed, or demanded by a given individual. Suppose this consumer has m dollars to spend and the price of the ith good is p_i. Frequently m is referred to as the consumer's *income*. Both prices and income appear as independent variables in the consumer's demand function. The usual assumption is that the individual has no control over them and hence, in so far as his decision making is concerned, regards them as "fixed." There are I goods, so that $i = 1, \ldots, I$. The demand function, h^i, for the ith good indicates, for each collection of positive prices $p_1, \ldots, p_I$ and income m, the quantity x_i chosen by the consumer. It is written

$$x_i = h^i(p_1, \ldots, p_I, m),$$

and there is one for each $i = 1, \ldots, I$. Using the vector notation $x = (x_1, \ldots, x_I)$, $p = (p_1, \ldots, p_I)$ and $h = (h^1, \ldots, h^I)$, this can be shortened to

$$x_i = h^i(p, m), \qquad i = 1, \ldots, I,$$

and the entire system of functions for the individual consumer can be

the literature relating to both the testing of demand theory and the estimation of demand.
[4]   Chapters 4 and 5, and Chapter 6 apporoach, respectively, the theory of the firm and the theory of an isolated market in the same way.

abbreviated as

$$x = h(p, m). \qquad (2.0\text{-}1)$$

The vector x often is called a "basket" or "bundle" of commodities. Because in practice only a finite number of points of h can ever be seen, the observable domain and range of h are finite.

The purpose of the theory of demand, then, is to explain observed demand functions and in so doing to provide insight into consumer choice. But it does much more than focus on only a finite number of observations. Rather it attempts to provide an understanding of all conceivable observations which could arise for the same person. Thus, although only bits and pieces of it can actually be seen, the theory explains a demand function whose domain is $\{(p, m) : (p, m) > 0\}$, and whose range is $\{x : x \geqslant 0\}$. In particular, it describes what commodities the consumer will purchase and in what quantities at any possible $(p, m) > 0$, and how these commodities and quantities change when (p, m) varies.

Much (though by no means all) of the analysis of the theory of demand can be identified with either of two lines of argument. In the first instance, it is assumed that the consumer has preferences among baskets of commodities, that these preferences have certain characteristics, and that in demanding baskets the consumer is "rational." From the economist's point of view, none of these elements — preferences, their properties, or rationality — can be seen directly. Furthermore, different kinds of preferences satisfying the "certain characteristics" generate different behavior. But in all such cases, regardless of the specific preferences involved, the same general properties of demand functions are always implied. Thus if, in fact, an individual's demand behavior were observed, it would be possible to tell if the demand functions actually describing that behavior were consistent with these assumptions without knowing anything about his preferences at all. If a consumer's observed functions do not exhibit the required properties, then the theory provides no insight into his behavior. This line of reasoning moves from preferences to demand. It places heavy emphasis on the derivation of the characteristics of demand implied by the characteristics of preferences, and it is the main concern of the present chapter.

The second line of reasoning (considered briefly with other items in Chapter 3) pursues the opposite direction from demand functions back to preferences. It reconstructs unseeable preferences and their characteristics from those demand functions satisfying the properties derived in the first line of argument.[5] Because they explain his behavior, the reconstructed preferences can be taken to be those of the consumer in question — even though they might not, in fact, be his. In the same way, the model of the clock in Section 1.2 can be taken to describe the workings of the clock, regardless of whether that is actually the case, because the observed behavior of each is identical.

Of course, the proposition that a consumer's observable behavior can be understood as if he were a utility maximizer is quite different from the statement that, in fact, the intent of his behavior is to maximize utility. The former is an assertion about the possible relevance of a model; the latter says something unknowable to the economist about what actually goes on in the consumer's mind. Still, the stage is now set for the introspective inference that there is such a purpose behind the consumer's activity. Introspection has already been discussed in Section 1.2. It arises here in the application of demand theory to individual welfare analysis in Section 3.4.

Subsequent development begins with a background discussion in Section 2.1 of the nature of utility functions, preference orderings, and the relationships between them. The ways in which properties of one arise as properties of the other are explored. Next, Section 2.2 digresses to examine the old distinction between ordinal and cardinal utility, and the meaning of interpersonal utility comparisons. The presentation of the first few paragraphs is somewhat terse and is based on more advanced mathematics than that employed elsewhere in this volume. The remainder of the section is more intuitive. Although Section 2.1 is needed for the analysis of revealed preference as developed in Section 3.2, and Section 2.2 provides a foundation for the notions of welfare (Section 3.4 and Chapter 12) and utility, neither is required to follow the reasoning of the so-called "classical" theory of demand examined in Sections 2.3 and 2.4. Of the four sections in this chapter, only Section 2.3 is a part of the particular grand view outlined in Section 1.4. For the time being, the possibilities that the consumer might save income for future consumption or spend a portion of previous savings are ignored.

2.1   PREFERENCES AND UTILITY[6]

In any Walrasian system, individual wants and desires define the ends or goals of that system. The totality of economic activity is, in the final analysis, di-

---

[5]   The idea of constructing preferences from observed behavior dates at least to Jevons' suggestion of it [6, pp. 11, 12]. Jevons himself did not attempt such a construction.

[6]   The reader may wish to peruse appendix Sections A.1 – A.3 before beginning this section.

rected towards their satisfaction. Regardless, to make analytical headway necessitates restricting these wants and desires to satisfy certain properties. The properties imposed represent key assumptions about the nature of individuals.

All relevant information about a consumer's wants and desires is assumed to be summarized in her preference ordering. A *preference ordering*, written $\succsim$, is a binary relation defined on the *commodity space* X, which is reflexive and transitive.[7] To keep matters simple, suppose $X = \{x : x \geqslant 0\}$, where, recall, x is a vector or basket of commodities. The symbol $x' \succsim x''$ is to be read "x' is preferred or indifferent to x''." *Preference* $\succ$ and *indifference* $\approx$ relations can be separated out from $\succsim$ as follows: For all x' and x'' in X,

$$x' \succ x'' \quad \text{if and only if} \quad x' \succsim x'' \text{ and not } x'' \succsim x', \tag{2.1-1}$$

and

$$x' \approx x'' \quad \text{if and only if} \quad \text{both } x' \succsim x'' \text{ and } x'' \succsim x'. \tag{2.1-2}$$

When $x' \succ x''$ or $x' \approx x''$ read, respectively, "x' is preferred to x''," or "x' is indifferent to x''."

The reflexivity and transitivity of $\succsim$ imply that $\succ$ is irreflexive, transitive, and asymmetric, and that $\approx$ is an equivalence relation, that is, reflexive, transitive, and symmetric.[8] To illustrate the reasoning required to establish these properties, consider the problem of demonstrating the transitivity of preference from the assumed transitivity of the preference ordering $\succsim$. Suppose $x' \succ x''$ and $x'' \succ x'''$ for some baskets x', x'', and x''' in X. It is necessary to show $x' \succ x'''$. First notice that $x' \succ x''$ and $x'' \succ x'''$ imply, by (2.1-1), that $x' \succsim x''$ and $x'' \succsim x'''$. Hence $x' \succsim x'''$ from the transitivity of $\succsim$. If it were also true that $x''' \succsim x'$, then combining $x''' \succsim x'$ and $x' \succsim x''$, the transitivity of $\succsim$ would imply that $x''' \succsim x''$. But according to (2.1-1), this last statement is contrary to the assumption that $x'' \succ x'''$. Therefore it cannot be the case that $x''' \succsim x'$. Putting $x' \succsim x'''$ and not $x''' \succsim x'$ together gives $x' \succ x'''$, again by (2.1-1). Hence $\succ$ is transitive. Proofs of the remaining properties are left to the reader (Exercise 2.1).

It is useful to group commodity bundles comparable to each x^0 of X

---

[7] The notions of binary relation, reflexivity, and transitivity are defined in appendix Section A.2.

[8] These concepts also are defined in appendix Section A.2.

under $\succsim$ in specific sets as follows:

$$C_{x^0}^{>} = \{x : x \succ x^0\},$$

$$C_{x^0}^{\geq} = \{x : x \succsim x^0\},$$

$$C_{x^0}^{<} = \{x : x^0 \succ x\},$$

$$C_{x^0}^{\leq} = \{x : x^0 \succsim x\},$$

$$C_{x^0}^{=} = \{x : x \approx x^0\},$$

where x is in X. These are, respectively, the collection of points "better than," "at least as good as," "worse than," "at least as bad as," and "indifferent to" x^0. When $C_{x^0}^{=}$ shrinks to an $I - 1$ dimensional surface in X it is called the *indifference surface* through x^0. If there is exactly one indifference surface through every basket in X, then the class of all such surfaces is referred to as the *indifference map*. For the special case in which $I = 2$, indifference surfaces become one-dimensional curves called *indifference curves*.

In practically all cases, economists translate preference information into a utility function context before doing anything with it. This is because the substitution of a numerical function for $\succsim$ permits use of mathematical techniques that are more familiar and that historically have provided simple derivations of certain standard results. Although such translations necessitate restrictions on $\succsim$ in addition to reflexivity and transitivity, these extra conditions usually are required anyway to derive typical conclusions directly when avoiding the utility function route. To understand what is involved in passing from preference orderings to utility functions, the logical connection between them has to be clarified.

A preference ordering $\succsim$ is called *representable* whenever there exists a function u mapping X into the real line such that for all x' and x'' in X,

$$x' \succsim x'' \quad \text{if and only if} \quad u(x') \geq u(x''). \tag{2.1-3}$$

The function u representing $\succsim$ is referred to as a *utility function* or *representation*. Denote the image of x under u by μ and write $\mu = u(x)$. It is clear (Exercise 2.2) from (2.1-1) – (2.1-3) that representability of $\succsim$ implies that for all x' and x'' in X,

$$x' \succ x'' \quad \text{if and only if} \quad u(x') > u(x''),$$

and

$$x' \approx x'' \quad \text{if and only if} \quad u(x') = u(x'').$$

Suppose $\succsim$ is represented by u. Let $\tau(\mu)$ be any *increasing transformation* (not necessarily linear) of the range of u into the reals, that is,

$$\mu' \geqslant \mu'' \quad \text{if and only if} \quad \tau(\mu') \geqslant \tau(\mu''), \qquad (2.1\text{-}4)$$

for all μ' and μ''. Consider any x' and x'' in X and set $\mu' = u(x')$ and $\mu'' = u(x'')$ for appropriately chosen μ' and μ''. Then from (2.1-3) and (2.1-4),

$$x' \succsim x'' \quad \text{if and only if} \quad u(x') \geqslant u(x''),$$

$$\text{if and only if} \quad \mu' \geqslant \mu'',$$

$$\text{if and only if} \quad \tau(\mu') \geqslant \tau(\mu''),$$

$$\text{if and only if} \quad \tau(u(x')) \geqslant \tau(u(x'')).$$

Hence, according to (2.1-3), the composite function $\tau \circ u$, where $\tau \circ u(x) = \tau(u(x))$ for all x, also represents $\succsim$, and the following proposition has been established:

Theorem 2.1-5 u represents $\succsim$ if and only if $\tau \circ u$ represents $\succsim$ where τ is any increasing transformation of the range of u.

Note also that with u representing $\succsim$, the utility of all baskets of commodities is determinate. Hence given any two baskets, it is possible to tell which is preferable by looking at their utility values. From (2.1-3), then, all baskets x in X are comparable under $\succsim$. In other words $\succsim$ is total.[9] Thus, although totality is not required in the definition of $\succsim$, totality must be present when $\succsim$ is representable. However, reflexivity, transitivity, and totality by themselves are still not sufficient to guarantee that $\succsim$ is representable. This is illustrated by the *lexicographic* ordering characterized for $I = 2$ as

$$x' \succsim x'' \quad \text{if and only if} \quad \text{either} \begin{cases} x_1' > x_1'', \quad \text{or} \\ \\ x_1' = x_1'' \quad \text{and} \quad x_2' \geqslant x_2'', \end{cases} \qquad (2.1\text{-}6)$$

for all $x' = (x_1', x_2')$ and $x'' = (x_1'', x_2'')$ in X. A picture appears in Figure 2.1 in which both bundles x' are preferred to x''. Observe that (2.1-6) implies that

---

[9] Totality is defined in appendix Section A.2.

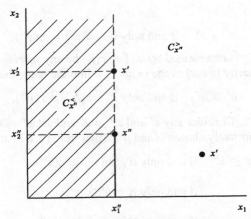

Figure 2.1 Lexicographic preferences

no two distinct points of X can be indifferent. The lexicographic ordering is reflexive, transitive, and total. Yet a real-valued function representing it cannot exist. Loosely speaking, to represent such an ordering requires, because no distinct points can be indifferent, the assignment of a unique real number to each point in X. However, because every vertical line in Figure 2.1 would then have to be mapped into a disjoint interval, and because the number of such intervals is countable but the number of vertical lines is uncountable, there are not enough real numbers to go around.[10] Therefore, to ensure representability in general, it is necessary to assume that $\succsim$ has properties in addition to reflexivity, transitivity, and totality. One form these extra conditions may take appears in the assertion below. It is stated without proof. In that statement, the *interior* of X is the subset $\{x : x > 0\}$.

Theorem 2.1-7 Let $\succsim$ be a total preference ordering on X. If either $C_x^>$ is open relative to the interior of X for every x, or $C_x^<$ is open relative to the interior of X for every x, then $\succsim$ is representable.[11]

In the lexicographic case described in Figure 2.1, neither $C_{x''}^<$ (the shaded region including the heavy line above x_1'' up to x'') nor $C_{x''}^>$ (the unshaded region plus the dashed line above x'') are relatively open because the "interior"

---

[10]   A formal proof is given by Katzner [7, p. 18].

[11]   For a proof see Katzner [7, p. 19]. Relatively open sets are defined in appendix Section A.1.

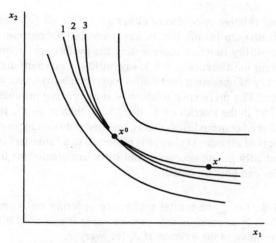

Figure 2.2 Indifference map obtained from a utility
function with a discontinuity at x^0

boundary dividing them is partly in one set and partly in the other. Hence Theorem 2.1-7 does not apply. It should also be emphasized that representability
does not require the relative openness of both $C_x^>$ and $C_x^<$ for every x in X.
A two dimensional example is provided in Figure 2.2. The indifference curves
pictured there can be thought of as derived from a utility function with a discontinuity at x^0. The underlying preference ordering, then, is representable.
As drawn, x^0 lies on the indifference curve labeled 1. Curves like 2 and 3
would be tangent to 1 at x^0 were they defined there. But they are not. Each has
a "hole" at x^0. All other indifference curves are of the usual variety. Although
$C_x^>$ is open (and hence relatively open) for every x, the set, say, $C_{x'}^<$ contains
x^0 and cannot, therefore, be open relative to the interior of X. A similar illustration is secured by placing x^0 on curve 3 and leaving holes in curves 1 and 2.
Now all $C_x^<$ are relatively open, but certain $C_x^>$ contain x^0. These latter sets
are not open relative to the interior of X.

It turns out, however, that representability is still not enough. For most
purposes, utility functions normally are taken to be at least continuous.[12] A
preference ordering is said to be *continuously representable* whenever there
exists a continuous utility function representing it. (However, not all representations can be continuous. See Exercise 2.4) The previous example shows

---

[12]   A definition of continuity appears in appendix Section A.3.

that totality and relative openness of either all $C_x^>$ or all $C_x^<$ (and hence representability itself) are insufficient to imply continuous representability. Regardless of the utility function representing the preference ordering shown in Figure 2.2, along indifference curve 3, say, utility is constant until it jumps at x^0. A simple way of obtaining continuous representability starts with a preliminary definition: The preference relation $\succ$ is *increasing* provided that for all distinct x' and x'' in the interior of X, if $x' \geqslant x''$, then $x' \succ x''$. In other words a "larger" basket of commodities (that is, one that contains more of at least one good and no less of all others) always is preferred to a "smaller" one. A formal proposition actually giving necessary and sufficient conditions for continuous representability can now be stated:

Theorem 2.1-8 Let $\succsim$ be a total preference ordering on X such that $\succ$ is increasing. Then $\succsim$ is continuously representable if and only if both $C_x^>$ and $C_x^<$ are open relative to the interior of X for every x.

Although the mathematics needed to establish Theorem 2.1-8 is too advanced for presentation here, it is still worth sketching two methods of constructing continuous utility functions, either of which could be employed as the basis for a proof.[13] The lack of detail below, however, should not obscure the fact that neither construction yields a continuous representation of $\succsim$ unless the hypotheses of the theorem are in force. Referring to Figure 2.3, let x be any bundle in X. Because $\succ$ is increasing, no two indifference curves in the interior of X can touch or intersect (Exercise 2.29). Hence the indifference map partitions the interior of the commodity space into mutually exclusive and exhaustive sets (*i.e.*, the indifference curves). Moreover, the indifference curve through x, namely $C_x^=$, must intersect the 45° ray at some point x^0. Hence the utility of x can be defined as either the last, say, coordinate of x^0 or the linear distance from x^0 to the origin. In both cases the utility function described can be shown to be continuous. Note that these constructions do not depend on the second-order dimensionality of the commodity space employed in Figure 2.3.

Continuity, of course, is not the only general property that utility functions might have. Thus u would be

    i) *quasi-concave*[14] if for any x' and x'' in X and any real number θ where $0 \leqslant \theta \leqslant 1$, the equality $u(x') = u(x'')$ implied $u(\theta x' + [1 - \theta]x'') \geqslant u(x')$.

---

13   A proof of Theorem 2.1-8 using one of these constructions appears in Katzner [7, p. 22].
14   This concept is discussed and illustrated in appendix Section A.3.

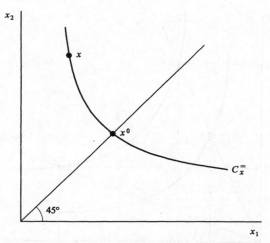

Figure 2.3 Utility of x defined as the distance from
the origin to x^0 or as the value of the second
coordinate of x^0

ii) *strictly quasi-concave* on the interior of X if for any distinct x' and x''
in the interior of X and any real number θ where $0 < \theta < 1$, the equality $u(x') = u(x'')$ implied $u(\theta x' + [1 - \theta]x'') > u(x')$.

iii) *linearly homogeneous* if $u(\alpha x) = \alpha u(x)$ for all x in X and any real
number $\alpha > 0$.

iv) *increasing* if for any x' and x'' in the interior of X which are distinct,
$x' \geqslant x''$ implied $u(x') > u(x'')$.

Observe that definitions (ii) and (iv) are restricted to the interior of the commodity space. If this were not done, then no two points on the same hyperplane
bounding X could be indifferent as long as the utility function were increasing
or strictly quasi-concave.

These characteristics all have counterparts in terms of preference orderings. The idea of an increasing $\succ$ has already been introduced a few paragraphs
back. Furthermore, $\succsim$ is

i) *convex* if for any x' and x'' in X and any real number θ where $0 \leqslant \theta \leqslant$
1, the statement that $x' \approx x''$ implies $\theta x' + (1 - \theta)x'' \succsim x'$.

ii) *strictly convex* on the interior of X if for any distinct x' and x'' in
the interior of X and any real number θ where $0 < \theta < 1$, the state-

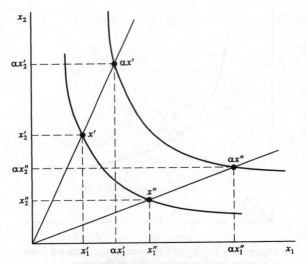

Figure 2.4 Homothetic preferences

ment that $x' \approx x''$ implies $\theta x' + (1 - \theta)x'' \succ x'$.

   iii) *homothetic* if for any x' and x'' in X, the statement $x' \approx x''$ implies $\alpha x' \approx \alpha x''$ for any real number $\alpha > 0$.

The same reason given in terms of utility functions for restricting definition (ii) and that of increasingness to the interior of X applies here. Note that homotheticity means that any pair of indifferent points each on a separate ray from the origin remain indifferent upon modification in like proportion or, loosely speaking, that indifference curves are "parallel" with respect to the origin. See Figure 2.4 for a two-dimensional illustration. (In this diagram the symbols x', x'', and α refer to the definition of homothetic preferences given above.)

   When $\succsim$ is representable, increasingness of $\succ$ and convexity and strict convexity of $\succsim$ are equivalent, respectively, to increasingness, quasi-concavity and strict quasi-concavity of all representations. Convexity of $\succsim$ also implies that $C_x^{\succeq}$ and $C_x^{\succ}$ are convex sets[15] for every x. Furthermore, if u is a concave function,[16] then it is also quasi-concave (Exercise 2.7), but not conversely: The utility function

$$u(x_1, x_2) = (x_1 x_2)^2,$$

---

[15]   Convex sets are defined in appendix Section A.1.

[16]   Concave functions are defined and discussed in appendix Section A.3.

is quasi-concave but not concave. Although in this case there is an increasing transformation, namely,

$$\tau(\mu) = \mu^{1/4},$$

which upon application to u yields a concave representation, such transformations do not exist in general.[17] Finally, for the case in which $\succsim$ is continuously representable and $\succ$ is increasing, it may be asserted that $\succsim$ is homothetic if and only if there exists a linearly homogeneous representation of it.[18] But regardless of whether $\succ$ is increasing, not all representations of homothetic preference orderings can be linearly homogeneous. For example, the square of any linearly homogeneous representation is a distinct representation of the same preference ordering that is not linearly homogeneous.

  Further properties of preference orderings and representations will be introduced as needed.

2.2   ORDINAL UTILITY, CARDINAL UTILITY, AND INTERPERSONAL COMPARISONS[19]

The questions of whether the utility of a basket of commodities (or some other object) can be measured on a cardinal scale as opposed to an ordinal scale, and whether these scales are comparable across persons, have only recently been asked. Before the twentieth century few economists had concerned themselves with such issues. From the Benthamites to Marshall, utility was thought of as a cardinal measure of pleasure, and this view tended to persist even after the 1890s when Fisher [5] and Pareto [10] showed that increasing transformations of the utility function have no impact on demand. Indeed, analyses implicitly (if not explicitly) requiring cardinal utility and interpersonal utility comparisons continue today. It was the positivists emerging after the First World War who argued that, because cardinality could not be expressed in terms of economic data knowable to the economist, it should not be assumed. Moreover, they went on, because of the necessity to rely on value judgments, interpersonal utility comparisons should not be made either. Although not germane to the argument of the present chapter, the ideas involved become important

---

[17]   Katzner [7, p. 218].
[18]   Katzner [7, p. 24].
[19]   Because this section is (insofar as the argument of Chapter 2 is concerned) a digression, and because it is, in part, mathematically demanding, the reader may want to postpone it until Chapter 2 has been completed. Doing so will not make Sections 2.3 and 2.4 more difficult to follow.

in Section 3.4 and Chapter 12. The following, then, is a digression concerned with the meaning of the notions of ordinal and cardinal utility and interpersonal utility comparisons.

Before addressing the main issues, it is well to consider a brief outline of the mathematics of measurement. Unfortunately there is not space enough to define all terms employed and to develop proofs. The interested reader is referred to Pfanzagl [11].

Let A be a collection of objects of which it is desired to measure the appearance of a given property in each. Suppose the property induces a relation ρ ordering the elements of A. Assume ρ is reflexive, transitive, and total. (Thus, in the same way that $\succsim$ generates $\approx$ in (2.1-2), ρ determines an equivalence relation which, in turn, partitions A into mutually exclusive and exhaustive equivalence classes.) Suppose further that the property also induces a closed operation, $\cdot$, on A. Such an operation is called *additive* if it is associative, commutative, cancellable, and continuous in each variable separately.

A *scale* is a function σ mapping A into the reals such that $a' \rho \, a''$ if and only if $\sigma(a') \geqslant \sigma(a'')$, for all a' and a'' in A. It is referred to as *ordinal* if it is (i) continuous and (ii) unique up to continuous and increasing transformations of its range into the reals. The scale is *cardinal* (or *interval*) if it is continuous and unique up to increasing linear transformations of its range into the reals.[20] Two results central to the present discussion are as follows:

---

[20]   Two additional types of scales are worthy of note. First, if ρ has the property that it assigns elements of A to categories but does not order the members of one category with respect to those of any other (this could be so if totality were dropped and, along with reflexivity and transitivity, ρ were also symmetric), then σ is called *nominal*. Nominal scales are completely arbitrary and, in the present context, always exist. To obtain the second, observe that a linear transformation

$$\tau(\mu) = \alpha\mu + \beta,$$

where α and β are real numbers, is called a *positive dilation* whenever $\alpha > 0$ and $\beta = 0$. Now σ is a *ratio* scale if it is continuous and unique up to positive dilations of its range into the reals. Ratio scales are also cardinal, ordinal, and nominal; cardinal scales are ordinal and nominal; and ordinal scales are nominal. The extra sufficient conditions beyond those securing cardinality (Theorem 2.2-2) which ensure the existence of ratio scales express the idea, at the level of the set A, that all admissible transformations of scale leave the zero unchanged.

The differences between nominal, ordinal, cardinal, and ratio scales can be illuminated by an example. Think of two pieces of wood and suppose piece R is 2 feet long and piece S is 10 feet long. Consider the following statements: (i) R and S have different lengths. (ii) S is longer than R. (iii) S is 8 feet longer than R. (iv) S is five times as long as R. Since longness, in fact, is measured as length on a ratio scale, all four statements are valid. If only the first three were meaningful (as in the case of temperature scales such as Fahrenheit), then length would be a cardinal (not ratio) measure of longness. When just (i) and (ii) hold, the scale is ordinal. And with (i) alone it is nominal.

Theorem 2.2-1 An ordinal scale representing ρ on A exists if and only if the interval topology for the equivalence classes under ρ has a countable base.

Theorem 2.2-2 Let A be connected and contain at least two elements. If $\cdot$ is additive, then there exists a cardinal scale such that for all a' and a'' in A,

$$\sigma(a' \cdot a'') = \alpha\sigma(a') + \beta\sigma(a'') + \gamma,$$

where α, β, and γ are constants, and α and β are determined uniquely.

As an example, suppose "longness" of the elements of A is the property to be measured. Then ρ orders A's objects according to their longness and the operation $\cdot$ reflects the lining up of these objects end to end. The scale σ measures longness in units of length. Its ordinality guarantees that objects with greater longnesses are assigned more units of length when measured. The cardinality of σ ensures that when two objects are lined up end to end, the length of the combined objects is the sum of the lengths of each separately. Having scales on which to measure properties like height (length) and weight, functions relating, say, the weights of individuals to their heights can be investigated. Note that both height and weight are measured on independent scales. Such relations between them (that is, between the scale numbers) can take on any relevant characteristics and assume any appropriate shape.

The question of whether utility is ordinal or cardinal has to do with the kind of scale upon which the elements of the range of u are measured. As with length and weight, it is not at all related to the shape of the graph u describes in mapping commodity bundles into utility (that is, real) numbers.[21]

Let A be a collection of objects capable of providing what historically has been called "pleasure" to the consumer. The sets X (the commodity space) and A are not related in any particular way. The set A is merely a general set to be used as the basis for constructing a scale on which pleasure is measured in units of "utils." Assume that some relation ρ (in the mind of the consumer) orders the objects of A by pleasure. Suppose ρ is reflexive, transitive, and total. If the additional requirement of Theorem 2.2-1 also is fulfilled, then there exists an ordinal scale for measuring pleasure. The scale is unique up to increasing and continuous transformations. When a utility function u is present, it maps baskets of X into measured pleasure μ. As indicated in Section 2.1, u is associated with a preference ordering, $\succsim$, that it represents. In representing $\succsim$, u over X is unique up to increasing transformations. But that fact is

---

[21]   This approach to cardinal utility is quite different from that proposed by Debreu [3, p. 21], which turns on additivity of the utility function.

not connected to the independent fact that, in representing ρ, the ordinal scale over A is unique up to increasing, continuous transformations, even though the elements of the range of u are measured on this same ordinal scale.

Now suppose that a closed, additive operation $\cdot$ (again, present only in the mind of the consumer) also is defined on A. Then under the appropriate conditions, Theorem 2.2-2 certifies the existence of a cardinal scale. Thus the measurement of pleasure is unique up to increasing linear transformations while, at the same time, the elements of the range of u, which are measured on the same scale, are generated by a function (representing $\succsim$ over X) that is unique only up to arbitrary increasing transformations.

This introduces a conceptual difficulty into the utility measurement problem. For there is something wrong with thinking of the elements of the range of u as determined up to linear transformations by virtue of the cardinality of the scale on which they are measured, while the utility function itself is determined only up to arbitrary increasing transformations (Theorem 2.1-5). To see why, note that because subtraction on A can be defined in terms of addition (that is, $\cdot$), "differences" in pleasure are ordered by ρ and measured on the cardinal scale. To be consistent, then, the same should be true of pleasure derived from baskets of commodities in X. But if u is unique only up to increasing transformations, then in spite of the cardinal scale, the ordering of differences such as

$$u(x') - u(x''),$$

where x' and x'' are in X, depends on the choice of the utility representation. The problem disappears if all nonlinear transformations are excluded (Exercise 2.9). Therefore, in addition to hypotheses yielding the cardinality of the scale upon which pleasure is measured, it is necessary to assume further that u is determined up to increasing linear transformations.

It turns out that insofar as observable behavior is concerned, the assumptions implying cardinal utility are of little help in understanding demand activity. Neither the type of utility scale nor the particular utility representation employed seems to matter. Information of this sort is not expressible in terms of preferences and hence is lost in the theoretical passage from utility to demand. Nevertheless, cardinality does play a role in the analysis of individual and group welfare, as it also does in certain formulations of utility functions representing preference orderings defined over uncertain outcomes. The latter issue has been extensively investigated following the work of von Neumann and Morgenstern [9], but exploration of it lies beyond the scope of the present volume. In addition, cardinality is often bound up in the notion of interpersonal comparisons of utility. These kinds of comparisons are considered next.

Beyond the following discussion, however, ordinal utility always is assumed unless otherwise stated.

Consider the utility scales on A of two persons, say,

$$\sigma^1 : A \to B^1,$$

$$\sigma^2 : A \to B^2,$$

where

$$b_1 = \sigma^1(a),$$

$$b_2 = \sigma^2(a),$$

for a in A, b_1 in B^1, and b_2 in B^2, and where B^1 and B^2 are sets of real numbers. If these scales are cardinal in the sense of Theorem 2.2-2, then for all a' and a'' in A,

$$\sigma^1(a' \cdot a'') = \alpha_1 \sigma^1(a') + \beta_1 \sigma^1(a'') + \gamma_1, \qquad (2.2\text{-}3)$$

$$\sigma^2(a' \cdot a'') = \alpha_2 \sigma^2(a') + \beta_2 \sigma^2(a'') + \gamma_2, \qquad (2.2\text{-}4)$$

where α_1, α_2, β_1, β_2, γ_1 and γ_2 are appropriate constants.

Let a function for combining scales be defined on the Cartesian product of the ranges of σ^1 and σ^2:

$$\nu : B^1 \times B^2 \to B^3,$$

where B^3 is a collection of reals. Write $\sigma = (\sigma^1, \sigma^2)$ and consider the function

$$\nu \circ \sigma : A \to B^3,$$

where

$$\nu \circ \sigma(a) = \nu(\sigma^1(a), \sigma^2(a)),$$

for all a in A. Define a social ordering ρ^* on A by setting, for all a' and a'' in A,

$$a' \rho^* a'' \quad \text{if and only if} \quad \nu \circ \sigma(a') \geqslant \nu \circ \sigma(a'').$$

These definitions ensure that $\nu \circ \sigma$ is an ordinal scale preserving the social ordering ρ^*.

Observe that cardinality of σ^1 and σ^2 is not needed to define $\nu \circ \sigma$ and hence ρ^*. Even if σ^1 and σ^2 were assumed cardinal so that these scales become unique up to continuous linear maps, ρ^* would still depend on the particular choice of them (Exercise 2.24). Thus to obtain a meaningful ordering of the elements of A according to social pleasure by combining scales in which individual pleasure is measured, fixed scales σ^1 and σ^2 must be adopted. Once $\sigma = (\sigma^1, \sigma^2)$ is chosen, the selection of ν can only be made on the basis of value judgments concerning the relative significance of the two individuals in defining the social pleasure scale. (The alternative approach of defining ρ^* directly from the orderings ρ^1 and ρ^2 underlying σ^1 and σ^2 respectively, without using ν or σ, requires equivalent value judgments. Value judgments would also be involved if ρ^* were obtained independently of ρ^1 and ρ^2.) Of course, fixing σ^1 and σ^2 does not mean that $\nu \circ \sigma$ will be cardinal. The following proposition shows how cardinality of $\nu \circ \sigma$ might be derived from that of σ^1 and σ^2.

Theorem 2.2-5 Let σ^1 and σ^2 be cardinal scales in the sense of Theorem 2.2-2. If ν is linear on $B^1 \times B^2$ with $\nu(0) = 0$, and the constants in (2.2-3) and (2.2-4) have the property that $\alpha_1 = \alpha_2$ and $\beta_1 = \beta_2$, then $\nu \circ \sigma$ is cardinal.

Proof: Using, in order, the definition of $\nu \circ \sigma$, equations (2.2-3) and (2.2-4) with $\alpha_1 = \alpha_2$ and $\beta_1 = \beta_2$, the linearity of ν, and the definition of $\nu \circ \sigma$ once again, gives the following string of equalities for any a' and a'' in A:

$$\nu \circ \sigma(a' \cdot a'') = \nu(\sigma^1(a' \cdot a''), \sigma^2(a' \cdot a'')),$$

$$= \nu(\alpha_1 \sigma^1(a') + \beta_1 \sigma^1(a'') + \gamma_1, \alpha_1 \sigma^2(a') + \beta_1 \sigma^2(a'') + \gamma_2),$$

$$= \alpha_1 \nu(\sigma^1(a'), \sigma^2(a')) + \beta_1 \nu(\sigma^1(a''), \sigma^2(a'')) + \nu(\gamma_1, \gamma_2),$$

$$= \alpha_1 [\nu \circ \sigma(a')] + \beta_1 [\nu \circ \sigma(a'')] + \nu(\gamma_1, \gamma_2).$$

This property is preserved only under continuous linear transformations; therefore $\nu \circ \sigma$ is cardinal.

Q.E.D.

Thus the combined social pleasure of persons 1 and 2 can be measured ordinally or cardinally (as the case may be) on the scale $\nu \circ \sigma$ depending, as shown above, on the assumptions employed. Using this scale, social welfare can be studied in terms of a function W mapping, for example, commodity distributions among these two persons into B^3 (see Section 11.1). None of the above imposes any restrictions on W except that if (as argued earlier) $\nu \circ \sigma$ is to be cardinal, then W would be unique up to continuous linear transformations. The graph of W can take on any shape or satisfy any property. The generalization of the argument to more than two persons is obvious.

Note that the choice of the linearity property of scales (that is, equation (2.2-3) or (2.2-4)) as a part of the notion of cardinality — both for pleasure and longness — is arbitrary. In the case of longness, it is easy and convenient (and justifiable by the linearity property) to measure longness with a ruler whose unit length is constant everywhere. More importantly, no problems of meaning arise by doing so. But when dealing with utility, subjective human feelings are involved. There is no obvious rationale for insisting that the units in which pleasure is measured remain constant along the utility scale. Furthermore, why should measured pleasure derived from combining two objects in A be exactly the weighted sum of the measured pleasures of each and not more or less? Such requirements are needed neither for the theory of demand nor to make interpersonal utility comparisons (the definitions ν and $\nu \circ \sigma$ do not rest on the linearity property). Hence there is no compelling reason to use the arbitrary assumption of linearity.

But there is a reason for not assuming linearity. For the kind of utility scale an individual may have is a matter of fact. Such a fact can never be tested against economic data known to the economist; the individual's scale can only be taken to be what he says it is (if, indeed, he is able to say). Thus, because making unnecessary assumptions renders analysis more restrictive than it has to be, alternative notions of cardinality that do not involve linearity ought to be explored. One possibility is to call an ordinal utility scale cardinal if and only if utility differences on that scale are viewed everywhere as meaningful by the consumer. If, for example, $\sigma^1(a') - \sigma^1(a'') = 5$ for some a' and a'' in A, then object a' simply provides 5 more units of pleasure to consumer 1 than a''. It does not matter that the units of measurement may not be constant over the entire scale. Although an ordinal $\nu \circ \sigma$ is obtained as before, cardinality of the social utility scale could be secured similarly at the community level.

Discussion now returns to the main theme of this chapter, namely, the line of argument connecting preferences and utility functions to demand functions.

2.3   THE CLASSICAL MODEL OF UTILITY MAXIMIZATION

Begin with the assumption that the consumer has a representable preference ordering defined on the commodity space. It is implicit that those preferences and all (utility) representations of them are taken to be fixed and invariant with respect to market price and income values. The remaining hypotheses employed in models of utility maximization fall into two categories. First are technical restrictions limiting the preference orderings about which the analysis has something to say. Their purpose is to provide an appropriate setting for the development of the model's line of argument. Thus, for example, relying on the maximization of utility would make no sense if utility functions representing the preferences in question did not possess the required maxima. It is the role of the technical restrictions to ensure that such maxima exist. The model based on the technical restrictions introduced below may be called "classical." It is primarily due to Slutsky [13].

The second category of hypotheses contains but a single assumption, namely, the postulate of rationality. This appears as a maximization type of decision rule employed by the consumer to choose baskets of commodities under various market conditions. It serves as a link connecting preferences with behavior and permits the translation of the technical restrictions into empirically testable properties of demand.

The technical restrictions of the classical model are as follows: Assume the utility function u maps X into the extended real line (that is, the real line plus the "point at infinity").[22] Denote its first- and second-order partial derivatives by, respectively, u_i and u_{in} for $i, n = 1, \ldots, I$.[23] The former, although not independent of the scale on which utility is measured, often are referred to as *marginal utilities*. Suppose further that

(2.3-1) u is continuous where finite on X, where not finite $u(x) = -\infty$ and u declines continuously to $-\infty$ through interior points of X, and u has continuous, second-order partial derivatives everywhere in the interior of X.

(2.3-2) $u_i(x) > 0$, for $i = 1, \ldots, I$ and all x in the interior of X.

(2.3-3) u is strictly quasi-concave on the interior of X.

(2.3-4)   For any distinct x' and x'' in X such that $u(x') = u(x'')$, if $x' > 0$ then $x'' > 0$.

In what follows, these properties of utility functions are called, respectively, continuity and differentiability, differential increasingness, strict quasi-concavity, and the boundary condition.

It may be inferred from (2.3-1) that the underlying preference ordering $\succsim$ is continuously representable at least on the interior of X, and from (2.3-2)

---

[22]   The fact that the extended real line is used here instead of the unextended real line employed in conjunction with (2.1-3) is of no consequence because (2.3-1) ensures that $u(x)$ can only be (negatively) infinite on the boundary of X.

[23]   That is, $u_i(x) = \partial \mu / \partial x_i$ and $u_{in}(x) = \partial^2 \mu / \partial x_i \partial x_n$.

that $\succ$ is increasing. The presence of differentiability in (2.3-1) and (2.3-2), however, precludes the converse assertions. In other words, the existence of differentiable representations introduces something extra about preference orderings that has not been explored. The issue is very complex and not taken up here. The main reason to include differentiability is for the convenience of being able to focus on tangency maxima and employ the Lagrange constrained maximization theorem. As will be seen in the next chapter, alternative means of analysis when differentiability might not be present are entirely possible. The equivalence of (2.3-3) and strict convexity of $\succsim$ has already been mentioned in Section 2.1. Property (2.3-4) prevents indifference surfaces in the interior of the commodity space from touching the boundary of X. This is also an assumption of convenience. It ensures that all maxima lie in the interior of X and is easily dispensed with. In fact, the presence of both differentiability and (2.3-4) are the distinguishing features of the classical approach. Finally, the point at infinity is included in the range of u so as not to exclude common utility representations such as $u(x_1, x_2) = \ln x_1 + \ln x_2$.

Solving the equation

$$\mu = u(x), \tag{2.3-5}$$

for any x_i, say,

$$x_I = w(x_1, \ldots, x_{I-1}, \mu), \tag{2.3-6}$$

(by (2.3-2) and the inverse function theorem discussed in appendix Section A.4, a twice continuously differentiable solution always exists for all $x > 0$) yields an explicit equation for the indifference surface through x, where μ is fixed. The first- and second-order partial derivatives of w with respect to quantities of commodities are denoted, as with u, by subscripts i and n.

Suppose for a moment that $I = 2$ and consider the point $\mu = u(x_1, x_2)$. Assume x_1 and x_2 are changed, respectively, by the small increments Δx_1 and Δx_2. Since u is differentiable, the resulting change in utility $\Delta \mu$ can be approximated by[24]

$$\Delta \mu \simeq u_1(x_1, x_2)\Delta x_1 + u_2(x_1, x_2)\Delta x_2.$$

If it is further required that Δx_1 and Δx_2 are chosen so as to remain on the original indifference curve, that is, so $\Delta \mu = 0$ (see Figure 2.5), then

$$\frac{\Delta x_2}{\Delta x_1} \simeq -\frac{u_1(x_1, x_2)}{u_2(x_1, x_2)}.$$

---

[24]   Apostol [1, p. 348]. See also equations (A.3-6) and (A.3-7) in appendix Section A.3.

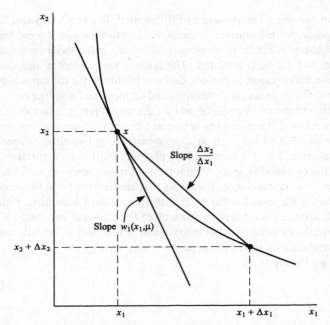

Figure 2.5 Slope of an indifference curve at x approximated
by the slope of a chord connecting x with another point on
the curve

Hence, passing to the limit along the same indifference curve,

$$w_1(x_1, \mu) = \lim_{\Delta x_1 \to 0} \frac{\Delta x_2}{\Delta x_1},$$

$$= \lim_{\Delta x_1 \to 0} -\frac{u_1(x_1, x_2)}{u_2(x_1, x_2)}, \tag{2.3-7}$$

$$= -\frac{u_1(x_1, x_2)}{u_2(x_1, x_2)},$$

where $\mu = u(x)$. Thus the slope $w_1(x_1, \mu)$ of the indifference curve at x —
that is, the rate at which the consumer would be willing to substitute good 1 for
good 2 while maintaining the same level of utility — is the negative of the ratio
of marginal utilities. Without the minus sign, this ratio of marginal utilities is

called the *marginal rate of substitution* of good 1 for good 2. It clearly depends on the point along the indifference curve in question. In any case, because u_1, and u_2 are positive by differential increasingness (2.3-2), the marginal rate of substitution is always positive and $w_1(x_1, \mu) < 0$. The argument is easily extended to indifference and utility functions of higher dimension. In that case, one formulation of the marginal rates of substitution is as the negative of

$$w_n(x_1, \ldots, x_{I-1}, \mu) = -\frac{u_n(x)}{u_I(x)}, \quad n = 1, \ldots I.$$

The ratios of marginal utilities $u_i(x)$, then, have meaning in terms of the underlying preference ordering $\succsim$. Recall, however, that, because u is an ordinal function, $u_i(x)$ by itself does not.

The curvature of an indifference curve expresses the ease or difficulty with which one commodity can be substituted for another along it. The easier substitution is, the less the marginal rate of substitution is affected by movement on the curve. At the extreme, the marginal rate of substitution is constant or, in other words, the indifference curve is linear (Figure 2.6(a)). In this case the commodities under consideration are called *perfect substitutes*. As an illustration, 5 pennies are usually a perfect substitute for 1 nickel. *Perfect complements* are at the other extreme. These kinds of goods cannot be substituted at all and must be consumed in a certain proportion. Indifference curves consist of a vertical and horizontal segment meeting at the ray of proportionality (the dashed line in Figure 2.6(b)). Shoes and shoe laces are an

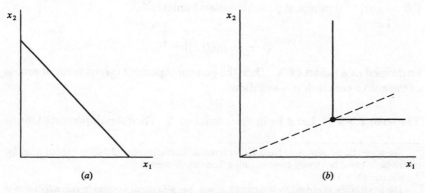

Figure 2.6 Perfect substitutes and complements: (*a*) perfect substitutes; (*b*) perfect complements

example. No utility representation associated with either extreme can satisfy all of assumptions (2.3-1) – (2.3-4). Perfect substitutes always leave the strictness of the quasi-concavity and the boundary condition violated, while perfect complements infringe on differentiability, (differential) increasingness, and the strictness of the quasi-concavity.

The curvature of indifference curves obtained from utility functions satisfying (2.3-1) – (2.3-4) falls in between. Properties (2.3-2) and (2.3-3) guarantee that for each value of μ, the indifference function w is strictly convex. [25] It follows that the second derivative $w_{11}(x_1, \mu) > 0$ most everywhere with exceptions permitted at "isolated" points.[26] Such exceptions arise for the same reason that the second-order derivative of the ordinary parabola $y = z^4$, which is strictly convex, vanishes at $z = 0$. Now define the *bordered Hessian matrix*

$$U(x) = \begin{bmatrix} 0 & u_1(x) & \cdots & u_I(x) \\ u_1(x) & u_{11}(x) & \cdots & u_{1I}(x) \\ \vdots & \vdots & & \vdots \\ u_I(x) & u_{I1}(x) & \cdots & u_{II}(x) \end{bmatrix}$$

at each x in the interior of X. Then, continuing with $I = 2$, the curvature of the indifference curve as stated in terms of $w_{11}(x_1, \mu)$ is related to that of the utility function as expressed by the determinant $|U(x_1, x_2)|$ according to the formula

$$|U(x_1, x_2)| = w_{11}(x_1, \mu)[u_2(x_1, x_2)]^3, \tag{2.3-8}$$

where $\mu = u(x)$. This is proved by differentiation of (2.3-7) and is left to the reader as Exercise 2.11. Therefore, assumptions (2.3-2) and (2.3-3) imply that $|U(x_1, x_2)| > 0$ except at possible isolated points of X.

Let

$$\mathcal{D} = \{x : |U(x)| \neq 0\}$$

be defined as a subset of X. Then the general statement (given without proof) of the above conclusion is as follows:

Theorem 2.3-9[27]   Let x be in the interior of X. Then for all permutations of

---

[25]   See appendix Section A.3. Note that differential increasingness (2.3-2) is needed here, for otherwise w could be strictly concave rather than strictly convex.
[26]   Katzner [7, p. 189].
[27]   The proposition is proved by Katzner [7, p. 40]. See also the discussion in appendix Section A.3.

the rows and columns containing u_{in} of $U(x)$,

$$\begin{vmatrix} 0 & u_1(x) & u_2(x) \\ u_1(x) & u_{11}(x) & u_{12}(x) \\ u_2(x) & u_{21}(x) & u_{22}(x) \end{vmatrix} \geqslant 0,$$

$$\begin{vmatrix} 0 & u_1(x) & u_2(x) & u_3(x) \\ u_1(x) & u_{11}(x) & u_{12}(x) & u_{13}(x) \\ u_2(x) & u_{21}(x) & u_{22}(x) & u_{23}(x) \\ u_3(x) & u_{31}(x) & u_{32}(x) & u_{33}(x) \end{vmatrix} \leqslant 0,$$

$$\vdots$$

and these inequalities are strict on $\mathcal{D}$.

Note that by differential increasingness (2.3-2) alone,

$$\begin{vmatrix} 0 & u_1(x) \\ u_1(x) & u_{11}(x) \end{vmatrix} < 0,$$

for every x in the interior of X. Thus the sequence of inequalities in Theorem 2.3-9 is extended one to the left with a strict inequality. Also, although avoided here, the notion that the points of X not in $\mathcal{D}$ are isolated can, in fact, be stated with considerable precision.[28] This is important because any $(I-1)$-dimensional surface in I-dimensional space must be taken here as isolated. For example, the bordered Hessian of the utility function of Exercise 2.14 vanishes over the entire line $x_2 = x_1$ in the interior of the two-dimensional commodity space $X = \{(x_1, x_2) : x_1 \geqslant 0 \text{ and } x_2 \geqslant 0\}$.

Now let prices $p = (p_1, ..., p_I)$ and the consumer's income m be introduced. Only positive vectors (p, m) are considered. Once such a (p, m) is given, the baskets of commodities x available to the consumer are limited to those satisfying the *budget inequality*

$$p \cdot x \leqslant m,$$

where the abbreviation

$$p \cdot x = \sum_{i=1}^{I} p_i x_i.$$

---

[28]   Katzner [7, p. 40], Debreu [4, pp. 391, 392].

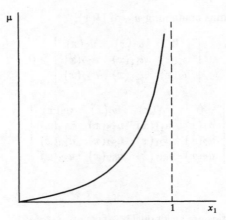

Figure 2.7 Utility function for which
no constrained maximum exists

The equation $p \cdot x = m$ is called the consumer's *budget constraint*. Geometrically, it appears as a straight line in two dimensions (that is, with two goods) and as an $(I - 1)$-dimensional hyperplane in I dimensions. In the context of demand theory, the rationality postulate requires that out of those bundles of commodities available to her, the consumer selects (purchases or demands) that which provides the greatest utility. Alternatively put, the consumer chooses so as to maximize her utility subject to the budget constraint.

The first issue raised by the postulate of rationality is whether, under assumptions (2.3-1) – (2.3-4), it is always possible to be rational; that is, does there exist a utility maximizing basket for every positive (p, m)? To illustrate in the one-dimensional case, what is to prevent the utility function from appearing as it does in Figure 2.7? In this diagram the points available to the consumer lie in the interval $(0, 1)$ and the utility function runs off asymptotically to the dashed vertical line above $x_1 = 1$. No maximum exists and rationality as defined here cannot be achieved. Theorem 2.3-10 shows that such situations have been ruled out.

Theorem 2.3-10   Let $(p, m) > 0$ be given. Then there exists a basket $x > 0$ such that $p \cdot x = m$ and $u(x) > u(x')$ for any $x' \neq x$ satisfying $p \cdot x' \leqslant m$.

Proof: Let $(p, m) > 0$ be given and choose any $x^0 > 0$ in X satisfying $p \cdot x^0 \leqslant m$. Then the collection of all points B that satisfy the budget inequality and also lie in $C_{x^0}^{\geqslant}$, is a nonempty compact set. Because any continuous function

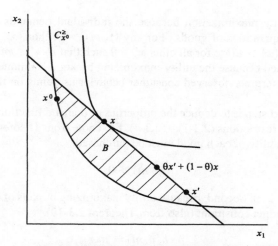

Figure 2.8 Utility maximization subject to the budget constraint

defined over a compact set always attains a maximum on that set,[29] there is an x in B such that $u(x) \geqslant u(x')$ for all x' in B. It is now shown that x satisfies the conclusions of the theorem. The argument may be followed in Figure 2.8.

From the boundary condition (2.3-4), $x > 0$ because $x^0 > 0$. If x did not satisfy the budget constraint, then it would lie in the interior of B. Hence there would be a basket of commodities larger than x in B. But then, by the differential increasingness assumption (2.3-2), that basket would have greater utility than x. This contradicts the maximality of x. Hence $p \cdot x = m$.

If there were another point x' in B such that $u(x') = u(x)$, the above indicates that it too must satisfy the budget constraint. Furthermore, if θ is between 0 and 1, then $\theta x + (1 - \theta)x'$ is also in B and satisfies the budget constraint. By the strict quasi-concavity assumption (2.3-3), $u(\theta x' + [1 - \theta]x) > u(x)$, again contradicting the maximality of x. Therefore $u(x) > u(x')$ for all $x' \neq x$ in B. This last assertion is extended to all $x' \neq x$ satisfying $p \cdot x' \leqslant m$ and $x' \geqslant 0$ by the continuity and increasingness of u (that is, assumptions (2.3-1) and (2.3-2)).

Q.E.D.

The general demand functions of (2.0-1) may now be characterized in

---

[29]   This proposition is discussed, along with the idea of compact sets, in appendix Section A.3.

terms of utility maximization because the individual demands only utility-maximizing quantities of goods. For any $(p, m) > 0$, then, $x = h(p, m)$ if and only if $u(x) > u(x')$ for all other $x' \geqslant 0$ such that $p \cdot x' \leqslant m$. Note that h is single-valued because the utility-maximizing basket x is unique. The theory of demand interprets observed consumer behavior as points on these demand functions.[30]

The next step is to deduce the properties of demand functions implied by the technical restrictions (2.3-1) – (2.3-4). First note from Theorem 2.3-10 that a positive quantity of each good must be purchased:

$$h(p, m) > 0, \tag{2.3-11}$$

for all $(p, m) > 0$. Second, because utility maximizing baskets of commodities satisfy the budget constraint (also from Theorem 2.3-10),

$$p \cdot h(p, m) = m, \tag{2.3-12}$$

again, for all $(p, m) > 0$. Thus the consumer must spend all of his income and any one demand function can be derived from those remaining. Third, because proportionate variations in all prices and income leave both budget inequality and constraint unchanged, and because such variations have no impact on preferences, h is homogeneous of degree 0. In other words, for all $(p, m) > 0$,

$$h(\alpha p, \alpha m) = h(p, m), \tag{2.3-13}$$

for any real $\alpha > 0$. Doubling, say, all prices and the consumer's income leaves purchases unchanged. Fourth, although not done so here, it can be shown

---

[30]   Long ago, the impulse to distinguish between "value in use" and "value in exchange" seems to have given rise to the notion of utility. Although traceable to Aristotle, the distinction was placed in economic perspective by Davanzati in 1588 who applied it to explain the "paradox" that usefulness is not necessarily reflected in price. The example made famous by Adam Smith in 1776 stated the argument in terms of diamonds and water: In spite of the fact that they are of little practical use, diamonds are dear (high value in exchange) because they are scarce, while water, being a requisite for life (high utility or value in use), is cheap because of its abundance. This hints at the possibility of a relationship between utility and demand — but it hardly gives an explicit description or derivation. In spite of the fact that the notion of demand expressed as an inverse relation between price and quantity goes back at least to King in 1696, and in spite of the fact that the idea of diminishing marginal utility was used by Bernoulli in 1738 to resolve the St. Petersburg paradox, no formal accounting of a relationship between utility and demand was provided until the end of the 19th century. Although Jevons in 1871 made, perhaps, the first attempt to bridge the gap between utility and demand through constrained maximization of the former, it was Walras in 1874 who was the first to succeed. Details and references may be found in Katzner [7, pp. 5-8].

that[31]

$$h \text{ is continuous where defined.} \qquad (2.3\text{-}14)$$

Note that the set $\mathcal{D}$ in X translates through h into a corresponding subset, Ω, of price-income space given by

$$\Omega = \{(p, m) : x = h(p, m) \text{ and } x \text{ is in } \mathcal{D}\}.$$

These restrictions already rule out large numbers of potential candidates for demand functions consistent with utility maximization. Alternatively put, the assumptions of this section do not explain observed behavior that violates (2.3-11) – (2.3-14). But the hypotheses underlying utility maximization impose still more restrictions. Further properties of demand in the classical model all turn on the ability to locate utility maximizing baskets of commodities at tangencies of budget hyperplanes and indifference surfaces.[32] The mathematical expression of such tangencies can be obtained from the constrained maximization theorem of Lagrange.

As applied in the present context, Lagrange's theorem[33] asserts that under assumptions (2.3-1) – (2.3-4), if x maximizes u subject to the budget constraint corresponding to a given $(p, m) > 0$, that is, if $x = h(p, m)$, then there exists a real number λ which is positive due to (2.3-2) and such that

$$u_i(x) = \lambda p_i, \quad i = 1, \ldots, I. \qquad (2.3\text{-}15)$$

(Here, maximization subject to the budget constraint can be used in place of maximization subject to the budget inequality because the utility maximizing bundle x lies on the budget hyperplane (Theorem 2.3-10).) It turns out (see Section 3.4) that the value of λ emerging from the constrained utility-maximization problem is the partial derivative of μ with respect to m. This value of λ, then, indicates the extent to which, at the margin, the level of utility is altered with changes in income. That λ is actually a continuously differentiable function of (p, m) can be seen by substituting $h(p, m)$ for x in (2.3-15). Equations (2.3-15) can be derived by differentiation of the so-called

---

[31]   Katzner [7, p. 44].

[32]   With two goods, for example, a budget line is said to be *tangent* at x to the indifference curve described by $x_2 = w(x_1, \mu)$ if the two touch at x and if the slope of the budget line is the same as the derivative $w_1(x_1, \mu)$ at x.

[33]   Theorem A.3-16 in appendix Section A.3. In the notation of that theorem, where the theorem's x is now the I-dimensional vector $(x_1, \ldots, x_I)$, the single constraint is $g^1(x) = p \cdot x - m$, and the constraint qualification is satisfied since $g_i^1(x) = p_i > 0$ for every i.

Lagrangian expression

$$u(x) - \lambda(p \cdot x - m),$$

with respect to the x_i and setting these derivatives equal to zero. Dividing the Ith equation of (2.3-15) into those remaining gives the result that the subjective marginal rate of substitution equals the objectively given price ratio:

$$\frac{u_i(x)}{u_I(x)} = \frac{p_i}{p_I}, \quad i = 1, \ldots, I - 1. \tag{2.3-16}$$

This, along with the budget constraint,

$$p \cdot x = m, \tag{2.3-17}$$

characterizes the location of x as at a tangency between an indifference surface and a budget hyperplane[34] (Figure 2.8). Taken together, (2.3-16) and (2.3-17) constitute a system of I equations in I "unknown" x_i's. Wherever its Jacobian does not vanish, the inverse function theorem implies that the system can be solved for a continuously differentiable h. It turns out that this Jacobian and $|U(x)|$ differ by the multiple $[u_I(x)]^{I+1}$. Hence, from differential increasingness (2.3-2), the Jacobian is never zero on $\mathcal{D}$, so the solution of (2.3-16) and (2.3-17) yields h at points of Ω. Moreover,

$$h \text{ is continuously differentiable on, and only on, } \Omega.^{[35]} \tag{2.3-18}$$

Recall, however, that h has already been obtained from Theorem 2.3-10 for all positive prices and incomes. Off of Ω, then, h is defined and continuous but not differentiable. In practice the Lagrangian method is frequently a very easy and convenient (if not the only) way of explicitly deriving demand functions from utility maximization.

Note that equations (2.3-15) are first-order conditions for unique maximization under a linear constraint. The second-order condition necessarily flowing from such a maximization is, in the two-good case,

$$|U(x_1, x_2)| \geqslant 0, \tag{2.3-19}$$

for all x_1 in some neighborhood of the maximum, where the inequality in (2.3-19) is strict except possibly at isolated points. In light of (2.3-8) and the fact that $u_2(x_1, x_2) > 0$ for all $(x_1, x_2) > 0$, condition (2.3-19) or the first inequality of Theorem 2.3-9 is equivalent to the statement that $w_{11}(x_1, \mu) > 0$

---

[34]   The characterization of tangency points is both necessary and sufficient. Katzner [7, p. 42].
[35]   All of this is rigorously proved by Katzner [7, p. 46]. Jacobians are defined and the inverse function theorem discussed in appendix Section A.4.

except for isolated points. (Were $u_1(x_1, x_2) < 0$ and $u_2(x_1, x_2) < 0$ at some unique under-constraint-minimizing $(x_1, x_2) > 0$, then the inequality of (2.3-19) would be reversed and $w_{11}(x_1, \mu)$ would remain positive except for isolated points where it could vanish. Alternatively, $u_1(x_1, x_2) < 0$, $u_2(x_1, x_2) < 0$ and, except for isolated points, $w_{11}(x_1, \mu) < 0$, would leave the inequality of (2.3-19) as it is but would reflect a unique constrained maximum. This latter situation arises in at y'' in Figure 4.9 upon translation of that diagram into the present context.) The general necessary second-order conditions, after all, merely assert in differential form that the shape of the indifference surfaces is consistent with unique constrained utility maximization. The same thing is said by stating that u is strictly quasi-concave. Again, there may occasionally be points at which the determinants of Theorem 2.3-9 vanish for the same reason that the second derivative of $y = -z^4$ is zero, even though it has a unique maximum, at $z = 0$. There is no reason to assume the stronger, sufficient second-order condition for a unique constrained maximum, namely, that the determinants of Theorem 2.3-9 are nonzero everywhere on X. This would only ensure the existence of maxima whose existence has already been established on weaker grounds and, moreover, would also exclude many ordinary utility functions, such as that of Exercise 2.14, from consideration.

2.4 DIFFERENTIAL PROPERTIES OF DEMAND

The remaining properties of demand derived within the classical framework are attributes of the derivatives of demand functions. All emerge from the first-order maximization conditions (2.3-15) and the budget constraint, which for convenience are repeated here:

$$u_i(x) = \lambda p_i, \quad i = 1, \dots, I,$$

$$p \cdot x = m,$$

(2.4-1)

As indicated earlier, (2.4-1) characterizes utility maximizing baskets of commodities x whenever x appears at a tangency between an indifference surface and a budget hyperplane. Recall that h is defined for all $(p, m) > 0$ but differentiable (since it is also the solution of (2.4-1) with λ eliminated) only on Ω. Hence the differential properties of demand are stated just for (p, m) in Ω.

Because the issues involved are so complex, only the simplest of cases is examined thoroughly here. All inessential details are eliminated. General

results are stated at the end. Thus the argument focuses on the demand curve
for good 1. This curve is obtained by fixing the prices of all other goods and
income at, say, $p_i = p_i^0$ for $i = 2, \ldots, I$, and $m = m^0$. The *demand curve*
for good 1, then, is the graph (with the independent variable placed on the
vertical axis and the dependent variable on the horizontal axis as described on
pp. 19-20 above) of the function

$$x_1 = h^1(p_1, p_2^0, \ldots, p_I^0, m^0).$$

The reciprocal of its slope at the point p_1 is given by the partial derivative
$h_1^1(p_1, p_2^0, \ldots, p_I^0, m^0)$. To simplify matters still further, the number of commodities is limited to $I = 2$.

   The relationship connecting the reciprocal of the slope of the demand
curve with tangencies between indifference curves and budget lines is pictured
in the two diagrams of Figure 2.9. Start at the (initial) point α on the demand
curve of Figure 2.9(b). Because p_2^0 and m^0 are fixed in advance, and because
p_1^α is the price coordinate of α, the budget line

$$p_1^\alpha x_1 + p_2^0 x_2 = m^0$$

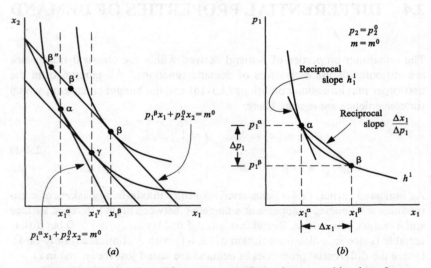

(a)   *(b)*

Figure 2.9 Derivation of the consumer's demand curve and its slope from
constrained utility maximization: (*a*) constrained utility maximization; (*b*)
demand curve

is determined. This budget line is tangent to an indifference curve at a point (also labeled α) in Figure 2.9(a) whose x_1-coordinate is the same as that corresponding to α in Figure 2.9(b). Now suppose p_1^α falls to p_1^β with p_2^0 and m^0 remaining fixed. Then the new (or final) point β is established in both diagrams. The reciprocal of the slope of the demand curve (the curve labeled h^1 in Figure 2.9(b)) evaluated at α, namely $h_1^1(p_1^\alpha, p_2^0, m^0)$, is approximated by

$$\frac{\Delta x_1}{\Delta p_1}$$

where

$$\Delta x_1 = x_1^\alpha - x_1^\beta,$$
$$\Delta p_1 = p_1^\alpha - p_1^\beta. \tag{2.4-2}$$

It is clear that the slope of the demand curve in Figure 2.9(b), which carries the same sign as the reciprocal of that slope, depends on the location of the point β in Figure 2.9(a). As drawn, the demand curve slopes downward. But if the indifference map were such that β fell at β'' instead, then the demand curve would have to slope upward. (Exercise 2.16 provides a simple illustration of this possibility but it is limited to a subset of X on which only continuity and differentiability (2.3-1), differential increasingness (2.3-2), and strict quasi-concavity (2.3-3) hold. The boundary condition (2.3-4) is not met.) Thus the assumptions of the classical model are not enough to guarantee demand curves that slope downward throughout their domains. It is necessary to look elsewhere for differential properties applying to all demand curves generated by utility functions satisfying (2.3-1) – (2.3-4).

One way to proceed is to break up the movement from α to β into income and substitution effects. There are several ways to do this, each incorporating the idea that a fall in the price of good 1 (a) makes good 1 cheaper relative to good 2 hence encouraging substitution of the former for the latter, and (b) results in an increase in the consumer's "real" income and consequently modifies demand. But because in the limit as price changes approach zero all decompositions turn out to be equivalent,[36] only one is considered here. Loosely speaking it is as follows: The *substitution effect* describes the reallocation of the consumer's demands if a price change is compensated (positively or negatively) by a simultaneous adjustment in his income, forcing the consumer (after utility maximization) to remain on the same indifference curve on which he began. The discrepancy between the consumer's position after compensation and

---

[36]   Katzner [7, pp. 56-58].

the final point reflects the *income effect*. Thus, in Figure 2.9(a), the movement from α to γ is the substitution effect; that from γ to β, the income effect. Note that in progressing from α to γ both p_1 and m are modified. Hence the slope of the budget line and its x_2 intercept change. (Compare the budget line through α with that through γ in Figure 2.9(a).) Variation in the consumer's income is the only modification from γ to β. Here the budget line shifts with constant slope.

Mathematically, using (2.4-2),

$$\frac{\Delta x_1}{\Delta p_1} = \frac{x_1^\alpha - x_1^\beta}{\Delta p_1} = \frac{x_1^\alpha - x_1^\gamma}{\Delta p_1} - \frac{x_1^\beta - x_1^\gamma}{\Delta p_1}, \qquad (2.4\text{-}3)$$

with reference again to Figure 2.9. The terms on the right-hand side of the right-hand equality are called, respectively, the *substitution ratio* and the *income ratio*. They can be viewed as measures of substitution and income effects. The geometry of Figure 2.9(a) suggests that these terms have certain signs, indicated in Table 2.1, which depend on the location of the final tangency between indifference curve and budget line. The interesting thing is that in spite of the variation in sign of the actual and reciprocal slopes of the demand curve, the substitution ratio is always negative. This is obviously a consequence of the downward sloping and strictly convex shape of the indifference curve. The latter, as has been pointed out, derives from the assumptions of differential increasingness (2.3-2) and strict quasi-concavity (2.3-3).

Table 2.1 Possible signs of income and substitution ratios and reciprocal slopes of demand curves from Figure 2.9

Final tangency in Fig. 2.9	Substitution ratio: $\dfrac{x_1^\alpha - x_1^\gamma}{\Delta p_1}$	Income ratio: $\dfrac{x_1^\beta - x_1^\gamma}{\Delta p_1}$	Approximate reciprocal slope of demand curve: $\dfrac{\Delta x_1}{\Delta p_1}$	Type of good as classified by	
				Income ratio	Slope of demand curve
β	negative	positive	negative	superior	normal
β'	negative	negative	negative	inferior	normal
β''	negative	negative	positive	inferior	Giffen

Note that Table 2.1 also classifies goods according to the signs of their income ratios and those of the reciprocal slopes of their demand curves. The idea is that, other things being equal, a good is *superior* (or *inferior*) if larger (or, respectively, smaller) quantities are demanded with larger incomes. In the present context this means that the income ratio is positive (or negative). The good is *normal* or *Giffen* according as the slope or the reciprocal of the slope of its demand curve is, respectively, negative or positive.[37] Normal goods can be either superior or inferior; Giffen goods are only inferior. In general, for any particular good these classifications can vary across the commodity space.

Passing to the limit in (2.4-3),

$$h_1^1(p_1^\alpha, p_2^0, m^0) \ = \ \lim_{\Delta p_1 \to 0} \frac{\Delta x_1}{\Delta p_1},$$

(2.4-4)

$$= \ \lim_{\Delta p_1 \to 0} \frac{x_1^\alpha - x_1^\gamma}{\Delta p_1} - \lim_{\Delta p_1 \to 0} \frac{x_1^\beta - x_1^\gamma}{\Delta p_1}.$$

The previous argument concerning the negativity of the substitution ratio also suggests

$$\lim_{\Delta p_1 \to 0} \frac{x_1^\alpha - x_1^\gamma}{\Delta p_1} \leqslant 0.$$

(2.4-5)

Inequality (2.4-5) would seem to hold for any utility function satisfying (2.3-1) − (2.3-4). It is therefore a candidate to replace the unreliable sign of h_1^1 as a property of demand behavior. But the problem with (2.4-5) is that to be able to compute $x_1^\alpha - x_1^\gamma$, it is necessary to know the indifference map. The indifference map, however, is not observable. The major contribution of Slutsky [13] was to show how to circumvent this impasse by expressing (2.4-5) in terms of the derivatives of demand functions. In so doing, the stronger assertion of strict inequality is obtained.

---

[37]   The identification of the name of Sir Robert Giffen (a contemporary of Marshall's) with the upward sloping demand curve is curious. As Stigler [14] points out, the responsibility appears to lie with Marshall, who first made the connection in the third edition of his Principles (1895) and included it in all subsequent editions. Marshall's statement of the reason for the upward slope required that a high portion of the individual's income be spent on the Giffen good. Thus in the more modern version, a rise in the price of that good (say, bread) reduces real income sufficiently so that the individual can no longer afford to consume as much of other commodities (such as, say, meat) and is forced to increase consumption of the Giffen good. That the high-portion-of-income condition is neither necessary nor sufficient for the more general notion of Giffen good defined here is clear from the example of Exercise 2.16. Moreover, according to Stigler, the idea that demand curves may slope upward is traceable back 70 more years or so before the publication of Marshall's third edition, to Simon Gray.

To see what is involved, it is necessary to go back to conditions (2.4-1) obtained, in part, from Lagrange's theorem. With $I = 2$ and (p, m) in Ω, substitution of $x = h(p, m)$ into (2.4-1) gives

$$p_1 h^1(p, m) + p_2 h^2(p, m) = m,$$

$$-\lambda p_1 + u_1(h(p, m)) = 0, \qquad (2.4\text{-}6)$$

$$-\lambda p_2 + u_2(h(p, m)) = 0,$$

where, as described in the discussion following equation (2.3-15), λ is thought of as a function of (p, m). Differentiating (2.4-6) with respect to m,

$$p_1 h_m^1 + p_2 h_m^2 = 1,$$

$$-\lambda_m p_1 + u_{11} h_m^1 + u_{12} h_m^2 = 0,$$

$$-\lambda_m p_2 + u_{21} h_m^1 + u_{22} h_m^2 = 0,$$

where the subscript m denotes a partial derivative with respect to m, and functional arguments (p, m) have been dropped to simplify notation. Elimination of p_1 and p_2 by substitution from (2.4-1) yields

$$u_1 h_m^1 + u_2 h_m^2 = \lambda,$$

$$-\frac{\lambda_m}{\lambda} u_1 + u_{11} h_m^1 + u_{12} h_m^2 = 0,$$

$$-\frac{\lambda_m}{\lambda} u_2 + u_{21} h_m^1 + u_{22} h_m^2 = 0,$$

Solving for h_m^1 with Cramer's rule,[38]

$$h_m^1 = \frac{\begin{vmatrix} 0 & \lambda & u_2 \\ u_1 & 0 & u_{12} \\ u_2 & 0 & u_{22} \end{vmatrix}}{\begin{vmatrix} 0 & u_1 & u_2 \\ u_1 & u_{11} & u_{12} \\ u_2 & u_{21} & u_{22} \end{vmatrix}} = -\frac{\lambda}{|U|} \begin{vmatrix} u_1 & u_{12} \\ u_2 & u_{22} \end{vmatrix}. \qquad (2.4\text{-}7)$$

---

[38]   Theorem A.4-2 in appendix Section A.4.

Now differentiate (2.4-6) with respect to p_1:

$$p_1 h_1^1 + p_2 h_1^2 = -h^1,$$

$$-\lambda_1 p_1 + u_{11} h_1^1 + u_{12} h_1^2 = \lambda,$$

$$-\lambda_1 p_2 + u_{21} h_1^1 + u_{22} h_1^2 = 0,$$

Substituting from (2.4-1) to eliminate the p_i and using Cramer's rule to solve for h_1^1 results in

$$h_1^1 = \frac{\lambda \begin{vmatrix} 0 & u_2 \\ u_2 & u_{22} \end{vmatrix} + \lambda h^1 \begin{vmatrix} u_1 & u_{12} \\ u_2 & u_{22} \end{vmatrix}}{|U|}.$$

Combining this with (2.4-7),

$$h_1^1 = \frac{\lambda}{|U|} \begin{vmatrix} 0 & u_2 \\ u_2 & u_{22} \end{vmatrix} - h^1 h_m^1. \tag{2.4-8}$$

Equation (2.4-8) is beginning to look something like (2.4-4). Before any conclusions can be drawn, however, it is necessary to know more about the term

$$\frac{\lambda}{|U|} \begin{vmatrix} 0 & u_2 \\ u_2 & u_{22} \end{vmatrix}.$$

Toward this end, consider the point x' in Figure 2.10 and denote its utility value by μ'. Suppose that instead of maximizing utility subject to the budget constraint, the consumer were to choose baskets of commodities so as to minimize expenditure $p \cdot x$ while at the same time securing a utility level at least as high as μ'. The consumer now is constrained by the set $C_{x'}^{\geqq}$ instead of by the budget inequality. The result is a unique choice $\overline{x}$, again located at a tangency between an indifference curve and an expenditure (or budget) line. (Obviously $\overline{x}$ can still be viewed as the result of maximizing utility subject to a budget constraint, where the latter is taken to be the line $p_1 x_1 + p_2 x_2 = m'$.) In fact, under assumptions (2.3-1) − (2.3-4), the entire discussion of Section 2.3 can be reformulated in these terms. Conclusions such as Theorem 2.3-10 are modified accordingly. The demand functions h^* so obtained depend on prices and utility:

$$x = h^*(p, \mu).$$

Thus, with μ fixed, h^* indicates quantities demanded as prices vary and the

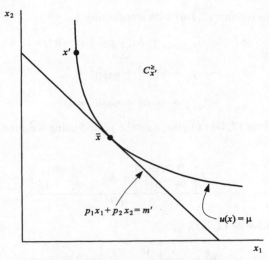

Figure 2.10 Expenditure minimization subject
to an indifference curve

consumer remains on the same indifference curve. Economists often refer to
h^* as the *compensated* demand function. The Lagrangian conditions[39] for
expenditure minimization are

$$p_i = \eta u_i(x), \quad i = 1, \ldots, I, \qquad (2.4\text{-}9)$$

where η, a continuously differentiable function of p and μ, plays the same role
as λ in (2.3-15). The subset of price-utility space corresponding to $\mathcal{D}$ (defined
analogously to Ω) is denoted by Υ. The system of equations that can be solved
to obtain h^* differentially on Υ consists of the ratios of Lagrangian conditions
and the utility constraint:

$$\frac{p_i}{p_I} = \frac{u_i(x)}{u_I(x)}, \quad i = 1, \ldots, I - 1,$$

$$\mu = u(x).$$

---

[39]   Here the single constraint (in the notation of Theorem A.3-16 with $x = (x_1, \ldots, x_I)$ as
before) is $g^1(x) = u(x) - \mu$. Because $g_i^1(x) = u_i(x) > 0$ for $i = 1, \ldots, I$ by (2.3-2), the
constraint qualification (A.3-17) is in force. Cf., n. 33 on p. 63.

It is also clear that for each $p > 0$, if

$$\bar{x} = h^*(p, \mu'),$$

then

$$\bar{x} = h(p, m'),$$

where $u(\bar{x}) = \mu'$ and $p \cdot \bar{x} = m'$ (see Figure 2.10). In other words, if μ and m are selected appropriately for each p, then the outcome of utility maximization and expenditure minimization are identical. This defines a 1–1 correspondence[40] between values of μ and m, given p. Moreover, combining (2.4-1) and (2.4-9),

$$\lambda = \frac{1}{\eta}. \tag{2.4-10}$$

Since λ is a function of (p, m) and η is a function of (p, μ), equation (2.4-10) only makes sense in light of the 1–1 correspondence mentioned above. Thus from (2.4-9) and (2.4-10) a system analogous to (2.4-1) is derived:

$$u_i(x) = \lambda p_i, \quad i = 1, \ldots, I,$$

$$u(x) = \mu, \tag{2.4-11}$$

Upon elimination of λ, (2.4-11) yields the same equations obtained from (2.4-9) and the constraint $u(x) = \mu$, and these, as before, can be solved to secure h^* on Υ.

Returning to the two-good world, substitute $x = h^*(p, \mu)$ into (2.4-11) so that

$$u(h^*(p, \mu)) = \mu,$$

$$-\lambda p_1 + u_1(h^*(p, \mu)) = 0,$$

$$-\lambda p_2 + u_2(h^*(p, \mu)) = 0.$$

Differentiation with respect to p_1 leaves

$$u_1 h_1^{*1} + u_2 h_1^{*2} = 0,$$

$$-\lambda_1 p_1 + u_{11} h_1^{*1} + u_{12} h_1^{*2} = \lambda,$$

$$-\lambda_1 p_2 + u_{21} h_1^{*1} + u_{22} h_1^{*2} = 0,$$

---

[40] A definition of the concept of 1–1 correspondence is given in appendix Section A.3.

Using (2.4-11) to substitute for p_i and applying Cramer's rule once again,

$$h_1^{*1} = \frac{\lambda}{|U|} \begin{vmatrix} 0 & u_2 \\ u_2 & u_{22} \end{vmatrix}. \tag{2.4-12}$$

Thus the expression involving derivatives of the utility function in (2.4-8) turns out to be the partial derivative of the compensated demand function. Putting (2.4-12) and (2.4-8) together yields Slutsky's equation

$$h_1^1(p, m) = h_1^{*1}(p, \mu) - h^1(p, m)h_m^1(p, m), \tag{2.4-13}$$

where both h and h^{*1} are differentiable.

The significance of (2.4-13) will be considered momentarily. First, however, recall that the construction of the substitution ratio from Figure 2.9(a) leaves little doubt that it must approach h_1^{*1} as $\triangle p_1$ declines to zero. More precisely, if μ^0 is the utility level of the indifference curve through α in Figure 2.9(a), then in the notation of equations (2.4-3) – (2.4-5),

$$h_1^{*1}(p_1^\alpha, p_2^0, \mu^0) = \lim_{\triangle p_1 \to 0} \frac{x_1^\alpha - x_1^\gamma}{\triangle p_1}, \tag{2.4-14}$$

provided p_1^α, p_2^0, μ^0 is in Υ. It follows that, with (p_1^α, p_2^0, m^0) in Ω, the limit of the income ratios and the second term on the right-hand side of (2.4-13) are related:

$$h^1(p_1^\alpha, p_2^0, m^0)h_m^1(p_1^\alpha, p_2^0, m^0) = \lim_{\triangle p_1 \to 0} \frac{x_1^\beta - x_1^\gamma}{\triangle p_1},$$

from (2.4-4), (2.4-13), and (2.4-14). In other words, h_1^{*1} and $h^1 h_m^1$ measure, respectively, substitution and income effects for arbitrarily small price changes, and the reciprocal of the slope of the demand curve is the difference between them.

Moreover, (2.4-5), which has not yet been rigorously demonstrated, and (2.4-14) imply

$$h_1^{*1}(p_1^\alpha, p_2^0, \mu^0) \leqslant 0. \tag{2.4-15}$$

Actually, as will be seen below, the weak inequality of (2.4-15) can be replaced by a strict one. But in either case the domain of h_1^{*1} includes the range of the utility function, and therefore h_1^{*1} cannot be seen. The importance of Slutsky's equation (2.4-13), however, is that it translates (2.4-15) from this "hidden" state into a form that can be observed in demand behavior. That is, define the

Slutsky function

$$s^{11}(p,m) = h_1^1(p,m) + h^1(p,m)h_m^1(p,m), \qquad (2.4\text{-}16)$$

for all (p,m) in Ω. Then, because s^{11} is derived only from the ordinary demand function, it is everywhere observable. Combining (2.4-13), (2.4-15) and (2.4-16), gives

$$s^{11}(p_1^\alpha, p_2^0, m^0) \leqslant 0. \qquad (2.4\text{-}17)$$

Regardless of the slope of the demand curve, if s^{11} as computed from (2.4-16) fails to exhibit this property, the classical model of utility maximization cannot be used to explain the behavior of the consumer in question.

In general, the *Slutsky functions* are defined as follows:

$$s^{in}(p,m) = h_n^i(p,m) + h^n(p,m)h_m^i(p,m), \quad i,n = 1,\ldots,I,$$

for all (p,m) in Ω. Note that h_n^i refers to the partial derivative of h^i with respect to its nth price. Inequality (2.4-17) is only a small part of one of two kinds of properties that assumptions (2.3-1) – (2.3-4) force upon the compensated demand functions and hence, through Slutsky's equation, upon the s^{in}. To state them let

$$S(p,m) = \begin{bmatrix} s^{11}(p,m) & \cdots & s^{1I-1}(p,m) \\ \vdots & & \vdots \\ s^{I-11}(p,m) & \cdots & s^{I-1I-1}(p,m) \end{bmatrix},$$

and

$$S^*(p,m) = \begin{bmatrix} s^{11}(p,m) & \cdots & s^{1I}(p,m) \\ \vdots & & \vdots \\ s^{I1}(p,m) & \cdots & s^{II}(p,m) \end{bmatrix},$$

on Ω. The differential properties of demand are given by the next two propositions.

Theorem 2.4-18[41]   (Negative definiteness.) For every (p,m) in Ω, $S(p,m)$ is negative definite and $|S^*(p,m)| = 0$.

Theorem 2.4-19[42]   (Symmetry.) For every (p,m) in Ω, $S^*(p,m)$ is symmetric.

---

[41]   See appendix Section A.4 for a definition of negative definite.
[42]   The notion of symmetry also is defined in Section A.4.

Although the proofs of these two theorems are beyond the scope of present considerations,[43] it should be understood that the negative definiteness property follows directly from the inequalities of Theorem 2.3-9. In essence, the reasoning is a generalization and formalization of the heuristic argument indicating why

$$s^{11}(p_1^{\alpha}, p_2^0, m^0) \leqslant 0.$$

The fundamental assumptions behind both this inequality and Theorem 2.4-18 are differential increasingness (2.3-2) and strict quasi-concavity (2.3-3). Thus negative definiteness is an observable characterization of the shape of indifference surfaces or, equivalently, of the necessary (not sufficient) second-order conditions for unique constrained maxima. In addition, it is easy to see (Exercise 2.22) that the negative definiteness of $S(p, m)$ implies

$$s^{11}(p, m) < 0, \qquad\qquad (2.4\text{-}20)$$

on Ω, thus strengthening (2.4-17). (In fact, $s^{ii}(p, m) < 0$ on Ω for $i = 1, \ldots, I$.)

To illustrate the formal derivation of negative definiteness as described above, it is worth drawing together the argument that yields (2.4-20) from differential increasingness and strict quasi-concavity in the two-good case. There are four steps: (i) Differential increasingness (2.3-2) and strict quasi-concavity (2.3-3) imply that for all μ,

$$x_2 = w(x_1, \mu)$$

is a strictly convex function of x_1 (see p. 58 above). (ii) Hence, $w_{11}(x_1, \mu) > 0$ except at isolated points (also p. 58). (iii) It follows from (2.3-8) that the determinant $|U(x_1, x_2)| > 0$ on $\mathcal{D}$. (iv) Therefore, combining (2.4-8) and (2.4-16),

$$s^{11}(p, m) = \frac{\lambda}{|U|} \begin{vmatrix} 0 & u_2 \\ u_2 & u_{22} \end{vmatrix},$$

$$(2.4\text{-}21)$$

$$= -\frac{\lambda(u_2)^2}{|U|} < 0,$$

on Ω, because $\lambda > 0$ from the differential increasingness. With more than 2 goods, s^{11} is λ times the ratio of a subdeterminant of $|U|$ to $|U|$, and the signs of the numerator and denominator of this ratio are obtained from Theorem 2.3-9.

---

[43] Proofs are given by Katzner [7, p. 48].

Table 2.2 Properties of demand implied by utility maximization under assumptions (2.3-1) – (2.3-4)

Name	Property	Textual source
positivity	$h(p,m) > 0$, for all $(p,m) > 0$	(2.3-11)
budget constraint	$p \cdot h(p,m) = m$, for all $(p,m) > 0$	(2.3-12)
homogeneity	$h(\alpha p, \alpha m) = h(p,m)$, for all $(p,m) > 0$ and $\alpha > 0$	(2.3-13)
continuity	h is continuous, for all $(p,m) > 0$	(2.3-14)
differentiability	h is continuously differentiable on Ω	(2.3-18)
negative definiteness	$S(p,m)$ is negative definite and $|S^*(p,m)| = 0$ on Ω	Theorem 2.4-18
symmetry	$S^*(p,m)$ is symmetric on Ω	Theorem 2.4-19

Generally, the symmetry property is deduced from the fact that the second-order cross partial derivatives of any twice, continuously differentiable function are independent of the order of differentiation.[44] In terms of a utility function u satisfying continuity and differentiability (2.3-1),

$$u_{in}(x) = u_{ni}(x), \quad i, n = 1, \ldots, I, \qquad (2.4\text{-}22)$$

for all x in the interior of X. There does not seem to be a simple economic interpretation of the symmetry property except as it relates to the differentiability of the utility function. Moreover, when $I = 2$ derivation of the symmetry property does not require (2.4-22), as can be seen from Exercise 2.23.

The properties of demand implied by utility maximization under assumptions (2.3-1) – (2.3-4) are summarized in Table 2.2. Each is identified with a name for future reference and a citation to its development in the text. Continuity and differentiability are sometimes lumped together under the heading "smoothness." Application of the classical model to understand the observed behavior exhibited by consumers is inappropriate unless all properties of Table 2.2 are consistent with that behavior.

---

[44]   Rudin [12, p. 236]. See Theorem A.3-3 in appendix Section A.3.

EXERCISES

2.1 Prove that $\succ$ is irreflexive and asymmetric, and that $\approx$ is an equivalence relation.

2.2 Show that if $\succsim$ is representable then for all x' and x'' in X,

$$x' \succ x'' \quad \text{if and only if} \quad u(x') > u(x''),$$

and

$$x' \approx x'' \quad \text{if and only if} \quad u(x') = u(x'').$$

2.3 Suppose it were desirable to develop the theory of demand from utility functions instead of from preference orderings. Given such a utility function, how could the preference ordering then be defined? Prove that this preference ordering would still be reflexive, transitive, and total.

2.4 Let $\succsim$ be a continuously representable preference ordering. Give an example to show that not all representations of it can be continuous.

2.5 What contradictions would arise in the definition of a strictly quasi-concave utility function if x' and x'' were not distinct or if θ were permitted to be zero or one?

2.6* Without using derivatives, show that a linear function is both concave and convex. (See appendix Section A.3 for definitions of these concepts.) Prove the converse assertion for functions of a single variable.

2.7 Show that any concave function is also quasi-concave.

2.8 Without using derivatives, express the property of linearity of a utility representation in terms of its underlying preference ordering.

2.9** Let u be a continuous utility function and let τ be a continuous transformation defined on the range of u. Show that the property

$$u(x^1) - u(x^2) \geqslant u(x^3) - u(x^4)$$

if and only if

$$\tau(u(x^1)) - \tau(u(x^2)) \geqslant \tau(u(x^3)) - \tau(u(x^4)),$$

for all x^1, x^2, x^3, x^4 in X, is equivalent to the assertion that τ is linear.

2.10 Let assumptions $(2.3\text{-}1) - (2.3\text{-}4)$ be satisfied for some utility function u. Using $(2.3\text{-}2)$, prove that no two indifference surfaces can touch or intersect. Can the same result be proved in the absence of $(2.3\text{-}2)$?

2.11 Let $I = 2$. Show that for all x in the interior of X,

$$|U(x_1, x_2)| = w_{11}(x_1, \mu)[u_2(x_1, x_2)]^3,$$

where $\mu = u(x_1, x_2)$.

2.12 The mathematical proposition that a continuous function defined on a compact set always achieves its maximum on that set cannot be applied directly to the compact set of nonnegative commodity bundles satisfying the budget inequality in the proof of Theorem 2.3-10. Why? If it were possible to do this the proof could be simplified by eliminating the set B.

2.13 Show by differentiation that demand functions are invariant under positively differentiable transformations of their utility generators.

2.14 Derive the sets $\mathcal{D}$ and Ω for the utility function $u(x_1, x_2) = (x_1)^3 x_2 + (x_2)^3 x_1$.

2.15 In spite of the fact that assumptions $(2.3\text{-}1) - (2.3\text{-}4)$ are not satisfied completely, derive the demand functions corresponding to the utility functions

    a) $u(x_1, x_2) = \alpha x_1 + \beta x_2$,

    b) $u(x_1, x_2) = \min(\alpha x_1, \beta x_2)$,

    c) $u(x_1, x_2) = \max(\alpha x_1, \beta x_2)$,

    d) $u(x_1, x_2) = \max(\alpha x_1, \beta x_2) + \min(\alpha x_1, \beta x_2)$,

where α and β are positive constants. Note that (a) and (b) illustrate the cases of, respectively, perfect substitutes and perfect complements.

2.16* Suppose $u(x_1, x_2) = (x_1 - 1)(x_2 - 2)^{-2}$ for $x_1 > 1$ and $0 < x_2 < 2$. Prove that u satisfies $(2.3\text{-}1) - (2.3\text{-}3)$ relative to its domain and derive h. Show that good 2 is superior and $h_2^2 < 0$ on its domain. For which prices and incomes is good 1 Giffen?[45]

---

[45]   This example is due to Wold and Juréen [15, p. 102].

2.17 Show that the utility function $u(x_1, x_2) = x_1 x_2$ satisfies (2.3-1) − (2.3-4) on X. Derive the demand and compensated demand functions from it. Show that all properties of Table 2.2 are satisfied. Determine the set Ω and verify Slutsky's equation (2.4-13).

2.18 Let $u(x_1, x_2)$ satisfy (2.3-1) − (2.3-3) on X. Suppose further that u is additive and exhibits diminishing marginal utility; that is,

$$u(x_1, x_2) = u^1(x_1) + u^2(x_2),$$

for some functions u^1 and u^2, and $u_{ii}(x) < 0$ on X for $i = 1, 2$. These additional assumptions were often imposed by nineteenth-century economists. Using (2.4-7) and (2.4-8), show that, under them, demand curves always slope downward everywhere.

2.19 Let $I = 2$. Using Euler's theorem,[46] deduce $|S^*(p, m)| = 0$ on Ω from the homogeneity of h.

2.20 Show that at each point of Ω there always must be at least one superior good.

2.21 Let

$$\varepsilon^{in}(p, m) = -h_n^i(p, m)[p_n / h^i(p, m)],$$

for $i, n = 1, \ldots, I$, and

$$\varepsilon^{im}(p, m) = h_m^i(p, m)[m / h^i(p, m)],$$

for $i = 1, \ldots, I$, be price and income elasticities of demand, respectively. Let $\beta^i(p, m)$ be the ratio of expenditure on good i to total income; that is,

$$\beta^i(p, m) = p_i[h^i(p, m) / m],$$

where $i = 1, \ldots, I$. Prove the following:

a) $\displaystyle\sum_{n=1}^{I} \varepsilon^{in} = \varepsilon^{im}$, for $i = 1, \ldots, I$.

b) $\displaystyle\sum_{i=1}^{I} \beta^i \varepsilon^{in} = \beta^n$, for $n = 1, \ldots, I$.

c) $\displaystyle\sum_{i=1}^{I} \beta^i \varepsilon^{im} = 1$.

---

[46]   Theorem A.3-9 in appendix Section A.3.

2.22 Show for the general case of $I > 2$ goods that the inequality $s^{11}(p, m) < 0$ can be derived from the negative definiteness of $S(p, m)$, for all (p, m) in Ω.

2.23 Prove that when $I = 2$,

$$s^{12}(p, m) = s^{21}(p, m) = \frac{\lambda u_1 u_2}{|U|},$$

on Ω. Combine this with (2.4-21) to conclude that $|S^*(p, m)| = 0$ on Ω, and compare the present proof of the latter result with that of Exercise 2.19.

2.24 Let $A = \{a', a''\}$ and suppose persons 1 and 2 measure the pleasure they obtain from the elements of A on scales σ^1 and σ^2, respectively, according to

$$\sigma^1(a') = 1, \quad \sigma^1(a'') = 4,$$

$$\sigma^2(a') = 3, \quad \sigma^2(a'') = 1.$$

Define $\nu : B^1 \times B^2 \to B^3$ such that

$$\nu(b_1, b_2) = b_1 + b_2,$$

for all b_1 in B^1 and b_2 in B^2. Verify that

$$\nu \circ \sigma(a'') > \nu \circ \sigma(a').$$

Show also that this inequality is reversed if the scale values of person 1 are halved.

2.25 Consider the utility function defined implicitly by the equation

$$(x_1 - \mu)^2 + (x_2 - \mu)^2 = \mu^2,$$

where $0 \leqslant x_1 \leqslant \mu$, $0 \leqslant x_2 \leqslant \mu$, and $\mu \geqslant 0$. Show that (2.3-1) – (2.3-3) are satisfied but that (2.3-4) is not. Explain why the property of positivity of demand (2.3-11) remains in force in spite of the failure of the utility function to satisfy the boundary condition (2.3-4).

2.26 Let $I = 3$ and consider the demand functions

$$h^1(p, m) = \frac{p_2}{p_1 + p_2 + p_3} \left[\frac{m}{p_1} \right],$$

$$h^2(p, m) = \frac{p_3}{p_1 + p_2 + p_3} \left[\frac{m}{p_2} \right],$$

$$h^3(p, m) = \frac{p_1}{p_1 + p_2 + p_3} \left[\frac{m}{p_3} \right],$$

defined for all $(p, m) > 0$. Show that these demand functions (a) satisfy the budget constraint, (b) are homogeneous of degree zero, and (c) are *not* consistent with constrained utility maximization.

2.27 Show that the utility function

$$u(x_1, x_2) = x_1 + \ln x_2$$

satisfies (2.3-1) – (2.3-3) but violates (2.3-4). Describe the geometric relationship between the indifference curves generated by u. Derive the demand functions and determine the domain on which these functions have nonnegative functions values (that is, the set on which $h(p, m) \geqslant 0$).

2.28 Imagine a world with $I = 4$ goods and partition these goods into two groups $\{1,2\}$ and $\{3,4\}$. The utility function u is said to be *weakly separable* with respect to this partition if and only if there exist functions ψ^1, ψ^2, and Ψ such that

$$u(x) = \Psi(\psi^1(x_1, x_2), \psi^2(x_3, x_4)),$$

for all x in X. Assume that u satisfies all requirements introduced in Section 1.3 and suppose that $\mathcal{D} = X$. If u is also weakly separable, show that:

a) The marginal rates of substitution between within-group goods depends only on the goods in that group and not on goods outside it.

b) The demand functions for goods in any group can be expressed as functions of the prices of only those goods in the group and expenditure on the group as a whole. Other prices and the consumer's income do not explicitly appear in this formulation.

REFERENCES

1. Apostol, T. M., *Mathematical Analysis*, 2nd ed. (Reading, Mass.: Addison-Wesley, 1974).
2. Deaton, A. and J. Muellbauer, *Economics and Consumer Behavior* (Cambridge: Cambridge University Press, 1980).
3. Debreu, G., "Topological Methods in Cardinal Utility Theory," *Mathematical Methods in the Social Sciences*, K. J. Arrow, S. Karlin and P. Suppes, eds. (Stanford: Stanford University Press, 1960), pp. 16-26.
4. ——, "Economies with a Finite Set of Equilibria," *Econometrica* 38 (1970), pp. 387-392.
5. Fisher, I., *Mathematical Investigations in the Theory of Value and Prices*, (New York: Kelley, 1965).
6. Jevons, W. S., *The Theory of Political Economy*, 5th ed. (New York: Kelley, 1965).
7. Katzner, D. W., *Static Demand Theory* (New York: Macmillan, 1970).
8. Lloyd, C. L., "The Northern Stores Project," *Collected Works* (Burnaby: School of Business Administration and Economics, Simon Fraser University, 1980), unpublished paper no. 1.
9. von Neumann, J. and O. Morgenstern, *Theory of Games and Economic Behavior* (Princeton: Princeton University Press, 1944).
10. Pareto, V., *Cours d' économie politique* (Lausanne: Rouge, 1896).
11. Pfanzagl, J., *Theory of Measurement*, 2nd ed. (Würzburg-Vienna: Physica-Verlag, 1971).
12. Rudin, W., *Principles of Mathematical Analysis*, 3rd ed. (New York: McGraw-Hill, 1976).
13. Slutsky, E. E., "On the Theory of the Budget of the Consumer," *Giornale degli economisti* 51 (1915), pp. 1-26. English translation: The American Economic Association's *Readings in Price Theory*, v. 4, G. J. Stigler and K. Boulding, eds. (Homewood: Irwin, 1952), pp. 27-56.
14. Stigler, G. J., "Notes on the History of the Giffen Paradox," *Journal of Political Economy* 55 (1947), pp. 152-156.
15. Wold, H. and L. Juréen, *Demand Analysis* (New York: Wiley, 1953).

Chapter 3

Topics in Demand Theory

There are several important issues arising with regard to the classical model described in Chapter 2. These include the possibility of reconstructing preferences from demand behavior, the effects of weakening hypotheses, expansion to permit the supply of factors of production by consumers, and the analysis of individual welfare. The third (Section 3.3) is an element of the particular grand view described in Section 1.4, and the fourth (Section 3.4) provides a basis for the presentation of (aggregate) economic welfare in Chapter 12. Before briefly discussing each, one additional point should be considered.

It is possible to give definitions of substitute and complementary goods alternative to the characterizations of perfect substitutes and perfect complements discussed in Section 2.3. The idea is that coffee and tea, say, would be substitutes if a rise in the price of one is accompanied by an increase in demand for the other. The higher price leads to substitution in favor of the competing good. On the other hand, coffee and cream would be complements when a price rise for one is associated with lower demand for both, because one is used with the other and the higher price decreases its demand. These statements would appear to express substitutability and complementarity in terms of the signs of cross partial derivatives of demand functions. But derivatives of the ordinary demand functions h cannot be used for such a purpose because, as in the example of Exercise 2.16, it is possible to have both $h_n^i(p, m) > 0$ and $h_i^n(p, m) < 0$ at the same (p, m). Looking at h_n^i, goods i and n would appear to be substitutes, whereas h_i^n would indicate that they are complements. This, however, cannot happen with compensated demand functions h^*. The symmetry property ensures that for all i and n,

$$s^{in}(p, m) = h_n^{*i}(p, \mu) = h_i^{*n}(p, \mu) = s^{ni}(p, m),$$

where $\mu = u(x)$ and $x = h(p, m)$. Therefore, an individual can be said to regard the pair i and n $(i \neq n)$ as, respectively, (net) substitute goods or (net) complementary[1] goods at (p, m), according as the derivatives of his Slutsky function

$$s^{in}(p, m) \gtrless 0. \tag{3.0-1}$$

One problem with employing the criterion of (3.0-1) is that the logic of utility maximization precludes the existence of complementarity in any two-commodity world (Exercise 3.1).[2]

3.1   INTEGRABILITY

The last chapter explored the implications for observable demand behavior derived by imputing properties to unobservable utility functions. This line of reasoning is schematically depicted along the upper arrow in Figure 3.1. The classical analysis of utility maximization provides little insight into the behavior of any consumer whose demand functions are inconsistent with these implications. But suppose a consumer's demand functions satisfy the observable properties of demand in Figure 3.1. In what sense, if at all, can it be said that utility maximization explains such an individual's behavior? The answer is subtle. For under no circumstances is it ever going to be possible to assert by observing a consumer's economic activity that he is, in fact, a utility maximizer. If it were possible, however, to construct from his observed demand functions a utility function (and hence preference ordering) which, when maximized subject to appropriate budget constraints, reproduces these same demand functions, then regardless of whether the consumer actually maximizes utility to determine demands, his behavior may be viewed as if he did. Analogously with the clock example of Section 1.2, the observable behavior of the

---

[1]   The word "net" is sometimes used here to emphasize the distinction between these notions of substitutes and complements and the "gross" concepts introduced in Sections 9.3 and 9.4. See n. 27 on p. 366.
[2]   For a discussion of additional problems with this definition and an alternative approach that avoids them, see Katzner [10, Sect. 7.4].

individual and that produced by the classical model are indistinguishable. It matters not that the "workings" of the model may be different from the real "workings" of the individual. The latter can never be known. But the model still provides a way of understanding what is seen.

Because the line of reasoning required to build a utility function satisfying (2.3-1) – (2.3-4) from demand involves the integration of a system of partial differential equations, it is often given the name "integrability." (Note the lower arrow in Figure 3.1.) The argument has three main parts. First, given demand functions exhibiting the observed properties of demand listed in Figure 3.1 or Table 2.2, the existence of a utility function has to be established through integration. Next, the unobservable properties (2.3-1) – (2.3-4) must be inferred for the utility function from the observable properties of demand. Finally, it must be shown that maximization of this utility function subject to budget constraints generates the demand functions with which the argument began. Because a more complete account is provided in the revealed preference context of Section 3.2, only the briefest of outlines is presented here. Details may be found in Katzner [10, Ch. 4].

It is convenient to begin with a utility function u in the two-commodity case in which $\mathcal{D} = \{x : x > 0\}$ and $\Omega = \{(p, m) : p > 0 \text{ and } m > 0\}$. With the utility function available, demand functions on Ω are often obtained by solving (2.3-16) and (2.3-17) on $\mathcal{D}$ for $x = (x_1, x_2)$ in terms of (p_1, p_2, m). An equivalent way of writing these equations is to divide the budget constraint

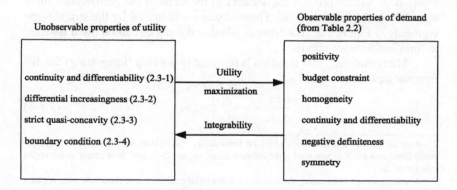

Figure 3.1 Classical model of consumer demand

by p_2 and replace p_1/p_2, by u_1/u_2:

$$\frac{u_1(x_1, x_2)}{u_2(x_1, x_2)} = \frac{p_1}{p_2},$$

$$\frac{u_1(x_1, x_2)}{u_2(x_1, x_2)} x_1 + x_2 = \frac{m}{p_2}.$$

(3.1-1)

Inversion of (3.1-1) also yields h. Furthermore, the negative of the ratio of marginal utilities at $x > 0$ is the slope of the indifference curve through x or

$$w_1(x_1, u(x_1, x_2)) = -\frac{u_1(x_1, x_2)}{u_2(x_1, x_2)},$$

where $\mu = u(x_1, x_2)$ has been substituted for μ in (2.3-7). Thus if the utility function is not known and if demand functions with the properties of Table 2.2

$$x_i = h^i(p, m), \quad i = 1, 2$$

(3.1-2)

are given which, in particular, are homogeneous of degree zero and satisfy the budget equality,[3] then solving (3.1-2) on Ω for p_1/p_2 and m/p_2 as functions of x, yields the inverse demand function $h^{-1} = (h^{-1^1}, h^{-1^2})$ on $\mathcal{D}$, or

$$\frac{p_1}{p_2} = h^{-1^1}(x),$$

$$\frac{m}{p_2} = h^{-1^2}(x),$$

where h^{-1^1} should provide the negative of the slope of the indifference curve at each x in the interior of X. These slopes are indicated by the straight-line segments in Figure 3.2. The issue is whether the slopes can be fitted together to form indifference curves.

Mathematically this question is resolved by solving (integrating) the differential equation[4]

$$\frac{dx_2}{dx_1} = -h^{-1^1}(x_1, x_2).$$

(3.1-3)

---

[3]   As with the demand functions obtained from utility maximization in Chapter 2, these demand functions are also assumed to be defined for all $(p, m) > 0$, and their image is the entire interior of X.

[4]   A more general, but related, discussion of differential equations and their solutions appears in Section 9.1.

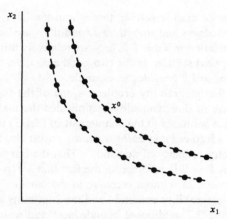

Figure 3.2 Integration of slopes of indifference curves

To say (3.1-3) has a solution through x^0 in the interior of X (see Figure 3.2) means that there exists a continuous function w such that $x_2 = w(x_1, x^0)$,

$$\frac{dw(x_1, x^0)}{dx_1} = -h^{-1^1}(x_1, w(x_1, x^0)),$$

and

$$x_2^0 = w(x_1^0, x^0).$$

With x^0 held fixed, $x_2 = w(x_1, x^0)$ is the equation of an indifference curve, the first of the above conditions asserting that its slope is $-h^{-1^1}$, and the second that it passes through the point x^0. Varying x^0 produces an entire indifference map and a utility function can be constructed from it. (Recall, for example, Theorem 2.1-8 on continuous representability.)

Now (3.1-3) has a solution under very weak circumstances. The only restriction is that h^{-1^1} be continuous, and the latter follows from the continuity of h. Because it is necessary that one and only one indifference curve pass through each point of X, solutions must also be unique. To obtain this uniqueness requires an additional property (namely, the so-called Lipschitz condition[5]) that is implied by, but not equivalent to, boundedness of the derivative $\partial h^{-1^1}/\partial x_2$. Still further smoothness-type characteristics are needed to ensure

---

[5]   The Lipschitz condition ensuring that there is only one indifference curve through the point $x^0 = (x_1^0, x_2^0)$ in X is as follows: There exists a number $\varepsilon > 0$ such that for every (x_1, x_2') and

that the indifference map is defined throughout the interior of X. Although these extra boundedness and smoothness conditions are beyond those implied by utility maximization in Table 2.2, they are relatively minor and disappear in the setting of the next section. In the two-good case then, the integration issue is resolved. Exercise 3.2 provides an example.

However, the integrability problem is one of the few in economics for which an increase in dimensionality complicates the mathematics considerably. For to obtain solutions to the counterpart of (3.1-3) when there are more than two goods, a further *integrability condition* must also hold. This turns out to be the symmetry property of demand.[6] (That the integrability condition is not needed when $I = 2$ is reflected in the fact that $s^{12}(p, m) = s^{21}(p, m)$ is proved in Exercise 2.23 without recourse to the equality $u_{12}(x) = u_{21}(x)$.) Along with the integrability condition and the continuity and differentiability indicated in Figure 3.1, additional boundedness and smoothness restrictions similar to those described for the two-good world are required here too. In general, then, a utility function can be obtained from any observed demand functions exhibiting the characteristics of Table 2.2 along with the additional boundedness and smoothness properties.

Turn now to the second and third parts of the integrability argument as outlined above. Because, from their very definition, solutions of differential equations can always be differentiated, smoothness of at least one utility representation — restriction (2.3-1) — follows from the process of integration and the differentiability of h. Utility characteristics (2.3-2) – (2.3-4) are derived from the remaining observable properties of demand. Thus differential increasingness (2.3-2) emerges from the integration argument because the budget property holds. Similarly, the strict quasi-concavity (2.3-3) and the boundary condition (2.3-4) are obtained, respectively, from negative definiteness and positivity.[7] Lastly, it is obvious that this utility function, u, generates the de-

---

(x_1, x_2'') in X,

$$\left| h^{-1^1}(x_1, x_2') - h^{-1^1}(x_1, x_2'') \right| \leqslant \varepsilon \left| x_2' - x_2'' \right|.$$

See Hurewicz [8, Ch. 1].

[6]   Awareness of the integrability condition by economists dates to Antonelli [1]. Chipman [5, pp. 321-322] describes how Antonelli's work, written in 1886, was lost and accidentally rediscovered by Herman Wold in 1943. It is also interesting that in discussing integrability, a mathematical economist as competent as Pareto conspicuously omitted the symmetry condition in the earlier Italian version of his *Manuale* [12]. Pareto's now-famous error was corrected by Volterra [16].

[7]   In light of the example of Exercise 2.25, the positivity of h by itself is not enough to ensure that the boundary condition (2.3-4) is satisfied. But positivity together with the extra smoothness-type conditions mentioned above is sufficient.

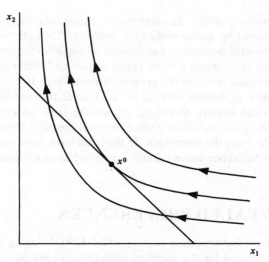

Figure 3.3 Constrained "maximization" with
lexicographic-type curves

mand functions given at the outset, because u was constructed from the same
equations (in the two-commodity case, equations (3.1-1)) that would result
from its maximization subject to the budget constraint.

One more word. The solutions obtained by integrating (3.1-3) and its
generalized counterpart in higher dimensions have been thought of as indifference curves and surfaces. Indeed, the utility function constructed above assigns
to each such curve (or surface) exactly one utility value. Care, however, should
be exercised. For suppose the consumer in question had the preference ordering pictured in Figure 3.3 such that if baskets on the curves of Figure 3.3 were
indifferent, then a utility representation satisfying (2.3-1) – (2.3-4) would exist. But instead, along each curve bundles closer to the x_2-axis are preferred
to those farther away. (Arrows indicate directions of higher preference along
each curve.) This is a lexicographic type of preference ordering with curves
that are smooth, strictly convex, do not touch the boundary of X, and for which
all points on curves to the upper right are preferred to all points on curves to
the lower left. No utility function can exist representing such an ordering. Yet,
given the budget constraint drawn in Figure 3.3, if the consumer selects the
"most preferred" basket of commodities available, he will choose x^0 — the
identical bundle he would pick if the curves were true indifference curves and

he were maximizing utility. In other words, exactly the same demand functions are generated by either preference ordering. Because the integrability argument starts with demand in the absence of any information about preferences, it cannot be assumed that the result will be an indifference map rather than a lexicographic one. In the present context, there is not enough information contained in seeable demand behavior to distinguish between them.[8] Two equally valid models, therefore, explain the same observable phenomenon. The investigator can either choose one over the other for reasons of, say, convenience, or leave the issue open. In the latter case, what would otherwise be called an indifference curve usually is referred to as a *pseudo-indifference* curve.

3.2   REVEALED PREFERENCES

The importance of assumptions (2.3-1) – (2.3-4) in deducing the observable properties of demand for the classical model should not be underestimated. The role of each can be summarized as follows: Continuity of u (the first part of assumption (2.3-1)) guarantees the existence of utility-maximizing baskets of commodities, thus legitimizing the explanation of demand in terms of utility. Differentiability (the last part of assumption (2.3-1)) prevents indifference surfaces from having kinks. The presence of such kinks would mean that utility-maximizing baskets of commodities might be the same for different budget hyperplanes (Figure 3.4(a)). Demand functions might then have regions in their domains, beyond those implied by the homogeneity, over which they are constant so their inverses there, apart from scalar multiples of (p, m), need not be single-valued functions. Differentiability is also the basis for the geometric tangency characterization (between indifference surfaces and budget hyperplanes) of utility-maximizing baskets of commodities and hence the proofs of symmetry and negative definiteness described in Chapter 2. Differential increasingness (2.3-2) implies that utility-maximizing baskets lie on budget hyperplanes and not in the interior of the budget set as pictured in Figure 3.4(b). From it the budget constraint property of h is derived. Differential increasingness along with quasi-concavity (part of assumption (2.3-3)) form a kind of "second-order" condition ensuring that indifference surfaces have the proper shape so that their tangencies to budget hyperplanes do, indeed, correspond to constrained maxima. Minima along the budget line (Figure 3.4(c)),

---

[8]   In a choice theory setting, with the individual permitted to choose from appropriate finite choice sets (rather than from budget sets with nondenumerable numbers of points), observable choice behavior can identify points that are indifferent. See, for example, Arrow [3].

saddle or inflection points (Figure 3.4(d)), and still other possibilities (such as Figure 3.4(e)) are ruled out. Strictness of the quasi-concavity (the rest of assumption (2.3-3)) keeps indifference surfaces from containing linear segments and being tangent to a single budget hyperplane at more than one point (Figure 3.4(f)). Otherwise, uniqueness of utility-maximizing bundles and the single-valuedness of h would be impaired. Recall also that strict quasi-concavity

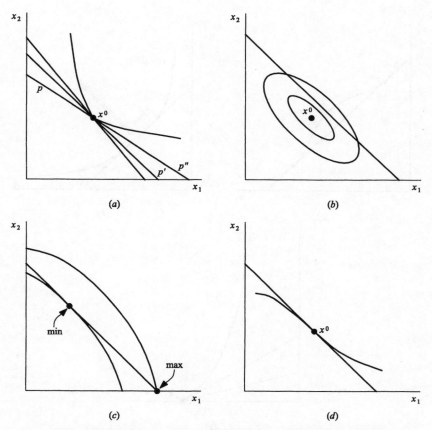

Figure 3.4 Weakening the assumptions of the classical model of consumer demand: (*a*) kink in an indifference curve; (*b*) utility-maximizing basket in the interior of the budget set; (*c*) strictly concave indifference curves; (*d*) indifference curve with an inflection point; (continued overleaf)

combined with differential increasingness are responsible for the negative definiteness condition. Lastly, the boundary assumption (2.3-4) precludes indifference surfaces from touching the boundary of X and leads to the positivity of
demand (that is, the statement that the consumer must always demand something of every good). In its absence, multiple budget hyperplanes could again
yield identical utility-maximizing baskets (Figure 3.4(g)) and inverse demand

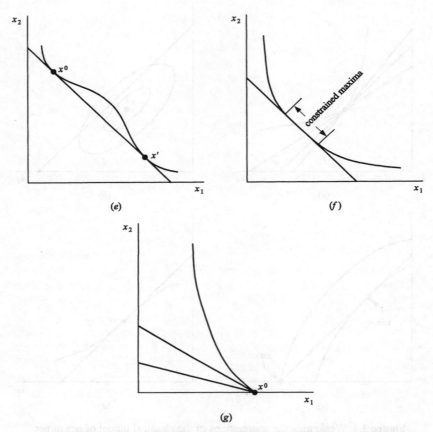

Figure 3.4 (continued) (e) indifference curve tangent to a budget line at
exactly two points; (f) linear segment in an indifference curve; (g) utility-
maximizing basket on the boundary of the commodity space

functions would then, in addition to scalar multiples of (p, m), be multivalued at those baskets.

It is abundantly clear, however, that even if one or more of the above assumptions are not fulfilled, as long as continuity is intact, the first part of the proof of the theorem on the existence of utility-maximizing baskets of commodities (Theorem 2.3-10) holds up and demand functions can be defined in the usual way (Section 2.3). But, depending on the manner in which (2.3-1) − (2.3-4) are breached, the properties of demand listed in Table 2.2 must be modified. Thus, for example, if differential increasingness were discarded and the utility function had a global maximum at the origin, then

$$h^i(p, m) = 0, \quad i = 1, \ldots, I,$$

for all $(p, m) > 0$. Positivity, budget constraint and negative definiteness properties of demand no longer apply. Nevertheless these are logically correct, if somewhat uninteresting, demand functions derived from utility maximization. Concrete illustrations are provided by the utility functions violating various assumed conditions in Exercises 2.15, 2.16, 2.25, 2.27, and 3.15.

To be more systematic in throwing away assumptions, consider a utility function, u, satisfying only

(3.2-1) u is continuous on the interior of X, continuous where finite on X and, where not finite, $u(x) = -\infty$ and u declines continuously to $-\infty$ through interior points of X.

(3.2-2) u is increasing.

(3.2-3) u is strictly quasi-concave on the interior of X.

Properties (3.2-1) − (3.2-3) differ from those of the classical model in the absence of both differentiability and the boundary condition. Thus kinks in indifference surfaces, maxima on the boundary of X, and multivalued inverse demand functions beyond that permitted by the homogeneity are possible. The theorem of Lagrange no longer applies. There are three reasons for examining such utility functions in some detail. First, weakening the assumptions of the classical model is worthwhile because it enlarges the number of preference orderings, and hence observed behaviors, covered by the analysis. Although less can be said about each, the loss does not seem to be significant. Second, unlike the classical model, assumptions (3.2-1) − (3.2-3) all have been given equivalent expressions in terms of preference orderings in Section 2.1. There is nothing extra in the utility function — namely, differentiability — that does not readily appear as a property of preferences. Third, it is in this context that the important and often used notion of revealed preference naturally arises.

Proceeding along the utility maximization line of argument from utility to demand, note (as suggested, in part, above) that except for the positivity of utility-maximizing baskets of commodities (which now becomes *nonnegativity*[9] because the boundary condition has been dropped), Theorem 2.3-10 on the existence of such baskets and its proof carry over without change. Stripping away differentiability of the utility function has no impact. Thus demand functions are obtained as before. Moreover, although nonnegativity is substituted for positivity, these functions still exhibit the original budget constraint (2.3-12) and homogeneity (2.3-13) properties. It is also possible, but not pursued here, to show them to be continuous for all $(p, m) > 0$.[10]

Because the first-order maximization conditions (2.3-15) are not available, an alternative way must be found to translate the information contained in the symmetry and negative definiteness restrictions from its initial state in terms of utility to demand. A basis for doing so is provided by Samuelson's revealed preference concept.[11] For any pair x' and x'' in X, write $x' \widetilde{R} x''$ and say that x' is *directly revealed preferred* to x'' whenever the following three conditions are met:

a) $x' \neq x''$.

b) There exist vectors $(p', m') > 0$ and $(p'', m'') > 0$ such that $x' = h(p', m')$ and $x'' = h(p'', m'')$.

c) $p' \cdot x' \geqslant p' \cdot x''$.

In words, $x' \widetilde{R} x''$ means that x' and x'' are distinct baskets, demanded by the consumer at some prices and income, such that with those prices and income at which x' is demanded, the consumer is able to demand x'' but does not. Thus the consumer "reveals a preference" for x' over x''. (Note, however, that revealed preferences are not the same as preferences defined in Section 2.1. The former are observable because they are characterized in terms of demand functions; the latter are never observable to the economist.) An illustration is given in Figure 3.5. Call x' *indirectly revealed preferred* to x''', or $x' \bar{R} x'''$, if there is a finite sequence of commodity bundles $x^1, \ldots, x^N$ in X (the empty sequence obtained when $N = 0$ is included as a possibility) such that $x' \widetilde{R} x^1$, $x^1 \widetilde{R} x^2, \ldots, x^{N-1} \widetilde{R} x^N$, and $x^N \widetilde{R} x'''$. In Figure 3.5, $x' \widetilde{R} x''$ and $x'' \widetilde{R} x'''$ so

---

[9]   Here nonnegativity means that both $x = h(p, m) \geqslant 0$ and $x = h(p, m) \neq 0$ for all $(p, m) > 0$. As long as $(p, m) > 0$, increasingness (3.2-2) ensures that at least one component of $x = h(p, m)$ is always positive.

[10]   Katzner [10, pp. 106, 107].

[11]   Samuelson [13, p. 65].

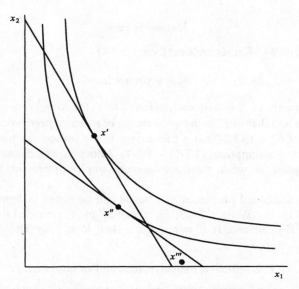

Figure 3.5 Direct and indirect revealed preference

that $x' \bar{R} x'''$. Note that $x' \widetilde{R} x''$ implies $x' \bar{R} x''$ but not conversely ($x' \bar{R} x'''$ in Figure 3.5 and yet x' is not directly revealed preferred to x''').

In deducing restrictions on $\widetilde{R}$ and $\bar{R}$ implied by utility maximization, a link between these relations and u would be useful. It is easily seen (Exercise 3.3) that for any x' and x'' in X, if $x' \widetilde{R} x''$ then $u(x') > u(x'')$. But the converse assertion cannot hold. Although x' in Figure 3.5 has larger utility value than that of x''', x' is not directly revealed preferred to x'''. A more significant result, stated below without proof,[12] concerns $\bar{R}$:

Theorem 3.2-4   For all x' and x'' in X, $x' \bar{R} x''$ if and only if $u(x') > u(x'')$.

This theorem plays the same role here as the equation of Slutsky does in the classical model. It is the vehicle by which properties of utility or preferences are translated into observable properties of revealed preferences. For Theorem 3.2-4 surely means that $\bar{R} = \succ$ and hence that these relations share the same properties. In particular,

$$\bar{R} \text{ is increasing,} \qquad (3.2\text{-}5)$$

---

[12]   A proof can be found in Katzner [10, pp. 108, 109].

$$\bar{R} \text{ is asymmetric.} \tag{3.2-6}$$

Moreover, (3.2-6) further implies (Exercise 3.4)

$$\widetilde{R} \text{ is asymmetric.} \tag{3.2-7}$$

The asymmetry of $\bar{R}$ is frequently referred to as the *strong axiom of revealed preference* and that of $\widetilde{R}$ as the *weak axiom of revealed preference*. However, neither (3.2-6) nor (3.2-7) is a true axiom in the present context. Both are deduced from assumptions (3.2-1) – (3.2-3). Although, as indicated, the strong axiom implies the weak, there are counterexamples disproving the converse statement.[13]

Still additional properties of demand can be stated in terms of a third relation R on X. Write $x'R\,x''$, for x' and x'' in X, provided that either (a) $x'\bar{R}\,x''$ or (b) neither $x'\bar{R}\,x''$ nor $x''\bar{R}\,x'$. Then $R = \underset{\sim}{\succeq}$ by Theorem 3.2-4 so that

$$R \text{ is reflexive, transitive, total and strictly convex.} \tag{3.2-8}$$

Furthermore, letting $C_{x^0}^{+} = \{x : x\,\bar{R}\,x^0\}$ and $C_{x^0}^{-} = \{x : x^0\bar{R}\,x\}$ be subsets of X for each x^0, it follows that $C_{x^0}^{+} = C_{x^0}^{\geq}$ and $C_{x^0}^{-} = C_{x^0}^{\leq}$. The continuity of u and Theorem 2.1-8 now imply

$$C_{x^0}^{+} \text{ and } C_{x^0}^{-} \text{ are open relative to the interior of } X, \text{ for all } x^0 \text{ in } X. \tag{3.2-9}$$

The observable properties of demand obtained thus far are not all independent. It has already been noted above that the strong axiom of revealed preference implies the weak. Exercise 2.1 indicates that the strong axiom, in turn, follows from the reflexivity and transitivity of R. Moreover, it can be shown that the homogeneity of h is a consequence of the weak axiom (Exercise 3.5). Hence the observable properties of demand reduce to nonnegativity, continuity, (3.2-5), (3.2-8), (3.2-9), and the budget constraint (2.3-12). The argument of the revealed preference model running from utility to demand is summarized in Figure 3.6. If, in addition to (3.2-1) – (3.2-3), u were also twice continuously differentiable in the interior of, and indifference surfaces did not touch the boundary of X, then the assumptions of the classical model would be satisfied. The observable properties of demand would then include the additional characteristics listed in Table 2.2 along with those indicated here.[14]

---

[13]   Gale [7].

[14]   Even if u is not differentiable, it is possible to show that (3.2-1) – (3.2-3) still imply symmetry and negative definiteness where h is differentiable. See Katzner [10, pp. 110-112].

It is important to remember that all three relations $\widetilde{R}$, $\bar{R}$, and R are defined solely in terms of h, that is, in terms of seeable demand phenomena. Given appropriate preferences or utility functions, h, $\widetilde{R}$, $\bar{R}$, and R are manifestations of constrained utility maximization. This is the source of the restrictions on demand listed in Figure 3.6. If the actual activity of a consumer is inconsistent with these properties, then the revealed preference model does not explain that consumer's behavior.

If, on the other hand, the consumer's behavior does exhibit the requisite properties, it is still necessary to ask, for the same reasons as in the classical model, whether a preference ordering can be reconstructed from that behavior. The line of reasoning needed to answer this question in the revealed preference model parallels the integrability argument in the classical model and usually goes under the heading "revealed preference theory." (See Figure 3.6. The terminology is subtle here: Revealed preferences as defined by $\bar{R}$, $\bar{R}$, and R arise in both the utility maximization and revealed preference theory progressions of thought.) Actually, in the present context, the logic involved is quite simple. For if an h defined for all $(p, m) > 0$ is given having X as its image and satisfying the observable properties of demand in Figure 3.6, then $\succsim$ can be taken to be R. It follows that $\succ = \bar{R}$ and, by the theorem on continuous representability (Theorem 2.1-8), a continuous utility function u representing $\succsim$ exists. Clearly u must satisfy (3.2-1) – (3.2-3), and maximization of u subject to the budget constraint yields the original h. Note that, unlike the integrability argument, no extra smoothness conditions have to be imposed on h. The implications of utility maximization are sufficient by themselves.

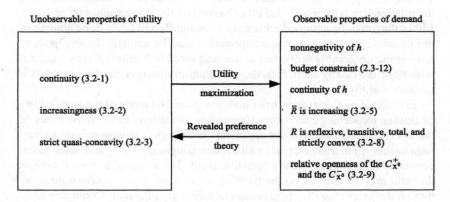

Figure 3.6 Revealed preference model of consumer demand

It is instructive to consider a geometric method (in two dimensions) for building $\succsim$ (or R) up from $\widetilde{R}$ and $\bar{R}$. Let $x^0 = h(p^0, m^0)$ for a fixed $(p^0, m^0) > 0$. Since each x in X is demanded at some $(p, m) > 0$ (a property implicit in the present definition of h and implied by utility maximization under (3.2-1) – (3.2-3)), for all x with $p^0 \cdot x < m^0$, $x^0 \widetilde{R} x$, and hence $x^0 \succ x$. Also if $x \geqslant x^0$ and $x \neq x^0$, then $x \, \bar{R} \, x^0$ (Exercise 3.6) so that $x \succ x^0$. Thus the preference relationship of x^0 to other points of X is obtained except for the shaded region of Figure 3.7(a). All points in the budget triangle are worse than x^0 and all points in the upper quadrant above x^0 are better. To narrow the shaded region from below, choose any x' such that $p^0 \cdot x' = m^0$. Then $x' = h(p', m')$ for some $(p', m') > 0$ and $x^0 \widetilde{R} x'$. By the weak axiom, $p' \cdot x^0 > m'$ or, in words, x^0 lies outside of the (p', m') budget set in Figure 3.7(b). Moreover, for any x'' outside the (p^0, m^0) budget line but still with $p' \cdot x'' < m'$ (see Figure 3.7(b)), $x' \widetilde{R} x''$. Hence $x^0 \bar{R} x''$ or $x^0 \succ x''$. Such x'' can therefore be removed from the shaded region.

The shaded region can also be narrowed from above. Choose any price vector $p^* > 0$ such that $p^* \neq \alpha p^0$ for all $\alpha > 0$, and let $m^* = p^* \cdot x^0$. Then at (p^*, m^*) a basket of commodities, say x^* (Figure 3.7(b)), is demanded: $x^* = h(p^*, m^*)$. By the weak axiom x^* must lie outside of the (p^0, m^0) budget set. Because $p^* \cdot x^* = p^* \cdot x^0$, $x^* \widetilde{R} x^0$ and $x^* \succ x^0$. Furthermore, for any $\bar{x} \geqslant x^*$, where $\bar{x} \neq x^*$ (Figure 3.7(b)), $\bar{x} \, \bar{R} \, x^*$. Hence $\bar{x} \, \bar{R} \, x^0$ and $\bar{x} \succ x^0$. Points such as $\bar{x}$ can also be dropped from the shaded region.

Continuing in this fashion, the shaded region (on both sides of x^0) becomes smaller and smaller. In the limit it is compressed to a downward sloping, strictly convex curve through x^0. All points above the curve are preferred to x^0, and x^0 is preferred to all points below it. But as in the integrability case, the relationship between x^0 and other baskets on the curve cannot be deduced. Either they may be assumed arbitrarily to be indifferent (as is done above), or the pseudo-indifference curve interpretation may be applied. In any case, as long as the observable properties of demand listed in Figure 3.6 are consistent with what is actually seen, then the consumer in question can be treated as if he were a utility maximizer.

In concluding this section brief mention should be made of the possibilities of further weakenings and other types of modifications in the hypotheses of the utility-maximization line of argument. With respect to weakenings, several implications of discarding part or all of increasingness (3.2-2) and strict quasi-concavity (3.2-3) have already been discussed. The result is demand functions that still may be defined on the basis of constrained utility maximization, although the properties they possess can be strikingly different. Continuity (3.2-

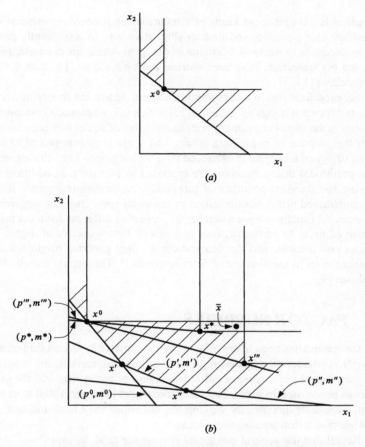

Figure 3.7 Construction of a pseudo-indifference curve from revealed preferences: (*a*) region of unknown preferences; (*b*) narrowing the region of unknown preferences

1) and the qualities of $\succsim$ that permit its representation by a utility function may also be weakened. But then the theory of demand itself may, of necessity, take on a rather different character. For in that case, even if a utility function continues to exist, the previously required constrained maxima of it might not. That is, the form of the postulate of rationality employed above might not

be applicable. Under these kinds of circumstances it becomes imperative to reconstitute that postulate and find an alternative way of analytically passing from preferences to demand. Methods of doing so when, for example, preferences are not transitive, have been worked out by Katzner [10, Sect. 6.4] and Sonnenschein [14].[15]

Other modifications in its assumption content permit the theory of demand to account for such things as Veblen's [15] notion of *conspicuous consumption*. The latter is the use of consumer goods as a display of social and economic status for the purpose of impressing others, and it has been interpreted to imply that the utility of an object is enhanced by a higher price. Thus the arguments of the traditional utility function are extended to include p in addition to x. Applying the standard postulate of rationality, demand functions are derived from constrained utility maximization in the usual way. But, not surprisingly, those demand functions have a number of properties different from the properties derived here. In particular, they may not be homogeneous of degree zero in prices and income, and the demand curves they generate might not slope downward even in the absence of inferior goods.[16] The details may be found in Kalman [9].

3.3 FACTOR SUPPLIES

Thus far income has been taken to be a fixed parameter in the maximization of utility. No consideration has been given to its sources, namely, the lending of money capital, the provision of entrepreneurship or enterprise, and the sale of factors of production to firms. Nor have consumers been permitted to exercise control over their incomes by varying the quantities they lend and sell. The following discussion pursues these ideas.

Recall that the general categories at issue are land, labor, money capital, and enterprise. They provide, respectively, rents, wages, returns, and profits to their owners. To simplify matters, the introduction of money capital and the returns on it are put off until Chapter 13. Enterprise is handled easily by supposing that each consumer receives a fractional share (inclusively from 0 to 1) of the profit of every firm according to her entrepreneurial contribution to that firm (exclusive of whatever money capital she may have supplied). For now, entrepreneurial contributions and hence profit shares are taken to be exogenous

---

[15] In Katzner's approach, preferences might not only be nontransitive, but might also be defined only locally at each point of the commodity space. See Sect. 15.2 below.
[16] Recall from the discussion of Section 2.4 that, in the context of that section, it is the presence of inferiority that permits demand curves to have a positive slope.

parameters of the model which go into the determination of actual and equilibrium time-paths of the economy. Profits received by the individual, then, depend on the resolution of market forces (that is, equations of the model) at the time in question. (The possibility of no profits beyond "normal" levels accruing to all firms and hence to all individuals is not ruled out.) Thus, for the maximization of utility, profits received can be viewed as fixed income beyond the influence of the consumer.

Land and labor can be treated in at least two ways. One view takes the supplies of these factors to be fixed. Each type and grade of land is identified as a separate good whose quantity in use is exogenous. Land not available for economic purposes is excluded from consideration. Alterations in land usage, that is, some land in economic employment becomes idle (because, say, its owner decides to hold it for recreational activities) or idle land is brought into production, necessitate corresponding changes in the equations and parameters of the model. Any land in use owned by a consumer yields a rent determined in the market for land. For purposes of utility maximization, then, rent received (like profits received) can be regarded as fixed income. Similarly, each type and quality of labor can be seen as an independent commodity with an exogenously found quantity in use. The rationale for this assumption is based on the fact that most people who work do so for the same amount of time in the same job day after day. Changes in jobs, working hours, or skills, of course, require associated modifications in equations and parameters. But again, wages received depend on market prices and can be taken to be given when maximizing utility. Therefore, accepting the view that land and labor supplied by consumers is determined exogenously, the income available to consumers for constrained utility maximization is fixed. Hence either the classical or revealed preference model of utility maximization is applicable as is, with m being the sum of income from every source. The case of fixed factor supplies is important for the analysis of the general economy and is discussed in that context in subsequent chapters.

The alternative approach permits the consumer to choose endogenously the number of units he works and the quantity of land he lets. For the moment continue to take the quantity of land rented to be fixed. To come to grips with labor, interpret one "commodity," say good $I + 1$, as leisure, and suppose that the consumer has Λ units of leisure to dispose of. Labor supplied is then given by $\Lambda - y_{I+1}$, where y_{I+1} varies over quantities of leisure units.[17] As-

---

[17]   This analysis of labor supply is intended for the continuous-time context described in Section 1.3. It is clearly an abstraction from the parallel argument set in discrete time. In the latter case, suppose the common interval of time is taken to be the day. Then Λ may be expressed

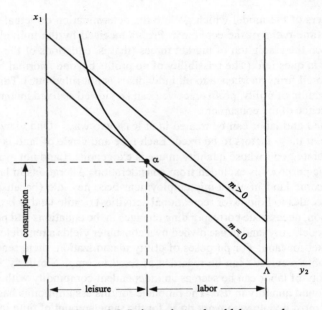

Figure 3.8 Leisure demand and labor supply

sume all labor supplied by the individual is homogeneous. With goods $1, \ldots, I$ remaining as final commodities, the budget constraint becomes

$$p_1 x_1 + \cdots + p_I x_I = p_{I+1}(\Lambda - y_{I+1}) + m, \qquad (3.3\text{-}1)$$

where p_{I+1} is labor's wage and m is nonwage income from entrepreneurship and land rentals as described earlier. Rewriting (3.3-1),

$$p \cdot x + p_{I+1} y_{I+1} = \Lambda p_{I+1} + m. \qquad (3.3\text{-}2)$$

Figure 3.8 provides an illustration when there is only one final commodity, namely, good 1. The slope of each budget line is $-p_2/p_1$, the negative of the ratio of the factor price to the price of the consumption good. If the consumer has no nonwage income and does not work, then he is unable to consume and the budget line meets the y_2-axis where $y_2 = \Lambda$. The possession of positive nonwage income permits positive consumption of good 1 at $y_2 = \Lambda$. The

---

as, say, 24 hours. If the individual reserved $y_{I+1} = 16$ hours for leisure, then $\Lambda - y_{I+1} = 8$ hours would be left for work. Transposing to the continuous framework, y_{I+1} and $\Lambda - y_{I+1}$ are, respectively, quantities of leisure units and labor units per instant of time.

possibility of a negative nonwage income (arising, perhaps, because a loan has to be repaid) is not considered.

In general, the commodity space is the collection of all nonnegative commodity baskets of the form (x, y_{I+1}). (The inequality $y_{I+1} > \Lambda$ means that the individual "adds" to his leisure time through the acquisition of someone else's labor.) Over this space impose the assumptions of either the classical or revealed preference model. Analysis now proceeds in the usual way. Thus utility is maximized subject to the budget constraint at α in Figure 3.8. Because only utility-maximizing quantities are demanded, the demand functions obtained and now denoted by $h = (h^1, \ldots, h^{I+1})$ are

$$(x, y_{I+1}) = h(p, m),$$

where the parameter Λ is subsumed in the symbol h, and the component h^{I+1} is the demand function for leisure. The supply function for labor is $\Lambda - h^{I+1}(p, m)$. The observable properties of these functions are similar, but obviously not identical, to those derived earlier.[18] In particular, labor supply curves may slope upward or downward depending on the location of the tangencies (in, for example, Figure 3.8) between indifference curves and budget lines before and after a change in the wage.

Note that if all labor of all persons is assumed to be homogeneous, then the aggregate supply of labor for the entire economy is obtained by summing the supply functions of all individuals. The mechanics of this summation are suggested, but not explicitly stated, in Section 6.1. Supply functions for separate industries cannot be found without further suppositions concerning the industry in which each person works at each wage. Relaxation of the homogeneity requirement would allow for distinct categories of labor, such as skilled and unskilled, even at the individual level. A separate supply function for each kind of labor would then be secured and, in this case, a single economy-wide labor supply function could not be defined.

An analogous argument could be made for the factor land (assuming a fixed labor supply) by thinking of, say, y_{I+2}, as quantities of land "consumed" or held back from the market by the consumer. In this case p_{I+2} is the rental price per unit of land. Land supplied is then the difference between what the consumer owns and what he consumes. The latter is determined by utility maximization. Of course, every type and grade of land is a distinct commodity with its own rental price. (The same is true of different kinds of labor when labor is not homogeneous.) Each requires its own supply function. The simul-

---

[18]   A precise statement of the observable properties (classical model) in this case can be found in Katzner [10, Sect. 7.1].

taneous derivation of such multiple supply functions (together with multiple supply functions for labor) is described in Section 7.2.

3.4   INDIVIDUAL WELFARE

In economics, to analyze the welfare of an individual is to compare various circumstances in order to determine those in which the individual is better off. Usually the term "circumstances" refers to baskets of commodities or price-income vectors, and the phrase "better off" is understood with respect to utility. Thus only consumers whose activity exhibits the observable properties of demand in Figure 3.1 or Figure 3.6 can be considered. If these properties are satisfied, the consumer's behavior can be explained as if she maximized a utility function obtainable, in principle, from her demand functions. (For convenience, lexicographic possibilities are excluded here: Any two points on the same pseudo-indifference curve are taken to be indifferent.) Only then is it certain that there is a utility function available for use in analyzing welfare. However, to say that a consumer's behavior may be explained with a given utility function is one thing. To further assert that this utility function actually indicates her welfare and represents what she considers to be her true wants and desires (preferences) is quite another. Yet, to make any headway at all, it is essential that such an introspective assumption be made. The only justification is that in light of the cultural backgrounds and values of both the investigator and individual in question, the investigator feels it reasonable to infer utility-maximizing intent behind the observed behavior of the consumer. (Recall Section 1.2.)

Although welfare comparisons are sometimes made by computing the utility of alternative commodity bundles in X, it is often more convenient to compare the utility associated with various vectors $(p, m) > 0$. Of course, the latter utility arises only because at every $(p, m) > 0$ the consumer demands a commodity bundle already having a utility number assigned to it. Thus the (p, m) must first be transformed into commodity baskets according to the given demand functions before utility as a function of (p, m) is determined. More precisely, let $\mu = u(x)$ be the consumer's utility function and $x = h(p, m)$ the demand functions generated from it. Then the *indirect utility function*[19] $v(p, m)$ is defined by

$$v(p, m) = u(h(p, m)) = \mu, \qquad (3.4\text{-}1)$$

---

[19]   In the same paper dealing with the integrability condition mentioned in n. 6 on p. 90, Antonelli [1] also introduced the indirect utility function.

for all $(p, m) > 0$. Observe that if u is twice, continuously differentiable on the interior of X, then h, and hence v, is continuously differentiable on Ω. Also v is homogeneous of degree zero. Additional properties of v have to do, in part, with the partial derivatives v_i and v_m of v with respect to p_i (for $i = 1, \ldots, I$) and m, and the relationship between v and h.

Three results are of interest. First, differentiating (3.4-1) with respect to m, for (p, m) in Ω,

$$v_m = \sum_{i=1}^{I} u_i h_m^i,$$

and, upon application of the first-order Lagrangian constrained maximization conditions (2.3-15),

$$v_m = \lambda \sum_{i=1}^{I} p_i h_m^i.$$

But differentiation of the budget constraint $p \cdot h(p, m) = m$ with respect to m yields

$$\sum_{i=1}^{I} p_i h_m^i = 1.$$

Hence

$$v_m = \lambda. \tag{3.4-2}$$

In other words, as suggested (but not proved) near the end of Section 2.3, λ is the marginal utility of income in the sense of being the derivative of the indirect utility function with respect to m. Because λ is always positive, so is $v_m(p, m)$. The second result is stated as follows:

Theorem 3.4-3 For all (p, m) in Ω,

$$h^i(p, m) = -\frac{v_i(p, m)}{v_m(p, m)}, \quad i = 1, \ldots, I.$$

Proof: Let i and (p, m) in Ω be given. Differentiating (3.4-1) with respect to p_i and using (3.4-2) yields

$$-\frac{v_i}{v_m} = \frac{\sum_{n=1}^{I} u_n h_i^n}{\lambda}.$$

Substitution of the first-order Lagrangian constrained maximization conditions (2.3-15) gives

$$-\frac{v_i}{v_m} = -\sum_{n=1}^{I} p_n h_i^n.$$

The conclusion now follows because differentiation of $p \cdot h(p, m) = m$ with respect to p_i results in

$$-\sum_{n=1}^{I} p_n h_i^n = h^i.$$

Q.E.D.

Theorem 3.4-3 asserts that demand functions can be computed from v without any reference to u at all. Implicit in that calculation, however, is the utility function u and its constrained maximization, which are required in the first place to obtain v from (3.4-1).

The third result, namely, that $v(p, m)$ is quasi-convex[20] for all $(p, m) > 0$, is the subject-matter of Exercise 3.17.

Returning to the analysis of individual welfare, it is clear that welfare comparisons would be quite simple if u and v were obtainable from observed market behavior. But the integrability and revealed preference arguments guarantee only the existence of these functions. As a practical matter, it is often impossible to find out what they are. Hence recourse must be made to welfare statements based on utility without having any idea of the nature of the actual utility functions.

There are several ways to proceed. Let u be twice, continuously differentiable on the interior of X and consider only (p, m) in Ω. First, it may be concluded from (3.4-2), the positivity of λ, and Theorem 3.4-3 that

$$v_i(p, m) < 0, \quad i = 1, \ldots, I,$$

for all (p, m) in Ω. This, together with the already established fact and, respectively, assumption that $v_m(p, m) > 0$ on Ω and $u_i(x) > 0$ on X, mean that lowering prices, increasing incomes, or adding to the consumer's quantities of commodities all make him better off. But all prices need not move in identical directions; higher incomes might accompany higher prices; and so on. To infer directions of welfare change under such circumstances, let ζ be a parameter beyond the influence of the consumer which affects prices, incomes, and hence

---

[20]   For a definition of quasi-convexity see appendix section A.3.

quantities through a continuously differentiable route. In appropriate contexts, ζ may be thought of as a policy control to be used by government in achieving various ends. The impact of small changes in ζ on the individual can be determined by differentiating (3.4-1) totally:

$$\frac{d\mu}{d\zeta} = \sum_{i=1}^{I} u_i \frac{dx_i}{d\zeta} = v_m \frac{dm}{d\zeta} + \sum_{i=1}^{I} v_i \frac{dp_i}{d\zeta}, \tag{3.4-4}$$

where $d\cdot/d\cdot$ indicates a total derivative and $x = h(p, m)$. There are two ways, then, to determine $d\mu/d\zeta$. On one hand, combining (3.4-4) and the first-order Lagrangian constrained maximization conditions (2.3-15) gives

$$\frac{d\mu}{d\zeta} = \lambda \sum_{i=1}^{I} p_i \frac{dx_i}{d\zeta}. \tag{3.4-5}$$

On the other hand, from (3.4-2), (3.4-4), and Theorem 3.4-3,

$$\frac{d\mu}{d\zeta} = \lambda \left(\frac{dm}{d\zeta} - \sum_{i=1}^{I} h^i \frac{dp_i}{d\zeta} \right). \tag{3.4-6}$$

Each of the terms on the right-hand sides of these last two expressions is observable except, typically, for λ. But in any case, because $\lambda > 0$ for all $(p, m) > 0$, the sign of $d\mu/d\zeta$ may be computed from either equation. The direction of welfare (utility) change for small variation in ζ can therefore be inferred.

However, a substantial portion of welfare analysis is concerned with finite incremental rather than arbitrarily small variations. Again let u be given. Instead of derivatives, attention focuses on

$$\Delta\mu = v(p', m') - v(p'', m''),$$

or

$$\Delta\mu = u(x') - u(x'').$$

Now the approach of (3.4-5) and (3.4-6) can only be applied to approximate welfare changes when x' is close to x'' and (p', m') is close to (p'', m''). To see why, replace derivatives by finite increments in (3.4-5) and (3.4-6). Then $\Delta\mu/\Delta\zeta$ may be approximated by

$$\lambda \sum_{i=1}^{I} p_i \frac{\Delta x_i}{\Delta\zeta},$$

and

$$\lambda \left(\frac{\Delta m}{\Delta \zeta} - \sum_{i=1}^{I} h^i \frac{\Delta p_i}{\Delta \zeta} \right).$$

If the increments Δx, Δp_i, Δm, and $\Delta \zeta$ are large enough, then these approximations may not have the same sign as each other. Under such conditions, not much information about $\Delta \mu / \Delta \zeta$ can be deduced from either approximation. Hence an alternative approach is needed.

Note also that ordinal utility is adequate as long as only signs of $\Delta \mu$ or $\Delta \mu / \Delta \zeta$ are of interest. As soon as magnitudes become important it is necessary to impose the further assumption that the utility function derived from observable behavior (that is, the utility function with which the analysis of welfare is carried out) is cardinal. For only in this case is the ordering of increments $\Delta \mu$ independent of the particular utility representation employed (Section 2.2).

In what follows utility differences are expressed in terms of the indirect utility function. The first result, stated without proof,[21] is the analogue in the absence of differentiability of the proposition established above that $v_i < 0$ and $v_m > 0$.

Theorem 3.4-7 For all $(p', m') > 0$ and $(p'', m'') > 0$, if either

a) $p'' \geqslant p'$, $p'' \neq p'$, and $m' \geqslant m''$, or

b) $p'' \geqslant p'$ and $m' > m''$,

then $v(p', m') > v(p'', m'')$.

A second proposition relates finite utility increments to certain integrals involving demand functions. Its proof is also omitted.[22]

Theorem 3.4-8 Let v be differentiable where defined. Then for any $(p', m') > 0$, and $(p'', m'') > 0$,

$$v(p', m') - v(p'', m'') = \int_{m''}^{m'} v_m(p'', m)dm$$

$$- \sum_{i=1}^{I} \int_{p_i''}^{p_i'} v_m(p^i, m')h^i(p^i, m')dp_i,$$

---

[21]   A proof is given by Katzner [10, p. 151].
[22]   A proof appears in Katzner [10, p. 152].

where $p^i = (p_1'', \ldots, p_{i-1}'', p_i, p_{i+1}', \ldots, p_I')$ for each i.

The main problem with the formula of Theorem 3.4-8 is that, even knowing that the marginal utility of income is always positive, neither the sign nor the magnitude of $v(p', m') - v(p'', m'')$ can be determined in ignorance of the function $v_m = \lambda$. Although the h^i are observable, v_m is usually not. In general, then, without being able to compute v, Theorem 3.4-8 is of little help. There is, however, at least one special case in which this problem disappears. Suppose

$$v_m(p, m) = \lambda = \frac{1}{m}, \qquad (3.4\text{-}9)$$

for all $(p, m) > 0$. In words, the marginal utility of income is independent of all prices and varies inversely with income. An example of a utility function with such a characteristic appears in Exercise 3.9. It turns out that all preference orderings, and only those, having a utility representation whose marginal utility of income $\lambda = 1/m$, are homothetic.[23] Substitution of (3.4-9) into the formula of Theorem 3.4-8 and performing the first integration gives

$$v(p', m') - v(p'', m'') = \ln m' - \ln m'' - \frac{1}{m'} \sum_{i=1}^{I} \int_{p_i''}^{p_i'} h^i(p^i, m') dp_i. \quad (3.4\text{-}10)$$

All elements on the right-hand side of the equality of (3.4-10) are observable. Furthermore the absolute value of the integral, say,

$$\int_{p_1''}^{p_1'} h^1(p^1, m') dp_1, \qquad (3.4\text{-}11)$$

is the shaded area "under" (*i.e.*, to the left of) the demand curve between p_1' and p_1'' in Figure 3.9. Note that the demand curve is drawn for $p_i = p_i'$, where $i = 2, \ldots, I$ and $m = m'$. Thus, with ordinal utility, the sign of $\Delta\mu = v(p', m') - v(p'', m'')$ indicates which of (p', m') or (p'', m'') the consumer prefers. If the particular utility representation having $v_m(p, m) = 1/m$ also is assumed cardinal, then the magnitude $\Delta\mu$ becomes meaningful.

Areas under the demand curve in Figure 3.9 may be given a "consumer's surplus" interpretation. Suppose the consumer were to purchase x_1' at p_1'. Then for the increment Δx_1, she must pay only $p_1' \Delta x_1$, when, according to her demand curve, she is willing to pay approximately (actually, in the diagram, considerably more than) $p_1'' \Delta x_1$. The difference, area $abcd$, may be considered as

---

[23] Combine Theorems 2.3-2 and 5.4-4 in Katzner [10, pp. 24, 92].

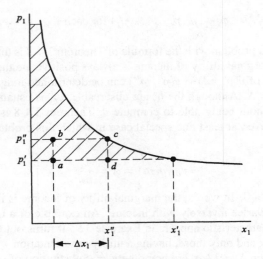

Figure 3.9 Consumer's surplus

a surplus derived by purchasing Δx_1 at the lower price. *Consumer's surplus* at
x_1' is the sum of all incremental surpluses up to x_1' as the interval between x_1'
and the origin is partitioned into smaller and smaller incremental units Δx_1, or
the entire shaded area under the demand curve.[24] The loss in consumer's surplus in moving from x_1' to x_1'' or the gain from going in the opposite direction
is the shaded area between p_1' and p_1''. This is given by the integral (3.4-11).
Hence the utility increment of (3.4-10) is the net total of all such gains and
losses between (p', m') and (p'', m'') adjusted, as indicated, with respect to m'
and m''.

There is, however, another method by which incremental comparisons
can be obtained in the absence of homothetic preferences.[25] Let $\mu = u(x)$
represent $\succsim$ with differentiable indirect utility function $\mu = v(p, m)$. Fix $p =
p''$. Because $v_m(p'', m) > 0$ for all $m > 0$, the inverse function is $m =
v^*(p'', \mu)$ with derivative

$$v_\mu^*(p'', \mu) > 0. \tag{3.4-12}$$

But (3.4-12) states that $v_\mu^*(p'', \mu)$ is an increasing transformation of μ. Hence
$v^*(p'', u(x))$ also represents $\succsim$. Now the indirect utility function correspond-

24   This notion of consumer's surplus is attributable to Dupuit [6] in 1844.
25   The idea is due to McKenzie and Pearce [11].

ing to the latter representation is

$$\overline{v}(p, m) = v^*(p'', v(p, m)),$$

where

$$\overline{v}(p'', m) = m, \tag{3.4-13}$$

for all $m > 0$. The reason for going to so much trouble to obtain $\overline{v}$ is that at p'' its marginal utility of income (obtained by differentiating equation (3.4-13)) is unity:

$$\overline{v}_m(p'', m) = 1, \tag{3.4-14}$$

for every $m > 0$. (Note that equation (3.4-14) does not help compute utility differences in the formula of Theorem 3.4-8 because it is valid for one and only one price vector. Vary p'' and the entire representation $\overline{v}$ changes.) Furthermore, when they exist, all higher order derivatives of $\overline{v}$ with respect to m vanish:

$$\overline{v}_{m...m}(p'', m) = 0, \tag{3.4-15}$$

again for all $m > 0$. Subsequent argument proceeds under the supposition that all derivatives required exist.

Consider any $(p', m') > 0$ and $(p'', m'') > 0$. The utility difference $\overline{v}(p', m') - \overline{v}(p'', m'')$, where the representation $\overline{v}$ depends on the vector p'' in question, has a differential expression according to Taylor's formula with remainder.[26] The first term of Taylor's formula contains only first-order derivatives evaluated at (p'', m''); the second employs derivatives of the second-order at (p'', m''); and so on. As terms with derivatives of higher and higher order at (p'', m'') are added, the remainder may or may not become small.[27] If the remainder disappears upon passing to the limit, then $\overline{v}(p', m') - \overline{v}(p'', m'')$ can be written as a convergent infinite series involving derivatives of all orders each evaluated at (p'', m''). In this case utility differences can be approximated as closely as desired by discarding the remainder and including terms with derivatives at (p'', m'') of sufficiently high order. The earlier restriction that (p', m') be near (p'', m'') is not needed. As is illustrated below, such an approximation can always be stated in the vocabulary of observable behavior. Hence it can be used to determine the sign or magnitude, as the case may be, of $\overline{v}(p', m') - \overline{v}(p'', m'')$. Although still requiring the existence of all higher-order derivatives and convergence of the remainder to zero, this analysis of

---

[26]   Apostol [2, pp. 241-244, 361, 362]. See also (A.3-6) – (A.3-8) in appendix Section A.3.

[27]   *Ibid.* An example in which the remainder does not approach zero is given by Buck [4, p. 79].

incremental welfare is not confined to those conditions (such as equation (3.4-9)) under which the unobservable "pieces" of the marginal utility of income can be eliminated from the formula of Theorem 3.4-8.

Ignoring the remainder (and assuming it goes to zero), the Taylor approximation up to the terms involving only first- and second-order partial derivatives is,[28] because $\bar{v}_{im} = \bar{v}_{mi}$,

$$\bar{v}(p', m') - \bar{v}(p'', m'') \simeq \bar{v}_m(p'', m'')\Delta m + \sum_{i=1}^{I} \bar{v}_i(p'', m'')\Delta p_i$$

$$+ \frac{1}{2} \sum_{i,j=1}^{I} \bar{v}_{ij}(p'', m'')\Delta p_i \Delta p_j + \sum_{i=1}^{I} \bar{v}_{im}(p'', m'')\Delta p_i \Delta m \quad (3.4\text{-}16)$$

$$+ \frac{1}{2}\bar{v}_{mm}(p'', m'')[\Delta m]^2,$$

where $\Delta p_i = p_i' - p_i''$ and $\Delta m = m' - m''$. Now from (3.4-14) and Theorem 3.4-3,

$$\bar{v}_i(p'', m'') = -h^i(p'', m''), \quad i = 1, \ldots, I,$$

$$\bar{v}_m(p'', m'') = 1. \quad (3.4\text{-}17)$$

Using Theorem 3.4-3 to differentiate $\bar{v}_i$ with respect to m, and employing (3.4-15) and (3.4-17) gives

$$\bar{v}_{im}(p'', m'') = -\bar{v}_{mm}h^i - \bar{v}_m h_m^i,$$

$$= -h_m^i(p'', m''). \quad (3.4\text{-}18)$$

Again differentiating $\bar{v}_i$, this time with respect to p_j noting that $\bar{v}_{mj} = \bar{v}_{jm}$, and substituting from (3.4-18) and (3.4-17) gives

$$\bar{v}_{ij}(p'', m'') = -\bar{v}_{mj}h^i - \bar{v}_m h_j^i,$$

$$= h^i(p'', m'')h_m^j(p'', m'') - h_j^i(p'', m''). \quad (3.4\text{-}19)$$

Due to the minus sign and a rearrangement of superscripts the last expression is not the Slutsky function of Section 2.4. Combining (3.4-15), and (3.4-17) –

---

[28]   Without remainder, the Taylor approximation using only derivatives of the first- and second-order is identical to that of equation (A.3-8) in appendix Section A.3.

(3.4-19) with (3.4-16), yields

$$\bar{v}(p', m') - \bar{v}(p'', m'') \simeq \Delta m + \sum_{i=1}^{I} h^i(p'', m'')\Delta p_i$$

$$+ \frac{1}{2} \sum_{i,j=1}^{I} \left[h^i(p'', m'')h_m^j(p'', m'') \right.$$

(3.4-20)

$$\left. -h_j^i(p'', m'') \right] \Delta p_i \Delta p_j$$

$$+ \sum_{i=1}^{I} h_m^i(p'', m'')\Delta p_i \Delta m.$$

All terms on the right-hand side of the approximation sign are observable. Hence the sign and magnitude of $\bar{v}(p', m') - \bar{v}(p'', m'')$ can always be calculated, no matter how far (p', m') is from (p'', m''). A similar conclusion can be deduced for Taylor approximations up to arbitrary numbers of terms.

EXERCISES

3.1 Prove that with $I = 2$, both goods must be substitutes as defined by the appropriate inequality of (3.0-1).

3.2 Find, by integration, a utility generator for the demand functions

$$h^i(p_1, p_2, m) = \frac{m}{2p_i}, \quad i = 1, 2,$$

defined for all $(p_1, p_2, m) > 0$.

3.3 Assuming a utility function u generating h exists, show that for all x' and x'' in X, if $x' \widetilde{R} x''$ then $u(x') > u(x'')$. Using this result (and not Theorem 3.2-4) prove that $x' \bar{R} x''$ implies $u(x') > u(x'')$ for any x' and x'' in X.

3.4 Show that asymmetry of $\bar{R}$ implies asymmetry of $\widetilde{R}$.

3.5 Use the weak axiom of revealed preference to deduce the homogeneity of h.

3.6 Prove directly from the definition of $\bar{R}$ (without recourse to Theorem 3.2-4) that $\bar{R}$ is increasing and transitive.

3.7 Let $u(x)$ be a utility function, and $h(p, m)$ and $v(p, m)$ the demand and indirect utility functions, respectively, generated by $u(x)$. Show that for all (p, m) in Ω,

$$h^i(p, m) = m \frac{v_i(p, m)}{\sum\limits_{n=1}^{I} p_n v_n(p, m)},$$

for $i = 1, \ldots, I$.

3.8 Prove that the marginal utility of income λ is not independent of the particular utility representation under discussion.

3.9 Find the marginal utility of income as a function of (p, m) and the indirect utility function for $u(x_1, x_2) = \ln(x_1 x_2)^{1/2}$.

3.10 Verify (3.4-13), namely, that $\bar{v}(p'', m) = m$ for all $m > 0$.

3.11 In a two-good world, a consumer is observed to purchase $x_1 = 20$ and $x_2 = 10$ at prices $p_1 = \$2$ and $p_2 = \$6$. He is also seen to buy $x_1 = 35$ and $x_2 = 4$ at prices $p_1 = \$3$ and $p_2 = \$5$. Is this behavior consistent with utility maximization? Why or why not?

3.12 Let $x' = h(p', m')$ and $x'' = h(p'', m'')$, where $x' \neq x''$ and h is derived from the constrained maximization of a utility function u satisfying (3.2-1) – (3.2-3). The value of the Laspeyre quantity index at (x', x'') (see Section 12.4) is given by $\mathcal{L} = p' \cdot x'' / p' \cdot x'$. Show that if $\mathcal{L} \leqslant 1$, then $u(x') > u(x'')$.

3.13 Let $v(p, m)$ be the indirect utility function of (3.4-1). Show that for all $(p, m) > 0$ and any $\theta > 0$,

$$v_m(\theta p, \theta m) = \theta^{-1} v_m(p, m).$$

Thus v_m is homogeneous of degree minus one.

3.14* Let $u(x_1, x_2)$ be the utility function described in Exercise 2.18. Suppose its associated indirect utility function has the property that

$$v_m(p, m) = \frac{1}{m},$$

everywhere. Show that the elasticities

$$-h_i^i(p, m)\frac{p_i}{h^i(p, m)} = 1, \quad i = 1, 2,$$

for all $(p, m) > 0$.

3.15 Let $I = 2$ and consider the commodity space

$$\bar{X} = \{(x_1, x_2) : x_1 \geqslant 0, \ x_2 \geqslant -x_2^0\},$$

where x_2^0 is a positive constant. Define a utility function on $\bar{X}$ which satisfies (2.3-1) – (2.3-3) on $\bar{X}$ and the following modified boundary condition:

For any distinct (x_1', x_2') and (x_1'', x_2'') in X such that $u(x_1', x_2') = u(x_1'', x_2'')$, if $(x_1', x_2') > (0, -x_2^0)$ then $(x_1'', x_2'') > (0, -x_2^0)$.

How, if at all, are the budget constraint, the maximization of utility subject to that constraint, and the properties of the derived demand functions of Figure 3.1 affected by permitting x_2 to take on zero and negative values as described here?

3.16 Consider a function $v(p, m)$ defined for all $(p, m) > 0$ such that

i) v is twice, continuously differentiable,

ii) v is homogeneous of degree zero, and

iii) the partial derivative $v_m(p, m) \neq 0$,

everywhere. Define the demand function h by the equation of Theorem 3.4-3. From conditions (i) – (iii) alone show that h and its derivatives satisfy:

a) the budget constraint $p \cdot h(p, m) = m$, and

b) the symmetry condition $s^{in}(p, m) = s^{ni}(p, m)$, for all i and n and all (p, m) in Ω.

3.17* Show that $v(p, m)$ is quasi-convex for all $(p, m) > 0$.

3.18 In contrast with the definition of the indirect utility function in (3.4-1), define the *expenditure function*

$$e(p, \mu) = p \cdot h^*(p, \mu),$$

for all $p > 0$ and μ appearing as function values of u, where h^* is the compensated demand function of Section 2.4. Note that e is continuous where defined and continuously differentiable on the set Υ (also introduced in Section 2.4). Denote the partial derivatives of e with respect to p_i by e_i, for $i = 1, \ldots, I$, and that with respect to μ by e_μ. Proofs identical (except for notation) to those of Theorems 4.5-2, 4.5-4, and 4.5-8 below demonstrate, respectively, that $e_i(p, \mu) = h^{*i}(p, \mu)$, for $i = 1, \ldots, I$, that $e(p, \mu)$ is concave in p for each μ, and that $e_\mu(p, \mu) = \eta$ (the Lagrange multiplier of the expenditure minimization problem in Section 2.4). Using these facts and others previously established in Section 2.4 show that

a) e is homogeneous of degree 1 in p for each μ, and

b) $e_\mu(p, \mu) > 0$ and $e_i(p, \mu) > 0$, for $i = 1, \ldots, I$ on Υ.

What is the relationship between $v(p, m)$ and $e(p, \mu)$?

REFERENCES

1. Antonelli, G. B., *Sulla teoria matematica della Economia politica* (Pisa: nella Tipografia del Folchetto, 1886). English translation: "On the Mathematical Theory of Political Economy," *Preferences, Utility and Demand*, J. S. Chipman, *et al.*, eds. (New York: Harcourt Brace Jovanovich, 1971), pp. 333-360.
2. Apostol, T. M., *Mathematical Analysis* 2nd ed. (Reading: Addison-Wesley, 1974).
3. Arrow, K. J., "Rational Choice Functions and Orderings," *Economica*, n.s. 26 (1959), pp. 121-127.
4. Buck, R. C., *Advanced Calculus* (New York: McGraw-Hill, 1956).
5. Chipman, J. S., "Introduction to Part II," *Preferences, Utility and Demand*, J. S. Chipman, *et al.*, eds., (New York: Harcourt Brace Jovanovich, 1971), pp. 321-331.
6. Dupuit, J., "De la Mesure de l'Utilité des Travaux Publics," *Annales des Ponts et Chaussées*, 2nd series, 8 (1844). English translation by R. H. Barback: "On the Measurement of the Utility of Public Works," *International Economic Papers* 2 (1952), pp. 83-110.
7. Gale, D., "A Note on Revealed Preference," *Economica*, n.s. 27 (1960), pp. 348-354.
8. Hurewicz, W., *Lectures on Ordinary Differential Equations* (New York: Wiley and the Technology Press of the Massachusetts Institute of Technology, 1958).
9. Kalman, P., "The Theory of Consumer Behavior when Prices Enter the

Utility Function," *Econometrica* 36 (1968), pp. 497-510.

10. Katzner, D. W., *Static Demand Theory* (New York: Macmillan, 1970).

11. McKenzie, G. and I. F. Pearce, "Exact Measures of Welfare and the Cost of Living," *Review of Economic Studies* 43 (1976), pp. 465-468.

12. Pareto, V., *Manuale di economia politica* (Milan: Societa Editrice Libraria, 1906).

13. Samuelson, P. A., "A Note on the Pure Theory of Consumer's Behavior," *Economica*, n.s.. 5 (1938), pp. 61-71.

14. Sonnenschein, H., "Demand Theory without Transitive Preferences, with Application to the Theory of Competitive Equilibrium," *Preferences, Utility and Demand*, J. S. Chipman, *et al.*, eds. (New York: Harcourt Brace Jovanovich, 1971), pp. 215-223.

15. Veblen, T., *The Theory of the Leisure Class* (London: George Allen & Unwin, 1989).

16. Volterra, V., "L'economia matematica ed il nuovo manuale del prof. Pareto," *Giornale degli Economisti* 32 (1906), pp. 296-301. English translation: "Mathematical Economics and Professor Pareto's New Manual," *Preferences, Utility and Demand*, J. S. Chipman, *et al.*, eds. (New York: Harcourt Brace Jovanovich, 1971), pp. 365-369.

Chapter 4

Production and Cost

As described earlier, a firm is an institution that combines inputs to produce outputs. More specifically, it decides what inputs to hire, how the inputs are to be employed, and hence the outputs secured. In reality, of course, much of the output produced by inputs hired today is finished and sold in the future. And since today's inputs of both variable factors and physical capital have to be paid today,[1] the financing of production compels the expenditure of money capital raised by the firm through the issuance and sale of appropriate monetary instruments. It follows that the cost of output, in addition to the cost of inputs, necessarily includes the cost of carrying the money capital required for that production to take place.

However, for pedagogical reasons, discussion of the role of money capital is postponed until Chapter 13. (Changes in subsequent results required upon the introduction of money capital are indicated in due course.) Present purposes, then, permit the residual left over from sales revenue after all inputs are paid to be viewed as profit that accrues to the firm's owners. In addition, the firm is assumed to view input and output prices as fixed parameters. Social interaction among employees is ignored. And, although in reality a variety of outputs may be produced, only the single-output firm is considered

---

[1]   Of course, compensation for the services of physical capital may be provided for differently through the appropriate timing of rental payments. But, as indicated earlier, this possibility is ignored.

(except in Exercise 5.21).

This chapter and the next are concerned with the operation of such a firm. Chapter 4 deals with technical relations between cost and production. Production functions are defined first and their properties explored. These properties are then translated into characteristics of cost functions through the mechanism of cost minimization. Thus, for example, the sign of the slope of the average variable cost curve at any output is seen to rest in many instances on the nature of the "local" returns to scale of the production function at the basket of inputs used to produce that output. Detailed discussions of returns to scale in general and of CES production functions in particular also are provided. Material relevant for the particular grand view of Section 1.4 appears in Sections 4.1, 4.4, and 4.5. Based on the technical apparatus developed here, Chapter 5 presents models of short- and long-run behavior of the firm. As with the models of the theory of demand, only timeless activity is described.

There are some striking similarities between the formal analysis of demand and that of the firm. Replacing the utility function is the production function with many of the same properties. The linear budget constraint is supplanted by a linear cost equation involving the sum of prices times quantities. Rather than maximizing utility subject to the budget constraint or, equivalently, minimizing linear expenditure given the level of utility, linear cost is minimized given the level of output. It is not surprising, then, that significant portions of subsequent presentation parallel corresponding derivations encountered in the theory of demand.

On the other hand, the theory of the firm (Chapter 5) deals with the maximization of profit in addition to cost minimization. To be sure that profit can actually be maximized it is necessary to consider the shape of the production surface (Sections 4.1 and 4.2). This goes well beyond a discussion, such as that found in demand theory and also relevant for cost minimization here, of the properties of the level contours (isoquants) of these surfaces. Recall that in the theory of demand there is no parallel to profit maximization, and hence only the shapes of the indifference surfaces (that is, the level contours of the utility surface), not so much the shape of the utility surface itself, were important.

Furthermore, the distinction between observables and unobservables (that is, between what can be seen in economic data and what cannot) drawn in the theory of demand plays no role in the theory of the firm. Production, cost, demand, and supply functions of the firm are, in principle, all observable.[2] Nevertheless it is still important to comprehend precisely the

---

[2]   There has been considerable effort devoted to the estimation of production and cost

theoretical nature of these functions, their properties, and their relationships to each other. Otherwise our understanding of the model of the firm would be incomplete, and the characteristics required of any collection of economic data to be consistent with the model would be uncertain. Moreover, there may be practical barriers limiting the information collectable on particular firms. It would then be important to know what the obtainable facts imply, in theory, about the remaining unavailable data.

4.1   PRODUCTION FUNCTIONS

Consider an isolated firm producing a particular output. The *technology* for that output is the collection of all available information concerning ways in which inputs can be combined to produce it. Let x be a scalar variable ranging over units of output, that is, $x \geqslant 0$. Now technology dictates that some goods ought to be used in production while others should not. Suppose J inputs are to be used, and denote quantities of them by the variables y_j, where $j = 1, \ldots, J$. Write $Y = \{y : y \geqslant 0\}$. Often Y is called the *input space* and y a basket or bundle of inputs. The firm's *production function*, f, is a functional relation between flows of output x and (for the present) flows of inputs y per unit of time indicating, given technology, the maximum quantity of output obtainable from every bundle of inputs. Mathematically,[3]

$$x = f(y), \qquad (4.1\text{-}1)$$

for y in Y. The *production surface* is the $(J + 1)$-dimensional graph of the production function. Note that by insisting output quantities be maximal with respect to each basket of inputs, the production function presupposes a technical (not economic) efficiency on the operation of the firm.[4] As before, first- and second-order derivatives are denoted with subscripts as in, respectively, $f_j(y)$ and $f_{jn}(y)$ and the functional arguments y frequently are dropped to simplify notation.

Activities of the firm arise in both long-run and short-run contexts. In the long run, all inputs entering the production function are taken to be variable.

---

functions. A good place to begin reading in this area is Walters [13].

[3]   The mathematical form of the production function dates to Wicksteed [15, p. 4]. Immediately after writing down his version of equation (4.1-1), Wicksteed also gives a mathematical specification of the notion of constant returns to scale. The latter concept is defined here by equation (4.2-17) in Section 4.2.

[4]   Economic efficiency refers, for example, to the attainment of the minimum cost of producing an output volume, or the maximum achievable profit.

Thus the long-run production function is given by (4.1-1). Over the short run at least one, but not all inputs are fixed. (To say that an input is fixed implies nothing about its durability — only that the firm has no power of decision over the quantity to be employed. The possibility that the fixed inputs may include physical capital is ignored until Chapter 13.) The precise nature of the short run depends on which inputs may vary. If a short run is specified by designating, say, the last $J - \delta$ inputs as fixed, or

$$y_j = y_j^0, \quad j = \delta + 1, \ldots, J,$$

for some integer $\delta \geqslant 1$, then the short-run production function for this period is given by

$$x = f(y_1, \ldots, y_\delta, y_{\delta+1}^0, \ldots, y_J^0),$$

defined for all $(y_1, \ldots, y_\delta) \geqslant 0$. Clearly any alteration in the fixed inputs (either in their numbers or in their indicated values) modifies the short-run production function and all conclusions based upon it. Confusion will not arise, however, by using the notation of (4.1-1) for both long- and short-run production functions. The major interest is in variable inputs anyway and, with respect to these, argument derived from (4.1-1) clearly applies to either context. In the short-run case the fixed inputs are subsumed in the functional symbol f.

It should be understood that the concepts of long and short run do not necessarily refer to time periods of specific length. Of course, in reality, different inputs require different amounts of time to adjust their quantities in production. Thus the long run can be interpreted as a period of time sufficiently long so that all inputs can be varied by the firm, and the short run as a sufficiently short time frame so that none of the designated fixed input values can be modified while values of the variable inputs may. But it is equally valid to think of the long-run and short-run concepts merely as a means for specifying which inputs are fixed and which inputs the firm is able to vary. On this view, the actual length of time it takes to change a variable input is irrelevant. Thus both long-run and short-run analyses can proceed in terms of continuous time with stationary states referring, respectively, to either long-run or short-run solutions. (Recall Section 1.3.) In either case, the long-run activities of the firm can be thought of in terms of planning, whereas those arising in the short run as more relevant for day-to-day operations.

Only production functions (long or short run) exhibiting the following properties are considered here:

(4.1-2) $f(0) = 0$, and $f(y) \geqslant 0$ for all y in Y.

(4.1-3) f is continuous on Y and twice, continuously differentiable in the interior of Y.

(4.1-4)   There exists an open, connected subset, D, of Y having the origin
as a limit point,[5] on which $f_j(y) > 0$ for $j = 1, \ldots, J$, and all y
in D.

(4.1-5) f is strictly quasi-concave on the interior of Y.

Note that the symbol 0 refers to both scalar and vector origins. Even though
"$f(y) \geqslant 0$ for all y in Y" is already implicit in the definition of f, for future
referencing purposes it is repeated in (4.1-2).

Properties (4.1-3) and (4.1-5) are similar to those required of utility functions in the classical model. One difference is that, unlike some utility functions, production functions are always finite on the boundary of Y. Continuity
can therefore be imposed everywhere. Assumption (4.1-4) is a weak form
of differential increasingness insisting only that at least for small changes in
some directions from the origin, employment of more inputs increases output.
Of course, any production function such that $f_j(y) > 0$ everywhere for each
j also satisfies (4.1-4). But in general f_j is permitted to vanish and become
negative off of D. Observe also that whereas utility values in the range of u
are measured on an ordinal scale, output values in the range of f are measured
on a ratio scale. (Ratio scales are cardinal scales for which the position of the
zero is fixed. See n. 20 on p. 48.) Evidently, the first part of (4.1-2), which has
no counterpart in the assumptions placed on utility functions, states that output
cannot be obtained without input.

Analogously to the classical model of utility maximization, if $f_J(y) \neq 0$,
then at this y, the equation $x = f(y)$ can be solved to secure

$$y_J = w(y_1, \ldots, y_{J-1}, x), \qquad\qquad (4.1\text{-}6)$$

whose derivatives

$$w_j(y_1, \ldots, y_{J-1}, x) = -\frac{f_j(y)}{f_J(y)}, \quad j = 1, \ldots, J - 1. \qquad (4.1\text{-}7)$$

Ratios of first-order derivatives of f are called *marginal rates of technical substitution* between the factors with respect to which the derivatives are taken.
Where defined, (4.1-6) is one representation of the *isoquant* associated with
output x, that is, $\{y : f(y) = x\}$. Thus (4.1-7) asserts that the negatives of
partial derivatives of isoquants are marginal rates of technical substitution.

Analysis of the curvature of isoquants is similar to that of indifference
surfaces. In general, strict quasi-concavity (which precludes linear isoquants)

---

[5]   The concepts of connectedness and limit point are defined in appendix Section A. 1.

and $f_j(y) \neq 0$, where $j = 1, \ldots, J$, imply for most $y > 0$ that

$$\begin{vmatrix} 0 & f_1 \\ f_1 & f_{11} \end{vmatrix} < 0, \qquad \begin{vmatrix} 0 & f_1 & f_2 \\ f_1 & f_{11} & f_{12} \\ f_2 & f_{21} & f_{22} \end{vmatrix} > 0,$$

$$\begin{vmatrix} 0 & f_1 & f_2 & f_3 \\ f_1 & f_{11} & f_{12} & f_{13} \\ f_2 & f_{21} & f_{22} & f_{23} \\ f_3 & f_{31} & f_{32} & f_{33} \end{vmatrix} < 0, \ldots$$

(4.1-8)

for all permutations of the numbers $1, \ldots, J$ identified with the J inputs. (Recall Theorem 2.3-9 and the discussion following it.) Excluding the first, these determinants may vanish at "isolated" points. (The important case in which inputs must be used in fixed proportions is ruled out here by the assumption of differentiability. An example of this does arise, however, in Section 4.3.)

Denote the bordered Hessian matrix of f at y by $F(y)$. To simplify matters and avoid repetition of the details required in Sections 2.3 and 2.4, from now on it is supposed, except where $f_j(y) = 0$ for at least one $j = 1, \ldots, J$, that $|F(y)| \neq 0$ throughout the interior of Y. Hence the inequalities of (4.1-8) also hold for every y in the interior of Y such that all $f_j(y) \neq 0$. For the same reasons, it is assumed further that isoquants, where nonnegatively sloped (in the sense of nonnegative first-order partial derivatives) and strictly convex, do not touch the boundary of Y. Production functions violating one or both of these conditions can be handled by modifying subsequent reasoning as suggested by the parallel arguments for demand analysis in Chapters 2 and 3.

Total product functions are obtained from the production function by holding all inputs but one fixed. Let input j be designated as variable and set $y_n = y_n^0 > 0$ for $n \neq j$. Then the *total product* with respect to j is

$$TP^j(y_j) = f(y_1^0, \ldots, y_{j-1}^0, y_j, y_{j+1}^0, \ldots, y_J^0),$$

for all $y_j \geqslant 0$. *Average product* per unit of input is given by

$$AP^j(y_j) = \frac{TP^j(y_j)}{y_j},$$

where $y_j > 0$. *Marginal product* is the derivative of the total product function or the partial derivative of the production function:

$$MP^j(y_j) = \frac{dTP^j(y_j)}{dy_j} = f_j(y_1^0, \ldots, y_{j-1}^0, y_j, y_{j+1}^0, \ldots, y_J^0),$$

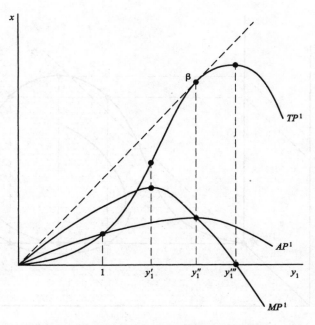

Figure 4.1 Total product, average product, and marginal product

for $y_j > 0$. Graphs of these functions are provided in Figure 4.1 where $j = 1$ and the x-axis has the appropriate scales superimposed upon it. The shape of TP^1 has been chosen because it is consistent with (4.1-2) – (4.1-5) and, at the same time, illustrates a variety of possibilities. The shapes of AP^1 and MP^1 are derived from it according to five principles:

i) MP^1 is zero where TP^1 has its maximum — at y_1'''.

ii) MP^1 has a maximum where TP^1 has its inflection point — at y_1'.

iii) AP^1 reaches its maximum where a ray from the origin is tangent at β to TP^1 (Exercise 4.1) — at y_1''.

iv) MP^1 intersects AP^1 from above where AP^1 has its maximum (Exercise 4.2) — at y_1''.

v) AP^1 intersects TP^1 from above — at $y_1 = 1$.

All functions and curves change with variations in any of the y_n^0, but as long as the general shape of the graph of TP^1 does not vary, the five principles remain.

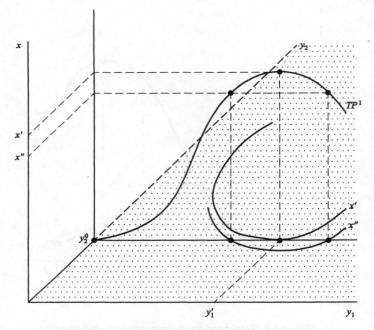

Figure 4.2 Total product curve and isoquants

The geometry of the relationship between total product curves (as pictured in Figure 4.1) and isoquants is illustrated for the two input case ($J = 2$) in Figure 4.2. The TP^1 curve in the diagram is that portion of the production surface (the graph of the production function) appearing in the plane parallel to the y_1-x plane through the fixed-input value y_2^0 on the y_2-axis. The x' and x'' isoquants appear in the shaded y_1-y_2 plane. Clearly, the x' isoquant corresponds to a higher level of output than does the x'' isoquant and is tangent at (y_1', y_2^0) to the line parallel to the y_1-axis through y_2^0. Indeed, x' is the largest output attainable when $y_2 = y_2^0$, that is, along the TP^1 total product curve. Likewise the same x' isoquant is also tangent to the left of y_1' to an appropriate line (not shown in the diagram) parallel to the y_2-axis where the TP^2 curve over that line (y_1 being fixed or given for that purpose) has a maximum. Provided that all total product curves (TP^1 and TP^2) have shapes similar to that of Figure 4.1, all isoquants in the interior of Y have at least two such tangencies — one with respect to a line parallel to the y_1-axis and the other with respect

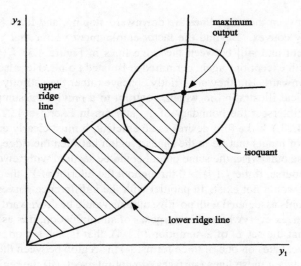

Figure 4.3 Ridge lines and an isoquant for a
production function with a maximum

to a line parallel to the y_2-axis. Moreover, if there were a tangency to a line
parallel to the y_2-axis along the x' isoquant to the right of y_1', it would also
correspond to a maximum of the appropriate TP^2 over that line.

The loci of points at which, as x varies, isoquants in Figure 4.2 are tangent to lines parallel to the y_1-axis and tangent to lines parallel to the y_2-axis
are called *ridge lines* (Figure 4.3). Using the relationship between these points
and maxima along total product curves, the *lower* ridge line can be defined as

$$\{y : y > 0 \quad \text{and} \quad f_1(y) = 0\},$$

and the *upper* ridge line by

$$\{y : y > 0 \quad \text{and} \quad f_2(y) = 0\}.$$

(In general, a *ridge surface* is defined in Y for each $j = 1, \ldots, J$ by $\{y : y > 0$
and $f_j(y) = 0\}$.) Where the ridge lines meet (if they do — and if they do so
at a single point), the production function itself has a unique, global maximum and the isoquant associated with that level of output degenerates to a
single point. Between the ridge lines and up to the global maximum if it exists
(*i.e.*, the shaded area in Figure 4.3), $f_j(y) > 0$ for each j, except at possible
isolated points where the f_j may vanish. Hence by (4.1-7), segments of iso-

quants between the ridge lines are downward sloping, and from (4.1-5), they are strictly convex. Beyond the factor-employment vector that yields maximum output and still between the ridge lines in Figure 4.3, $f_j(y) < 0$ for each j, with exceptions again permitted at isolated points. Here isoquants also slope downward. But they are strictly concave rather than strictly convex.[6] A mathematical illustration in which, contrary to a previous assumption, some isoquants intersect the boundary of Y, appears in Exercise 4.22. (See also Exercise 4.23.) If the firm desires to be efficient, it must clearly employ combinations of inputs that lie in the shaded region between the ridge lines. Were it to choose otherwise, the same output could be secured with fewer inputs.

Of course, if the $f_j(y) > 0$ throughout the interior of Y, then ridge lines (surfaces) would not exist. In parallel with the indifference curves of Section 2.3, isoquants associated with positive outputs would be downward sloping and strictly convex everywhere. For purposes of simplification, it is assumed from here on that the set D of assumption (4.1-4), that is, the set on which all f_j are positive, takes on one of three forms: (i) the region between the ridge lines (surfaces) when those lines (surfaces) do not intersect, (ii) the region between the ridge lines (surfaces) up to a unique, global maximum when the ridge lines (surfaces) intersect at a single point, and (iii) the entire interior of Y when there are no ridge lines (surfaces) at all. Isolated points at which some $f_j(y) = 0$ are not permitted in D. Moreover, all inequalities of (4.1-8) necessarily hold on D.

Previous discussion clearly imparts significance to the shapes that total product curves can assume. Among many possibilities TP^1, say, can be strictly convex, strictly concave, or linear. In other words, MP^1 is, respectively, increasing, decreasing, or constant over an appropriate portion of its domain. This could also be described in terms of the sign of the second derivative of the total product function or dMP^1/dy_1. Employing the second of these three equivalent characterizations over the region in question, TP^1 is said to exhibit *increasing, decreasing,* or *constant returns to the fixed factors* $y_j = y_j^0$ where $j \neq 1$, according as MP^1 is increasing, decreasing, or constant. Thus statements about returns to fixed factors are assertions about the shape of the production function over lines parallel to the coordinate axes. The example of Figure 4.1 illustrates increasing returns up to y_1' and decreasing returns thereafter.

The *law of diminishing returns* is the assertion that all total product curves derived from any real-world production function eventually exhibit de-

---

[6]   See the discussion at the end of appendix Section A.3.

creasing returns to the fixed factors as the variable input increases.[7] The curve may be convex to begin with but sooner or later output starts increasing at a decreasing rate. Thereafter the marginal product continues to decline. The law of diminishing returns is plausible because as one input is increased with all others held fixed, the fixed inputs become more scarce in production relative to the variable one. Thus additional units of the variable input will crowd the remaining units and will be more and more at a disadvantage in contributing to output. But plausibility aside, the law of diminishing returns is an empirical statement that can be checked against reality. Wherever it withstands such scrutiny, it provides valuable information in the analysis of actual production.

4.2   RETURNS TO SCALE

Given the input basket $y > 0$ in Y, the *ray* from the origin through y is described by

$$\{\alpha y : \alpha \geqslant 0\},$$

where α is a real number. In moving along this ray, if $\alpha = 2$, say, then all inputs of basket y have been doubled; if $\alpha = \frac{1}{2}$ they have been halved. Just as notions of returns to fixed factors have to do with the shapes of production surfaces over lines parallel to the coordinate axes, concepts of returns to scale focus on shapes of production surfaces over rays from the origin. Because of its importance in subsequent chapters, the idea of returns to scale is explored in some detail here. Both local and global characterizations are considered. The former looks at a single point on a single ray in isolation, and the latter focuses on all points and rays simultaneously. It turns out that the relationships between returns to scale and the slopes of average variable cost curves have significant local as well as global facets. Since mathematically and geometrically it is easier to understand what is happening at isolated points along single rays before expanding to the entire input space, local notions are considered first. Also for reasons of pedagogy, the assumptions of the previous section are relaxed somewhat by letting f take on negative values and permitting $f(0) \neq 0$. The remaining properties of f, namely (4.1-3) – (4.1-5), continue in force.

Before proceeding, note that because movement along any ray from the origin requires all input quantities to vary, it is natural to think of returns-to-

---

[7]   A clear statement of the law of diminishing returns appears in Mill [7, p. 174]. Brue [2, p. 186] traces the origins of the law back through Ricardo, Malthus, and others to Turgot in 1767.

scale notions in the long-run context. But formally, there is nothing in the definitions that prevents returns to scale from also applying to short-run production functions with the fixed inputs subsumed in the functional symbol f, and this possibility is not precluded in subsequent discussion.

Let α be a nonnegative scalar and $y > 0$ a given input basket in Y Then f is said to exhibit *local decreasing returns to scale* at y whenever there exist real numbers α' and α'' such that $0 < \alpha' < 1 < \alpha''$ and

$$f(\alpha y) > \alpha f(y), \quad \text{for all } \alpha' < \alpha < 1, \tag{4.2-1}$$

$$f(\alpha y) < \alpha f(y), \quad \text{for all } 1 < \alpha < \alpha''. \tag{4.2-2}$$

Thus, for example, if $\alpha'' > 2$ and $\alpha' < \frac{1}{2}$ then doubling all inputs less than doubles output, whereas halving all inputs diminishes output by less than one half. Similarly, f exhibits *local increasing returns to scale* at y if there exist α' and α'' such that $0 < \alpha' < 1 < \alpha''$ and

$$f(\alpha y) < \alpha f(y), \quad \text{for all } \alpha' < \alpha < 1, \tag{4.2-3}$$

$$f(\alpha y) > \alpha f(y), \quad \text{for all } 1 < \alpha < \alpha''. \tag{4.2-4}$$

And f exhibits *local constant returns to scale* at y provided that there exist α' and α'' such that $0 < \alpha' < 1 < \alpha''$ and

$$f(\alpha y) = \alpha f(y), \tag{4.2-5}$$

for all $\alpha' < \alpha < \alpha''$. Note that each part of the definition of local decreasing (or increasing) returns restricts f "locally" on one side of y over the ray from the origin through y. Although intuition suggests a connection between concave, convex, and linear forms for f and, respectively, local decreasing, increasing, and constant returns to scale, the actual relationships present turn out, as will be seen, to be rather complex. Thus, for example, certain strictly convex functions may exhibit local decreasing returns to scale at y in Y. The geometry of these concepts can be understood with the aid of the following propositions.

Theorem 4.2-6 If f exhibits local decreasing returns to scale at $y > 0$ in Y, then

$$f(y) \geqslant \sum_{j=1}^{J} y_j f_j(y).$$

Proof: By L'Hôpital's rule,[8]

$$\lim_{\alpha \to 1} \frac{f(\alpha y) - \alpha f(y)}{\alpha - 1} = \lim_{\alpha \to 1} \left[\sum_{j=1}^{J} y_j f_j(\alpha y) - f(y) \right],$$

$$= \sum_{j=1}^{J} y_j f_j(y) - f(y).$$

Using (4.2-1) when $\alpha' < \alpha < 1$ and (4.2-2) when $1 < \alpha < \alpha''$ gives

$$\frac{f(\alpha y) - \alpha f(y)}{\alpha - 1} < 0.$$

Therefore

$$\lim_{\alpha \to 1} \frac{f(\alpha y) - \alpha f(y)}{\alpha - 1} \leqslant 0,$$

whence

$$\sum_{j=1}^{J} y_j f_j(y) - f(y) \leqslant 0.$$

Q.E.D.

The proofs of Theorems 4.2-7 and 4.2-8 are analogous to that of Theorem 4.2-6.

Theorem 4.2-7   If f exhibits local increasing returns to scale at $y > 0$ in Y, then

$$f(y) \leqslant \sum_{j=1}^{J} y_j f_j(y).$$

Theorem 4.2-8   If f exhibits local constant returns to scale at $y > 0$ in Y, then

$$f(y) = \sum_{j=1}^{J} y_j f_j(y).$$

---

[8]   Rudin [8, p. 109].

To interpret the above theorems consider the facts that with $y > 0$ given,

$$\frac{\partial f(\alpha y)}{\partial \alpha}\bigg|_{\alpha=1} = \sum_{j=1}^{J} y_j f_j(y),$$

and

$$\frac{\partial \alpha f(y)}{\partial \alpha} = f(y),$$

for all α. Now

$$\frac{\partial f(\alpha y)}{\partial \alpha}\bigg|_{\alpha=1}$$

is the derivative of f expressed as a function of the scalar variable α for fixed y and evaluated at $\alpha = 1$.[9] Geometrically it is the slope of the graph of f at y thought of as a one-dimensional curve over the ray from the origin through y in Y. Similarly

$$\frac{\partial \alpha f(y)}{\partial \alpha}$$

is the slope of the line $x = \alpha f(y)$, with y fixed, as α varies over the same ray. According to Theorems 4.2-6, 4.2-7, and 4.2-8, then, each concept of local returns to scale implies something about the relationship between these slopes: If f exhibits local decreasing (increasing or constant) returns to scale at y, then the slope of this one-dimensional curve derived from f at $\alpha = 1$ is no larger than (no smaller than or, respectively, equal to) that of the line $x = \alpha f(y)$, where y is fixed.

A two-input example of local decreasing returns to scale at y appears in Figure 4.4(a). The plane formed by the x-axis and the ray in the input space through y is reproduced in Figure 4.4(b). Observe here that the left-hand αy on the horizontal axis is the point obtained from y when $\alpha' < \alpha < 1$; the right-hand αy applies for $1 < \alpha < \alpha''$. Two further instances of local decreasing returns to scale at y, showing only the plane over the ray through y, are pictured in Figures 4.4(c) and (d). In each case, a ray from the origin through the graph of f at $(y, f(y))$ cuts the graph from below as required by (4.2-1) and (4.2-2). (Parallel illustrations of local increasing returns would have this ray cutting the graph from above as, for example, at y' in Figure 4.6.) The aforementioned slope conditions also are satisfied. Note that if the horizontal axis in Figures

---

[9]   This derivative (evaluated at $\alpha = 1$) differs from the directional derivative defined in appendix Section A.3 only in that here $|y|$ need not be unity. See Theorem A.3-3.

4.4(b), (c), and (d) were labeled in terms of the variable α, then along those axes, y would be replaced by the number 1. Either way, it matters not that the graph at $(y, f(y))$ slopes upward or downward, or has a convex or concave shape.

The definition of local constant returns to scale at y given in (4.2-5) as-

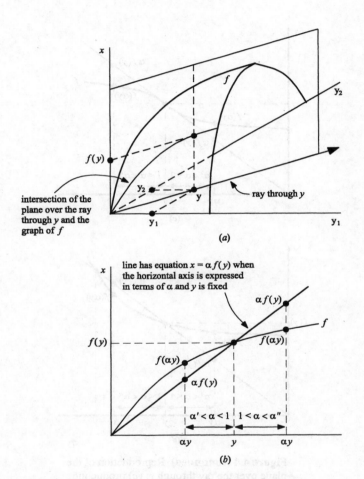

(a)

(b)

Figure 4.4 Local decreasing returns to scale: (*a*) strictly concave production function; (*b*) reproduction of the plane over the ray through y from (*a*); (continued overleaf)

serts that

$$f(\alpha y) = \alpha f(y),$$

for all α such that $\alpha' < \alpha < \alpha''$. Because y is fixed and α varies, along the subset $\{\alpha y : \alpha' < \alpha < \alpha''\}$ of the ray from the origin through y, f is the

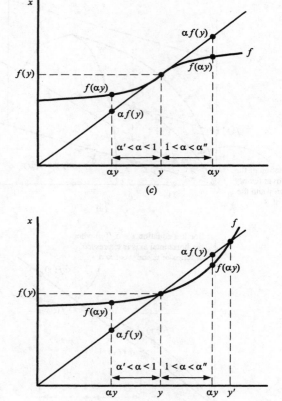

Figure 4.4 (continued) Reproduction of the plane over the ray through y: (c) production function with strictly concave and strictly convex regions; (d) strictly convex production function

product of α times a constant term. Hence f is linear through the origin over this subset. If, on the other hand, over the same subset containing y,

$$f(\alpha y) = \alpha b,$$

for $\alpha' < \alpha < \alpha''$, where b is a positive constant, then (4.2-5) holds with $b = f(y)$. The following result has therefore been demonstrated:

Theorem 4.2-9 f exhibits local constant returns to scale at y if and only if, for suitable α' and α'' such that $0 < \alpha' < 1 < \alpha''$, f is linear through the origin over the subset $\{\alpha y : \alpha' < \alpha < \alpha''\}$ of the ray extending from the origin through y.

Note that the converses of Theorems 4.2-6, 4.2-7, and 4.2-8 do not hold. If

$$f(y) = \sum_{j=1}^{J} y_j f_j(y),$$

at some $y > 0$ in Y, then f could be linear and hence exhibit local constant returns to scale at y. But in this case f could also appear as in Figure 4.4(c), exhibiting local decreasing returns to scale at y. There are other possibilities as well. Observe also that for similar reasons the weak inequalities of Theorems 4.2-6 and 4.2-7 cannot be strengthened. However, local decreasing and increasing returns to scale can be inferred from the strong form of these inequalities:

Theorem 4.2-10   If for some $y > 0$ in Y,

$$f(y) > \sum_{j=1}^{J} y_j f_j(y),$$

then f exhibits local decreasing returns to scale at y.

Proof: Let

$$f(y) > \sum_{j=1}^{J} y_j f_j(y), \quad \text{for } y > 0 \text{ in } Y.$$

Then by the continuity of f and the f_j there exist α' and α'' such that $0 < \alpha' <$

$1 < \alpha''$ and

$$f(\alpha y) > \sum_{j=1}^{J} \alpha y_j f_j(\alpha y), \qquad (4.2\text{-}11)$$

for all $\alpha' < \alpha < \alpha''$. Define the function

$$\psi(\alpha) = f(y) - \frac{f(\alpha y)}{\alpha}, \qquad \alpha' < \alpha < \alpha''. \qquad (4.2\text{-}12)$$

Then ψ is continuously differentiable,

$$\psi(1) = 0,$$

and from (4.2-11),

$$\frac{d\psi(\alpha)}{d\alpha} = \frac{f(\alpha y) - \sum_{j=1}^{J} \alpha y_j f_j(\alpha y)}{\alpha^2} > 0, \qquad \alpha' < \alpha < \alpha''.$$

Hence

$$\psi(\alpha) \begin{cases} < 0, & \text{for } \alpha' < \alpha < 1, \\ > 0, & \text{for } 1 < \alpha < \alpha'', \end{cases}$$

so that, according to (4.2-12), (4.2-1), and (4.2-2), f exhibits local decreasing returns to scale at y.

Q.E.D.

Theorem 4.2-13   If for some $y > 0$ in Y,

$$f(y) < \sum_{j=1}^{J} y_j f_j(y),$$

then f exhibits local increasing returns to scale at y.

The proof of Theorem 4.2-13 is similar to that of Theorem 4.2-10.

Global notions of returns to scale are secured by imposing local returns to scale at each interior point of Y. Thus f is said to exhibit (global) *decreasing*, *increasing*, or *constant returns to scale* on Y whenever, for every $y > 0$ in Y, there exist appropriate α' and α'' such that (4.2-1) and (4.2-2), (4.2-3) and (4.2-4), or (4.2-5) are satisfied, respectively. Actually if f exhibits local decreasing returns to scale at all $y > 0$ in Y, then applying Theorem 4.2-6 to positive vectors in Y of the form αy, where $y > 0$ and $\alpha > 0$, gives

$$f(\alpha y) \geqslant \sum_{j=1}^{J} \alpha y_j f_j(\alpha y).$$

Hence, as in the proof of Theorem 4.2-10, the function $\psi(\alpha)$ defined by (4.2-12) for all $\alpha > 0$ given $y > 0$ in Y is *nondecreasing* (that is, $\overline{\alpha} \geqslant \overline{\overline{\alpha}}$ implies $\psi(\overline{\alpha}) \geqslant \psi(\overline{\overline{\alpha}})$ for every $\overline{\alpha} > 0$ and $\overline{\overline{\alpha}} > 0$). It follows that (4.2-1) and (4.2-2) must remain in force beyond the limits imposed by α' and α'', or in other words, that

$$f(\alpha y) > \alpha f(y), \quad \text{for all } 0 < \alpha < 1, \tag{4.2-14}$$

$$f(\alpha y) < \alpha f(y), \quad \text{for all } \alpha > 1, \tag{4.2-15}$$

at each $y > 0$ in Y. Moreover, in the global (not local) case, (4.2-14) is equivalent to (4.2-15). For suppose (4.2-14) is in force for all $y > 0$ in Y. Consider any $\alpha > 1$. Then $0 < 1/\alpha < 1$, and (4.2-14) applies to $\alpha y > 0$ in Y using $1/\alpha$, that is,

$$f\left(\frac{1}{\alpha}[\alpha y]\right) > \frac{1}{\alpha} f(\alpha y),$$

or

$$f(\alpha y) < \alpha f(y).$$

This is the inequality of (4.2-15). In the same way, (4.2-15) implies (4.2-14). Thus to define decreasing returns to scale it is only necessary to require that one of these inequalities holds for all y.

Similarly, generalized versions of (4.2-3) and (4.2-4) are equivalent as well. Hence (global) increasing returns to scale is characterized by either

$$f(\alpha y) < \alpha f(y), \quad \text{for all } 0 < \alpha < 1, \tag{4.2-16}$$

or

$$f(\alpha y) > \alpha f(y), \quad \text{for all } \alpha > 1,$$

at every $y > 0$ in Y. In the same way f exhibits (global) constant returns to scale if and only if

$$f(\alpha y) = \alpha f(y) \tag{4.2-17}$$

for all $\alpha > 0$ and $y > 0$ in Y. Constant returns to scale production functions also are called linearly homogeneous or homogeneous of degree one.[10] Observe that in a one-input world there is no difference in functional geometry between constant returns to scale and local constant returns to scale at any $y > 0$ as long as (4.2-5) holds for all $\alpha > 0$. Either way the graph of f lies on a straight line through the origin with the same slope.

In general, the differential implications of global returns to scale are (not surprisingly) stronger than those of local returns to scale. These differential properties are described in the next three propositions. Note that the discrepancy between necessary and sufficient requirements for local decreasing and increasing returns evident, respectively, in Theorems 4.2-6 and 4.2-10, and also in Theorems 4.2-7 and 4.2-13, disappears here. The proof of Theorem 4.2-20 parallels that of Theorem 4.2-18 and is omitted.

Theorem 4.2-18 f exhibits decreasing returns to scale on Y if and only if the following two conditions hold:

i) For all $y > 0$ in Y,

$$f(y) \geqslant \sum_{j=1}^{J} y_j f_j(y).$$

ii) For all $y > 0$ in Y and any pair of real numbers α' and α'', where $\alpha'' > \alpha' > 0$,

$$f(\alpha y) = \sum_{j=1}^{J} \alpha y_j f_j(\alpha y)$$

cannot hold for every α such that $\alpha' < \alpha < \alpha''$.

Proof: Assume f exhibits decreasing returns to scale on Y. Then (i) is established by applying Theorem 4.2-6 to all $y > 0$ in Y. Now suppose for some $y > 0$ in Y and $\alpha'' > \alpha' > 0$ that

$$f(\alpha y) = \sum_{j=1}^{J} \alpha y_j f_j(\alpha y),$$

---

[10]   Recall the definition of linear homogeneity in Section 2.1. A general definition of homogenous functions is given in appendix Section A.3. As pointed out in n. 3 on p. 123, the mathematical statement of constant returns to scale was brought into economics by Wicksteed [15, p. 4].

for every α between α' and α''. Without loss in generality, it can be assumed that $\alpha' < 1 < \alpha''$. Consider again the function of (4.2-12), namely,

$$\psi(\alpha) = f(y) - \frac{f(\alpha y)}{\alpha}, \quad \alpha' < \alpha < \alpha''. \tag{4.2-19}$$

Then $\psi(1) = 0$ and, as in the proof of Theorem 4.2-10,

$$\frac{d\psi(\alpha)}{d\alpha} = 0$$

for all $\alpha' < \alpha < \alpha''$. Hence, for every α between α' and α'', $\psi(\alpha) = 0$, that is,

$$f(\alpha y) = \alpha f(y),$$

contrary to the decreasing returns to scale of f on Y. This proves (ii).

   To go the other way, let (i) and (ii) be satisfied. Fix $y > 0$ in Y and define ψ as in (4.2-19) for all $\alpha \geqslant 1$. As before, $\psi(1) = 0$ and

$$\frac{d\psi(\alpha)}{d\alpha} \geqslant 0, \quad \alpha \geqslant 1,$$

from (i). But (ii) implies that between any pair α' and α'', where $\alpha'' > \alpha' > 0$, there always exists an α such that

$$\frac{d\psi(\alpha)}{d\alpha} > 0.$$

From this it may be concluded[11] that $\psi(\alpha) > 0$ for all $\alpha > 1$, thus establishing (4.2-15). Because y was chosen arbitrarily f exhibits decreasing returns to scale on Y.

Q.E.D.

Theorem 4.2-20 f exhibits increasing returns to scale on Y if and only if the following two conditions hold:
   i) For all $y > 0$ in Y,

$$f(y) \leqslant \sum_{j=1}^{J} y_j f_j(y).$$

   ii) For all $y > 0$ in Y and any pair of real numbers α' and α'', where

---

[11]   The previous sentence ensures that ψ is an increasing function of α. See Katzner [6, p. 186].

$$\alpha'' > \alpha' > 0,$$

$$f(\alpha y) = \sum_{j=1}^{J} \alpha y_j f_j(\alpha y)$$

cannot hold for every α such that $\alpha' < \alpha < \alpha''$.

Theorem 4.2-21 f exhibits constant returns to scale on Y if and only if the partial derivatives, $f_j(y)$ for $j = 1, \ldots, J$, are homogeneous of degree zero and

$$f(y) = \sum_{j=1}^{J} y_j f_j(y),$$

for all $y > 0$ in Y.

Proof: Suppose first that f exhibits constant returns to scale on Y. Differentiating (4.2-17) with respect to y_j and cancelling α gives

$$f_j(\alpha y) = f_j(y),$$

for all $y > 0$ and all $\alpha > 0$. Hence the f_j are homogeneous of degree zero. Now, differentiating (4.2-17) with respect to α gives

$$\sum_{j=1}^{J} y_j f_j(\alpha y) = f(y),$$

for all $y > 0$ and all $\alpha > 0$. The required conclusion is obtained either by setting $\alpha = 1$ or by employing the just-deduced homogeneity of the f_j.

Conversely, suppose $f(y) = \sum_{j=1}^{J} y_j f_j(y)$, where the f_j are homogeneous of degree zero. Then for any $y \neq 0$ and all $\alpha > 0$,

$$f(\alpha y) = \sum_{j=1}^{J} \alpha y_j f_j(\alpha y),$$

$$= \alpha \sum_{j=1}^{J} y_j f_j(y),$$

$$= \alpha f(y).$$

Q.E.D.

Theorem 4.2-21 usually is referred to as *Euler's theorem* for linearly homogeneous functions.[12] The general statement of Euler's result for functions that are homogeneous of any degree appears as Theorem A.3-9 of appendix Section A.3.

Further insight into the nature and geometry of global returns to scale is provided by the next five propositions. These results link global returns to the possibilities of strict concavity, strict convexity, and linearity of the production function.

Theorem 4.2-22   If f is strictly concave on Y and $f(0) \geqslant 0$, then f exhibits decreasing returns to scale on Y.

Proof: Consider any $y > 0$ in Y and choose α so that $0 < \alpha < 1$. Then by the strict concavity,

$$f(\alpha y) = f(\alpha y + [1 - \alpha]0),$$

$$> \alpha f(y) + [1 - \alpha]f(0),$$

$$\geqslant \alpha f(y),$$

because $f(0) \geqslant 0$. This proves (4.2-14) for all $y > 0$ in Y.

Q.E.D.

The converse of Theorem 4.2-22 cannot be true. Figure 4.5 provides a one-variable-input example of a function exhibiting decreasing returns to scale which is not concave. As drawn, f has the property that all rays from the origin meet its graph from below. In addition, the hypothesis of Theorem 4.2-22 that $f(0) \geqslant 0$ cannot be dispensed with. The one-variable-input example pictured in Figure 4.6 is the graph of a strictly concave function that does not exhibit decreasing returns to scale. This is so because the ray from the origin through $(y_1', f(y_1'))$ does not cut the graph of f at $(y_1', f(y_1'))$ from below. As the next proposition shows, the differential inequality of Theorem 4.2-6 and the first

---

[12]   The first appearance of Euler's theorem in the economics literature is in Flux's [5, p. 311] 1894 review of Wicksteed's *An Essay on the Coordination of the Laws of Distribution*. (The latter book, recall n. 3 on p. 123 above, introduced economists to the mathematical specifications of the production function and the notion of constant returns to scale.) Flux uses Euler's theorem to shorten Wicksteed's derivation of the "adding-up" or "product exhaustion" theorem. A version of that theorem that dispenses with the constant-returns-to-scale assumption appears towards the end of Section 5.2 below.

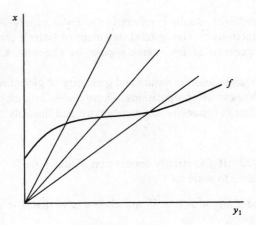

Figure 4.5 Nonconcave production
function exhibiting decreasing returns to
scale

part of Theorem 4.2-18 can be strengthened in the presence of strict concavity
— something that is not possible with decreasing returns to scale alone.

Theorem 4.2-23 If f is strictly concave on Y and $f(0) \geqslant 0$, then

$$f(y) > \sum_{j=1}^{J} y_j f_j(y),$$

for all $y > 0$ in Y.

Proof: From the strict concavity it follows that[13]

$$f(y') - f(y) < \sum_{j=1}^{J} (y'_j - y_j) f_j(y),$$

for all $y' \neq y$ in the interior of Y. Actually, the inequality also holds when

---

[13]   Katzner [6, p. 183].

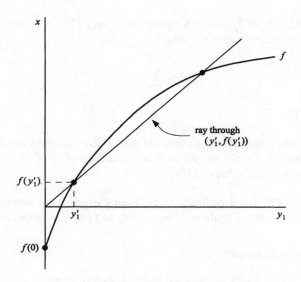

Figure 4.6 Strictly concave production function
that does not exhibit decreasing returns to scale

$y' = 0.$[14] Thus, with $y' = 0$,

$$f(y) - f(0) > \sum_{j=1}^{J} y_j f_j(y).$$

The conclusion now is deduced from the requirement that $f(0) \geqslant 0$.

Q.E.D.

The word "strictly" can be struck from Theorem 4.2-23 upon replacement of the strong by the weak inequality. In either case the converse assertion does not hold for the same reason that there is no converse to Theorem 4.2-22: Everywhere in Figure 4.5 the appropriate inequality is satisfied (all rays cut the graph of f from below) but f is not strictly concave.

Results corresponding to Theorems 4.2-22 and 4.2-23 for strictly convex functions are derived from the fact that a function f is strictly convex on Y if and only if $-f$ is strictly concave there. They are stated without proof as follows:

---

[14]   Katzner's proof cited in n. 13 on the previous page is easily extended to cover this case.

Theorem 4.2-24 If f is strictly convex on Y and $f(0) \leqslant 0$, then f exhibits increasing returns to scale on Y and

$$f(y) < \sum_{j=1}^{J} y_j f_j(y),$$

for all $y > 0$ in Y.

Note that constant returns to scale production functions can be concave or convex but not strictly so. When f is linear, the nature of global returns to scale depends on the value of $f(0)$.

Theorem 4.2-25 Let f be linear on Y. Then f exhibits decreasing, constant, or increasing returns to scale on Y according as $f(0)$ is positive, zero, or negative.

Proof: Linearity means

$$f(y) = \sum_{j=1}^{J} \gamma_j y_j + \delta,$$

for some constants $\gamma_1, \ldots, \gamma_J$ and δ. Thus $f(0) = \delta$. It is easy to verify (4.2-14), (4.2-16), or (4.2-17) according to the sign of δ (Exercise 4.3).

Q.E.D.

Moreover, Theorem 4.2-9 has an obvious generalization:

Theorem 4.2-26 f exhibits constant returns to scale on Y if and only if f is linear through the origin over every ray from the origin into Y.

Because of the analytical convenience it affords, the hypothesis of constant returns to scale has received considerable attention. A typical two-input example appears in Figure 4.7. (Observe the linearity of f over the ray drawn from the origin into Y.) It is tempting to argue that real world production functions should approximate constant returns to scale because doubling, say, all inputs by building a carbon copy of any existing plant should double output. Moreover output should be tripled, quadrupled, and so on by simply reproducing the same plant over and over again. But this argument misses the point. For production functions are defined subject to technical efficiency requiring maximum output to be identified with each input basket. There is no *a priori* guarantee, then, that the combined output of the original and replicated plants

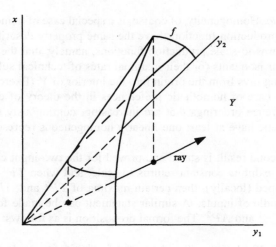

Figure 4.7 Constant returns to scale production
function

is the maximum obtainable when all inputs are doubled. The maximum could
more than double the original output, technology permitting, or less than double it if the operation of the replicated plant "interferes," as specified by the
technology, with that of the original. Like the law of diminishing returns, the
issue of whether a real production function exhibits constant returns to scale is
an empirical question.

Two further implications of constant returns to scale are worth considering here. First, because the f_j are homogeneous of degree zero (Theorem
4.2-21), the partial derivatives of the isoquants from (4.1-7), namely,

$$w_j(y_1, \ldots, y_{J-1}, f(y)) = w_j(y_1, \ldots, y_{J-1}, x),$$

are also homogeneous of degree zero. Hence these derivatives remain constant
along rays from the origin into the interior of Y. With two inputs, then, the
slopes of all isoquants intersecting any ray are, at the points of intersection,
identical. More generally, let $\tau(x)$ be any increasing, differentiable transformation defined on the range of f whose derivative $\tau'(x) > 0$ everywhere, and
let f be homogeneous of any (real-number) degree κ, that is,

$$f(\alpha y) = \alpha^\kappa f(y),$$

for all y in the interior of Y and any $\alpha > 0$. Then $\tau \circ f(y) = \tau(f(y))$ is said to be *homothetic*. Homogeneity, of course, is a special case of homotheticity. All homothetic production functions have the same property described above for constant-returns-to-scale production functions, namely, that the partial derivatives of their isoquants (or their marginal rates of technical substitution) are constant along rays from the origin into the interior of Y (Exercise 4.8). This parallels the case of homothetic preferences in the theory of demand since, recall, preference orderings that are increasing, continuously representable, and homothetic have at least one linearly homogeneous representation (Section 2.1).

The second result is stated and proved for the two-input case. It asserts that when f exhibits constant returns to scale, and when TP^1 and TP^2 are properly shaped (locally), then certain maxima of TP^2 and AP^1 occur over the same bundle of inputs. A similar statement can be made for appropriate maxima of TP^1 and AP^2. The formal proposition is as follows:

Theorem 4.2-27 Let $J = 2$ and assume f exhibits constant returns to scale on Y. Suppose, at some point $y^0 = (y_1^0, y_2^0) > 0$, the second partial derivatives $f_{11}(y^0) < 0$ and $f_{22}(y^0) < 0$. Define TP^1 and TP^2 by setting, respectively, $y_2 = y_2^0$ and $y_1 = y_1^0$. Then $AP^1(y_1)$ has a unique maximum at $y_1 = y_1^0$ if and only if $TP^2(y_2)$ has a unique maximum at $y_2 = y_2^0$.

Proof: If

$$\frac{dAP^1(y_1^0)}{dy_1} = 0,$$

then differentiating

$$AP^1(y_1) = \frac{f(y_1, y_2^0)}{y_1}$$

at $y_1 = y_1^0$ results in

$$\frac{y_1^0 f_1(y^0) - f(y^0)}{(y_1^0)^2} = 0.$$

Application of Euler's theorem (Theorem 4.2-21) gives

$$\frac{-y_2^0 f_2(y^0)}{(y_1^0)^2} = 0.$$

Since $(y_1^0, y_2^0) > 0$,

$$f_2(y^0) = 0.$$

Reversing these steps proves the converse implication. Hence

$$\frac{dAP^1(y_1^0)}{dy_1} = 0$$

if and only if $MP^2(y_2^0) = f_2(y^0) = 0$.

That y_2^0 corresponds to a unique maximum of TP^2 is clear because $f_{22}(y0) < 0$. To show that AP^1 has a unique maximum where

$$\frac{dAP^1(y_1)}{dy_1} = 0,$$

differentiate

$$\frac{dAP^1(y_1)}{dy_1}$$

and evaluate the derivative at $y_1 = y_1^0$. Using the fact established above that $f_2(y^0) = 0$ yields

$$\frac{d^2 AP^1(y_1^0)}{(dy_1)^2} = \frac{(y_1^0)^3 f_{11}(y^0) + 2y_1^0 y_2^0 f_2(y^0)}{(y_1^0)^4},$$

$$= \frac{1}{y_1^0} f_{11}(y^0) < 0.$$

Because $f_{11}(y^0) < 0$, the conclusion is immediate.

Q.E.D.

Theorem 4.2-27 is illustrated in Figure 4.8 under the assumption that the relevant total product curves are shaped as depicted in Figure 4.1. When all total product curves take on this form in a constant-returns-to-scale environment,[15] the theorem implies that both TP^2 and AP^1, which appear in perpendicular planes, have maxima over the same basket of inputs. Moreover, the lower ridge line

$$\left\{ y : y > 0 \text{ and } f_1(y) = MP^1(y_1) = 0 \right\} = \left\{ y : y > 0 \text{ and } \frac{dAP^2(y_2)}{dy_2} = 0 \right\},$$

---

[15]   That such shapes of total product curves are consistent with constant returns to scale has amply been demonstrated by a series of communications in the *American Economic Review* 53 (1963), pp. 1084-1085, and 54 (1964), pp. 739-753.

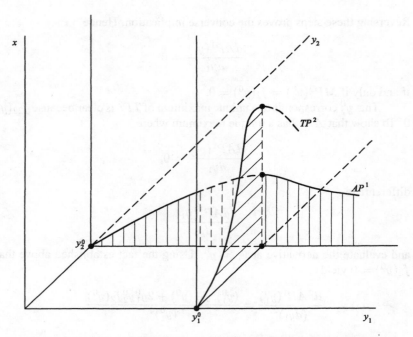

Figure 4.8 Average and total product curves illustrating Theorem 4.2-27

and the upper ridge line

$$\{y : y > 0 \text{ and } f_2(y) = MP^2(y_2) = 0\} = \left\{y : y > 0 \text{ and } \frac{dAP^1(y_1)}{dy_1} = 0\right\}.$$

In other words, both ridge lines can be determined either from TP^1 or from TP^2. A mathematical example appears in Exercise 4.23.

From here on, the assumptions that $f(y) \geqslant 0$ on Y and $f(0) = 0$ are reimposed.

4.3   THE ELASTICITY OF SUBSTITUTION

One useful way of thinking about the curvature or shape of isoquants is in terms of the elasticity of substitution. This is a unitless number (like all elasticities) measuring changes in the ratio of inputs employed relative to the rate at which substitution between inputs takes place along an isoquant. Only a two-input world is considered. It will be seen that constancy in the elasticity of substitution, when present, is the primary defining characteristic of an important class of production functions.

Let $x = f(y)$ be a production function where $y = (y_1, y_2)$ and suppose

$$y_2 = w(y_1, x), \tag{4.3-1}$$

is an isoquant derived from it. Then from (4.1-7),

$$w_1(y) = -\frac{f_1(y)}{f_2(y)}, \tag{4.3-2}$$

where $f(y)$ replaces the functional argument x in w_1. The *elasticity of substitution* at y, written $\sigma(y)$, is defined along an isoquant at points of D as the ordinary elasticity (Section 1.5) of the input ratio y_2/y_1 with respect to the marginal rate of technical substitution f_1/f_2, or

$$\sigma(y) = \frac{f_1(y)/f_2(y)}{y_2/y_1} \frac{d(y_2/y_1)}{d(f_1(y)/f_2(y))}, \tag{4.3-3}$$

for all $y > 0$. As usual, the symbol $d \cdot / d \cdot$ refers to the total derivative.

From (4.3-1), both

$$\frac{y_2}{y_1} = \frac{w(y_1, x)}{y_1} \tag{4.3-4}$$

and

$$\frac{f_1(y)}{f_2(y)} = \frac{f_1(y_1, w(y_1, x))}{f_2(y_1, w(y_1, x))} \tag{4.3-5}$$

are functions of y_1 when x is fixed. Therefore, because σ relates to the rate of substitution along an isoquant, that is, because x is fixed, application of the implicit function theorem[16] permits (4.3-3) to be written in a form more amenable to manipulation:

$$\sigma(y) = \frac{f_1(y)/f_2(y)}{y_2/y_1} \frac{\dfrac{d(y_2/y_1)}{dy_1}}{\dfrac{d(f_1(y)/f_2(y))}{dy_1}}. \tag{4.3-6}$$

---

[16]   Rudin [8, pp. 224-228].

Now substitute (4.3-4) and (4.3-5) into (4.3-6), carry out the indicated differentiations, and replace w_1 according to (4.3-2). Then (4.3-6) reduces to

$$\sigma(y) = \frac{f_1(y)f_2(y)[y_1 f_1(y) + y_2 f_2(y)]}{y_2 y_1 |F(y)|}, \qquad (4.3-7)$$

where $|F(y)|$ is the determinant of the bordered Hessian of f. Recall that $|F(y)|$ has been assumed to be nonvanishing where all $f_j(y) \neq 0$ on the interior of Y, that is, in particular, on the set D (Section 4.1).

As an illustration, the production function

$$f(y_1, y_2) = B(y_1)^{\beta_1}(y_2)^{\beta_2}, \qquad (4.3-8)$$

where B, β_1, and β_2 are positive constants, can be shown to have $\sigma(y) = 1$ for all $y > 0$ (Exercise 4.6). Observe that $\beta_1 + \beta_2 \gtreqless 1$ according as f exhibits increasing, constant, and decreasing returns to scale, respectively. (This is a special case of Exercise 4.19.) When $\beta_1 + \beta_2 = 1$, that is, when f is homogeneous of degree 1, the production function is called *Cobb–Douglas*.[17] Sometimes (4.3-8) itself is referred to as the *generalized* Cobb-Douglas production function.

In the general case of constant returns to scale (of which equation (4.3-8) with $\beta_1 + \beta_2 = 1$ is a special instance), further simplification of (4.3-7) is possible. By using the results of Exercise 4.4 and the fact that $f_{12}(y) = f_{21}(y)$ everywhere (Theorem A.3-3 of appendix Section A.3),

$$|F(y)| = \frac{1}{y_1 y_2} f_{12}(y)[y_1 f_1(y) + y_2 f_2(y)]^2.$$

Hence from (4.3-7) and Euler's theorem,

$$\sigma(y) = \frac{f_1(y)f_2(y)}{f(y)f_{12}(y)},$$

for all $y > 0$ in D.

Note that the collection of all generalized Cobb-Douglas production functions is rigid in its specification that $\sigma = 1$ for all y in Y, regardless of the values of β_1 and β_2. On the other hand, precisely because β_1 and β_2 do vary over its members, this class is flexible with respect to the nature of the returns to scale it imposes. By contrast, the collection of production functions considered next is flexible in allowing σ (though still constant over Y) to vary from

---

[17]   The Cobb-Douglas production function was actually introduced by Wicksell [14, p. 286] in 1923, some five years before the initial paper employing the same function by C. W. Cobb and P. H. Douglas [3] appeared in 1928.

one function to another, but is rigid in insisting on linear homogeneity for all of them.

A function f is said to be a member of the *CES class* (that is, the *constant elasticity of substitution class*) of production functions whenever (i) f is homogeneous of degree one, and (ii) $\sigma(y)$ is constant for all $y > 0$. Violation of either (i) or (ii) disqualifies f from membership. Over the interior of Y, it turns out that all production functions in the CES class are of the form[18]

$$f(y_1, y_2) = A[\alpha(y_1)^{-\rho} + (1 - \alpha)(y_2)^{-\rho}]^{-1/\rho}, \qquad (4.3\text{-}9)$$

where A, α, and ρ are constants such that $A > 0$, $0 < \alpha < 1$, and $\rho \geqslant -1$. Because f is continuous on the interior of Y, it can be continuously extended to the boundary. Confusion will not arise by using the same symbol f to denote both (4.3-9) and its continuous extension. Ignoring the special cases $\rho = -1$, $\rho = 0$, and $\rho = \infty$, which are considered shortly (actually, some parts of the following apply either as they stand or as slightly modified in these situations), f is smooth as described in (4.1-3), and $f(y) > 0$ on Y. To determine the value of $f(0)$, it is sufficient (because f is continuous) to consider function values along the ray $y_2 = y_1$. Substitution of $y_2 = y_1$ into (4.3-9) and taking the limit as y_1 goes to zero gives

$$f(0) = \lim_{y_1 \to 0} Ay_1 = 0,$$

satisfying the remainder of (4.1-2). Property (4.1-4) holds because

$$f_1(y) = \frac{\alpha}{A^\rho} \left(\frac{x}{y_1} \right)^{1+\rho} > 0,$$

$$\qquad\qquad\qquad (4.3\text{-}10)$$

$$f_2(y) = \frac{1 - \alpha}{A^\rho} \left(\frac{x}{y_2} \right)^{1+\rho} > 0,$$

for all $y > 0$ where $x = f(y)$ (Exercise 4.7). From (4.3-10) the slopes of the isoquants running through the interior of the input space Y are

$$w_1(y) = -\frac{\alpha}{1 - \alpha} \left(\frac{y_2}{y_1} \right)^{1+\rho}. \qquad (4.3\text{-}11)$$

Differentiation of (4.3-11) yields

$$w_{11}(y) = -\frac{\alpha(1 + \rho)}{1 - \alpha} \left(\frac{y_2}{y_1} \right)^{\rho} \left[\frac{y_1 w_1(y) - y_2}{(y_1)^2} \right],$$

---

[18]   Arrow *et al.* [1, pp. 229, 230].

and, because $w_1(y) < 0$,

$$w_{11}(y) > 0, \tag{4.3-12}$$

for all $y > 0$ as long as $\rho \neq -1$. Thus isoquants interior to Y are strictly convex and f is strictly quasi-concave: Property (4.1-5) remains intact. Moreover, adapting equation (2.3-8) (relating the bordered Hessian determinant to the second derivative of the indifference function) to the present context, (4.3-12) ensures $|F(y)| \neq 0$ throughout the interior of Y. Verification that f is homogeneous of degree one and

$$\sigma(y) = \frac{1}{1+\rho}, \tag{4.3-13}$$

for every $y > 0$ is left to Exercise 4.7. Therefore the production function of (4.3-9) with $\rho \neq -1$, $\rho \neq 0$, and $\rho \neq \infty$ satisfies the basic properties listed in Section 4.1 and both characteristics of the CES class. Because $\sigma(y)$ is constant for all $y > 0$, the symbol for the functional argument, y, can be dropped.

The shape of interior isoquants derived from production functions of the CES class depends on the value of ρ (or σ). If $\rho = -1$ (or $\sigma = \infty$) then (4.3-9) becomes

$$f(y_1, y_2) = A[\alpha y_1 + (1 - \alpha)y_2].$$

Both f and its isoquants are linear, and the slopes of the isoquants, which (with y_1 as the independent variable) all reduce to $-\alpha/(1 - \alpha)$ everywhere, are negative. As with indifference curves, this can be called the case of perfect substitutes. When $-1 < \rho < 0$ (or $1 < \sigma < \infty$) the exponents of (4.3-9) are all positive. Along the isoquant $x = f(y)$, if $y_1 = 0$, then

$$y_2 = \frac{x}{A}(1 - \alpha)^{1/\rho},$$

and if $y_2 = 0$, then

$$y_1 = \frac{x}{A}(\alpha)^{1/\rho}.$$

Hence each isoquant intersects both y_1- and y_2-axes. (This violates one of the extra restrictions imposed in the discussion following inequalities 4.1-8.) On the other hand, for $0 < \rho < \infty$ (or $0 < \sigma < 1$) the exponents of (4.3-9) are negative. Write (4.3-9) as

$$f(y_1, y_2) = A \left[\frac{(y_1 y_2)^\rho}{\alpha(y_2)^\rho + (1 - \alpha)(y_1)^\rho} \right]^{1/\rho},$$

$$= \frac{A y_1 y_2}{[\alpha(y_2)^\rho + (1 - \alpha)(y_1)^\rho]^{1/\rho}}.$$

Then, excluding the origin (for which $f(0) = 0$), it follows that $f(y) = 0$ if and only if either $y_1 = 0$ or $y_2 = 0$. Here interior isoquants cannot intersect the boundary of Y. Indeed, they are asymptotic to lines parallel to the y_1- and y_2-axes (Exercise 4.7). To evaluate the case in which $\rho = \infty$ (or $\sigma = 0$), take the limit of (4.3-11) as $\rho \to \infty$ to obtain

$$w_1(y_1, y_2) = \begin{cases} -\infty, & \text{if } y_2 > y_1, \\ \\ 0, & \text{if } y_2 < y_1. \end{cases}$$

Thus with $\rho = \infty$ (or $\sigma = 0$) each isoquant must consist of a horizontal half-line and a vertical half-line meeting on the ray $y_1 = y_2$. There is no substitution. Parallel to demand theory, the inputs can be referred to as perfect complements. They are employed only in a 1-1 ratio.

The last possibility to consider is $\rho = 0$ (or $\sigma = 1$). From (4.3-9),

$$\ln f(y_1, y_2) - \ln A = \frac{-\ln \left[\alpha(y_1)^{-\rho} + (1 - \alpha)(y_2)^{-\rho} \right]}{\rho}.$$

Both numerator and denominator to the right of the equality sign tend to zero with ρ. By L'Hôpital's rule,

$$\lim_{\rho \to 0} \left[\ln f(y_1, y_2) - \ln A \right] = \lim_{\rho \to 0} \frac{\alpha(y_1)^{-\rho} \ln y_1 + (1 - \alpha)(y_2)^{-\rho} \ln y_2}{\alpha(y_1)^{-\rho} + (1 - \alpha)(y_2)^{-\rho}},$$

$$= \alpha \ln y_1 + (1 - \alpha) \ln y_2,$$

$$= \ln (y_1)^\alpha (y_2)^{1-\alpha}.$$

Thus (4.3-9) with $\rho = 0$ is the Cobb-Douglas production function

$$f(y_1, y_2) = A(y_1)^\alpha (y_2)^{1-\alpha}.$$

Note that the Cobb-Douglas function satisfies (4.1-2) – (4.1-5); none of its interior isoquants touches the boundary of Y and all are asymptotic to the y_1-

and y_2-axes; and $|F(y)| \neq 0$ everywhere in the interior of Y.

Functions of the CES class are frequently used in empirical studies that require statistical estimation of the parameters of production. This is because the parameters of these functions are relatively easy to estimate, and the functional form (4.3-9) defining the CES class imposes relatively few *a priori* restrictions on them. There are not many other known production functions having such convenient properties.

4.4 COST MINIMIZATION

Just as the relationship between inputs and output in the production function hinges on technical efficiency, that between output and cost rests on economic efficiency. One aspect of economic efficiency has already been introduced in the exclusion of areas outside of that between the ridge lines. Another arises in the context of selecting cost minimizing combinations of inputs to produce a given output.

Let f be a production function satisfying (4.1-2) – (4.1-5) on Y. The assumptions that the set D of (4.1-4) is either the region between the ridge surfaces (up to a unique global maximum output — if that maximun exists) or the entire interior of Y, that $|F(y)| \neq 0$ for all $y > 0$ such that $f_j(y) \neq 0$ where $j = 1, \ldots, J$, and that isoquants, where nonnegatively sloped and strictly convex, do not touch the boundary of Y, are continued. Write Γ for the interior of the image of Y under f. Thus if f has a maximum (it has already been assumed that when one exists it is both global and unique) or, more generally, if the image of Y under f has a least upper bound, then

$$\Gamma = \{x : 0 < x < \overline{x}\},$$

where $\overline{x}$ is the least upper bound or maximum output. Otherwise, Γ is unbounded:

$$\Gamma = \{x : 0 < x\}.$$

The reason for introducing Γ is to isolate the interior outputs for which isoquants exist. These outputs constitute the domain of the firm's cost function defined in Section 4.5.

Denote the price of input j by r_j and set $r = (r_1, \ldots, r_J)$. In accordance with earlier discussion, y is the vector of variable inputs; fixed inputs (if any) are subsumed under the functional symbol f. Hence total cost, TC, is given by

$$TC = r \cdot y + b, \tag{4.4-1}$$

where $b > 0$ is total fixed cost, that is, prices times quantities of the fixed inputs subsumed in f. (In the absence of fixed inputs, $b = 0$.) Assume the firm takes r and b to be determined by market forces beyond its control and views them, therefore, as fixed parameters. Given its output x, if the firm were to hire inputs so as to produce x as efficiently as possible, then it would choose its input bundle y to minimize

$$r \cdot y + b,$$

subject to

$$f(y) = x, \tag{4.4-2}$$

where x is taken as another fixed parameter.

Formally, the problem is identical to that of the consumer selecting commodity baskets by minimizing expenditure for a given level of utility, and much of the corresponding analysis of Section 2.4 applies. Thus it can be shown that unique cost minimizing solutions y exist in D for all $r > 0$ and all x in Γ. For these vectors (r, x), functions g^* can be defined in the usual way:

$$y = g^*(r, x), \tag{4.4-3}$$

if and only if y minimizes $r \cdot y + b$ subject to $f(y) = x$. It is not necessary to include b as a functional argument of g^* because cost-minimizing baskets are the same regardless of the value of b and, in any case, unlike r and x, the parameter b will not be permitted to vary. Note that g^* is a vector of functions $g^* = (g^{*1}, ..., g^{*J})$. The two-input geometric solution is identical to that pictured in Figures 2.8 and 2.10 with indifference curves labeled as isoquants and budget lines replaced by constant-total-cost or *isocost* lines. Analogously to the first-order Lagrangian expenditure minimization conditions (2.4-9), the equations obtained from Lagrange's theorem are[19]

$$r_j = \eta f_j(y), \quad j = 1, ..., J, \tag{4.4-4}$$

where the multiplier $\eta > 0$ is a continuously differentiable function of r and x. In parallel to the interpretation of λ in the constrained utility-maximization problem described earlier, the value of η obtained in the present constrained

----

[19]   As in n. 39 on p. 72, the constraint qualification (A.3-17) is satisfied since the f_j are nonvanishing throughout D.

cost-minimization problem turns out to be the partial derivative of total cost with respect to output. (See Theorem 4.5-8 below.) Dividing the last equation of (4.44) into those remaining gives

$$\frac{r_j}{r_J} = \frac{f_j(y)}{f_J(y)}, \qquad j = 1, \ldots, J - 1, \tag{4.4-5}$$

which, together with (4.4-2), is the mathematical statement of the tangency between isocost hyperplanes and isoquants. As in the argument used to derive the differentiability of h on Ω (statement 2.3-18), the Jacobian of the system consisting of (4.4-5) and (4.4-2) is nonzero where $f_j(y) \neq 0$ for all j because at these points $|F(y)| \neq 0$. Solving, therefore, provides an explicit formulation of g^* which, under present assumptions, is continuously differentiable throughout its domain.

If the production function has non-intersecting ridge surfaces, or ridge lines when there are only two factors, the assumption of cost minimization clearly precludes choices by the firm of input baskets beyond the region within the ridge surfaces. Furthermore, if the ridge surfaces intersect uniquely (that is, if the production function has a unique global maximum) so that isoquants take on ellipsoidal shapes, then there are actually two isocost hyperplanes tangent to the isoquant of (4.4-2) and two solutions of the system (4.4-2), (4.4-5). A two-dimensional possibility is illustrated in Figure 4.9. The tangency (and solution) at y'' in the diagram is discarded because it lies outside the area of efficiency between the ridge lines, *i.e.*, the set D, and is associated with maximum, not minimum, cost. (Exercise 4.22 illustrates the mathematics involved.) All of this is reflected in the inequalities of (4.1-8) and by the fact that the f_j are all positive only between the ridge surfaces up to the unique maximum. Conditions (4.1-8), stated as they are with strong inequalities are the sufficient second-order restrictions ensuring, since they are in force, a unique constrained minimum of $r \cdot y + b$ where (4.4-4) is satisfied.

To provide an interpretation of the function g^*, observe that for each $r > 0$ the locus

$$\left\{ y : \frac{r_j}{r_J} = \frac{f_j(y)}{f_J(y)}, \text{ for } j = 1, \ldots, J - 1 \text{ and } y \text{ in } D \right\},$$

is the collection of all input baskets at which isoquants are tangent to parallel isocost hyperplanes as x varies over Γ. This locus is called the *expansion path* given r (see Figure 4.9), and the equations describing it are (4.4-5).[20] Thus g^*

---

[20] Introduction of a money capital requirement into the model of the firm necessitates significant modification of equations (4.4-4) and (4.4-5) and the present definition of the expansion

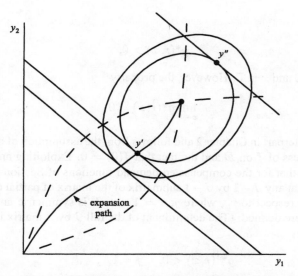

Figure 4.9 Ridge lines, isoquants, and the expansion path for a production function with a maximum

can be understood as a function that maps vectors (r, x) into points on expansion paths. That is, with r given, $y = g^*(r, x)$ indicates the least-cost combination of inputs associated with x as the firm moves along the r-expansion path. It should also be pointed out that g^* is not really a demand function for the firm's inputs because it has, as a functional argument, the variable x, which is endogenously determined within the firm. In other words, g^* does not provide a full statement of the firm's behavior in response to relevant market variables. (Generally, firm input demand functions do give complete behavioral specifications. They depend on input and output prices and are studied in detail in the next chapter.) But because g^* furnishes a basis for defining cost functions and examining their properties in Section 4.5, further exploration of it is worthwhile here.

Several of the properties of g^* are derived in much the same way as the corresponding properties of consumer compensated demand functions in Chapter 2. Thus, for example, g^* is homogeneous of degree zero in r for each

path. See Section 13.3.

x in Γ, and

$$g^*(r, x) > 0, \tag{4.4-6}$$

for all $r > 0$ and x in Γ. However, the property

$$\lim_{x \to 0} g^*(r, x) = 0 \tag{4.4-7}$$

has no counterpart in Chapter 2 and follows from the assumption of differential increasingness of f on D and the fact that $f(0) = 0$. Exploiting an argument identical to that for the compensated demand functions of Section 2.4, it can be shown that any $J - 1$ by $J - 1$ submatrix of the matrix of partial derivatives of g^{*j} with respect to r_n, where $j, n = 1, \ldots, J$, is symmetric and negative definite where defined. (The determinant of the full J by J matrix is zero.) In particular,

$$g_j^{*j}(r, x) < 0, \quad j = 1, \ldots, J,$$

for all $r > 0$ and x in Γ. Thus the graph of the single-variable "input-demand" function relating y_j to r_j, as derived from g^* with all other input prices and x held fixed, is downward sloping. But the signs of the other input-price derivatives as well as those with respect to x, namely g_x^{*j}, cannot be pinned down. The latter, however, merit further attention. For the signs of the g_x^{*j} turn out to hinge on the signs of the derivatives of the firm's expansion path.

Begin by substituting $y = g^*(r, x)$ into the production function $x = f(y)$ to obtain

$$f(g^*(r, x)) = x,$$

for all x in Γ and $r > 0$. Upon differentiation with respect to x,

$$\sum_{j=1}^{J} f_j(g^*(r, x)) g_x^{*j}(r, x) = 1, \tag{4.4-8}$$

again on Γ and with $r > 0$. Because $f_j(g^*(r, x)) > 0$ on Γ, where $j = 1, \ldots, J$, it follows that at least one g_x^{*j} is positive at each x. But even though a minimum of one input must be increased, expansion of output at any x in Γ could still result in either more or less employment of any particular input.

To see what is involved, consider a two-input world. Explicit expressions for the derivatives g_x^{*j} are easy to derive. Putting (4.4-3) into (4.4-4) and (4.4-

2) and setting $\lambda = 1/\eta$ leaves (for $J = 2$) the system

$$f(g^{*1}(r,x), g^{*2}(r,x)) = x,$$

$$-\lambda r_1 + f_1(g^{*1}(r,x), g^{*2}(r,x)) = 0,$$

$$-\lambda r_2 + f_2(g^{*1}(r,x), g^{*2}(r,x)) = 0.$$

As in Section 2.4, differentiating with respect to x, substituting $f_j = \lambda r_j$ for $j = 1, 2$ into the result, and dropping functional arguments:

$$f_1 g_x^{*1} + f_2 g_x^{*2} = 1,$$

$$-\frac{\lambda_x}{\lambda} f_1 + f_{11} g_x^{*1} + f_{12} g_x^{*2} = 0, \qquad (4.4\text{-}9)$$

$$-\frac{\lambda_x}{\lambda} f_2 + f_{21} g_x^{*1} + f_{22} g_x^{*2} = 0,$$

where λ_x is the partial derivative of λ (a function of r and x) with respect to x. (Since η is positive and continuously differentiable, $\lambda = 1/\eta$ is also.) By Cramer's rule [21]

$$g_x^{*1} = \frac{1}{|F|}(-f_1 f_{22} + f_2 f_{12}), \qquad (4.4\text{-}10)$$

and

$$g_x^{*2} = \frac{1}{|F|}(f_1 f_{21} - f_2 f_{11}). \qquad (4.4\text{-}11)$$

Using these expressions, the signs of the g_x^{*j} can be related to the slope of the expansion path in Y. Recall from (4.4-5) that the expansion path is characterized (between ridge lines when they exist, and possibly up to a unique maximum) by

$$\frac{f_1(y_1, y_2)}{f_2(y_1, y_2)} = \frac{r_1}{r_2}. \qquad (4.4\text{-}12)$$

It is clear that (4.4-12) implicitly describes a function relating y_2 to y_1 along the r-expansion path. The derivative of this function, written dy_2/dy_1, gives the slope of the expansion path and is found upon implicit differentiation of

---

[21]   See Theorem A.4-2 of appendix Section A.4.

(4.4-12) with r_1/r_2 held fixed:

$$\frac{\partial(f_1/f_2)}{\partial y_1} + \frac{\partial(f_1/f_2)}{\partial y_2}\frac{dy_2}{dy_1} = 0. \qquad (4.4\text{-}13)$$

Evaluating the partial derivatives of (4.4-13) and solving for dy_2/dy_1, it can be verified that

$$\frac{dy_2}{dy_1} = \frac{f_1 f_{21} - f_2 f_{11}}{f_2 f_{12} - f_1 f_{22}}. \qquad (4.4\text{-}14)$$

Combining (4.4-10), (4.4-11), and (4.4-14),

$$\frac{dy_2}{dy_1} = \frac{g_x^{*2}}{g_x^{*1}}. \qquad (4.4\text{-}15)$$

If both numerator and denominator on the right-hand side of (4.4-15), are positive, then so is dy_2/dy_1. Conversely, if $dy_2/dy_1 > 0$ then the right-hand-side numerator and denominator are of the same sign. In the latter case, (4.4-8) with $J = 2$ implies, as has previously been indicated, that at least one of g_x^{*1} and g_x^{*2} must be positive. Therefore they both are. The following proposition has now been established.

Theorem 4.4-16 Let $J = 2$, $r > 0$, and x be in Γ. Then the expansion path given r is upward sloping if and only if

$$g_x^{*j}(r, x) > 0, \quad j = 1, 2.$$

Thus the slope of the expansion path in Y determines the signs of the g_x^{*j}. An expansion path negatively inclined at some y would mean that one (but not both) of the g_x^{*j} is negative at the associated r and x. This would be analogous to the case of an inferior good in demand theory as described in Section 2.4: As output rises with input prices remaining fixed, the use of one input in production falls.

It is left as Exercise 4.8 to verify that if $x = f(y_1, y_2)$ is homogeneous of any degree or, more generally, if f is homothetic, then all expansion paths are rays from the origin into the interior of Y. (Hence $g_x^{*j}(r, x) > 0$ for $j = 1, 2$ by Theorem 4.4-16.)

One final result will be useful later on. Denote the partial derivative of the Lagrange multiplier η with respect to x by η_x. The *Hessian* matrix, $\bar{F}(y)$, associated with f at y is the bordered Hessian without its first row and column:

$$\bar{F}(y) = \begin{bmatrix} f_{11}(x) & \cdots & f_{1J}(x) \\ \vdots & & \vdots \\ f_{J1}(x) & \cdots & f_{JJ}(x) \end{bmatrix}.$$

Just as the signs of the principal minors of the bordered Hessian of f are related to the quasi-concavity of f (recall inequalities 4.1-8 and Theorem 2.3-9), so are the signs of the principal minors of the (unbordered) Hessian of f related to the concavity of f.[22] The proposition of interest here is stated in general and proved in the two-input world. The general proof is not difficult.

Theorem 4.4-17   For all $r > 0$ and x in Γ,

$$\eta_x = \eta \frac{|\bar{F}(y)|}{|F(y)|},$$

where $\eta = r_j / f_j(y)$ for any j, and $y = g^*(r, x)$.

Proof: Using Cramer's rule to solve (4.4-9) for $-\lambda_x / \lambda$, and noting that with $r > 0$, all $f_j(y) > 0$, and hence $|F(y)| \neq 0$ for cost-minimizing y corresponding to each x in Γ, it follows that:

$$-\frac{\lambda_x}{\lambda} = \frac{|\bar{F}(y)|}{|F(y)|}.$$

Moreover, because $\lambda = 1/\eta$,

$$\lambda_x = -\frac{1}{\eta^2} \eta_x.$$

The conclusion of the theorem is obtained by combining these results.

Q.E.D.

The next section demonstrates, in part, that η, as it depends on x, is the firm's marginal cost function. The slope of the marginal cost curve is therefore given by η_x. It also establishes the link between returns to scale and the slopes

---

22   See Theorem A.3-10 in appendix Section A.3 and Katzner [6, Sect. B.5].

of the average variable cost curve.

4.5   COST FUNCTIONS

Given fixed input prices, the total cost of a particular output is the total cost of
the least-cost combination of variable inputs used to produce that output plus
the cost of the fixed inputs. Thus, to determine the cost of x, first secure the
least-cost combination of inputs from the intersection of the x-output isoquant
and the expansion path given r. This information already is contained in the
functions $g*$. Then compute total cost from (4.4-1). Using the same symbol for
both the function and the variable, the *total cost* function $TC(r, x)$, therefore,
is given by

$$TC(r, x) = r \cdot g*(r, x) + b, \qquad (4.5\text{-}1)$$

for all x in Γ and all $r > 0$.

Consider first the properties of $TC(r, x)$ as a function of r for fixed x.
Those relating to $TC(r, x)$ as a function of x for fixed r will be taken up subsequently. To begin with, $TC(r, x) - b$ is homogeneous of degree one because
$g*(r, x)$ is homogeneous of degree zero in r. Because $g*$ is continuously differentiable and hence continuous, $TC(r, x)$ is too. The partial derivatives of
TC with respect to the jth input price, that is, the $TC_j(r, x)$ can be calculated
according to a proposition due to Shephard [10, p. 11]:

Theorem 4.5-2   For all $r > 0$ and x in Γ,

$$TC_j(r, x) = g^{*j}(r, x), \quad j = 1, \ldots, J.$$

Proof: Choose $r^0 > 0$ and x^0 in Γ and set $y^0 = g*(r^0, x^0)$. Define the
function

$$\xi(r) = TC(r, x^0) - r \cdot y^0 - b, \qquad (4.5\text{-}3)$$

for $r > 0$. Then the continuous differentiability of TC implies that ξ is also
continuously differentiable. Moreover, because $TC(r, x^0)$ is the total cost of
the cheapest way of producing x^0 given r (see Figure 4.10),

$$\xi(r) \begin{cases} \leqslant 0. & \text{if } r \neq r^0, \\ = 0, & \text{if } r = r^0. \end{cases}$$

It follows that ξ has a maximum at $r = r^0$ and hence its partial derivatives

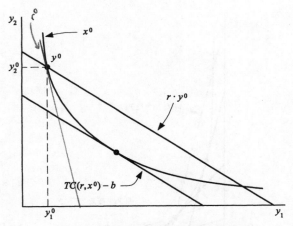

Figure 4.10 Definition of the function ξ

$$\xi_j(r^0) = 0, \quad j = 1, \ldots, J.$$

Reckoning ξ_j from (4.5-3),

$$TC_j(r^0, x^0) - y_j^0 = 0, \quad j = 1, \ldots, J,$$

which, because $y^0 = g^*(r^0, x^0)$, proves the theorem.

Q.E.D.

The positivity of g^* (inequality 4.4-6) together with Theorem 4.5-2 imply

$$TC_j(r, x) > 0, \quad j = 1, \ldots, J,$$

for all $r > 0$. Thus increases in one or more input prices raise the total cost of each output. Another property of the total cost function is that of concavity in r. It is stated as the next theorem.

Theorem 4.5-4   On the domain of positive input-price vectors, $TC(r, x)$ is a concave function[23] of r for each fixed x in Γ.

Proof: Let x in Γ be fixed and choose any $r' > 0$ and $r'' > 0$. Without loss of generality, the firm's fixed cost b can be taken to be zero. Write $y' = g^*(r', x)$

---

[23]   A definition of concave functions appears in appendix Section A.3.

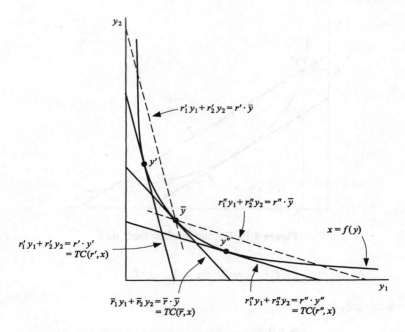

Figure 4.11 Concavity of $TC(r,x)$ as a function of x

and $y'' = g^*(r'', x)$. Then y' minimizes $r' \cdot y$ and y'' minimizes $r'' \cdot y$, each subject to the constraint $x = f(y)$. (The argument can be followed in Figure 4.11.) Hence

$$TC(r', x) = r' \cdot y',$$

$$TC(r'', x) = r'' \cdot y''.$$

Let θ be any number between zero and one and consider the input price vector $\overline{r} = \theta r' + [1 - \theta]r''$. Setting $\overline{y} = g^*(\overline{r}, x)$, it is clear that $\overline{y}$ minimizes $\overline{r} \cdot y$ subject to the same constraint $x = f(y)$ and that $TC(\overline{r}, x) = \overline{r} \cdot \overline{y}$. Note that the definition of $\overline{y}$ in terms of cost minimization for the same fixed x ensures that

$$r' \cdot \overline{y} \geqslant r' \cdot y',$$

$$r'' \cdot \overline{y} \geqslant r'' \cdot y''.$$

Therefore,

$$TC(\theta r' + [1 - \theta]r'', x) = (\theta r' + [1 - \theta]r'') \cdot \overline{y},$$

$$\geqslant \theta r' \cdot y' + [1 - \theta]r'' \cdot y'',$$

$$= \theta TC(r', x) + [1 - \theta]TC(r'', x),$$

and hence $TC(r, x)$ is concave in r.

Q.E.D.

Given a total cost function $TC(r, x)$ with the properties described above, it is sometimes possible to construct the production function from which $TC(r, x)$ can be derived. To see how this is done, assume without loss of generality that $b = 0$. Note first that Theorem 4.5-2 permits the calculation of

$$y_j = g^{*j}(r, x), \quad j = 1, \ldots, J,$$

as the partial derivatives of the given total cost function. Next, because linear homogeneity of $TC(r, x)$ implies that the $TC_j = g^{*j}$ are homogeneous of degree zero in r,

$$y_j = g^{*j}\left(\frac{r_1}{r_J}, \ldots, \frac{r_{J-1}}{r_J}, 1, x\right), \quad j = 1, \ldots, J,$$

for all $r > 0$ and x in Γ. Therefore, when these last equations can be solved to express x as a function of the y_j, that is, when $J - 1$ equations can be used to eliminate the $J - 1$ input price ratios r_j/r_J, the result is the production function generator of $TC(r, x)$. Exercise 4.13 provides an illustration. Although the actual arguments given employ different methods of execution, note the parallel between the recreation of production functions from total cost functions described here and the reconstructions of utility functions from demand functions presented in Sections 3.1 and 3.3.

The remainder of this section is concerned with total cost as a function of x for fixed r. It is often convenient to subsume the fixed r in the functional symbol for total cost. Thus the total cost function is written as $TC(x)$. Before examining its properties, which are often expressed in terms of average and marginal costs, it is necessary to introduce the variable and fixed cost functions. Now, *variable cost* (that is, the cost of the variable inputs alone) as a function of x is

$$VC(x) = r \cdot g^*(r, x), \tag{4.5-5}$$

on Γ. The *fixed cost* function, of course, is

$$FC(x) = b, \qquad\qquad (4.5\text{-}6)$$

again on Γ. Combining (4.5-1), (4.5-5), and (4.5-6),

$$TC(x) = VC(x) + FC(x), \qquad\qquad (4.5\text{-}7)$$

for all x in Γ.

Clearly, from (4.4-6), $TC(x) > 0$ and $VC(x) > 0$ for all x in Γ, and (4.4-7) implies

$$\lim_{x \to 0} TC(x) = b,$$

and

$$\lim_{x \to 0} VC(x) = 0.$$

Both functions are continuously differentiable on Γ because g^* is continuously differentiable. Further properties are established momentarily.

Average total cost, *average variable cost*, *average fixed cost*, and *marginal cost* are defined in the usual way.[24] Respectively, they are

$$ATC(x) = \frac{TC(x)}{x},$$

$$AVC(x) = \frac{VC(x)}{x},$$

$$AFC(x) = \frac{FC(x)}{x},$$

$$MC(x) = \frac{dTC(x)}{dx},$$

for all x in Γ. Equations (4.5-1) and (4.5-5) imply that $MC(x)$ is the same whether it is defined as the derivative of $TC(x)$ or of $VC(x)$. From (4.5-7),

$$ATC(x) = AVC(x) + AFC(x),$$

---

[24]   According to Scherer [9], average cost functions were calculated by a German music publishing firm and used for internal decision making almost a century before their first appearance in the economics literature. The latter appearance occurred in 1886 in the work of W. von Nördling. Cournot [4, p. 57], of course, had used total — not average – cost functions in 1838.

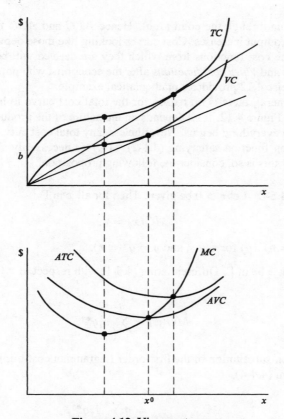

Figure 4.12 Viner cost curves

on Γ. Figure 4.12 depicts the graph of a total cost function frequently used to illustrate these ideas, and the variable, average, and marginal cost curves deduced from it. The horizontal axes are lined up so that passing from one to the other along a vertical does not change output. The vertical axes have the appropriate scales superimposed upon them. The rules relating these curves are analogous to those employed in deriving average and marginal curves from total product curves in Section 4.1. Proofs are similar to proofs required for Exercises 4.1 and 4.2. Thus ATC and AVC have respective minima and intersect MC where rays from the origin in the upper diagram are tangent to TC and VC. Marginal cost has a minimum at the inflection point on TC and VC. The AFC curve is not drawn, but its shape would be that of a rectangular hyperbola through the point $(1, b)$. Hence ATC and AVC become closer together as output increases. Cost curves looking like those depicted in Figure 4.12 and the cost functions from which they are derived will be called *Viner cost curves* and *Viner cost functions* after the economist who popularized them [12]. Exercise 4.12 provides a mathematical example.

In general, there is no reason for the total cost curve to have the shape pictured in Figure 4.12. It all depends on the nature of the production function with which everything begins. Nevertheless, any total cost curve generated by a production function satisfying (4.1-2) – (4.1-5) necessarily slopes upward. To see why this is so, consider the following proposition.

Theorem 4.5-8 Let $r > 0$ be given. Then for all x in Γ,

$$MC(x) = \eta,$$

where $r_j = \eta f_j(y)$ for any j, and $y = g^*(r, x)$.

Proof: Let x be in Γ. Differentiating (4.5-1) with respect to x for fixed $r > 0$ gives

$$MC(x) = \sum_{j=1}^{J} r_j g_x^{*j},$$

which, upon substitution of the first-order Lagrangian cost-minimization conditions from (4.4-4),

$$= \eta \sum_{j=1}^{J} f_j g_x^{*j}.$$

Application of equation (4.4-8) completes the proof.

Q.E.D.

Because $\eta > 0$ for every x in Γ, Theorem 4.5-8 implies that the derivative of the total cost function with respect to x is positive. Hence the model is consistent with the empirically obvious observation that, other things being equal, additions to output always cost more to produce. The next result provides a basis for relating the shape of the production surface to the shapes of the cost functions it generates. This is done by linking slopes of average variable cost curves to associated quantities of outputs relative to sums of corresponding quantities of inputs, weighted by the partial derivatives of the production function evaluated at the inputs in question.

Theorem 4.5-9   For all x in Γ,

$$\frac{dAVC(x)}{dx} \gtreqless 0 \quad \text{if and only if} \quad f(y) \gtreqless \sum_{j=1}^{J} y_j f_j(y),$$

respectively, where $y = g^*(r, x)$ and $r > 0$ is given.

Proof: Let x in Γ be given. From (4.5-5),

$$AVC(x) = \frac{r \cdot g^*(r, x)}{x}.$$

Differentiating with respect to x for fixed $r > 0$, replacing the r_j according to the first-order Lagrangian cost-minimization conditions of (4.4-4), and applying (4.4-8) yields

$$\frac{dAVC(x)}{dx} = \frac{\eta \left[f(y) - \sum_{j=1}^{J} y_j f_j(y) \right]}{x^2}.$$

Because η and x are positive, the conclusion is immediate.

Q.E.D.

The connections between returns to scale and concavity of production functions on one hand and the slopes of average variable cost curves on the other are obtained by combining Theorem 4.5-9 with previous results. Several of these are listed in Table 4.1. (In perusing the table, the reader might recall the relationships developed in Section 4.2 between local returns and global returns, and between returns to scale and concavity or convexity. As a reminder, strict concavity, say, implies (because $f(0) = 0$) global decreasing returns to scale, which, in turn, implies local decreasing returns to scale at each y in Y.) Actually, the table provides only one-way implications from the properties of the production function to those of the average variable cost function. Converse assertions are subtle. If the inequality on line 1 (or 2) or 4 (or 5) of Table 4.1 were strict, then combining Theorem 4.5-9 with Theorem 4.2-10 (or 4.2-13) would yield, respectively, local or global decreasing (or increasing) returns to scale at the appropriate y or on Γ. But, in general, there are no converses of lines $1 - 3$, 7, and 8 for the same reasons that Theorems 4.2-$6 - 4.2$-8, 4.2-23, and 4.2-24 do not have converses. Furthermore, due to the possibility that $dAVC(x)/dx = 0$ on lines 4 and 5, and the requirement that $dAVC(x)/dx$ vanishes identically on line 6, lines $4 - 6$ cannot have converses either: For

Table 4.1 Implications for average variable cost functions of various returns to scale and concavity restrictions on productions functions satisfying (4.1-2) − (4.2−5)

When $y = g^*(r,x)$ for x in Γ and a given $r > 0$,		
if f	then $\dfrac{dAVC(x)}{dx}$	The result follows from
1. exhibits local decreasing returns to scale at y	$\geqslant 0$ at x	Theorems 4.5-9 and 4.2-6
2. exhibits local increasing returns to scale at y	$\leqslant 0$ at x	Theorems 4.5-9 and 4.2-7
3. exhibits local constant returns to scale at y	$= 0$ at x	Theorems 4.5-9 and 4.2-8
4. exhibits (global) decreasing returns to scale on Y	$\geqslant 0$ on Γ	application of line 1 above to each x in Γ, or Theorems 4.5-9 and 4.2-18
5. exhibits (global) increasing returns to scale on Y	$\leqslant 0$ on Γ	application of line 2 above to each x in Γ, or Theorems 4.5-9 and 4.2-20
6. exhibits (global) constant returns to scale on Y	$= 0$ on Γ	application of line 3 above to each x in Γ, or Theorems 4.5-9 and 4.2-21
7. is strictly concave on Y	> 0 on Γ	Theorems 4.5-9 and 4.2-23
8. is strictly convex on Y	< 0 on Γ	Theorems 4.5-9 and 4.2-24

with respect to line 4, say, $dAVC(x)/dx = 0$ could be a consequence of constant returns to scale. And with respect to line 6, decreasing returns to scale still permits the eventuality of

$$f(y^0) = \sum_{j=1}^{J} y_j^0 f_j(y^0),$$

at every y^0 of a relatively open, connected subset N of some expansion path, where N also does not lie along any ray from the origin into Y. That is, over the ray from the origin through each y^0 in N (every such ray intersects N in exactly one point), the production function could be similar to that shown in Figure 4.4(c) (except that now $f(0)$ would have to equal zero), with the inflection point (above y in the diagram) always occurring over y^0 in N. Inspite of the decreasing returns to scale, then, Theorem 4.5-9 forces

$$\frac{dAVC(x)}{dx} = 0$$

on the corresponding open, connected subset of Γ. (An illustration apears in Exercise 4.18.) Thus, contrary to intuition, a decreasing returns to scale production function might still be associated with constant average variable costs. This shows that line 6 of Table 4.1 cannot have a converse and, in addition, that the weak inequality of line 4 cannot be strengthened. The reason for the existence of such counterintuitive possibilities is that assumptions of returns to scale restrict the shapes of production surfaces only over rays from the origin into the interior of Y. The shapes of average variable cost curves, however, depend on the shapes of productions functions over expansion paths. Hence, as long as expansion paths are *not* rays from the origin, "anomalies" of this sort can arise. Evidently these "difficulties" are eliminated when focusing attention on the points of N in the special case in which the latter (still a relatively open, connected subset of an expansion path) is contained in some ray from the origin into the interior of Y.

Formally, let N be a relatively open, connected subset of the r-expansion path for $r > 0$, and Γ_N, the open, connected subset of Γ associated with N under f.

Theorem 4.5-10 Let $r > 0$ be fixed, and suppose N lies on some ray from the origin into Y. Then $AVC(x)$ is decreasing, constant, or increasing[25] on

---

[25] The concept of increasing function (transformation) is defined by (2.1-4) in Chapter 2. To characterize the notion of *decreasing* function, reverse the right-hand inequality in that state-

Γ_N, if and only if f exhibits local increasing, constant, or decreasing returns to scale, respectively, for all y in N.

Proof: As in line 4 of Table 4.1, if f exhibits local decreasing returns to scale on N, then from Theorem 4.5-9 and part (i) of Theorem 4.2-18 restricted to N,

$$\frac{dAVC(x)}{dx} \geqslant 0,$$

on Γ_N. Because N lies on a ray from the origin into Y, an argument similar to that establishing the second part of Theorem 4.2-18 as applied to N guarantees that there is no open, connected subset of Γ_N, on which equality can hold. This is enough to ensure that $AVC(x)$ is increasing on Γ_N.[26] Conversely, if $AVC(x)$ is increasing on Γ_N, then

$$\frac{dAVC(x)}{dx} \geqslant 0,$$

on Γ_N, and there is no open, connected subset of Γ_N, on which equality can hold.[27] Application of Theorems 4.5-9 and 4.2-18 (again restricting the latter to N) now leads to the conclusion that f exhibits local decreasing returns to scale at all y in N.

The remaining parts of the theorem are deduced analogously.

Q.E.D.

Thus, under the hypotheses of Theorem 4.5-10, increasing returns to scale, say, results in falling average variable costs, and conversely. More specifically, the segments of the curves in Figure 4.12 to the left of x^0 can be identified with local increasing returns to scale. The curvature of those portions of the curves to the right of x^0 may arise with local decreasing returns to scale. Note also that constant returns to scale production functions beget (and are implied by) linear TC and VC curves, the latter of which declines to the origin as x approaches zero. Theorem 4.5-10 is illustrated by Exercise 4.11 (see also Exercise 4.19) with reference to the class of generalized Cobb-Douglas production functions, whose members are all homogeneous of different degrees.

At this point, having translated various possible shapes of production surfaces into corresponding shapes of average variable cost curves, the stage

---

ment. The idea of *constant* function can be described by replacing the same right-hand inequality with an equals sign.

[26] Katzner [6, p. 186].

[27] *Ibid.*

has now been set for a discussion of the kinds of production functions that permit profit to be maximized. The issue is taken up in Chapter 5.

EXERCISES

4.1 Why does AP^1 in Figure 4.1 achieve its maximum at y_1'' where a ray from the origin is tangent at β to the total product curve?

4.2 Prove, in conjunction with Figure 4.1, that if $AP^1(y_1)$ has a maximum at $y_1 = \overline{y}_1$, then $AP^1(\overline{y}_1) = MP^1(\overline{y}_1)$.

4.3 Let $f(y) = \sum_{j=1}^{J} \gamma_j y_j + \delta$ where the γ_j and δ are fixed constants. Show that if $\delta > 0$, then (4.2-14) and (4.2-15) are satisfied.

4.4 Suppose $x = f(y_1, y_2)$ exhibits constant returns to scale. Show that for all $(y_1, y_2) > 0$,

$$f_{11}(y_1, y_2) = -\frac{y_2}{y_1} f_{21}(y_1, y_2),$$

$$f_{22}(y_1, y_2) = -\frac{y_1}{y_2} f_{12}(y_1, y_2).$$

Prove, as a result, that $\left| \bar{F}(y) \right| = 0$ for all $y > 0$.

4.5 Comment on the following: "If proportional changes of land and labor [always] lead to [the same] proportional changes in the output of wheat, and if labor yielded increasing marginal products, the world's wheat could be grown in a flower pot, if the pot were small enough."[28]

4.6 Prove that if $f(y_1, y_2) = B(y_1)^{\beta_1}(y_2)^{\beta_2}$, where B, β_1, and β_2 are positive constants, then the elasticity of substitution $\sigma(y) = 1$, for all $y > 0$.

4.7* Show that the production function of (4.3-9) is homogeneous of degree one, and verify formulas (4.3-10) and (4.3-13). Show also that when $0 < \sigma < 1$, all isoquants interior to Y are asymptotic to lines parallel to the y_1- and y_2-axes. Note how the latter compares to the Cobb-Douglas case ($\sigma = 1$).

4.8 Prove that, for homothetic production functions with J inputs, all marginal rates of technical substitution are constant along rays from the origin into

---

28   Stigler [11, p. 132].

the interior of Y, and hence that all expansion paths are also rays from the origin into the interior of Y.

4.9* Imagine a firm with production function

$$x = \begin{cases} \frac{3}{10}y_1 + \frac{1}{5}y_2, & \text{if } y_1 \leqslant y_2, \\[2mm] \frac{1}{6}y_1 + \frac{1}{3}y_2, & \text{if } y_1 \geqslant y_2. \end{cases}$$

Which of properties (4.1-2) – (4.1-5) are violated? Do isoquants intersect the boundaries of Y? Given any output $x > 0$, geometrically describe the least-cost combinations of inputs for producing x associated with all input price vectors $r = (r_1, r_2) > 0$. Define the function $g^*(r, x)$ for all $r > 0$ and $x > 0$.

4.10 Verify the formula of (4.4-14).

4.11* Consider the production function of Exercise 4.6. Express the expansion path (i) by deriving g^* and (ii) by determining y_2 as a function of y_1. Verify the hypothesis and conclusion of Theorem 4.4-16. Find $TC(x)$ and $AVC(x)$. Show that for all $x > 0$,

$$\frac{dAVC(x)}{dx} \gtreqqless 0 \quad \text{according as} \quad \beta_1 + \beta_2 \lesseqqgtr 1,$$

and relate this assertion to Table 4.1 and Theorem 4.5-10. Graph $TC(x)$, $AVC(x)$ and $MC(x)$ for the special case in which $\beta_1 + \beta_2 = \frac{1}{2}$.

4.12 Imagine a firm that employs only one variable input. What is the relationship between this firm's production function and its total cost function? Suppose the firm's production function f is defined implicitly on Y by

$$y = x^3 - 4x^2 + 8x,$$

where y is the scalar input variable. Show that f satisfies (4.1-2) – (4.1-5) and that the cost curves derived from f are Viner curves.

4.13 Find the production function from which the cost function

$$TC(r, x) = 2x^4 \sqrt{r_1 r_2} + b$$

is derived.

4.14 Let $x = f(y_1, y_2)$ be a production function that is homogeneous of degree one. Show that for any $y^0 = (y_1^0, y_2^0) > 0$,

$$\frac{dAP^1(y_1^0)}{dy_1} \gtreqless 0 \quad \text{according as} \quad MP^2(y_2^0) \lesseqgtr 0.$$

4.15 Let $f(y)$ be a production function and $TC(r, x)$ its associated total cost function. Suppose f is homogeneous of degree one. Demonstrate the existence of a function $\xi(r)$ such that

$$TC(r, x) = x\xi(r) + b,$$

for all $r > 0$ and x in Γ.

4.16* Give an example to show that, under the assumptions of this chapter, the concavity of $TC(r, x)$ in Theorem 4.5-4 cannot be strengthened to strict concavity. What would be wrong with the argument in the proof of Theorem 4.5-4 if it used the uniqueness of cost-minimizing baskets of inputs (which follows from the strict quasi-concavity of f) to replace the weak inequalities by strong inequalities, and hence infer strict concavity?

4.17* Let $J = 2$ and define the *relative expenditure on factors* by the firm (or the *relative income share* of the firm's factors) at cost-minimizing combinations of inputs by

$$\zeta(y) = \frac{r_1 y_1}{r_2 y_2} = \frac{y_1 f_1(y)}{y_2 f_2(y)}.$$

Show that the elasticity of $\zeta(y)$ with respect to the marginal rate of technical substitution along an isoquant is $1 - \sigma(y)$. Hence a constant elasticity of substitution implies a constant elasticity of factor shares.

4.18** Let $J = 2$ and set

$$f(y_1, y_2) = A + 3y_1 + y_2 + \arctan(y_2 - y_1 - A),$$

on

$$\Xi = \{(y_1, y_2) : y_1 \geqslant 1, y_2 \geqslant 0, \text{ and } y_2 \leqslant y_1 + A\},$$

where the number $A \geqslant 2$. Show that throughout Ξ, f is twice continuously differentiable and strictly quasi-concave, $f(y) \geqslant 0$ and $f_j(y) \geqslant 0$ for $j = 1, 2$. Demonstrate also that f exhibits local decreasing returns to scale at every (y_1, y_2) in Ξ, and that over the ray $y_2 = \gamma y_1$ in Ξ, f is strictly convex when

$0 < \gamma < 1$, linear when $\gamma = 1$, and shaped as in Figure 4.4(c) when $1 < \gamma < A + 1$. Note that the inflection point above y in Figure 4.4(c) always occurs where the ray $y_2 = \gamma y_1$ intersects the line $y_2 = y_1 + A$, and that at each such point,

$$f(y) = \sum_{j=1}^{2} y_j f_j(y).$$

Let f be extended to Y in a continuously differentiable manner such that assumptions (4.1-2) – (4.1-5) are satisfied. Let a vector of input prices $r = (r_1, r_2)$ be given with $r_1 = r_2$. Verify that the expansion path for outputs $x > 2A + 4$ is

$$N = \{(y_1, y_2) : y_1 > 1 \text{ and } y_2 = y_1 + A\},$$

and that the average variable cost function on

$$\Gamma_N = \{x : x > 2A + 4\}$$

is

$$AVC(x) = \tfrac{1}{2}r_1.$$

Thus, in spite of the local decreasing returns to scale on Ξ,

$$\frac{dAVC(x)}{dx} = 0,$$

identically on Γ_N.

4.19 Consider a production function that is homogeneous of degree κ, where κ is any positive number. Demonstrate that f exhibits decreasing returns to scale if and only if $0 < \kappa < 1$, and that f exhibits increasing returns to scale if and only if $\kappa > 1$.

Show that the graphs of average variable cost functions derived from a production function that is homogeneous of degree κ, where $0 < \kappa < 1$, always slopes upward.

4.20 Let f exhibit constant returns to scale. Show for every $y^0 > 0$ that, as the firm expands production along the ray $\{\alpha y^0 : \alpha \geqslant 0\}$, output and all inputs grow at the same rate. (The rate of growth of output is defined as

$$\frac{dx/d\tau}{x},$$

where τ denotes time. The growth rate of each input is defined similarly.)

4.21 Give an alternative proof of Theorem 4.5-2 that does not require use of the function ξ.

4.22 Although it violates the assumption (p. 126) that isoquants, where non-negatively sloped and strictly convex, do not touch the boundary of the input space, consider the production function

$$f(y_1, y_2) = 8y_1 + 6y_2 - (y_1)^2 - (y_2)^2,$$

defined on Y.

   a) Find the maximum output that can be produced with this production function and the unique basket of inputs that provides it. Describe the geometry of the production function, its total product curves, and its isoquants.

   b) Find equations for the upper and lower ridge lines and, for any $(r_1, r_2) > 0$, the equation characterizing the expansion path.

   c) Assuming $r_1 = r_2$, find the least-cost combination of inputs for producing an output of $x = 23$.

4.23 Although it, too, violates the assumption that isoquants, where nonnegatively sloped and strictly convex, do not touch the boundary of the input space, consider the production function

$$f(y_1, y_2) = 10\sqrt{y_1 y_2} - y_1 - y_2$$

defined for all $(y_1, y_2) \geqslant 0$.

   a) Show that f exhibits constant returns to scale.

   b) Find equations for the lower and upper ridge lines from, respectively, TP^1 and TP^2.

   c) Derive the lower ridge line from TP^2.

REFERENCES

1. Arrow, K. J., *et al.*, "Capital-Labor Substitution and Economic Efficiency," *Review of Economics and Statistics* 43 (1961), pp. 225-250.

2. Brue, S. L., "Retrospectives: The Law of Diminishing Returns," *Journal of Economic Perspectives* 7, no. 3 (Summer, 1993), pp. 185-192.

3. Cobb, C. W. and P. H. Douglas, "A Theory of Production," *American Economic Review, Papers and Proceedings Supplement* 18 (March, 1928), pp. 139-165.

4. Cournot, A., *Researches into the Mathematical Principles of the Theory of Wealth*, N. T. Bacon, trans. (New York: Kelley, 1960).

5. Flux, A. W., "Review of P. H. Wicksteed's *Essay on the Coordination of the Laws of Distribution*," *Economic Journal* 4 (1894), pp. 305-313.

6. Katzner, D. W., *Static Demand Theory* (New York: Macmillan, 1970).

7. Mill, J. S., *Principles of Political Economy with Some of Their Applications to Social Philosophy*, V. W. Bladen and J. M. Robson, eds. (Toronto: University of Toronto Press, 1965).

8. Rudin, W., *Principles of Mathematical Analysis*, 3rd ed. (New York: McGraw-Hill, 1976).

9. Scherer, F. M., "An Early Application of the Average Total Cost Concept," *Journal of Economic Literature* 39 (2001), pp. 897-901.

10. Shephard, R. W., *Cost and Production Functions* (Princeton: Princeton University Press, 1953).

11. Stigler, G. J., *The Theory of Price*, revised ed. (New York: Macmillan, 1952).

12. Viner, J., "Cost Curves and Supply Curves," *Zeitschrift für Nationalökonomie* 3 (1931), pp. 23-46. Reprinted with a supplementary note in The American Economic Association's *Readings in Price Theory*, G. J. Stigler and K. E. Boulding, eds. (Chicago: Irwin, 1952), pp. 198-232.

13. Walters, A. A., "Production and Cost Functions: An Econometric Survey," *Econometrica* 31 (1963), pp. 1-66.

14. Wicksell, K., "Real Capital and Interest," *Ekonomisk Tidskrift* 1923 (nos. 5,6), pp. 145-180. English translation reprinted in K. Wicksell, *Lectures on Political Economy*, v. 1 (New York: Kelley, 1967), pp. 258-299.

15. Wicksteed, P. H., *An Essay on the Coordination of the Laws of Distribution* (London: Macmillan, 1894).

Chapter 5

Models of the Firm

Consider a firm having a production function f with properties (4.1-2) – (4.1-5) as described in Chapter 4. The money capital necessary for production to take place continues, for now, to be ignored. Suppose this firm views the input and output prices it faces as set parameters over which it has no control. Suppose also that all inputs employed by the firm are used up in production during the period (or instant) of time in question. In particular, the firm maintains no inventory of inputs and there is no input with the durability of physical capital. (As has previously been noted, such capital inputs along with money capital are introduced in Chapter 13.) To these assumptions, add the requirement that all output produced is sold. Hence there is no inventory of output either. The models presented below are intended to explain the behavior of the firm under these conditions.

As in the theory of demand, behavior is summarized in terms of demand and supply functions. The *demand function* for the firm's inputs indicates, for each collection of input and output prices, the basket of inputs the firm would hire for production. Similarly, the *supply function* for its output associates the same input and output price vectors to quantities of output produced and hence supplied. Only the output price and the prices of those inputs included in the firm's production function (that is, those inputs which, according to technology, the firm is able to use in production) appear as arguments in the firm's input demand and output supply functions. Hence the analysis is distinctly partial-equilibrium. There is an implicit assumption that the prices and quantities of all other goods in the economy are fixed.

The models developed here differ in that some include fixed inputs and costs (Section 5.1), whereas others do not (Section 5.2). The former thus focus on the short run; the latter cover the long run. In a parallel fashion, Section 5.1 or 5.2 is a part of the particular grand view of Section 1.4 when taken in, respectively, the short- or long-run context. Each model deals with timeless behavior and can be applied to describe the stationary path of an appropriate but unspecified dynamic system. But these models are also relevant to dynamic worlds in which behavior varies with time. In those latter environments, the partial derivatives of, say, output supply functions may be interpreted as the rates of change of output in moving from one position to another due to arbitrarily small price shifts as time passes. Sufficient assumptions may be imposed (Chapter 9 suggests some possibilities in an economy-wide setting) so that behavior generated by these models along nonstationary paths eventually converges to that on stationary ones.

A central concept figuring in the analysis of the firm, but which has not yet been introduced, is profit. Profit, π, is the difference between total revenue and total cost or, in terms of the symbolism of the previous chapter,

$$\pi = px - r \cdot y - b, \tag{5.0-1}$$

where p denotes output price. In the long run, profit is defined by (5.0-1) with $b = 0$. All models considered below are based on a rationality postulate, specifically, that the firm hires inputs and produces (and sells) output so as to maximize profit. Note that for the firm to maximize profit it must hire input vectors lying between the ridge lines or surfaces (when they exist) and produce each output with the least-cost combination of inputs. In other words, the firm must produce somewhere on the cost curves derived in Section 4.5.

Of course, reality for a firm is usually more complex than the simple maximization of profit (even when the presence of money capital is left out of the picture). In corporations, for example, where the functions of management and ownership often reside with different groups of people, the aims of managers need not be the same as those of owners. Here and in other cases, profit maximization may appear as one among many goals pursued by the firm (such as growth of its market share or development of a reputation for technical excellence or social progressiveness). Still the maximization of profit has a special importance because a firm that does not concern itself with profitability runs a significantly greater risk of being eliminated by competition. Moreover, even if profit-maximization is not its main concern, the firm nevertheless needs to know its profit-maximization position so that it

can calculate the true economic cost (that is, profit sacrificed) of its real
objective. With this in mind, the following abstracts from all other aims of the
firm and focuses on profit maximization alone. As pointed out in Section 1.2,
attention thus is directed toward a specific, underlying, pure economic force
that arises in actuality only as modified by attendant circumstances.

Analogously to the theory of consumer demand, it is not necessary that
firms in fact be profit maximizers. The only requirement is that their behavior
be consistent with profit maximization. Thus observed input demand
functions and output supply functions should exhibit certain properties. It is
possible to develop dual lines of argument — one obtaining the implications
of profit maximization from the properties of production functions and the
other reconstructing production functions from behavior — but there is little
incentive to do so here. First, a parallel discussion has already been presented
for consumer demand theory and is not worth repeating in the context of the
firm. Second, the thrust of the analysis of the firm is somewhat different from
that of the consumer. The latter employs hypotheses relating to what is
unseeable to explain seeable behavior. By contrast, it has already been
pointed out that there is nothing potentially unobservable about production,
cost, output supply, and input demand functions. Certainly the analysis of the
firm focuses on the links connecting these functions and attempts to provide a
coherent setting in which they and their interrelatedness can be understood.
But because production and cost functions are both observable, it is not
necessary to go through a reconstruction argument to conclude that the firm
(in parallel to the consumer) can be viewed as if it were a profit maximizer.
Such a conclusion may be inferred directly upon verification that the
production function has characteristics as assumed, and input demand and
output supply functions exhibit the properties implied by profit maximization.
Hence even though the reconstruction of production functions from firm
behavior is not so consequential, the characteristics of input demand and
output supply functions are still as important to the theory of the firm as the
traits of demand functions are to the analysis of consumer activity.

Furthermore there is often little difficulty in employing the introspective
assumption that firms actually do choose inputs and outputs so as to
maximize profits. In addition to earlier discussion, it should also be noted that
although real world firms often appear to produce as much as they can sell,
and price their output by "marking up" from unit cost, as long as such policies
are flexibly applied, mark-up procedures can still bring firms to the point of
profit maximization.[1] In this case, mark-up policies can be understood as

---

[1]   Pearce [4].

firms' practical methods of achieving maximum profits.

Except for $f(y) \geqslant 0$ on Y and $f(0) = 0$, the characteristics required of production functions in Chapter 4 parallel those assumed for utility functions. In each instance some form of smoothness, increasingness, and strict quasi-concavity is present. Earlier comments already have suggested that, although these properties are sufficient to resolve the principal issues of demand theory, they are not enough to complete the analysis of the firm. This is because (4.1-2) – (4.1-5) do not by themselves restrict the slopes of cost curves. As indicated by Theorem 4.5-9, at each x in Γ, both positively and negatively sloped average variable cost curves are possible. Without further hypotheses, it cannot be guaranteed that the shape of the graph of f permits the firm to maximize profit. To make profit maximization meaningful, then, something further must be assumed about the curvature of the production surface over expansion paths. Three alternatives are considered below: (i) f is strictly concave on the interior of Y and its first-order partial derivatives range over all positive real numbers above every expansion path; (ii) f exhibits constant returns to scale on Y; and (iii) f is such that the cost curves it generates are Viner curves like those drawn in Figure 4.12.

Along with (4.1-2) – (4.1-5), subsequent discussion continues the assumptions that $f_j(y) > 0$, where $j = 1, \ldots, J$, for all y within the region bounded by the ridge lines (surfaces) up to a unique global maximum output if one is present or, when no ridge lines (surfaces) exist, for all $y > 0$; that $|F(y)| \neq 0$ for y in the interior of Y such that all $f_j(y) \neq 0$; and that isoquants, where nonnegatively sloped and strictly convex, do not touch the boundary of Y. (This last assumption, of course, excludes all constant elasticity of substitution production functions for which $\sigma > 1$. The CES cases $\sigma = \infty$ and $\sigma = 0$ are also ruled out.)

5.1 THE SHORT RUN

Recall that Γ is the collection of positive outputs (under the production function f) less than any maximum output that might exist. Define the *total revenue* function by

$$TR(x) = px, \qquad (5.1\text{-}1)$$

for x in Γ, where $p > 0$ is the given output price. According to (5.1-1), $TR(x)$ is differentiable everywhere. Its derivative, called the *marginal revenue* function, is

$$MR(x) = \frac{dTR(x)}{dx} = p, \tag{5.1-2}$$

on Γ. The general expression for *profit* as a function of output is written

$$\pi(x) = TR(x) - TC(x), \tag{5.1-3}$$

for all x in Γ, where $TC(x)$ is the cost function of (4.5-1) and the symbol π is used now to denote the function rather than function values. At maximum profit,

$$\frac{d\pi(x)}{dx} = 0,$$

or, from (5.1-3),[2]

$$MC(x) = MR(x). \tag{5.1-4}$$

Application of (5.1-2) reduces (5.1-4) to[3]

$$MC(x) = p. \tag{5.1-5}$$

An illustration using Viner cost curves (Figure 4.12) with the variable cost and average variable cost curves omitted appears in Figure 5.1.[4] Note in that diagram that $ATC(x) = p$ at the same level of output for which $TR(x) = TC(x)$.

Two issues concerning (5.1-5) immediately arise. First, the question of the existence of an x in Γ which equates marginal cost with price is clearly of paramount importance. However, even after such an x is found, the problem of whether it actually identifies a maximum (instead of a minimum or inflection point) still remains. This second issue comes up, for example, in Figure 5.1 where marginal cost intersects marginal revenue at x' and x'' with only the former corresponding to maximum profit. The sufficient second-order condition

---

[2]   Theorem A.3-12 in appendix Section A.3. Cournot [1, p. 57] derived a similar equation in the context of monopoly (see Sect. 11.2 below).

[3]   Cournot [1, p. 90] and Marshall [3, pp. 428, 499]. Like equations (4.4-4) and (4.4-5), taking money capital into account requires modification of (5.1-5). See Section 13.3.

[4]   Were $\pi = 0$ at x' in Figure 5.1, then at that output value, the total cost and total revenue curves would be tangent, as would the marginal revenue and average total cost curves. This could be the case, for example, if π were interpreted as profit in excess of normal profit, and normal profit were included in total cost. Such a possibility is illustrated, in part, in Figure 13.2(a) of Chapter 13. Normal profit itself is defined in the next section.

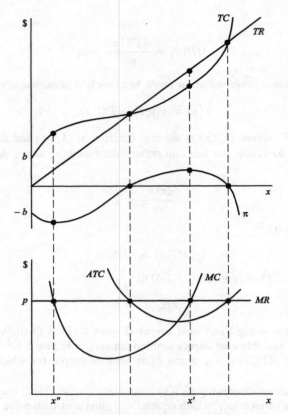

Figure 5.1 Profit maximization with Viner cost curves

ensuring a maximum at x is[5]

$$\frac{d^2\pi(x)}{dx^2} < 0,$$

or, in light of (5.1-3) and (5.1-2),

$$\frac{dMC(x)}{dx} > 0.$$

---

[5]   Theorem A.3-13 in appendix Section A.3.

To have maximum output, then, marginal cost should be rising in the neighborhood of the x satisfying (5.1-5) — as it does at x' in Figure 5.1. This implies, of course, that $TC(x)$ is strictly convex over such a neighborhood. Thus if the production function generates a total cost curve with a shape similar to that in Figure 5.1, and if the given output price provides a profit function with a maximum, then there is no problem. But observe that if output price were to fall below minimum marginal cost, a positive profit-maximizing output could not exist.

Before considering these issues more generally, note that for all x in Γ and $r > 0$, the marginal cost function is continuously differentiable with respect to x and $r_1, \ldots, r_J$. (Recall that $MC(x)$ depends on r as well as on x even though the symbol r is subsumed in the functional notation $MC(x)$.) To see why and make explicit an argument that was only suggested earlier, combine Theorem 4.5-8 with the first-order Lagrangian cost-minimization conditions (4.4-4) and the definition of the function g^* in (4.4-3). Thus

$$MC(x) = \frac{r_j}{f_j(g^*(r, x))},$$

for any $j = 1, \ldots, J$, and all x in Γ and $r > 0$, that is, marginal cost is the unit cost of any factor divided by its marginal product. Because each f_j is positive on the set D (recall p. 130) and continuously differentiable with respect to $y_1, \ldots, y_J$ on the interior of Y, and because g^* is continuously differentiable with respect to x and $r_1, \ldots, r_J$ at all vectors (x, r) where x is in Γ and $r > 0$, it follows that for all x in Γ and $r > 0$ marginal cost is also continuously differentiable with respect to x and $r_1, \ldots, r_J$.[6] Sufficient conditions guaranteeing an everywhere upward-sloping marginal cost curve can now be given. This provides one resolution of the issue of maximum versus minimum, raised above: If there exists an x at which marginal cost equals price, then under the stated hypotheses, x must maximize profit. The profit function can have neither a minimum nor an inflection point at x.

Theorem 5.1-6 Let $r > 0$ be given. If f is strictly concave on the interior of Y and $\left| \bar{F}(y) \right| \neq 0$ for all $y > 0$, then

$$\frac{dMC(x)}{dx} > 0,$$

for all x in Γ.

---

6 This is a consequence of the chain rule. Rudin [5, p. 214].

Proof: Combining Theorems 4.4-17 and 4.5-8,

$$\frac{dMC(x)}{dx} = MC(x)\frac{|\bar{F}(y)|}{|F(y)|},$$ (5.1-7)

for all x in Γ, where $y = g^*(r, x)$. Now the sign of $|F(y)|$ depends on the dimensionality of y according to (4.1-8). Because f is strictly concave and $|\bar{F}(y)| \neq 0$ in the interior of Y, for all $y > 0$,

$$|\bar{F}(y)| = \begin{cases} f_{11} < 0, \\[2ex] \begin{vmatrix} f_{11} & f_{12} \\ f_{21} & f_{22} \end{vmatrix} > 0, \\[3ex] \begin{vmatrix} f_{11} & f_{12} & f_{13} \\ f_{21} & f_{22} & f_{23} \\ f_{31} & f_{32} & f_{33} \end{vmatrix} < 0, \\[4ex] \vdots \end{cases}$$

according as $y = (y_1)$, $y = (y_1, y_2)$, $y = (y_1, y_2, y_3)$, ..., respectively.[7] This, together with (4.1-8), indicates that $|F(y)|$ and $|\bar{F}(y)|$ always have the same sign. Furthermore $MC(x) > 0$ on Γ (remember the discussion following Theorem 4.5-8). Therefore

$$\frac{dMC(x)}{dx} > 0,$$

for every x in Γ.

Q.E.D.

Theorem 5.1-6 is illustrated in Figure 5.2. In the special instance pictured there, f is assumed to be strictly concave on the interior of Y so that $TC(x)$ is strictly convex and $\pi(x)$ is strictly concave (Exercise 5.16). Also, $AVC(x) = p$ where $\pi(x) = -b$, marginal cost slopes upward everywhere, and $MC(x) = p$ at a unique x for each p. As with Viner cost curves, the difference between $ATC(x)$ and $AVC(x)$ becomes smaller as x increases and fixed cost is spread over more units of output. For all $p > 0$, a unique profit-maximizing output exists in this case. Recall that strictly concave production functions generate

---

[7]   This follows from Katzner [2, p. 200] and the fact that f is strictly concave if and only if $-f$ is strictly convex. See Theorem A.3-10 of appendix Section A.3.

average variable cost curves that slope upward over their entire domains (Table 4.1). It should be further noted that, although the marginal cost curve as drawn in Figure 5.2 is strictly convex, Exercise 5.14 indicates that a strictly concave marginal cost curve is consistent with the shapes of the remaining curves in that diagram, as well as with the assumptions on the production function behind it.

But as the example of Exercise 5.14 also shows, strict concavity of f together with the nonvanishing of its Hessian is still not enough to ensure, in

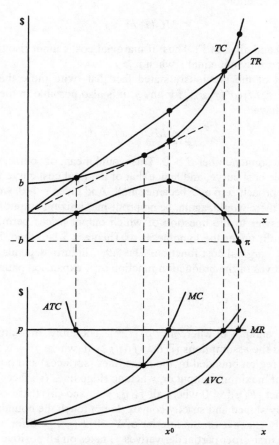

Figure 5.2 Profit maximization with a strictly concave production function

general, that at least one profit-maximizing output always exists for each $p > 0$ (the first issue noted above). The production function in this one-input situation is twice continuously differentiable for all $y > 0$, has positive first-order and negative second-order derivatives everywhere, is therefore strictly concave on the interior of Y, and satisfies the condition that zero input produces zero output. Nevertheless there is no profit-maximizing output for any $p > r$, where r is the input price. The reason is simple: Each $MC(x)$ in the example is bounded by the input price upon which the derivation of that marginal cost function is based. In other words, explicitly writing r as an argument of the marginal cost function,

$$MC(r, x) < r,$$

for all $r > 0$ and all x in Γ. Thus, if marginal cost cannot rise to or above r, then it can certainly not equal p when $p \geqslant r$.

In light of the previously stated fact that, with more than one input, $MC(r, x) = r_j / f_j(g^*(r, x))$, for any j, it is also possible in the strictly concave case to have

$$\lim_{x \to 0} MC(r, x) = \beta,$$

for $r > 0$ and some number $\beta > 0$. This would mean, of course, that the slope of the variable cost curve, and hence that of the total cost curve in Figure 5.2, would not approach zero as x became small. And given $r > 0$, were the output price $p < \beta$, there would, again, be no profit-maximizing output for that (r, p).

The answer to the question of which output prices permit the firm to maximize profit under the hypotheses of Theorem 5.1-6, then, hinges on the image of the marginal cost function. The latter, in turn, depends on the image of the derivatives of the production function over expansion paths because

$$MC(x) = \frac{r_j}{f_j(y)}, \quad j = 1, \ldots, J,$$

for all x in Γ and $r > 0$, where $y = g^*(r, x)$. Therefore, in addition to (4.1-2) – (4-1-5) and the assumptions (i) that $f_j(y) > 0$, where $j = 1, \ldots, J$, for all y within the region bounded by the ridge lines (surfaces) and possibly up to a unique global maximum output or, when no ridge lines (surfaces) exist, for all $y > 0$; (ii) that $|F(y)| \neq 0$ where all $f_j(y) \neq 0$; and (iii) that isoquants where nonnegatively sloped and strictly convex do not touch the boundary of Y; if f is also strictly concave on the interior of Y, if $|\bar{F}(y)| \neq 0$ for all $y > 0$, and if each of its first-order partial derivatives f_j takes on all positive real numbers as function values over every expansion path, then for all $(r, p) > 0$ a unique profit-maximizing output exists as the solution of the first-order maximization equation (5.1-5) on Γ.

In the absence of strict concavity of f everywhere on the interior of Y, let Γ^* be that subset of Γ on which $dMC(x)/dx > 0$. Consider only production functions that generate Viner cost functions with graphs as drawn in Figure 5.1. Thus Γ^* is nonempty. Suppose further that the first-order partial derivatives of f take on values that are arbitrarily close to zero for some input baskets $y > 0$ along every expansion path. Hence $MC(x)$ is unbounded on Γ^* for all $r > 0$. Now if the output price p is smaller than the minimum value $MC(x)$ can assume on Γ, then (5.1-5) has no solution and the firm sets $x = 0$. Otherwise, the firm's profit-maximizing output exists uniquely and is obtained by solving (5.1-5) for x in Γ^*. (A continuously differentiable solution always exists because $dMC(x)/dx > 0$ on Γ^*.)

However, even in this case the firm would not produce any output when price falls below

$$\widetilde{p} = \min_{x \text{ in } \Gamma} AVC(x).$$

At such a point the firm's profit is negative. It would lose less by setting $y = 0$ and wiping out its variable cost (fixed cost necessarily remains) than it would by producing where $MC(x) = p < \widetilde{p}$ at the "loss minimizing" x in Γ^*. For with $p < \widetilde{p}$, all of its fixed cost would be lost along with some (if not all) of its variable cost. Losses could be cut by eliminating the variable cost entirely, and so the firm would not produce. When profit is negative with an output price larger than $\widetilde{p}$, the firm is recovering all of its variable cost and some of its fixed cost. Thus it should continue to operate where $MC(x) = p > \widetilde{p}$ at the optimal x in Γ^*. Setting $y = 0$ would only increase losses to the amount of the fixed cost. For the borderline case in which $p = \widetilde{p}$, adopt the convention that the firm produces its profit-maximizing output $\widetilde{x}$. Call $\widetilde{p}$ the firm's *shut-down point* and note that it depends on r because

$$\widetilde{p} = AVC(\widetilde{x}) = MC(\widetilde{x}) = \frac{r_j}{f_j(g^*(r, \widetilde{x}))},$$

for any $j = 1, \ldots, J$. Notice also that with a strictly concave production function having cost functions whose graphs are pictured in Figure 5.2, $\widetilde{p} = 0$, $\widetilde{x} = 0$, and $\Gamma^* = \Gamma$, no matter what the value of r. Clearly the situation of Figure 5.2, in which the firm remains in operation at all positive prices, may be regarded, in so far as expressing the profit-maximizing output as the solution of the first-order maximization equation (5.1-5) is concerned, as a special case of the Viner circumstance discussed above. With respect to the latter, to say that the firm remains "open" when $p = \tilde{p} = 0$ still means that it hires no variable input and produces no output.

Recall that the input prices r, taken by the firm to be fixed, have been subsumed in the functional notation MC. Making them explicit once again, the firm's output supply function defined earlier may, because the firm supplies only profit-maximizing outputs, now be characterized as

$$x = \begin{cases} g^{J+1}(r,p), & \text{if } r > 0, p \geqslant \tilde{p}, \\ \\ 0, & \text{if } r > 0, \tilde{p} > p > 0, \end{cases} \tag{5.1-8}$$

where g^{J+1} is the solution of the first-order maximization equation (5.1-5) and $\tilde{p}$ depends on r. The reason for the superscript $J+1$ on g is that the nonzero parts of the input demand functions derived momentarily are denoted by $g^1, \ldots, g^J$. Observe first, however, that with $r = r^0$, the *output supply curve* obtained from

$$x = g^{J+1}(r^0, p)$$

is, in light of the reversal of axes described earlier on pp. 19-20, the upward sloping portion of the marginal cost curve at and above $\tilde{p}$. If $\tilde{p} = 0$, as in the strictly concave case of Figure 5.2, then there is no p between $\tilde{p}$ and 0, and (5.1-8) simplifies to

$$x = g^{J+1}(r, p),$$

for all $(r, p) > 0$.

Given output produced from (5.1-8), and using the assumption that only profit-maximizing quantities of inputs are employed, demands for the firm's inputs are obtained from the expansion path functions (4.4-3). Thus the input demand functions described in the introduction to this chapter, and whose nontrivial parts are written $g^1, \ldots, g^J$, are derived by substituting (5.1-8) into (4.4-3):

$$y_j = \begin{cases} g^j(r,p) = g^{*j}(r, g^{J+1}(r,p)), & \text{if } r > 0, p \geqslant \tilde{p}, \\ \\ 0, & \text{if } r > 0, \tilde{p} > p > 0, \end{cases} \tag{5.1-9}$$

for $j = 1, \ldots, J$ and $\tilde{p}$ again dependent on r.

To summarize, let $r > 0$ and $p \geqslant \tilde{p}$ be given and start with the entire input space as pictured, say, in Figure 5.3. From the shape of the production function, locate ridge lines (if, as in Figure 5.3, they are present) and exclude the area beyond them. Next, by introducing input prices and cost minimization, restrict attention still further to the expansion path. Express cost as a function of output, and then use output price information and profit maximization to determine the output x^0 and the isoquant $f(y) = x^0$ on which the firm should operate. Finally, the intersection of this isoquant and the expansion path identifies the input basket y^0 it should hire. The result is a unique point satisfying the output supply and input demand functions of (5.1-8) and (5.1-9).

An alternative approach that winds up at the same place begins by expressing profit as a function of y. Substituting $x = f(y)$ into (5.0-1), and using π to denote the resulting function yields

$$\pi(y) = pf(y) - r \cdot y - b, \qquad (5.1\text{-}10)$$

for all y in Y. With p, r, and b given, $\pi(y)$ has a maximum at $y = y^0$ if and only if $\pi(x)$ of (5.1-3) has a maximum at $x = x^0$, where $x^0 = f(y^0)$ and $y^0 = g^*(r, x^0)$ (see Exercise 5.1). Hence for any $(p, r) > 0$, strict concavity of f on the interior of Y together with the requirements that its first-order partial derivatives take on all positive real numbers as function values over every expansion path and that $\left| \bar{F}(y) \right| \neq 0$ for all $y > 0$, or (when p is at least as large as the minimum value of $MC(x)$) the conditions on f underlying Viner curves (Figure 5.1) and the unboundedness of $MC(x)$ ensure that $\pi(y)$

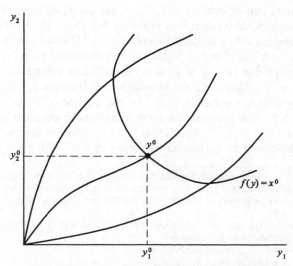

Figure 5.3 Determination of the profit-maximizing input basket given x^0

can be maximized uniquely. At the maximum, the partial derivatives

$$\pi_j(y) = 0, \quad j = 1, \ldots, J,$$

or

$$p f_j(y) = r_j, \quad j = 1, \ldots, J. \tag{5.1-11}$$

Note that, upon division of the Jth equation of (5.1-11) into those remaining, the characterization of the expansion path of (4.4-5) is obtained. Also, dividing any equation of (5.1-11), say the jth, by $f_j(y)$, and invoking the previously derived equality $MC(x) = r_j/f_j(y)$ yields the statement of (5.1-5) that $MC(x) = p$. The term $p f_j(y)$ is called the *value of the marginal product* with respect to input j. Loosely speaking, it is the value to the firm (measured in terms of the extra revenue it receives) of hiring the last increment of the jth input in the basket y. Equations (5.1-11) state that at profit maximization, the extra value created by the last increment of each input employed should equal its unit cost.[8]

The necessary second-order conditions supposing a maximum exists are

$$f_{11} \leqslant 0, \quad \begin{vmatrix} f_{11} & f_{12} \\ f_{21} & f_{22} \end{vmatrix} \geqslant 0, \quad \begin{vmatrix} f_{11} & f_{12} & f_{13} \\ f_{21} & f_{22} & f_{23} \\ f_{31} & f_{32} & f_{33} \end{vmatrix} \leqslant 0, \ldots, \tag{5.1-12}$$

for all permutations of inputs $j = 1, \ldots, J$, and all y satisfying (5.1-11).[9] The sufficient second-order conditions ensuring that (5.1-11) identifies a unique maximum require strong inequalities in (5.1-12).[10] If maximum profit is known to exist at $y = y'$ (as pictured, say, at the corresponding x' in Figure 5.1) and if it is assumed that $|\bar{F}(y)| \neq 0$, then the sufficient second-order conditions hold for $y = y'$. Moreover, the hypotheses of Theorem 5.1-6, namely, that f is strictly concave and $|\bar{F}(y)| \neq 0$ on the interior of Y (as in, for example, Figure 5.2), guarantee that the same sufficient second-order conditions are satisfied for all $y > 0$.[11] (Recall that these hypotheses also ensure that the second-order condition for maximizing $\pi(x)$, or $dMC(x)/dx > 0$, is in force

---

[8]   Marshall [3, p. 406]. Actually, the idea that, restating (5.1-11) in the single-input case, the profit-maximizing firm should hire "... workers until the last employed worker brings forth only such increase [in output] as is equal to his [real] wage" goes back at least to von Thünen [8, p. 317] in 1850.

Equations (5.1-11), too, need revision, as indicated in Section 13.3, when money capital is injected into the analysis of firm behavior.

[9]   Theorem A.3-14 in appendix Section A.3.

[10]   Theorem A.3-15 in appendix Section A.3.

[11]   See the proof of Theorem 5.1-6.

on Γ.) Note the similarity between (5.1-12) and the inequalities listed in the proof of Theorem 5.1-6.

Now (5.1-11) can be viewed as a system of J equations in J unknown input quantities. The Jacobian of the system is $|\bar{F}(y)|$. Hence, if $|\bar{F}(y)| \neq 0$ for all $y > 0$ (as assumed in Theorem 5.1-6), then (5.1-11) can be solved everywhere to secure y as a continuously differentiable function of (r, p).[12] For $p \geqslant \tilde{p} > 0$, where $\tilde{p}$ is dependent on r, these functions must be identical to $g^1, \ldots, g^J$ of the input demand functions described in (5.1-9). Even if solutions exist, they are ignored when they imply negative inputs or outputs, when solutions lie outside the area between the ridge lines and (or) beyond the unique global maximum when the latter are present, and when p falls below $\tilde{p}$. To obtain an equivalent formulation of the output supply function (5.1-8), insert the input demands just secured into the production function:

$$
x = \begin{cases} g^{J+1}(r,p) = f(g^1(r,p), \ldots, g^J(r,p)), & \text{if } r > 0, p \geqslant \tilde{p}, \\ \\ 0, & \text{if } r > 0, \tilde{p} > p > 0, \end{cases} \tag{5.1-13}
$$

for $\tilde{p}$ dependent on r. Thus, without explicitly introducing expansion paths and cost functions, input demand functions for $p \geqslant \tilde{p} > 0$ can be derived by solving the first-order maximization conditions (5.1-11). The output supply function for $p \geqslant \tilde{p} > 0$ then is obtained by substituting these solutions into the production function. But expansion paths and cost functions have not gone away. They are implicit in the above derivations. The output supply curve secured from (5.1-13) with $r = r^0$ is still the inverse of the upward sloping portion of the marginal cost curve at and above $\tilde{p}$. And cost functions certainly are needed to determine the specific value of $\tilde{p}$.

Just as the supply curve obtained from $x = g^{J+1}(r^0, p)$ with r^0 fixed has a geometric interpretation as the upward sloping portion of the marginal cost curve, the *input demand curve* derived from, say,

$$
y^1 = g^1(r_1, r_2^0, \ldots, r_J^0, p^0),
$$

where $r_2^0, \ldots, r_J^0$ and $p^0 > \tilde{p}$ are fixed, can be interpreted in terms of the value of marginal product curves. The argument follows the two-input illustration of Figure 5.4. With $r_2 = r_2^0$ and $p = p^0$, choose an r_1'. The resulting inputs (y_1', y_2') and output x' are determined from the firm's demand and supply functions (5.1-8) and (5.1-9). Hence the isoquant, $f(y) = x'$, and the value of marginal product curve, that is, the graph of $p^0 f_1(y_1, y_2') = r_1$, are known. These are drawn in Figure 5.4 with the isoquant tangent to the cost line at the

---

[12]   See the discussion of the inverse function theorem in appendix Section A.4.

point of maximum profit (and minimum cost). Now suppose r_1 falls to r_1'' with r_2^0 and p^0 constant. Then new inputs (y_1'', y_2'') and output x'' obtain. It will be shown below that, although y_1 generally rises, no such statement can be made for y_2 and x. Each of

$$x'' \gtreqless x' \quad \text{and} \quad y_2'' \gtreqless y_2'$$

is possible. Suppose things turn out so that the new isoquant, $f(y) = x''$, is as drawn in the lower diagram of Figure 5.4. Because $y_2'' \neq y_2'$, the total product curve TP^1, and hence the value of marginal product curve, have changed. The new $r_1 = p^0 f_1(y_1, y_2'')$ curve appears in the upper diagram of Figure 5.4. Thus,

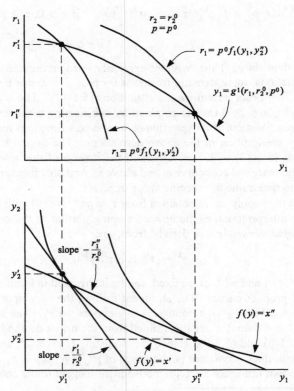

Figure 5.4 Derivation of the firm's input demand curve from profit maximization

in general, each point on the demand curve, $y_1 = g^1(r_1, r_2^0, p^0)$, is also a point on a distinct value of marginal product curve.

Consider now the properties of the firm's input demand and output supply functions as implied by profit maximization. According to (5.1-8) and (5.1-9), these functions vanish identically when $p < \widetilde{p}$. Hence it is only necessary to analyze the characteristics of $g^1, \ldots, g^{J+1}$, defined for all $r > 0$ and $p \geqslant \widetilde{p} > 0$. (Recall that in the strictly concave case of Figure 5.2, the inequality $p \geqslant \widetilde{p} > 0$ is replaced by $p > 0$.) Because the g^j are obtainable by different methods, there are correspondingly alternative ways of deriving each trait. On one hand, the properties of the g^j can be inferred from the properties of g^*, equations (5.1-9), and the properties of solution (5.1-8) of (5.1-5). On the other hand, they also follow from the properties of the solution of (5.1-11) and the properties of f in (5.1-13). Only one approach is employed for each case below.

It has already been noted that $g^1, \ldots, g^J$, as the solution of (5.1-11), are continuously differentiable. Because f is also continuously differentiable from (4.1-3), the chain rule[13] guarantees that g^{J+1} in (5.1-13) is too. Thus all input demand and output supply functions are continuously differentiable, and hence continuous, when $r > 0$ and $p \geqslant \widetilde{p} > 0$. That $g^j(r, p) > 0$, for $r > 0$ and $p \geqslant \widetilde{p} > 0$, where $j = 1, \ldots, J$, follows from (5.1-9) since g^* is known to be positive by (4.4-6). Because Γ^* is the range of g^{J+1} according to the derivation of (5.1-8),[14] $g^{J+1}(r, p) > 0$ for $r > 0$ and $p \geqslant \widetilde{p} > 0$. The fact that $g^1, \ldots, g^{J+1}$ are homogeneous of degree zero in (r, p) is left to the reader as Exercise 5.4.

Let $g_n^j(r, p)$ denote the partial derivative of g^j with respect to r_n, where $j = 1, \ldots, J + 1$, and $n = 1, \ldots, J$. The partial derivative with respect to p is written g_p^j for each j. Under conditions ensuring that profit maximization is possible, it can be demonstrated that all demand curves slope downward and all supply curves slope upward. In addition, the matrix of partial derivatives of the input demand functions with respect to input prices, that is the g_n^j, have properties analogous to those of the $I - 1$ by $I - 1$ Slutsky matrix of demand theory (Theorems 2.4-18 and 2.4-19). The restrictions imposed to arrive at these conclusions apply in both strictly-concave-production-function and Viner-cost-curve cases. In the former instance, the hypotheses of Theorem 5.1-6 imply those restrictions for all price vectors $(r, p) > 0$. (Recall that here the Viner-case inequality $p \geqslant \widetilde{p} > 0$ reduces to $p > 0$.) In the latter, the production function has to be strictly concave over appropriate sub-regions

---

[13]   Rudin [5, p. 214].
[14]   Note that when the hypotheses of Theorem 5.1-6 are satisfied, $\Gamma^* = \Gamma$.

of Y in order to guarantee the shapes that characterize Viner cost curves, and such production functions will often satisfy the restrictions referred to for all $r > 0$ and $p \geqslant \widetilde{p} > 0$. The results themselves are stated in general, although Theorem 5.1-14 is proved only for $J = 2$.

Theorem 5.1-14 For all $r > 0$ and $p \geqslant \widetilde{p} > 0$ with $\widetilde{p}$ dependent on r, if $|\bar{F}(y)| \neq 0$ and second-order condition inequalities (5.1-12) are satisfied for every y such that $y_j = g^j(r, p)$ where $j = 1, \ldots, J$, then

$$g_n^j(r, p) = g_j^n(r, p), \quad j, n = 1, \ldots, J,$$

and for all permutations of inputs,

$$g_1^1 < 0, \quad \begin{vmatrix} g_1^1 & g_2^1 \\ g_1^2 & g_2^2 \end{vmatrix} > 0, \quad \begin{vmatrix} g_1^1 & g_2^1 & g_3^1 \\ g_1^2 & g_2^2 & g_3^2 \\ g_1^3 & g_2^3 & g_3^3 \end{vmatrix} < 0, \ldots,$$

Proof: For $p \geqslant \widetilde{p} > 0$, substitution of (5.1-9) into (5.1-11) gives, with two inputs,

$$f_j(g^1(r, p), g^2(r, p)) = \frac{r_j}{p}, \quad j = 1, 2. \tag{5.1-15}$$

Differentiating with respect to r_1 and dropping functional arguments to simplify notation gives

$$f_{11}g_1^1 + f_{12}g_1^2 = \frac{1}{p},$$

$$f_{21}g_1^1 + f_{22}g_1^2 = 0.$$

By Cramer's rule,[15]

$$g_1^1 = \frac{1}{p} \frac{f_{22}}{|\bar{F}|},$$

$$\tag{5.1-16}$$

$$g_1^2 = -\frac{1}{p} \frac{f_{21}}{|\bar{F}|}.$$

---

[15] See Theorem A.4-2 of appendix Section A.4.

Similarly, differentiating (5.1-15) with respect to r_2 gives

$$g_2^2 = \frac{1}{p}\frac{f_{11}}{|\bar{F}|},$$

$$g_2^1 = -\frac{1}{p}\frac{f_{12}}{|\bar{F}|}.$$

Application of (5.1-12) and the fact that $\left|\bar{F}(y)\right| \neq 0$ for appropriate $y > 0$ leads to

$$g_1^1(r,p) < 0,$$

$$g_2^2(r,p) < 0,$$

because the inequalities in (5.1-12) are now strict. Moreover,

$$\begin{vmatrix} g_1^1 & g_2^1 \\ g_1^2 & g_2^2 \end{vmatrix} = \frac{1}{p^2\,|\bar{F}|} > 0.$$

Finally

$$g_n^j(r,p) = g_j^n(r,p), \quad j,n = 1,2,$$

because $f_{12} = f_{21}$.[16]

Q.E.D.

Theorem 5.1-17   For all $r > 0$ and $p \geqslant \tilde{p} > 0$ with $\tilde{p}$ dependent on r, if $\left|\bar{F}\right|(y) \neq 0$ and second-order condition inequalities (5.1-12) are satisfied for every y such that $y_j = g^j(r,p)$ where $j = 1,\ldots,J$, then

$$g_p^{J+1}(r,p) > 0.$$

Proof: Because $x = g^{J+1}(r,p)$ is the inverse of $MC(x) = p$ for $p \geqslant \tilde{p}$ and each $r > 0$, by the inverse function theorem,[17]

$$g_p^{J+1}(r,p) = \frac{1}{\dfrac{dMC(x)}{dx}},$$

---

[16]   See Theorem A.3-3 of appendix Section A.3.
[17]   Rudin [5, pp. 221-223].

where $x = g^{J+1}(r, p)$. Hence, from (5.1-7),

$$g_p^{J+1}(r, p) = \frac{|F(y)|}{MC(x)\,|\bar{F}(y)|}. \tag{5.1-18}$$

Using (5.1-12) and $|\bar{F}(y)| \neq 0$ at appropriate y in Y, an argument similar to that of Theorem 5.1-6 establishes the conclusion.

Q.E.D.

Generally, it is impossible to deduce in advance the signs of g_n^j for $n \neq j$. As seen in the two-input proof of Theorem 5.1-14, the signs of g_2^1 and g_1^2 turn on those of f_{12} and f_{21}. In parallel to the situation with respect to the functions g^*, the signs of the $g_j^3(r, p)$ depend on the slope of the expansion path at (r, p). For differentiating (5.1-13) with respect to, say, r_1:

$$g_1^3 = f_1 g_1^1 + f_2 g_1^2,$$

whence, employing (5.1-16),

$$g_1^3 = \frac{f_1 f_{22} - f_2 f_{21}}{p\,|\bar{F}|}.$$

Similarly,

$$g_2^3 = \frac{f_2 f_{11} - f_1 f_{12}}{p\,|\bar{F}|}.$$

Combining the last two equations with (4.4-10) and (4.4-11) and using the fact that $f_{12} = f_{21}$,

$$g_1^3 = -\frac{|F|}{p\,|\bar{F}|}\,g_x^{*1}$$

and

$$g_2^3 = -\frac{|F|}{p\,|\bar{F}|}\,g_x^{*2}.$$

Now, with $J = 2$, the determinant $|F| > 0$ on D. Furthermore, from Theorem 4.4-16, both g_x^{*1} and g_x^{*2} are positive if and only if the expansion path is positively sloped. In that event, with $|\bar{F}| > 0$ (as is implied by the hypotheses of Theorems 5.1-14 and 5.1-17 that $|\bar{F}(y)| \neq 0$ and inequalities 5.1-12 hold),

$$g_j^3(r, p) < 0, \quad j = 1, 2.$$

The following proposition has therefore been proved.

Theorem 5.1-19 Let $J = 2$, $r > 0$, and $p \geqslant \widetilde{p} > 0$ with $\widetilde{p}$ dependent on r. If the expansion path is positively sloped at (r, p) and $\left| \bar{F}(y) \right| > 0$ for y with $y_j = g^j(r, p)$ where $j = 1, 2$, then

$$g_j^3(r, p) < 0, \quad j = 1, 2.$$

Based on the discussions following equation (4.4-8) and Theorem 4.4-16, and using the above relationships between the g_x^{*j} and the g_j^3, a negatively sloped expansion path would reverse the sign of g_j^3 for one, but not both, inputs j. A parallel between a positive g_j^3 and the inferior good case in demand theory is also apparent.

Complications arise in the argument of this section when f exhibits (global) constant returns to scale. In that case, the total cost function is linear, and average variable cost and marginal cost are constant and equal for all x (Table 4.1). Although there is no problem with cost minimization, unique interior maxima of the profit function do not exist. The possibilities are illustrated in Figure 5.5. If output price is larger than the constant average variable cost, total revenue is increasing faster than total cost as output rises (Figure 5.5(a)). No profit maximizing output can be found. With p less than that average variable cost, maximum profit occurs at $x = 0$ (Figure 5.5(b)). Only when p is the same as the average variable cost, that is, when TR and TC are parallel, is the firm able to maximize profit (minimize loss) in the interior of Γ. But then every x in Γ maximizes profit (Figure 5.5(c)). In this last case, if $b = 0$ then $TR = TC$ throughout Γ. It should be observed that under circumstances like those depicted in Figures 5.5(a) and 5.5(c) there is nothing internal to the profit-maximizing firm that limits the quantities of inputs it hires and the quantity of output it produces. Outside forces or boundaries, however, can impose such limits, and examples of their imposition appear in Exercise 5.20 and Chapters 8 and 11.

It is not surprising that much of the analysis of the present section does not hold up under conditions of constant returns to scale. Conclusions fail because the hypotheses upon which they are based do not apply. As indicated in Exercise 4.4, $\left| \bar{F}(y) \right| = 0$ everywhere on the interior of Y. Hence one of the differential characteristics associated with unique maxima is absent. Theorems 5.1-6, 5.1-14, 5.1-17, and 5.1-19 cannot be utilized, and in formulas such as (5.1-16) that provide expressions for the derivatives of input demand and output supply functions, denominators vanish. Except for the circumstance described in Figure 5.5(c) where marginal cost is identically equal to price, there are no points satisfying the first-order profit-maximization conditions (5.1-5)

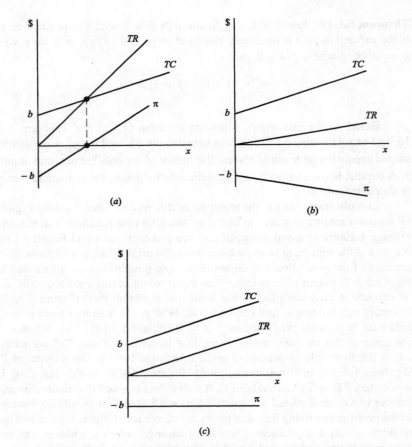

Figure 5.5 Profit, total revenue, and total cost curves with constant returns to scale production functions: (*a*) output price greater than average variable cost; (*b*) output price less than average variable cost; (*c*) output price equal to average variable cost

or (5.1-11). In the exceptional situation, when many points satisfy these equations for the same (r, p), the Jacobian of each system vanishes identically, and the inverse functions are set-valued.

The input demand and output supply functions of the firm with a constant returns to scale production function, and with $\tilde{p}$ dependent on r and equal to the constant average variable cost are, respectively,

$$
y_j = \begin{cases} \infty, & \text{if } r > 0, p > \widetilde{p}, \\ g^j(r,p) = \{y_j : y_j \geqslant 0\}, & \text{if } r > 0, p = \widetilde{p}, \\ 0, & \text{if } r > 0, 0 < p < \widetilde{p}, \end{cases} \quad (5.1\text{-}20)
$$

for $j = 1, \ldots, J$, and

$$
x = \begin{cases} \infty, & \text{if } r > 0, p > \widetilde{p}, \\ g^{J+1}(r,p) = \{x : x \geqslant 0\}, & \text{if } r > 0, p = \widetilde{p}, \\ 0, & \text{if } r > 0, 0 < p < \widetilde{p}. \end{cases} \quad (5.1\text{-}21)
$$

These functions are clearly quite different from those described earlier in this section.

Let f be subject to constant returns to scale and suppose the firm has no fixed cost. Then according to Table 4.1 (and reintroducing the variable r into cost function notation) $AVC(r, x)$ and hence $ATC(r, x)$ are independent of x. It follows that there exists a function Θ of r such that

$$
ATC(r, x) = \Theta(r), \quad (5.1\text{-}22)
$$

for all $r > 0$ and x in Γ (recall Exercise 4.15). Because $TC(r, x)$ is homogeneous of degree one in r for each x, $\Theta(r)$ is homogeneous of degree one. Now if, in addition, total revenue and total cost are everywhere identical, then output price is always the same as $ATC(r, x)$. Hence for all $r > 0$, (5.1-22) implies

$$
p = \Theta(r),
$$

where $p = \widetilde{p}$. Applying the homogeneity of Θ gives

$$
1 = \Theta\left(\frac{r_1}{p}, \ldots, \frac{r_J}{p}\right), \quad (5.1\text{-}23)
$$

again for all $r > 0$ and $p = \widetilde{p}$. Equation (5.1-23) implicitly defines a relation, called the *factor-price frontier*, between r_J/p, say, and $r_1/p, \ldots, r_{J-1}/p$. An example is provided in Exercise 5.17.

This section has considered short-run input demand and output supply functions of the firm as defined by profit maximization under three alternative sets of assumptions on production functions. In all cases the properties of the input demand and output supply functions have been studied. The following propositions recapitulate the three sets of conditions given above which ensure that these functions exist. To emphasize the structure of previous argument, the minor overlap of restrictions occurring in their hypotheses is not eliminated. Since constant returns to scale production functions cannot have unique global maxima in the interior of Y, that possibility is eliminated in the statement of Theorem 5.1-26. It is also convenient to avoid those parts of the input demand and output supply functions that map points of their respective domains into zero or infinity. Hence the propositions are stated in terms of the g^j of (5.1-8) and (5.1-9), or with reference to the set-valued g^j of (5.1-20) and (5.1-21). Each proposition describes a particular situation that frequently arises in subsequent chapters.

Theorem 5.1-24 Assume that (4.1-2) – (4.1-5) are satisfied; that $f_j(y) > 0$ where $j = 1, \ldots, J$, for all y within the region bounded by the ridge lines (surfaces) and up to a unique global maximum output (if it exists) or, when no ridge lines (surfaces) exist, for all $y > 0$; that $|F(y)| \neq 0$ for y in Y with $f_j(y) \neq 0$ for every $j = 1, \ldots, J$; and that isoquants where nonnegatively sloped and strictly convex do not touch the boundary of Y. If f is strictly concave on the interior of Y, if $|\bar{F}(y)| \neq 0$ on the interior of Y, and if each of the f_j takes on all positive real numbers as function values over every expansion path, then the g^j are defined for all $(p, r) > 0$, and $j = 1, \ldots, J+1$.

Theorem 5.1-25 Assume that (4.1-2) – (4.1-5) are satisfied; that $f_j(y) > 0$ where $j = 1, \ldots, J$, for all y within the region bounded by the ridge lines (surfaces) and up to a unique global maximum output (if it exists) or, when no ridge lines (surfaces) exist, for all $y > 0$; that $|F(y)| \neq 0$ for y in Y with $f_j(y) \neq 0$ for every $j = 1, \ldots, J$; and that isoquants where nonnegatively sloped and strictly convex do not touch the boundary of Y. If, for each $r > 0$, f generates Viner cost functions as graphed in Figure 5.1 and if the first-order partial derivatives of f take on (positive) values that are arbitrarily close to zero for some input baskets $y > 0$ along every expansion path, then the g^j are defined for all $r > 0$, $p \geqslant \tilde{p}$, and $j = 1, \ldots, J+1$, where $\tilde{p}$ is dependent on r.

Theorem 5.1-26 Assume that (4.1-2) – (4.1-5) are satisfied; that $f_j(y) > 0$ where $j = 1, \ldots, J$, for all y within the region bounded by the ridge lines (surfaces) or, when no ridge lines (surfaces) exist, for all $y > 0$; that $|F(y)| \neq 0$ for y in Y with $f_j(y) \neq 0$ for every $j = 1, \ldots, J$; and that isoquants where nonnegatively sloped and strictly convex do not touch the boundary of Y. If f exhibits constant returns to scale on Y, and if profit vanishes identically on

Γ, then the g^j are defined as set-valued functions for all $r > 0$, $p = \widetilde{p}$, and $j = 1, \ldots, J + 1$, where $\widetilde{p}$ is dependent on r.

Although earlier reasoning employed to establish the above theorems was based on a characterization of the g^j as solutions of first-order maximization equations (for example, equation (5.1-5)), it is clear that these functions could also be defined in terms of the outcome of a general maximization procedure without any reliance on derivatives at all. The approach would be similar to that used to define consumer demand functions in Section 2.3. A proposition analogous to Theorem 2.3-10 would have to be proved in which the existence of profit-maximizing x and y would be guaranteed for certain values of r and p. Once the g^j were secured in this way their properties could then be studied. Of course, under the additional hypotheses of Theorem 5.1-24, 5.1-25, or 5.1-26, the same g^j implied by these respective theorems would obtain.

For ease of reference, the structures outlined by Theorems 5.1-24, 5.1-25, and 5.1-26 are referred to as, respectively, the *strictly concave model*, the *Viner model*, and the *constant returns to scale model* of the firm. As these theorems indicate, (finite, nonzero) input demand and output supply functions are defined for all positive input and output prices in the strictly concave model, for all positive input and output prices such that output price is at least as large as minimum average variable cost in the Viner model, and are set-valued in the constant returns to scale model. No models containing a strictly convex or a globally increasing returns to scale production function are considered because, like the constant returns to scale case of Figure 5.5(a), these production functions are incompatible with profit maximization when input and output prices are taken to be fixed — unless outside-the-firm limits are placed on the quantities of inputs the firm is able to employ or the quantity of output it is permitted to produce. And, in any case, such constructions are beyond the purview of present discussion.

5.2   THE LONG RUN

In light of the distinction between the short and long run set out at the beginning of Section 4.1, there are two ways to obtain the long-run analogues of the models of Section 5.1. The first is to take the subscript j to range over all inputs permitted by the firm's technology. Hence the production function f is not subject to fixed inputs hidden in the background. Fixed cost $b = 0$ and the analysis of the previous section can be applied as it stands. Except for the zero-profit qualification to be introduced shortly, the input demand and output supply functions so obtained are long-run relations and their properties are those described previously.

A more common procedure, which permits detailed explication of the relationship between short- and long-run cost functions, but which still leads to the same result, begins by reintroducing fixed inputs explicitly into the production function and deriving short-run cost functions as before. In the notation of Section 4.1, the production function becomes

$$x = f(y_1, \ldots, y_\delta, y_{\delta+1}, \ldots, y_J),$$

where $y_{\delta+1}, \ldots, y_J$ designate quantities of fixed inputs. Frequently each fixed vector $(y_{\delta+1}, \ldots, y_J)$ is interpreted as identifying an *associated plant* that the firm constructs and with respect to which it hires variable inputs to produce its output. (In this terminology, the word "plant" refers to the structure that houses the firm's entire operation.) Under certain conditions (such as, for example, the existence of an ordering relation among associated plants that gives meaning to the notion of relative "bigness," and which has, in part, properties similar to those of a representable preference ordering in Section 2.1), it is possible to assign a number to each associated plant that indicates, in light of that plant, the *size* or *scale* of operation of the firm. Of course, when there is only one fixed input, it is obvious that the quantity of that input in use automatically serves this purpose. Regardless, applying the argument of Sections 4.4 and 4.5 with $y_{\delta+1}, \ldots, y_J$ regarded as fixed, the short-run total cost function (4.5-1) can be rewritten as

$$TC(r, x, y_{\delta+1}, \ldots, y_J) = \sum_{j=1}^{\delta} r_j g^{*j}(r_1, \ldots, r_\delta, x, y_{\delta+1}, \ldots, y_J)$$

$$(5.2\text{-}1)$$

$$+ \sum_{j=\delta+1}^{J} r_j y_j.$$

The only difference between (4.5-1) and (5.2-1) is that the presence of fixed inputs is not hidden in the symbols TC, g^*, and b. As before, explicit reference to r as an argument of the function TC (and also as arguments of ATC and MC below) is not necessary and is therefore dropped. The definitions of short-run average total cost, $ATC(x, y_{\delta+1}, \ldots, y_J)$, and short-run marginal cost, $MC(x, y_{\delta+1}, \ldots, y_J)$, are similarly adjusted.

The *long-run average cost* of a given output, say x, is the minimum short-run average total cost of producing x over all relevant values of $(y_{\delta+1}, \ldots, y_J)$.

Denoting the long-run average cost function by $LRAC(x)$ yields

$$LRAC(x) = \min ATC(x, y_{\delta+1}, \ldots, y_J), \qquad (5.2\text{-}2)$$

where for each x the minimum is taken over all associated plants $(y_{\delta+1}, \ldots, y_J)$ > 0 capable of producing output x. Enough continuity has been assumed on the production function to ensure that a minimum in (5.2-2) always exists. Thus each point on the (Viner) $LRAC$ curve in Figure 5.6(a) is tangent to a short-run ATC curve corresponding to a different associated plant.[18] Note that where $LRAC$ is rising or falling, the tangency cannot occur at the minimum (with respect to x) of short-run average total cost. Only at the minimum long-run average cost are the two curves tangent at their minimum points.[19] (If the long-run average cost curve were a horizontal line, as would be the case with a long-run constant-returns-to-scale production function, then all tangencies between short-run curves and the long-run curve would occur at the minimum values of the short-run average total cost curves. See Exercise 5.11.) Moreover, there may be short-run average total cost curves that are not tangent to the long-run average cost curve at any point (like ATC^* in Figure 5.6(a)). Such a curve would arise if quantities of the fixed inputs could be reduced without having any impact on output at any x in Γ. (Thus, for example, the fixed inputs y_j^0 for $j > \delta$ might be such that $(y_1, \ldots, y_\delta, y_{\delta+1}^0, \ldots, y_J^0)$ lies outside of the area between the long-run ridge surfaces for all $(y_1, \ldots, y_\delta)$ on the short-run expansion path.) Alternatively, ATC^* could obtain in conjunction with Figure 5.6(d) discussed below. Excluding all nontangent short-run curves, the long-run average cost curve often appears as the envelope[20] of the remaining short-run curves. It is left as Exercise 5.10 to demonstrate that $LRAC(x)$ as characterized by (5.2-2) is identical to that obtained from the first method

---

[18]   Apart from the possibility, in relation to the firm's production function, of variations in returns to scale as output increases, the initial decline and subsequent rise in long-run average cost along the LRAC curve in Figure 5.6(a) is explainable in parallel to the standard explanation of the U-shape of the short-run average total cost curve. In the latter case, with fixed costs present, falling average fixed cost per unit of output tends to dominate average variable cost at low levels of output, while expanding average variable cost generally overrides average fixed cost at high levels of output. A similar effect for the long-run average cost curve may obtain by thinking of normal profit (to be defined shortly) as a fixed cost in the long run.

[19]   There is a famous battle over this point reported in the economics literature by Professor Viner between himself and his draftsman, Mr. Wong. Apparently Professor Viner wanted Mr. Wong to draw a U-shaped long-run average cost curve so that at each point it would be tangent to a short-run average total cost curve at the minimum point of the short-run curve. Viner believed that only Wong's "scruples" as a craftsman prevented him from doing so [9, reprinted version pp. 214, 227].

[20]   The notion of envelope is defined in appendix Section A.4.

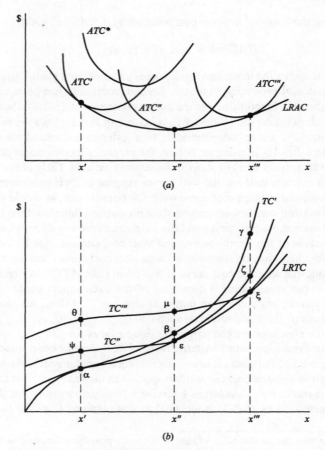

Figure 5.6 Long-run and short-run costs: (*a*) long-run and short-run average cost curves; (*b*) long-run and short-run total cost curves

described above by setting $b = 0$. A specific example is provided in Exercise 5.11.

A definition similar to (5.2-2) can be given for the *long-run total cost function* $LRTC(x)$. (See the example of Figure 5.6(b), in which x', x'', and x''' are intended to be the same as in Figure 5.6(a), and in which TC', TC'', and TC''' correspond, respectively, to ATC', ATC'', and ATC''', also in Figure

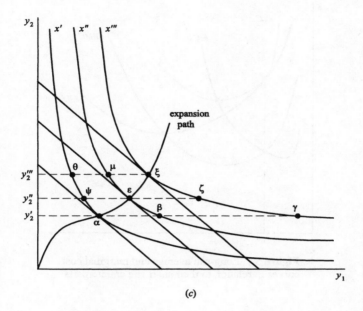

expansion
path

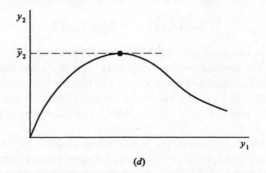

Figure 5.6 (continued) (*c*) long-run and short-run costs in
relation to isoquants and the expansion path; (*d*) expansion
path yielding short-run cost curves that are not tangent to the
associated long-run cost curves

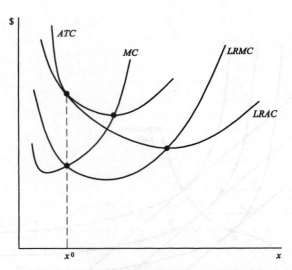

Figure 5.7 Long-run average and marginal cost
curves in relation to their short-run counterparts

5.6(a).) On the other hand, $LRTC(x)$ can be obtained simply as the product

$$LRTC(x) = x[LRAC(x)],$$

on Γ. *Long-run marginal cost* $LRMC(x)$ is the derivative of $LRTC(x)$ with respect to x. The relationship between long- and short-run average and marginal curves is illustrated in Figure 5.7. Notice that the intersection of short-run MC and $LRMC$ lies exactly below the tangency between the corresponding short-run ATC and $LRAC$. Also $LRMC$ cuts short-run MC from above. (See Exercise 5.12.)

For the two-input world, the long-run and short-run total cost curves of Figure 5.6(b) are also related to tangencies between isocost lines and isoquants as shown in Figure 5.6(c). These diagrams assume that input 1 varies in the short run while input 2 remains fixed, and that TC', TC'', and TC''' are the short-run total cost curves obtained, respectively, for the associated plants or, since there is only one fixed input, the scales of operation y'_2, y''_2, and y'''_2. The long-run total cost curve is derived from the firm's expansion path determined by r. In the short run, given the scale y''_2, say, x' is produced with input basket ψ in Figure 5.6(c), x'' with input basket ε, and x''' with input basket ζ. Since ψ does not lie on the expansion path, the (short-run) cost of producing x' at

ψ is larger than the (long-run) cost of producing x'at α. This is depicted by the points α (on TC') and ψ (on TC'') in Figure 5.6(b). All production points labeled with Greek letters in Figure 5.6(c) are similarly identified in terms of their relative cost positions in Figure 5.6(b). Thus, apart, from the earlier characterization of the long-run total cost of producing output x as the minimum total cost as associated plants vary, this provides another way of arriving at the conclusion that, except at the tangency (in which case both long-run and short-run output are produced with the same input basket on the expansion path), short-run total cost is always greater than long-run total cost.

. Observe that, since the short-run total cost curve for any scale of operation, say y_2'' from Figure 5.6(c), is tangent to the long-run curve at ε in Figure 5.6(b) only in conjunction with the intersection of the line through y_2'' parallel to the y_1-axis and the firm's expansion path at ε in Figure 5.6(c), the shape of the expansion path determines the pattern of short-run cost curves in relation to the long-run cost curve. With respect to the expansion path shown in Figure 5.6(d), the short-run total cost curve associated with any scale of operation larger than $\overline{y}_2$ is seen to lie everywhere above the long-run total cost curve. This produces short-run average cost curves similar to ATC^* in Figure 5.6(a). Likewise, for $y_2 < \overline{y}_2$, each short-run curve (total or average) is tangent to the relevant long-run curve at two distinct points. Further possibilities arise with different expansion paths.

Because, as already pointed out, the two approaches to long-run cost curves described here are equivalent, the long-run input demand and output supply functions generated in both cases are the same. Either way, the discussion of Section 5.1 applies. In particular, $(y_{\delta+1}, \ldots, y_J)$, or the associated plant, can be determined along with everything else from long-run profit maximization given r and p.

It should also be noted that long-run profit maximization implies short-run profit maximization, but the converse is not true. Choosing y so as to maximize long-run profit clearly determines optimal values for both variable and fixed short-run inputs. Optimal values for the latter, of course, define the *optimal associated plant*. However, since firms can produce output only with a plant that has actually been built and that usually cannot be altered in the short run, it is still possible for a firm to maximize short-run profit with a nonoptimal associated plant. For example, suppose a firm chooses all input and output values, and hence its associated plant, so as to maximize long-run profit given some $(r, p) > 0$. Suppose further that after production with this associated plant begins, (r, p) changes. Then in the short-run, the firm can modify only its variable inputs so as to maximize short-run profit with its now inefficient associated plant. Long-run profit cannot be maximized again until the firm is able to adjust its associated plant appropriately.

When the firm maximizes profit in both contexts simultaneously, certain relationships arise between the short-run input demand functions for variable inputs $g^j(r, p)$, where $j = 1, \ldots, \delta$, and their long-run counterparts. (Note that for the long-run case, the functional argument $r = (r_1, \ldots, r_J)$, whereas for the short run, $r = (r_1, \ldots, r_\delta)$, in accordance with equation (5.2-1).) Similar links between the short-run and long-run functions $g^{*j}(r, x)$ secured from cost minimization also obtain. To separate things notationally, denote the short-run and long-run versions of these functions, respectively, by $[SR]g^j$ and $[LR]g^j$ in the first instance, and by $[SR]g^{*j}$ and $[LR]g^{*j}$ in the second. Consider the functions g^{*j} first. Suppose that the price of one variable input, say r_j, rises while all others remain unchanged. With output set and all factors variable (that is, the long run), cost minimization requires substitution away from input j. But upon introducing the short-run constraints that certain other inputs are fixed, the opportunity for substitution may decrease. Surely the presence of such constraints cannot increase the substitution possibilities. Hence it is natural to expect that at any $r > 0$,

$$[SR]g^{*j}_j(r, x) \geqslant [LR]g^{*j}_j(r, x), \qquad (5.2\text{-}3)$$

for all inputs j that are variable in the short run. (The inequality in (5.2-3) appears as it is because, according to the discussion following equation (4.4-7), the g^{*j}_j are always negative. In absolute terms, then, the greater change necessarily occurs in the long run.) Moreover, a similar conclusion should hold for the g^j when p is held constant and x is permitted to vary. Thus

$$[SR]g^j_j(r, p) \geqslant [LR]g^j_j(r, p), \qquad (5.2\text{-}4)$$

for the same j and all $(p, r) > 0$ such that p is at least as large as short-run minimum average variable cost (which depends on r). Multiplication of both sides of, say, (5.2-4) by $-r_j/y_j$ leads to the assertion that the long-run input demands are generally more elastic than their short-run counterparts.

These propositions have their origins in the Le Chatelier principle of thermodynamics.[21] Although a general proof[22] is beyond the scope of present discussion, it is worth considering an illustration with two inputs. In the long run, of course, both inputs must be permitted to vary. Let the short run be defined

---

[21]   The relevance of the Le Chatelier principle in economic contexts of this sort was first noticed by Samuelson [6, p. 38, n. 13].
[22]   See Silberberg [7, pp. 293-298].

by fixing, say, input 2. Referring again to the argument following (4.4-7),

$$[LR]g_1^{*1}(r, x) < 0, \qquad (5.2\text{-}5)$$

where x is given and $r > 0$. But in the short run, there is only one variable input. Hence the tangency condition (4.4-5), which arises from cost minimization and is the basis upon which (5.2-5) is derived, does not apply. In fact, when there are only two inputs and when x (that is, an isoquant) and input 2 are fixed, so is input 1. Hence

$$[SR]g_1^{*1}(r, x) = 0, \qquad (5.2\text{-}6)$$

for all $r > 0$, and (5.2-3) follows as a strict inequality from the combination of (5.2-5) and (5.2-6).

To deduce (5.2-4), recall from (5.1-16) that

$$[LR]g_1^1 = \frac{f_{22}}{p[f_{11}f_{22} - (f_{12})^2]}, \qquad (5.2\text{-}7)$$

where functional arguments have been dropped to simplify notation. When there is only one variable input y_1 (and $y_2 = y_2^0$), profit maximization implies

$$pf_1(y_1, y_2^0) = r_1, \qquad (5.2\text{-}8)$$

as in (5.1-11). Solving (5.2-8) for y_1 (assuming it is possible to do so) yields

$$y_1 = [SR]g^1(r_1, p), \qquad (5.2\text{-}9)$$

where y_2^0 is subsumed in the symbol g^1. Substitution of (5.2-9) into (5.2-8) and differentiating the result with respect to r_1 gives

$$[SR]g_1^1 = \frac{1}{pf_{11}}. \qquad (5.2\text{-}10)$$

Thus if $f_{12} = 0$, then (5.2-4) follows as an equality from (5.2-7) and (5.2-10). Similarly, when $f_{12} \neq 0$ and $f_{22} < 0$ (the latter inequality always obtains if, say, f is strictly concave and $|\bar{F}(y)| \neq 0$ on the interior of Y), the inequality of (5.2-4) is strict.

As indicated earlier, the reasoning of Section 5.1 can be applied to determine the long-run behavior of the firm. But in addition to that argument, there are frequently circumstances in which an additional constraint, namely that long-run profit be zero, is required to complete the analysis. The source of this constraint is considered in Section 6.2. For the present, interest centers on the impact of introducing such a zero-profit condition on the long-run input demand and output supply functions of the firm.

The first question to be considered is why, if profit is zero in the long-run, should the firm produce at all. Indeed, as described here, there is little reason for it to do so. But if, as indicated earlier, a *normal profit*, that is, the minimum return to the owners of the firm which is needed to induce them to keep the firm going,[23] were somehow already included in the expense of operating the firm, then there would be no difficulty with zero profit. To anticipate subsequent discussion, this can be accomplished by combining the reward of entrepreneurship with the return to money capital and including them as an extra cost to the firm. Normal profit, then, would be accounted for as the sum the firm must pay for the use of the money capital it requires. There would be no distinction between the owners of the firm and the owners of the firm's money capital. A positive difference between revenues and production plus money capital costs would be regarded as additional, *abnormal* profit rewarding entrepreneurship and money capital beyond what is necessary. The fact that abnormal profit might vanish is irrelevant to the question of whether the firm should continue to operate. All that matters is that the difference between total revenue and total production plus money capital cost not be negative. The details are postponed until money capital is brought formally into the picture in Chapter 13 (see especially Section 13.3).

Return to the long-run analysis developed above with normal profit excluded. Restrict attention to production functions that exhibit constant returns to scale or yield Viner cost curves. Now adding the requirement that profit be zero (or that long-run average cost equal output price) to the assumption of profit maximization (output price equals long-run marginal cost) forces the firm to settle on an output x for which

$$LRAC(x) = LRMC(x).$$

Clearly this can happen only when the firm operates with an output price p such that

$$p = \min_{x \text{ in } \Gamma} LRAC(x).$$

But as demonstrated above, input prices (and the production function) are the sole determinants of minimum long-run average cost. In long-run analysis, then, invoking both profit maximization and zero profit means that output price can no longer be thought of as an independent variable. Instead, output price

---

[23]   The idea goes back to Marshall [3, p. 411].

necessarily becomes a function of r. Note also that according to Theorem 4.5-9, minimum long-run average cost at x is identified by the equation[24]

$$f(y) = \sum_{j=1}^{J} y_j f_j(y),$$ (5.2-11)

where $x = f(y)$ and $y = g^*(r, x)$. Recall, too, that the first-order conditions for long-run profit maximization appear in (5.1-11) as

$$pf_j(y) = r_j, \quad j = 1, \ldots, J.$$ (5.2-12)

Because $x = f(y)$, multiplying (5.2-11) by p and combining the result with (5.2-12) leads to

$$px = r \cdot y,$$

thus returning to the zero-profit condition from which this line of reasoning began. In other words, paying all inputs the values of their marginal products at minimum long-run average cost exhausts the firm's proceeds in that all revenue received by it is distributed exactly to the inputs employed, leaving nothing over with which to reward the entrepreneur. This version of the so-called *adding-up* or *product-exhaustion* theorem appears in Wicksell [10, pp. 129-130]. Contrary to that of Wicksteed (recall n. 12 on p. 143 above), it holds regardless of whether the production function itself exhibits (global) constant returns to scale.

If the firm has a strictly concave production function, however, minimum long-run average cost always occurs at zero output. Hence, with the zero-profit condition in force, the Section 5.1 approach to profit maximization based on the strictly concave production function (Theorem 5.1-24) is irrelevant for explaining the long-run behavior of an operating firm. (Such a conclusion will generally not hold when money capital and normal profit are put into the picture.) Of course the other two approaches requiring, respectively, that f exhibit constant returns to scale (Theorem 5.1-26) or that f generate long-run Viner cost curves shaped as in Figures 4.12 or 5.1 (Theorem 5.1-25) still apply. But in the Viner situation, because it implies the dependence of p on r, the zero-profit constraint alters the firm's input demand and output supply functions considerably. The character of these changes is now explored.

Combining (5.2-11) and (5.2-12) or, equivalently, the statement of long-run zero profit $px = r \cdot y$ with the production function $x = f(y)$, the precise

---

[24]   Theorem 4.5-9 applies here because in the long run all inputs are variable and hence long-run average cost is the same as average variable cost.

nature of the relation between p and r is obtained:

$$p = \frac{r \cdot y}{f(y)}. \tag{5.2-13}$$

Long-run input demand, as a function of r and not p, is derived by solving (5.2-12) after replacing p by (5.2-13), or

$$r_j = \frac{r \cdot y}{f(y)} f_j(y), \quad j = 1, \ldots, J. \tag{5.2-14}$$

(The Jacobian of equations (5.2-14) is nonvanishing wherever $\left| \bar{F}(y) \right| \neq 0$. Evidently unique solutions need not exist in cases of constant returns to scale because $\left| \bar{F}(y) \right|$ is then identically zero. Recall Exercise 4.4.) Use the notation

$$y_j = \bar{g}^j(r), \quad j = 1, \ldots, J, \text{ and } r > 0, \tag{5.2-15}$$

to denote the resulting input demand functions. Then long-run output supply, namely,

$$x = \bar{g}^{J+1}(r),$$

where $r > 0$, is secured upon substitution of (5.2-15) into the production function as in (5.1-13). Like the long-run input demand functions (5.2-15), $\bar{g}^{J+1}$ cannot be a function of output price. The latter is determined as a function of r by using (5.2-15) to eliminate y in (5.2-13). Analogously to other input demand and output supply functions derived in Section 5.1, the g^j, for $j = 1, \ldots, J + 1$, are homogeneous of degree zero, continuous, continuously differentiable where $\left| \bar{F}(y) \right| \neq 0$, and have nonnegative function values for all $r > 0$.

However, signs of the derivatives of the $\bar{g}^j$ cannot be deduced *a priori*. To see what is involved, consider a two-input case. Observe first that (5.2-13) becomes

$$p = \frac{r_1 y_1 + r_2 y_2}{f(y)}.$$

Employing (5.2-12), the derivatives of p with respect to r_1 and r_2 can be shown (Exercise 5.13) to be

$$\frac{\partial p}{\partial r_j} = \frac{y_j}{f(y)}, \quad j = 1, 2, \tag{5.2-16}$$

for all y associated with production at minimum long-run average cost (given some $r > 0$). At these y, of course, $f(y) > 0$ so that

$$\frac{\partial p}{\partial r_j} > 0, \quad j = 1, 2.$$

In words, provided that the firm adjusts production to maintain maximum profit (that always turns out to be zero), a small rise in any input price increases the minimum long-run average cost and hence output price.

An expression for the derivative of $\bar{g}^1$ with respect to r, written $\bar{g}_1^1(r)$, is found by substituting (5.2-15) into (5.2-12) and differentiating with respect to r_1. Using (5.2-16), this yields

$$p(f_{11}\bar{g}_1^1 + f_{12}\bar{g}_1^2) + \frac{\bar{g}^1}{f}f_1 = 1,$$

$$p(f_{21}\bar{g}_1^1 + f_{22}\bar{g}_1^2) + \frac{\bar{g}^1}{f}f_2 = 0,$$

where functional arguments have been dropped to simplify notation, and p depends on r as defined by the substitution of (5.2-15) into (5.2-13). Dividing by p, moving the terms immediately to the left of the equal sign to the other side, and invoking Cramer's rule gives

$$\bar{g}_1^1 = \frac{1}{pf} \left[\frac{(f - \bar{g}^1 f_1)f_{22} + \bar{g}^1 f_2 f_{12}}{|\bar{F}|} \right],$$

as long as $|\bar{F}| \neq 0$. Hence, from the combination of (5.2-11) and (5.2-15),

$$\bar{g}_1^1 = \frac{f_2}{pf} \left[\frac{\bar{g}^2 f_{22} + \bar{g}^1 f_{12}}{|\bar{F}|} \right].$$

Now $p > 0$ and $f(y) > 0$ by assumption, and $f_2 > 0$ because all relevant vectors y lie in the set D described on p. 130. Furthermore, if profit maximization is to be possible and if $|\bar{F}| \neq 0$, then (5.1-12) must hold with strict inequalities. Hence $f_{22} < 0$ and $|\bar{F}| > 0$. The sign of $\bar{g}_1^1$ therefore turns on the sign of f_{12} and the magnitude of $\bar{g}^1 f_{12}$. Only when

$$y_1 f_{21}(y) + y_2 f_{22}(y) < 0,$$

(where, recall, $(y_1, y_2) = (\bar{g}^1(r), \bar{g}^2(r))$ and $f_{12} = f_{21}$) is $\bar{g}_1^1(r) < 0$.[25] This

---

[25]   Note that if $y_1 f_{21}(y) + y_2 f_{22}(y) = 0$, then the derivative f_2 would satisfy the Euler theorem condition for zero-degree homogeneity at y.

conclusion is quite different from that of Theorem 5.1-14 as applied to long-run input demand functions in the absence of any zero-profit constraint. Thus the addition of a zero-profit restriction introduces modifications into that which would be obtained from a straightforward transference of the Viner model of Section 5.1 into a long-run context by eliminating all fixed inputs and setting $b = 0$.

EXERCISES

5.1* Let p, r, and b be given. Assume conditions (4.1-2) – (4.1-5) of Chapter 4. Without using first-order maximization conditions, prove that $\pi(y)$ has a maximum at $y = y^0$ if and only if $\pi(x)$ has a maximum at $x = x^0$, where $x^0 = f(y^0)$ and $y^0 = g*(r, x^0)$.

5.2 Redraw Figure 5.1 for the case in which output price is smaller than the minimum value that the marginal cost function is permitted to assume.

5.3 Without employing the properties of solutions of (5.1-11) or the properties of f in (5.1-13), show that input demand functions (5.1-9) and the output supply function (5.1-8) are continuously differentiable for $r > 0$ and $p \geqslant \widetilde{p} > 0$.

5.4 Prove that the input demand and output supply functions generated by the strictly concave and Viner models are homogeneous of degree zero.

5.5 In a two-input world, differentiation of (5.1-13) for $r > 0$ and $p \geqslant \widetilde{p} > 0$ gives

$$g_p^{J+1} = f_1 g_p^1 + f_2 g_p^2.$$

Using this, verify formula (5.1-18) by differentiating (5.1-11) to compute g_p^1 and g_p^2.

5.6 What is the relationship between the firm's value of marginal product curve and its input demand curve when the firm uses only one variable input?

5.7 Let f exhibit constant returns to scale. Prove in two different ways that $dMC(x)/dx = 0$.

5.8* Derive the short-run input demand and output supply functions for the production function of Exercises 4.6 and 4.11 when $\beta_1 + \beta_2 < 1$. Verify that

$g_j^j(r,p) < 0$ for $j = 1,2$, and $g_p^3(r,p) > 0$. What about the sign of $g_j^3(r,p)$ for $j = 1,2$? What happens when $\beta_1 + \beta_2 \geqslant 1$?

5.9 Consider a firm whose production function is given by

$$f(y_1, y_2) = (\min[y_1, y_2])^{1/2},$$

on Y. Are assumptions $(4.1\text{-}2) - (4.1\text{-}5)$ and any of the restrictions imposed in Section 5.1 to ensure that profits can be maximized satisfied? Derive the firm's short-run input demand and output supply functions. Show in this case that a small rise in output price, or a small fall in the price of either input, increases both output supply and the demand for each input.

5.10 Prove that the two derivations of the long-run average cost function in Section 5.2 are equivalent.

5.11 Imagine the long-run production function

$$f(y_1, y_2) = \sqrt{y_1 y_2},$$

defined for all $(y_1, y_2) \geqslant 0$. For a given, nonnegative value of input 2, say $y_2^0 \geqslant 0$, let

$$f(y_1) = \sqrt{y_1 y_2^0},$$

defined for all $y_1 \geqslant 0$, be a short-run production function derived from the long-run function. Show that the average total cost function obtained from the long-run production function through equation $(4.5\text{-}1)$ with $b = 0$ is the same as that secured by using the short-run production functions in conjunction with $(5.2\text{-}2)$. Hence, in this case, the long-run average cost curve is the envelope of the family of short-run average total cost curves. Show also that each short-run average total cost curve is U-shaped as in Figure 5.6 and tangent to the long-run average cost curve at the minimum value on the short-run curve.

5.12 Give a geometric argument based on Figure 5.6(b) to show that, in reference to Figure 5.7, if $ATC(x^0) = LRAC(x^0)$, then $MC(x^0) = LRMC(x^0)$. Also show geometrically

$$MC(x) < LRMC(x), \quad \text{if } x < x^0,$$

and

$$MC(x) > LRMC(x), \quad \text{if } x > x^0.$$

5.13   Verify equation (5.2-16).

5.14**   Consider the production function $f(y)$ defined implicitly on Y by

$$y = x - \ln(1+x),$$

where y is a scalar variable. Show that $f(y) \geqslant 0$ for $y \geqslant 0$, $f(0) = 0$, $f'(y) > 1$ for $y > 0$ (f' is the first-order derivative of f), and that f is strictly concave on the interior of Y. Find the marginal cost function and prove that

$$0 < MC(r, x) < r,$$

and

$$\frac{dMC(x)}{dx} > 0,$$

for all $x > 0$ and $r > 0$. (Recall that the notation $MC(r, x)$ makes explicit the implicit r in $MC(x)$.) Graph TC, VC, ATC, AVC, and MC in a diagram similar to Figure 4.12. Derive the firm's output supply and input demand functions and specify their domains of definition.

5.15   Let $f(y_1, y_2)$ satisfy (4.1-2) – (4.1-5). Suppose also that f is linearly homogeneous and, except along rays from the origin (over which it is linear), strictly concave. Set $z = y_1/y_2$. Dividing $x = f(y_1, y_2)$ by y_2, obtain the equation

$$\frac{x}{y_2} = \nu(z),$$

where

$$\nu(z) = f(z, 1),$$

for all $z > 0$. Show that with $r_1 > 0$ and $r_2 > 0$ given, and with $p = \tilde{p} = 1$, profit maximization implies

$$r_1 = \nu'(z),$$

$$r_2 = \nu(z) - z\nu'(z),$$

where ν' is the derivative of ν, and z is evaluated at the maximum.

A picture of a typical ν appears in Figure 5.8. Let $z^0 > 0$ denote the profit maximizing point for some $r_1^0 > 0$ and $r_2^0 > 0$, where $p = 1$. Then the slope of the line tangent to the graph of ν at $(z^0, \nu(z^0))$ is equal to r_1^0. Convince yourself that the vertical intercept (at $z = 0$) of the same line is equal to r_2^0.

5.16* Prove that if f is strictly concave on the interior of Y, then so is the profit function $\pi(y)$ of (5.1-10). Without using the results of Table 4.1, show also that strict concavity of f (and $\left|\bar{F}(y)\right| \neq 0$ for all $y > 0$) implies strict convexity of $TC(x)$ and hence strict concavity of the profit function $\pi(x)$ of (5.1-3) on Γ.

5.17 Assuming $b = 0$ and $\pi(x) = 0$ for all x in Γ, derive the factor-price frontier for the production function of Exercises 4.6 and 4.11 with $\beta_1 + \beta_2 = 1$.

5.18 Derive the short-run total cost, input demand, and output supply functions for the profit-maximizing firm whose production function is

$$f(y_1, y_2) = \sqrt{y_1} + \sqrt{y_2}.$$

5.19 Consider a firm with production function

$$f(y_1, y_2) = a_1 y_1 + a_2 y_2 + c,$$

where $a_1 > 0$, $a_2 > 0$, and $c > 0$. In spite of the violation of (4.1-2) and (4.1-5), derive $TC(r, x)$ for $r_1/r_2 < a_1/a_2$.

Suppose the maximum amount of each input available to the firm is c/a_1. With $r_1/r_2 < a_1/a_2$ and $p > r_1/a_1$, what is the firm's profit-maximizing output?

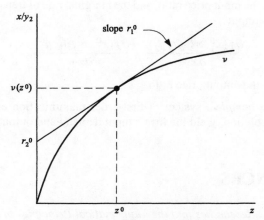

Figure 5.8 Profit maximization expressed in terms of the function v

5.20* Imagine a profit-maximizing firm with constant-returns-to-scale production function

$$f(y_1, y_2) = \sqrt{y_1 y_2},$$

and with zero fixed cost ($b = 0$). Assume the firm is able to sell all it produces at the price $p = 10$. Suppose the prices of its inputs are $r_1 = 1$ and $r_2 = 4$, and at those prices, the firm is only able to buy as much of them as it wants up to $y_1 = 5$ and $y_2 = 20$. How much of each input will the firm employ, and how much output will it produce? (Note that, in this case, the limitations on input availability permit the firm to uniquely maximize profit despite the constant returns to scale. But the profit-maximizing basket of inputs does *not* lie on the expansion path.)

5.21 Consider a firm that produces two outputs, x_1 and x_2, using two inputs, y_1 and y_2, according to the implicitly defined production function

$$f(x_1, x_2, y_1, y_2) = 0.$$

Assume f has sufficient properties to support the following:

a) Show that, at the profit-maximizing vector $(x_1^0, x_2^0, y_1^0, y_2^0)$, the marginal rate of technical substitution between inputs,

$$\frac{\partial f(x_1^0, x_2^0, y_1^0, y_2^0)}{\partial y_1} \bigg/ \frac{\partial f(x_1^0, x_2^0, y_1^0, y_2^0)}{\partial y_2},$$

equals the input price ratio, and the marginal rate of transformation between outputs,

$$\frac{\partial f(x_1^0, x_2^0, y_1^0, y_2^0)}{\partial x_1} \bigg/ \frac{\partial f(x_1^0, x_2^0, y_1^0, y_2^0)}{\partial x_2},$$

equals the output price ratio.

b) Give a *complete* system of first-order maximization equations that, upon solution, yield the firm's input demand and output supply functions.

REFERENCES

1. Cournot, A., *Researches into the Mathematical Principles of the Theory of Wealth*, T. Bacon trans. (New York: Kelley, 1960).

2. Katzner, D. W., *Static Demand Theory* (New York: Macmillan, 1970).
3. Marshall, A., *Principles of Economics*, 8th ed. (New York: Macmillan, 1948).
4. Pearce, I. F., "A Study in Price Policy," *Economica*, n.s. 23 (1956), pp. 114-127.
5. Rudin, W., *Principles of Mathematical Analysis*, 3rd ed. (New York: McGraw-Hill, 1976).
6. Samuelson, P. A., *Foundations of Economic Analysis* (Cambridge: Harvard University Press, 1947).
7. Silberberg, E., *The Structure of Economics* (New York: McGraw-Hill, 1978).
8. von Thünen, J. H., *The Isolated State in Relation to Agriculture and Political Economy*, v. 2, B. W. Dempsey, trans. In B. W. Dempsey, *The Frontier Wage* (Chicago: Loyola University Press, 1960), pp. 187-367.
9. Viner, J., "Cost Curves and Supply Curves," *Zeitschrift für Nationalökonomie* 3 (1931), pp. 23-46. Reprinted with a supplementary note in The American Economic Association's *Readings in Price Theory*, G. J. Stigler and K. E. Boulding, eds. (Chicago: Irwin, 1952), pp. 198-232.
10. Wicksell, K., *Lectures on Political Economy*, v. 1 (New York: Kelley, 1967).

Chapter 6

Markets in Isolation

Consumers buying outputs and selling factors and firms buying inputs and selling outputs all do so in markets. Indeed, as described earlier, a market is nothing more than an institutional arrangement to facilitate such exchanges. But markets do vary in size, procedures, and disposition. They may be economy-wide in scope or confined to small numbers of persons in a single room. In some markets exchange takes place directly between buyers and sellers. In others, brokers, agents, and auctioneers operate as intermediaries. And written contracts may or may not be a part of the exchange procedures.

The Walrasian view, however, abstracts from most of these details (Section 1.1). The only market elements taken into account are the numbers and size of buyers and sellers, whether the goods exchanged on the market are standardized (homogeneous), the cost of entering the market as a buyer or seller, and the information available to market participants concerning products, production, and prices. Recall that a market with a "large" number of "small" buyers and sellers, a single homogeneous or standardized commodity, free entry and exit, and the same product and price information available to everyone is called *perfectly competitive*. For present purposes, the phrase "large number of small buyers and sellers" is defined vaguely to mean each unit is sufficiently small and there are a sufficiently large number of them so that each believes its economic decisions have no effect on market price. The fact that such an impact might actually exist and be significant is ignored (see Chapter 11). Both buyers and sellers therefore view market prices as fixed parameters given to them and each thinks he is able to buy or sell as much as he wants at these prices. The cost of entry or exit is the cost of, respectively, starting up production from scratch or going out of business (the former is characterized more rigorously in Section 13.2). "Free entry and exit" means zero start-up and going-out-of-business costs as well as the absence of all other barriers (such as patents held by already existing firms, or government prohibitions against exit that prevent significant economic or social damage) to the entry of new and exit of old firms. The information requirement often is intended to imply that different prices for the market's good cannot simultaneously arise, and sometimes that production and hence cost functions of all firms in the market are identical.

It should be pointed out that the notion of perfect competition employed in this volume frequently incorporates the more moderate form of information availability that permits differences among firms. But, for the sake of simplicity, there is little reason not to focus attention in the present chapter on the extreme case in which all firms in any market are carbon copies of each other. Be aware, however, that for the most part this is a simplifying assumption only and does not significantly alter the general nature of the results.

Furthermore, the presence of market intermediaries, for example auctioneers, is assumed to have no impact on the final outcome achieved in a market. Because only final outcomes are relevant in the study of timeless activity and comparative statics (that is, the comparison of stationary states), such intermediaries between buyers and sellers may be ignored for now. However, the role of institutional arrangements surrounding auctioneers and the like becomes significant when the path by which the market achieves (or fails to achieve) its final outcome is examined. Discussion of this is postponed to Chapter 9.

It should also be clear that the models of Chapters 2 – 5 are entirely consistent with the assumptions of perfect competition in that firms and consumers regard prices as fixed. Moreover, implicit in the notion of goods and their prices in these models is the idea that the market for any commodity contains a single, homogeneous good. That is, each good is associated with a unique quantity and price variable. Any good corresponding to a different price variable must also have a different quantity variable and different demand and supply functions, and must be traded in a different market. These models of consumer and firm behavior, then, are taken to describe the behavior of individual units in a perfectly competitive market. Of course, free entry and exit and an appropriate information-availability requirement must be added to complete the picture.

Perfect competition, obviously, is a hypothetical structure that does not exist in actuality. Economists study it because (recall Section 1.2) it supplies an explanation of certain behaviors in their purest form, because it provides a standard for comparison with reality, and because it furnishes a basis for exploring modified and, perhaps, more realistic forms of market structures. The latter frequently are derived by altering those characteristics of perfect competition concerned with the standardization of goods in a market and the numbers and size of individual buying and selling units. Specifically, permitting variation in the market commodity (that is, a heterogeneous good) with all remaining elements intact yields *monopolistic competition*.[1] Retaining all characteristics of perfect competition except allowing sellers to be "large" enough to believe their decisions do influence market price results in *perfect oligopoly*. *Monopolistic oligopoly* arises upon introducing the above two modifications simultaneously. A market with a single seller (and hence with a homogeneous good and blocked entry of other potential sellers) is a *monopoly*. Other ways in which the characteristics of perfect competition might be transformed include buyers who believe they are large enough to influence market price (*monopsony*, that is, one buyer facing many small sellers, is one example), the possibility of nonfree entry in general, and the withholding of various kinds of information from certain buyers or sellers. Several nonperfect or imperfect forms of market structure are considered in Chapter 11.

The present chapter is concerned only with the partial-equilibrium analysis of the perfectly competitive market. As is implicit in the above discussion, this market has a single good that passes from sellers to buyers in return for certain numbers of units of a medium of exchange. The medium of exchange can be thought of either as another good or as "money" (see Chapter 7). In both cases, market price is the number of units of the medium of exchange traded per unit of the market commodity. When the sellers in a market are firms, remember, they constitute an industry. Only markets having firms as sellers, buyers, or both are discussed here. Section 7.1 considers perfectly competitive markets in which all participants are consumers.

Section 6.1 describes the short-run case and Section 6.2 deals with the long run. The former is a component of the short-run rendition of the particular grand view outlined in Section 1.4; the latter belongs to the long-run

---

[1]   Actually, the analysis of Section 11.3, which (in part) introduces a monopolistically competitive market into a model of an entire economy, treats this heterogeneity of the market commodity as an illusion on the part of the firm.

version. Section 6.3 is concerned with the effects on both input and output markets of imposing profits or sales taxes on the firms of an isolated industry.

6.1 THE SHORT-RUN PERFECTLY COMPETITIVE MARKET

Market demand and supply functions under perfect competition are obtained by summing, respectively, the demand and supply functions of all buyers and sellers in the market. When buyers are consumers, explicit characterization of market demand necessitates the introduction of the subscript and superscript k running over all individuals, $k = 1, \ldots, K$. Let x_{ik} denote quantities of good i for person k, and $h^k = (h^{1k}, \ldots, h^{Ik})$ represent k's demand function as defined in Section 2.3. For now, think of

$$x_i = \sum_{k=1}^{K} x_{ik}.$$

(The symbol x_i referred to individual rather than market quantities of good i in Chapters 2 and 3). Then the *market demand function*, H^i, for good i is given by

$$x_i = H^i(p, m_1, \ldots, m_K), \tag{6.1-1}$$

where m_k is the income[2] of person k, and

$$H^i(p, m_1, \ldots, m_K) = \sum_{k=1}^{K} h^{ik}(p, m_k).$$

The *market demand curve* for, say, good 1 is the graph of

$$x_1 = H^1(p_1, p_2^0, \ldots, p_I^0, m_1^0, \ldots, m_K^0),$$

where the superscript 0 denotes a fixed variate, and values of x_1 are measured along the horizontal axis with those of p_1 appearing on the vertical. Evidently, changes in the prices of other goods, namely, $p_2^0, \ldots, p_I^0$, or a variation in any

---

2 The interpretation of m_k varies according to the context in which the analysis is set. Recall that in Chapter 2 it was simply the amount person k had to spend, whereas in Section 3.3 it took the form of "nonwage" income. In subsequent chapters m_k will often disappear as an argument of consumer demand (and factor supply) functions because it is recognized there that m_k depends on prices.

person's income may induce a shift in the market demand curve. Market demand functions (6.1-1) are considered further in Section 8.3. A similar procedure yields market supplies of the factors of production from the individual supply functions described in Section 3.3.

If firms are the buyers or sellers, then the appropriate summation is over the demand or supply functions of the firm derived in Chapter 5. To illustrate, focus attention on the final commodity i. Suppose there are L_i firms in the industry, and let $x_{i\ell}$ represent quantities of good i produced and supplied by firm ℓ, where $\ell = 1, ..., L_i$. Write

$$x_i = \sum_{\ell=1}^{L_i} x_{i\ell}.$$

Confusion will not arise by using the same symbol x_i to denote both market quantities demanded and supplied. In any particular case, context implies the appropriate meaning. Firm ℓ's supply function is given by

$$x_{i\ell} = \begin{cases} g^{i\ell J+1}(r, p_i), & \text{if } r > 0, p_i \geqslant \widetilde{p}_i, \\ \\ 0, & \text{if } r > 0, \widetilde{p}_i > p_i > 0, \end{cases}$$

where $\widetilde{p}_i$ depends on r, and where $g^{i\ell J+1}$ and $\widetilde{p}_i$ are, respectively, the g^{J+1} and $\widetilde{p}$ of (5.1-8).[3] The components of r consist of the prices of only those inputs appearing in the production functions of the firms producing good i. The *market supply function*, G^i, is the sum of these individual functions over ℓ. But because the production, cost, and hence supply functions of each firm are identical (from the information availability requirement), the market supply

---

[3]   Of course, the assumptions underlying the derivation of (5.1-8) must hold. Thus, in addition to (4.1-2) − (4.1-5), the positivity of all marginal products either between the ridge lines (surfaces) up to a unique global maximum output if such a maximum exists, or throughout the interior of Y, the nonvanishing of the bordered Hessian determinant where marginal products are positive, and isoquants that do not touch the boundary of Y where nonnegatively sloped and strictly convex, either the production function generates cost functions as pictured in Figure 5.1 and the first-order partial derivatives of f take on (positive) values that are arbitrarily close to zero for some input baskets $y > 0$ along every expansion path (the Viner model of Theorem 5.1-25), or the production function is strictly concave, its Hessian determinant is nonvanishing everywhere, and its first-order partial derivatives take on all positive real numbers as function values over every expansion path (the strictly concave model of Theorem 5.1-24). As noted in Section 5.1, the latter assumptions imply $\widetilde{p} = 0$ for all $r > 0$ and simplify the supply function to

$$x_{i\ell} = g^{i\ell J+1}(r, p_i),$$

for all $(r, p) > 0$. In this case, (6.1-2) below must be modified accordingly.

equation reduces to

$$x_i = G^i(p_i, r) = \begin{cases} L_i g^{i\ell J+1}(r, p_i), & \text{if } r > 0, p_i \geqslant \widetilde{p}_i, \\ \\ 0, & \text{if } r > 0, \widetilde{p}_i > p_i > 0, \end{cases} \tag{6.1-2}$$

for any ℓ. The market supply curve is drawn, therefore, for fixed values of input prices r. More general formulations of firms' market supply functions are presented in Sections 7.2 and 8.2 in different contexts. Market input demand functions are obtained similarly by summing across firms and industries.

Consider now a market, say for good 1, in which buyers are consumers and sellers are firms. To set the partial-equilibrium context, let the prices of all other goods and the incomes of all consumers be fixed. As shown in Section 1.3, upon restricting attention to positive prices, market equilibrium occurs where, and only where, supply and demand intersect.[4] Hence equilibrium price is obtained as the solution of

$$H^1(p_1, p_2^0, \ldots, p_I^0, m_1^0, \ldots, m_K^0) = G^1(p_1, r^0), \tag{6.1-3}$$

where the superscript 0 indicates the variable values taken to be fixed. (If $\overline{p}_1$ is any equilibrium price, then $\overline{p}_1 \geqslant \widetilde{p}_1$ where, recall, $\widetilde{p}_1$ is the minimum value of average variable cost, dependent on r, in all of the industry's identical firms. This follows from the fact that when $p_1 < \widetilde{p}_1$, market supply is zero but market demand, which is generated by utility functions as described in Section 2.3, is positive. Hence no p_1 both smaller than $\widetilde{p}_1$ and satisfying equation (6.1-3) can exist.) Equilibrium quantity is found upon substitution of the equilibrium price and the fixed values of other prices and incomes into (6.1-1) or (6.1-2). A picture of this market in equilibrium along with a representative firm[5] in relation to the equilibrium is drawn in Figure 6.1 for the case in which the representative firm has Viner cost curves (Theorem 5.1-25). The same scale appears

---

[4]   It is interesting that in Ricardo's time there was some confusion as to whether the interaction of demand and supply did, indeed, determine market price. Ricardo, in fact, flatly stated that, "The opinion that the price of commodities depends solely on the proportion of supply to demand ... has been the source of much error ..." and argued instead that marked price is set by the cost of production [3, p. 382]. Shortly thereafter economists recognized that both propositions are true: Price is governed by supply and demand in the short run but by the cost of production in the long run. (See Mill [2, pp. 467, 468, 471]. The long-run case is discussed in Section 6.2.) Still later, Marshall colorfully likened demand and supply to the blades of a pair of scissors [1, p. 348].

[5]   The notion of the representative firm is due to Marshall. Although there is not much to it in the case of identical firms, this concept is quite useful in general when differences in production and cost functions are allowed. See Marshall [1, pp. 317, 342, 459-460] and n. 6 on the next page.

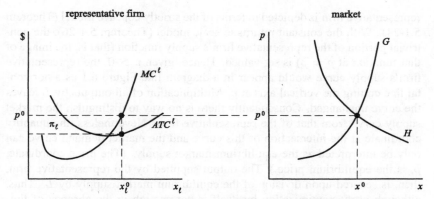

Figure 6.1 Market and representative firm in short-run equilibrium

on each vertical axis. These are lined up so that movement from one to the other along a horizontal line does not change the scale value. To simplify notation the subscript and superscript 1 is dropped. The demand curve is labeled H, and the supply curve is labeled G. (Recall that G is the sum of L identical marginal cost curves for p at least as large as minimum average variable cost.) Market quantities are denoted by the scalar x and firm ℓ's quantities by the scalar x_ℓ. Market equilibrium occurs at (p^0, x^0). Here firm ℓ is producing at x_ℓ^0 and earning a short-run profit identified by the rectangle with the symbol π_ℓ. Note that $L x_\ell^0 = x^0$ and that the two horizontal axes in Figure 6.1 have different scales for measuring quantities imposed upon them. In keeping with an earlier convention (Section 1.3), it is not necessary that the number of firms, L, be an integer. The spirit of perfect competition is preserved as long as a "small" change, say an increase, in L is always accompanied by a "small" increase in market supply. (This is certainly true of equation (6.1-2) because in that formulation the number of firms is multiplied by the supply of the representative firm.[6]) Moreover, as suggested above, the market demand curve in Figure 6.1 has to be sufficiently far out from the origin so that multiplication of the representative firm's supplies by L yields a market supply curve that intersects the market demand curve above the shut-down point $\widetilde{p}$.

An appropriately modified diagram based on Figure 5.2 applies when the

---

[6]   If firms were not identical and L could be any real number rather than only an integer, then the proper formulation of (6.1-2) would be either to interpret firm ℓ as Marshall's representative or average firm (recall n. 5 on the previous page) from which market totals could be calculated upon multiplication by L, or to write (6.1-2) in terms of an integral of the individual supply functions over ℓ.

representative firm is depicted in terms of the strictly concave model (Theorem 5.1-24). With the constant returns to scale model (Theorem 5.1-26), the non-trivial portion of the representative firm's supply function (that is, the image of that function at $p = \widetilde{p}$) is set-valued. Hence, given $r > 0$, the representative firm's supply curve would appear in a diagram like Figure 6.1 as a horizontal line cutting the vertical axis at $\widetilde{p}$. Multiplication of all outputs by L leaves the curve unchanged. Consequently there is no way to distinguish the market supply curve from that of the representative firm. Nevertheless, the quantity coordinate at the intersection of this curve and the market demand curve can only be interpreted as the equilibrium market supply. (The price coordinate, $\widetilde{p}$, is the equilibrium price.) The output supplied by the representative firm, then, is secured upon division of the equilibrium market supply by L. Thus, although profit maximization by itself is not enough in the absence of limitations on input availability (recall Exercise 5.20), profit maximization plus interaction with market demand is sufficient to determine a unique output for constant returns to scale firms under perfect competition.

Equation (6.1-3) emphasizes the partial-equilibrium character of the analysis of isolated markets. (Recall Section 1.3.) Equilibrium price and quantity are determined for the fixed values $p_2^0, \ldots, p_I^0, m_1^0, \ldots, m_K^0$, and r^0. There is no guarantee that other markets are in equilibrium at these values. Changes in any of them generally modify equilibrium in the market for good 1 by inducing shifts in demand or supply. Ignored is the possibility that this latter modification of equilibrium in the market for good 1 may impact on other markets, causing still further variation in the "fixed" values, and hence affecting again the equilibrium in the market for good 1. Moreover, the components of the input price vector r include only prices of those inputs used in the production of good 1. Nothing is said in (6.1-3) about the prices of excluded inputs. Such prices are presumed independent of demand, supply, and hence equilibrium in the market for good 1.

Each kind of market considered in this volume, namely, the final commodity, intermediate commodity, and factor markets of Table 1.1, can be viewed similarly. In all final commodity markets, of course, firms are sellers, and hence a picture similar to that of Figure 6.1 applies. When attention centers on intermediate goods markets where firms are both buyers and sellers, a corresponding diagram in which the demand curve is based on the representative buying firm's value of marginal product curve (as in Figure 5.4) is relevant. And, in the case of factor markets, the demand side emerges from firms' value of marginal product curves while the supply side either derives from consumer utility maximization or reflects fixed factor quantities as described in Section

3.3. As also indicated in Section 3.3, only factor markets for the particular types of land and labor in use are considered for now. In general, markets (and associated functions and equations) appear and disappear according as goods enter and exit the circular flow of commodities around the economy described in Figure 1.1. The interactions occurring among existing markets in such an economy are taken up upon discarding the partial equilibrium approach in Chapter 7.

6.2 PERFECTLY COMPETITIVE MARKETS IN THE LONG RUN

When sellers are firms, market equilibrium in the long run under perfect competition requires more than maximization on the part of individual units and the equality of supply and demand. For as long as sellers are earning positive profits (and information availability, that is, the identical-firms supposition, ensures everyone receives the same profit), new firms are attracted to the industry. Under the assumption of free entry (another of the characteristics defining perfect competition) there are no cost or other barriers preventing these firms from entering as additional producers and sellers. The presumption is, then, that entry does take place. Although the dynamic rules governing the entry of new firms are not considered here, it is still clear that p^0 in Figure 6.1 cannot be a long-run equilibrium price. With producing units entering, the short-run supply curve shifts outward. This continues until all profits disappear and equilibrium is achieved at a price equal to the minimum long-run average cost of all firms. (The assumption of identical firms ensures that the minimum long-run average cost is the same in all firms.) A similar argument applies to firms leaving the industry when long-run profits are negative. Again, the dynamic rules determining which firms depart are not specified.[7] The fact that profits vanish and the issue of why firms should produce under such conditions have been mentioned in Section 5.2. As indicated there, the latter is taken up once more

---

[7] One way to frame the dynamics involved and, at the same time, enrich the description of the conditions of exit and entry, is by dropping the assumption of identical firms. In that case, some firms in the perfectly competitive industry may in fact be realizing positive profits at long-run equilibrium by reason of lower costs arising from differing production functions. Under such conditions, it may be only the "marginal firms" whose minimum long-run average cost equals the output-market price and therefore generate zero profit. These firms would be the first to exit the industry were the market price to start to fall; the remaining firms would, at least initially, merely realize diminished, but still positive profits. On the other hand, with price increases, higher-cost firms would be attracted into the industry.

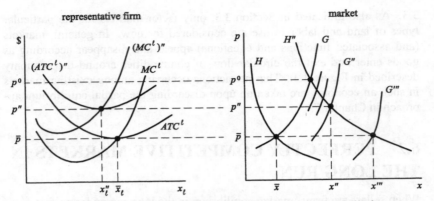

Figure 6.2 Market and representative firm in long-run equilibrium

in Section 13.3.

The representative firm and the market in long-run equilibrium appear in Figure 6.2 with the representative firm having Viner cost curves in both the short run and the long run. Again, the vertical axes are lined up in the usual way and the quantity scales on the two horizontal axes are distinct. Subscripts and superscripts indicating the particular good in question have been dropped. Long-run market demand, H, is obtained from, say, utility maximization by consumers in the appropriate long-run context. The analysis is identical to that of Chapters 2 and 3 except for an extended time frame. Short-run market supply is labeled G. Short-run average total cost, ATC^ℓ, is that curve tangent to the long-run average cost curve at the latter's minimum point. Short-run marginal cost is denoted by MC^ℓ. (Recall that G is made up of the sum of short-run marginal cost curves.) It is not necessary to include the long-run cost curves in the diagram. Long-run equilibrium price is $\overline{p}$, and the associated firm and market long-run equilibrium quantities are, respectively, $\overline{x}_\ell$ and $\overline{x}$. At long-run equilibrium, $\overline{p}$, the minimum long-run average cost of each firm, and the minimum short-run average total cost of each firm are all the same.

Like the discussion of the long-run behavior of the individual firm at the end of Section 5.2, addition of the long-run zero-profit condition here requires alteration of the original conception of the model. For in this particular case, attaching that condition overdetermines the usual system of equations describing market equilibrium price. The equality of demand and supply cannot determine price if price has already been set at the minimum long-run average cost of each firm. Internal consistency, then, requires that either one equation has to be dropped or a "new" variable must be inserted into the system. Because both equations are essential to the ordinary characterization of long-run equilibrium, the only alternative is the latter.

To be more precise, consider the market for good 1. Because all firms are identical, the representative firm can be taken to be firm 1. Let input prices r^0 be given. Assume that the production function of firm 1 is such that its long-run average cost has a unique minimum with respect to x_{11}, namely, min $LRAC^{11}$. Then long-run market equilibrium price, $\bar{p}_1$, is found from

$$\bar{p}_1 = \min LRAC^{11}. \tag{6.2-1}$$

Clearly, long-run equilibrium price depends only on the given values of input prices and the production function. With market price known, the equality of short-run supply and long-run demand at $\bar{p}_1$, (written as equation (6.1-3) with $p_1 = \bar{p}_1$ and H^1 interpreted in long-run terms, and pictured in Figure 6.2 with the superscripts on H and G dropped) adds independent information to (6.2-1) if L_1, the number of firms in the industry, is interpreted as a variable determined by (6.1-3). That is, making the identical-firm assumption explicit by substituting from (6.1-2) with $i = 1$ into (6.1-3), L_1 is found from:

$$H^1(\bar{p}_1, p_2^0, \ldots, p_I^0, m_1^0, \ldots, m_K^0) = L_1 g^{11J+1}(r^0, \bar{p}_1). \tag{6.2-2}$$

(Observe that the superscript on g indicates, as in equation (6.1-2), the $J + I^{\text{st}}$ function — that is, the (short-run) supply function — of firm 1 in industry 1.) Long-run market equilibrium quantity is obtained upon substitution of $\bar{p}_1, p_2^0, \ldots, p_I^0, m_1^0, \ldots, m_K^0$ into (6.1-1) with $i = 1$, or $\bar{p}_1$, r^0, and the previously determined value for L_1 into (6.1-2), again with $i = 1$. Thus addition of the long-run zero profit condition permits determination of the number of firms in the industry. As pointed out in Section 1.3, solutions of (6.2-2) producing a noninteger value for L_1, although empirically irrelevant, do not invalidate the model.

Note that long-run equilibrium cannot be thought of in terms of an intersection of the long-run demand and supply curves in the usual way. This is because the long-run supply of the firm is inexpressible as a single-valued function of output price given fixed values of input prices (Section 5.2). To each collection of input price values there corresponds only one market output price. Variation of quantity in response to output price modification is impossible. Thus in Figure 6.2 long-run market supply can be represented in one of two ways: either by taking the dependent variable x in the typical supply relation as fixed for all values of the "independent" variable p, which produces a vertical straight line through, say, (p'', x''); or by taking p (now actually de-

pendent on r) as fixed for all values of x, which gives a horizontal straight line
through the same (p'', x'').

It has already been pointed out in Section 5.2 that long-run equilibrium
with strictly concave production functions (that is, with the strictly concave
model of Theorem 5.1-24 set in the long-run context) is not important because, in such a case, equation (6.2-1) implies a market price of zero. If firm
production functions exhibit constant returns to scale (the long-run version of
the constant returns to scale model of Theorem 5.1-26), then long-run average costs are constant over all levels of output (Table 4.1). Long-run marginal
costs are identical to long-run average costs and, with profits vanishing, are
everywhere equal to output price. Hence, like the short-run constant returns to
scale regime, market price can be set as in (6.2-1) and market quantity can be
obtained from the demand function. This defines long-run market equilibrium.
Nevertheless, there is still not enough information to deduce both the output of
each firm and the number of firms in the industry. Specification of the number
of firms as in short-run analysis, then, permits inference of the output of each
firm in the present situation. Rather than the entry and exit of firms, in this
case it is the size of the output of existing firms that adjusts to achieve long-run
equilibrium.

Now suppose long-run market equilibrium at $(\overline{p}, \overline{x})$ in Figure 6.2 is dis-
turbed by a shift in demand from H to H''. Then market price rises to p^0,
and firms immediately begin to experience positive profits. As new firms enter, the short-run supply curve moves outward, and prices and profits start to
fall. The point at which this process stops and long-run equilibrium is re-
established depends on what is happening in the markets where firms are purchasing their inputs.[8] If input prices stay constant (perhaps increases in input
demand are offset by increases in input supply as new firms enter the input
industries, or perhaps production in these industries is subject to constant returns to scale), the cost curves of the representative firm are not changed and
the long-run equilibrium price remains at $\overline{p}$. Long-run quantity supplied by
the representative firm is still $\overline{x}_\ell$. The additional firms in the industry boost
the short-run supply curve to G''' and the long-run market equilibrium quantity to x'''. If, on the other hand, input prices rise, then costs go up. Hence
entry of new firms squeezes profits between declining revenues and increasing costs. The new long-run equilibrium must therefore settle at a price such
as p'', where $\overline{p} < p'' < p^0$, with short-run supply curve G'' and short-run av-

---

[8]   Even if it is assumed that no firm by itself can have an impact on the market price of any
input, the expansion of an industry by the entry of new firms is potentially of a different order
of magnitude and can still cause input prices to change.

erage and marginal cost curves $(ATC^\ell)''$ and $(MC^\ell)''$. Although Figure 6.2 shows $\overline{x}_\ell > x''_\ell$, the new output supplied by the representative firm x''_ℓ may, in general, be greater than, less than or equal to the old output $\overline{x}_\ell$, depending on the manner in which the cost curves of the repesentative firm shift. Likewise, were input prices and hence cost curves to fall, long-run equilibrium would reappear at a price below $\overline{p}$ (not shown in Figure 6.2). These three situations are referred to, respectively, as cases of *constant input costs*, *external diseconomies*, and *external economies*. The word "external" reflects the fact that the final long-run equilibrium depends on factors outside of the market, and hence of the firms, in question.

6.3   TAXATION

The analysis of taxing an isolated, perfectly competitive market usually is concerned with the immediate effects of the tax upon the individual consumers and firms in the market and upon market equilibrium.[9] Of course, changes in input prices resulting from induced variations in factor demands due to the tax tend to transform firms' costs and hence have a further impact on output markets, whereas alterations in output price from a tax similarly impose modifications in input markets. Moreover, to the extent that the government employs revenues obtained from the tax in a manner that alters market demand and supply (either directly or by forcing changes in the prices of other goods), the final outcome cannot be determined until all relevant government behavior is also known. An example is provided in Section 14.2. For isolated markets, however, it is customary to dismiss all secondary or feedback developments and concentrate on the initial impact. This will be the first approach taken here; thereafter limited feedback effects will be introduced. Only profits and sales taxes imposed on firms are considered, and their effects on both output and input markets are explored. Once again, the method of analysis is comparative statics. Stationary states reflecting short-run or long-run equilibria are compared with and without the tax.

A firm's profit can be taxed directly by exacting a fixed sum over the instant (or period) in question or, more commonly, by assessing a fraction of the difference between revenue and cost. The former levy requires payment of a particular amount regardless of the quantity of output produced and can be thought of as an additional fixed cost, possibly arising because the firm must purchase a license in order to operate; the latter tax, which is proportional to

---

[9]   Subsidies or negative taxes are handled analogously.

profit, is collected only when profit is positive. In neither case does the imposition of the tax modify the firm's profit maximizing output or input quantities
(Exercise 6.3). For the short run, then, there is no change in behavior on the
part of the firm. Hence market equilibrium price and quantity are unaffected.
Firms' profits, of course, are lowered by the amount of the tax paid. In the
long run, because the difference between revenues and costs vanishes at equilibrium, the fraction-of-profits tax is of no consequence. If the market starts
at long-run equilibrium, however, the fixed-sum tax, which adds a fixed cost
where none formerly existed, initially results in negative profits. Hence this
tax drives some firms from the industry, thereby reducing market quantity and
raising market price.[10] Long-run equilibrium is restored when market price
rises to the level of the minimum of the new (if input prices have changed)
long-run average cost plus tax paid per unit of output.

The markets for the industry's inputs are affected similarly. Because
there is no change in behavior by individual firms (that is, buyers) in the short
run, market demand is, at least initially, unaltered. The tax has no impact on
short-run input prices and quantities. But if, as described above for the long
run, the tax drives some firms out of the industry, and if the demand for inputs
by the taxed industry constitutes significant portions of the market demands for
those inputs, then the latter input demands will decline. In that case, long-run
equilibrium input prices and quantities fall. The feedback consequences on
firms' costs and hence on output are ignored.

There are two kinds of sales taxes to be examined. The first is a *specific*
tax of, say, τ dollars per unit of output sold. Dropping the subscript i indicating
the industry and output in question, market quantities are denoted by the scalar
x. The output of firm ℓ is x_ℓ, where $\ell = 1, \ldots, L$. As in Chapters 4 and 5,
production functions are given by

$$x_\ell = f^\ell(y_\ell), \quad \ell = 1, \ldots, L, \tag{6.3-1}$$

where y_ℓ is the vector of inputs employed by the ℓth firm. Expressing profit
as a function of output given fixed input prices (recall equations (5.1-1) and
(5.1-3)),

$$\pi^\ell(x_\ell) = p x_\ell - TC^\ell(x_\ell) - \tau x_\ell,$$

where the superscript ℓ identifies π and TC for the firm in question. If firm ℓ
chooses output so as to maximize profit, then

$$p = MC^\ell(x_\ell) + \tau. \tag{6.3-2}$$

---

[10] Recall the discussion on p. 233 including that of n. 7.

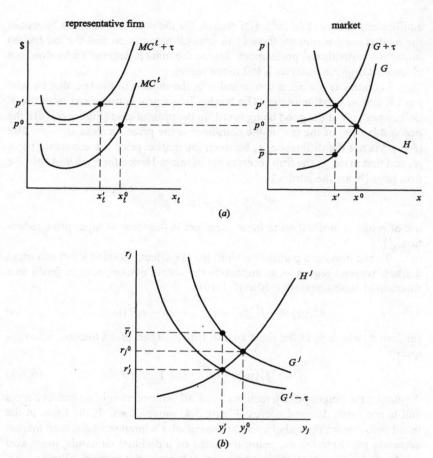

Figure 6.3 Specific tax imposed on the output of an isolated industry –
short-run equilibrium before and after the tax: (*a*) output market and
representative firm; (*b*) an input market

A short-run case is illustrated in Figure 6.3(a). Before-tax equilibrium is
at (p^0, x^0) with the representative firm producing x_ℓ^0. Upon imposition of the
tax, the relevant firm and industry short-run supply curves (the latter, recall, is
the sum of the former) are labeled, respectively, $MC^\ell + \tau$ and $G + \tau$. These,
again respectively, are vertically parallel to MC^ℓ and G, having been shifted
upward by τ everywhere. Equation (6.3-2) is satisfied at (p', x_ℓ'), and market

equilibrium occurs at (p', x'). (Of course, for the case in which the buyers in the market are consumers, there is an implicit assumption that the tax has no impact on individuals' preferences. Hence the market demand curve does not change.) Long-run analysis is left to the reader.

Economists are often concerned with the *burden* of the tax, that is, who pays it and in what amounts. The burden frequently is measured in terms of dollars per unit of the good being taxed. In the present case (Figure 6.3(a)), the per-unit burden of the tax on the consumer is the price increase $p' - p^0$. But $p' - p^0$ is not the difference, τ, between the market price the consumer pays, p', and that price, $\overline{p}$, the firm receives net of taxes. Hence for each unit sold the firm pays (bears the burden)

$$p^0 - \overline{p} = \tau - (p' - p^0)$$

out of profit or shifts it on to input suppliers in the form of input price reductions.[11]

To see how, in a parallel fashion, the tax affects isolated short-run input markets without regard to its impact on the output market, rewrite profit as a function of inputs analogously to (5.1-10):

$$\pi^\ell(y_\ell) = p f^\ell(y_\ell) - r \cdot y_\ell - b_\ell - \tau f^\ell(y_\ell),$$

for firm ℓ, where b_ℓ is the fixed cost in firm ℓ. Then profit maximization requires

$$[p - \tau] f_j^\ell(y_\ell) = r_j, \quad j = 1, \ldots, J. \tag{6.3-3}$$

Assuming the output price p remains fixed, all value of marginal product curves and hence input demand curves (Figure 5.4) move down. If the firms in the taxed industry are the only buyers in the industry's input markets, then market demands for these inputs, being the sums of individual demands, must also fall to the same extent. (Were there other buyers, the market effects would be reduced accordingly.) These changes are pictured for input j in Figure 6.3(b). The before-tax equilibrium occurs at (r_j^0, y_j^0) with demand curve G^j and supply curve H^j. After-tax results are (r_j', y_j'). (Notice that although G^j has shifted downward to the curve labeled $G^j - \tau$ in Figure 6.3(b), equation (6.3-3) implies that the vertical lengths between these curves vary with y_j.)

---

[11]   As a matter of social policy, governments may decide to impose taxes on certain commodities and provide subsidies to others. The extent to which this is done may depend, for example, on the manner in which the burden of a tax, or the benefit of a subsidy, falls on the supplier of the commodity. That, in turn, as is illustrated in Table 6.2 below, will depend on the slopes of the market demand and market supply curves.

The tax has forced sellers to accept a lower price; their tax burden per unit of input j is $r_j^0 - r_j'$. Again, the difference $\overline{r}_j - r_j^0$ comes out of profit or is shifted to the buyers of the firm's output. Of course, to the extent that the firms in the taxed industry constitute less than the full complement of buyers in any input market, the impact of the tax on that market is reduced accordingly. Extension of this argument to the long-run case is not considered.

Observe that the mathematical expressions for after-tax output supply and input demand functions are obtained by solving, respectively, (6.3-2) and (6.3-3) to express quantities as appropriate functions of $r = (r_1, \ldots, r_J)$, and $p - \tau$. Thus, for example, the output supply function for firm ℓ corresponding to (5.1-8) would be

$$
x_\ell = \begin{cases} g^{\ell J+1}(r, p - \tau), & \text{if } r > 0, p - \tau \geqslant \widetilde{p}, \\[2mm] 0, & \text{if } r > 0, \widetilde{p} > p - \tau > 0, \end{cases}
$$

where $\widetilde{p}$ depends on r, and the sum of the $g^{\ell J+1}$ over the L firms would generate the market supply function $G(p - \tau, r)$. The market curve labeled $G + \tau$ in Figure 6.3(a) is the graph of G with $r_1, \ldots, r_J$ and τ fixed. Market equilibrium after imposition of the tax is described by the equality of supply and demand as in (6.1-3).

As noted, the geometric analysis of the effect of imposing a specific tax on an isolated output market (Figure 6.3(a)) is based on the supposition that input prices remain constant. Likewise, the parallel geometric approach to the impact of the same tax on those isolated markets in which the firms that produce the taxed output purchase their inputs (Figure 6.3(b)) rests on an unchanging output price. But these diagrams tell only part of the story because, as previously indicated, both input and output prices are modified by the tax. Indeed, changes in output price cause changes in the values of marginal products and hence changes in input demands; and changes in input prices cause changes in costs and hence changes in output supplies. The complete picture for an isolated combination of an output market and the input markets to which that output relates is secured by removing the requirements that first input and then output prices are fixed, and by letting all resulting feedback effects work themselves out. This can be accomplished with a mathematical calculation of the final positions of the firms and of the input and output markets which accounts for all simultaneous interactions among input demands, output supply, input prices, and output price. (The after-tax input demand and output supply functions obtained above are implicit in such a calculation.) Moreover, by comparing before-tax profits with profits after both the specific tax is imposed and all market price and quantity adjustments have occurred, the extent to which firms are able to shift the burden of the tax to buyers of their output and sellers of their inputs can be determined. It is instructive to examine a simple short-run illustration. Suppose firms employ but one input. Then the equations describing the behavior of the representative firm under taxation are, from (6.3-1) and (6.3-3),

$$x = f(y),$$

$$[p - \tau]f'(y) = r,$$

(6.3-4)

where, for convenience, subscripts and superscripts ℓ and j have been dropped and f' denotes the derivative of f. Because all L firms are identical, the output market is in equilibrium (with market demand function H) when

$$xL = H(p).$$

(6.3-5)

Notice that fixed values of incomes and other final commodity prices are subsumed in the symbol H. Moreover, H is taken to be independent of r. Assuming, again to keep matters simple, that the industry under scrutiny is the sole buyer of its input, equilibrating demand and supply in the input market gives

$$yL = Z(r),$$

(6.3-6)

where the input-market supply function Z is supposed independent of p. (Neither the symbol G nor the symbol H is used to denote the supply function in equations (6.3-6) in order to avoid confusion with previous notation.) Equations (6.3-4) − (6.3-6) form a system of four equations in the four unknowns x, p, y, r, and two parameters τ and L. When unique solutions exist, values of the variables can be computed and compared for different values of τ. In particular, before-tax and after-tax situations can be contrasted by solving the system for $\tau = 0$ and $\tau = \tau^0 > 0$.

When (6.3-4) − (6.3-6) are solved, profit of the representative firm is given by

$$\pi = (p - \tau)x - ry - b.$$

(6.3-7)

If π at $\tau = 0$ is larger than π at $\tau = \tau^0 > 0$, then firms are unable to shift all of the burden of the tax onto buyers of their output and sellers of their input.

Alternatively, calculations can be expressed in terms of rates of change. Of interest here are the derivatives

$$\frac{dx}{d\tau}, \ \frac{dp}{d\tau}, \ \frac{dy}{d\tau}, \ \frac{dr}{d\tau},$$

(6.3-8)

as determined by (6.3-4) – (6.3-6). Evaluation of them at τ^0 indicates modulations in x, p, y, and r generated by small changes in τ from τ^0. Setting $\tau^0 = 0$, before-tax and after-tax comparisons are achieved. Once the derivatives of (6.3-8) are known, $d\pi/d\tau$ can be obtained by differentiating (6.3-7):

$$\frac{d\pi}{d\tau} = (p - \tau)\frac{dx}{d\tau} + x\left(\frac{dp}{d\tau} - 1\right) - r\frac{dy}{d\tau} - y\frac{dr}{d\tau}. \qquad (6.3\text{-}9)$$

If $d\pi/d\tau$ turns out to be negative for some (x, p, y, r, τ), then at that (x, p, y, r, τ), profit declines as a result of imposing (or increasing) the tax, and hence at least part of the burden of the tax (or of increasing the tax) is borne by the firm.

Computation of the above derivatives is not difficult. Differentiation of (6.3-4) – (6.3-6) and listing the differentiated version of equation (6.3-5) first yields

$$-L\frac{dx}{d\tau} \; + H'(p)\frac{dp}{d\tau} \qquad\qquad\qquad\qquad = 0,$$

$$\frac{dx}{d\tau} \qquad\qquad -f'(y)\frac{dy}{d\tau} \qquad\qquad = 0,$$

$$f'(y)\frac{dp}{d\tau} \; + [p - \tau]f''(y)\frac{dy}{d\tau} \qquad -\frac{dr}{d\tau} = f'(y),$$

$$L\frac{dy}{d\tau} \; -Z'(r)\frac{dr}{d\tau} = 0,$$

where H', f', and Z' are first-order derivatives and f'' is the derivative of second order. Applying Cramer's rule and simplifying gives

$$\frac{dx}{d\tau} = \frac{1}{|A|} H'Z'[f']^2,$$

$$\frac{dp}{d\tau} = \frac{1}{|A|} LZ'[f']^2,$$

$$\frac{dy}{d\tau} = \frac{1}{|A|} H'Z'f', \qquad\qquad (6.3\text{-}10)$$

$$\frac{dr}{d\tau} = \frac{1}{|A|} LH'f',$$

where

$$|A| = \begin{vmatrix} -L & H' & 0 & 0 \\ 1 & 0 & -f' & 0 \\ 0 & f' & [p-\tau]f'' & -1 \\ 0 & 0 & L & -Z' \end{vmatrix},$$

and functional arguments have been eliminated to simplify notation. Upon expansion,

$$|A| = [p-\tau]H'Z'f'' + LZ'[f']^2 - LH'. \tag{6.3-11}$$

Combining (6.3-9) with (6.3-10), (6.3-4), and (6.3-11) yields

$$\frac{d\pi}{d\tau} = \frac{H'}{|A|}(xL - x[p-\tau]Z'f'' - yLf'). \tag{6.3-12}$$

Clearly the differential expressions of (6.3-10) and (6.3-12) are valid only when $|A| \neq 0$. One way of inferring their signs is provided by the following proposition.

Theorem 6.3-13 Suppose f is strictly concave where defined and $f(0) = 0$. Let (x^0, p^0, y^0, r^0) be a solution of (6.3-4) − (6.3-6) given $\tau = \tau^0 \geqslant 0$. If $f'(y^0) > 0$, $H'(p^0) < 0$, and $Z'(r^0) > 0$, and if $p^0 > \tau^0$, then evaluated at (x^0, p^0, y^0, r^0) and τ^0, the derivatives $dx/d\tau < 0$, $dp/d\tau > 0$, $dy/d\tau < 0$, $dr/d\tau < 0$, and $d\pi/d\tau < 0$.

Proof: The strict concavity of f and the sign conditions assumed in the theorem ensure, according to (6.3-11), that $|A| > 0$. Hence, from (6.3-10), $dx/d\tau < 0$, $dp/d\tau > 0$, $dy/d\tau < 0$, and $dr/d\tau < 0$. Moreover, the strict concavity of f and the property $f(0) = 0$ imply, by Theorem 4.2-23, that

$$f(y) > yf'(y), \tag{6.3-14}$$

for all y in the domain of f. Using the hypotheses of the theorem together with (6.3-12), (6.3-14), and the first equation of (6.3-4), $d\pi/d\tau < 0$.

Q.E.D.

Thus if the output demand curve slopes downward, the input supply curve upward, $f(0) = 0$, marginal productivity is positive, f is strictly concave, and if the tax is less than the market price, then all of the price-quantity results illustrated by the diagrams of Figure 6.3 are established for the imposition of a small tax by setting $\tau^0 = 0$. In addition, the inequality $d\pi/d\tau < 0$ means that firms are unable to shift all of the burden of the tax to buyers of their output and sellers of their input.

Table 6.1 Possible combinations of slopes of output demand and input supply curves

Output market	Input market		
	$Z'(r0) = 0$	$0 < Z'(r0) < \infty$	$Z'(r0) = \infty$
$H'(p^0) = 0$	1	2	3
$-\infty < H'(p^0) < 0$	4	5	6
$H'(p^0) = -\infty$	7	8	9

Similar, if not identical, results are obtained upon altering the hypotheses of Theorem 6.3-13 in various ways. Of special concern are situations in which, assuming $f''(y) < 0$ for all $y > 0$, output demand or input supply curves could be vertical or horizontal. The possibilities are assigned numbers in Table 6.1. (Due to the usual inversion of axes when drawing demand and supply curves as described on pp. 19-20 above, zero derivatives correspond to vertical curves; whereas "infinite" derivatives imply horizontal ones.) For each case, and assuming appropriate limits exist, the signs of the differential expressions of (6.3-10) and (6.3-12) can be read from Table 6.2 (see Exercise 6.4). These are based on the same hypotheses as Theorem 6.3-13 except for the obvious modifications in the sign conditions on $H'(p^0)$ and $Z'(r^0)$. Note that the indeterminacy of circumstance 1 is to be expected. In this case firms can shift the burden of the tax to output buyers or input sellers or both. Any magnitudes of these shifts (as long as they do not exceed the amount of the tax) are consistent with profit maximization and market equilibrium under perfect competition, and leave input and output quantities unchanged. The model of (6.3-4) – (6.3-6) in case 1 cannot, by itself, determine p and r uniquely. Notice also that only in situations 2 and 3 is $d\pi/d\tau = 0$. Here (and in case 1 if they so choose) firms are able to avoid any burden from the tax.

In concluding this chapter, very brief mention should be made of the ad valorem tax. This is the second (and empirically more common) form of the sales tax alluded to earlier. Unlike the specific tax characterized as so many dollars per unit of output sold, the *ad valorem* tax is expressed as a fraction, ν, of the output price or revenue of the firm. The ℓth firm's profits become

$$\pi^\ell(x_\ell) = px_\ell - TC^\ell(x_\ell) - \nu px_\ell,$$

Table 6.2 Effect of tax changes in alternative situations

Situation from Table 6.1	Derivatives of (6.3-10) and (6.3-12)				
	$dx/d\tau$	$dp/d\tau$	$dy/d\tau$	$dr/d\tau$	$d\pi/d\tau$
1	0	indeterminate	0	indeterminate	indeterminate
2	0	1	0	0	0
3	0	1	0	0	0
4	0	0	0	negative	negative
5 (Th. 6.3-13)	negative	positive	negative	negative	negative
6	negative	positive	negative	0	negative
7	0	0	0	negative	negative
8	negative	0	negative	negative	negative
9	negative	0	negative	0	negative

and the maximizing first-order condition is

$$p(1 - \nu) = MC^{\ell}(x_{\ell}).$$

Solving for x_{ℓ} as a function of $p(1 - \nu)$ and input prices yields the supply function of the firm's output. Analysis now proceeds in much the same way as before. Details are left to the reader.

EXERCISES

6.1 Let p_2, r_1, r_2 and m be fixed parameters. Under perfectly competitive conditions, determine the short-run market demand and supply functions for output 1, and the market equilibrium values for p_1 and x_1 when the market consists of

a) K consumers with identical incomes m and identical utility functions

$$u^k(x_{1k}, x_{2k}) = x_{1k}x_{2k}, \quad k = 1, \dots, K;$$

b) L_1 firms with identical production functions (from Exercise 5.9)

$$f^{1\ell}(y_{1\ell1}, y_{1\ell2}) = (\min[y_{1\ell1}, y_{1\ell2}])^{1/2}, \quad \ell = 1, \dots, L_1,$$

where $y_{1\ell j}$ represents input j of firm ℓ.

How much of output 1 is produced by each firm and consumed by each person?

6.2 Let good 1 be produced by identical firms and sold to consumers in a perfectly competitive market. Suppose the prices of all other commodities are fixed. Assume input prices are specified as numerical values in such a manner that, together with the production function, the long-run total cost curve of firm 1 in this market is (from Exercise 4.12)

$$LRTC^1(x_{11}) = (x_{11})^3 - 4(x_{11})^2 + 8x_{11}.$$

Let the long-run market demand curve be given by

$$x_1 = 200 - 25p_1.$$

Find the long-run market equilibrium price and quantity and the number of firms in the industry.

6.3 Show that the imposition of either a fixed-sum or a fraction-of-profits tax on the perfectly competitive individual firm has no effect on its profit maximizing output or input quantities.

6.4* Assuming all limits exist as $H'(p^0)$ and $Z'(r^0)$ approach zero and plus or minus infinity, verify the results of Table 6.2.

6.5 In Exercise 6.1, let $K = 10$, $L_1 = 100$, $m = 10$, $r_1 = 4$, and $r_2 = 2$. Suppose a specific tax of $\tau = 1$ is imposed on the output sold in the market for good 1. Compute approximate market equilibrium values for p_1 and x_1 both before and after imposition of the tax. Calculate approximate market equilibrium values of p_1 and x_1 if the output sold in the market is subjected to an ad valorem tax of $\nu = 0.4$ instead.

REFERENCES

1. Marshall, A., *Principles of Economics*, 8th ed. (New York: Macmillan, 1948).
2. Mill, J. S., *Principles of Political Economy with Some of Their Applications to Social Philosophy*, V. W. Bladen and J. M. Robson, eds. (Toronto: University of Toronto Press, 1965).
3. Ricardo, D., *On the Principles of Political Economy and Taxation*, P. Sraffa and M. H. Dobb, eds. (London: Cambridge University Press, 1951).

Chapter 7

Interacting Markets

As described in the previous chapter, the analysis of equilibrium in a model of an isolated market takes the behavior of individuals with respect to that market (*i.e.*, their demand and supply curves) as given and requires that certain outside variables such as prices in other markets be fixed. These assumption are the source of the model's partial-equilibrium nature. In general, however, because market demand and supply are functions of many prices, equilibrium in one market is intimately related to equilibrium in others. To illustrate, suppose a blight on tea leaves reduces the supply of tea and raises its market price. Then, because the demand for coffee depends in part on the price of tea, consumers may shift demand from tea to coffee. The result is a lowering of the price of tea and a higher price for coffee. These last price variations, along with potential impacts on factor markets due to the possibility of factor substitutions, have still further effects on the demand and supply curves for coffee and tea. And so on. Although at each stage (that is, after each sequential shift of a demand or supply curve), the two markets could be thought of as in isolated partial equilibrium, it is clear that equilibrium "between" them cannot reappear until all changes cease.

For now, the process by which equilibrium might be re-established is not important. Consideration of it is postponed to the discussion of dynamics in Chapter 9. Instead, present argument continues to focus on timeless activity or comparative statics. In the comparative statics interpretation, recall, equations depict the equilibrium, or stationary state, of a dynamic system. But rather than dealing with individual economic units in isolation as in previous sections, the models of this and the next five chapters are intended to describe some Walrasian perspectives on the entire economy with consumers, firms, and markets all interacting simultaneously. The analysis of equilibrium thus takes on a more general character.

The behavior of consumers, firms, and markets is that developed in Chapters 2 – 6. Indeed, the purpose of the present chapter is to offer three systems of equations, each depicting simultaneous interaction among these units as they behave, and to begin an inquiry into the overall equilibrium and its properties that each system might generate. The first to be considered (Section 7.1) is a two-person, two-good, exchange (that is, productionless) economy. The study of this simple world provides an ideal vehicle for gaining a clear and uncluttered understanding of some of the ideas involved in simultaneous economic behavior and also paves the way for an examination of the general production economy considered in Section 7.2. With respect to the latter, both short-run and long-run circumstances are considered. In the short-run case, fixed inputs and costs are present, and there is no pressure that forces the profits of firms to vanish. For the long-run, fixed inputs and costs are absent, and firms' profits are driven to zero. The model of Section 7.2 is relevant for the particular grand view of Section 1.4. It summarizes and links together the behavior of individuals, firms, and markets already presented as parts of that grand view in Sections 2.3, 3.3, 4.1, 4.4, 4.5, 5.1 (short run) or 5.2 (long run), and 6.1 (short run) or 6.2 (long run). Section 7.3 adds a restricted notion of "money" to the system of Section 7.2. Note that the exchange model (Section 7.1) and the model with money (Section 7.3) can be conceived, respectively, as a special case of and as a simple extension of the production model of Section 7.2.

Except for capital inputs, which are ignored until Chapter 13, the general production economy being modeled by the equations of Section 7.2 is the same as that depicted in Section 1.1. The model itself consists of utility-maximizing consumers and profit-maximizing firms who buy and sell commodities and factors in markets. Equilibrium can occur in the model only when all consumers, firms, and markets are at rest and there is no tendency for anything to change. That is, equilibrium prevails at a particular collection of input and output prices (and, implicitly, quantities) whenever, at these prices,

a) all consumers are buying outputs and selling factors so as to maximize utility subject to their budget constraints,

b) all firms are hiring inputs and producing outputs so as to maximize profits, and

c) supply equals demand in all markets.[1]

In the long run, of course, it is required in addition that the profits of all firms be zero. The timeless activity or comparative statics equations of Section 7.2 are precisely the equations that spell out these equilibrium conditions. If this system has a unique solution, then equilibrium prices and quantities are determined for all units in the economy. Just as an understanding of the original clock in the example of Section 1.2 was secured by building a model whose outward behavior duplicated what was seen, an understanding of the economy can be obtained here by interpreting solution values of the system (that is, the outward behavior of the economic model) as those actually observed in the production economy from which the model is drawn (recall the discussions of market equilibrium in Section 1.3). Other interpretations, of course, are also possible. The issue is taken up again in Section 9.1.

Because the assumptions of Chapters 2 – 6 lying behind the behavior of individual firms and consumers are retained, the models of interacting markets considered here apply to the circumstance in which each of the actual markets in the economy is perfectly competitive. The assumption of identical firms within industries, imposed for convenience in Chapter 6, is dropped. In this case, the "real world" as described in Section 1.1 is called a *perfectly competitive economy* and equilibrium in the model often is referred to as *competitive equilibrium*.

A useful way to conceptualize the operation of simultaneously interacting markets in a perfectly competitive economy is in terms of an auctioneer. One common auctioneer conceptualization or "story" in the simple context of a productionless world is as follows: Let each consumer begin with an initial basket of commodities, called the individual's *initial endowment*, which is taken to a central market place. There an auctioneer announces a collection of market prices, one for each good. Consumers then value their initial endowments at these prices, check their preferences, and declare the quantities of each good they wish to buy and sell. Adding over individuals, the auctioneer obtains market demand and supply quantities for each good. If demand equals supply in every market, equilibrium is realized throughout the economy, goods are exchanged at the announced prices, and everyone goes home. If not, no exchange takes place and the auctioneer provides another set of prices. The process continues until competitive equilibrium is achieved and only then is actual exchange permitted.[2] Note

---

[1]   See Walras [9, pp. 172, 173, 253-255].
[2]   The assumption that no market trades are effected at nonequilibrium prices is frequently referred to as the absence of "false trading." The present approach also involves the further

that the auctioneer is not rewarded for her services.

The above auctioneer story may be expressed in terms of either continuous or discrete time and can easily be generalized to include production. Thus the comparative statics or timeless equilibrium equations presented below can be thought of as describing the outcome of this auctioneer process. In so doing they would depict utility maximization by consumers, profit maximization by firms (if production is present), and the equalities of supply and demand or, in other words, a competitive equilibrium. Observe that this auctioneer story is incomplete in that no indication is given of the rule by which the auctioneer adjusts her price announcement when market-demand-equals-market-supply does not prevail everywhere. Actually, were such a rule to be specified, the auctioneer story would then provide the basis for an explanation of how equilibrium is achieved and prices are determined from out-of-equilibrium positions. That is, it would describe, at least informally, the dynamic movement of the Walrasian system through time and set out a foundation upon which a theory of price determination could be built. But, as suggested, in part, earlier, questions of dynamics and price determination are deferred to Chapters 9 and 10.

7.1   SIMPLE EXCHANGE

An *exchange economy* is one in which there is no production. Each consumer has an initial endowment of goods that can be traded or exchanged in markets, but the total quantity of goods distributed in the economy cannot be modified. In the simplest case there are two consumers and two goods.

To model such a situation formally, recall that x_{ik} denotes quantities of good i for person k, where $i, k = 1, 2$. Let initial commodity endowments be indicated by

$$(x_{1k}^0, x_{2k}^0) \geqslant 0,$$

where at least one of x_{1k}^0 and x_{2k}^0 is positive for each k, and at least one of x_{i1}^0 and x_{i2}^0 is positive for each i. The excess demand, q_{ik}, for good i by person k is the difference between what that person would like to have of good i and

---

supposition that the final multi-market equilibrium position is independent of, or not affected by, the process leading to it. In particular, the "notional" or out-of-equilibrium price vectors announced by the auctioneer are taken to have no impact on market participants' preferences. This, of course, is consistent with the earlier imposition of the requirement that prices do not appear as arguments in consumer utility functions.

what he actually has, or

$$q_{ik} = x_{ik} - x_{ik}^0, \quad i, k = 1, 2. \tag{7.1-1}$$

This is one specification of the notion of *excess demand*, which generally is defined in a variety of contexts as quantity demanded minus quantity supplied. (Clearly, with respect to the consumer, the phrase "quantity supplied" refers to the largest quantity that might be supplied.)

Once market prices p_1 and p_2 are given (perhaps by an auctioneer) the consumer is able to value his initial endowment at m_k^0:

$$m_k^0 = p_1 x_{1k}^0 + p_2 x_{2k}^0, \quad k = 1, 2. \tag{7.1-2}$$

Hence his budget constraint is given by

$$p_1 x_{1k} + p_2 x_{2k} = m_k^0, \quad k = 1, 2. \tag{7.1-3}$$

Upon combination of (7.1-1) – (7.1-3), the consumer's budget constraint can be expressed in terms of excess demands:

$$p_1 q_{1k} + p_2 q_{2k} = 0, \quad k = 1, 2. \tag{7.1-4}$$

Geometrically, the budget constraint appears as usual in Figure 7.1. Equation

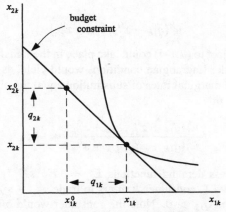

Figure 7.1 Excess demand formulation of utility maximization subject to the budget constraint

(7.1-3) is the mathematical form in which it was introduced originally in Section 2.3. Equation (7.1-4) expresses the same constraint when the coordinate axes are translated so that the origin falls at the initial endowment (x_{1k}^0, x_{2k}^0).

It is possible that at the given prices the consumer is satisfied with his initial endowment. On the other hand, there may be a basket of commodities lying on (or below) his budget line which he prefers. In that case he attempts to obtain the better basket by offering to trade.

Suppose each consumer chooses the commodity basket he would like to achieve through trade by maximizing, subject to his budget constraint, a utility function $u^k(x_{1k}, x_{2k})$ with properties as described in Section 2.3. Demand functions $h^k = (h^{1k}, h^{2k})$ would obtain in the usual manner employing (7.1-3). By use of (7.1-2) to eliminate m_k^0 from the h^{ik}, excess demand functions $E^k = (E^{1k}, E^{2k})$ could then be defined from (7.1-1) by

$$q_{ik} = E^{ik}(p), \quad i, k = 1, 2, \tag{7.1-5}$$

where

$$E^{ik}(p) = h^{ik}(p, p_1 x_{1k}^0 + p_2 x_{2k}^0) - x_{ik}^0,$$

for all $p > 0$ and $i, k = 1, 2$, and where $p = (p_1, p_2)$ and the initial endowment vector (x_{1k}^0, x_{2k}^0) is subsumed in the functional symbol E^{ik}. The properties of E^k can be derived directly from its definition in (7.1-5) and the properties of h^k (see Exercise 7.6). In particular, E^k is continuous and homogeneous of degree zero. Alternatively, (7.1-1) could be substituted into the utility function to give

$$u^k(q_{1k} + x_{1k}^0, q_{2k} + x_{2k}^0);$$

maximization subject to (7.1-4) could take place in the transformed coordinate space; the first-order Lagrangian conditions would yield, as before, the result that the subjective marginal rates of substitution equal the objectively market-given price ratios, or

$$\frac{u_1^k(q_{1k} + x_{1k}^0, q_{2k} + x_{2k}^0)}{u_2^k(q_{1k} + x_{1k}^0, q_{2k} + x_{2k}^0)} = \frac{p_1}{p_2};$$

and the same excess demand functions $E^k = (E^{1k}, E^{2k})$ would arise. As pictured in Figure 7.1, consumer k offers to trade $x_{2k}^0 - x_{2k}$ for $x_{1k} - x_{1k}^0$. Hence $q_{2k} < 0$ and $q_{1k} > 0$. Note the consumer would offer no trade at all (that is, $q_{1k} = q_{2k} = 0$) if the utility-maximizing basket of commodities fell at the initial endowment.

Market excess demand functions are the sums of the individual functions or

$$q_i = E^i(p), \quad i = 1, 2,$$

where, for each i,

$$q_i = q_{i1} + q_{i2},$$

and

$$E^i(p) = E^{i1}(p) + E^{i2}(p). \tag{7.1-6}$$

Because each of the E^{ik} are continuous and homogeneous of degree zero, the market excess demand functions are too. Partial equilibrium in, say, the market for good 1 separately, occurs if the price of good 2 is fixed at some $\bar{p}_2$ and supply equals demand for good 1. In other words

$$E^1(p_1, \bar{p}_2) = 0. \tag{7.1-7}$$

Similarly, partial equilibrium in the market for good 2, when isolated and when $p_1 = \bar{p}_1$, is described by

$$E^2(\bar{p}_1, p_2) = 0. \tag{7.1-8}$$

Both markets are in equilibrium simultaneously provided that[3]

$$E^i(p) = 0, \quad i = 1, 2. \tag{7.1-9}$$

Clearly, if (7.1-9) is satisfied for some $\bar{p} = (\bar{p}_1, \bar{p}_2)$, then both (7.1-7) and (7.1-8) are also satisfied at $\bar{p}$. The converse assertion, however, cannot be true. Partial equilibrium in each market in isolation does not imply (7.1-9) because in either market the price of the other good may not be fixed at the level that implies equilibrium in the other market.[4] That is, given the initial endowments of both individuals, if (7.1-7) holds for $p_1 = \tilde{p}_1$ and if (7.1-8) obtains with $p_2 = \tilde{p}_2$, then the two markets, although each in partial equilibrium separately, are not in simultaneous equilibrium unless it happens to be the case that $\tilde{p}_1 = \bar{p}_1$ and $\tilde{p}_2 = \bar{p}_2$.

---

[3]   It is implicit in (7.1-9) that all dynamic interaction, such as that described in the introduction to the present chapter between the markets for coffee and tea, has ceased. This is made explicit in Section 9.1 with the supposition that "equilibrium in the economic" coincides with "equilibrium in the (complete) dynamic system as a whole."

[4]   Walras' law (equation (7.1-11)) and Theorem 7.1-12 below do not apply here since, in the partial equilibrium context, the two markets are isolated and independent of each other.

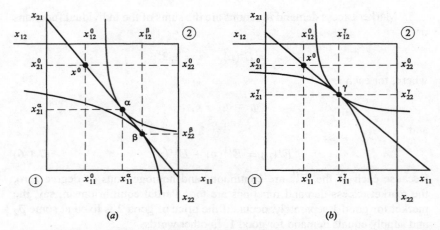

Figure 7.2 Two-commodity, two-person exchange: (*a*) nonequilibrium price ratio; (*b*) equilibrium price ratio

Equilibrium in this simple exchange model can be pictured in a diagram known as the (consumption) Edgeworth box.[5] Figures 7.2(a) and (b) exhibit the coordinate system of individual 1 drawn in the usual manner. Its origin is indicated by the encircled symbol 1. But the coordinate system of individual 2 is turned upside down with origin at encircled 2 so that the axis measuring good 1 is parallel to that for person 1, and similarly for good 2. The length and height of the box equal, respectively, the sum of the initial endowments of good 1 and good 2. Thus every point in the box reflects a possible distribution of the total endowment among the consumers. The initial endowment distribution is denoted by x^0. With prices given, budget lines can be drawn through initial endowments. Although each consumer views his own budget line in terms of his own coordinate axes, these lines coincide in the box. Suppose (Figure 7.2(a)) that person 1 maximizes utility subject to his budget constraint at α, and person 2 maximizes at β. Then person 1 will want to supply $x_{21}^0 - x_{21}^\alpha$ in the market for good 2 and demand $x_{11}^\alpha - x_{11}^0$, in the market for good 1. Similarly, person 2 will attempt to demand $x_{22}^\beta - x_{22}^0$ in the market for good 2

---

[5] According to Jaffé [3, p. 1190n], posterity seems to have dealt frivolously with Edgeworth and Pareto: The box diagram attributed to Edgeworth (Figure 7.2) cannot be found anywhere in his work but makes its first appearance in Pareto's Manuel [5, Ch. 3, §116]. Pareto is "compensated" by receiving credit for the notion of Pareto optimality even though it was actually introduced (in consumption only) by Edgeworth. See n. 5 on p. 470.

and supply $x_{12}^0 - x_{12}^\beta$ in the market for good 1. Although both individuals are maximizing utility subject to their respective budget constraints, supply does not equal demand in either market. Indeed, the excess demand for good 1 is negative, and the excess demand for good 2 is positive. Therefore equilibrium does not prevail at these prices. Equilibrium can occur in the model only at prices for which indifference curves are tangent to budget lines at the same point, as illustrated at γ in Figure 7.2(b).

In terms of excess demands, the comparative statics or timeless equations describing equilibrium are

$$\frac{u_1^k(q_{1k} + x_{1k}^0, q_{2k} + x_{2k}^0)}{u_2^k(q_{1k} + x_{1k}^0, q_{2k} + x_{2k}^0)} = \frac{p_1}{p_2}, \quad k = 1, 2,$$

$$p_1 q_{1k} + p_2 q_{2k} = 0, \qquad k = 1, 2, \qquad (7.1\text{-}10)$$

$$E^i(p_1, p_2) = 0, \qquad i = 1, 2.$$

The first four equations ensure that each consumer is buying and selling goods so as to maximize utility subject to his budget constraint, and the last two guarantee that demand and supply are equal in both markets. This is a system of six equations in the six unknowns q_{11}, q_{21}, q_{12}, q_{22}, p_1, and p_2. One might hope, then, that it would be possible to solve the system simultaneously to obtain equilibrium values for prices and quantities. However, substitution of (7.1-5) into (7.1-4), summing the result over the two consumers, and then using (7.1-6) gives

$$p_1 E^1(p) + p_2 E^2(p) = 0, \qquad (7.1\text{-}11)$$

for all $p > 0$. Thus the following proposition is obtained:

Theorem 7.1-12   Suppose $p > 0$. Then $E^1(p) = 0$ if and only if $E^2(p) = 0$.

Theorem 7.1-12 says that, in this two-commodity model, one market cannot be in equilibrium without the other. The geometry of Figure 7.2 suggests a similar conclusion. Equation (7.1-11), from which Theorem 7.1-12 comes, is referred to as *Walras' law*.[6] Note that Walras' law is stronger than the statement of Theorem 7.1-12; that is, (7.1-11) implies Theorem 7.1-12 but not conversely. Furthermore, Walras' law, because it holds for all $p > 0$, ensures that even when out of equilibrium, the sum of the values of excess demands (*i.e.*, prices times excess demand quantities) over all markets exactly balance each

---

6   Walras [9, p. 170].

other out. Thus there are no "leakages" in the system: All goods and payments flow between the two consumers, none being "lost" to third parties such as foreign countries. Walras' law also implies via Theorem 7.1-12 that not all of the equations of (7.1-10) are unrelated. In particular, the subsystem of equations that determines the values of the two equilibrium prices, namely (7.1-9), actually consists of only a single independent equation. Hence, even if a solution exists, it is not possible to determine both absolute price values (measured in terms of a counter such as money [recall Section 1.3]) uniquely.

One way to interpret the indeterminacy raised by Walras' law is to rewrite (7.1-10) so as to be dependent on the ratio of prices. Thus, using the homogeneity of E^1,

$$\frac{u_1^k(q_{1k} + x_{1k}^0, q_{2k} + x_{2k}^0)}{u_2^k(q_{1k} + x_{1k}^0, q_{2k} + x_{2k}^0)} = \frac{p_1}{p_2}, \quad k = 1, 2,$$

$$\frac{p_1}{p_2}q_{1k} + q_{2k} = 0, \quad k = 1, 2, \quad (7.1\text{-}13)$$

$$E^1\left(\frac{p_1}{p_2}, 1\right) = 0.$$

The equation describing equilibrium in market 2 is dropped because it is redundant. This can be thought of as a system of five equations in five unknowns, namely, q_{11}, q_{21}, q_{12}, q_{22}, and the ratio p_1/p_2. When unique solutions exist, then, equilibrium quantities and the price ratio are obtained. The fact that only the ratio of prices is determinate and not their absolute levels is hardly surprising. Analytically, the form of the budget constraint (which is, in part, also reflected in the homogeneity of the E^i and the first-order Lagrangian maximization conditions) implies, as previously indicated, that if p is an equilibrium price vector satisfying (7.1-10) or (7.1-13), then so is σp where σ is any positive number. In ratio form this indeterminacy is eliminated. Geometrically, in terms of Figure 7.2(b), one does not need to know the absolute level of prices to draw the equilibrium at γ. It is necessary to have only the rate at which one commodity exchanges for another at equilibrium, that is, the equilibrium price ratio or slope of the budget line. Furthermore, absolute price values cannot be inferred from Figure 7.2(b). Equations (7.1-10) and (7.1-13) are merely formalizations of the information contained in this diagram. They cannot be expected by themselves to determine the absolute levels of p_1 and p_2. And lastly, all prices in the real world are actually expressed relative to the price of a single good anyway — that single good being the commodity known as money.[7] (The ways in which several functions of money can be accounted for in the Walrasian system are considered in Section 7.3.)

An alternative to eliminating the indeterminacy of (7.1-10) by combining the two prices into one ratio is to add an extra equation restricting the price space to some subset of $\{p : p > 0\}$ without constraining the price ratio determined at equilibrium. Such an equation is called a *normalization*. Examples of normalizations are

$$p_2 = 1,$$

$$p_1 + p_2 = 1,$$

and

$$(p_1)^2 + (p_2)^2 = 1.$$

The first limits the price space to the line above the p_2-axis parallel to the p_1-axis through $p_2 = 1$, the second to the straight line connecting the points $(0, 1)$ and $(1, 0)$ in the positive quadrant, and the third to the quarter circle (again in the positive quadrant) of radius 1 whose center lies at the origin. The equation

$$p_1 = p_2,$$

is not a normalization because it forces the price ratio to be identically 1 regardless of the ratio's true equilibrium value.

Provided they are uniquely solvable, equilibrium quantities and the price ratio can be found from (7.1-13) or (7.1-10) in a two-stage process. The equilibrium price ratio can be obtained in (7.1-13) from the market equilibrium condition alone. It then can be substituted into the remainder of the system to determine the distribution of goods among consumers. In the case of (7.1-10), the first step is to solve one of the market equilibrium equations together with a normalization. This yields values for both p_1 and p_2 which can be used in a second step identical to that employed for (7.1-13). Clearly the equilibrium quantities and price ratio, if they exist, are the same with either (7.1-13) or (7.1-10) regardless of the normalization chosen for the latter. The issue of existence of solutions (that is, the conditions under which there are equilibrium quantities and a price ratio) is pursued in Chapters 8 and 9 in more general contexts.[8]

---

[7]   Thinking of money as an actual commodity involves much more than its above use as an abstract counter that is independent of the economic system.

[8]   Note that the Jacobian "test" for solvability of (7.1-10) or (7.1-13) is not applicable here because the implicit function theorem, apart from whatever restrictions it may place on Jacobians, already assumes that a solution exists. See Apostol [1, p. 374] and appendix Section A.4.

Only when the normalization $p_2 = 1$ is employed does (7.1-10) become formally identical to (7.1-13), although as indicated above, equilibrium quantities and the price ratio are coincident anyway. In this case, the solution value of p_1, in (7.1-10) is the same as the solution value of p_1/p_2 in (7.1-13). The setting of p_2 at unity means that good 2 becomes a standard of value with respect to which the value of good 1 (that is, its price) is measured. Under such circumstances, good 2 is taking on one of the functions of money, namely that of the counter, and is called the *numéraire*. Of course, it is always possible to employ different normalizations for different purposes. Thus, for example, a particular normalization may be chosen to simplify complicated mathematical manipulations.

Although the geometry of the Edgeworth box breaks down with more than two persons, it should be noted that the exchange model (that is, the mathematical equations) of this section generalizes in the obvious way to include I goods and K consumers, for any I and K.[9] Details are left to the reader. The model of the next section not only permits arbitrary numbers of goods and consumers but includes production as well.

7.2 THE GENERAL PRODUCTION ECONOMY

All previous discussion has, in one way or another, been concerned with the analysis of specific pieces or special cases of the general production economy. It is now appropriate to pull these threads together and write down the complete system of timeless equilibrium equations of the model. The short-run case is considered first.

Without sacrificing generality, several convenient notational conventions are introduced. Recall that the index $i = 1, \ldots, I$ varies over produced goods while $j = 1, \ldots, J$ runs over inputs and factors. Intermediate goods, then, because they are produced to be used as inputs, appear as both an i and a j. To avoid this double counting, restrict j to only nonproduced factors. Let n index all goods in the economy by listing first produced goods and then factors in order. Thus

$$n = 1, \ldots, I, I + 1, \ldots, I + J.$$

---

9   Radford [6] has observed that certain World War II prisoner-of-war camps appear to have many of the (generalized) characteristics described above. For example, there is no production in these camps, initial endowments in the form of rations provided by the camp and parcels from the Red Cross and home arrive periodically and, immediately upon arrival, become the objects of intense trading among the prisoners. Hence the I-good, K-person version of the model of this section would seem to provide an explanation of how such exchange economies operate.

As before, each $i = 1, \ldots, I$ also represents an industry. The number of firms in industry i is written L_i, and the firms in the industry are indexed by $\ell = 1, \ldots, L_i$. For the time being, L_i is taken to be fixed. Consumers, as usual, are denoted by $k = 1, \ldots, K$.

The most general form of the production function for firm ℓ in industry i is

$$x_{i\ell} = f^{i\ell}(x_{i\ell 1}, \ldots, x_{i\ell I}, y_{i\ell I+1}, \ldots, y_{i\ell I+J}), \qquad (7.2\text{-}1)$$

where $x_{i\ell n}$ and $y_{i\ell n}$ describe, respectively, quantities of produced good and factor n used by firm $i\ell$. Now, as indicated in Section 4.1, not all of the $x_{i\ell n}$ and $y_{i\ell n}$ need be relevant for the production of good i. Technology determines which inputs actually appear as arguments in $f^{i\ell}$. Moreover, $x_{i\ell}$ and $x_{i\ell i}$ represent the same good. To take explicitly into account these details would complicate matters unnecessarily. If all the $x_{i\ell n}$ and $y_{i\ell n}$ were left as arguments of $f^{i\ell}$, then most cost-minimizing points would have to lie on a boundary of the input space where some inputs are not used. This would render substantial portions of Chapters 4 and 5 inapplicable because the usual first-order maximization conditions (such as input price ratios equal to ratios of marginal products as in equation (4.4-5) and input prices equal to values of marginal products as in equation (5.1-11)) would become inadmissible. If the irrelevant $x_{i\ell n}$ and $y_{i\ell n}$ were excluded from $f^{i\ell}$, then the intricate notation required to specify which inputs are in and which are out would tend to obscure the main argument. Both extremes can be avoided by agreeing to another notational convention: The production function of firm $i\ell$ will continue to be written as in (7.2-1) with the understandings that (a) $x_{i\ell}$ is taken to be net output, that is, gross output less whatever quantity of output is used by $i\ell$ as input, and the input variable $x_{i\ell i}$ is eliminated, though its elimination is not explicitly indicated notationally, as an argument of $f^{i\ell}$; and (b) although their omission is also not indicated notationally, the irrelevant input variables are additionally excluded as arguments of $f^{i\ell}$. (Alternatively, in place of (b), one might suppose the technology of each firm is such that cost minimization requires the employment of positive amounts of every good, $n = 1, \ldots, I + J$, in the production of each output. The following discussion applies to this case without modification.)

The production function (7.2-1) can also be expressed in terms of firm excess demands. These are variables indicating quantities demanded by the firm minus quantities it supplies. Let $q_{i\ell}$ and $q_{i\ell n}$ denote, respectively, the excess demand of firm $i\ell$ for its output and for input n. Then, because $x_{i\ell}$ is taken as net output and because firms are assumed to have no initial stocks of goods,

$$q_{i\ell} = -x_{i\ell},$$

$$q_{i\ell n} = \begin{cases} x_{i\ell n}, & \text{when } n = 1, \ldots, I, \\ y_{i\ell n}, & \text{when } n = I+1, \ldots, I+J. \end{cases}$$

Substituting these variables into (7.2-1) gives

$$-q_{i\ell} = f^{i\ell}(q_{i\ell 1}, \ldots, q_{i\ell I+J}). \tag{7.2-2}$$

Profit maximization can be based equivalently on either (7.2-1) or (7.2-2). Subsequent argument employs the latter under appropriate subsets of assumptions of Chapters 4 and 5 that ensure that unique profit maximization is possible. (Recall the strictly concave model of Theorem 5.1-24 and the Viner model of Theorem 5.1-25. The modifications required in the following to permit use of the constant returns to scale model of Theorem 5.1-26 are left to the reader.) Let

$$P_n = \begin{cases} p_n, & \text{if } n = 1, \ldots, I, \\ r_n, & \text{if } n = I+1, \ldots, I+J, \end{cases}$$

and set $P = (P_1, \ldots, P_{I+J})$. Then the profit of firm $i\ell$ is

$$\pi_{i\ell} = P_i f^{i\ell}(q_{i\ell 1}, \ldots, q_{i\ell I+J}) - \sum_{n=1}^{I+J} P_n q_{i\ell n} - b_{i\ell}, \tag{7.2-3}$$

where terms $q_{i\ell n}$ that do not appear as arguments of $f^{i\ell}$ also are excluded from the sum on the right, and the parameter $b_{i\ell}$ is the firm's fixed cost. As in Section 5.1, profit maximization yields the firm's output and input excess demand functions:

$$q_{i\ell} = E^{i\ell}(P), \tag{7.2-4}$$

$$q_{i\ell n} = E^{i\ell n}(P), \quad n = 1, \ldots, I+J. \tag{7.2-5}$$

The $E^{i\ell n}$ corresponding to commodities not appearing as arguments in $f^{i\ell}$ vanish identically for all P. The properties of these functions carry over from those of the ordinary firm input demand and output supply functions (Exercise 7.6). In particular, they are continuous and homogeneous of degree zero.

Industry excess demand functions are derived by summing over the excess demand functions of the individual firms. Thus in industry i,

$$q_i = \widetilde{E}^i(P), \tag{7.2-6}$$

for output and

$$q_{in} = E^{in}(P), \quad n = 1, \ldots, I + J, \tag{7.2-7}$$

for inputs, where, for all n,

$$q_i = \sum_{\ell=1}^{L_i} q_{i\ell}, \quad q_{in} = \sum_{\ell=1}^{L_i} q_{i\ell n},$$

$$\widetilde{E}^i(P) = \sum_{\ell=1}^{L_i} E^{i\ell}(P), \quad E^{in}(P) = \sum_{\ell=1}^{L_i} E^{i\ell n}(P).$$

The symbol $\widetilde{E}^i$ is used in place of E^i to distinguish, later on, industry from consumer excess demand. With the extra supposition (beyond the presently assumed requirements for perfect competition) of identical firms, (7.2-6) reduces to

$$q_i = L_i E^{i1}(P), \tag{7.2-8}$$

and (7.2-7) becomes

$$q_{in} = L_i E^{i1n}(P), \quad n = 1, \ldots, I + J. \tag{7.2-9}$$

Regardless, because they are sums of individual firm excess demand functions, industry excess demand functions, too, are at least continuous and homogeneous of degree zero.

Turning to the consumer, it is convenient to suppose that person k possesses a utility function

$$\mu^k = u^k(x_{1k}, \ldots, x_{Ik}, y_{I+1k}, \ldots, y_{I+Jk}), \tag{7.2-10}$$

exhibiting the classical properties described in Sections 2.3 and 3.3, and having all goods as arguments. Thus produced goods may be either consumed or used as inputs in production. Quantities of the y_{nk} reflect units of good n (such as leisure and land) consumed or demanded by person k. The difference between demand and endowment is supplied to firms (Section 3.3). More precisely, let

$$y_k^0 = (y_{I+1k}^0, \ldots, y_{I+Jk}^0) \geqslant 0$$

be the vector of initial factor endowments of person k. Assume that at least one $y^0_{I+jk} > 0$ for each j as k varies, and for each k as j varies. Because consumers are not endowed with produced goods, the excess demand of k for commodity n, namely q_{nk}, is, as in (7.1-1),

$$q_{nk} = \begin{cases} x_{nk}, & \text{for } n = 1, \ldots, I, \\ \\ y_{nk} - y^0_{nk}, & \text{for } n = I+1, \ldots, I+J. \end{cases}$$

(There is nothing to prevent $y_{nk} - y^0_{nk} > 0$ for $n > I$, in which case person k enters factor market n as a buyer rather than as a seller.) Substitution back into (7.2-10) transforms utility into a function of excess demands:

$$\mu^k = u^k(q_{1k}, \ldots, q_{I+Jk}), \tag{7.2-11}$$

where y^0_k is subsumed in the functional symbol u^k.

In addition to income earned from the sale of factors, consumers receive profits distributed from firms. Let $\theta_{ki\ell}$ be the fraction of profit from firm $i\ell$ accruing to person k (Section 3.3). For now, the $\theta_{ki\ell}$ are taken to be fixed, nonnegative parameters with

$$\sum_{k=1}^{K} \theta_{ki\ell} = 1,$$

for all i and ℓ. It also is assumed, to keep matters simple, that all fixed costs are paid directly to consumers in the same proportion as profits. Hence, as in the previous section, the budget constraint faced by person k is

$$\sum_{n=1}^{I+J} P_n q_{nk} - \sum_{i=1}^{I} \sum_{\ell=1}^{L_i} \theta_{ki\ell}(\pi_{i\ell} + b_{i\ell}) = 0. \tag{7.2-12}$$

Note that, except for context, (7.2-12) is the same budget constraint as (3.3-1).

Parallel to the arguments of Sections 2.3, 3.3, and 7.1, maximization of utility in (7.2-11) subject to the budget constraint (7.2-12) yields excess demand as a function of P and the $\pi_{i\ell} + b_{i\ell}$. But as can be seen upon substitution of (7.2-4) and (7.2-5) into (7.2-3), each $\pi_{i\ell}$ itself depends on P. Moreover, the $b_{i\ell}$ are fixed parameters. Hence the excess demand functions for person k can be written as

$$q_{nk} = E^{nk}(P), \quad n = 1, \ldots, I+J,$$

where the $\theta_{ki\ell}$ and the $b_{i\ell}$ are subsumed in the functional notation E^{nk}. The properties of these functions are easily obtained (Exercise 7.6). As is true for firm excess demands, the E^{nk} are, among other things, continuous and homogeneous of degree zero. Adding across persons gives the excess demand functions for all consumers or

$$q_n = E^n(P), \quad n = 1, \ldots, I + J, \tag{7.2-13}$$

where, for each n,

$$q_n = \sum_{k=1}^{K} q_{nk},$$

$$E^n(P) = \sum_{k=1}^{K} E^{nk}(P).$$

As before at the aggregate level, the E^n are, at a minimum, continuous and homogeneous of degree zero.

To write down the market equilibrium conditions for produced commodity markets, it is first necessary to rename the index over industries in the industry output excess demand equations. Thus (7.2-6) becomes

$$q_n = \widetilde{E}^n(P), \quad n = 1, \ldots, I. \tag{7.2-14}$$

This involves no real change because the index n, for $n = 1, \ldots, I$, has the same meaning as i. Loosely speaking, produced commodity markets are in equilibrium when consumer demand for consumption plus firm demand for use in production exactly offsets firm supply. Mathematically,

$$E^n(P) + \left[\sum_{i=1}^{I} E^{in}(P) \right] + \widetilde{E}^n(P) = 0, \quad n = 1, \ldots, I. \tag{7.2-15}$$

Note that the distinction made in Section 1.4 between final and intermediate goods markets (recall Table 1.1) does not apply here because firms can sell their output to both consumers and other firms simultaneously. Likewise, factor markets are in equilibrium when firm demand for use in production equals consumer supply:

$$\left[\sum_{i=1}^{I} E^{in}(P) \right] + E^n(P) = 0, \quad n = I + 1, \ldots, I + J. \tag{7.2-16}$$

Equations (7.2-15) and (7.2-16) constitute a system of $I + J$ equations for determining $I + J$ equilibrium prices. Equilibrium quantities are found, as in the exchange model of Section 7.1, from appropriate first-order maximization conditions and constraints. But once again Walras' law or, more precisely, one of its implications, intrudes:

Theorem 7.2-17   Simultaneous equilibrium in any $I+J-1$ markets at $P > 0$ implies equilibrium in the remaining market.

Proof: Elimination of the production function from the profit equation by substitution of (7.2-2) into (7.2-3), adding over all firms, then substituting industry excess demand functions for industry excess demand quantities, and splitting up the right hand summation,

$$\sum_{i=1}^{I}\sum_{\ell=1}^{L_i}\pi_{i\ell} + b_{i\ell}$$

$$= -\sum_{n=1}^{I}P_n\widetilde{E}^n(P) - \sum_{n=1}^{I}P_n\left[\sum_{i=1}^{I}E^{in}(P)\right] \tag{7.2-18}$$

$$- \sum_{n=I+1}^{I+J}P_n\left[\sum_{i=1}^{I}E^{in}(P)\right],$$

where the index i on $\widetilde{E}^i$ has been changed to n as in (7.2-14). On the other hand, summing all budget constraints over k, and replacing consumer excess demand quantities by consumer excess demand functions gives, because $\sum_{k=1}^{K}\theta_{ki\ell} = 1$,

$$\sum_{n=1}^{I+J}P_nE^n(P) - \sum_{i=1}^{I}\sum_{\ell=1}^{L_i}(\pi_{i\ell} + b_{i\ell}) = 0. \tag{7.2-19}$$

Substituting (7.2-18) into (7.2-19) and rearranging terms yields, for all $p > 0$,

$$\sum_{n=1}^{I}P_n\left\{E^n(P) + \left[\sum_{i=1}^{I}E^{in}(P)\right] + \widetilde{E}^n(P)\right\}$$

$$+ \sum_{n=I+1}^{I+J}P_n\left\{\left[\sum_{i=1}^{I}E^{in}(P)\right] + E^n(P)\right\} = 0. \tag{7.2-20}$$

Because the expressions within the braces are precisely the left-hand sides of the market equilibrium conditions of (7.2-15) and (7.2-16), the theorem follows immediately.

Q.E.D.

Thus, as in the exchange model, not all equations determining equilibrium prices are independent. When solvable, (7.2-15) and (7.2-16) yield at best unique equilibrium price ratios. The discussions in Section 7.1 of this problem and of leakages, normalizations, and the numéraire apply (with obvious but minor modification) here. In the production context, equation (7.2-20) is Walras' law.[10] The fact that (7.2-20) can hold for all $p > 0$ only without leakages as goods and payments for them flow between consumers and firms is a reflection in the present model of the identical property described in Section 1.1 for the simplified economy without physical and money capital. The same absence of leakages there could have been pictured, as was indicated, in an appropriately modified version of Figure 1.1.

Due to the presence of fixed costs, the possibility of nonvanishing profits, and the treatment of the number of firms in each industry as a given parameter, the model presented thus far is, as indicated at the outset, of the short-run variety. To convert it into a long-run system of comparative statics, or timeless, equations,

a) set

$$b_{i\ell} = 0,$$

for all i and ℓ,

b) make appropriate adjustments in the equations of the model so as to be able to use the explicit form of industry excess demand functions provided in (7.2-8) and (7.2-9) (that is, assume all firms within industries are identical)[11] with the number of firms L_i interpreted as a variable to be determined by the system at equilibrium,

c) add the long-run equilibrium conditions

$$\pi^{i1}(P) = 0, \quad i = 1, \dots, I, \tag{7.2-21}$$

where π^{i1} is the function obtained from the substitution of (7.2-4) and (7.2-5) into (7.2-3).

---

[10]   Walras [9, p. 248].
[11]   For an illustration see the last part of Section 11.1 below.

This adds I new variables L_i and the I new equations of (7.2-21) and excludes the strictly concave model from consideration for all firms. The consumer side of the model also must be reinterpreted in long-run terms, but significant modification of the short-run equations or the introduction of new ones is not required. (Of course, because fixed inputs no longer exist, income from them is eliminated from budget constraints. Income from profit remains in the constraints but is reduced to zero upon imposition of the long-run equilibrium conditions of equations (7.2-21).) Alternatively, as described on p. 236, one might require (a), the first part of (b), and (c); retain the L_i as fixed parameters; and assume that all production functions are subject to constant returns to scale. As long as there is at least one positive profit-maximizing level of output for one firm in each industry, the last assumption implies that marginal cost is everywhere equal to price throughout the economy, thus rendering the marginal conditions ensuring profit maximization redundant. Dropping them from the model offsets the addition of (7.2-21), leaving the number of equations the same as the number of variables (see Section 11.1 below).

7.3   CIRCULATING MONEY

For the most part, the model of the general production economy of Section 7.2 is not really designed as a framework within which to analyze the unique features of money. At equilibrium, there is no vital or necessary economic role for money to play. In particular, money is not needed to transport purchasing power through time or across space; nor can it become involved in the creation of wealth since such creation cannot occur. Still, it is possible to interpret the model as implicitly containing a commodity performing two of the more elementary functions that money typically discharges. The first is, as previously noted, the existence of a standard of value against which the values (prices) of commodities are measured. This can be made explicit by the choice of a numéraire (Section 7.1). The second is the existence of a medium of exchange, because any commodity can be used as the basis for payment in all trades. The medium of exchange function can also be made explicit by adding a good having no purpose other than to serve as the means for making payments. For want of a better term refer to it as *circulating money* or, for short, just *money*.[12] But because it omits "precautionary" and "speculative" functions, circulating money is not the same thing as that which is actually present

---

[12]   In the prisoner-of-war camps described by Radford [6] (see n. 9 on p. 260), cigarettes took on these standard-of-value and medium-of-exchange functions and hence served as circulating money.

in the modern world.[13]

   Although circulating money can be introduced in a variety of ways, it is worth keeping the approach here as simple as possible. To that end, it will be assumed that amounts of money are placed in the hands of consumers as part of their initial endowments. Consumers use that money (and only money) to purchase goods. Firms return all money received (and nothing more) to consumers in payment for the factors (including entrepreneurship) employed in production. Clearly, the solution values of what will be called money prices in the full model will now generally turn not only on factor endowments but also on endowments of money.

   Assuming, then, that individuals are willing to hold money only for the purpose of facilitating exchange, let x_{0k} vary over quantities of money to be held or demanded by person k. Circulating money also is taken to be the numéraire by setting its price at unity. The *money price* of any good n is the ratio of P_n, to the price of money, or just P_n. Supposing each person to be endowed with an initial stock of money $x_{0k}^0 \geqslant 0$, where $x_{0k}^0 > 0$ for at least one k, person k's excess demand for money is

$$q_{0k} = x_{0k} - x_{0k}^0. \tag{7.3-1}$$

Her budget constraint is the same as (7.2-12) except for the presence of q_{0k}:

$$q_{0k} + \sum_{n=1}^{I+J} P_n q_{nk} - \sum_{i=1}^{I} \sum_{\ell=1}^{L_i} \theta_{ki\ell}(\pi_{i\ell} + b_{i\ell}) = 0. \tag{7.3-2}$$

Assume that the possession of money provides no utility so that q_{0k} does not appear in k's utility function,

$$\mu^k = u^k(q_{1k}, \ldots, q_{I+Jk}),$$

which is identical to (7.2-11).

---

[13]   In actual fact, money serves a precautionary function in that by holding it, one is able to cover unforeseen irregularities in the timing of income receipts and expenditures. In this sense, money performs as a store of value and as a means of transferring purchasing power through time. The speculative function of money arises in the possibility of increasing wealth by holding money. Such an increase would be realized (i) if a decline in the prices of goods, reflecting an increase in the purchasing power of money, occurs during the period for which money is held, and (ii) if the prices of income-earning assets that substitute for money fall and the purchase of these assets for one's portfolio is delayed (that is, the money is held) until after the price reduction. It is possible to argue that realism in addressing the precautionary and speculative functions requires appeal to the notions of historical time and nonprobabilistic uncertainty described in Ch. 15 below. See, for example, Vickers [8, pp. 72-73].

Maximization of u^k subject to (7.3-2) leads to the first-order conditions

$$\frac{u_n^k(q_k)}{u_{I+J}^k(q_k)} = \frac{P_n}{P_{I+J}}, \quad n = 1, \ldots, I + J - 1, \qquad (7.3-3)$$

where $q_k = (q_{1k}, \ldots, q_{I+Jk})$. But there are not enough equations in (7.3-2) and (7.3-3) to determine all excess demands $q_{0k}, q_{1k}, \ldots, q_{I+Jk}$ as functions of $P = (P_1, \ldots, P_{I+J})$ and the $\pi_{i\ell} + b_{i\ell}$. Thus it is necessary to add an assumption describing the demand for money. An easy way to do this is to suppose that money demand is proportional to the value of nonmonetary initial endowment, or[14]

$$x_{0k} = \delta \left[\sum_{n=I+1}^{I+J} P_n y_{nk}^0 \right], \qquad (7.3-4)$$

where $y_k^0 = (y_{I+1k}^0, \ldots, y_{I+Jk}^0)$ is the initial endowment vector and $\delta > 0$ is a constant of proportionality which, for convenience, is assumed given and independent of k. Substitution of (7.3-4) into (7.3-1) provides the missing expression, namely, the excess demand relation for money:

$$q_{0k} = E^{0k}(P), \qquad (7.3-5)$$

where

$$E^{0k}(P) = \delta \left[\sum_{n=I+1}^{I+J} P_n y_{nk}^0 \right] - x_{0k}^0.$$

Equations (7.3-2), (7.3-3), and (7.3-5) can now be solved (provided the requisite Jacobian is nonzero[15]) to obtain the remaining excess demand functions $E^{nk}(P)$. The terms $\pi_{i\ell} + b_{i\ell}$ are eliminated as functional arguments of E^{nk} in the same manner as in Section 7.2.

Firms, on the other hand, neither produce nor hold circulating money. As soon as they receive money they pass it along to consumers and other firms in payment for inputs and in distributing profits. Thus the firm excess demand functions of the previous section are unaffected by the presence of money.

Given all of the individual excess demand functions, aggregation proceeds as in Section 7.2. Market equilibrium conditions for produced goods

---

[14]   This assumption, which is imposed for pedagogical reasons, removes from consideration many important features that more realistic versions of the demand for money might exhibit. The analysis of those features is well beyond the scope of the present volume.

[15]   See Apostol [1, p. 374] and appendix Section A.4.

and factors are the same as those of (7.2-15) and (7.2-16). The equilibrium condition in the money market as presently conceived is

$$E^0(P) = 0,$$

where

$$E^0(P) = \sum_{k=1}^{K} E^{0k}(P).$$

Hence there are $I + J + 1$ market-equilibrium equations to determine only $I + J$ prices, because the price of money has been normalized to 1. Walras' law (see Exercise 7.7) ensures that the extra equation is redundant. When solvable, equilibrium money prices are obtained for all produced goods and factors. Equilibrium quantities are found from the remaining equations of the system. Note that Walras' law also indicates that equilibrium in all commodity and factor markets implies equilibrium in the money market, but equilibrium in the money market alone implies only that any value-of-excess-demand imbalances in commodity and factor markets (if they exist) must offset each other and sum to zero. This last assertion, namely, that money market equilibrium implies offsetting imbalances in commodity and factor markets is one interpretation of what is referred to as *Say's law*.[16]

The total quantity of money or the *money supply*, namely,

$$\sum_{k=1}^{K} x_{0k}^0,$$

is a fixed, positive parameter of the model. However, it is shown in the context of the fixed-factor-supply economy of the next chapter that changing money endowments to vary the money supply in any proportion alters each equilibrium money price (the price of money excluded) in that same proportion but leaves equilibrium quantities (excluding money) and equilibrium price ratios among goods (again, excluding money) and factors unaffected (Theorem 8.4-6). Thus there is a separation or dichotomy between the real (non-money equilibrium price ratios and quantities) and monetary (equilibrium money prices and the quantity of money) sectors of the model. When solvable, equilibrium price ratios and quantities are determined in the real sector by utility functions, production functions, and initial factor endowments. Money prices are determined in the monetary sector by the quantity of money. This is the basis for the view that money, as narrowly defined here, is a "veil" that hides but does not

---

[16]   See, for example, Schumpeter [7, p. 619].

affect "real" economic processes. The veil must be drawn aside to understand the determination of quantities and relative prices.[17]

EXERCISES

7.1 Consider a two-person, two-good exchange model with utility functions

$$u^1(x_{11}, x_{21}) = x_{11}x_{21},$$

$$u^2(x_{12}, x_{22}) = x_{12}x_{22}.$$

Suppose the initial endowment of person 1 is $(x_{11}^0, x_{21}^0) = (1, 3)$, whereas that of person 2 is $(x_{12}^0, x_{22}^0) = (4, 2)$. Derive the individual and market excess demand functions. Solve the system for equilibrium price ratios and quantities.

7.2 Show that the Jacobian of the system of market excess demand functions in Exercise 7.1, namely,

$$E^1(p_1, p_2) = 0,$$

$$E^2(p_1, p_2) = 0,$$

vanishes for all $(p_1, p_2) > 0$, whereas that of the system consisting of the single equation, say,

$$E^1\left(\frac{p_1}{p_2}, 1\right) = 0,$$

in the single variable p_1/p_2 is nonzero everywhere. What is the meaning of the vanishing of the first Jacobian and the nonvanishing of the second?

7.3 Add the normalization

$$p_1 + p_2 = 1$$

to the system of Exercise 7.1 and solve for equilibrium prices and quantities. How does the equilibrium price ratio compare to that of Exercise 7.1?

---

[17] The idea that money operates as a veil, *i.e.*, that changes in the quantity of money have no effect on the allocation of resources, the production and distribution of goods, and relative commodity prices, is tantamount to the classical notion of "money neutrality." It arises here as a consequence of the highly restrictive assumption content of the Walrasian model developed on preceding pages.

7.4* The consumer's *offer curve* is defined to be the locus of tangencies between indifference curves and budget lines as prices vary and the budget line rotates around the point of initial endowment. Express the offer curve of each person in Exercise 7.1 in terms of the quantities of commodities he consumes. Show that the intersection of the two offer curves, each expressed in terms of the coordinates of the same person, coincides with competitive equilibrium. Illustrate this coincidence geometrically in the Edgeworth box diagram.

7.5 Add circulating money to the model of Exercise 7.1 as follows: Let $x_{01}^0 = 4$, $x_{02}^0 = 6$, and suppose $\delta = 1$ (that is, money demand equals the value of nonmonetary initial endowment). Resolve the system to determine equilibrium money prices and quantities. Show that money prices double without change in the real sector if the money endowment doubles to $x_{01}^0 = 8$ and $x_{02}^0 = 12$. Demonstrate also that the equilibrium money price ratio p_1/p_2 is invariant over all vectors $(x_{01}^0, x_{02}^0) > 0$ and that at equilibrium, the quantities of commodities demanded by individuals are the same for all values $(x_{01}^0, x_{02}^0) > 0$ such that x_{01}^0/x_{02}^0 remains constant.

7.6 Describe the properties of the excess demand functions for output and inputs of the isolated firm. How do they relate to the firm's ordinary output supply and input demand functions. Do the same thing for the nondifferential properties of the excess demand functions for final goods and factors of the isolated consumer.

7.7 Derive Walras'law for the circulating money model of Section 7.3.

7.8** In an exchange model, a redistribution of initial endowments across individuals is in the *core* if no subset of persons is able, by trading among themselves alone, to increase each of their utilities above that which they would received in the redistribution.

    a) Find the core of the exchange model of Exercise 7.1 and note that it contains the equilibrium distribution. Draw an Edgeworth box diagram depicting the core.

Equilibria in exchange models are generally in the core.[18]

    Now expand the model of Exercise 7.1 by adding second persons with the same preferences and initial endowments as, respectively, persons 1 and 2.

---

[18] Hildenbrand and Kirman [2, p. 83]. The proof of this proposition is similar to that of Theorem 12.3-11.

Denote the two persons identical to person 1 by 1_A and 1_B, and those identical to person 2 by 2_A and 2_B Write redistributions of the four initial endowments as

$$x = (x_{11_A}, x_{21_A}, x_{11_B}, x_{21_B}, x_{12_A}, x_{22_A}, x_{12_B}, x_{22_B}),$$

where, say, (x_{11_A}, x_{21_A}) is the component of x going to person 1_A.

b) By comparing each of $(x_{11_A}, x_{21_A}) = (1, 2)$ and $(x_{11_B}, x_{21_B}) = (2, 1)$ to the basket at the midpoint of the straight line segment connecting $(1, 2)$ and $(2, 1)$, show that the redistribution

$$(1, 2, 2, 1, x_{12_A}, x_{22_A}, x_{12_B}, x_{22_B})$$

cannot be in the core of the expanded model regardless of the components going to persons 2_A and 2_B.

c) By comparing $(x_{11_A}, x_{21_A}) = (3, 1)$ to the basket at the midpoint of the straight line segment connecting $(3, 1)$ and $(2, 4)$, and comparing $(x_{12_A}, x_{22_A}) = (2, 1)$ to the basket at the midpoint of the straight line segment connecting $(2, 1)$ and $(3, 4)$ show that the redistribution

$$(3, 1, 2, 4, 2, 1, 3, 4)$$

also cannot be in the core of the expanded model.

The results of 7.8(b) and 7.8(c) suggest the general proposition that identical persons receive equal treatment in the core.[19] Thus the core in the four-person model can be pictured in the Edgeworth box diagram drawn for 7.8(a).

d) Show that the components $(x_{11_A}, x_{21_A}, x_{12_A}, x_{22_A})$ and $(x_{11_B}, x_{21_B}, x_{12_B}, x_{22_B})$ of every x in the core of the four-person model are also in the core of the two-person model of 7.8(a).

e) By comparing $(x_{11_A}, x_{21_A}) = (1.8, 1.8)$ to a basket near the midpoint of the straight line segment connecting 1_A's initial endowment with $(1.8, 1.8)$, by making the same comparison for 1_B, and by comparing $(x_{12_A}, x_{22_A}) = (3.2, 3.2)$ to an appropriate nearby basket, show that the redistribution

$$(1.8, 1.8, 1.8, 1.8, 3.2, 3.2, 3.2, 3.2),$$

---

[19]   For a proof see Hildenbrand and Kirman [2, p. 167].

whose respective components are in the core of 7.8(a), is *not* in the core of the four-person model.

The last result also suggests a general proposition, namely, that as the number of persons identical to the original collection of individuals increases, the core shrinks towards the collection of all equilibrium distributions.[20]

7.9** In a two-good, two-person exchange model, the distribution $\bar{x} = (\bar{x}_{11}, \bar{x}_{21}, \bar{x}_{12}, \bar{x}_{22})$ is a *Nash two-person-bargaining equilibrium*[21] if it maximizes the product

$$[u^1(x_{11}, x_{21}) - u^1(x_{11}^0, x_{21}^0)][u^2(x_{12}, x_{22}) - u^2(x_{12}^0, x_{22}^0)]$$

over all distributions $x = (x_{11}, x_{21}, x_{12}, x_{22}) > 0$ such that

$$u^k(x_{1k}, x_{2k}) \geqslant u^k(x_{1k}^0, x_{2k}^0), \quad k = 1, 2,$$

and

$$x_{i1} + x_{i2} = x_{i1}^0 + x_{i2}^0, \quad i = 1, 2,$$

where $x = (x_{11}^0, x_{21}^0, x_{12}^0, x_{22}^0)$ is the vector of initial endowments. Show that, in the model of Exercise 7.1, a Nash two-person-bargaining equilibrium exists and is in the core (as derived in Exercise 7.8(a)), but is different from the competitive equilibrium distribution. (Note: the calculation of $\bar{x}$ is both difficult and unnecessary in this exercise.)

REFERENCES

1. Apostol, T. M., *Mathematical Analysis*, 2nd ed. (Reading: Addison-Wesley, 1974).
2. Hildenbrand, W., and A. P. Kirman, *Equilibrium Analysis: Variations on Themes by Edgeworth and Walras* (Amsterdam: North-Holland, 1988).
3. Jaffé, W., "Pareto Translated: A Review Article," *Journal of Economic Literature* 10 (1972), pp. 1190-1201.
4. Nash, J. F., Jr., "The Bargaining Problem," *Econometrica* 18 (1950), pp. 155-162.

---

[20] Hildenbrand and Kirman [2, p. 167]. In the case of Exercise 7.8 here, there is only one equilibrium distribution.

[21] Nash [4, p. 159]. This concept of equilibrium is different from the Nash equilibrium described towards the end of Section 15.2.

5. Pareto, V., *Manuel d'économie politique*, trans. into French by A. Bonnet (Geneva: Droz, 1966). English translation from the French: *Manual of Political Economy*, A. S. Schwier, trans. (New York: Kelley, 1971).

6. Radford, R. A., "The Economic Organisation of a P.O.W. Camp," *Economica*, n.s. 12 (1945), pp. 189-201.

7. Schumpeter, J. A., *History of Economic Analysis* (New York: Oxford University Press, 1954).

8. Vickers, D., *Economics and the Antagonism of Time* (Ann Arbor: University of Michigan Press, 1994).

9. Walras, L., *Elements of Pure Economics*, W. Jaffé trans. (Homewood: Irwin, 1954).

Chapter 8

The Fixed-Factor-Supply Economy

The fixed-factor-supply economy, that is, one in which individual factor supplies are viewed as fixed parameters, is a special case of the general production economy. Models of it have received widespread application in economics for several reasons. First, these models are especially useful because they permit simple and explicit expression of the notion of final commodity opportunity cost in terms of trade-offs along a transformation surface. Second, the two-dimensional geometry of equilibrium and the economy's production possibilities (the area on and under the transformation curve) is straightforward and easy to visualize. Last, the model's simplicity extends to its mathematical structure. These same reasons also provide the present pedagogic rationalization for examining the model in some detail before attempting the more complex problems of the general case. Because of the model's simplified and special nature, none of Sections 8.1 – 8.4 are appropriate for the particular grand view set out in Section 1.4. Still, it should be understood, the fixed-factor-supply economy serves as the basis for the analysis of imperfect competition, welfare, and capital in subsequent chapters.

For each person k, let $a_{jk} \geqslant 0$ denote his fixed supply of factor j, and suppose a_{jk} does not exceed his initial endowment y^0_{I+jk}, where $j = 1, \ldots, J$. Then the quantity of factor j that person k keeps for himself, namely y_{I+jk}, is related to his initial endowment and fixed supply of that factor by

$$y_{I+jk} = y_{I+jk}^0 - a_{jk}, \qquad \begin{matrix} j = 1, \ldots, J, \\ k = 1, \ldots, K. \end{matrix}$$

Evidently, individual k is permitted to consume nonnegative, fixed amounts of his initial endowment including, of course, leisure time. Hence to obtain the fixed-factor-supply model from that of the (perfectly competitive) general production economy, it is necessary only to add the above equations to those of Section 7.2 and to restrict consumer maximization of utility to the determination of demand for produced goods $i = 1, \ldots, I$. Consumer factor excess demands thus become fixed for all j and k at

$$q_{nk} = -a_{jk},$$

where $n = I + j$; utility functions can be written with the a_{jk} and initial endowment parameters subsumed in the functional symbol u^k:

$$\mu_k = u^k(q_{1k}, \ldots, q_{Ik});$$

and consumer excess demand functions for factors reduce to the constant functions

$$E^{nk}(P) = -a_{jk}, \quad n = I + j, \ j = 1, \ldots, J,$$

for each k and all $P > 0$. Assume that at least one $a_{jk} > 0$ for each k, and for each j.

It is an enormous convenience and, at the same time, has no significant impact on the central ideas of this chapter to suppose also that there are no intermediate commodities. In other words, all goods are either nonproduced factors or sold as final commodities to consumers. Without such an assumption the number and complexity of equations becomes excessive, notation becomes unnecessarily detailed, and the main results tend to be obscured. Thus the firm production functions of (7.2-1) can be truncated to

$$x_{i\ell} = f^{i\ell}(y_{i\ell 1}, \ldots, y_{i\ell J}),$$

for all i and ℓ, where $y_{i\ell j}$ is written in place of $y_{i\ell I+j}$ because it is no longer required to list quantities of goods $x_{i\ell n}$, as arguments of $f^{i\ell}$. It is also expedient to drop the excess demand notation of Chapter 7 and rely on the symbols of earlier chapters. The excess demand notation is employed again in Chapter 9.

Matters can be further simplified by noting that each industry in the model can be treated as if it were a single firm. The easiest way to see how the firms in an industry can be combined to achieve the latter end is to observe that if (as is assumed throughout) all firms within an industry are identical, then they always employ the same quantities of inputs and produce the same quantity of output. Hence with L_i denoting the number of firms in industry i, and with

$$x_i = \sum_{\ell=1}^{L_i} x_{i\ell} \quad \text{and} \quad y_{ij} = \sum_{\ell=1}^{L_i} y_{i\ell j},$$

for every i and j, the *industry production function* can be written as

$$x_i = f^i(y_{i1}, \ldots, y_{iJ}),$$

where

$$f^i(y_{i1}, \ldots, y_{iJ}) = L_i f^{i1}\left(\frac{y_{i1}}{L_i}, \ldots, \frac{y_{iJ}}{L_i}\right), \tag{8.0-1}$$

for each i. Firm $i1$, then, appears as the representative firm in industry i. In the long-run context, the symbolism f^i must be used with care because the number of firms in industry i is variable. In short-run models, however, the L_i are given parameters and this ambiguity does not arise. That industry production functions can still be defined in the absence of the identical-firms assumption is left as Exercise 8.1.

It follows upon differentiation of (8.0-1) that

$$f_j^i(y_{i1}, \ldots, y_{iJ}) = f_j^{i1}\left(\frac{y_{i1}}{L_i}, \ldots, \frac{y_{iJ}}{L_i}\right), \tag{8.0-2}$$

or, in words, that industry marginal products are the same as those of the representative firm. Moreover, if $TC^i(x_i)$ and $TC^{i1}(x_{i1})$ denote the total cost functions of, respectively, industry i and firm $i1$, then

$$TC^i(x_i) = [L_i] TC^{i1}\left(\frac{x_i}{L_i}\right).$$

Hence the marginal cost of the industry and representative firm are also identical:

$$MC^i(x_i) = MC^{i1}\left(\frac{x_i}{L_i}\right). \tag{8.0-3}$$

Therefore industry output supply and input demand functions can be obtained either by multiplying the functions of representative firm $i1$ by L_i as in

(6.1-2) or by directly applying the analysis of Chapters 4 and 5 in terms of industry profit maximization to the industry production function f^i.

This chapter begins by showing how, under certain conditions, all relevant technological information contained in industry production functions can be combined in the so-called transformation function. Section 8.2 then demonstrates that the ordinary industry supply functions in final goods (output) markets, secured on the basis of profit maximization by individual firms as described in Chapters 5 and 6, can be derived in a more general form directly from a maximization problem in which the transformation function appears as a constraint. Correspondingly, the aggregate consumer demand functions in these markets also turn out to be related, again under suitable conditions, to the constrained maximization of something referred to as the community utility function (Section 8.3). Like the transformation function which encapsulates all supply behavior of firms, the community utility function distills all demand behavior of consumers. Using the transformation and community utility functions, Section 8.4 provides conditions under which competitive equilibrium in the fixed-factor-supply model exists and is unique. In two dimensions both the uniqueness conditions and the equilibrium itself have simple and appealing geometric interpretations.

8.1   THE TRANSFORMATION SURFACE

Based on the foregoing, the production side of the fixed-factor-supply model is described by the I industry production functions

$$x_i = f^i(y_i), \quad i = 1, \ldots, I, \tag{8.1-1}$$

where $y_i = (y_{i1}, \ldots, y_{iJ})$ and all of the economy's factors are represented in the index $j = 1, \ldots, J$. Assume each f^i is defined for all $y_i \geqslant 0$ such that

(8.1-2) $f^i(0) = 0$ and $f^i(y_i) \geqslant 0$ for all $y_i \geqslant 0$.

(8.1-3) f^i is continuous everywhere and twice continuously differentiable where $y_i > 0$.

(8.1-4)   The first-order partial derivatives $f^i_j(y_i) > 0$ for all $y_i > 0$ and $j = 1, \ldots, J$.

(8.1-5) f^i is concave for all $y_i \geqslant 0$, and strictly quasi-concave for all $y_i > 0$.

Note that by not requiring the concavity of f^i in (8.1-5) to be strict in the interior of the input space, constant returns to scale production functions are possible in subsequent analysis. Thus both strictly concave and constant returns to scale models can be employed at the industry level. Condition (8.1-5), however, precludes production functions that generate Viner cost curves. (Some of the consequences of permitting such production functions are explored in Exercise 8.17.) For convenience it is supposed further that each industry's bordered Hessian determinant (based on the partial derivatives of the f^i) is nonzero where defined and that its isoquants associated with positive outputs do not intersect the boundaries of its input space. Observe that under these assumptions no cost-minimizing industry can produce a positive output without employing a positive amount of each input. Hence the convention adopted in Section 7.2, which permits the exclusion of inputs from the production function, is not relevant here. Subsequent discussion must be modified in the obvious way when certain industries never employ specific factors or when no usage of particular factors is one among many outcomes of cost-minimization.

Abbreviate (8.1-1) with the symbolism

$$x = f(y), \qquad\qquad (8.1\text{-}6)$$

where $x = (x_1, \ldots, x_I)$, $y = (y_1, \ldots, y_I)$ and $f = (f^1, \ldots, f^I)$. Note that y is also short for

$$y = (y_{11}, \ldots, y_{1J}, y_{21}, \ldots, y_{2J}, \ldots, y_{I1}, \ldots, y_{IJ}).$$

Let a_j be the aggregate fixed supply of the jth factor and $a = (a_1, \ldots, a_J)$. In terms of the previous notation,

$$a_j = \sum_{k=1}^{K} a_{jk}.$$

For any $a > 0$, let $\mathcal{A}_a$ be the collection of available input vectors, namely,

$$\mathcal{A}_a = \left\{ y : y \geqslant 0 \text{ and } \sum_{i=1}^{I} y_{ij} \leqslant a_j, \text{ for } j = 1, \ldots, J \right\}.$$

Then the *production possibility set* given a is defined by

$$\mathcal{T}_a = \{ x : x = f(y) \text{ and } y \text{ is in } \mathcal{A}_a \}.$$

Let X^I denote the following subset of one of the $(I-1)$-dimensional coordinate hyperplanes bounding $\mathcal{T}_a$:

$$X^I = \{ (x_1, \ldots, x_{I-1}) : (x_1, \ldots, x_{I-1}, 0) \text{ is in } \mathcal{T}_a \}.$$

The "interior" boundary of $\mathcal{T}_a$, that is, that portion of the boundary of $\mathcal{T}_a$ which does not intersect any coordinate hyperplane together with all limit points of this boundary portion, is called the *transformation surface*[1] given a. Assumption (8.1-4) implies that on the transformation surface the fixed factor supplies are used to their fullest extent. In explicit functional form the transformation surface is written

$$x_I = t(x_1, \ldots, x_{I-1}),$$

for all $(x_1, \ldots, x_{I-1})$ in X^I, where the given factor supply vector a is subsumed in the functional symbol t. These ideas are illustrated in two dimensions in Figure 8.1(a). Because $a > 0$ and f is continuous (assumption (8.1-3)), both $\mathcal{A}_a$ and $\mathcal{T}_a$ are nonempty, contain positive vectors, and are compact, and hence the transformation surface (the interior boundary of $\mathcal{T}_a$) exists.[2] Also

$$t(x_1, \ldots, x_{I-1}) \geqslant 0$$

on X^I.

An alternative way to define the transformation surface and function is to find, for each $(x_1, \ldots, x_{I-1})$ in X^I, the vector y_I that maximizes

$$x_I = f^I(y_I),$$

subject to the constraints

$$f^i(y_i) = x_i, \quad i = 1, \ldots, I-1,$$

and y is in $\mathcal{A}_a$. Adding to each vector $(x_1, \ldots, x_{I-1})$ in X^I the Ith component x_I obtained from the above maximization, where $x_1, \ldots, x_{I-1}$ are the numbers on the right-hand sides of the $I - 1$ production function constraints, yields the transformation surface. In functional terms, the maximization associates to every $(x_1, \ldots, x_{I-1})$ in X^I a unique x_I, thereby providing an explicit characterization of t. The continuity of the f^i (assumption (8.1-3)) and the definition of $\mathcal{A}_a$ ensure that the set over which the maximization of f^I is to take place after the constraints have been imposed is compact. Because a continuous function defined over a compact set always has a maximum function

---

[1] Although antecedents of the notion of transformation surface (along with many other ideas subsequently discussed in this chapter) make verbal appearances far back in the economics literature, Chipman [3, p. 685] credits von Haberler with its explicit introduction. See, for example, von Haberler [5, p. 176].

[2] With $a > 0$, the definition of $\mathcal{A}_a$ ensures its compactness. Because f is continuous and the continuous image of a compact set is compact [Rudin, 11, p. 89], $\mathcal{T}_a$ is compact. And since compact sets are closed and bounded, their boundaries exist.

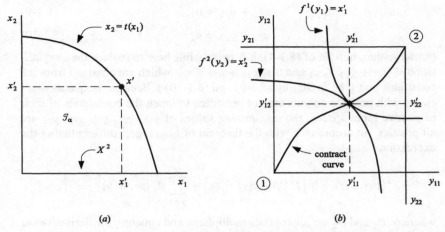

(a)   (b)

Figure 8.1 Production in a fixed-factor supply model: (a) production possibility set and transformation curve; (b) contract curve in the production Edgeworth box

value,[3] such x_I exist. Furthermore, the assumption of positive marginal productivity (8.1-4) guarantees that the maximum x_I is unique and lies on the interior boundary of the production possibility set. Hence the transformation surface and function can always be defined in this way, and the two approaches given here (namely, that based on the interior boundary of $\mathcal{T}_a$ and that derived from the constrained maximization of f^I) are, in so far as characterizing the transformation surface and function is concerned, equivalent.

Before considering the properties of transformation surfaces in general, it is worth examining the two-output, two-factor case in some detail. With $I = J = 2$, the transformation function

$$x_2 = t(x_1),$$

is derived by maximizing

$$x_2 = f^2(y_{21}, y_{22}), \tag{8.1-7}$$

subject to

$$f^1(y_{11}, y_{12}) = x_1, \tag{8.1-8}$$

---

[3]   See Theorem A.3-1 in appendix Section A.3 and the discussion following it.

$$y_{11} + y_{21} = a_1, \tag{8.1-9}$$

$$y_{12} + y_{22} = a_2. \tag{8.1-10}$$

(Observe that, in light of (8.1-4), it is permissible here to replace the inequalities $0 \leqslant y_{11} + y_{21} \leqslant a_1$ and $0 \leqslant y_{12} + y_{22} \leqslant a_2$, which are obtained from the constraint that y be in $\mathcal{A}_a$, by (8.1-9) and (8.1-10).) Because isoquants associated with positive outputs are not permitted to touch the boundaries of their respective input spaces, the maximizing values of y_{11}, y_{21}, y_{12}, and y_{22} are all positive. In accordance with the theorem of Lagrange,[4] differentiating the expression

$$f^2(y_{21}, y_{22}) + \alpha \left[f^1(y_{11}, y_{12}) - x_1 \right] + \sum_{j=1}^{2} \beta_j \left[y_{1j} + y_{2j} - a_j \right],$$

where α, β_1 and β_2 are appropriate multipliers, and equating the derivatives to zero leads to

$$\frac{f_1^1(y_{11}, y_{12})}{f_2^1(y_{11}, y_{12})} = \frac{f_1^2(y_{21}, y_{22})}{f_2^2(y_{21}, y_{22})}. \tag{8.1-11}$$

(Since at constrained maxima $(y_{11}, y_{12}) > 0$ and $(y_{21}, y_{22}) > 0$, all of these derivatives are defined.) When a solution exists, solving $(8.1-7) - (8.1-11)$ to eliminate the y_{ij} produces t. An illustration is provided by Exercise 8.2.

The equality of (8.1-11) is between familiar ratios. It asserts that the industry isoquants associated with the outputs derived from the constrained maximization of f^2 have identical slopes at the respective input vectors for which the maximum occurs.[5] In other words, the marginal rates of technical substitution identified with the industry production functions are equal at the maximum. This can be pictured in a (production) Edgeworth box diagram similar to that for consumption in Section 7.1. Figure 8.1(b) depicts such a box on whose coordinate axes are measured inputs for industries 1 and 2, and whose overall length and height sum to, respectively, the fixed-factor supplies a_1 and a_2. Parallel to the two-consumer case, any point in the box identifies a distribution of the available factor supplies between the industries. If $x' = (x_1', x_2') > 0$ is on the transformation curve (Figure 8.1a), then x_2' is the maximum output attainable for industry 2 under the constraints $(8.1-8) - (8.1-10)$. The isoquants corresponding to x_1' and x_2' appear in Figure 8.1(b).

---

[4] Theorem A.3-16 in appendix Section A.3. It is easy to see that the constraint qualification (A.3-17), in this case, involving the determinant of a 3×3 matrix, is satisfied since $f_1^1(y_{11}, y_{12}) \neq 0$ for all $(y_{11}, y_{12}) > 0$.
[5] The analysis of Chapter 4 applies to industry as well as firm production functions.

The strictness of the quasi-concavity of the f^i (assumption (8.1-5)) implies that the tangency (necessarily in the interior of the box and expressed, in part, in equation (8.1-11)) of these isoquants at the input vector obtained from the maximization, namely $(y'_{11}, y'_{12}, y'_{21}, y'_{22})$ is unique.

Thus each $x > 0$ on the transformation curve in Figure 8.1(a) must correspond to a unique tangency in the interior of the box of Figure 8.1(b). Conversely, each tangency in the interior of the box is associated with a unique $x > 0$ on the transformation curve[6] because isoquants are strictly convex, marginal products are positive, and at these tangencies the total quantity of fixed factor supplies is used up. The locus of all such tangencies in the box is called the *(production) contract curve*. Note that this curve must connect (but not include) the origins of the two industries. In terms of the coordinates of, say, industry 1, an expression identifying the behavior of that industry in relation to the contract curve is obtained by substituting (8.1-9) and (8.1-10) into (8.1-11):

$$\frac{f_1^1(y_{11}, y_{12})}{f_2^1(y_{11}, y_{12})} = \frac{f_1^2(a_1 - y_{11}, a_2 - y_{12})}{f_2^2(a_1 - y_{11}, a_2 - y_{12})}.$$

To sum up, the above argument establishes a 1–1 correspondence[7] between points on the contract curve and points on the transformation curve in the two-output, two-factor model.

The generalization of this proposition to any number of goods I and factors J is not difficult. But it does require a broader conceptualization of the notion of contract curve that permits I and J to be larger than 2. Thus let the *(production) contract set* be the collection of all vectors $y > 0$ such that for all $(x_1, \ldots, x_{I-1}) > 0$ in X^I, the vector y_I maximizes $x_I = f^I(y_I)$ subject to $f^i(y_i) = x_i$ for $i = 1, \ldots, I - 1$ and the constraint that y be in $\mathcal{A}_a$. Clearly the contract curve defined above is a special instance of the contract set.

Theorem 8.1-12[8]   There is a 1–1 correspondence between vectors $x = (x_1, \ldots, x_I) > 0$ on the transformation surface and vectors $y = (y_1, \ldots, y_I) > 0$ in the contract set.

Proof: The definitions of the transformation surface and the contract set ensure that each positive vector on the former is associated with at least one positive vector in the latter and vice versa. It remains to show that this correspondence is 1–1.

---

6   This relationship has been described by Samuelson [12, pp. 233, 234]. See also Bator [2].

7   The notion of a 1–1 correspondence is defined in appendix Section A.2.

8   This theorem and its proof is due to R. Bausor.

First, since f is a function, only one $x > 0$ on the transformation surface can be associated with each $y > 0$ in the contract set. Second, suppose that $y' > 0$ and $y'' > 0$ in the contract set were both associated with the same $x^0 > 0$ on the transformation surface. Then $x^0 = f(y')$ and $x^0 = f(y'')$. Since $y' = (y'_{11}, \ldots, y'_{1J}, y'_{21}, \ldots, y'_{IJ})$ and $y'' = (y''_{11}, \ldots, y''_{1J}, y''_{21}, \ldots, y''_{IJ})$ must be in $\mathcal{A}_a$, $\sum_{i=1}^{I} y'_{ij} \leqslant a_j$ and $\sum_{i=1}^{I} y''_{ij} \leqslant a_j$, where $j = 1, \ldots, J$. Now, for each θ such that $0 < \theta < 1$, these latter inequalities imply

$$\sum_{i=1}^{I} \{\theta y'_{ij} + [1 - \theta] y''_{ij}\} = \theta \sum_{i=1}^{I} y'_{ij} + [1 - \theta] \sum_{i=1}^{I} y''_{ij} \leqslant a_j, \quad j = 1, \ldots, J,$$

so that $\theta y' + [1 - \theta] y''$ is in $\mathcal{A}_a$ for all θ, where $0 < \theta < 1$. Hence, by the strict quasi-concavity of (8.1-5),

$$f(\theta y' + [1 - \theta] y'') > \theta f(y') + [1 - \theta] f(y'') = x^0.$$

Thus there would be an input vector, $\theta y' + [1 - \theta] y''$ in $\mathcal{A}_a$, which yielded an output vector, $f(\theta y' + [1 - \theta] y'')$ in the production possibility set, each of whose components are larger then those of x^0. But then x^0 could not lie on the transformation surface. This is a contradiction.

Q.E.D.

When the constraint qualification (A.3-17) is satisfied, and sometimes when it is not,[9] the method of Lagrange can be applied to the constrained maximization problem that characterizes the contract set to obtain the $(I - 1)(J - 1)$ equations

$$\frac{f_j^i(y_i)}{f_J^i(y_i)} = \frac{f_j^I(y_i)}{f_J^I(y_i)}, \qquad \begin{matrix} i = 1, \ldots, I - 1, \\ j = 1, \ldots, J - 1. \end{matrix} \tag{8.1-13}$$

These, together with the J input constraints (which may, as (8.1-9) and (8.1-10), be expressed as equalities)

$$\sum_{i=1}^{I} y_{ij} = a_j, \quad j = 1, \ldots, J, \tag{8.1-14}$$

constitute a system of $IJ - I + 1$ equations in the IJ unknowns y_{ij}. Conversely, should argument begin with the satisfaction of (8.1-13) and (8.1-14),

---

9   The constraint qualification is a sufficient — not a necessary — condition to be able to employ Lagrange multipliers. See Theorem A.3-16 and the discussion following it in appendix Section A.3.

it will be convenient to avoid discussion of all second-order maximization issues and simply take those equations to define the contract set as the outcome of the maximization problem from which it was initially derived. In either case, when solvable, the $IJ - I + 1$ equations of (8.1-13) and (8.1-14) can be used to eliminate $IJ - I$ unknowns. And regardless of whether $I = J$, $I > J$, or $I < J$, these latter relations with some of the y_{ij} removed, in parallel to the two-output, two-factor situation discussed above, often express the contract set in reference to one-dimensional curves in the input spaces (*i.e.*, with respect to the input variables) of each industry. (See Exercises 8.2, 8.4, 8.6, and 8.8. An example in which this kind of reduction is not possible appears in Exercise 8.5.) Such *implied curves*, derived from the contract set as they are, are not themselves contract sets or curves because they only account for what is happening in a single industry. In any case, equations (8.1-13) and (8.1-14), whether solvable or not, are frequently used as the defining characteristics of the contract set, under the assumption, of course, that the vectors y satisfying them are, in fact, appropriately maximizing (as opposed to, say, minimizing) values.

Clearly, the contract set may not identify a one-dimensional curve in the input space of each industry if the solvability of (8.1-13) and (8.1-14) mentioned above fails. Thus, for example, each of the industry production functions

$$f^1(y_{11}, y_{12}) = y_{11} + y_{12},$$

$$f^2(y_{21}, y_{22}) = y_{21} + y_{22},$$

yield linear isoquants with the same slope, and the contract set is the entire Edgeworth box. Note in this illustration that the strictness of the quasiconcavity assumption (8.1-5) along with the restriction that isoquants associated with postive outputs do not touch the boundary of their respective input spaces are violated. Even so, the transformation function still exists and is given by

$$x_2 = t(x_1) = a_1 + a_2 - x_1,$$

for $0 \leqslant x_1 \leqslant a_1 + a_2$.

The relationship between contract sets and transformation surfaces is explored further in the following proposition.

Theorem 8.1-15   Suppose all industry production functions are homogeneous of degree one. Then the transformation surface is linear if and only if the curve implied by the contract set in the input space of each industry is a one-dimensional ray from the origin.

Proof: Suppose the transformation surface is linear. Then any point on it can be written as

$$(\gamma_1 x_1^0, \ldots, \gamma_I x_I^0),$$

where the γ_i are numbers such that

$$0 \leqslant \gamma_i \leqslant 1,$$

$$\sum_{i=1}^{I} \gamma_i = 1,$$

and

$$x_i^0 = f^i(a_1, \ldots, a_J).$$

Now consider any $(\gamma_1 x_1^0, \ldots, \gamma_I x_I^0)$ on the transformation surface. By the homogeneity,

$$\gamma_i x_i^0 = \gamma_i f^i(a) = f^i(\gamma_i a_1, \ldots, \gamma_i a_J),$$

for each I. Because

$$\sum_{i=1}^{I} \gamma_i a_j = a_j, \quad j = 1, \ldots, J,$$

the vectors $(\gamma_1 a_1, \ldots, \gamma_1 a_J, \gamma_2 a_1, \ldots, \gamma_I a_J)$ must also lie in the contract set, and the component vectors $(\gamma_i a_1, \ldots, \gamma_i a_J)$ must lie on the implied curves in the input spaces of each industry i. Since this is true for any $\gamma_1, \ldots, \gamma_I$ and, hence, for all points on the transformation surface and in the contract set (which correspond as indicated in Theorem 8.1-12), the curves implied by the contract set must all be rays from the origin. (Note that the vector of fixed input supplies $a = (a_1, \ldots, a_J)$ lies at the end of the implied curve in the input space of each industry i because the points $(0, \ldots, 0, x_i^0, 0, \ldots, 0)$ are all on the transformation surface.)

Assume, on the other hand, that all implied curves are rays from the origin. Because each of the latter connects the origin with the point a, every component y_{ij} of any given vector $(y_{11}, \ldots, y_{1J}, y_{21}, \ldots, y_{IJ})$ in the contract set, where each subvector $(y_{i1}, \ldots, y_{iJ})$ lies on the implied curve in the input space of industry i, can be written as

$$y_{ij} = \delta_i a_j,$$

subject to $0 \leqslant \delta_i \leqslant 1$ and

$$\sum_{i=1}^{I} \delta_i = 1.$$

Let $x = (x_1, \ldots, x_I)$ be the vector of outputs associated with y. Of course, x must lie on the transformation surface. Invoking the homogeneity yields

$$x_i = f^i(\delta_i a_1, \ldots, \delta_i a_J) = \delta_i f^i(a), \quad i = 1, \ldots, I.$$

Hence

$$\sum_{i=1}^{I} \frac{x_i}{f^i(a)} = 1,$$

which is the equation of the transformation surface. Therefore the transformation surface is linear.

$$\text{Q.E.D.}$$

Thus, in the presence of constant returns to scale at the industry level, linearity of the transformation surface and linearity of the curves implied by the contract set in the input space of each industry go hand in hand. Observe that the first part of the proof of Theorem 8.1-15 breaks down if the production functions are homogeneous of any degree other than one. Even with all remaining hypotheses in force, the absence of linear homogeneity destroys the validity of the theorem, as the example of Exercise 8.6 shows.

Continuing with the hypotheses of Theorem 8.1-15 in place, it is also true that the transformation surface is linear if and only if along the transformation surface inputs are employed in the same fixed proportions by all industries. (See Exercise 8.16 and the example of Exercise 8.2.) Thus with constant returns to scale and everywhere varying input proportions, the transformation surface cannot be even partly linear. The only alternative in such a case is, according to the next result (Theorem 8.1-16) and the fact that industry production functions are still concave, for the transformation surface to be strictly concave. Actually Theorem 8.1-16 is not restricted to the situation of constant returns to scale alone. Rather, the proposition explores the implications of concavity of the f^i under the general requirements of this section, namely, that all industry production functions satisfy (8.1-2) – (8.1-5).

Theorem 8.1-16   The transformation surface (that is, the function t) is concave. If, in addition, all production functions are strictly concave in the interiors of their domains, then the concavity of the transformation surface is also strict.

Proof: Clearly the vectors $f(0)$ and $(0, \ldots, 0, \overline{x}_i, 0, \ldots, 0)$ for $i = 1, \ldots, I$, where $\overline{x}_i = f^i(a_1, \ldots, a_J)$, are in $\mathcal{T}_a$. Since f is continuous everywhere, and since $f_j^i(y_i) > 0$ for all $y_i > 0$, where $i = 1, \ldots, I$ and $j = 1, \ldots, J$, to produce a positive amount of any good or goods other than good i when all factor supplies are already devoted to the production of good i, requires some shifting of those factor supplies away from industry i, and hence the lowering of $\overline{x}_i$. It follows that to prove that the transformation surface is concave, it is sufficient to show that the production possibility set $\mathcal{T}_a$ is convex.

Thus let x' and x'' be in $\mathcal{T}_a$. Using the notation of (8.1-1) and (8.1-6), this means $x' = f(y')$ and $x'' = f(y'')$, where

$$\sum_{i=1}^{I} y'_{ij} \leqslant a_j, \quad j = 1, \ldots, J,$$

$$(8.1\text{-}17)$$

$$\sum_{i=1}^{I} y''_{ij} \leqslant a_j, \quad j = 1, \ldots, J,$$

and $y' = (y'_{11}, \ldots, y'_{1J}, y'_{21}, \ldots, y'_{IJ}) \geqslant 0$ and $y'' = (y''_{11}, \ldots, y''_{1J}, y''_{21}, \ldots, y''_{IJ}) \geqslant 0$. Convexity of $\mathcal{T}_a$ follows once it is established that all points on the line segment connecting x' and x'', namely,

$$\theta f(y') + [1 - \theta] f(y'')$$

for any θ such that $0 < \theta < 1$, lie in $\mathcal{T}_a$.

To that end, let θ with $0 < \theta < 1$ be given. Then as in the proof of Theorem 8.1-12, the vector $\theta y' + [1 - \theta] y''$ lies in $\mathcal{A}_a$. Hence $f(\theta y' + [1 - \theta] y'')$ is in $\mathcal{T}_a$. Furthermore, the concavity of f (assumption (8.1-5)) ensures

$$f(\theta y' + [1 - \theta] y'') \geqslant \theta f(y') + [1 - \theta] f(y''). \qquad (8.1\text{-}18)$$

Because f is continuous and because marginal products are positive (assumptions (8.1-3) and (8.1-4)), by reducing the components of $\theta y' + [1 - \theta] y''$, a vector $y^0 = (y^0_{11}, \ldots, y^0_{1J}, y^0_{21}, \ldots, y^0_{IJ})$ can be found such that

$$y^0_{ij} \leqslant \theta y'_{ij} + [1 - \theta] y''_{ij}, \quad i = 1, \ldots, I, \quad j = 1, \ldots, J,$$

and

$$f(y^0) = \theta f(y') + [1 - \theta] f(y'').$$

But since this, together with (8.1-17), implies

$$\sum_{i=1}^{I} y_{ij}^0 \leqslant a_j, \quad j = 1, \ldots, J,$$

it follows that y^0 is in $\mathcal{A}_a$. Therefore $f(y^0)$ must lie in $\mathcal{T}_a$ and $\mathcal{T}_a$ is convex.

When the concavity of all production functions is strict, apply the above argument to points $x' > 0$ and $x'' > 0$ on the transformation surface. In this case the inequality of (8.1-18) becomes strict so that $f(y^0)$ falls in the interior of $\mathcal{T}_a$. Therefore the transformation surface is strictly concave.

Q.E.D.

The converse assertions of Theorem 8.1-16 do not generally hold. In particular, strictly concave transformation surfaces are consistent with concave production functions whose concavity is not strict (see Exercises 8.8 and 8.9). Furthermore, as the example of Exercise 8.2 shows, concavity of production functions without strictness is not enough to rule out the possibility of linear transformation surfaces. (Recall that linear transformation surfaces have been related to linear curves implied by contract sets in Theorem 8.1-15.) Of course, if the concavity of the f^i in (8.1-5) were dropped, as would be necessary if the Viner model were invoked for some industry, then the concavity of the transformation surface t would not be assured. Even so, it would still be possible for t to be strictly concave over subregions of its domain (see Exercise 8.17).

The last property of transformation surfaces to be considered here is already implicit in the first part of the proof of Theorem 8.1-16. It is now proved explicitly in terms of the transformation function

$$x_I = t(x_1, \ldots, x_{I-1}). \tag{8.1-19}$$

Using (8.1-1) and (8.1-14), rewrite (8.1-19) as

$$f^I\left(a_1 - \sum_{i=1}^{I-1} y_{i1}, \ldots, a_J - \sum_{i=1}^{I-1} y_{iJ}\right) = t\big(f^1(y_1), \ldots, f^{I-1}(y_{I-1})\big).$$

Assuming that t is differentiable in the interior of its domain X^I and differentiating with respect to y_{ij} gives

$$t_i(x_1, \ldots, x_{I-1}) = -\frac{f_j^I(y_I)}{f_j^i(y_i)}, \quad \begin{array}{l} i = 1, \ldots, I-1, \\ j = 1, \ldots, J, \end{array} \tag{8.1-20}$$

where $(x_1, \ldots, x_I) = \left(f^1(y_1), \ldots, f^I(y_I)\right)$ and t_i denotes the ith partial derivative of t. Because marginal products are positive (assumption (8.1-4)),

$$t_i(x_1, \ldots, x_{I-1}) < 0, \quad i = 1, \ldots, I - 1, \tag{8.1-21}$$

in the interior of X^I. The absolute value of t_i is the rate at which the economy converts good i into good I along the transformation surface, or the *marginal rate of transformation* between i and I. Applying the industry analogues of the cost-minimizing equations (4.4-4), and the relationship between marginal cost and the Lagrange multiplier of Theorem 4.5-8, equation (8.1-20) becomes

$$t_i(x_1, \ldots, x_{I-1}) = -\frac{MC^i(x_i)}{MC^I(x_I)}, \tag{8.1-22}$$

for $i = 1, \ldots, I - 1$. Thus when t is differentiable, its partial derivatives are negative and, in absolute value, express the relative cost at the margin (or *opportunity cost*) of each good with respect to the Ith.

8.2 OUTPUT SUPPLY AND FACTOR DEMAND

As pointed out in the introduction to this chapter, one way to derive industry output supply and factor demand functions is to apply the argument of Chapters 4 and 5 to industry production functions by invoking the assumption that industries as a whole are profit maximizers. In the short run, at outputs with rising marginal costs in industry i, the results are, respectively,

$$x_i = G^{iJ+1}(r, p_i),$$
$$y_{ij} = G^{ij}(r, p_i), \quad j = 1, \ldots, J, \tag{8.2-1}$$

where $p_i \geqslant \widetilde{p}_i > 0$, the input price vector $r > 0$, $\widetilde{p}_i$ is minimum industry average variable cost, and $\widetilde{p}_i$ depends on r. If $p_i < \widetilde{p}_i$, recall, $x_i = y_{i1} = \ldots = y_{iJ} = 0$. Note that here the lower-case g of (5.1-8) and (5.1-9) has been capitalized and the subscript and superscript i added to distinguish industry i from the isolated firm of Chapter 5. Of course, equations (8.2-1) with $\widetilde{p}_i > 0$ are associated with the Viner model of Theorem 5.1-25. Although that model has been ruled out by earlier assumptions in Section 8.1, it is included here because, as Exercise 8.17 shows, the transformation function and surface can still be defined in its presence. Further reference to the Viner case will be made towards the end of this section. Recall that (8.2-1) requires (in addition to assumptions 4.1-2 – 4.1-5, the nonvanishing of bordered Hessians,[10] and the nonintersecting of isoquants where nonnegatively sloped and strictly convex with boundaries of input spaces) that production functions determine a subset of output values for which marginal costs slope upward and are unbounded over every expansion path. Under these conditions the G^{ij} and G^{iJ+1} are discontinuous at $\widetilde{p}_i$. On the other hand, if the last condition above were replaced by the restrictions that production functions were strictly concave, that their (unbordered) Hessian determinants were nonzero everywhere, and that their partial derivatives took on all positive real numbers as function values over every expansion path (so, in particular, marginal costs are unbounded and everywhere upward sloping), then each $\widetilde{p}_i$ would vanish for every $r > 0$, and the G^{ij} and G^{iJ+1} would be defined and continuously differentiable for all $(r, p_i) > 0$ (the strictly concave model of Theorem 5.1-24). A third alternative in which production functions exhibited constant returns to scale and all profits vanished identically (the constant returns to scale model of Theorem 5.1-26) would result in the G^{ij} and G^{iJ+1} being the set-valued functions of (5.1-20) and (5.1-21) defined only for $p_i = \widetilde{p}_i$ and $r > 0$.

The demand and supply functions of (8.2-1) are close to those obtained for excess demands in Section 7.2. Apart from functional ranges consisting of excess demand quantities in the latter case, the main difference for the Viner and strictly concave models is in the appearance of output prices other than p_i as functional arguments in (7.2-4) and (7.2-5). There, the actual output prices included corresponded to those intermediate goods that, according to the particular industry's technology, arose as arguments in its production function.[11] Similar minor differences would arise if the model of Section 7.2 were enlarged to permit constant returns to scale production functions.

However, in the fixed-factor-supply model, industry output supplies and input demands may frequently be expressed as functions of output prices alone. Factor prices are not needed. The present section explains how this comes about. There are four parts to the discussion: First, a new kind of industry supply function is defined from the maximization of the value of the economy's (final) output subject to the transformation surface. Second, the properties of such a function (which turn out to be analogous to those of demand functions generated from the maximization of utility subject to the budget constraint) are explored. Third, the implicit determination of factor prices in constrained-

---

[10]   Actually, in Chapter 5 the bordered Hessian is taken to be nonzero only where all of its associated marginal products are also nonzero. But here, in light of assumption (8.1-4), this implies that bordered Hessians are nonvanishing everywhere.

[11]   Of course, some factor prices may be excluded as arguments of the G^{ij} if technology precludes the appearance of these factors in certain firm production functions.

value-of-output maximization is described. And fourth, the relationship of these new industry supply functions to the old industry supply functions of (8.2-1) is examined.

Retaining assumptions (8.1-2)–(8.1-5), consider the transformation function

$$x_I = t(x_1, \ldots, x_{I-1}),$$

mapping X^I into the nonnegative real numbers and suppose that

(8.2-2) t is continuous on X^I and twice, continuously differentiable in the interior of X^I.

(8.2-3)   The first-order partial derivatives $t_i(x_1, \ldots, x_{I-1}) < 0$ in the interior of X^I for $i = 1, \ldots, I - 1$.

(8.2-4) t is strictly concave.

Properties (8.2-3) and (8.2-4) could be obtained as derived earlier from characteristics of industry production functions (8.1-2) – (8.1-5). (Recall equation (8.1-21) and Theorem 8.1-16.) Note that the continuance of (8.1-5) eliminates industry Viner models from consideration. (As previously indicated, attention will return to the Viner case at the end of the section.) Moreover, (8.2-4) precludes some but not all circumstances with constant returns to scale production functions, as Exercises 8.2, 8.8, 8.9, and 8.16 show. In what follows, (8.2-3) is sometimes referred to as differential decreasingness.

Let input and output price vectors $r = (r_1, \ldots, r_J)$ and $p = (p_1, \ldots, p_I)$ be given. Then cost minimization in production implies

$$\frac{f_j^i(y_i)}{f_J^i(y_i)} = \frac{r_j}{r_J}, \qquad \begin{matrix} i = 1, \ldots, I, \\ j = 1, \ldots, J - 1. \end{matrix} \tag{8.2-5}$$

It follows that the first-order conditions (8.1-13) secured from maximizing f^I subject to output and factor constraints are met. When the latter factor constraints, namely (8.1-14) or

$$\sum_{i=1}^{I} y_{ij} = a_j, \quad j = 1, \ldots, J,$$

also are satisfied, that is, when the fixed factor supplies are fully employed, (8.2-5) must indeed, by an earlier convention imposed to avoid discussion of second-order maximization conditions, be associated with a constrained maximum value of $f^I(y_I)$. Hence any output vector identified with firm or industry cost minimization and (8.1-14) necessarily lies on the transformation surface.

Moreover, any point on the transformation surface may, under present assumptions, be interpreted as a vector of industry output supplies. To see why, observe first that such a point can also be viewed as one that uniquely maximizes, for an appropriate choice of p, the value of output $p \cdot x$ (the dot denotes inner product) subject to the production possibility set $\mathcal{T}_a$ or, equivalently, to $x_I = t(x_1, \ldots, x_{I-1})$. An argument similar to that of Theorem 2.3-10 for utility maximization indicates that a unique maximizer $x \geqslant 0$ exists for every $p > 0$. Hence a function associating maximizing x's to positive p's is defined:

$$x = \widehat{G}(p), \qquad (8.2\text{-}6)$$

where $\widehat{G} = (\widehat{G}^1, \ldots, \widehat{G}^I)$. To simplify notation, the superscript $J + 1$ that appears on the output supply function of (8.2-1) is discarded. It is reintroduced when needed toward the end of this section. Geometrically, x corresponds to p under $\widehat{G}$ if x lies on the transformation surface, and if the surface is tangent there to an iso-value-of-output hyperplane determined by p. A two-dimensional case is illustrated in Figure 8.2. The mathematics of the tangency in the interior of X^I, namely,

$$-t_i(x_1, \ldots, x_{I-1}) = \frac{p_i}{p_I}, \quad i = 1, \ldots, I - 1, \qquad (8.2\text{-}7)$$

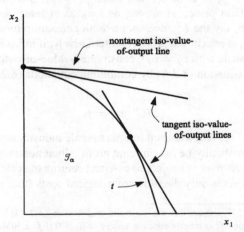

Figure 8.2 Value-of-output maximization subject to the production possibility set

is derived from Lagrange's constrained maximization theorem in the usual way.[12]

To show that x_i, in general, is supplied by industry i when

$$x_i = \widehat{G}^i(p) > 0$$

for every i and $(x_1, \ldots, x_{I-1})$ is in the interior of X^I, notice that if $p_i \geqslant \widetilde{p}_i$ where $i = 1, \ldots, I$, and if every industry is able to produce so as to maximize profit,[13] then

$$MC^i(x_i) = p_i, \quad i = 1, \ldots, I.$$

Upon dividing the Ith equation into those remaining,

$$\frac{MC^i(x_i)}{MC^I(x_I)} = \frac{p_i}{p_I}, \quad i = 1, \ldots, I-1. \tag{8.2-8}$$

Combining (8.2-8) and (8.1-22) yields (8.2-7). Therefore given p and r, industry profit maximization with full employment of the fixed factor supplies and value-of-output maximization subject to the transformation surface each yield the same vector x. The relationship between the supply function G^{iJ+1} of (8.2-1) and $\widehat{G}^i$ is discussed later on.

Recall that if the production function of some industry i exhibits constant returns to scale, a unique profit-maximizing output for that industry cannot exist when $p_i \geqslant \widetilde{p}_i$: For when $p_i = \widetilde{p}_i$, all outputs are profit maximizing and $MC^i(x_i) = p_i$ at each x_i; and when $p_i > \widetilde{p}_i$, marginal cost is everywhere smaller than price. However, as long as at least one industry's production function, say the Ith, does not exhibit constant returns to scale so that $MC^I(x_I) = p_I$, at maximum profit (or alternatively, if industry I exhibits constant returns to scale with $p_I = \widetilde{p}_I$), constrained-value-of-output maximization (which implies equation (8.2-8) by combining equations (8.2-7) and (8.1-22)) ensures

$$MC^i(x_i) = p_i,$$

for $i = 1, \ldots, I-1$. Any constant returns to scale industry among $1, \ldots, I-1$, then, must automatically be maximizing profit, albeit nonuniquely. When production in all industries is subject to constant returns to scale, value-of-output maximization reveals only the ratios of marginal costs (that is, the derivatives

---

[12]   Assumption (8.2-3) ensures that the constraint qualification (A.3-17) is satisfied.
[13]   Thus $p_i > 0$ when f^i is strictly concave, and $p_i = \widetilde{p}_i > 0$ if f^i exhibits constant returns to scale. Recall that the Viner case is not relevant under present assumptions.

of the transformation function). Marginal costs themselves continue to be in-
determinate. At the single-industry level in any of the above cases, as with all
constant-returns-to-scale industries in isolation, the problems of what quantities of output to produce and how many units of inputs to hire remain. But
once constrained-value-of-output maximization is assumed, all industries interact with each other and against the constraint imposed by the fixed factor
supplies so as to determine unique industry outputs and inputs, provided the
transformation surface is strictly concave. (See Exercises 8.7 – 8.9.)

The properties of $\widehat{G}$ parallel those of consumer demand functions. Thus
$\widehat{G}$ is nonnegative, continuous, homogeneous of degree zero, and satisfies the
transformation constraint

$$\widehat{G}^I(p) = t(\widehat{G}^1(p), \ldots, \widehat{G}^{I-1}(p)). \tag{8.2-9}$$

Observe, in particular, that the homogeneity implies

$$\widehat{G}^i(p) = \widehat{G}^i\left(\frac{p_1}{p_I}, \ldots, \frac{p_{I-1}}{p_I}, 1\right), \quad i = 1, \ldots, I,$$

for all $p > 0$. The differential properties of $\widehat{G}$ are obtained from the statement
of tangency between an iso-value-of-output hyperplane and the transformation
surface (8.2-7). Note that the tangency need not hold where the transformation
surface meets the boundary of the space $X = \{x : x \geqslant 0\}$. (See Figure 8.2.)
But to all other x on the transformation surface, there corresponds a unique
price-ratio vector

$$\left(\frac{p_1}{p_I}, \ldots, \frac{p_{I-1}}{p_I}\right),$$

defining the tangent iso-value-of-output hyperplane at x. Hence, using the
homogeneity of $\widehat{G}$, it follows that the vectors $(t_1, \ldots, t_{I-1})$ from (8.2-7) and
$(\widehat{G}^1, \ldots, \widehat{G}^{I-1})$ where

$$x_i = \widehat{G}^i\left(\frac{p_1}{p_I}, \ldots, \frac{p_{I-1}}{p_I}\right), \quad i = 1, \ldots, I - 1,$$

must be inverse functions. Therefore $\widehat{G}$ can be found by first inverting (8.2-
7) on the interior of X^I to secure $(\widehat{G}^1, \ldots, \widehat{G}^{I-1})$ and then substituting these
functions into the transformation function, as in (8.2-9), to produce $\widehat{G}^I$.

In general, $\widehat{G}$ is differentiable at prices p corresponding to vectors $x > 0$
on the transformation surface, and hence to interior vectors $(x_1, \ldots, x_{I-1})$ of

X^I, such that the determinant of the Jacobian of (8.2-7), namely,

$$T(x_1,\ldots,x_{I-1}) = \begin{bmatrix} -t_{11}(x_1,\ldots,x_{I-1}) & \cdots & -t_{1I-1}(x_1,\ldots,x_{I-1}) \\ \vdots & & \vdots \\ -t_{I-11}(x_1,\ldots,x_{I-1}) & \cdots & -t_{I-1I-1}(x_1,\ldots,x_{I-1}) \end{bmatrix},$$

is nonzero. By the strict concavity of t (assumption (8.2-4)), T is positive semidefinite on the interior of X^I and positive definite except for "isolated" points.[14] This means $|T(x_1,\ldots,x_{I-1})| \neq 0$ and hence that $\widehat{G}$ is differentiable "practically" everywhere.[15] In addition, throughout the interior of X^I the second-order continuous differentiability of t (assumption (8.2-2)) implies that T is symmetric.[16]

Now where $|T(x_1,\ldots,x_{I-1})| \neq 0$, the inverse matrix T^{-1}exists, and its elements are the derivatives of $(\widehat{G}^1,\ldots,\widehat{G}^{I-1})$.[17] That is, denoting the partial derivative of $\widehat{G}^i$ with respect to its nth argument by $\widehat{G}^i_n$ for $n = 1,\ldots,I-1$,

$$T^{-1}\left(\frac{p_1}{p_I},\ldots,\frac{p_{I-1}}{p_I},1\right) =$$
$$\begin{bmatrix} \widehat{G}^1_1\left(\frac{p_1}{p_I},\ldots,\frac{p_{I-1}}{p_I},1\right) & \cdots & \widehat{G}^1_{I-1}\left(\frac{p_1}{p_I},\ldots,\frac{p_{I-1}}{p_I},1\right) \\ \vdots & & \vdots \\ \widehat{G}^{I-1}_1\left(\frac{p_1}{p_I},\ldots,\frac{p_{I-1}}{p_I},1\right) & \cdots & \widehat{G}^{I-1}_{I-1}\left(\frac{p_1}{p_I},\ldots,\frac{p_{I-1}}{p_I},1\right) \end{bmatrix}.$$

But because T is symmetric and positive definite at these x's, so is T^{-1} at the corresponding price-ratio vectors.[18] An alternative way of saying the same thing is that the matrix

$$\begin{bmatrix} \widehat{G}^1_1(p) & \cdots & \widehat{G}^1_{I-1}(p) \\ \vdots & & \vdots \\ \widehat{G}^{I-1}_1(p) & \cdots & \widehat{G}^{I-1}_{I-1}(p) \end{bmatrix} =$$

---

[14]   See Katzner [7, pp. 183, 200, 202] and Debreu [4, pp. 391, 392]. A definition of positive definite is given in appendix Section A.4.

[15]   Apostol [1, p. 372]. Recall that a similar result was obtained (in property 2.3-18) for consumer demand functions.

[16]   Rudin [11, p. 236]. See Theorem A.3-3 in appendix Section A.3.

[17]   Apostol [1, p. 373]. See also appendix Section A.4 for a definition of the concept of inverse matrix.

[18]   See appendix Section A.4.

$$T^{-1}\left(\frac{p_1}{p_I},\dots,\frac{p_{I-1}}{p_I},1\right)\begin{bmatrix} \dfrac{1}{p_I} & 0 & 0 & \cdots & 0 \\[2mm] 0 & \dfrac{1}{p_I} & 0 & \cdots & 0 \\[2mm] 0 & 0 & \dfrac{1}{p_I} & \cdots & 0 \\[2mm] \vdots & \vdots & \vdots & \ddots & \vdots \\[2mm] 0 & 0 & 0 & & \dfrac{1}{p_I} \end{bmatrix},$$

is symmetric and positive definite where defined because, again by the homogeneity,[19]

$$\widehat{G}_n^i\left(\frac{p_1}{p_I},\dots,\frac{p_{I-1}}{p_I},1\right) = p_I\widehat{G}_n^i(p),\quad i,n = 1,\dots,I-1.$$

Recall, by comparison, that the $I-1$ by $I-1$ matrix of consumer Slutsky functions is symmetric and negative definite on Ω (Theorems 2.4-19 and 2.4-18).

If assumptions (8.2-2) – (8.2-4) are weakened to permit, say, kinks or linear segments in the transformation surface, then the above analysis must be modified along lines suggested in Section 3.2 where similar difficulties are introduced into the theory of demand.[20] An example is provided in Exercise 8.7.

To express industry input demands as a function of p alone, note that each $p > 0$ determines a unique supply vector x according to

$$x = \widehat{G}(p).$$

---

[19]   The equation that follows is secured upon partially differentiating

$$\widehat{G}^i\left(\frac{p_1}{p_I},\dots,\frac{p_{I-1}}{p_I},1\right) = \widehat{G}^i(p_1,\dots,p_I),\quad i = 1,\dots,I,$$

with respect to p_n. Although the symbol $\widehat{G}_n^i$ continues to indicate the partial derivative of $\widehat{G}^i$ with respect to its nth argument, the derivatives

$$\widehat{G}_n^i\left(\frac{p_1}{p_I},\dots,\frac{p_{I-1}}{p_I},1\right)$$

and $\widehat{G}_n^i(p_1,\dots,p_I)$ are different because the nth arguments of these functions are different. Thus, for example, if $I = 2$ and $\widehat{G}^1(p_1,p_2) = p_1/p_2$, then $\widehat{G}_1^1(p_1,p_2) = 1/p_2$. Nevertheless $\widehat{G}_1^1(p_1/p_2,1) = 1$.

[20]   The case in which linear segments can appear on the transformation surface is considered in general by Katzner [6, pp. 35-37, 39-42].

Because this $x = (x_1, \ldots, x_I)$ lies on the transformation surface, corresponding input demands for industry i can be found, as a function of p, from the 1–1
corespondence of Theorem 8.1-12. The properties of these input demand functions are not examined here except to note that they, too, are homogeneous of
degree zero. Thus value-of-output maximization leads to industry output supply and input demand functions of the form

$$x_i = \widehat{G}^{iJ+1}(p),$$

$$y_{ij} = \widehat{G}^{ij}(p),$$

(8.2-10)

where $i = 1, \ldots, I, j = 1, \ldots, J$, and the superscript $J+1$ has been reinstated
on the output supply functions to distinguish them clearly from input demand
functions. The surprising thing about (8.2-10) is that not only do output supply
functions but also input demand functions appear to be independent of input
prices. It is worth pausing for a moment to see what has happened.

Within the collections of positive output and input price-ratio vectors
define the sets:

$$\mathcal{P} = \left\{ \left(\frac{p_1}{p_I}, \ldots, \frac{p_{I-1}}{p_I} \right) : \text{there exists a vector } x > 0 \text{ such that } x_I = t(x_1, \right.$$

$$\left. \ldots, x_{I-1}) \text{ and } \frac{p_i}{p_I} = -t_i(x_1, \ldots, x_{I-1}), \text{ for } i = 1, \ldots, I-1 \right\}.$$

$$\mathcal{R} = \left\{ \left(\frac{r_1}{r_J}, \ldots, \frac{r_{J-1}}{r_J} \right) : \text{there exists a vector } y > 0 \text{ such that } \sum_{i=1}^{I} y_{ij} \right.$$

$$\left. = a_j \text{ and } \frac{r_j}{r_J} = \frac{f_j^i(y_i)}{f_J^i(y_i)}, \text{ for } i = 1, \ldots, I \text{ and } j = 1, \ldots J-1 \right\}.$$

Thus $\mathcal{P}$ is the set of all output-price-ratio vectors corresponding to the iso-
value-of-output hyperplanes tangent to the transformation surface. The smoothness and strict concavity of the transformation surface (assumptions (8.2-2)
and (8.2-4)) ensure that there is a 1–1 correspondence between positive vectors x on the transformation surface and the elements of $\mathcal{P}$. On the other hand,
$\mathcal{R}$ is the set of input-price-ratio vectors corresponding to iso-cost hyperplanes
tangent to isoquants at input distributions in the contract set. Although the
tangencies between isocost and isoquant are unique along any given isoquant
(from the smoothness and strict quasi-concavity of industry production functions — assumptions (8.1-3) and (8.1-5)), they may occur for any given vector
in $\mathcal{R}$ at more than one y in the contract set. This happens when iso-cost hy-

perplanes associated with the same input-price-ratio vector are tangent to more than one collection of isoquants (one for each firm). In other words, the contract set reduced to its implied curves in the input spaces of some industries must intersect at least one expansion path in those spaces at more than one point. (Intersections at the origins or at points associated with the origins of other industries under the fixed-factor-supply limitations do not count.) But if these multiple-intersection possibilities are ruled out, then there is a 1–1 correspondence between positive vectors y in the contract set and the elements of $\mathcal{R}$. Combining the 1–1 correspondences between outputs and output-price ratios and between inputs and input-price ratios, together with the 1–1 correspondence of Theorem 8.1-12 gives the result of Theorem 8.2-11.

Theorem 8.2-11   If the contract set, reduced to its implied curve in the input space of any industry, intersects no expansion path in that space at more than one point, then there is a 1–1 corespondence between $\mathcal{P}$ and $\mathcal{R}$.

Now suppose that there are only two industries and that both production functions are homothetic. Then in the input space of each industry (see Exercise 8.14), either

    a) the contract curve is linear and coincides with an expansion path, or

    b) no expansion path intersects the contract curve at more than one interior point.

When (b) holds in each industry, Theorem 8.2-11 applies and there is a 1–1 correspondence between $\mathcal{P}$ and $\mathcal{R}$. With (a) in force everywhere, $\mathcal{R}$ contains exactly one vector. If, in addition to (a) in each industry, it were also assumed that each production function were homogeneous of degree one, then the transformation surface would be linear by Theorem 8.1-15 (this, of course, would violate assumption 8.2-4), and hence $\mathcal{P}$ also would contain exactly one vector. The 1–1 correspondence of Theorem 8.2-11 would therefore be reduced to the trivial identification of two isolated points.

Thus, under the hypothesis of Theorem 8.2-11, the structure of the fixed-factor-supply model is such that the following property holds: Given any $p > 0$ whose associated vector of output-price ratios lies in $\mathcal{P}$, maximization of the value of output subject to the transformation surface determines input price ratios along with profit-maximizing market (industry) output supplies and industry (not market) input demands. By taking a different route, however, it is sometimes possible to go still further.

Abbreviate the input demand functions of (8.2-10) with the vector notation

$$y_i = \mathcal{G}^i(p), \quad i = 1, \ldots, I,$$

where $y_i = (y_{i1}, \ldots, y_{iJ})$ and $\mathcal{G}^i = (\widehat{G}^{i1}, \ldots, \widehat{G}^{iJ})$. Then, when the profit-maximizing conditions of (5.1-11), namely,

$$r_j = p_i f_j^i(y_i), \quad \begin{array}{l} i = 1, \ldots, I, \\ j = 1, \ldots, J, \end{array} \tag{8.2-12}$$

are applicable, it follows that

$$r_j = p_i f_j^i(\mathcal{G}^i(p)) \quad \begin{array}{l} i = 1, \ldots, I, \\ j = 1, \ldots, J, \end{array} \tag{8.2-13}$$

for all $p > 0$ whose associated output-price-ratio vector is in $\mathcal{P}$. Hence, for the same p.

$$\frac{r_j}{p_I} = f_j^I(\mathcal{G}^I(p)), \quad j = 1, \ldots, J, \tag{8.2-14}$$

and

$$\frac{r_j}{r_J} = \frac{f_j^i(\mathcal{G}^i(p))}{f_J^i(\mathcal{G}^i(p))}, \quad \begin{array}{l} i = 1, \ldots, I, \\ j = 1, \ldots, J - 1. \end{array} \tag{8.2-15}$$

Even though the $\mathcal{G}^i$ are homogeneous of degree zero, (8.2-13) still provides a unique r for each $(p_1/p_I, \ldots, p_{I-1}/p_I)$ in $\mathcal{P}$. Moreover, unique vectors $(r_1/p_I, \ldots, r_J/p_I)$ and $(r_1/r_J, \ldots, r_{J-1}/r_J)$ are associated to every $(p_1/p_I, \ldots, p_{I-1}/p_I)$ by, respectively, (8.2-14) and (8.2-15). As pointed out earlier, (8.2-12) may not be available in some cases of constant returns to scale. Furthermore, unless conditions such as the hypotheses of Theorem 8.2-11 obtain, (8.2-15) need not produce a 1–1 correspondence between input and output price ratios: Although each $(p_1/p_I, \ldots, p_{I-1}/p_I)$ is mapped into a single $(r_1/r_J, \ldots, r_{J-1}/r_J)$, many $(p_1/p_I, \ldots, p_{I-1}/p_I)$s might be identified with the same $(r_1/r_J, \ldots, r_{J-1}/r_J)$ and some $(r_1/r_J, \ldots, r_{J-1}/r_J)$'s might not be linked with any $(p_1/p_I, \ldots, p_{I-1}/p_I)$ at all. But provided that (8.2-12) holds for at least one i and all $j = 1, \ldots, J$, constrained-value-of-output maximization always determines an r from p according to (8.2-13). Input prices, then, have not "disappeared" from the input demand and output supply functions of (8.2-10). They are implicit in the $\widehat{G}^{ij}$ and can often be made explicit upon substitution from (8.2-13).

As noted in Section 8.1 and exemplified in Exercise 8.17, the presence of Viner models at the industry level need not completely destroy the strict concavity of the transformation surface. The argument of this section applies wherever the strict concavity remains intact. In these situations, input demand and output supply functions $\widehat{G}^{ij}$ are defined by constrained-value-of-output maximization for $p \geqslant (\widetilde{p}_1, \ldots, \widetilde{p}_I)$, where $\widetilde{p}_i > 0$ is the minimum average variable cost (that is, the shutdown point) in industry i. (Recall that the strictly concave model for any industry i can be regarded as a special case of the Viner model in which $\widetilde{p}_i = 0$ and positive output is supplied and positive input demanded for all $p_i > 0$.) It remains to consider the relationship between the $\widehat{G}^{ij}$ secured for strictly concave, constant returns to scale, and Viner model regimes and the G^{ij} of (8.2-1), which were derived for the same regimes by application of the analysis of Chapters 4 and 5 to industry production functions.

Except in cases of constant returns to scale, given any i and j, both $\widehat{G}^{ij}$ and G^{ij} relate profit-maximizing input or output to input and output prices linked by equations (8.2-13), for all p whose associated output vector x lies on the strictly concave portion of the transformation surface. As long as the same input and output prices are used for each, identical function values are obtained. (The exceptions with constant returns to scale are illustrated by industry 2 in Exercise 8.9.) In particular (with appropriate qualification for circumstances of constant returns to scale), substitution of (8.2-13) with, say $i = I$, into (8.2-1) and combining the result with (8.2-10), gives

$$\widehat{G}^{ij}(p) = G^{ij}\left(p_I f_1^I\left(\mathcal{G}^I(p)\right), \ldots, p_I f_J^I\left(\mathcal{G}^I(p)\right), p_i\right),$$

for $i = 1, \ldots, I$, $j = 1, \ldots, J + 1$, and all $p \geqslant (\widetilde{p}_1, \ldots, \widetilde{p}_I)$ such that the output-price ratio vector associated with p is in $\mathcal{P}$. Therefore, in the fixed-factor-supply model, the $\widehat{G}^{ij}$ of (8.2-10) and the G^{ij} of (8.2-1) often amount to the same thing.

To obtain long-run output supply and input demand functions equivalent to those of Section 5.2 and 6.2 requires some modification. To begin with, long-run industry production and cost functions cannot be derived as in the introduction to this chapter until the numbers of firms in each industry, the L_i, are either determined at long-run equilibrium or specified by assumption. (Recall equations (8.0-1) – (8.0-3).) Moreover, production functions could not be strictly concave for then the absence of fixed costs would imply that minimum long-run average cost would be zero, and hence long-run equilibrium output prices and quantities would have to vanish. One possibility is to skip over individual firms and to assume that all industry production functions are subject to constant returns to scale. Then industry profit maximization at positive outputs and the long-run zero-profit condition would guarantee that with $\widetilde{p}_i$, the minimum (and constant) long-run average cost in industry i and $p = (\widetilde{p}_1, \ldots, \widetilde{p}_I)$,

$$MC^i(x_i) = LRAC^i(x_i) = \widetilde{p}_i, \quad i = 1, \ldots, I,$$

for every x_i, and the derivation of long-run output supply and input demand functions could proceed in terms of the value-of-output maximization above. Notice that the number of firms in each industry is not determinate because the minimum average cost in the representative firm does not occur at a unique output. Hence the output of the representative firm remains unknown until the L_i, are assigned specific values. Under these circumstances it might also be appropriate to weaken the strictness of the concavity assumed in (8.2-4) and permit linear segments on the transformation surface and the consequent set-valuedness of the $\widehat{G}^{ij}$.

Recall that if the production function of the representative firm in an industry were of the Viner type, then it would be necessary to assign a value to L_i in order to specify the industry production function as defined in (8.0-1), and all previous discussion of the difficulties pursuant to industry Viner models would be relevant. However, if the long-run zero-profit condition forcing the representative firm always to produce at minimum long-run average cost were additionally imposed, then the long-run position of the industry would be identical to that which would obtain if a constant returns to scale industry production function were assumed having minimum long-run average cost for each $r > 0$ identical to that of the corresponding Viner average cost curves. Thus the industry can be thought of as possessing a technology distinct from the technology of its constituent firms. Assuming this to be so in every industry, an everywhere concave transformation surface for the economy can be found, and functions $\widehat{G}^{ij}$ can be derived that represent all long-run industry input demand and output supply functions. Therefore the Viner model has a role to play at the level of the individual firm in the long-run fixed-factor-supply framework even when the concavity of (8.1-5) is required of all industry production functions.

8.3   THE COMMUNITY UTILITY FUNCTION

Just as aggregate firm (that is, industry) behavior can be understood in terms of a transformation surface, it is convenient in the fixed-factor-supply model to analyze aggregate consumer behavior with reference to a *community utility function*. The latter is defined as a utility function which, when maximized subject to an aggregate budget constraint, produces the same market demand functions obtained by summing consumer demand functions derived from individual utility maximization.[21] The community utility function is united in the next section with the transformation surface to describe equilibrium in the fixed-factor-supply model and to provide a basis for proving existence and uniqueness of that equilibrium. There is no presumption here that the community utility function says anything at all about community "welfare." The special conditions under which the community utility function might indeed be viewed as a "welfare function" are noted at the end of this section and in Section 12.1.

The argument[22] begins with the short-run budget constraint facing person k. As described in the introduction to this chapter, consumer excess demands for factors, q_{nk}, are related to nonnegative fixed supplies:

$$q_{nk} = -a_{jk}, \qquad \begin{array}{l} j = 1, \ldots, J, \\ k = 1, \ldots, K, \end{array} \qquad (8.3\text{-}1)$$

where $n = I + j$. Assume at least one $a_{jk} > 0$ for each k as j varies, and for each j as k varies. The vector of fixed factor supplies attributed to person k is written $a_k = (a_{1k}, \ldots, a_{Jk})$. Furthermore, because there are no initial endowments of produced goods,

$$q_{nk} = x_{ik}, \qquad \begin{array}{l} n = i = 1, \ldots, I, \\ k = 1, \ldots, K. \end{array} \qquad (8.3\text{-}2)$$

Hence the budget constraint (7.2-12) can be written as

$$p \cdot x_k = m_k, \qquad (8.3\text{-}3)$$

where $x_k = (x_{1k}, \ldots, x_{Ik})$ and income is secured from the sale of the fixed factor supplies and the return of profits and fixed costs to consumers, that is,

$$m_k = r \cdot a_k + \sum_{i=1}^{I} \sum_{\ell=1}^{L_i} \theta_{ki\ell} \left(\pi_{i\ell} + b_{i\ell} \right), \qquad (8.3\text{-}4)$$

for each k. (The disaggregated $\pi_{i\ell}$ and $b_{i\ell}$ may be used in equation (8.3-4) because, even though present argument begins with industry production functions, those functions are still built up from firm production functions as indicated in the introduction to this chapter.) Because they are beyond his control, p and m_k are parameters to the consumer in the course of making his demand

---

[21]   The community utility function in its indifference map form appears in Lerner [9, p. 347n]. See also Viner [15, p. 521], especially n. 8.
[22]   It is based on Pearce [10, p. 118].

decisions. From the perspective of the entire system, however, m_k in (8.3-4) would appear to be a function of p and r because the a_k, $\theta_{ki\ell}$ and $b_{i\ell}$ are given, and because $\pi_{i\ell}$ depends on p_i and r as described in the discussion following (7.2-12). Furthermore, employing (8.2-13) and the assumptions upon which it rests, r is seen to vary with p. Hence, along the transformation surface determined by the a_k in combination, m_k is actually a function of p alone.

Based on (8.3-1) and (8.3-2), utility functions (7.2-11) are described by

$$\mu_k = u^k\left(x_{1k}, \ldots, x_{Ik}\right), \quad k = 1, \ldots, K,$$

where the vector of fixed factors $a_k = (a_{1k}, \ldots, a_{Jk})$ is subsumed in the symbol u^k. Let these functions satisfy the classical hypotheses: continuity and differentiability (2.3-1), differential increasingness (2.3-2), strict quasi-concavity (2.3-3), and the boundary condition (2.3-4). Then the demand functions generated by them, namely, $h^k = (h^{1k}, \ldots, h^{Ik})$ where

$$x_{ik} = h^{ik}(p, m_k), \quad \begin{array}{l} i = 1, \ldots, I, \\ k = 1, \ldots, K, \end{array}$$

have properties as listed in Table 2.2: positivity, budget constraint, homogeneity, continuity, differentiability, negative definiteness, and symmetry. The Slutsky functions relating to the last two properties are

$$s^{kin}(p, m_k) = h_n^{ik}(p, m_k) + h^{nk}(p, m_k)h_m^{ik}(p, m_k), \quad (8.3\text{-}5)$$

for $i, n = 1, \ldots, I$ and $k = 1, \ldots, K$. The same equality with all superscripts and subscripts k deleted defines the Slutsky functions in Section 2.4.

Summing over constraints (8.3-3) yields

$$p \cdot x = M, \quad (8.3\text{-}6)$$

where $x = (x_1, \ldots, x_I)$,

$$x_i = \sum_{k=1}^{K} x_{ik},$$

and

$$M = \sum_{k=1}^{K} m_k.$$

Sometimes M is called "aggregate income," and $p \cdot x$ is referred to as "aggregate expenditure." The aggregate constraint (8.3-6) asserts equality between them. (Note that x in equation (8.3-6) refers to quantities demanded by consumers, whereas x in the expression for value of output employed in the previous section relates to quantities supplied by industries.) Let d_k denote the fraction of aggregate income going to person k, that is,

$$d_k = \frac{m_k}{M},$$

for each k. The vector $(d_1, \ldots, d_K)$ describes the relative distribution of income among consumers.

It has been suggested earlier that although p and m_k (for any k) are fixed parameters in so far as individual decision-making is concerned, from the point of view of the system as a whole, m_k varies with p across the transformation surface. In the same way, M and d_k can also be regarded as dependent on p. However, to characterize market demand (like individual demand) as the outcome of constrained community utility maximization, p and M have to be thought of as fixed parameters at the community decision-making level. Analogously to p and m_k for individuals, these parameters are modified independently by market forces out of reach of community control. The m_k and d_k are still taken to be the functions of p described above with

$$m_k = d_k M, \quad k = 1, \ldots, K, \qquad (8.3\text{-}7)$$

even though the model does not permit actual achievement of those utility-maximizing market quantities demanded which do not lie on the transformation surface, but which arise nevertheless as a result of independent variation in M. As before, from the perspective of the entire system, M remains a function of p.

Market demand functions $H = (H^1, \ldots, H^I)$ are defined as in (6.1-1) and rewritten in terms of M by employing (8.3-7). Thus, for $(p, M) > 0$,

$$x_i = H^i(p, M), \qquad (8.3\text{-}8)$$

where p and M are independent variates,

$$H^i(p, M) = \sum_{k=1}^{K} h^{ik}(p, d_k M), \qquad (8.3\text{-}9)$$

and $i = 1, \ldots, I$. The distribution vector d does not appear as an argument of H^i because, in the present context, the d_k (but not M) are viewed as dependent on p. It is clear that H exhibits positivity, budget constraint (in terms of equation (8.3-6)), and homogeneity properties analogous to those of the individual

h^k. Moreover, if the d_k are continuously differentiable functions of p, then the continuity and differentiability properties of individual demand functions also are satisfied by H.

Letting H_n^i be the partial derivative of H^i with respect to the nth price, and H_M^i that with respect to income, *market Slutsky functions* s^{Hin} are defined at appropriate (p, M) by

$$s^{Hin}(p, M) = H_n^i(p, M) + H^n(p, M)H_M^i(p, M),$$

for $i, n = 1, \ldots, I$. Using (8.3-5) and (8.3-9), this reduces to

$$s^{Hin} = \sum_{k=1}^{K} s^{kin} + \sum_{k=1}^{K} h_m^{ik} \left(\frac{\partial m_k}{\partial p_n} - h^{nk} + \frac{m_k}{M} \sum_{k=1}^{K} h^{nk} \right), \qquad (8.3\text{-}10)$$

for every i and n, where functional arguments have been dropped to simplify notation. From (8.3-10) and the symmetry of individual Slutsky matrices, it follows that the I by I matrix of market Slutsky functions, S^{*H}, is symmetric where defined if and only if

$$\sum_{k=1}^{K} h_m^{ik} \left(\frac{\partial m_k}{\partial p_n} - h^{nk} + \frac{m_k}{M} \sum_{k=1}^{K} h^{nk} \right) =$$

$$\qquad\qquad\qquad\qquad\qquad\qquad\qquad\qquad\qquad\qquad (8.3\text{-}11)$$

$$\sum_{k=1}^{K} h_m^{nk} \left(\frac{\partial m_k}{\partial p_i} - h^{ik} + \frac{m_k}{M} \sum_{k=1}^{K} h^{ik} \right),$$

where $i, n = 1, \ldots, I$. From (8.3-10), the negative definiteness of individual Slutsky matrices, and the fact that the termwise sum of negative semidefinite matrices, at least one of which is negative definite, is also negative definite (Exercise 8.10), a sufficient condition for the $I - 1$ by $I - 1$ matrix of market Slutsky functions, S^H, to be negative definite where defined is that:

(8.3-12)   The matrix of terms

$$\sum_{k=1}^{K} h_m^{ik} \left(\frac{\partial m_k}{\partial p_n} - h^{nk} + \frac{m_k}{M} \sum_{k=1}^{K} h^{nk} \right),$$

is negative semidefinite.

Note that (8.3-12) is actually stronger than necessary to ensure that S^H is negative definite. Lastly, the homogeneity of H implies $|S^{*H}(p, M)| = 0$ where defined. (Recall Exercise 2.19.)

Clearly, affixing (8.3-11), (8.3-12), and continuous differentiability of each d_k as a function of p to the classical hypotheses (2.3-1) – (2.3-4) from which the properties (Table 2.2) of all individual demand functions are derived, yields, upon summation, market demand functions also satisfying all of the properties listed in Table 2.2. Attaching still further appropriate smoothness-type requirements, it is possible to infer (as suggested in Section 3.1) the existence of a utility function $u^H(x)$ defined for $x \geqslant 0$ and exhibiting the classical properties (2.3-1) – (2.3-4), which, when maximized subject to the constraint (8.3-6), generates the market demand functions H of (8.3-8). This u^H is the community utility function sought after. In the absence of yet additional hypotheses, conclusions concerning the welfare of the K persons across whom individual demand functions were summed cannot usually be deduced from u^H. In other words, the statement

$$u^H(x') > u^H(x'')$$

does not in general mean that, as a community, these K people prefer x' to x''. The issue of group welfare is taken up in Chapter 12.

It should also be pointed out that if

$$x_{Ik} = w^k(x_{1k}, \dots, x_{I-1k}, \mu_k)$$

denotes the indifference function (2.3-6) of person k, and if

$$x_I = w^H(x_1, \dots, x_{I-1}, \mu_H)$$

refers to that derived from u^H, then the partial derivatives

$$w_i^k(x_{1k}, \dots, x_{I-1k}, \mu_k) = w_i^H(x_1, \dots, x_{I-1}, \mu_H), \qquad (8.3\text{-}13)$$

where $i = 1, \dots, I - 1$, $k = 1, \dots, K$,

$$x_i = \sum_{k=1}^{K} x_{ik},$$

and

$$x_{ik} = h^{ik}(p, m_k),$$

for some $m_1, \dots, m_k$ and p, and all i and k. This assertion follows by applying the first-order Lagrangian maximization conditions to obtain the statement of (2.3-16) that ratios of marginal utilities equal the same price ratios for both the u^k and u^H, and then noting that the w_i^k and w_i^H are the negatives of ratios of marginal utilities (as in, for example, equation (2.3-7)). Loosely speaking,

(8.3-13) reflects the fact that if an aggregate budget hyperplane is tangent to an indifference surface of u^H at x, and if x is distributed according to the way it was obtained from summing over individual consumers in the first place, then at this distribution, a parallel individual budget hyperplane is tangent to an indifference surface of u^k for each k.

Furthermore, although conditions (8.3-11) and (8.3-12) express, in part, restrictions on the ways changes in output prices can affect the income distribution, the community utility function they help to secure does not have that distribution as an argument. In other words, at each x in its domain, a distribution of income and hence of x is implicit in u^H. This occurs precisely because the income distribution itself depends on p. And the latter dependence, recall, only arises because it is possible to link input prices to output prices through tangencies along the transformation surface (Section 8.2).

It is interesting that there are several well-known results concerning the construction of community utility functions which may be regarded as special cases of the above procedure.[23] For example, if all persons have identical, homothetic preference orderings so that their demand functions take the form[24]

$$h^{ik}(p, m_k) = m_k \zeta^i(p), \quad i = 1, \ldots, I, \quad k = 1, \ldots, K,$$

for some functions ζ^i, then it is easy to see that the second sum to the right of the equals sign in (8.3-10) vanishes identically for all i and n. Hence

$$s^{Hin}(p, M) = \sum_{k=1}^{K} s^{kin}(p, d_k M), \quad i, n = 1, \ldots, I,$$

and the existence of a community utility function is established as in previous argument. When, in this special case, all individuals also consume identical baskets of commodities, the community utility function can be thought of as a community "welfare function" (See Section 12.1).

Finally, the adjustments required to place the construction of u^H in a long-run context are quite trivial. Merely set the fixed cost parameters

$$b_{i\ell} = 0, \quad \begin{array}{l} i = 1, \ldots, I, \\ \ell = 1, \ldots, L_i, \end{array}$$

---

[23]   The assumption of identical and homothetic preferences discussed below is employed by Samuelson [13, p. 5n]. It and the alternative hypotheses of Eisenberg and of Gorman (not considered here) are shown to be special cases by Katzner [8, p. 436].

[24]   The derivation of (8.3-14) from homothetic preferences can be found in Katzner [7, pp. 24, 76]

in individual budget constraints (8.3-4). Equilibrium in the long run, of course, will ensure that the $\pi_{i\ell} = 0$. All demand and utility functions can then be thought of in long-run terms, that is, as the relevant functions for analyzing timeless equilibrium or the steady state of a long-run dynamic system.

8.4   EQUILIBRIUM

Consider a short-run fixed-factor-supply model in which utility functions exhibit continuity and differentiability (2.3-1), differential increasingness (2.3-2), strict quasi-concavity (2.3-3), and the boundary property (2.3-4). Let (8.3-11), (8.3-12), and the additional requirements needed to obtain a community utility function also be satisfied. Suppose that industry production functions exhibit nonnegativity (8.1-2), continuity and differentiability (8.1-3), differential increasingness (8.1-4), strict concavity (implying assumption (8.1-5)), and have everywhere nonvanishing Hessians and marginal products that take on all positive real numbers as function values over every expansion path. Isoquants associated with positive outputs are not permitted to touch the boundaries of their respective input spaces. (This is the case of the strictly concave model of Theorem 5.1-24 applied at the industry level.) Assume that the transformation function is differentiable as in (8.2-2). Note the above specification of industry production functions ensures that the transformation function also meets (8.2-3) and (8.2-4).

Equilibrium in this model is now quite easy to describe as long as $a > 0$ and each individual supplies a positive amount of at least one factor. Let $\mathcal{T}_a$ be the relevant production possibility set and u^H the community utility function. Suppose $\overline{x} > 0$ were to maximize uniquely $u^H(x)$ subject to the constraint that x be in $\mathcal{T}_a$. Clearly, $\overline{x}$ must lie on the transformation surface. From Lagrange's theorem,[25]

$$\frac{u_i^H(\overline{x})}{u_I^H(\overline{x})} = -t_i(\overline{x}_1, \ldots, \overline{x}_{I-1}), \quad i = 1, \ldots, I-1. \tag{8.4-1}$$

A two-good example is illustrated in Figure 8.3(a).[26] Now according to Theorem 8.1-12 and equations (8.1-13) and (8.1-14) there is a unique input vector

---

[25]   Because $\overline{x}$ is on the transformation surface, the constraint may be written as the equation $t(x_1, \ldots, x_{I-1}) - x_I = 0$. The constraint qualification (A.3-17) is satisfied since, for every i, the partial derivatives t_i are assumed negative on X^I.

[26]   A similar diagram in the context of international trade between two countries can be found in Lerner [9, p. 346]. See also Viner [15, p. 521], especially n. 8.

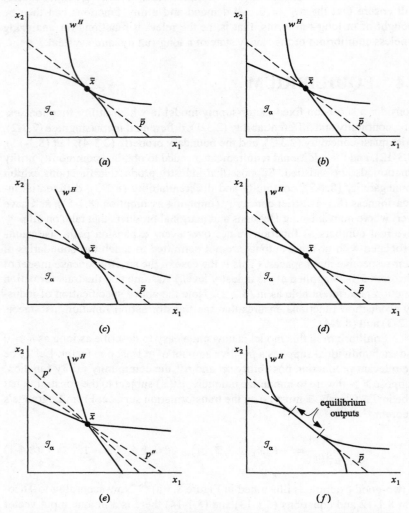

Figure 8.3 Equilibrium in a fixed-factor-supply model: (*a*) differentiable and strictly concave transformation curve, differentiable and strictly convex u^H-indifference curve; (*b*) linear and kinked transformation curve; (*c*) linear and kinked u^H-indifference curve; (*d*) linear segment in the u^H-indifference curve; (*e*) linear and kinked transformation and u^H-indifference curves; (*f*) linear segments in transformation and u^H-indifference curves

$\bar{y} = (\bar{y}_1, \ldots, \bar{y}_I) > 0$ corresponding to $\bar{x}$ such that

$$\frac{f^i_j(\bar{y}_i)}{f^i_J(\bar{y}_i)} = \frac{f^I_j(\bar{y}_I)}{f^I_J(\bar{y}_I)}, \qquad \begin{array}{l} i = 1, \ldots, I - 1, \\ j = 1, \ldots, J - 1, \end{array}$$

and

$$\sum_{i=1}^{I} \bar{y}_{ij} = a_j, \quad j = 1, \ldots, J. \tag{8.4-2}$$

Define prices $\bar{p}$ and $\bar{r}$ by first requiring

$$\frac{\bar{p}_i}{\bar{p}_I} = \frac{u^H_i(\bar{x})}{u^H_I(\bar{x})}, \quad i = 1, \ldots, I - 1,$$

and

$$\frac{\bar{r}_j}{\bar{r}_J} = \frac{f^I_j(\bar{y}_I)}{f^I_J(\bar{y}_I)}, \quad j = 1, \ldots, J - 1.$$

Then normalize by setting

$$\bar{p}_I = 1,$$

and fix $\bar{r}_J$ according to (8.2-12):

$$\bar{r}_J = f^I_J(\bar{y}_I).$$

Aggregate income is given by

$$\bar{M} = \bar{p} \cdot \bar{x}.$$

Clearly both $\bar{p}$ and $\bar{r}$ are positive.

   Now quantity demanded equals quantity supplied in all output markets at prices $\bar{p}$ and quantities $\bar{x}$. This is so because the iso-value-of-output hyperplane or, equivalently, the aggregate budget hyperplane

$$\bar{p} \cdot x = \bar{M},$$

is tangent to both the transformation surface and an indifference surface w^H (of u^H) at $\bar{x}$ (see Figure 8.3(a)). Quantity demanded also equals quantity supplied in all input markets at $\bar{r}$ and $\bar{y}$. The latter is deduced from (8.4-2), which asserts that the sum of demands by each industry (that is, the market demand) for factor j equals the fixed quantity of factor j supplied by consumers. The distribution of income is found from (8.3-4).[27] It has been shown, moreover, that at $\bar{p}$, $\bar{r}$, $\bar{x}$ and $\bar{y}$ each firm is hiring inputs and producing outputs so as to maximize its profit (Section 8.2), and each consumer is buying outputs so as to maximize utility subject to his budget constraint (Section 8.3). Therefore $\bar{p}$, $\bar{r}$, $\bar{x}$ and $\bar{y}$ are, respectively, equilibrium prices and quantities, and the distributions of $\bar{x}$ and $\bar{y}$ among, respectively, consumers and firms are determined.

The above argument is incomplete, however, because it rests on the as-yet-to-be-established fact that the $\bar{x} > 0$ maximizing u^H over $\mathcal{T}_a$ exists uniquely. But existence is a simple consequence of the compactness of the set $\mathcal{T}_a$, the continuity of u^H, and the mathematical proposition that a continuous function defined over a compact set always has a maximum value. That $\bar{x} > 0$ follows from the boundary condition (2.3-4) on individual utility functions. In addition, the strict concavity of the transformation function or the strict quasi-concavity of the community utility function guarantees that with the normalization $\bar{p}_I = 1$, the vectors $\bar{p}$, $\bar{r}$, $\bar{x}$ and $\bar{y}$, and hence the distributions of income and of $\bar{x}$, are all unique. The following theorem has therefore been proved:

Theorem 8.4-3 On the consumption side suppose consumers are utility maximizers with classical utility functions satisfying (2.3-1) – (2.3-4). Let nonnegative fixed factor supplies be given such that at least one $a_{jk} > 0$ for each k as j varies, and for each j as k varies. Assume that consumer behavior is constrained further by (8.3-11), (8.3-12), and the additional restrictions needed to obtain u^H as described in Section 8.3. On the production side let firms be profit maximizers. Suppose that industry production functions as defined by (8.0-1) fulfill (8.1-2) – (8.1-4), are strictly concave and have nonvanishing Hessians everywhere, that their marginal products take on as function values all positive real numbers over every expansion path, and that their positive-output isoquants do not touch the boundaries of their respective input spaces. Assume further that the transformation function exhibits (8.2-2) – (8.2-4). Then there exist unique, positive vectors $\bar{p}$, $\bar{r}$, $\bar{x}$ and $\bar{y}$, with $\bar{p}_I = 1$, and unique distributions of income and of $\bar{x}$ among consumers, and of $\bar{y}$ among firms, at which equilibrium prevails.

Of course, existence and uniqueness of equilibrium can be demonstrated under weaker conditions than those of Theorem 8.4-3. Figure 8.3 illustrates several possibilities for two outputs. Although differentiability of t and u^H at $\bar{x}$ are violated by the presence of kinks, and the strictness of concavity and quasi-concavity fails in the face of linearities, unique equilibrium quantities

---

[27]   In that equation, the $\pi_{i\ell}$ are obtained from profit maximization at $(\bar{p}, \bar{r})$, and the a_k, $\theta_{ki\ell}$, and $b_{i\ell}$ are known parameters.

and price ratios nevertheless exist in Figures 8.3(b) through 8.3(d). Uniqueness of equilibrium price ratios is destroyed in Figure 8.3(e) because both transformation and indifference curves have kinks at the still unique equilibrium output. Equilibrium price ratios are unique in Figure 8.3(f), but equilibrium outputs are not because the transformation and indifference curves coincide along a linear segment. Note that the appearance of kinks renders equations such as (8.4-1), representing differential tangencies, invalid because these tangencies no longer exist. In general, propositions analogous to Theorem 8.4-3 allowing for Viner and constant returns to scale industry models, as well as propositions set in long-run contexts, are also obtainable but not considered here.

Return now to the model of Section 7.3 with circulating money. Restrict it to the fixed-factor-supply context by the method described in the introduction to this chapter. Recall that initial endowments of money are written x_{0k}^0, and that from (7.3-4), individual demands for money are assumed to be proportional to the value of nonmonetary initial endowment:

$$x_{0k} = \delta \left[\sum_{j=1}^{J} r_j y_{I+jk}^0 \right],$$

for $k = 1, \ldots, K$, where $\delta > 0$ is the same for all k. The market demand for money is found by summing over k. Thus

$$\sum_{k=1}^{K} x_{0k} = \delta \left[\sum_{n=I+1}^{I+J} P_n z_n^0 \right], \tag{8.4-4}$$

where, as in Section 7.3, n replaces j in the symbol r_j,

$$P_n = \begin{cases} p_n, & \text{if } n = 1, \ldots, I, \\ r_n, & \text{if } n = I+1, \ldots, I+J, \end{cases}$$

$y_{nk}^0 = y_{I+jk}^0$ for $n = I+1, \ldots, I+J$, and

$$z_n^0 = \sum_{k=1}^{K} y_{nk}^0, \quad n = I+1, \ldots, I+J.$$

(Note that, in general, $y_{nk}^0 \neq a_{nk}$ for $n = I+1, \ldots, I+J$ and $k = 1, \ldots, K$.)

Similarly, the market supply of money (which is assumed positive) is

$$\sum_{k=1}^{K} x_{0k}^0.$$

The price of money, remember, is set at unity. As before, denote vectors of inputs and outputs excluding money by, respectively, y and x. The money prices of these goods (that is, their prices relative to the price of money) are $P = (p, r)$.

Suppose equilibrium prevails at positive P^0, x^0, and y^0 with money supply

$$\sum_{k=1}^{K} x_{0k}^0.$$

Let each initial endowment of money be altered in the proportion α, that is,

$$x_{0k}' = \alpha x_{0k}^0, \quad k = 1, \ldots, K.$$

Then the new money supply also is changed by α:

$$\sum_{k=1}^{K} x_{0k}' = \alpha \left[\sum_{k=1}^{K} x_{0k}^0 \right]. \tag{8.4-5}$$

Assume there are no other parameter changes in the model and that a new equilibrium arises at positive P', x', and y'. The relationship between the old and new equilibria is established by the following proposition.

Theorem 8.4-6 Under the hypotheses of Theorem 8.4-3, $x' = x^0$, $y' = y^0$, and $P' = \alpha P^0$.

Proof: Equating money demand (8.4-4) with money supply at the old equilibrium gives

$$\sum_{k=1}^{K} x_{0k}^0 = \delta \left[\sum_{n=I+1}^{I+J} P_n^0 z_n^0 \right], \tag{8.4-7}$$

and at the new equilibrium gives

$$\sum_{k=1}^{K} x_{0k}' = \delta \left[\sum_{n=I+1}^{I+J} P_n' z_n^0 \right]. \tag{8.4-8}$$

Define the terms

$$z_n^0 = 0, \quad n = 1, \ldots, I.$$

(This is consistent with the assumption that consumers have no initial endowments of produced goods.) Then the right-hand sums in (8.4-7) and (8.4-8) can run from $n = 1$ to $n = I + J$ without change in value. Thus, combining (8.4-7) and (8.4-8) with (8.4-5) and cancelling δ,

$$\sum_{n=1}^{I+J} P_n' z_n^0 = \alpha \left[\sum_{n=1}^{I+J} P_n^0 z_n^0 \right],$$

or

$$P_1' \left[z_1^0 + \sum_{n=2}^{I+J} \frac{P_n'}{P_1'} z_n^0 \right] = \alpha P_1^0 \left[z_1^0 + \sum_{n=2}^{I+J} \frac{P_n^0}{P_1^0} z_n^0 \right]. \tag{8.4-9}$$

Now, by the proof of Theorem 8.4-3 as applied to the fixed-factor-supply model with circulating money, quantities of goods other than money and money price ratios such as P_n/P_1 depend on appropriate ratios of marginal utilities and marginal products, and on the derivatives of the transformation surface. The latter, in turn, are independent of money endowments. Hence $x^0 = x'$, $y^0 = y'$ and, in particular

$$\frac{P_n'}{P_1'} = \frac{P_n^0}{P_1^0}, \quad n = 2, \ldots, I + J.$$

Equation (8.4-9) thus implies that

$$P_1' = \alpha P_1^0.$$

A similar argument applies to the money prices of the remaining goods $n = 2, \ldots, I + J$.

Q.E.D.

Theorem 8.4-6 reflects the dichotomy between real and monetary sectors of the model described in Section 7.3. It asserts that doubling, say, the money supply by doubling initial money endowments doubles money prices without affecting equilibrium money price ratios and equilibrium quantities. Note that the proof of the theorem remains valid regardless of how the doubled money supply is distributed in increased money endowments to consumers.[28]

---

[28]   It should also be pointed out that the invariance in the demand-for-money function (7.3-4) of the proportionality constant δ across individuals is crucial to the applicability of the proof

EXERCISES

8.1* As an alternative to the introduction of this chapter, define the industry production function $x_i = f^i(y_{i1}, \ldots, y_{iJ})$, as that which indicates the maximum output x_i associated with each vector of industry inputs $(y_{i1}, \ldots, y_{iJ})$. Assume differentiability, verify that the constraint qualification (A.3-17) is satisfied, and show that at this maximum, the input vector $(y_{i1}, \ldots, y_{iJ})$ must be distributed among the industry's firms so as to equalize the marginal product of each input over all firms. Find a system of equations whose solution (when it exists) is precisely the industry production function. Show that the industry production function of (8.0-1) is a special case of that derived here.

8.2 Show that the constraint qualification (A.3-17) is satisfied, and find equations for both the contract and transformation curves[29] when factor supplies are fixed and industry production functions are $f^i(y_{i1}, y_{i2}) = (y_{i1}y_{i2})^{1/2}$ for $i = 1, 2$. Express the contract-set-related behavior of industry 1 in terms of the input variables of that industry.

8.3 Draw an Edgeworth box diagram as in Figure 8.1(b) showing isoquants that force the contract curve to run along a portion of the boundary of the box. What assumptions of Section 8.1 are violated?

8.4 Let $I = 3$, $J = 2$, and suppose factor supplies are fixed. Consider the industry production functions $f^i(y_{i1}, y_{i2}) = (y_{i1}y_{i2})^{1/2}$ for $i = 1, 2, 3$. Demonstrate that the constraint qualification (A.3-17) is satisfied, and derive an equation in terms of industry 1's input variables for the curve identified with the contract set.

8.5 Let $I = 3$, $J = 2$, and suppose factor supplies are fixed. Consider the industry production functions

$$f^i(y_{i1}, y_{i2}) = \sqrt{y_{i1}y_{i2}}, \quad i = 1, 2,$$

$$f^3(y_{31}, y_{32}) = \left[y_{31}y_{32} + \tfrac{1}{2}(y_{32})^2\right]^{1/4}.$$

---

of Theorem 8.4-6. Without it, changes in the initial endowments of money may have different impacts on the demand for money of different persons. In that case, equation (8.4-9) may be modified sufficiently to vitiate the neutrality of money deduced from it. A parallel conclusion applies when wealth effects are considered by introducing the quantities of money held by individuals as arguments in their utility functions.

[29] As indicated in the discussion following equation (8.1-11), in two-good, two-firm cases such as these, the contract set is actually a curve.

Assume the constraint qualification is satisfied and show that an equation in terms of industry 1's input variables alone that represents a suitable curve identified with the contract set cannot be found using Lagrange's theorem (Theorem A.3-16 in appendix Section A.3).

8.6 Let $I = 2$, $J = 3$, and suppose factor supplies are fixed. Consider the industry production functions

$$f^i(y_{i1}, y_{i2}, y_{i3}) = (y_{i1}y_{i2}y_{i3})^{1/4}, \quad i = 1, 2.$$

Show that the constraint qualification (A.3-17) is satisfied and derive equations in terms of industry 1's input variables for the curve that is identified with the contract set. Find the equation for the transformation curve.

8.7 In spite of the failure of assumption (8.2-4) for this transformation curve, derive industry output supply as a function of output price $p = (p_1, p_2)$ over the domain $\{p : p > 0\}$ for the production functions and transformation curve of Exercise 8.2. Assume perfectly competitive conditions. If profits cannot be uniquely maximized by such industries in isolation (recall the discussion following Theorem 5.1-19 and Exercises 4.6, 4.11, and 5.8 with $\beta_1 = \beta_2 = \frac{1}{2}$ and $B = 1$), why do these supply functions exist? Relate points on these supply functions to points in the diagrams of Figure 5.5.

8.8 Let $I = J = 2$ and suppose factor supplies are fixed. Consider the industry production functions

$$f^1(y_{11}, y_{12}) = (y_{11})^{1/3} (y_{12})^{2/3},$$

$$f^2(y_{21}, y_{22}) = (y_{21})^{2/3} (y_{22})^{1/3}.$$

Show that the constraint qualification (A.3-17) is satisfied. Derive an equation in terms of industry 1's input variables for the curve identified with the contract set and deduce that, even with the linear homogeneity of both f^1 and f^2, the transformation curve is not linear.

8.9 Consider a perfectly competitive economy with two outputs and one input. Let industry production functions be

$$f^1(y_1) = \sqrt{2y_1}, \quad f^2(y_2) = y_2,$$

where y_1 and y_2 are scalars and $y_1 + y_2 = a$, for some constant $a > 0$. Derive the transformation curve and show that in spite of the constant returns to scale in industry 2, the transformation curve is strictly concave. For each industry, derive output supply and input demand as a function of output price $p = (p_1, p_2)$ over the domain $\{p : p > 0\}$. In light of the fact that profit cannot be uniquely maximized by industry 2, why do these output supply and input demand functions for industry 2 exist as single-valued functions? Compare these output supply and input demand functions for industry 2 to (5.1-20) and (5.1-21).

8.10 Prove that the termwise sum of negative semidefinite matrices, at least one of which is negative definite, is also negative definite.

8.11* In a model of a perfectly competitive economy, there are two factors, two outputs, and industry production functions

$$x_1 = \min\left(\frac{y_{11}}{4}, \frac{y_{12}}{2}\right),$$

$$x_2 = \min\left(\frac{y_{21}}{5}, \frac{y_{22}}{6}\right).$$

Input usage cannot exceed

$$y_{11} + y_{21} \leqslant 1260,$$

$$y_{12} + y_{22} \leqslant 840.$$

Derive the transformation curve. What output vector (x_1, x_2) corresponds to full employment of both factors? Assume that if a factor is not fully employed, its market price is zero. Find the output price ratio p_1/p_2 and the input-output price ratio r_1/p_2 or r_2/p_2 associated with positive outputs when (a) factor 1 is not fully utilized, and when (b) factor 2 is not fully utilized. What range of values for p_1/p_2 is consistent with the full employment of both factors simultaneously?

In a production Edgeworth box diagram, draw the contract set for this model. Which distributions in the contract set involve waste or inefficiency, and why are such distributions included in the contract set?

8.12 To Exercises 8.2 and 8.7 add the individual utility functions

$$u^k(x_{1k}, x_{2k}) = x_{1k}x_{2k}, \quad k = 1, 2.$$

Suppose person 1 supplies $\frac{1}{3}$ of a_1 and $\frac{1}{2}$ of a_2, while person 2 supplies the remainder. Derive market demand functions and a community utility function.

Determine long-run competitive equilibrium values for the x_{ik}, x_i, y_{ij} and for r_1, r_2, and p_1, assuming $p_2 = 1$. Are these equilibrium values unique?

8.13** Consider a model of a perfectly competitive economy with one factor, two outputs, and industry production functions

$$x_1 = f^1(y_1) = 2\sqrt{y_1},$$

$$x_2 = f^2(y_2) = 2\sqrt{y_2},$$

where y_1 and y_2 are scalars. The total quantity of the factor supplied is 25 so that its employment is limited by $y_1 + y_2 \leqslant 25$. Suppose consumer 1 owns all 25 units of the factor. Upon selling them to the two industries, she receives income that she uses to buy outputs according to the utility function

$$u^1(x_{11}, x_{21}) = \sqrt{x_{11}x_{21}}.$$

Assume consumer 2 owns both industries. His income is derived from profits, and his utility function is

$$u^2(x_{12}, x_{22}) = \sqrt{x_{12} + x_{22}}.$$

In spite of the fact that consumer 2's utility function has linear indifference curves that intersect the boundary of his commodity space, find a community utility function generating the market demand functions. Setting $p_2 = 1$, compute short-run equilibrium prices and quantities. Is the equilibrium unique?

8.14 Assume a world with only two industries. Under the assumptions of Section 8.2 show that if all industry production functions are homothetic, then in the input space of each industry, either the contract curve is linear and coincides with an industry expansion path, or no industry expansion path intersects the contract curve at more than one interior point.

8.15* Consider a fixed-factor-supply model with industry production functions $x_i = f^i(y_{i1}, y_{i2})$, $i = 1, 2$, and with sufficient properties to generate a 1–1 correspondence between input and output price ratios. Let the f^i be linearly homogeneous and, as in Exercise 5.15, define z_i and ν^i by

$$z_i = \frac{y_{i1}}{y_{i2}},$$

$$\nu^i(z_i) = f^i(z_i, 1),$$

for $i = 1, 2$. Assume differentiability as needed and suppose

$$\nu^i(z_i) > 0,$$

$$\frac{d\nu^i(z_i)}{dz_i} > 0,$$

$$\frac{d^2\nu^i(z_i)}{(dz_i)^2} < 0,$$

for each i and all $z_i > 0$. Use the results of Exercise 5.15 (modified by discarding the requirement that output price be unity) to show that for all relevant values of z_1, z_2, r_2/r_1, and p_2/p_1,

i) $$\frac{dz_i}{d\left(\dfrac{r_2}{r_1}\right)} > 0, \quad i = 1, 2,$$

and

ii) $$\frac{d\left(\dfrac{p_2}{p_1}\right)}{d\left(\dfrac{r_2}{r_1}\right)} \gtreqless 0 \quad \text{according as} \quad z_2 \lesseqgtr z_1.$$

The production of output 1 is said to be *more intensive* in factor 1 (than that of output 2) if $z_1 > z_2$. It is more intensive in factor 2 when $z_2 > z_1$. Analogous definitions apply to the production of output 2. Observe that because there are only two factors, the production of output 1 is more intensive in, say, factor 1 if and only if the production of output 2 is more intensive in factor 2. Deduce from (ii) the proposition that if the relative price of, say, output 2 rises, then the relative price of the factor used more intensively in the production of output 2 must also rise. This last result is due to Stopler and Samuelson [14, pp. 65, 66].

8.16 In addition to (8.1-2) – (8.1-5), suppose all industry production functions are homogeneous of degree one. Show that the transformation surface is linear if and only if along the transformation surface inputs are employed in the same fixed proportions by all industries.

8.17 Let a model of a perfectly competitive economy with two outputs and one factor have industry production functions

$$y_1 = \bar{f}^1(x_1) = (x_1)^3 - 4(x_1)^2 + 8x_1,$$

$$x_2 = f^2(y_2) = y_2,$$

where y_1 and y_2 are scalars and $\bar{f}^1(x_1)$ — the inverse of $f^1(y_1)$ — is the inverse production function of Exercise 4.12. Suppose $y_1 + y_2 \leqslant a$, for some constant $a > 1\frac{1}{3}$. Although (recall Exercise 4.12) f^1 satisfies (8.1-2) – (8.1-4) and the strict quasi-concavity part of (8.1-5), demonstrate that contrary to the rest of (8.1-5), f^1 is not concave. Note that Exercise 4.12 also indicated that the cost curves derived from f^1 are Viner curves. Derive the transformation curve t and show that t is strictly convex for $0 \leqslant x_1 \leqslant 1\frac{1}{3}$ and strictly concave over the remainder of its domain.

8.18   Reprove Theorem 8.4-3 for the fixed-factor-supply model of Section 8.4 with circulating money.

REFERENCES

1. Apostol, T. M., *Mathematical Analysis*, 2nd ed. (Reading: Addison-Wesley, 1974).
2. Bator, F. M., "The Simple Analytics of Welfare Maximization," *American Economic Review* 47 (1957), pp. 22-59.
3. Chipman, J. S., "A Survey of the Theory of International Trade: Part 2, The Neo-Classical Theory," *Econometrica* 33 (1965), pp. 685-760.
4. Debreu, G., "Economies with a Finite Set of Equilibria," *Econometrica* 38 (1970), pp. 387-392.
5. von Haberler, G., *The Theory of International Trade with Its Application to Commercial Policy*, A. Stonier and F. Benham, trans. (New York: Macmillan, 1937).
6. Katzner, D. W., "A General Approach to the Theory of Supply," *Economic Studies Quarterly* 19 (1968), pp. 32-45.
7. ——, *Static Demand Theory* (New York: Macmillan, 1970).
8. ——, "A Simple Approach to Existence and Uniqueness of Competitive Equilibria," *American Economic Review* 62 (1972), pp. 432-437.
9. Lerner, A. P., "The Diagrammatical Representation of Cost Conditions in International Trade," *Economica* 12 (1932), pp. 346-356.
10. Pearce, I. F., *A Contribution to Demand Analysis* (London: Oxford

University Press, 1964).

11. Rudin, W., *Principles of Mathematical Analysis*, 3rd ed. (New York: McGraw-Hill, 1976).

12. Samuelson, P. A., *Foundations of Economic Analysis* (Cambridge: Harvard University Press, 1947).

13. ——, "Social Indifference Curves," *Quarterly Journal of Economics* 70 (1956), pp. 1-22.

14. Stopler, W. F. and P. A. Samuelson, "Protection and Real Wages," *Review of Economic Studies* 9 (1941-42), pp. 58-73.

15. Viner, J., *Studies in the Theory of International Trade* (New York: Harper & Brothers, 1937).

Chapter 9

Dynamics and Equilibrium

As described in Section 1.3, the Walrasian theory of market behavior developed here views the outcomes observed in the real-world economy as the product of the working out of a dynamic system.[1] Previous argument, however, has focused only on timeless activity which can be interpreted as occurring along stationary states or equilibrium paths. It is now appropriate to consider the dynamic system as a whole and explicitly discuss its relationship to the equations of earlier chapters. It is also natural at this point to examine the questions raised in Section 1.3 concerning the general characteristics of the system, namely, the existence, uniqueness, and stability of equilibrium paths. Knowledge of any particular system is incomplete without an understanding of these properties as they appear within it.

The specific systems to be considered are essentially "dynamic versions" of the model of Section 7.2 which reduce, along stationary paths, to the timeless equations of that section. Consumer utility functions are assumed to have the continuity and differentiability, differential increasingness, strict quasi-concavity, and boundary properties of Section 2.3. Firm production functions are supposed to exhibit the nonnegativity, differentiability, and strict

---

[1]   Clearly, the explanatory significance of such a system need not be fully maintained as economic developments occur in reality over time. Cogent explanation may require modification in the parameter values or even the functional structure of that system to accommodate actual change.

quasi-concavity properties of Section 4.1. For simplicity, marginal products are taken to be positive everywhere, and isoquants associated with positive outputs are not permitted to touch the boundaries of input spaces. Conditions, as described for the strictly concave and Viner models in Chapter 5, ensuring the existence of unique profit-maximizing inputs and outputs also are assumed. Rationality is hypothesized for both consumers and firms; the excess demand notation of Chapter 7 is employed throughout; and the requisites for interpreting the model as one of a perfectly competitive economy are maintained.

There are, of course, many ways to convert this model into a dynamic system. Utility and production functions, initial endowments, consumer and firm decisions, and market prices and quantities generally change over time. To keep matters as simple as possible, however, utility and production functions and initial endowments are taken to be fixed. Elements such as speculation, inventories, and capital movements between industries continue to be ignored. Consumers and producers are assumed to react to changes in hypothetical market prices as discussed in Chapters 2 – 5 under the economic assumptions listed in the previous paragraph. Hence to obtain a dynamic model, it is necessary only to add to the equations of Section 7.2 a formal specification of the way prices vary. The behavior of individual consumers and firms over time, that is, individual (and hence market) quantities demanded and supplied, can then be deduced from the combination of economic assumptions and movements of market prices. Thus the dynamic systems investigated here consist of two parts: an "economic," which summarizes all economic behavior in the form of market excess demand functions, and a "dynamic," which describes how market prices modify in response to nonzero excess demands.

An alternative view is to think of the economic in terms of the inverses of the market excess demand functions and the dynamic as indicating how market quantities adjust when prices are not at their respective equilibrium values. Both perspectives are analyzed below.

Along with the specification of a market price or quantity dynamic, a story is frequently told to provide a way of concretizing the abstract, dynamic formalizations that determine equilibrium prices and quantities. The auctioneer concept of the introduction to Chapter 7 serves as one basis for such stories. In the particular auctioneer story of that introduction, recall, the auctioneer announces a set of prices, ascertains the market demand and supply for all goods and, if equilibrium does not prevail, announces a new set of prices. The story, as noted in Chapter 7, is complete except for a statement of how the auctioneer actually adjusts prices in response to nonzero market excess demands, and this response cannot be indicated without explicit stipulation of the nature of the dynamic (for example, equation (9.3-13), below). A *tâtonnement* dynamic is one exhibiting the characteristics of a story in which trading between buyers and sellers occurs (as in the auctioneer story of the introduction to Chapter 7) only after equilibrium has been established.[2] *Nontâtonnement* dynamics correspond to stories requiring buyers and sellers to trade as part of the process of establishing equilibrium. That is, at each announced set of prices (nonequilibrium or otherwise) trade takes place according to some prespecified rule. These trades, of course, may alter the initial endowments in place for the next price announcement and the trade that follows it. Not surprisingly, trading rules and changing initial endowments tend to make nontâtonnement dynamics considerably more complicated than tâtonnement dynamics. Only the latter are considered here.

Recall (from Section 3.1) that time in this volume is taken to be continuous rather than discrete. Thus the dynamic systems examined below are expressed in differential as opposed to difference equation form. Such an abstraction requires decisions and transformations to be accomplished instantaneously. For example, firms are thought of as selecting profit-maximizing outputs and inputs and converting the latter into the former at each moment of time. As prices modify across instants, decisions change and continuous "time-paths" emerge.

The entire chapter is an integral part of the particular grand view outlined in Section 1.4. It also provides the necessary background for the discussion of price determination in Chapter 10.

9.1   DYNAMIC ECONOMIC SYSTEMS

Consider first some purely mathematical ideas. Let $z = (z_1, \ldots, z_N)$ be a vector of variables ranging over an open connected set Z. Denote time by the scalar τ and let it vary across

$$[0, \infty) = \{\tau : 0 \leqslant \tau < \infty\}.$$

One way to describe movement of z in time is with the differential equation

$$\frac{dz_n}{d\tau} = \zeta^n(z, \tau), \quad n = 1, \ldots, N,$$

---

[2]   This was referred to as an absence of false trading in n. 2 on pp. 251-252.

where each ζ^n is defined over $Z \times [0, \infty)$. Writing $\zeta = (\zeta^1, \ldots, \zeta^N)$ and

$$\frac{dz}{d\tau} = \left(\frac{dz_1}{d\tau}, \ldots, \frac{dz_N}{d\tau} \right),$$

the equation can be abbreviated to

$$\frac{dz}{d\tau} = \zeta(z, \tau). \qquad (9.1\text{-}1)$$

A (*time-*) *path* or *solution* of (9.1-1) starting at z^0 in Z is a function

$$z = \nu(z^0, \tau),$$

such that

$$\frac{d\nu(z^0, \tau)}{d\tau} = \zeta(\nu(z^0, \tau), \tau),$$

for all $\tau > 0$, and

$$\nu(z^0, 0) = z^0.$$

In words, a path (solution) must have "slopes" (derivatives) that satisfy the differential equation, and must also start (with $\tau = 0$) at the initial point z^0. A one dimensional example is pictured in Figure 9.1. Note the symbol ν is short for the vector of functions $(\nu^1, \ldots, \nu^N)$. The main conditions ensuring that

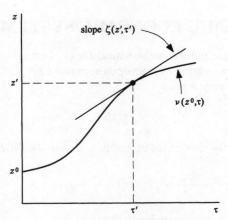

Figure 9.1 Solution of a differential equation

solutions exist and are unique (that is, that there is exactly one path through each z in Z) are that ζ be continuous and satisfy an appropriate Lipschitz condition.[3] The latter is guaranteed if Z is convex and the partial derivatives of ζ with respect to the z_i exist and are bounded on $Z \times [0, \infty)$.[4]

An *equilibriuim point* of (9.1-1) is a vector $\overline{z}$ in Z with

$$\nu(\overline{z}, \tau) = \overline{z},$$

for all τ. In words, were the system started at an equilibrium point, it would remain there for all time. The path described by the equation $\nu(\overline{z}, \tau)$ is called an *equilibrium path* or *stationary state*.

Let $\overline{z}$ in Z be an equilibrium point of (9.1-1). The equilibrium path associated with $\overline{z}$ is said to be *locally (asymptotically) stable* provided there exists a neighborhood $\mathcal{N}$ of $\overline{z}$ such that every solution of (9.1-1) starting at a z^0 in $\mathcal{N}$ converges to $\overline{z}$. Alternatively put,

$$\lim_{\tau \to \infty} \nu(z^0, \tau) = \overline{z},$$

for all solutions $\nu(z^0, \tau)$ whose initial point z^0 is in $\mathcal{N}$. Examples of paths converging to an equilibrium path appear in Figures 9.2(a) and (b). Two non-convergent paths are shown in Figures 9.2(c) and (d). Call the equilibrium path associated with $\overline{z}$ *globally (asymptotically) stable* whenever

$$\lim_{\tau \to \infty} \nu(z^0, \tau) = \overline{z},$$

for all z^0 in Z and every solution ν of (9.1-1). Equation (9.1-1) itself is (*asymptotically*) *stable* if and only if every solution no matter where it starts converges to some equilibrium point $\overline{z}$ in Z. Thus any differential equation with a globally stable equilibrium path is stable. Equations with one or more equilibria need not be stable even if all equilibrium paths themselves are locally stable.

When (9.1-1) has more than one equilibrium point, none of their associated equilibrium time-paths can be globally stable. For, starting the system off at any of the equilibria, the time-path generated remains there and cannot converge to any other equilibrium. Thus global stability of an equilibrium path (whether assumed or proved) must imply uniqueness of the correspond-

---

[3]   That is, there exists a constant $\delta > 0$ such that

$$|\zeta(z', \tau) - \zeta(z'', \tau)| < \delta|z' - z''|,$$

for all (z', τ) and (z'', τ) in $Z \times [0, \infty)$. Recall the discussion of Section 3.1 and see Hurewicz [5, Ch. 2].

[4]   Apostol [1, p. 356].

ing equilibrium point. Moreover, if (9.1-1) is stable and $\bar{z}$ in Z is a unique equilibrium point, then the associated equilibrium path is globally stable.

Turning to the economics, let $P = (P_1, \ldots, P_{I+J}) > 0$ represent vectors of prices and $Q = (Q_1, \ldots, Q_{I+J})$ denote aggregate market excess demand quantities. Thus for produced goods, Q_n, is the sum of consumer excess demand for n as a final commodity, firm excess demand for n to use in production, and firm excess demand (that is, supply) of n as output. For factors, Q_n is firm excess demand for n to use in production plus consumer excess de-

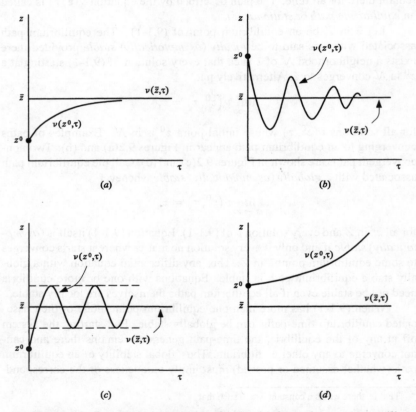

Figure 9.2 Convergence properties of paths: (a) damped convergence; (b) oscillatory convergence; (c) constant (nonconvergent) oscillations; (d) divergence

mand (that is, supply) of n out of initial endowments. Let the sum of the excess demand functions of all consumers and firms in market n be written

$$Q_n = \mathcal{E}^n(P), \quad n = 1, \ldots, I + J. \tag{9.1-2}$$

The $\mathcal{E}^n$ are often called *market* excess demand functions. In the notation of Section 7.2, the $\mathcal{E}^n$ are defined by

$$\mathcal{E}^n(P) = E^n(P) + \left[\sum_{i=1}^{I} E^{in}(P) \right] + \widetilde{E}^n(P), \quad n = 1, \ldots, I,$$

$$\mathcal{E}^n(P) = \left[\sum_{i=1}^{I} E^{in}(P) \right] + E^n(P), \quad n = I + 1, \ldots, I + J,$$

and, according to (7.2-15) and (7.2-16), simultaneous equilibrium in all markets occurs when

$$\mathcal{E}^n(P) = 0, \quad n = 1, \ldots, I + J. \tag{9.1-3}$$

Equations (9.1-2) and (9.1-3) can also be written, respectively, as

$$Q = \mathcal{E}(P), \tag{9.1-4}$$

and

$$\mathcal{E}(P) = 0, \tag{9.1-5}$$

where $\mathcal{E} = \left(\mathcal{E}^1, \ldots, \mathcal{E}^{I+J} \right)$. Note that $\mathcal{E}$ is continuous and homogeneous of degree zero.

Equations (9.1-3) or, equivalently, (9.1-5) describe, of course, the situation that exists when all market equilibrium conditions are satisfied. But, recall, in order to arrive at a multi-market, mutually-determined, and generalized equilibrium, the consumers and firms whose actions are implicit in the excess demand functions $\mathcal{E}(P)$ are assumed to have made optimizing decisions with respect to criteria described in earlier chapters. Before equilibrium is reached, the outcomes of the applications of those decision-making rules are to be understood as tentative and hypothetical in the sense that no realizable magnitudes of the relevant variables are specified. It is the simultaneous interaction of all relations of the system in determining the equilibrium prices and quantities that places these variables at their realizable equilibrium-solution values. That assumption of simultaneity, and the implied inability to identify the reaction of certain variables in response to changes in certain other variables, precludes the explicit derivation of the kinds of empirically testable patterns (such as, for example, those derivable for a consumer's demand behavior from the weak axiom of revealed preference) that might be obtained in partial-equilibrium or nonequilibrium situations.

Now introduce the normalization $P_{I+J} = 1$ and set

$$\mathcal{E}^{(I+J)} = \left(\mathcal{E}^1, \ldots, \mathcal{E}^{I+J-1}\right),$$

$$P^{(I+J)} = \left(P_1, \ldots, P_{I+J-1}\right),$$

$$Q^{(I+J)} = \left(Q_1, \ldots, Q_{I+J-1}\right),$$

where the components of $\mathcal{E}^{(I+J)}$ are thought of as functions of the first $I+J-1$ prices. Thus $\mathcal{E}^{(I+J)}$, $P^{(I+J)}$, and $Q^{(I+J)}$ are the same as $\mathcal{E}$, P, and Q except that $P_{I+J} = 1$ and the $I + J^{\text{th}}$ component of each vector has been removed. Since Walras' law (7.2-20) asserts that for any P,

$$\sum_{n=1}^{I+J} P_n \mathcal{E}^n(P) = 0, \tag{9.1-6}$$

or that $\mathcal{E}^{I+J}$ is determined by $\mathcal{E}^1, \ldots, \mathcal{E}^{I+J-1}$ when $P_{I+J} = 1$, all information contained in (9.1-4) can be summarized as

$$Q^{(I+J)} = \mathcal{E}^{(I+J)}(P^{(I+J)}). \tag{9.1-7}$$

Furthermore, equilibrium conditions (9.1-5) are stated equivalently as

$$\mathcal{E}^{(I+J)}(P^{(I+J)}) = 0. \tag{9.1-8}$$

Equation (9.1-7) is one form for the economic in the dynamic economic systems developed here.

If the inverse of $\mathcal{E}^{(I+J)}$ exists, then an alternative, equivalent expression of the economic (9.1-7) is

$$P^{(I+J)} = \mathcal{E}^{-1}(Q^{(I+J)}), \tag{9.1-9}$$

where the inverse $\mathcal{E}^{-1} = (\mathcal{E}^{-1^1}, \ldots, \mathcal{E}^{-1^{I+J-1}})$ and the superscript $(I + J)$ on $\mathcal{E}^{-1}$ has been dropped to simplify notation. The equilibrium conditions (9.1-8) in this context are

$$P^{(I+J)} = \mathcal{E}^{-1}(0).$$

Let the Jacobian matrix, $\mathcal{B}(P^{(I+J)})$ of $\mathcal{E}^{(I+J)}$ exist, and suppose its determinant

$$\left| \mathcal{B}(P^{(I+J)}) \right| \neq 0,$$

for all $P^{(I+J)}$. Then the Jacobian matrix of $\mathcal{E}^{-1}$ is precisely the inverse matrix $\mathcal{B}^{-1}$ of $\mathcal{B}$, and at each $P^{(I+J)}$,

$$\mathcal{B}(P^{(I+J)})\mathcal{B}^{-1}(Q^{(I+J)}) = \mathcal{I},$$

where $Q^{(I+J)} = \mathcal{E}^{(I+J)}(P^{(I+J)})$ and $\mathcal{I}$ denotes the $I + J - 1$ by $I + J - 1$ identity matrix.[5]

In attempting to describe the motion of prices and market excess demands over time, it is necessary to specify the dynamic behavior of only one. The other can then be deduced from the market excess demand function or its inverse. The approach that begins by hypothesizing the movement of prices is said to postulate a *Walrasian adjustment rule*; whereas that starting from the movement of quantities postulates a *Marshallian adjustment rule*.[6] Thus, suppose in conjunction with the auctioneer story, say, a Walrasian adjustment rule of the form of (9.1-1) is postulated for the motion of prices:

$$\frac{dP^{(I+J)}}{d\tau} = \xi^P(P^{(I+J)}, \tau), \tag{9.1-10}$$

where $dP^{(I+J)}/d\tau$ and ξ^P are appropriate $(I + J - 1)$-dimensional vectors. The complete dynamic economic system, then, contains two parts — the economic, which, as described earlier, encapsulates all economic behavior and consists of the market excess demand equations (9.1-7); and the dynamic or Walrasian adjustment rule (9.1-10). To secure an explicit expression for the movement of market excess demand quantities, differentiate (9.1-7) with respect to τ:

$$\frac{dQ^{(I+J)}}{d\tau} = \mathcal{B}(P^{(I+J)})\frac{dP^{(I+J)}}{d\tau}. \tag{9.1-11}$$

---

[5]   Apostol [1, pp. 372, 373]. See appendix Section A.4.

[6]   This usage of the adverbs Walrasian and Marshallian is somewhat more liberal than that which would be permissible if strict adherence to the writings of Walras and Marshall were maintained. Walras [13, p. 170] considers price adjustment only when excess demand arises as a function of price. Marshall [8, p. 345], on the other hand, describes quantity adjustment only in the context of Exercise 9.4 where "excess price" appears as a function of ordinary (not excess demand) quantity. These notions are extended here so that quantity adjustment with (inverse) excess demand functions is also called Marshallian adjustment, and price adjustment with (inverse) excess price functions is still referred to as Walrasian adjustment. (See Exercise 9.4.)

(In equation (9.1-11), $dQ^{(I+J)}/d\tau$ and $dP^{(I+J)}/d\tau$ are thought of as column vectors.) Substitution of (9.1-10) and (9.1-9) into (9.1-11) now yields

$$\frac{dQ^{(I+J)}}{d\tau} = \left[\mathcal{B}(\mathcal{E}^{-1}(Q^{(I+J)})) \right] \left[\xi^P(\mathcal{E}^{-1}(Q^{(I+J)}), \tau) \right]. \qquad (9.1\text{-}12)$$

Although it contains both the dynamic (appearing as ξ^P) and the economic (expressed as $\mathcal{B}$), (9.1-12) is still a differential equation in $Q^{(I+J)}$. From it the motion of prices can be recovered through (9.1-9). Thus (9.1-9) and (9.1-12) constitute an equivalent statement of the complete dynamic economic system. Equilibrium points of the two systems correspond, and one is stable if and only if the other is stable. An example is presented in Section 9.3.

Once the drift of market prices is set by a starting point and (9.1-10), the dynamic activity of individual consumers and firms can be inferred from their respective utility and production functions and their assumed desire to maximize. Another way of saying the same thing is that their behavior can be found by direct substitution of the path of price vectors generated by (9.1-10) into consumer and firm excess demand functions. The latter, of course, are the building blocks for (9.1-7) in the first place. It should also be remembered that the normalization $P_{I+J} = 1$ forces P_{I+J} to remain constant over time, and that the motion of Q_{I+J}, is implied by (9.1-10), (9.1-7), and Walras' law (9.1-6).

An alternative method of constructing a complete dynamic economic system is to postulate the motion of market excess demand quantities (that is, a Marshallian adjustment rule) by setting

$$\frac{dQ^{(I+J)}}{d\tau} = \xi^Q(Q^{(I+J)}, \tau), \qquad (9.1\text{-}13)$$

for some function ξ^Q. With this dynamic, the system is completed by adding the economic (9.1-9). Differentiation of (9.1-9) with respect to τ and employment of (9.1-7) and (9.1-13) yields the motion of prices

$$\frac{dP^{(I+J)}}{d\tau} = \left[\mathcal{B}^{-1}(\mathcal{E}^{(I+J)}(P^{(I+J)})) \right] \left[\xi^Q(\mathcal{E}^{(I+J)}(P^{(I+J)}), \tau) \right], \qquad (9.1\text{-}14)$$

which, together with (9.1-7), gives an equivalent formulation of the complete system (equations (9.1-13) and (9.1-9)) containing both the economic and the dynamic.

Regardless of the economic, independently postulating a Walrasian adjustment rule as opposed to independently postulating a Marshallian adjustment rule generally leads to distinct, if not contradictory, results.[7] Thus conditions ensuring stability depend on the approach employed. The same is true with different choices for ξ^P in (9.1-10) and ξ^Q in (9.1-13). Moreover, links between P and Q other than market excess demand functions (such as the excess price functions of Exercise 9.4) are theoretically permissible means for expressing the economic, and use of these furnishes still further conclusions. The selection of a Walrasian or Marshallian rule with a specific form for ξ^P or, respectively, ξ^Q, along with the specification of the type of market-level aggregates of individual consumer and firm behavior, is determined by the nature of the story that is being told about the manner in which the economy adjusts when out of equilibrium. Different stories evidently give rise to different explanations of how the same equilibrium in a tâtonnement environment is achieved.

Now let $\nu^Q(Q^{(I+J)}, \tau)$ denote the solution of (9.1-12) and $\nu^P(P^{(I+J)}, \tau)$ that of (9.1-14). In stipulating the dynamic (9.1-10) it is necessary to require that

$$\mathcal{E}^{(I+J)}(\bar{P}^{(I+J)}) = 0 \quad \text{if and only if} \quad \nu^Q(0, \tau) = 0, \text{ for all } \tau,$$

where $\bar{P}^{(I+J)} > 0$ is an equilibrium price vector. Similarly for (9.1-13),

$$\mathcal{E}^{-1}(0) = \bar{P}^{(I+J)} \quad \text{if and only if} \quad \nu^P(\bar{P}^{(I+J)}, \tau) = \bar{P}^{(I+J)}, \text{ for all } \tau.$$

Thus, in either case, the economic is in equilibrium when and only when the complete system is following an equilibrium path. Alternatively, all timeless equations of the model of Section 7.2 are assumed to be satisfied simultaneously only on equilibrium paths, and conversely. The "static equilibrium" and the "dynamic equilibrium" coincide. Without such concurrence, the notion of equilibrium would become ambiguous. Note that this assumption of coincidence imposes nontrivial restrictions on the dynamic. An example in which coincidence fails appears in Exercise 9.8.

Of course, it is not mandatory that the normalization $P_{I+J} = 1$ be used in the specification of dynamic economic systems. Other normalizations are possible (as is illustrated towards the end of Section 9.3) or the model can be structured in terms of price ratios. Generally, in the former instance, the simultaneous solution of the equations of the economic takes both Walras' law and the normalization into account. And from the point of view of the economic, the specific normalization employed is of little consequence except as it provides the context with respect to which equilibrium prices are expressed.

---

[7]   Unless, of course, the two dynamics happen to be related according to (9.1-11). In Section 9.3, the models of equations (9.3-13) and (9.3-15) are related in this way.

But once a dynamic is introduced, it becomes imperative to ensure not only that equilibrium in the economic coincides with equilibrium in the combined system as a whole, but also that, when out of equilibrium, the variable values along time paths generated by the dynamic satisfy the relevant equations of the economic including, in particular, Walras' law. Among other things, this can mean that restriction have to be imposed on the choice of the normalization. The issue is discussed on pp. 362-363 in relation to dynamic (9.3-32).

It is clear, then, that a dynamic system or model employed by the Walrasian theory of market behavior to comprehend economic reality as described in Section 1.1 consists of (9.1-10) (or (9.1-13)) together with (9.1-7) (or, respectively, (9.1-9)) and all timeless equations depicting consumer, firm and market behavior summarized in Section 7.2. It has already been pointed out in Section 1.3 that to gain a complete understanding of this system requires that certain issues be raised, namely, the questions of whether equilibrium paths exist and, if so, whether they are unique and globally stable. Whenever the answer to any of these questions is "not necessarily," it is essential to ask further if additional restrictions could be imposed on the system to ensure affirmative answers. Apart from the fact that such an investigation must be undertaken before a full understanding can be achieved and a complete theory of price determination (see Chapter 10) developed, there are separate motives, which stand on their own, for studying each question.

Several reasons for the importance of these questions have already been suggested, in Section 1.3, in the context of an isolated market. Rephrased to apply here, the argument runs as follows: Economists often interpret observations of the real economy as lying exactly or approximately on the equilibrium paths derived from the dynamic systems in their models. (It should be borne in mind, however, that the equilibrium in view is at all times a characteristic of a model and not necessarily that of the real world.) Clearly, equilibrium paths for these systems must exist if this interpretation is to have meaning. Moreover, because only one sighting of the world is available at any point in time, the existence of multiple equilibrium paths for the systems, each path with its own attendant properties, would render impossible the task of finding the appropriate theoretical properties that should be associated with the seen equilibrium. The latter difficulty cannot arise when equilibrium paths are unique. Lastly, with changing observations over time, each identified by its own equilibrium path and associated parameter values, economists frequently want to assert that those changes reflect the economy's movements from one equilibrium to another brought about by variations in parameter values. To be able to make such a statement requires that, upon leaving any "old" equilibrium, the time-path followed in the model converges to the "new" equilibrium.[8] Otherwise the passage between the equilibria cannot be explained. Moreover, convergence to the new equilibrium path from starting points "near" the new equilibrium point is not enough; the time-path must always converge to the new equilibrium path. It is necessary, therefore to know that the equilibrium path associated with each collection of parameter values is globally stable.

Note that with such an interpretation of equilibria as related to actual data in force, the dynamic workings of the theoretical model cannot be observed. Only the end result, namely the equilibrium, can be seen.[9] Hence the nonstationary time-paths along which the system converges as well as the auctioneer stories that go with them, although contributing to our understanding of how equilibrium is achieved, can have no basis in observable reality. Alternative interpretations need not share this property. Thus if sequential data drawn from the real economy were taken as points on nonstationary time-paths, then the dynamic laws that guide the course of the economy would, at least in principle, be capable of observation. But clearly, in that case, the equilibrium towards which that sequential data might be converging is always hidden from view. Regardless, the interpretation of observed data (which reflects trades that have already occurred) as equilibria can only be maintained with respect to a tâtonnement dynamic since it is the latter that delays trading until after equilibrium has been reached. The alternative interpretation necessitates a nontâtonnement dynamic because trades, as mirrored in actual data, occur outside of equilibrium. (However, as previously indicated, the analysis of nontâtonnement dynamics is not pursued here.)

Of course the first of the above interpretations often provides a convenient basis for empirical analysis. Moreover, by thinking of observations as falling along equilibrium paths that are unique and globally stable, the theory can be said to identify the forces and their interactions that "determine" what is seen. Certainly unique equilibrium paths must exist for this purpose. Lacking uniqueness the theory is incomplete because it does not explain why a particular observation (one equilibrium), and not some other observation (another equilibrium), is determined. And absent global stability, there is no explanation of the determination process, that is, of how observations emerge out of previously observed positions. (Recall that a more extensive discussion of price determination will be provided in Chapter 10.) With the alternative in-

---

[8]   The time-path that the model follows in moving from one equilibrium toward another is called a *traverse* by Hicks [4, pp. 81-82].

[9]   Recall that "seen phenomena," as the notion was introduced in Section 1.2, refers to phenomena that show up in economic data. Things that do not are unseeable in the sense of being unknown to the economist.

terpretation the theory can be viewed as determining the "end" (equilibrium) toward which the real economy (as seen by observing points on its actual non-stationary time-path) is moving. In such a case, stability is needed to guarantee that, were the relevant parameters and functions to remain fixed, the economy would eventually get there.

The question of existence of equilibrium paths is also significant because it furnishes a way of checking on the internal consistency of the model. If an equilibrium exists, then there is at least one vector of prices and quantities which satisfies all timeless equations simultaneously. Thus the system cannot be contradictory or overdetermined, and the Walrasian theory of market behavior is not vacuous. Another way of saying the same thing is that the demonstration of existence of equilibrium implies a meaningful coherency in the simultaneous behavior of (that is, the pursuit of self-interest by) all consumers and firms in the system.

It should also be noted that the question of uniqueness of equilibrium paths is important because of the relation of uniqueness to stability. For if an equilibrium path is not unique, then it is possible to have both stable and unstable equilibria. Furthermore, as noted earlier, in the absence of uniqueness no equilibrium path can be globally stable.

Even if observations of the real world are taken to be on time-paths that do not converge to an equilibrium path, in order to understand what is going on in the model, it is still necessary to know about the existence, uniqueness, and stability properties of equilibrium paths. Such information may also shed light on the route the nonconvergent time-path is taking.[10]

9.2   EXISTENCE OF EQUILIBRIUM PATHS

The dynamic economic systems pursued in Section 9.1 require equilibrium paths of the complete system to coincide with equilibrium in the economic. When considering equilibrium by itself, then, it is not necessary to account for the presence of adjustment rules or dynamic forces. Thus the usual method of proving existence of equilibrium paths is to demonstrate existence of equilibrium in the economic alone. The result then applies to any dynamic economic

---

[10]   It is surprising that although the Walrasian theory of market behavior described in the present volume dates to the publication of Walras' *Elements* [13] in 1874, the questions of existence, uniqueness, and stability of equilibria — so crucial to understanding this theory and its relevance and applicability to the real world — seem to have escaped the serious attention of economists until the 1930s. The major work on existence and uniqueness began with Wald [12], whereas that on stability started with Hicks [3]. A more detailed history is given by Arrow and Hahn [2, Ch. 1, and the notes following Chs. 5-7, 9, and 12].

system with the same economic, regardless of the particular form the dynamic assumes.

The economic considered here is precisely that of the previous section as described by the excess demand equations of (9.1-4), namely,

$$Q = \mathcal{E}(P) \tag{9.2-1}$$

where $\mathcal{E} = (\mathcal{E}^1, \ldots, \mathcal{E}^{I+J})$, along with the accompanying background assumptions and equations of Section 7.2. Thus $\mathcal{E}(P)$ is defined only for $P > 0$ at which all consumers are demanding produced goods and supplying factors so as to maximize utility subject to their budget constraints, and all firms are hiring inputs and producing outputs so as to maximize profits. Equilibrium occurs at $\bar{P} > 0$ such that (recall equation (9.1-5)),

$$\mathcal{E}(\bar{P}) = 0, \tag{9.2-2}$$

or supply equals demand in all markets. Walras' law, repeated from (9.1-6), is

$$\sum_{n=1}^{I+J} P_n \mathcal{E}^n(P) = 0, \tag{9.2-3}$$

for all $P > 0$. The functions $\mathcal{E}$ are homogeneous of degree zero and continous.

To prove the existence of equilibrium in this economy it is only necessary to find a $\bar{P} > 0$ satisfying (9.2-2). The remainder of the timeless or comparative statics equations are then solved as described at the end of Section 7.2. For a fixed-factor-supply model of Chapter 8, eqilibrium prices have already been shown to exist provided that certain extra condition are met. Although these extra conditions simplify matters considerably, they are not needed to prove the existance of an equilibrium $\bar{P}$. The following discussion demonstrates this for the general model of Section 7.2 and hence, by implication, for the special case of Chapter 8.

The particular assumptions under which equilibrium is shown to exist are these: Utility functions satisfy continuity and diffentiability (2.3-1), differential increasingness (2.3-2), strict quasi-concavity (2.3-3), and the boundary property (2.3-4). Initial endowments are given such that the aggregate endowment of each factor is positive and every consumer has a positive amount of at least one factor. Firm production functions exhibit nonnegativity (4.1-2), continuity and differentiability (4.1-3), positive marginal products throughout the interiors of their respective input spaces (implying the differential increasingness of (4.1-4)), and strict concavity (ensuring the strict quasi-concavity of (4.1-5)), with nonvanishing bordered and unbordered Hessians where the latter are defined. It is supposed futher that marginal products take on as function values all positive real numbers over every expansion path, and that isoquants for positive outputs do not touch the boundaries of their respective input spaces. (This, once again, is the strictly concave model of the firm from Theorem 5.1-24.) Note that these assumptions make certain that the minimum average variable cost in every firm is zero. Hence firm excess demand functions are defined continuously for all $P > 0$. Because the same thing is already true of consumer excess demand functions, the market excess demand functions of (9.2-1) also are defined continuously for all $P > 0$. Observe, however, that the present assumptions are not relevant for long-run circumstances because imposing the long-run equilibrium requirement that all profits vanish forces long-run equilibrium output to be zero in every firm.

The basic mathematical tool to be employed is Brouwer's theorem asserting that any continuous function Φ mapping a compact, convex set (of, say, price vectors) D into itself has at least one fixed point.[11] In other words, there is a $\bar{P}$ in D such that

$$\Phi(\bar{P}) = \bar{P}.$$

Using Brouwer's theorem, four steps are needed to prove the existence of an equilibrium price vector:

1. Find an appropriate compact, convex set D.

2. Define a suitable continuous function Φ mapping D into itself.

3. Apply Brouwer's theorem to obtain a fixed point $\bar{P}$.

4. Show that $\bar{P}$ is a positive equilibrium price vector.

An example of a simple application of these steps to demonstrate the existence of equilibrium in a single, isolated market appears in Exercise 9.1.

Turning to step 1, it is clear that the domain of definition of $\mathcal{E}$, namely

$$\{P : P > 0\},$$

is neither closed nor bounded. Hence it is not compact. A compact subset can be secured, however, by permitting zero prices and choosing the normalization

$$\sum_{n=1}^{I+J} P_n = 1.$$

---

[11]   See Theorem A.3-2 of appendix Section A.3 and the discussion following it.

Thus

$$D = \left\{ P : \sum_{n=1}^{I+J} P_n = 1 \quad \text{and} \quad P \geqslant 0 \right\} \tag{9.2-4}$$

is compact. It is also convex (Exercise 9.2). Note the vector $P = 0$ is not in D.

An appropriate continuous function mapping D into itself (step 2) is not as easy to construct. The continuous excess demand function $\mathcal{E}$ might appear to be a natural candidate, but there is no reason why $\mathcal{E}$ should map D into itself. Moreover, $\mathcal{E}$ is not even defined on the boundary of D where one or more (but not all) of the P_n are zero. This is because the boundary condition on indifference surfaces and the assumption of positive marginal utilities together imply that if the price of a consumer good is zero, a constrained utility-maximizing basket of commodities cannot exist. Corresponding assumptions on production functions render profit maximization by firms impossible with vanishing input prices. None of these difficulties is insurmountable, although each requires some effort to overcome.

The problem of existence of utility-maximizing and profit-maximizing points on the boundary of D can be skirted by taking into account the limits placed on production and consumption by the size of the initial endowment. In the pre-excess-demand notation of Section 7.2 recall that $y^0_{jk} = y^0_{I+jk} \geqslant 0$ is the initial endowment of factor j held by person k. Let

$$\Lambda_j = 1 + \sum_{k=1}^{K} y^0_{jk}, \quad j = I+1, \ldots, I+J. \tag{9.2-5}$$

It has already been assumed in Section 7.2 that at least one $y^0_{jk} > 0$ for each k as j varies, and for each j as k varies. From the latter, $\Lambda_j > 1$ for every j. Now with $n = 1, \ldots, I$ set

$$\Lambda_n = 1 + \max \sum_{\ell=1}^{L_n} f^{n\ell}(x_{n\ell 1}, \ldots, x_{n\ell I}, y_{n\ell I+1}, \ldots, y_{n\ell I+J}),$$

where the maximum is subject to all remaining production functions (7.2-1) outside of industry n, namely,

$$x_{i\ell} = f^{i\ell}(x_{i\ell 1}, \ldots, x_{i\ell I}, y_{i\ell I+1}, \ldots, y_{i\ell I+J}), \quad i \neq n,$$

and the constraints

$$\sum_{\varepsilon=1}^{I}\sum_{\ell=1}^{L_\varepsilon} y_{\varepsilon\ell I+j} \leqslant \Lambda_j, \quad j = 1,\dots,J,$$

and

$$\sum_{\varepsilon=1}^{I}\sum_{\ell=1}^{L_\varepsilon} x_{\varepsilon\ell i} \leqslant \sum_{\ell=1}^{L_i} x_{i\ell}, \quad i = 1,\dots,I.$$

Thus Λ_j is one more than the aggregate quantity of factor j available, and Λ_n is one more than the maximum output of produced good n obtainable if all resources were devoted either directly or indirectly to its production.[12] Define Λ to be the largest of all the Λ_j and Λ_n. Then

$$\sum_{n=1}^{I}\sum_{\ell=1}^{L_n} y_{n\ell I+j} < \Lambda, \quad j = 1,\dots,J,$$

$$\sum_{\ell=1}^{L_n} x_{n\ell} < \Lambda, \quad n = 1,\dots,I,$$

(9.2-6)

and from the definition of profit (equation (7.2-3)) and from (9.2-6),

$$\sum_{n=1}^{I}\sum_{\ell=1}^{L_n} (\pi_{n\ell} + b_{n\ell}) \leqslant \sum_{n=1}^{I}\sum_{\ell=1}^{L_n} P_n x_{n\ell} < \Lambda \left[\sum_{n=1}^{I} P_n\right]. \qquad (9.2\text{-}7)$$

Suppose, for P in D, consumers were to choose produced goods and factor supplies so as to maximize their utility functions

$$u^k(x_{1k},\dots,x_{Ik}, y_{I+1k},\dots,y_{I+Jk}),$$

subject to the usual budget constraint (7.2-12) in inequality form (and in non-excess-demand notation),

$$\sum_{n=1}^{I} P_n x_{nk} + \sum_{n=I+1}^{I+J} P_n\left(y_{nk} - y_{nk}^0\right) \leqslant \sum_{i=1}^{I}\sum_{\ell=1}^{L_i} \theta_{ki\ell}\left(\pi_{i\ell} + b_{i\ell}\right), \qquad (9.2\text{-}8)$$

---

[12]   That Λ_n exists for each $n = 1,\dots,I$ follows from the continuity of the sum to be maximized, the compactness of the set over which the maximum is to take place, and Theorem A.3-1 in appendix Section A.3. Of course, even though Λ_n exists, no output of size $\Lambda_n - 1$ can actually be produced because there are not enough resources in the economy for the firm to hire Λ_j of each input j.

and also subject to

$$x_{nk} \leqslant \Lambda, \quad n = 1, \ldots, I,$$

$$y_{nk} \leqslant \Lambda, \quad n = I + 1, \ldots, I + J,$$

(9.2-9)

where $k = 1, \ldots, K$ and the index n runs over all goods as in Section 7.2. Depending on circumstances, the latter commodity constraints may or may not be effective in this maximization. But it is not hard to see that the budget constraint is always effective. To do so requires showing that for each k, and any P in D, the associated budget hyperplane intersects the set

$$R^k = \{(x_{1k}, \ldots, x_{Ik}, y_{I+1k}, \ldots, y_{I+Jk}) :$$

$$0 \leqslant x_{nk} \leqslant \Lambda \text{ and } 0 \leqslant y_{nk} \leqslant \Lambda, \text{ for all } n\} .$$

The assumption of positive marginal utilities then ensures that person k necessarily achieves her maximum somewhere on this intersection. Hence the budget constraint identified with P is effective. Proceeding with the needed demonstration, observe that for any P in D, the budget hyperplane shifts away from the origin as initial endowments and profit-plus-fixed-cost income rise. According to (9.2-6) – (9.2-8), therefore, no budget hyperplane (given P) for any consumer can be farther from the origin than that given by

$$\sum_{n=1}^{I} P_n x_{nk} + \sum_{n=I+1}^{I+J} P_n (y_{nk} - \Lambda) = \Lambda \left[\sum_{n=1}^{I} P_n \right] .$$

But the above equation is certainly satisfied by the point whose coordinates are

$$x_{nk} = \Lambda, \quad n = 1, \ldots, I,$$

$$y_{nk} = \Lambda, \quad n = I + 1, \ldots, I + J,$$

and which lies in R^k. Hence all budget hyperplanes intersect R^k and the budget constraint is always effective.

Using the proposition that a continuous function defined on a compact set achieves a maximum on that set, and combining the above argument with one similar to the proof of Theorem 2.3-10, the existence of unique utility-maximizing baskets of commodities can be established for each consumer k. Thus for all P in D there is a vector $(x_{1k}, \ldots, x_{Ik}, y_{I+1k}, \ldots, y_{I+Jk})$ in R^k

satisfying the budget equality

$$\sum_{n=1}^{I} P_n x_{nk} + \sum_{n=I+1}^{I+J} P_n \left(y_{nk} - y_{nk}^0 \right) = \sum_{i=1}^{I} \sum_{\ell=1}^{L_i} \theta_{ki\ell} \left(\pi_{i\ell} + b_{i\ell} \right), \qquad (9.2\text{-}10)$$

and such that any other vector in R^k satisfying (9.2-8) has lower utility associated with it. Several possibilities are illustrated for the one factor, one final-good world in Figure 9.3. In each case the constrained utility maximizing basket is indicated by the symbol α. Note that ordinary tangency maxima appear in Figures 9.3(a) and (c). Since the tangency maximum occurs outside of R^k in Figure 9.3(b), the constraint on y_{1k} (in addition to the budget constraint) is effective and the point of constrained maximum utility occurs where the line $y_{1k} = \Lambda$ intersects the budget line. A similar conclusion obtains in Figure 9.3(d), illustrating a situation in which the price of the factor is zero. Here, in the absence of the constraint $y_{1k} = \Lambda$, the consumer would choose a basket (x_{1k}, y_{1k}) such that y_{1k} is infinite.

Because utility-maximizing baskets of commodities always exist, "demand" functions can be defined and their properties deduced as in Sections 2.3 and 2.4. The translation into excess demand functions is the same as that of Section 7.2. Since these functions are different from those originally defined in Sections 2.3 and 7.2 in that their domain includes zero prices and in that their characterization requires the extra constraints (9.2-9), they are often referred to as, respectively, *pseudo demand* or *pseudo excess demand functions*. Using the excess-demand notation of Section 7.2, the latter are written as

$$q_{nk} = \widehat{E}^{nk}(P), \quad n = 1, \ldots, I+J,$$

defined on D for each k. The $\widehat{E}^{nk}$ are continuous, homogeneous of degree zero, and (since the budget constraint is always effective) satisfy the budget constraint equality (9.2-10) on D.

Note that for each $(x_{1k}, \ldots, x_{Ik}, y_{I+1k}, \ldots, y_{I+Jk})$ in the interior of R^k, that is for which

$$0 < x_{nk} < \Lambda, \quad n = 1, \ldots, I,$$

$$0 < y_{nk} < \Lambda, \quad n = I+1, \ldots, I+J,$$

there is a P in D such that $(x_{1k}, \ldots, x_{Ik}, y_{I+1k}, \ldots, y_{I+Jk})$ maximizes u^k subject to (9.2-8) and (9.2-9), and such that the maximum occurs at a tangency (Figure 9.3(a)). In other words, the first-order Lagrangian constrained maximization conditions are met. Let D^k be the collection of all price vectors P

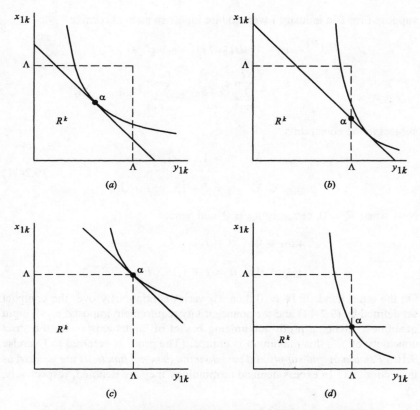

Figure 9.3 Utility maximization subject to budget and Λ-availability constraints: (a) utility maximizing basket in the interior of R^k; (b) utility maximizing basket on the boundary of R^k with all prices positive; (c) utility maximizing basket as large as possible; (d) utility maximizing basket on the boundary of R^k with the price of factor 1 at zero

in D associated with tangency maxima in the interior of R^k. Then the pseudo excess demand functions and the ordinary excess demand functions (Section 7.2) coincide on D^k, or

$$\widehat{E}^{nk}(P) = E^{nk}(P), \quad n = 1, \ldots, I + J,$$

for all P in D^k and $k = 1, \ldots, K$.

Pseudo excess demand functions for firms are obtained similarly. Thus suppose firm ℓ in industry i were to hire inputs so as to maximize

$$\pi_{i\ell} = P_i f^{i\ell}(x_{i\ell 1}, \ldots, x_{i\ell I}, y_{i\ell I+1}, \ldots, y_{i\ell I+J})$$

$$- \sum_{n=1}^{I} P_n x_{i\ell n} - \sum_{n=I+1}^{I+J} P_n y_{i\ell n} - b_{i\ell},$$

subject to the constraints

$$x_{i\ell n} \leqslant \Lambda, \quad n = 1, \ldots, I,$$

$$(9.2\text{-}11)$$

$$y_{i\ell n} \leqslant \Lambda, \quad n = I+1, \ldots, I+J.$$

Now when $P_i = 0$, certainly $x_{i\ell} = 0$, and hence

$$x_{i\ell n} = 0, \quad n = 1, \ldots, I,$$

$$y_{i\ell n} = 0, \quad n = I+1, \ldots, I+J.$$

On the other hand, if $P_i > 0$ then $\pi_{i\ell}$ varies continuously over the compact set defined by (9.2-11) and the nonnegativity requirement imposed on all input quantities. Hence a profit-maximizing basket of inputs exists. By the strict concavity of $f^{i\ell}$, this maximum is unique. (The proof is deferred to Exercise 9.10.) *Pseudo output supply* and *pseudo input demand functions* are secured as in Section 5.1. In excess demand terminology they are denoted, respectively, by

$$q_{i\ell} = \widehat{E}^{i\ell}(P),$$

$$q_{i\ell n} = \widehat{E}^{i\ell n}(P), \quad n = 1, \ldots, I+J,$$

on D. These pseudo excess demand functions are continuous and homogeneous of degree zero everywhere in D.

Analogously with consumers, to any point in the interior of the set defined by (9.2-11) and the boundaries of the input space for firm $i\ell$, there corresponds a $P > 0$ in D for which the differential first-order maximization conditions are satisfied. Letting $D^{i\ell}$ represent the set of all such price vectors,

$$\widehat{E}^{i\ell}(P) = E^{i\ell}(P),$$

$$\widehat{E}^{i\ell n}(P) = E^{i\ell n}(P), \quad n = 1, \ldots, I+J,$$

on $D^{i\ell}$, where $E^{i\ell}$ and $E^{i\ell n}$ are the ordinary excess demand functions of (7.2-4) and (7.2-5).

It has already been pointed out that at maximum profit for firm $i\ell$, if $P_i = 0$ then output and all input quantities vanish. Hence $\pi_{i\ell} = 0$. However, if P is in $D^{i\ell}$, then where profits are maximized (recall (5.1-11))

$$P_n = P_i f_n^{i\ell}(x_{i\ell 1}, \ldots, x_{i\ell I}, y_{i\ell I+1}, \ldots y_{i\ell I+J}),$$

with $n \neq j$ and $n = 1, \ldots, I + J$. Thus for firm $i\ell$,

$$\pi_{i\ell} + b_{i\ell} = P_i x_{i\ell} - \sum_{n=1}^{I} P_n x_{i\ell n} - \sum_{n=I+1}^{I+J} P_n y_{i\ell n}$$

$$= P_i \left[f^{i\ell} - \sum_{n=1}^{I} x_{i\ell n} f_n^{i\ell} - \sum_{n=I+1}^{I+J} y_{i\ell n} f_n^{i\ell} \right],$$

where the functional arguments of $f^{i\ell}$ and its derivatives have been dropped to simplify notation. (Recall from the notational convention adopted in Section 7.2, that the above sums need not contain all terms indicated by the summation symbolism because not all possible inputs are necessarily included as arguments in the firms' production functions. In particular, $x_{i\ell i}$ is not an argument of $f^{i\ell}$ and therefore not contained in these sums.) It follows from the strict concavity of $f^{i\ell}$ and Theorem 4.2-23 that

$$\pi_{i\ell} + b_{i\ell} > 0.$$

This means that as long as P_i is in $D^{i\ell}$ and $P_i > 0$ for every i and ℓ, no firm has to produce a positive output when it cannot recover in revenue its variable cost. Furthermore, at least one consumer has a positive profit-plus-fixed-cost income.

Aggregate all consumer and firm pseudo excess demand functions as in Sections 7.2 and 9.1 to obtain the pseudo market excess demand counterpart to the ordinary market excess demand functions $\mathcal{E}$ of (9.2-1). Denote them by

$$Q = \widehat{\mathcal{E}}(P),$$

where $\widehat{\mathcal{E}} = (\widehat{\mathcal{E}}^1, \ldots, \widehat{\mathcal{E}}^{I+J})$ Let D^* be the intersection of all sets D^k and $D^{i\ell}$, namely,

$$D^* = \left[\bigcap_{k=1}^{K} D^k \right] \cap \left[\bigcap_{i=1}^{I} \left(\bigcap_{\ell=1}^{L_i} D^{i\ell} \right) \right].$$

Clearly D^* is a subset of D. The following properties of market pseudo excess demand functions are needed:

(9.2-12) $\widehat{\mathcal{E}}$ is defined on D.

(9.2-13)   For all P in D^*

$$\mathcal{E}(P) = \widehat{\mathcal{E}}(P).$$

(9.2-14) $\widehat{\mathcal{E}}$ is continous where defined.

(9.2-15)   Walras' law applies to $\widehat{\mathcal{E}}$. Thus, on D,

$$\sum_{n=1}^{I+J} P_n \widehat{\mathcal{E}}^n(P) = 0.$$

(9.2-16)   For all $(P_1, \ldots, P_{n-1}, 0, P_{n+1}, \ldots, P_{I+J})$ in D,

$$\widehat{\mathcal{E}}^n(P_1, \ldots, P_{n-1}, 0, P_{n+1}, \ldots, P_{I+J}) > 0,$$

where $n = 1, \ldots, I + J$.

Proofs of these properties are left to the reader (Exercise 9.3).

It is now possible to construct the required function for step 2 in the application of Brouwer's theorem. Define

$$\Upsilon^n(P) = \max \left[P_n + \widehat{\mathcal{E}}^n(P), \tfrac{1}{2} P_n \right], \qquad (9.2\text{-}17)$$

on D. (This definition is made possible by property (9.2-12)). Then for each n, Υ^n is continuous from (9.2-14) and, by (9.2-16), $\Upsilon^n(P) > 0$ where defined. Let

$$\Psi(P) = \sum_{n=1}^{I+J} \Upsilon^n(P), \qquad (9.2\text{-}18)$$

also on D. Then $\Psi(P)$, too, is continuous and $\Psi(P) > 0$ on D. Finally, set

$$\Phi^n(P) = \frac{\Upsilon^n(P)}{\Psi(P)}, \quad n = 1, \ldots, I + J, \qquad (9.2\text{-}19)$$

and $\Phi = \left(\Phi^1, \ldots, \Phi^{I+J} \right)$, for all P in D. Clearly Φ is continuous and $\Phi(P) > 0$ on D. Because

$$\sum_{n=1}^{I+J} \Phi^n(P) = 1,$$

Φ maps D into itself. Therefore Φ on D satisfies the hypotheses of Brouwer's theorem.

According to Brouwer's theorem (step 3), there exists a vector $\bar{P}$ in D such that

$$\Phi(\bar{P}) = \bar{P},$$

or, from (9.2-19),

$$\bar{P}_n = \frac{\Upsilon^n(\bar{P})}{\Psi(\bar{P})}, \quad n = 1, \dots, I + J. \tag{9.2-20}$$

Evidently, $\bar{P} > 0$. It remains to show (step 4) that $\bar{P}$ is an equilibrium price vector. This requires a preliminary result:

Lemma 9.2-21   For each $n = 1, \dots, I + J$,

$$\Upsilon^n(\bar{P}) = \bar{P}_n + \widehat{\mathcal{E}}^n(\bar{P}).$$

Proof: Note first from (9.2-17) that the smallest value $\Upsilon^n(\bar{P})$ can assume is $\frac{1}{2}\bar{P}_n$. Setting each $\Upsilon^n(\bar{P})$ at this minimum value, and using (9.2-18) and the fact that $\bar{P}$ is in D

$$\Psi(\bar{P}) = \sum_{n=1}^{I+J} \tfrac{1}{2}\bar{P}_n = \tfrac{1}{2}.$$

Hence

(9.2-22)   If $\Upsilon^n(\bar{P}) > \frac{1}{2}\bar{P}_n$ for at least one n, then $\Psi(\bar{P}) > \frac{1}{2}$.

The proof of the lemma now proceeds by contradiction.

Suppose $\Upsilon^n(\bar{P}) = \frac{1}{2}\bar{P}_n$ for every n. Then from (9.2-17),

$$\widehat{\mathcal{E}}^n(\bar{P}) < 0, \quad n = 1, \dots, I + J.$$

Thus

$$\sum_{n=1}^{I+J} \bar{P}_n \widehat{\mathcal{E}}^n(\bar{P}) < 0,$$

contrary to Walras' law (9.2-15). On the other hand, suppose $\Upsilon^1(\bar{P}) = \frac{1}{2}\bar{P}_1$, say, and that $\Upsilon^n(\bar{P}) > \frac{1}{2}\bar{P}_n$, for at least one $n \neq 1$. Then, in view of (9.2-20) and (9.2-22),

$$\bar{P}_1 = \frac{\frac{1}{2}\bar{P}_1}{\Psi(\bar{P})} < \bar{P}_1,$$

which, again, is a contradiction. By (9.2-17), the only other possibility is

$$\Upsilon^n(\bar{P}) = \bar{P}_n + \widehat{\mathcal{E}}^n(\bar{P}),$$

for all n.

Q.E.D.

Now combining (9.2-20) with the lemma,

$$\bar{P}_n = \frac{\bar{P}_n + \widehat{\mathcal{E}}^n(\bar{P})}{\Psi(\bar{P})}, \quad n = 1, \ldots, I + J.$$

Multiplying by $\widehat{\mathcal{E}}^n(\bar{P})$ and adding over n,

$$\sum_{n=1}^{I+J} \bar{P}_n \widehat{\mathcal{E}}^n(\bar{P}) = \frac{\sum_{n=1}^{I+J} \bar{P}_n \widehat{\mathcal{E}}^n(\bar{P}) + \sum_{n=1}^{I+J} \left[\widehat{\mathcal{E}}^n(\bar{P})\right]^2}{\Psi(\bar{P})}.$$

By Walras' law (9.2-15), both the sum on the left-hand side of the equality and the left-hand sum in the numerator vanish, so that

$$\sum_{n=1}^{I+J} \left[\widehat{\mathcal{E}}^n(\bar{P})\right]^2 = 0.$$

Hence

$$\widehat{\mathcal{E}}^n(\bar{P}) = 0, \quad n = 1, \ldots, I + J.$$

In other words, the vector $\bar{P}$ satisfies all utility maximization, profit maximization, and pseudo-excess-demand market equilibrium conditions simultaneously. But because there are not enough resources to get there, none of the components of the individual consumer and firm vectors of quantities of commodities associated with $\bar{P}$ can lie on the Λ-boundaries in their respective commodity and input spaces. Hence the definition of $\widehat{\mathcal{E}}$ ensures that all relevant first-order constrained maximization conditions are satisfied. Thus $\bar{P}$ is in D^*, and (9.2-13) implies

$$\mathcal{E}(\bar{P}) = 0.$$

Therefore $\bar{P}$ is a competitive equilibrium. The preceding argument is summarized by the following proposition:

Theorem 9.2-23   Let nonnegative initial endowments be given such that at least one $y_{jk}^0 > 0$ for each k as j varies, and for each j as k varies. Suppose consumer utility functions exhibit the continuity and differentiability, differential increasingness, strict quasi-concavity, and boundary properties of Section 2.3. Let firm production functions have the nonnegativity, continuity, and differentiability properties of Section 4.1. Assume further that marginal products are positive throughout the interiors of their respective input spaces and take on as function values all positive real numbers over every expansion path, that isoquants associated with positive outputs do not touch the boundaries of their respective input spaces, and that production functions are strictly concave with nonvanishing bordered and unbordered Hessians where the latter are defined. Then the dynamic model of Section 9.1 has an equilibrium path.

Existence theorems can be proved under modified and even weaker hypotheses. Thus, for example, constant returns to scale production functions and Viner models of the firm can be permitted, and theorems for long-run models with zero profits and zero fixed costs also are possible. However, none of these alternatives is pursued here.[13]

9.3   STABILITY OF EQUILIBRIUM PATHS

The dynamic systems under consideration here are comprised of two parts: an economic and a dynamic. The economic embodies timeless behavior of all individual consumers and firms in the economy; the dynamic is a supposed specification of the movement of market prices or quantities over time. These two parts are linked together so that equilibrium in the economic corresponds to equilibrium paths in the dynamic economic system as a whole. In other words, consumers are maximizing utility subject to budget constraints, firms are maximizing profits, and supply equals demand in all markets if and only if market prices and quantities are not changing over time.

The two approaches introduced in Section 9.1 can be summarized as follows: One specification of the dynamic economic system takes the Walrasian form of (9.1-7) and (9.1-10):

$$Q^{(I+J)} = \mathcal{E}^{(I+J)}\left(P^{(I+J)}\right), \qquad (9.3\text{-}1)$$

---

[13]   See, for example, Arrow and Hahn [2].

$$\frac{dP^{(I+J)}}{d\tau} = \xi^P(P^{(I+J)}, \tau),$$ (9.3-2)

where (9.3-1) represents the economic and (9.3-2) the dynamic and, recall, $P_{I+J} = 1$. An equivalent formulation of the same thing is, from (9.1-12),

$$\frac{dQ^{(I+J)}}{d\tau} = \left[\mathcal{B}(\mathcal{E}^{-1}(Q^{(I+J)}))\right]\left[\xi^P(\mathcal{E}^{-1}(Q^{(I+J)}), \tau)\right],$$ (9.3-3)

along with the inverse excess demand function (equation (9.3-4), below). The alternative Marshallian specification consists of (9.1-9) and (9.1-13), namely,

$$P^{(I+J)} = \mathcal{E}^{-1}(Q^{(I+J)}),$$ (9.3-4)

$$\frac{dQ^{(I+J)}}{d\tau} = \xi^Q(Q^{(I+J)}, \tau),$$ (9.3-5)

or equivalently, using (9.1-14),

$$\frac{dP^{(I+J)}}{d\tau} =$$ (9.3-6)

$$\left[\mathcal{B}^{-1}(\mathcal{E}^{(I+J)}(P^{(I+J)}))\right]\left[\xi^Q(\mathcal{E}^{(I+J)}(P^{(I+J)}), \tau)\right],$$

together with the excess demand function of (9.3-1). Equations (9.3-1) and (9.3-2) and equations (9.3-4) and (9.3-5) constitute distinct systems. Although they are based on the same economic (recall that $\mathcal{E}^{(I+J)}$ and $\mathcal{E}^{-1}$ are inverse functions), they cannot themselves be equivalent without some restraint on the choice of ξ^P or ξ^Q. Given ξ^P, say, it is of course possible to choose ξ^Q so that the two systems are identical. An example is provided below.

Clearly, as examination of (9.3-3) and (9.3-6) shows, stability of either system turns on both economic and dynamic characteristics. With the same economic, an equilibrium path could be stable or not depending on the properties of the dynamic. Similarly, for a given dynamic, an equilibrium path would be stable or not according to the properties of the economic. Thus there appears to be three focal points for stability analysis: the economic, the dynamic, and the combined system taken as a whole. Loosely speaking, it sometimes turns out that assumptions on any two permit inferences about the third. An interesting consequence of this observation is that properties of the economic may occasionally be inferred by combining hypotheses on the dynamic with hypotheses on the complete system. The latter proposition is known as Samuelson's *correspondence principle*.[14]

---

[14] Samuelson [11, pp. 258ff, 284ff].

To see what stability analysis involves, two simple examples are explored first. Both assume linear excess demand functions and in both cases the normalization employed (namely $P_{I+J} = 1$) introduces no difficulties in relation to the conjunction of Walras' law and the dynamic.[15] It should be understood, however, that these examples are presented for pedagogic purposes alone. Although many of the ideas of stability analysis find convenient illustration when excess demand functions are linear, utility and profit maximization as described here are not generally capable of producing an $\mathcal{E}^{(I+J)}$ that is completely linear.[16] More general results that do not require the assumption of linearity are presented later on.

Consider initially an economic with two goods (that is, $I + J = 2$). Then $P^{(I+J)} = P_1$, $Q^{(I+J)} = Q_1$, and $\mathcal{E}^{(I+J)} = \mathcal{E}^1$. Since confusion cannot arise, the subscript and superscript 1 are dropped for the remainder of this example. Suppose market demand and supply equations are, respectively,

$$x_d = \alpha P + \beta,$$

$$x_s = \gamma P + \delta,$$

where x_d represents market quantity demanded, x_s denotes market quantity supplied, and α, β, γ, and δ are constants such that $\alpha \neq \gamma$ and

$$\frac{\delta - \beta}{\alpha - \gamma} > 0.$$

Although γ would normally be required to be positive, for the sake of argument no such restriction is imposed here. With $Q = x_d - x_s$, aggregate market excess demand is

$$Q = \mathcal{E}(P), \tag{9.3-7}$$

where

$$\mathcal{E}(P) = (\alpha - \gamma) P + (\beta - \delta). \tag{9.3-8}$$

Furthermore,

$$P = \mathcal{E}^{-1}(Q), \tag{9.3-9}$$

---

where

$$\mathcal{E}^{-1}(Q) = \frac{1}{\alpha - \gamma}Q + \frac{\delta - \beta}{\alpha - \gamma}. \tag{9.3-10}$$

Note that the Jacobians are nonzero and reduce to

$$\mathcal{B}(P) = \alpha - \gamma, \tag{9.3-11}$$

and

$$\mathcal{B}^{-1}(P) = \frac{1}{\alpha - \gamma}. \tag{9.3-12}$$

Equilibrium exists and is unique. It occurs at

$$\bar{Q} = 0,$$

$$\bar{P} = \frac{\delta - \beta}{\alpha - \gamma},$$

with $\bar{P} > 0$.

Assume the dynamic is given in Walrasian form by

$$\frac{dP}{d\tau} = \theta\mathcal{E}(P), \tag{9.3-13}$$

where $\theta \neq 0$ is a constant. Thus the auctioneer, in the typical story associated with this case, adjusts price in proportion to excess demand when out of equilibrium. If $\theta > 0$, price rises (or falls) with positive (or, respectively, negative) excess demand. Note that $|\theta|$ may be thought of as the "speed" of adjustment.

From (9.3-7), (9.3-11), and (9.3-13), the system (9.3-3) becomes

$$\frac{dQ}{d\tau} = (\alpha - \gamma)\theta Q, \tag{9.3-14}$$

whose solution or path through Q^0 is[17]

$$\nu^Q(Q^0, \tau) = Q^0 e^{\theta(\alpha - \gamma)\tau}.$$

Because $\bar{Q} = 0$ is a unique equilibrium point of (9.3-14), the restriction that equilibrium in the system as a whole coincides with equilibrium in the economic is satisfied. Moreover, the equilibrium path is

$$\nu^Q(0, \tau) = 0.$$

---

[17]   See appendix Section A.5.

As long as $\theta(\alpha - \gamma) < 0$, not only is the equilibrium path globally stable, but also the system itself is stable.

Now suppose the dynamic were taken to be in the Marshallian form

$$\frac{dQ}{d\tau} = \theta\left[(\alpha - \gamma)^2 \mathcal{E}^{-1}(Q) + (\beta - \delta)(\alpha - \gamma)\right]. \tag{9.3-15}$$

Then from (9.3-9), (9.3-12), and (9.3-15), the system (9.3-6) would appear as

$$\frac{dP}{d\tau} = \theta(\alpha - \gamma) P + \theta(\beta - \delta). \tag{9.3-16}$$

The general path through P^0 would be[18]

$$\nu^P(P^0, \tau) = \left(P^0 - \frac{\delta - \beta}{\alpha - \gamma}\right) e^{\theta(\alpha - \gamma)\tau} + \frac{\delta - \beta}{\alpha - \gamma},$$

and the unique equilibrium path would be given by

$$\nu^P\left(\frac{\delta - \beta}{\alpha - \gamma}, \tau\right) = \frac{\delta - \beta}{\alpha - \gamma}.$$

Once again, equilibrium in the economic is uniquely identified with equilibrium in the system as a whole, and global stability of the equilibrium path and stability of the system would require $\theta(\alpha - \gamma) < 0$.

Because substitution of (9.3-8) into (9.3-13) produces (9.3-16), and substitution of (9.3-10) into (9.3-15) yields (9.3-14), the systems based on the dynamics (9.3-13) and (9.3-15) are identical. The Walrasian and Marshallian approaches have thus been rendered equivalent through judicious choice of the rules of adjustment. In fact, (9.3-15) was derived by substituting (9.3-8) into (9.3-13) and then factoring out the Jacobian expression (9.3-12) as required by (9.3-6). Any other specification of (9.3-15) would force the two systems to be distinct.

It has been demonstrated in either case that stability depends on the sign of $\theta(\alpha - \gamma)$. Now θ is a parameter of the dynamic, $(\alpha - \gamma)$ is an expression involving parameters of the economic, and $\theta(\alpha - \gamma)$ relates to the dynamic economic system as a whole. Imposing assumptions on the sign of any two of θ, $(\alpha - \gamma)$, and $\theta(\alpha - \gamma)$ permits inference of the sign of the third. Postulating only that $\theta(\alpha - \gamma) < 0$, say, is insufficient for such inference because both $(\alpha - \gamma) < 0$ and $(\alpha - \gamma) > 0$ would obtain according to the sign of θ. Four possibilities for the economic are illustrated in Figure 9.4. Each graph, recall, actually depicts the inverse demand curve (labeled H) and the inverse supply

---

[18] *Ibid.*

curve (labeled G) because, conforming to tradition, the dependent variable has been placed on the horizontal axis. Thus if $\theta > 0$, Figures 9.4(a) and (b) reflect globally stable situations; if $\theta < 0$, they do not. Likewise, Figures 9.4(c) and (d) exhibit global stability when $\theta < 0$ and a lack thereof when $\theta > 0$. The absence of global stability in these circumstances may be referred to as "global instability" in that, for example, $\lim_{\tau \to \infty} \nu^Q(Q^0, \tau) = \infty$ for all $Q^0 \neq 0$. Remember also that global stability in this market implies global

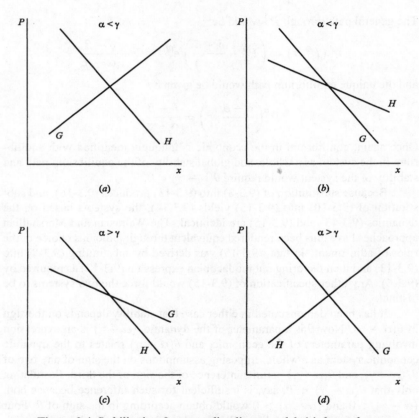

Figure 9.4 Stability in a 2-commodity, linear model: (a) demand curve slopes downward, supply curve slopes upward; (b) slope of (inverse) demand curve greater than slope of (inverse) supply curve; (c) slope of (inverse) demand curve less than slope of (inverse) supply curve; (d) demand curve slopes upward, supply curve slopes downward

stability in the remaining market by Walras' law.

The correspondence principle can also be illustrated here. For assuming global stability of the system as a whole (that is, $\theta(\alpha - \gamma) < 0$) and, say, $\theta > 0$ in the dynamic, it follows that $\alpha < \gamma$ in the economic. Thus the comparative static or timeless statement that the slope of the demand curve should be less than the slope of the supply curve can be derived as a proposition from dynamic hypotheses. A situation in which the correspondence principle does not apply can be found in Exercise 9.9.[19]

The two-good system examined above is quite simple. But like the integrability problem of demand theory (Section 3.1), the mathematics of stability changes substantially in passing to higher dimensions. Because the main alterations occur when the number of goods is increased by one, many of the difficulties present in general stability analysis (with linear excess demand functions) can be illustrated in a three-good world. Several of these are suggested by the second example offered below.

Let x_{nd} denote quantities demanded and x_{ns} quantities supplied in market n, where $n = 1, 2$. (The third market can be ignored by Walras' law.) In this case $I + J = 3$, $P^{(3)} = (P_1, P_2)$, $Q^{(3)} = (Q_1, Q_2)$, and $\mathcal{E}^{(3)} = (\mathcal{E}^1, \mathcal{E}^2)$. Take market demand and supply function to be

$$x_{nd} = \alpha_{n1} P_1 + \alpha_{n2} P_2 + \beta_n,$$

$$x_{ns} = \gamma_{n1} P_1 + \gamma_{n2} P_2 + \delta_n,$$

for $n = 1, 2$, where the α_{ni}, β_n, γ_{ni}, and δ_n are constants. Setting

$$Q_n = x_{nd} - x_{ns},$$

$$a_{ni} = \alpha_{ni} - \gamma_{ni},$$

$$c_n = \beta_n - \delta_n,$$

$$c = (c_1, c_2),$$

and

$$A = \begin{bmatrix} a_{11} & a_{12} \\ a_{21} & a_{22} \end{bmatrix},$$

---

[19]   Another example is given by Arrow and Hahn [2, pp. 320-321].

the market excess demand functions are

$$Q^{(3)} = \mathcal{E}^{(3)}(P^{(3)}), \tag{9.3-17}$$

where

$$\mathcal{E}^{(3)}(P^{(3)}) = AP^{(3)} + c. \tag{9.3-18}$$

(In this equation $\mathcal{E}^{(3)}$, $P^{(3)}$, and c are all column vectors.) Market equilibrium occurs at $\bar{Q}^{(3)} = 0$. Assuming the Jacobian determinant

$$\left| \mathcal{B}(P^{(3)}) \right| = |A| \neq 0, \tag{9.3-19}$$

the equilibrium price vector $\bar{P}^{(3)}$ is obtained by combining (9.3-17) and (9.3-18), setting $Q^{(3)} = 0$, and solving with Cramer's rule. Thus

$$\bar{P}_1 = \frac{c_2 a_{12} - c_1 a_{22}}{|A|},$$

$$\bar{P}_2 = \frac{c_1 a_{21} - c_2 a_{11}}{|A|}.$$

Supposing that the right-hand sides of these equations are positive, $\bar{P}^{(3)} > 0$.
   As in the previous example, let the dynamic be

$$\frac{dP^{(3)}}{d\tau} = \theta \mathcal{E}^{(3)}(P^{(3)}), \tag{9.3-20}$$

where $\theta \neq 0$ is a scalar constant. For simplicity, the speed of adjustment has been assumed identical in both markets. Putting together (9.3-17), (9.3-19) in matrix form, and (9.3-20), the dynamic economic system (9.3-3) is

$$\frac{dQ^{(3)}}{d\tau} = \theta A Q^{(3)}. \tag{9.3-21}$$

(Here $Q^{(3)}$ and $dQ^{(3)}/d\tau$ are column vectors.) It is not necessary to write down the formula for the general solution of (9.3-21) — a description of it can be found for a particular case in appendix Section A.5 — but it should be pointed out that to do so requires knowledge of the roots of the following quadratic equation in χ:

$$|\theta A - \chi \mathcal{I}| = \chi^2 - \theta (a_{11} + a_{22}) \chi + \theta^2 (a_{11} a_{22} - a_{12} a_{21}) = 0.$$

These roots can be secured from the standard formula

$$\chi = \frac{\theta}{2}\left\{(a_{11} + a_{22}) \pm \sqrt{(a_{11} + a_{22})^2 - 4(a_{11}a_{22} - a_{12}a_{21})}\right\}. \quad (9.3\text{-}22)$$

Now $\bar{Q}^{(3)} = 0$ can be shown to be the unique equilibrium point of (9.3-21) so that equilibrium in the complete system is again identified with equilibrium in the economic. Moreover, the stability of (9.3-21) turns out to depend on the sign of the real parts of the roots in (9.3-22). In particular, (9.3-21) is stable when they are negative.[20]

Sufficient conditions for stability can be expressed in terms of θ and the parameters and derivatives of the economic. Recall that $P_3 = 1$ and that the excess demand function for market 3 is determined according to Walras' law (9.1-6):

$$P_1\mathcal{E}^1(P^{(3)}) + P_2\mathcal{E}^2(P^{(3)}) = -\mathcal{E}^3(P^{(3)}), \quad (9.3\text{-}23)$$

for all $P^{(3)} > 0$. In general $\mathcal{E}^3$ is nonlinear. Assume the partial derivatives evaluated at $\bar{P}^{(3)}$,

$$\mathcal{E}_i^3(\bar{P}^{(3)}) > 0, \quad i = 1, 2. \quad (9.3\text{-}24)$$

It is now shown that, in addition to (9.3-24), the restrictions

$$\theta > 0,$$
$$\quad (9.2\text{-}25)$$
$$a_{ni} > 0, \quad n \neq i,$$

where $n, i = 1, 2$, are enough to guarantee that the real parts of each root of (9.3-22) are negative. Under these conditions, then, (9.3-21) is stable. Because the equilibrium point $\bar{Q}^{(3)} = 0$ is unique, the equilibrium path is globally stable.

Differentiating the identity (9.3-23) with respect to P_1 and evaluating it at the equilibrium $\bar{P} > 0$ gives, from (9.3-18) and the fact that $\mathcal{E}^1(\bar{P}^{(3)}) = 0$,

$$a_{11}\bar{P}_1 + a_{21}\bar{P}_2 = -\mathcal{E}_1^3(\bar{P}^{(3)}).$$

A similar differentiation with respect to P_2, because $\mathcal{E}^2(\bar{P}^{(3)}) = 0$, yields

$$a_{12}\bar{P}_1 + a_{22}\bar{P}_2 = -\mathcal{E}_2^3(\bar{P}^{(3)}).$$

Thus from (9.3-24) and (9.3-25) it follows that

$$a_{nn} < 0, \quad n = 1, 2, \quad (9.3\text{-}26)$$

---

20   See appendix Section A.5.

and

$$-a_{11}\bar{P}_1 > a_{21}\bar{P}_2,$$

$$-a_{22}\bar{P}_2 > a_{12}\bar{P}_1.$$

Because both sides of the last two inequalities are positive (from inequalities (9.3-25) and (9.3-26)),

$$a_{11}a_{22}\bar{P}_1\bar{P}_2 > a_{12}a_{21}\bar{P}_1\bar{P}_2,$$

or

$$a_{11}a_{22} > a_{12}a_{21}. \tag{9.3-27}$$

If the term under the radical in (9.3-22) is positive so that the roots are real, then (9.3-27) implies

$$|a_{11} + a_{22}| > \left| \sqrt{(a_{11} + a_{22})^2 - 4(a_{11}a_{22} - a_{12}a_{21})} \right|.$$

Hence, from (9.3-26) and the fact that θ is assumed positive, both roots are negative. On the other hand, if the term under the radical is negative, then the roots are complex. The real part of each is

$$\frac{\theta}{2}(a_{11} + a_{22}),$$

which, again by (9.3-26), is negative.

When the excess demand functions $\mathcal{E}^1(P^{(3)})$ have the properties recorded in (9.3-24) – (9.3-25), namely that for $n \neq 3$ and $i \neq 3$,

$$a_{ni} > 0, \quad n \neq i,$$

and

$$\mathcal{E}_i^3(\bar{P}^{(3)}) > 0, \quad i \neq 3,$$

then goods n and i (for $i \neq n$) are called gross substitutes (everywhere), and goods i and 3 are gross substitutes at $\bar{P}$.[21] Furthermore, the inequalities

$$a_{11} < 0, \quad a_{22} < 0, \quad a_{11}a_{22} - a_{12}a_{21} > 0,$$

---

[21]   A definition of gross substitutes for excess demand functions in general is given in Section 9.4. See also n. 27 on pp. 366.

are a special case of what are sometimes called *Hicksian stability conditions*.[22] Thus, under the very particular circumstances considered here, the preceding argument establishes two propositions:

Theorem 9.3-28   If goods n and i, for $n \neq i$, $n \neq 3$, and $i \neq 3$, are gross substitutes, and if goods 3 and $i \neq 3$ are gross substitutes at the equilibrium $\bar{P} > 0$, then the Hicksian stability conditions are satisfied.

Theorem 9.3-29   If the dynamic (9.3-20) has the property that $\theta > 0$, and if the economic (9.3-17) satisfies the Hicksian stability conditions, then the equilibrium path of the system as a whole (that is, equations (9.3-17) and (9.3-20)) is globally stable.

Combining these results, it is clear that if $\theta > 0$ and if the gross substitutability hypothesis of Theorem 9.3-28 is met, then the equilibrium path of the dynamic economic system of (9.3-17) and (9.3-20) is globally stable. Of course, when $\theta < 0$ in the dynamic, then neither the Hicksian stability conditions nor strict gross substitutability guarantee stability.

The generalizations of Theorems 9.3-28 and 9.3-29 to linear excess demand functions with more than three goods is not pursued here.[23] A further generalization of their combination that, although it applies only to exchange economies, dispenses with the linearity requirement itself is deferred to Section 10.2. In the remainder of this section, alternative sufficient conditions, also for not-necessarily-linear systems, are developed which ensure global stability of the equilibrium path, and which do not require explicit examination of solutions. The theorem so obtained provides, among other things, a basis for the generalization in Section 10.2 mentioned above.

Begin by removing the restriction that $I + J = 3$ and the normalization $P_{I+J} = 1$. Combine $\mathcal{E}^{I+J}$ with $\mathcal{E}^{(I+J)}$ so that the economic appears as in (9.1-4), namely,

$$Q = \mathcal{E}(P), \tag{9.3-30}$$

for $P > 0$. Normalize with

$$\sum_{n=1}^{I+J} (P_n)^2 = 1. \tag{9.3-31}$$

---

[22]   A general definition of Hicksian stability can be found in Hicks [3, p. 325].
[23]   See Metzler [9].

Consider a dynamic similar to those invoked previously and which permits equilibirum in the economic to coincide with that in the combined system as a whole:

$$\frac{dP}{d\tau} = \theta\mathcal{E}(P),\tag{9.3-32}$$

where $\theta \neq 0$ is a scalar constant. As before, Walras' law

$$\sum_{n=1}^{I+J} P_n\mathcal{E}^n(P) = 0\tag{9.3-33}$$

applies to all $P > 0$ whether in or out of equilibrium.

Now multiplying (9.3-32) by P and using Walras' law (9.3-33) results in

$$\sum_{n=1}^{I+J} P_n\frac{dP_n}{d\tau} = \theta\sum_{n=1}^{I+J} P_n\mathcal{E}^n(P) = 0.$$

It follows from this, (9.3-32), and Walras' law, that the $I + J^{\text{th}}$ equation of (9.3-32) can be derived from those remaining:

$$\frac{dP_{I+J}}{d\tau} = -\frac{1}{P_{I+J}}\sum_{n=1}^{I+J-1} P_n\frac{dP_n}{d\tau}$$

$$= -\frac{\theta}{P_{I+J}}\sum_{n=1}^{I+J-1} P_n\mathcal{E}^n(P)$$

$$= \theta\mathcal{E}^{I+J}(P).$$

Observe also that the normalization $\sum_{n=1}^{I+J} P_n = 1$ cannot be used with dynamic (9.3-32). For since differentiation of $\sum_{n=1}^{I+J} P_n = 1$ with respect to τ leads to the differential equation $\sum_{n=1}^{I+J} dP_n/d\tau = 0$ and not

$$\sum_{n=1}^{I+J} P_n\frac{dP_n}{d\tau} = 0,$$

price vectors along time paths generated by (9.3-32) cannot meet the requirements of that normalization.[24] However, normalization (9.3-31) is consistent

---

[24]   This would not happen of one of the dynamic equations of (9.3-32) were determined by the others in conjunction with Walras' law.

with $\sum_{n=1}^{I+J} P_n(dP_n/d\tau) = 0$ as can be seen upon differentiation of both sides of (9.3-31) with respect to τ. In view of (9.3-31), the path of prices generated by (9.3-32) and any initial starting price vector P^0 is confined to the domain

$$\widehat{D} = \left\{ P : P > 0 \quad \text{and} \quad \sum_{n=1}^{I+J}(P_n)^2 = 1 \right\}.$$

Let $\bar{P} = (\bar{P}_1, \ldots, \bar{P}_{I+J}) > 0$ be an equilibrium point of both (9.3-30) and the full system as a whole. To ensure global stability of the equilibrium path generated by $\bar{P}$, it is sufficient that $\theta > 0$ in the dynamic, and a "weak axiom" for market excess demand functions holds in the economic:

(9.3-34)   For all $P' = (P_1', \ldots, P_{I+J}') > 0$ and $P'' = (P_1'', \ldots, P_{I+J}'') > 0$ such that $\mathcal{E}(P') \neq \mathcal{E}(P'')$, if

$$\sum_{n=1}^{I+J} P_n' \mathcal{E}^n(P'') \leqslant \sum_{n=1}^{I+J} P_n' \mathcal{E}^n(P'),$$

then

$$\sum_{n=1}^{I+J} P_n'' \mathcal{E}^n(P'') < \sum_{n=1}^{I+J} P_n'' \mathcal{E}^n(P').$$

The reader should compare (9.3-34) with the weak axiom of revealed preference (3.2-7), taking cognizance of the parallels between them. From Walras' law (9.3-33), the right-hand side of the first inequality of (9.3-34) and the left-hand side of the second vanish. Hence (9.3-34) can be restated as

(9.3-35)   For all $P' = (P_1', \ldots, P_{I+J}') > 0$ and $P'' = (P_1'', \ldots, P_{I+J}'') > 0$ such that $\mathcal{E}(P') \neq \mathcal{E}(P'')$, if

$$\sum_{n=1}^{I+J} P_n' \mathcal{E}^n(P'') \leqslant 0,$$

then

$$\sum_{n=1}^{I+J} P_n'' \mathcal{E}^n(P') > 0.$$

It turns out (the demonstration is postponed to Theorem 9.4-8 in the next section) that (9.3-34) also implies the equilibrium price vector is "unique" in that only vectors of the form $\psi \bar{P}$ for scalars $\psi > 0$ can be equilibria.[25] Therefore, if P'' is set equal to the unique equilibrium vector $\bar{P}$ in the above, then because $\mathcal{E}(\bar{P}) = 0$ and $\mathcal{E}(\bar{P}) \neq \mathcal{E}(P')$ for all $P' > 0$ where $P' \neq \psi \bar{P}$ for every $\psi > 0$, (9.3-35) implies

$$\sum_{n=1}^{I+J} \bar{P}_n \mathcal{E}^n(P') > 0, \tag{9.3-36}$$

again for all $P' > 0$ such that $P' \neq \psi \bar{P}$ for every $\psi > 0$.

Due the normalization (9.3-31), $\psi \bar{P}$ is in $\widehat{D}$ for only one value of ψ. Without loss of generality it may be assumed that $\bar{P}$ is in $\widehat{D}$. In that case, $\bar{P}$ is unique in $\widehat{D}$ and (9.3-36) holds for all $P \neq \bar{P}$ in $\widehat{D}$. To establish the sufficiency of (9.3-34) and $\theta > 0$ for global stability, define the (continuous) function V by setting

$$V(P) = \sum_{n=1}^{I+J} \left(P_n - \bar{P}_n \right)^2,$$

on $\widehat{D}$. Then

(9.3-37) V is continuously differentiable on $\widehat{D}$,

and

(9.3-38) $V(\bar{P}) = 0$ and $V(P) > 0$ for all P in $\widehat{D}$ distinct from $\bar{P}$.

Furthermore,

$$\frac{dV(P)}{d\tau} = 2 \sum_{n=1}^{I+J} \left(P_n - \bar{P}_n \right) \frac{dP_n}{d\tau},$$

which, from (9.3-32) and Walras' law (9.3-33) reduces to

$$\frac{dV(P)}{d\tau} = -2\theta \sum_{n=1}^{I+J} \bar{P}_n \mathcal{E}^n(P),$$

on $\widehat{D}$. Therefore, by (9.3-36) and the fact that $\theta > 0$,

(9.3-39)   For all $P \neq \bar{P}$ in $\widehat{D}$,

$$\frac{dV(P)}{d\tau} < 0.$$

---

[25]   Recall that, from the homogeneity of $\mathcal{E}$, if $\mathcal{E}(\bar{P}) = 0$, then $\mathcal{E}(\psi \bar{P}) = 0$ for all $\psi > 0$.

The satisfaction of (9.3-37) – (9.3-39) means that V is a Liapunov function[26] with respect to $\bar{P}$. It follows from Theorem A.5-11 of appendix Section A.5 that the equilibrium path through $\bar{P}$ is globally stable. This result is now formally summarized:

Theorem 9.3-40   Let $\bar{P}$ in $\widehat{D}$ be an equilibrium point of the economic system described by (9.3-30) – (9.3-32). If $\theta > 0$ and (9.3-34) is met, then the equilibrium path generated by $\bar{P}$ is globally stable.

Observe that the choice of the dynamic in (9.3-32) introduces a high degree of specialization into the above discussion of stability. Indeed, Theorem 9.3-40 has been proved only for that particular case. If the functional form of the dynamic were altered, or if θ were to be made dependent on P, then the sufficient conditions for global stability established by the theorem need not retain their sufficiency.

9.4   UNIQUENESS OF EQUILIBRIUM PATHS

The issue of uniqueness of equilibrium prices and quantities, and hence of equilibrium paths, has already come up in several contexts. It should be clear by now that the meaning of the term "uniqueness" is subtle. Although there is no difficulty with the notion of unique equilibrium quantities at either market or individual levels, even under the strongest of conditions only equilibrium price ratios, and not absolute price values, can be unique. Indeed, if $\bar{P} > 0$ is an equilibrium price vector, then so is $\psi\bar{P}$ for all scalars $\psi > 0$. This multiplicity or indeterminacy of absolute equilibrium price values stems from the homogeneity of all demand and supply functions which, in turn, reflects the nature of budget constraints and the definition of profit. Introduction of a normalization does not eliminate the indeterminacy, but it does permit the location (when possible) of unique prices relative to that normalization. Thus, to talk about unique equilibrium prices, it is necessary to do so either with respect to some normalization or in terms of price ratios. Even so, it will still be convenient to employ the phrase "unique equilibrium price vector $\bar{P}$" when the many equilibrium price vectors are of the form $\psi\bar{P}$ for $\psi > 0$, as long as there is only one vector of equilibrium price ratios.

---

[26]   The notion of a Liapunov function is defined in appendix Section A.5. The interesting story of how the use of Liapunov functions in stability analysis found its way into economics has been told by Weintraub [14, Ch. 4].

Two sources of propositions concerning uniqueness have been suggested earlier. For the case in which factor supplies are fixed, conditions for uniqueness of equilibrium quantities and price ratios have been established in Section 8.4 in terms of the convexity and smoothness properties of transformation surfaces and community utility functions. Alternative theorems rest on the relationship, discussed in Section 9.1, between uniqueness of equilibrium paths and their global stability. Thus a demonstration of global stability turns out to be also a demonstration of uniqueness. Neither of these avenues, however, is pursued here. Instead, restrictions sufficient for uniqueness are presented which are unlike the latter in that they are couched in the economic alone, and at the same time, are more general than the former in that they do not require fixed factor supplies and conditions ensuring the existence of a community utility function.

Consider the economic of (9.1-4) and (9.3-30), namely

$$Q = \mathcal{E}(P),$$

and let $\mathcal{E}$ be continuously differentiable for all $P > 0$. No normalization of any kind is imposed. With $i \neq n$, good n is said to be a *gross substitute*[27] for good i at P provided that

$$\mathcal{E}_i^n(P) > 0, \tag{9.4-1}$$

where $\mathcal{E}_i^n$ denotes the partial derivative of $\mathcal{E}^n$ with respect to its ith argument. Thus a small increase in the price of good i increases the excess demand for good n. The characterization of gross substitutes given toward the end of Section 9.3 is exactly (9.4-1) applied to the special case in which $\mathcal{E}^{(3)}$ is linear. The first uniqueness result of this section is now stated and proved.

Theorem 9.4-2 Let $I + J > 1$. If all pairs of distinct goods are gross sub-

---

[27] The notion of gross substitutes seems to have been introduced by Mosak [10, p. 33] and Metzler [9]. The reason for the presence of the adjective "gross" stems from the possibility, described in the introduction of Chapter 3, of defining substitutability in demand in two distinct ways. Using the notation of Chapter 3, good i could be called a "gross substitute" for good n at (p, m) if the partial derivative of the ith demand function $h_n^i(p, m) > 0$. The goods would be "net substitutes" at (p, m) if the Slutsky function (which is h_n^i with the income effect netted out) $s^{in}(p, m) > 0$. Although it is not clear what effects should be removed from the "gross derivatives" $\mathcal{E}_n^i(P)$ to obtain "net derivatives," the expression "gross substitutes" seems to have been transferred to excess demand functions in general. And since the characterizations of substitutes in terms of, say, h^i and $\mathcal{E}^i$ are based on the signs of the partial derivatives of different functions, one characterization neither implies nor precludes the other. Furthermore, in parallel with the ordinary demand functions, h^i, to say only that $\mathcal{E}_n^i(P) > 0$ does not ensure that $\mathcal{E}_i^n(P) > 0$ at the same value $P > 0$. The possibility of these two derivatives having different signs, however, is ruled out in the hypothesses of Theorem 9.4-2.

stitutes (that is, inequality (9.4-1) holds for every i and n where $i \neq n$) for all $P > 0$, and if $\bar{P} = (\bar{P}_1, \ldots, \bar{P}_{I+J}) > 0$ is an equilibrium price vector, then the equilibrium ratios $\bar{P}_1/\bar{P}_{I+J}, \ldots, \bar{P}_{I+J-1}/\bar{P}_{I+J}$ are unique.

Proof: Let $P' = (P'_1, \ldots, P'_{I+J})$ be any price vector such that

$$\frac{\bar{P}_n}{\bar{P}_{I+J}} \neq \frac{P'_n}{P'_{I+J}},$$

for at least one n. The theorem is demonstrated upon showing that P' cannot be an equilibrium price vector.

Set

$$\sigma = \max_n \frac{P'_n}{\bar{P}_n}.$$

Then $\sigma > 0$,

$$\sigma \bar{P}_n \geqslant P'_n, \quad n = 1, \ldots, I + J, \tag{9.4-3}$$

and for at least one (but not the same) n,

$$\sigma \bar{P}_n > P'_n \quad \text{and} \quad \sigma \bar{P}_n = P'_n. \tag{9.4-4}$$

Also, by the homogeneity of $\mathcal{E}$ and the fact that $\bar{P}$ is an equilibrium price vector,

$$\mathcal{E}^n(\bar{P}) = \mathcal{E}^n(\sigma \bar{P}) = 0, \quad n = 1, \ldots, I + J. \tag{9.4-5}$$

Without loss of generality, suppose the equality of (9.4-4) holds for $n = 1$:

$$\sigma \bar{P}_1 = P'_1. \tag{9.4-6}$$

By the mean value theorem,[28] there exists a vector P'' such that

$$\mathcal{E}^1(P') - \mathcal{E}^1(\sigma \bar{P}) = \sum_{n=1}^{I+J} (P'_n - \sigma \bar{P}_n) \mathcal{E}^1_n(P''), \tag{9.4-7}$$

where P'' lies on the straight line segment connecting P' and $\sigma \bar{P}$. Because

$$(P'_1 - \sigma \bar{P}_1) \mathcal{E}^1_1(P'') = 0$$

by (9.4-6), because

$$\mathcal{E}^1_n(P'') (P'_n - \sigma \bar{P}_n) \leqslant 0, \quad n = 2, \ldots, I + J,$$

---

[28] . Theorem A.3-5 of appendix Section A.3.

by (9.4-3) and the gross substitutability hypothesis with $P = P''$ in (9.4-1), and because

$$\mathcal{E}_n^1(P'') \left(P_n' - \sigma \bar{P}_n \right) < 0$$

for at least one $n \neq 1$ by (9.4-4) and gross substitutability, it follows that the right-hand sum in (9.4-7) is negative. Therefore (9.4-5) implies

$$\mathcal{E}^1(P') < 0,$$

and so P' cannot be an equilibrium price vector.

Q.E.D.

When $\mathcal{E}_i^n(P) < 0$ with $i \neq n$, good n is called a *gross complement* with respect to good i. This notion of complementarity is not the same as either of those described in the introduction to Chapter 3 since, like the characterization of gross substitutes in (9.4-1), gross complementarity here is expressed with respect to the signs of the partial derivatives of excess rather than ordinary demand functions. (Recall n. 27 on pp. 366.) Gross complementarity is considered more fully in relation to stability analysis and price determination in Section 10.2 below. It is, of course, clearly precluded by the hypotheses of Theorem 9.4-2.

A second uniqueness result is based on the weak axiom of (9.3-34). Rather than employ price ratios, the uniqueness of $\bar{P}$ is characterized here by the equivalent statement that only vectors $\psi \bar{P}$ for scalars $\psi > 0$ are equilibria.

Theorem 9.4-8 Let $I + J > 1$ and assume (9.3-34) is in force. If $\bar{P} = (\bar{P}_1, \ldots, \bar{P}_{I+J}) > 0$ is an equilibrium price vector, then it is unique.

Proof: Suppose $P = (P_1, \ldots, P_{I+J}) > 0$ is any price vector such that $P \neq \psi \bar{P}$ for all $\psi > 0$. Since $\bar{P}$ is an equilibrium price vector,

$$\sum_{n=1}^{I+J} P_n \mathcal{E}^n(\bar{P}) = 0.$$

By Walras' law (9.3-33),

$$\sum_{n=1}^{I+J} P_n \mathcal{E}^n(P) = 0.$$

Hence

$$\sum_{n=1}^{I+J} P_n \mathcal{E}^n(\bar{P}) = \sum_{n=1}^{I+J} P_n \mathcal{E}^n(P).$$

Applying (9.3-34) with $P' = P$ and $P'' = \bar{P}$, and noting that $\sum_{n=1}^{I+J} \bar{P}_n \mathcal{E}^n(\bar{P}) = 0$,

$$\sum_{n=1}^{I+J} \bar{P}_n \mathcal{E}^n(P) > 0.$$

Therefore P cannot be an equilibrium price vector and $\bar{P}$ is unique.

Q.E.D.

Of course, under the hypotheses of either Theorem 9.4-2 or Theorem 9.4-8, equilibrium quantities are also unique because excess demand functions are single valued. Further discussion of uniqueness can be found in Arrow and Hahn [2, Ch. 9].

The uniqueness results of this section, along with Theorem 9.3-40 (the global stability proposition based on the existence of a Liapunov function at the end of the previous section), play an important role in the discussion of price determination in the next chapter.

EXERCISES

9.1 Consider a single market in isolation. Let $\mathcal{P}$ be a collection of positive prices and $\mathcal{X}$ a collection of positive quantities. For p in $\mathcal{P}$ and x in $\mathcal{X}$,

$$x = G(p),$$

$$p = H(x),$$

are, respectively, continuous market supply and (inverse) market demand functions. Assume $\mathcal{P}$ and $\mathcal{X}$ are compact and convex, and set

$$D = \mathcal{X} \times \mathcal{P},$$

$$\Phi = (G, H).$$

Prove that D and Φ satisfy the hypothesis of Brouwer's theorem. (Note: that D

is compact follows from Tychonoff's theorem.[29]) Then use Brouwer's theorem
to demonstrate the existence of a market equilibrium. Show geometrically that
if the domain of H is not all of $\mathcal{X}$ or if the domain of G is not all of $\mathcal{P}$, then
equilibrium need not exist. Show, also geometrically, that a similar assertion
does not apply to the ranges of G and H.

9.2 Prove that the set D of (9.2-4) is convex.

9.3 Prove properties (9.2-12), (9.2-13), (9.2-15), and (9.2-16) in the context
of Section 9.2.

9.4 Suppose the first market in a two-good economic has market demand and
supply equations

$$x = \alpha P_d + \beta,$$

$$x = \gamma P_s + \delta,$$

where P_d and P_s, denote, respectively, the price on the demand curve and that
on the supply curve corresponding to x. Assume $\alpha \neq 0$, $\gamma \neq 0$, $\alpha \neq \gamma$, and

$$\frac{\beta\gamma - \alpha\delta}{\gamma - \alpha} > 0.$$

Define the market "excess price" variable and function, respectively, by setting $\omega = P_d - P_s$ and letting Ξ be the difference between the inverse market
demand function and the inverse market supply function. Thus

$$\omega = \Xi(x),$$

for each x. Compute $\Xi(x)$ from the given market demand and supply functions. Find the unique equilibrium values for ω and x and compare them to
those of the two-good example of Section 9.3. Let the Marshallian dynamic be
specified as

$$\frac{dx}{d\tau} = \theta\Xi(x),$$

where $\theta \neq 0$ is a constant. Deduce the equivalent Walrasian dynamic describing the motion of excess price ω over time[30] and determine two equivalent
expressions for the dynamic economic system as a whole. Derive conditions

---

[29]   Kelley [7, p. 143].
[30]   Recall n. 6 on p. 333.

for the equilibrium paths of the complete systems to be stable and compare these conditions to those of the two-good example of Section 9.3.

9.5 Let the excess demand functions $\mathcal{E}^{(I+J)}(P^{(I+J)})$ of (9.1-7) be continuously differentiable on their domains. Suppose $\bar{P}^{(I+J)}$ is a unique equilibrium price vector and consider the dynamic

$$\frac{dP^{(I+J)}}{d\tau} = \theta \mathcal{B}^{-1}(\mathcal{E}^{(I+J)}(P^{(I+J)}))\mathcal{E}^{(I+J)}(P^{(I+J)}),$$

where $\theta < 0$ is a scalar constant and $\mathcal{B}^{-1}(Q^{(I+J)})$ is the nonsingular (inverse) Jacobian matrix of Section 9.1. Show that

$$V\left(P^{(I+J)}\right) = \sum_{n=1}^{I+J-1} \left[\mathcal{E}^n(P^{(I+J)})\right]^2$$

is a Liapunov function with respect to $\bar{P}^{(I+J)}$ and hence that the equilibrium path generated by $\bar{P}^{(I+J)}$ is globally stable.

9.6 Consider a pure exchange economy with two consumers and two goods. Assume utility functions are

$$u^k(x_{1k}, x_{2k}) = x_{1k} + \sqrt{x_{2k}},$$

for $k = 1, 2$. Let initial endowments be

$$(x_{1k}, x_{2k}) = (x_{1k}^0, x_{2k}^0), \quad k = 1, 2.$$

Show that if $\bar{P} = (\bar{P}_1, \bar{P}_2) > 0$ is an equilibrium price vector, then the equilibrium price ratio $\bar{P}_1/\bar{P}_2$ is unique.

9.7 Why would the proof of existence of equilibrium paths (Theorem 9.2-23) break down if, instead of (9.2-17), $\Upsilon^n(P)$ were defined as

$$\Upsilon^n(P) = P_n + \widehat{\mathcal{E}}^n(P), \quad n = 1, \ldots, I+J,$$

in anticipation of Lemma 9.2-21?

9.8 Consider an economic given by (9.3-8) and specify the dynamic as

$$\frac{dP}{d\tau} = [B + \mathcal{E}(P)]^{1-\theta},$$

for any scalars $B > 0$ and $0 < \theta < 1$. Find the differential equation expression for the rate of change in excess demand over time and show that equilibrium in the economic does not correspond to equilibrium in the dynamic economic system.

9.9 Consider an economic given by (9.3-8) and specify the dynamic as

$$\frac{dP}{d\tau} = \left(1 - \frac{\tau}{\alpha - \gamma}\right)\mathcal{E}(P).$$

Find the differential equation expression for the rate of change in excess demand over time and determine its solution. Show that equilibrium in the economic coincides with the equilibrium path in the complete system. Show also that the equilibrium path is globally stable regardless of the value of $(\alpha - \gamma)$. The latter assertion means that the correspondence principle is not relevant in this case.

9.10 Prove the assertion following (9.2-11) in the text that, "By the strict concavity of $f^{i\ell}$, this maximum is unique."

REFERENCES

1. Apostol, T. M., *Mathematical Analysis*, 2nd ed. (Reading: Addison-Wesley, 1974).
2. Arrow, K. J. and F. H. Hahn, *General Competitive Analysis* (San Francisco: Holden-Day, 1971).
3. Hicks, J. R., *Value and Capital*, 2nd ed. (London: Oxford University Press, 1939).
4. ———, *Capital and Time* (Oxford: Oxford University Press, 1973).
5. Hurewicz, W., *Lectures on Ordinary Differential Equations* (New York: Wiley and the Technology Press of Massachusetts Institute of Technology, 1958).
6. Katzner, D. W. and L. R. Klein, "On the Possibility of the General Linear Economic Model," *Economic Models, Estimation and Risk Programming*, K. A. Fox, J. K. Sengupta and G. V. L. Narasimham, eds. (Berlin: Springer-Verlag, 1969), Ch. 15.
7. Kelley, J. L., *General Topology* (Princeton: Van Nostrand, 1955).
8. Marshall, A., *Principles of Economics*, 8th ed. (New York: Macmillan, 1948).
9. Metzler, L. A., "Stability of Multiple Markets: The Hicks Conditions," *Econometrica* 13 (1945), pp. 277-292.

10. Mosak, J. L., *General-Equilibrium Theory in International Trade* (Bloomington: Principia Press, 1944).
11. Samuelson, P. A., *Foundations of Economic Analysis* (Cambridge: Harvard University Press, 1947).
12. Wald, A., "On Some Systems of Equations of Mathematical Economics," *Zeitschrift für Nationalökonomie* 7 (1936), pp. 637-670. English translation: *Econometrica* 19 (1951), pp. 368-403.
13. Walras, L., *Elements of Pure Economics*, W. Jaffé trans. (Homewood: Irwin, 1954).
14. Weintraub, E. R., *Stabilizing Dynamics: Constructing Economic Knowledge* (Cambridge: Cambridge University Press, 1991).

Chapter 10

Methodological Individualism and the Theory of Price Determination[1]

The Walrasian model articulates a vision that underlies one way in which economists are able to think about the micro-economy. In the form presented here, it consists of a dynamic mathematical system whose equations characterize, at each moment, the behavior of consumers, the behavior of firms, and the operation of markets. Consumer and firm behaviors emerge from, respectively, utility maximization subject to budget constraints, and profit maximization subject to technological production possibilities. For each vector of equilibrium and nonequilibrium price values announced by an auctioneer, the unique solutions of the relevant demand-side and supply-side equations of the model at a moment on the model's time-clock (assuming such solutions exist) represent the result of the simultaneous interaction of the consumers, firms, and markets at that moment in light of the endowments and technologies available. A collection of these solutions starting with a fixed

---

[1]   This chapter is an expanded and considerably revised version of my "Methodological Individualism and the Walrasian Tâtonnement," *Journal of Economic and Social Research* 1 (1999), pp. 5-33. It is reproduced here with permission.

initial endowment and generated by changing prices is called a time path. A time path along which there is neither change in economic behavior by any consumer or firm, nor change in economic value in any market, is an equilibrium path or just an "equilibrium." Sufficient, albeit not very general, assumptions are usually imposed in the Walrasian model to ensure a unique equilibrium exists that is globally stable. Since the presence of a unique and globally stable equilibrium implies that no matter where prices begin, they always end up at their equilibrium values, a theory of the *determination* of market equilibrium prices is provided. An additional property of the equilibrium is that all markets clear; thus it can be said that markets operate so as, at least eventually, to equilibrate demand and supply. And the dynamic market-price-adjustment mechanism generating the model's time paths is often taken to be a tâtonnement in that trade takes place only after market-clearing equilibrium is achieved. Of course, as parameters and other "fixed" elements modify, the equilibrium changes.

It is important to understand that to have a theory of price determination it is necessary to account for dynamic movement across time. For the main purpose of any such theory is to provide an explanation of how market prices that have been observed in reality have come to pass. Identifying those observations as equilibrium prices in a static Walrasian model (*i.e.*, a Walrasian model without a dynamic) and then simply asserting that they arose from the interaction of the forces of demand and supply is not enough. That is because the interaction itself needs to be explained in terms of the out-of-equilibrium behavior that brought the equilibrium about and, in the context of this volume, such behavior perforce arises as consumers and firms react to hypothetical market prices that change over time. Moreover, the way prices change over time can depend, among other things, on the latter reactions. Therefore it is only through the specification of a dynamic which, when combined with the economic fully characterizes the interactions in both directions between (hypothetical) prices and behaviors, that a complete explanation of observed prices is obtained.

Economists have always intended that the Walrasian model as described here be encompassed within the tradition of methodological individualism, which generally understands individuals, with given preferences and endowments, and firms, with given technologies, to enter the market process as autonomous entities. Among other things, this tradition imposes certain restrictions on the nature of the model that affect its relation to the reality it purports to explain. But the extent to which the model actually measures up to the standards set by these restrictions, and hence, by implication, its explanatory capability, is still open to doubt. This is because, in the words of

Hahn [12, p. 137], the typical market-price-adjustment rules attributed to the auctioneer are market-level prescriptions and generally do not constitute "... a theory of price formation based on the rational calculations of rational agents." Moreover, truly general conditions on individual-agent preferences and technologies guaranteeing the uniqueness and global stability of equilibria under those rules, conditions without which, economists have thought, the model's ability to explain real phenomenon is seriously impaired, are not known. Thus a full and theoretically satisfying explanation of price determination in a competitive economy does not yet seem to be within reach. And the issue is not so much whether the Walrasian model fits a particular collection of observed real-world facts but, rather, whether it is capable of explaining any such facts at all and still remain true to methodological individualism.

In a 1989 paper, Kirman [15] concluded, at least when the model employs a tâtonnement dynamic, that it cannot. His argument, in reference to an exchange economy, was that there is little hope of obtaining conditions that ensure uniqueness and global stability of equilibria from assumptions of "reasonable generality" on individual-agent preferences. Now a portion of this argument is implicit in the discussion of Sections 10.1 and 10.2 below. But the conclusion itself leaves something to be desired because it also rests, in part, on the postulation of standard price-adjustment rules at the aggregate or market level. And, as noted above, these rules are not explicitly expressed in terms of individual agent behavior. Thus the possibility remains that by postulating "individual-agent-" rather than market-price-adjustment rules, and hence returning the Walrasian model to its methodological-individualism roots, Kirman's negative conclusion might be overcome.[2] In addition, even if general uniqueness-and-global-stability conditions on agent preferences are unattainable, it is not clear that the viability and usefulness of the Walrasian model as an explanatory entity is actually threatened. For the special instances, some known, some not yet discovered, in which uniqueness and global stability prevail may be sufficiently general for all practical purposes. The aim of this chapter is to clarify some of these issues for the case of tâtonnement dynamics. Attention is focused primarily on the simplified world of an exchange economy.

---

[2]   Ways of overcoming the conclusion for the case of nontâtonnement adjustment rules, which permit trading out of equilibrium, have been suggested by Fisher [9] and Smale [24]. Other nontâtonnement methods that might be transferable from the single-market context in which they are developed are surveyed by Hahn [11, pp. 788-791]. Still additional approaches located somewhat beyond the confines of the standard Walrasian framework are described by Bénassy [2].

Briefly, the chapter begins with a discussion of methodological individualism and its significance for the Walrasian system. It then describes, in the context of an exchange economy, the ways in which many versions of the Walrasian model fail to meet the standards for explanation set by the desire to adhere to methodological individualism, and the kinds of modifications that need to be made to bring those versions in line with methodological individualism. Included at this point is a discussion relating to Kirman's argument, and a presentation of two sets of special-case-assumptions on individual-agent preferences from which uniqueness and global stability are known to follow. Next, a simple example of a Walrasian tâtonnement is described in which, consistent with methodological individualism, agent-price-adjustment rules are characterized in terms of "rational calculations of rational agents," and the afore-mentioned, special-case conditions ensuring uniqueness and stability of global equilibria in an exchange economy continue to apply. Not only, then, does this special-case model fall within the framework of methodological individualism, but it is also viable in so far as its explanatory capability is concerned. Finally it is argued that, as a practical matter, the special-case model's speciality does not stand in the way of its usefulness, whatever that might be, in understanding how the microeconomy operates. Sections 10.2 and 10.3 are required for the grand view set out in Section 1.4.

10.1 METHODOLOGICAL INDIVIDUALISM

Before considering the notion of methodological individualism in relation to economic actors, it will help to set the frame of reference by considering what has been referred to as the metaphysical theory of *mechanism* that largely directed the development of the physical sciences from the 17th to the middle of the 19th century. In that theory, the universe is made up of tiny particles, whose existence is unexplained, and which behave according to simple mechanical laws. Every physical thing is understood in terms of the configuration of the particles that make it up, and all physical behavior is a consequence of the basic mechanical laws governing the behavior of the individual particles. Like all metaphysical theories, mechanism is not empirically testable. Any physical phenomenon that does not seem to fit into the mechanism mold can be attributed to a lack of ability to come up with an appropriate mechanical model rather than to a mistaken approach to reality. But while mechanism is therefore compatible with any and all collections of observations that might come along, it is not consistent with all models of the physical world. For example, to think of light only in terms of waves is to abandon mechanism in favor of another metaphysical theory. Thus the adoption of mechanism as a world view restricts the kinds of models that are acceptable for understanding and explaining reality.[3]

Now, as has been suggested in Section 1.2, social science is quite different from mechanistic physical science. It deals with thinking, feeling, reacting, and evolving human beings — not inert and changeless particles. Nevertheless, from the perspective of the social sciences, *methodological individualism* is a meta-theory quite analogous to mechanism. According to it, society is made up of individual agents, whose existence is unexplained, and whose behavior conforms to "laws" in a manner that can be said to have been guided, approximately, by those agents' "dispositions" and their "understandings" of their own situations. Every social thing is understood in terms of the configuration of the agents that make it up, and all social behavior is a consequence of the basic behavior of its constituent agents and the interactive effects of that behavior. Methodological individualism, too, is not empirically testable. Any social phenomenon that does not seem to fit into its mold can be attributed to a lack of ability to come up with an appropriate model rather than to a mistaken approach to reality. And while methodological individualism is therefore compatible with any and all collections of observations that might come along, it is not consistent with all models of the social world.[4]

It should be emphasized that methodological individualism is made up of two components: first that macro or group objects and concepts are composed of individual (agent) objects and concepts, and second that macro behavior is derived from or determined by individual (agent) behavior. As the phrase is construed here, methodological individualism includes both, and not just one or the other, of these elements.[5] The possibility of, say, "herd" effects where, by reason of absorption into the mass, individuals follow some kind of herd instinct, is precluded.

Although the idea of methodological individualism dates at least to Epicurus[6] and, in its physical-world manifestation, was employed as the basis for mechanism by Descartes in his *Discours* of 1637,[7] its explicit introduction into economics was probably due to Menger. In the Preface to the first edition (1871) of his *Principles* (*Grundsätze*), Menger wrote [19, pp. 46-47], "... I

---

[3]   See, for example, Watkins [31, p. 270].

[4]   *Ibid.*, pp. 270-271.

[5]   *cf.*, Brodbeck [4, p. 286], and Sensat [23, pp. 190-194].

[6]   Strozier [28, pp. 117-118].

[7]   *e.g.*, Burtt [6, p. 103], and Levins and Lewontin [17, pp. 1-2]. The notion of mechanism goes back beyond even Epicurus. See Strodack [27, pp. 3-4].

have endeavored to reduce the complex phenomena of human economic activity to the simplest elements that can still be subjected to accurate observation, ... and ... to investigate the manner in which the more complex economic phenomena evolve from their elements according to definite principles." Evidently, Menger felt rather strongly that this was the only method for conducting economic inquiry.[8] Hayek [13, p. 6], moreover, took virtually the same position some 75 years later: "... there is no other way toward an understanding of social phenomena but through our understanding of individual actions ...." And this perspective, accepted with the same fervor of Menger and Hayek, seems to be shared by most economists today. It implies, in the final analysis, that the private economy can only be understood and explained in terms of consumers and firms; aggregate concepts, including the notion of "the economy" itself, have no independent existence or meaning apart from them.

Of course, from time to time, there appear to have been temporary "lapses" from the perspective of methodological individualism. The development of macroeconomics in terms of economy-wide aggregates during the middle of the 20th century, that is, the Keynesian Revolution through the Neoclassical Synthesis can be interpreted in this way.[9] But the more recent search for micro foundations of macroeconomics reveals a yearning for methodological individualism that carries over into the macroeconomic arena. Indeed, evidence suggests that economists never really gave up methodological individualism even throughout their mid-century focus on macroeconomic problems.[10] There always seems to have been the feeling that, in light of the possibilities of aggregation, the whole should somehow equal the "sum" of its parts.[11] Moreover, with little progress made by 1967 in uncovering suitable micro foundations, Arrow referred to the persisting gap between microeconomics and macroeconomics as a "major scandal" [1, p. 734]. In any event, it is widely thought that the economics of the Keynesian Revolution and the Neoclassical Synthesis lost its favor due, in part, to the inability to come up with appropriate micro foundations.[12]

Adherence to the tradition of methodological individualism has important bearing on the nature of the Walrasian model and on its relation to the real economic world it is attempting to explain.[13] Various aspects of the latter re-

---

[8] cf., Menger [20, p. 93-94].

[9] Blaug [3, p. 161].

[10] Hoover [14, pp. 3-4].

[11] e.g., Samuelson [21, p. 356].

[12] Hoover [14, p. 3].

[13] Evidently, the prefectly competitive atomism underlying the Walrasian system is sufficient for methodological individualism, but not necessary. For models with imperfectly competitive

lation have been described in Sections 1.2 and 1.3. To focus attention more
sharply on the issues involved, it is worth repeating and summarizing some
of that discussion here. Recall that a model of something — the thing was
called thing T — is a construct having enough in common with the observable facets of T that insight into T can be obtained by studying the construct.
The Einstein-Infeld illustration, in which a physical model of a clock is built
to explain how the clock works, is also relevant. In that example, remember,
the model built, and hence the explanation given, is not unique. And the explanation functions, as do all such explanations, by identifying something in
the model (the movement of the model's "hands") with what is observed (the
movement of the hands on the original clock). In economics, of course, models are usually not physical things. Rather they are mental constructs based on
assumptions, concepts, and relations among variables. They also abstract from
a multitude of possible forces to concentrate on the minimum number necessary for explanation, and their properties are their own and not properties of
that which is the object of explanation. Nevertheless, they function in much
the same way as in the Einstein-Infeld example.

The Walrasian model is properly understood in these terms. As previously indicated, it primarily focuses on the notion of equilibrium and is built
up by making assumptions about the preferences, endowments, and technologies of individual agents, $i.e.$, consumers and firms. Its purpose is to explain
and clarify the determination of observed prices and quantities, and the simultaneous, interacting behavior of real agents in the economy. To achieve this
purpose requires, among other things, that an investigation of the questions of
existence, uniqueness, and global stability of equilibria in the model be successfully undertaken. An obvious way to comprehend the urgency of such an
inquiry is to recall the account given earlier (Section 1.3) of a common method
of interpreting equilibrium in a single, real-world market in isolation: Suppose one were to observe that market at a particular moment of time. In that
case, one could see that so much of the market's commodity was traded at
such-and-such a price or, in other words, one would observe a single point
in commodity-price space. Subsequent observation at a later moment would
yield a second point with, to provide a concrete illustration, a higher price and
a larger quantity. In building a model to explain how these points came to be
seen, the economist could, for example, assume (i) that there exist two distinct
market demand curves each passing through one, but not the same, observed
point, and (ii) that there exists only one market supply curve passing through

markets and government institutions can be consistent with methodological individualism too.

them both.[14] Then, since each observed point is identified as a market equilibrium point in the model,[15] each could be explained as analogous to, or as if it were, the outcome of the interaction of supply and demand as characterized by implicit rules of price adjustment. The economist could also assert that the movement from the first point to the second occurred because of a "shift" in demand. Clearly, equilibrium must exist in the model for this explanation to work. If, moreover, the equilibrium in the model were not unique, then the explanation would be incomplete; it would allow the observed point to be identified with many equilibria, each with its own properties, and thus the reason for the movement between the two points would become clouded. Lastly, when the observed point changes from the old to the new, the equilibrium in the model would have to adjust accordingly. But if the latter equilibrium were not globally stable, then whatever dynamics there were in the model could prevent the new equilibrium from being reached and, in that circumstance, the explanation given for the observed movement from the one point to the other would break down. An alternative interpretation of reality would be to locate observed points along time-paths that converge to equilibria in the model rather than to identify them specifically as those equilibria. But in either case the questions of existence, uniqueness, and global stability have to be explored because that is the only way to be sure that the model can be linked to the real world.

A similar argument applies to the full Walrasian model with many goods, consumers, and firms (Section 9.1). Furthermore, to be consistent with the tenets of methodological individualism, the assumptions from which the existence of unique and globally stable equilibria are to be deduced have to be imposed at the level of individual agents. The problem is that, although the existence issue has been satisfactorily resolved in this way (Section 9.2), the dynamic adjustment rules defining the operation of markets, along with the sufficient conditions ensuring uniqueness and global stability, have tended to be expressed, as suggested above and described in Section 9.3 and the next section, in terms of market excess demand functions rather than with respect to individual preferences, technologies, and behaviors. Thus the distance it is possible to go in explaining and understanding economic reality in terms of a Walrasian model that is faithful to the tradition of methodological individualism in economics has remained an open question. And this is so without

---

[14]   These two assumptions lie in the tradition of methodological individualism because market demand and supply curves are built up from individual demand and supply curves.

[15]   Note that demand curves, supply curves, and equilibrium points cannot exist in reality. They can only be present in models. Similarly, to prove that equilibrium exists and is unique and stable in a model can never imply that unique and stable equilibria exist in the real world.

even questioning the realism of assumptions and the relevance of conclusions derived from them.

Before examining these issues in greater detail, it is worth pointing out that the Walrasian system is meant to explain the determination of prices and the allocation of resources at a particular moment of time or across a relatively brief time period. Describing the evolution of the economy over long periods of time is not within its purview. It follows that those elements of the economic world that modify very slowly, and require great expanses of time to do so, may be taken as part of the fixed background within which Walrasian models are constructed. Apart from preferences and technologies, the most important of these elements for present purposes is the institution of the market. Thus the attempt to construct explanations of market behavior in terms of the behavior of individual agents, that is, the search, at the level of the individual agent, for a definition of the operation of markets and for uniqueness and global stability conditions, must necessarily take place within a given institutional, market framework. The possibility that market institutions themselves might have been built up in the past as a consequence of agent behavior is relevant for the theory of the development of markets[16] — not for the characterization and analysis of Walrasian models.

10.2   THE WALRASIAN SYSTEM

Consider first the prospect of inferring uniqueness and global stability from the assumptions imposed in a typical Walrasian model. To simplify matters, attention is focused mostly on the case of an exchange economy similar to that of Section 7.1, but with $I > 1$ goods and $K > 1$ persons. (Thus the model of Section 7.1 is the special circumstance in which $I = K = 2$.) To generalize the notation of Section 7.1, write $q_{ik} = E^{ik}(p)$ for the excess demand function of person k for good i, where $i = 1, \ldots, I$, and $k = 1, \ldots, K$, and denote the market excess demand function for good i by $q_i = E^i(p)$, where

$$q_i = \sum_{k=1}^{K} q_{ik}, \quad E^i(p) = \sum_{k=1}^{K} E^{ik}(p),$$

and $i = 1, \ldots, I$. Set $q = (q_1, \ldots, q_I)$ and $E(p) = (E^1(p), \ldots, E^I(p))$ so that

$$q = E(p).$$

---

[16]   See, for example, Schotter [22].

Take the E^{ik} to be derived from constrained utility maximization in the usual way (as summarized in Section 7.1) where the endowment vector $x_k^0 = (x_{1k}^0, \ldots, x_{Ik}^0) \geqslant 0$ and has at least one of its components positive for each k. Assume also that for every i, at least one $x_{ik}^0 > 0$ as k varies. Equilibrium in this model can be shown to exist (along lines similar to those of Section 9.2 with production eliminated) provided that all utility functions are suitably continuous, differentiable, increasing, and strictly quasi-concave, and all interior indifference curves stay away from the boundaries of the commodity space. Hereafter, the latter properties are assumed to be in force.

Where subsequent discussion requires it, normalize according to

$$\sum_{i=1}^{I} (p_i)^2 = 1. \tag{10.2-1}$$

The fact that this normalization is different from those employed to prove the existence of equilibrium in Sections 8.4 and 9.2 is of no consequence. Once equilibrium is shown to exist in relation to one normalization, the same equilibrium, with adequate adjustments in absolute equilibrium prices (not price ratios), exists for all normalizations. The use of (10.2-1) here is appropriate in light of the particular dynamic employed below and its interaction with Walras' law as described on pp. 362–363 above. Recall also that the proofs of uniqueness in Section 9.4 did not require the use of a normalization.

Now the dynamic price-adjustment rule defining the operation of markets in a Walrasian model of this sort is often taken to be

$$\frac{dp}{d\tau} = \theta E(p), \tag{10.2-2}$$

where τ represents (continuous) time, and $\theta \neq 0$ is a scalar constant. Evidently, (10.2-2) is actually a special case of the more general formulation (recall (9.1-10))

$$\frac{dp}{d\tau} = \zeta(p, \tau),$$

for some function ζ, and either way is not really consistent with methodological individualism. The inconsistency arises in that (10.2-2), or the more general formulation, constitutes a specification of aggregate (market), rather than individual behavior. Koopmans [16, p. 179] put it this way: "If, ... [in accordance with (10.2-2)], the net rate of increase in price is assumed to be proportional to the excess of demand over supply, whose behavior is thereby expressed? And how is that behavior motivated?" The standard interpretation of (10.2-2) is that it characterizes the activity of a market-level auctioneer. In particular, it is assumed to indicate the information that that auctioneer has, namely, the aggregate excess demand quantities in every market at each positive price vector, and how he responds to that information when making price adjustments. No justification is provided for this response in terms of the rationality of individual agents. (A more complete statement of the auctioneer's activities has already been provided at the start of Chapters 7 and 9.) In spite of its non-methodological-individualism orientation, however, (10.2-2) is still employed, primarily for pedagogical reasons, as the basis for discussion in the remainder of this section. Later on, price-adjustment rules at the individual-agent level that fit into the framework of methodological individualism will be introduced. These latter rules will reflect the idea that individual agents are seeking to improve their situations or levels of utility.

Regardless, when derived, as described above, from constrained utility maximization, where utility functions are appropriately continuous, increasing, strictly quasi concave, and so on, the functions E^{ik} and E^i are continuous, homogeneous of degree zero, and satisfy, respectively, the budget equations

$$\sum_{i=1}^{I} p_i E^{ik}(p) = 0, \quad k = 1, \ldots, K, \tag{10.2-3}$$

and Walras' law

$$\sum_{i=1}^{I} p_i E^i(p) = 0, \tag{10.2-4}$$

throughout their domains.[17] Although not needed immediately below, it will be convenient to assume further that the E^{ik}, and hence the E^i, are continuously differentiable. Because it is known that, as a consequence of constrained utility maximization, the E^{ik} possess still further properties (such as the analogue of Slutsky negative definiteness and symmetry of ordinary demand functions), one might ask if any of these additional properties carry over to, or impose other restrictions on, the E^i. That is, when the E^i are an outgrowth of the constrained maximization of individual utility functions, do they necessarily, by dint of those maximizations, exhibit characteristics beyond continuity, homogeneity, and Walras' law that apply generally, regardless of the particular utility functions involved? Sonnenschein [25], [26], Mantel [18], and Debreu [7] have given answers to this question. Before stating Debreu's result, which is the strongest, two definitions are needed:

---

[17]   These properties are either stated or implied in the discussion of Section 7.1.

First, the function $E(p)$ is said to be *generated* on a collection of positive price vectors D in a model of an exchange economy with K agents, whenever there exist K initial endowment vectors x_k^0 and K corresponding continuous, increasing, and strictly quasi-concave utility functions whose constrained maximization leads, via the summing of individual agent excess demand functions, to $E(p)$, for all p in D. And second, for any real number $\varepsilon > 0$, set

$$D_\varepsilon = \{p = (p_1, \ldots, p_I) : p_i \geqslant \varepsilon, \text{ where } i = 1, \ldots, I\}.$$

Debreu's proposition is stated without proof as follows:

Theorem 10.2-5   Let $E(p)$ be continuous, homogeneous of degree zero, and satisfy Walras' law on $\{p : p > 0\}$. Then for any $\varepsilon > 0$, $E(p)$ is generated on D_ε in a model of an exchange economy with $K = I$ agents.

The significant implication of Debreu's theorem for the present argument[18] is derived from its statement that, loosely speaking, constrained utility maximization by all individuals does not, at least in the typical model of an exchange economy, generally imply anything at all about market excess demand functions beyond the already-established properties of continuity, homogeneity, and Walras' law. To obtain further restrictions on market excess demand functions would therefore require the imposition of additional postulates like, for example, the supposition that individual utility functions take on special forms. Moreover, the uniqueness and global stability of equilibria in Walrasian models of exchange economies turn on the presence of certain kinds of such further restrictions. Given the information possessed by the auctioneer, then, it follows that without additional postulates beyond the continuity, increasingness, and strict quasi-concavity of utility functions, exchange models do not have sufficient assumption content to permit the derivation of propositions that establish uniqueness and global stability. Uniqueness and global-stability analyses, then, can only proceed by adding extra hypotheses.[19]

---

[18]   The Sonnenschein and Mantel theorems alluded to above, but not stated, carry a similar implication.

[19]   It is important to recognize that the Sonnenschein-Mantel-Debreu theorems and their implication that constrained utility maximization imposes nothing more than continuity, homogeneity, and Walras' law on market excess demand functions, are relevant only to the excess demand functions as specified here. This formulation is based on fixed initial endowments, applies to both equilibrium and nonequilibrium price and quantity vectors, and is fundamental to the Walrasian tâtonnement considered here and in Chapter 9. However, it has been demonstrated by Brown and Matzkin [5] that with initial endowments varying, and with attention focusing on equilibria arising from finite numbers of initial endowment vectors, additional restrictions on market excess demand functions with respect to those equilibria and initial endowment vectors

One way of adding extra hypotheses is to introduce sufficient properties relating to individual behavior so as to ensure the existence of a community utility function $u^H(x)$ generating market demand vectors x. Those restrictions, although set out in terms of demand functions that depend on prices and incomes in Section 8.3, are not translated into excess demand language here.[20] Suffice it to say that if $x = H(p, M)$, where $H = (H^1, \ldots, H^I)$ is the vector of market demand functions of (8.3-8) that correspond to $q = E(p)$, then

$$E(p) = H(p, M) - x^0,$$

where $x^0 = \sum_{k=1}^K x_k^0$ and, invoking inner-product notation, $M = p \cdot x^0$. Of course, in the present exchange-economy context, there is no production, there are no factors, and individuals' supplies of goods are not fixed. Moreover, given $P > 0$, each component x_i of the vector of aggregate demands x may be more or less than the aggregate quantities of initial endowments x^0 depending on the outcome of constrained utility maximization at those prices. When $x^0 = H(p, M) = H(p, p \cdot x^0)$, then, $E(p) = 0$ and the exchange economy is in equilibrium.

Theorem 10.2-6 In the model of an exchange economy described above, let there exist a community utility function $u^H(x)$ generating the market demand functions $x = H(p, M)$. If

$$\sum_{i=1}^I p_i' E^i(p'') \leqslant \sum_{i=1}^I p_i' E^i(p'),$$

then

$$\sum_{i=1}^I p_i'' E^i(p'') < \sum_{i=1}^I p_i'' E^i(p'),$$

for all $p' = (p_1', \ldots, p_I') > 0$ and $p'' = (p_1'', \ldots, p_I'') > 0$ such that $E(p') \neq E(p'')$.

Proof: Let p' and p'' be given such that $E(p') \neq E(p'')$, and suppose

$$\sum_{i=1}^I p_i' E^i(p'') \leqslant \sum_{i=1}^I p_i' E^i(p').$$

can be obtained.

---

[20] Such a translation would employ the definition of E^{ik} in (7.1-5). Thus, for example, since $m_k = \sum_{i=1}^I p_i x_{ik}^0$, the term $[\partial m_k / \partial p_n] - h^{nk}$ in (8.3-10) reduces to $x_{nk}^0 - x_{nk} = -q_{nk}$.

With $q' = E(p')$ and $q'' = E(p'')$ this becomes, using inner-produce notation,

$$p' \cdot q'' \leqslant p' \cdot q', \qquad (10.2\text{-}7)$$

where $q' \neq q''$. Invoking the definitions of excess demand and income (equations (7.1-1) and (7.1-2)) applied at the aggregate level, set

$$x' = q' + x^0 \quad \text{and} \quad M' = p' \cdot x^0,$$

and

$$x'' = q'' + x^0 \quad \text{and} \quad M'' = p'' \cdot x^0,$$

so that $x' = H(p', M')$ and $x'' = H(p'', M'')$. Substituting into (10.2-7),

$$p' \cdot (x'' - x^0) \leqslant p' \cdot (x' - x^0),$$

or

$$p' \cdot x'' \leqslant p' \cdot x'. \qquad (10.2\text{-}8)$$

Let a community utility function generating H exist. Then the weak axiom of revealed preference (3.2-7) is satisfied. That is, the direct revealed preference relation defined in terms of H is asymmetric. It follows from that asymmetry and the definition of the direct revealed preference relation that, for all x' and x'' such that $x' \neq x''$, $x' = H(p', M')$, and $x'' = H(p'', M'')$, if $p' \cdot x' \geqslant p' \cdot x''$, then $p'' \cdot x'' < p'' \cdot x'$. Hence, for the particular p', x', p'', and x'' employed above, (10.2-8) implies

$$p'' \cdot x'' < p'' \cdot x'.$$

Subtracting $p'' \cdot x^0$ from both sides results in

$$p'' \cdot (x'' - x^0) < p'' \cdot (x' - x^0).$$

But since $x - x^0 = q = E(p) = (E^1(p), \ldots, E^I(p))$ at both (p', x') and (p'', x''), this is the statement that

$$\sum_{i=1}^{I} p_i'' E^i(p'') < \sum_{i=1}^{I} p_i'' E^i(p'),$$

Q.E.D.

Observe that the assertion of the second part of Theorem 10.2-6 is the analogue of (9.3-34) for models of exchange economies. Combining Theorems 10.2-6 and 9.4-8 with the exchange-model analogue of Theorem 9.3-40 (whose

proof is identical to that of Theorem 9.3-40 except for the exchange-model setting) and adding the exchange-model analogue of the argument demonstrating
the existence of equilibrium in Section 9.2 (the requisite restrictions on utility
functions have already been assumed to be in force), yields the following:[21]

Theorem 10.2-9   In the model of an exchange economy described above with
dynamic (10.2-2) and normalization (10.2-1), if the conditions on individual
behavior (given in Section 8.3) ensuring the existence of a community utility
function are satisfied, and if $\theta > 0$, then an equilibrium path exists that is
unique and globally stable.

A second method of adding extra hypotheses to ensure uniqueness and
global stability in exchange models is based on the next proposition.

Theorem 10.2-10   If $\bar{p} = (\bar{p}_1, \ldots, \bar{p}_I) > 0$ is an equilibrium price vector, if
all pairs of distinct goods are gross substitutes, and if $\lim_{p_i \to 0} E^i(p) = \infty$ for
all positive values of $p_1, \ldots, p_{i-1}, p_{i+1}, \ldots, p_I$, and all $i = 1, \ldots, I$, then

$$\sum_{i=1}^{I} \bar{p}_i E^i(p) > 0, \qquad (10.2\text{-}11)$$

for all $p \neq \psi \bar{p}$ where the scalar $\psi > 0$.

Proof: Since all pairs of distinct goods are gross substitutes, Theorem 9.4-2,
as it applies in the present exchange economy context, implies that $\bar{p}$ is a unique
equilibrium price vector or that, in other words, the vector of price ratios

$$\left(\frac{\bar{p}_1}{\bar{p}_I}, \ldots, \frac{\bar{p}_{I-1}}{\bar{p}_I} \right)$$

is unique. Let N be a compact, convex subset of $\{p : p > 0\}$ that contains $\bar{p}$ in
its interior. Then by Theorem A.3-1 of appendix Section A.3, the function

$$\sum_{i=1}^{I} \bar{p}_i E^i(p), \qquad (10.2\text{-}12)$$

which is continuous on N, attains a minimum at some not-necessarily-unique
p^0 in N. Since the quantities supplied in all markets are limited by the initial-
endowment holdings of the K individuals, since all quantities demanded are

---

[21] Recall that the uniqueness of the equilibrium price vector required in the argument establishing Theorem 9.3-40 is also provided by Theorem 9.4-8.

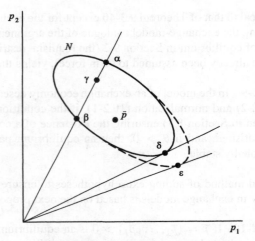

Figure 10.1 Enlargement of the set N

bounded from below by zero, and since $\lim_{p_i \to 0} E^i(p) = \infty$ for all positive values of $p_1, \ldots, p_{i-1}, p_{i+1}, \ldots, p_I$, and all $i = 1, \ldots, I$, it is possible to choose N large enough so that at least one p^0 lies in the interior of N. The latter statement may be illustrated in reference to the two-good example of Figure 10.1. For purposes of this illustration, the homogeneity property of the E^i will be invoked — although the previous assertion follows as stated without it. Observe first that if p^0 appeared on the boundary of N at points like α or β, then by the homogeneity, there will always be a point γ in the interior of N having the same minimum value as $\sum_{i=1}^{I} \bar{p}_i E^i(p^0)$. Moreover, were p^0 located at δ, then N may be enlarged by adding the area out to (and including) the dashed curve. It is, of course possible, that a new minimum will occur at point ε. But because the value of $\sum_{i=1}^{I} \bar{p}_i E^i(p)$ remains constant along the ray from the origin through ε (by the homogeneity), and because $\lim_{p_2 \to 0} E^2(p) = \infty$ for all positive values of p_1, eventually points such as ε will no longer minimize $\sum_{i=1}^{I} \bar{p}_i E^i(p)$, and the minimum will have to lie in the interior of the enlarged N. In any event, at such an interior p^0, partial differentiation of (10.2-12) with respect to each p_n gives

$$\sum_{i=1}^{I} \bar{p}_i E_n^i(p^0) = 0, \quad n = 1, \ldots, I.$$

Now consider the same system of equations, namely

$$\sum_{i=1}^{I} \overline{p}_i E_n^i(p) = 0, \quad n = 1, \ldots, I, \tag{10.2-13}$$

with p varying, as (10.2-13) permits, over N. Clearly $\overline{p}$ satisfies (10.2-13) since, upon partial differentiation of Walras' law (10.2-4) with respect to each p_n,

$$\sum_{i=1}^{I} \overline{p}_i E_n^i(\overline{p}) = -E^n(\overline{p}) = 0, \quad n = 1, \ldots, I.$$

Pick any p' in N such that $p' \neq \psi \overline{p}$ for all $\psi > 0$. Now define σ as in the proof of Theorem 9.4-2:

$$\sigma = \max_i \frac{p_i'}{\overline{p}_i},$$

where the maximum is now taken over $i = 1, \ldots, I$. Then $\sigma \overline{p}_i \geqslant p_i'$ for all i, with the weak inequality for at least one i being strict and that for at least one different i being an actual equality. Taking $i = 1$, say, to be a case of equality, the argument of the proof of Theorem 9.4-2 shows that $E^1(p') < 0$. Hence, using the equation that results from the partial differentiation of Walras' law with respect to p_1,

$$\sum_{i=1}^{I} \overline{p}_i E_1^i(p') = \frac{1}{\sigma} \sum_{i=1}^{I} \sigma \overline{p}_i E_1^i(p'),$$

$$> \frac{1}{\sigma} \sum_{i=1}^{I} p_i' E_1^i(p'),$$

$$= -\frac{1}{\sigma} E^1(p'),$$

$$> 0.$$

Since the same argument can be made for any i, other than multiples $\psi \overline{p}$ (where $\psi > 0$), $\overline{p}$ is the only vector in the interior of N that satisfies (10.2-13).

It follows that, excluding possible multiples $\psi \overline{p}$ in N, $p^0 = \overline{p}$ is the only minimizer of (10.2-12) in the interior of N. But then, with

$$\sum_{i=1}^{I} \bar{p}_i E^i(\bar{p}) = 0$$

as the smallest value that (10.2-12) can take on, it is clear that

$$\sum_{i=1}^{I} \bar{p}_i E^i(p) > 0,$$

for all $p \neq \psi\bar{p}$ in the interior of N with $\psi > 0$. Since N can be made large enough to include any $p > 0$ such that $p \neq \psi\bar{p}$ for all $\psi > 0$, the theorem is proved.

Q.E.D.

Let

$$\widehat{D} = \left\{ p : p > 0 \text{ and } \sum_{i=1}^{I}(p_i)^2 = 1 \right\}.$$

Then the hypotheses of Theorem 10.2-10 clearly imply that (10.2-11) holds for all $p \neq \bar{p}$ in $\widehat{D}$. Moreover, the uniqueness of the equilibrium price vector has already been asserted in the proof of that theorem. These facts, together with the exchange-model analogue of Theorem 9.3-40 that replaces the hypothesis (9.3-34) with (9.3-36),[22] provides a uniqueness and global stability result:

Theorem 10.2-14   In the model of an exchange economy described earlier in this section with dynamic (10.2-2) and normalization (10.2-1), if $\bar{p}$ in $\widehat{D}$ is an equilibrium price vector, if all pairs of distinct goods are gross substitutes, if $\lim_{p_n \to 0} E^n(p) = \infty$ for all positive values of $p_1, \ldots, p_{n-1}, p_{n+1}, \ldots, p_I$, and all $n = 1, \ldots, I$, and if $\theta > 0$, then the equilibrium path is unique and globally stable.

Theorem 10.2-14, in turn, may be combined with the exchange-model analogue of the existence of equilibrium argument of Section 9.2 (remember the necessary properties of utility functions have already been assumed) to obtain:

Theorem 10.2-15   In the model of an exchange economy described earlier in this section with dynamic (10.2-2) and normalization (10.2-1), if all pairs of

---

[22]   Recall that, under the assumptions made here, (9.3-36) is implied by (9.3-34).

distinct goods are gross substitutes, if $\lim_{p_n \to 0} E^n(p) = \infty$ for all positive values of $p_1, \ldots, p_{n-1}, p_{n+1}, \ldots, p_I$, and all $n = 1, \ldots, I$, and if $\theta > 0$, then an equilibrium path exists that is unique and globally stable.

It is instructive to consider the kinds of things that can happen when one or more of the inequalities in the definition of gross substitutes (9.4-1) are reversed and what has been called gross complementarity is present. For this purpose, imagine an exchange economy with only two markets that are simultaneously in (unique) equilibrium at prices $(\bar{p}_1, \bar{p}_2)$ and excess demand quantities $(q_1, q_2) = (0, 0)$. When out of equilibrium at (p'_1, p'_2), where $p'_1 \neq \bar{p}_1$ and $p'_2 \neq \bar{p}_2$, Walras' law implies that any positive excess demand, say, in the market for good 1 must be offset by negative excess demand (of equal value) in the market for good 2. The latter market is illustrated in Figure 10.2.

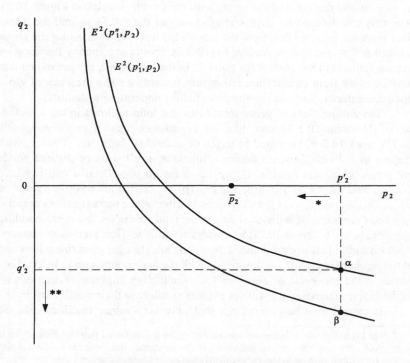

Figure 10.2 Possible undermining of stability in the presence of gross complementarity ($p''_1 > p'_1$)

In that diagram, the out-of-equilibrium situation is located on the graph of $q_2 = E^2(p_1', p_2)$ at point α where $q_2' = E^2(p_1', p_2') < 0$. Although appearing as downward sloping and strictly convex, the slope and curvature of that graph is actually arbitrary except for the requirement of Theorem 10.2-15 that $\lim_{p_2 \to 0} E^2(p_1', p_2) = \infty$. Regardless, according to the dynamic (10.2-2) with $\theta > 0$, the positive excess demand for good 1 and the negative excess demand for good 2 should lead from (p_1', p_2') to, respectively, a rise in p_1 and a fall in p_2 (in the latter case, p_2 should move the direction of the arrow with a single asterisk in Figure 10.2). To have stability, it is necessary in part that those price changes eventually reduce the excess demand in the market for good 1 and raise it (*i.e.*, render it less negative) in the market for good 2. But if $E_1^2(p_1, p_2) < 0$ at these price values, then the increase in p_1 to, say, p_1'' would, before any change in p_2 is taken into account, result in a lower (more negative) excess demand at point β on the graph of $q_2 = E^2(p_1'', p_2)$. Thus forces are created that tend to push excess demand farther from the equilibrium value $q_2 = 0$ (in the direction of the arrow with the double asterisk in Figure 10.2). And this effect could be large enough to offset the fall in p_2 and the attendant increase in q_2 arising from the associated travel from α along the curve labeled $E^2(p_1', p_2)$ that, according to (10.2-2), should accompany the negative excess demand in the market for good 2. In the latter case, the net movement may be away from equilibrium rather than towards it. The presence of gross complementarity, then, carries the potential for undermining stability.

The assumptions of gross substitutes and infinite limits in the hypotheses of Theorem 10.2-15 can, like the hypotheses relating to the economic in Theorem 10.2-9, be stated in terms of individual behavior. That is, with respect to individual excess demand functions, if all pairs of distinct goods are gross substitutes (that is, $E_n^{ik}(p) > 0$ for all $p > 0$, all i and n where $i \neq n$, and all k), and if $\lim_{p_n \to 0} E^{nk}(p) = \infty$ for all positive values of $p_1, \ldots, p_{n-1}, p_{n+1}, \ldots, p_I$, and all n and k, then since market excess demand functions are sums of individual excess demand functions, the corresponding hypotheses of Theorems 10.2-15 immediately follow. However, these assumptions on individual excess demand functions are stronger than those imposed at the market level. And the former, as with the assumptions on individual behavior in the economic of Theorem 10.2-9, although implying restrictions on individual preferences, are still not expressed solely in their vocabulary.[23]

It should also be pointed out that only very minor modifications are

---

[23]   Fisher [8] has provided necessary and sufficient conditions for all pairs of distinct goods to be gross substitutes that involve individual utility functions. But since his conditions also include restrictions relating to income elasticities and expenditure proportions, they, too, are not stated explicitly and fully in the language of individual preferences.

needed to extend Theorems 10.2-10, 10.2-14, and 10.2-15 to the model of a production economy that forms the basis of Chapter 9. Indeed, Theorems 9.3-40 and 9.4-2 on which those results depend, are already set in that framework. But whether the assumptions on the economic can, in this case, be set out in reference to the behavior of individual consumers and firms is an open question.

Returning to the model of an exchange economy, examples in which all of the hypotheses required of the economic in Theorem 10.2-9 and Theorem 10.2-15 are satisfied and can be explicitly and fully expressed with respect to individual preferences, are provided by certain circumstances in which every agent's utility function assumes a Cobb-Douglas form. First, suppose that, in addition to the Cobb-Douglas assumption, all utility functions are identical. That a community utility function exists in this case follows (recall p. 310) from the fact that Cobb-Douglas utility functions always represent homothetic preference orderings (Exercise 10.1). Second, it is not hard to establish that with arbitrary, non-identical Cobb-Douglas utility functions, all pairs of distinct goods are still gross substitutes. Recall that the utility function of agent k is written with the symbolism

$$\mu_k = u^k(x_k),$$

where μ_k varies over the range of u^k, and the first-order, partial derivatives of u^k are denoted by u_i^k, for $i = 1, \ldots, I$. For notational convenience, the following proposition employs the (equivalent) logarithmic version of the Cobb-Douglas configuration.

Theorem 10.2-16 Let utility functions be of the form

$$\mu_k = u^k(x_k) = \sum_{i=1}^{I} \alpha_i^k \ln x_{ik}, \quad k = 1, \ldots, K, \qquad (10.2\text{-}17)$$

where the α_i^k are constants such that $\sum_{i=1}^{I} \alpha_i^k = 1$, and $\alpha_i^k > 0$, for $i = 1, \ldots, I$, and $k = 1, \ldots, K$. Assume further that $x_k^0 = (x_{1k}^0, \ldots, x_{Ik}^0) \geqslant 0$ for each k, and that at least one $x_{ik}^0 > 0$ for every i as k varies and for every k as i varies. Then all pairs of distinct goods are gross substitutes.

Proof: The first-order conditions for constrained maximization of the u^k are

$$\frac{u_i^k(x_k)}{u_n^k(x_k)} = \frac{\alpha_i^k}{\alpha_n^k} \frac{x_{nk}}{x_{ik}} = \frac{p_i}{p_n}, \quad \begin{matrix} i, n = 1, \ldots, I, \ i \neq n, \\ k = 1, \ldots, K. \end{matrix}$$

Combining these equations with the budget constraints $m_k = p \cdot x_k$, where

m_k, remember, is the "income" or the value of initial endowment of person k at prices p, gives the individual demand functions h^{ik} such that

$$x_{ik} = h^{ik}(p, m_k) = \alpha_i^k \frac{m_k}{p_i}, \qquad \begin{matrix} i = 1, \dots, I, \\ k = 1, \dots, K. \end{matrix} \qquad (10.2\text{-}18)$$

Each $h^{ik}(p, m_k) > 0$ everywhere because $x_{ik}^0 \geqslant 0$ for all i and k, and at least one $x_{ik}^0 > 0$ for every k as i varies. Since $m_k = p \cdot x_k^0$ and $q_{ik} = x_{ik} - x_{ik}^0$ for each i and k, the excess demand functions of person k are

$$q_{ik} = E^{ik}(p) = \alpha_i^k \frac{p \cdot x_k^0}{p_i} - x_{ik}^0,$$

$$= \left[\alpha_i^k - 1 \right] x_{ik}^0 + \sum_{n \neq i} \alpha_i^k \frac{p_n}{p_i} x_{nk}^0,$$

for $i = 1, \dots, I$, and $k = 1, \dots, K$. Summing over k yields the market excess demand functions

$$q_i = E^i(p) = \sum_{k=1}^{K} \left[\alpha_i^k - 1 \right] x_{ik}^0 + \frac{1}{p_i} \sum_{n \neq i} p_n \left[\sum_{k=1}^{K} \alpha_i^k x_{nk}^0 \right], \qquad (10.2\text{-}19)$$

for $i = 1, \dots, I$. Therefore, since $x_{ik}^0 \geqslant 0$ for all i and k, and since at least one $x_{ik}^0 > 0$ for every i as k varies, partially differentiating (10.2-19) with respect to p_n for every $n \neq i$ gives, for all $p > 0$ and all i and n such that $i \neq n$,

$$E_n^i(p) = \frac{1}{p_i} \left[\sum_{k=1}^{K} \alpha_i^k x_{nk}^0 \right] > 0, \qquad (10.2\text{-}20)$$

which proves the theorem.

Q.E.D.

Note that with $x_{nk}^0 \geqslant 0$ for all n and k, and at least one $x_{nk}^0 > 0$ for every n as k varies, partial differentiation of (10.2-19) with respect to p_i results, as one would expect, in

$$E_i^i(p) = -\frac{1}{(p_i)^2} \sum_{n \neq i} p_n \left[\sum_{k=1}^{K} \alpha_i^k x_{nk}^0 \right] < 0, \qquad (10.2\text{-}21)$$

for $i = 1, \dots, I$, and all $p > 0$.

Turning back to the discussion concerning, in the Cobb-Douglas situation, the satisfaction of the hypotheses on the economic in Theorems 10.2-9 and 10.2-15, the third point to be made is that (10.2-19) clearly implies that $\lim_{p_n \to 0} E^n(p) = \infty$ for all positive values of $p_1, \ldots, p_{n-1}, p_{n+1}, \ldots, p_I$, and all $n = 1, \ldots, I$. (The roles of n and i have been reversed in (10.2-19) compared to their use here.) Finally, the Cobb-Douglas utility functions, whether the same for all individuals or not, evidently have sufficient properties for the existence-of-equilibrium argument to hold. Therefore, as long as $\theta > 0$, under either Theorem 10.2-9 when all Cobb-Douglas functions are identical or Theorem 10.2-15, a unique and globally stable equilibrium path exists.

It should be emphasized that the assumption of Cobb-Douglas utility functions (10.2-17), with the added requirement of identical utility functions when appropriate, permits the expression of all hypotheses imposed on the economic in Theorems 10.2-9 and 10.2-15 directly in terms of individual preferences alone. And in this respect, it brings the Walrasian model into partial compliance with the requirements of methodological individualism. (The dynamic (10.2-2), of course, remains a market-level construction.) Although not entirely stated with explicit reference to individual preferences, in the absence of Cobb-Douglas functions a similar partial compliance may be asserted for the more general assumptions on individual behavior of Theorem 10.2-9 and those that could be imposed on individual behavior to secure the hypotheses of Theorem 10.2-15. But each set of assumptions also reduces the Walrasian model to a highly specialized case. If that were the only way to obtain uniqueness and global stability, it might be argued, then the usefulness of the Walrasian model in studies that adhere to methodological individualism would be doubtful. Apart from the challenge to this argument given at the end of the next section, the questions of whether there are other conditions on agent utility functions and initial endowments sufficient for uniqueness and global stability, or other conditions relating to market-level adjustment rules different from (10.2-2) that lead to a similar result, are largely unresolved. In this regard, it is worth noting that Flaschel [10] has shown that the price adjustment rule (10.2-2) can be modified so as to make at least local stability fully dependent on the properties of the rule alone. Restrictions that might be imposed on utility functions beyond continuity, increasingness, and strict quasi-concavity are not needed.[24] Such questions, however, are not pursued further here. In addition, and as was pointed out earlier, the use of (10.2-2) itself removes the Walrasian model from lying within the boundaries dictated by the requisites of the methodological-individualism tradition. Subsequent discussion, then,

---

[24]   Flaschel's approach is to make price adjustment dependent, in addition to excess demands, on the rates of change of those excess demands. For example, greater adjustments in prices might occur where potential movements away from equilibrium are faster.

considers the possibility of adjustment rules that permit the restoration of the methodological individualism foundation of the Walrasian exchange model in its entirety.

10.3   THE DETERMINATION OF PRICE

The typical story that goes with dynamic adjustment rules like (10.2-2) depicts the Walrasian tâtonnement and the price determination it implies in terms of the market-level auctioneer mentioned earlier. According to that story, recall, the auctioneer announces a vector of prices, maximizing agents (who are price takers and, to be general, are either consumers or firms) respond with statements of their excess demand quantities which are then summed, and if market excess demand vanishes everywhere, the stated trades are then consummated. Otherwise, the auctioneer announces a new vector of prices as dictated by the adjustment rule, and the process continues. Only when zero excess demand in all markets is achieved, is trade permitted to take place. Of course, the auctioneer of this story is neither a consuming nor a producing agent in the economy. He is, rather, a fictitious being whose sole purpose is to guide the operation of the markets and, as such, is part of the given institutional structure that characterizes the markets themselves.   And since the activities of the auctioneer reflect price behavior that is not explainable in terms of the actions or decisions of individual agents, like equation (10.2-2) that the story accompanies, the auctioneer is also inconsistent with methodological individualism.

Moreover, the auctioneer story and the adjustment rules that are associated with it may not describe the kind of market organization and operation that Walras actually had in mind. According to Walker [29, p. 1721], Walras never mentioned an auctioneer. Rather, in full confluence with methodological individualism, he told an alternative story in which "buyers and sellers or their agents ... cry out prices and change them up or down when they discover that they cannot buy or sell all they wish."[25] In any case, it is reasonable and appropriate to ask about the possibility of introducing stories and adjustment rules for a Walrasian tâtonnement that do not rely on the standard auctioneer or something similar, and are more faithful to the tradition of methodological individualism. The remainder of this section provides a simple illustration, in line with the above quotation, of how this might be done.

---

[25]   Walker [29, p. 1721]. This is consistent with Walras' own description [30, pp. 83-86]. But it should be noted that, at one point in the passage cited here (p. 83), Walras does explicitly employ the term "auction," thus suggesting, if Walker's interpretation is accepted, the concept of an "auction without an auctioneer."

The story describing the operation of markets and the determination of market prices to be developed is based on the idea that individual agents, although retaining their price-taking characteristics, are the ones who (simultaneously) cry out prices. As before, trade is not permitted until equilibrium is achieved, perfect competition prevails everywhere, and individuals, in spite of their role as price proposers, still believe that their behavior (including that of announcing prices) has no impact on the final determination of market prices. Each agent, then, announces his own vector of suggested market prices to all other market participants. The latter respond as price takers by stating their desired excess demand quantities, derived from appropriate maximization, at those prices. In this way, each agent answers the price announcements of all other agents.[26] Even though it has been assumed that all agents make price announcements simultaneously, it may turn out in practice that agents make announcements sequentially. In such a case, the order in which agents take turns in making those announcements could influence individual expectations of future price-vector announcements. But although different orders might then result in different sequences of announced price vectors and different sequences of initial-endowment evaluations, and might also affect the time it takes for equilibrium to be achieved, the implicit assumption (carried over from the previous section) that utility functions remain fixed ensures, as long as a unique and globally stable equilibrium exists, that the end result will be independent of the particular order actually in play. This is because prices will end up at their equilibrium levels anyway, and trade will not take place until they do. For the same reasons, the initial price announcement of each agent does not matter either.

Continuing with the development of the story, return to the point at which each agent has responded to the simultaneous price-vector announcements of all other agents. Consider a representative agent participating in this process. Were trade actually to take place at the prices announced by that agent, the agents who responded to the price announcement would consummate their trades first, and the agent making that announcement would accept the residue of remaining demand and supply of each commodity. But if the announced prices were not equilibrium prices, then the announcing agent would find that he is unable to buy and sell what he wants at those prices. Since the announcing agent can deduce this without the occurrence of trade from the statement of excess demands by the individuals responding to his price-vector announcement, on the next round of announcements he changes his suggested price vec-

---

[26]   A clearing-house may be included that collects and disseminates all of the relevant information relating to these announcements and responses.

tor according to an agent-specific adjustment rule. This rule, though generally different for different agents, always reflects the following: When the agent is unable to buy as much as he would like of a particular good at the price he has announced, he raises his announced price; when he cannot sell as much as he would like, he lowers it. When the agent is able to buy more than he would like of a particular good at the price he has announced, he lowers his announced price; when he can sell more than he would like, he raises it. Proceeding in such a manner, the agent continues to modify his suggested price vector on succeeding rounds until it coincides with the market equilibrium price vector or, in other words, the price vector at which the residual the announcing agent would be required to accept is identical to that which he wants. With all agents doing the same thing, and with equilibrium unique, change would cease everywhere when all participating individuals arrive at the same equilibrium vector.[27] At that point, since no agent would announce a new price, all agents would know that equilibrium has been reached, and trade would take place.[28] Henceforth, to distinguish it from the auctioneer story described earlier, this story will be referred to as the "agent-price-adjustment story."

It is evident that every agent in the agent-price-adjustment story is, at the same time, both a price taker and his own "auctioneer," and that price-adjustment rules accompanying the story are necessarily postulated at the in-dividual level. Although related to maximizing behavior in a manner to be subsequently indicated, these adjustment rules as such are not objects of choice derivable from agent preferences and maximization *per se*. Instead they emerge independently, in the same way as agent preferences and maximization, from current dispositions and understandings developed in light of a long evolution of historical experiences, and, again like agent preferences and maximization, are taken as given at the start of the analysis. Indeed, for present purposes, such

---

[27]   The assumption of perfect divisibility, introduced earlier for analytical purposes, eliminates the possibility that, at equilibrium, some agents could be buying and selling exactly what they want, while others are not.

[28]   If there were a mechanism, such as a random draw, to determine which agent would be *the* price anouncer, then, as long as that person maintained the belief that his price announcements did not influence the final outcome, it would not be necessary to require that all agents announce suggested prices. Price announcements by the designated price announcer would suffice. In this case, the designated price announcer would function as a market-level auctioneer except that his price announcement would be based on the possibility of improving his own utility position as described below, and the process of adjustment to equilibrium would be fully consistent with methodological individualism.

In addition, the process of convergence could be shortened in the multi-price announcer case by having the first agent to reach the equilibrium price vector identify it as the equilibrium price vector for everyone. Since the other agents know that this is where they will end up, they immediately move to it.

price-adjustment rules along with agent maximization are lumped together in what might be regarded as an expanded "postulate of rationality," and the price-determining behavior the adjustment rules describe is considered as part of the "rational calculations of rational agents." In any case, the hypothesizing of price-adjustment rules like these clearly falls within the framework of methodological individualism.

It is additionally evident that in the agent-price-adjustment story markets retain their perfectly-competitive character with zero transactions and information-gathering costs. But the informational requirements for price adjustment to proceed are clearly greater than those of the standard, market-level, auctioneer story in that many more messages have to be sent than when there is only a single auctioneer. This is because each auctioneer makes his own price announcements and gathers his own responses to them. If, however, only a single agent played the role of auctioneer as described in n. 28 (on the previous page), then the informational requirements would reduce to those of the market-level auctioneer case.

Pursuing the characteristics and implications of the agent-price-adjustment story still further, and returning the focus of attention exclusively to the world of exchange, consider, for a moment, agent k (who is not necessarily the designated price announcer of n. 28 referred to above). Set $\widetilde{q}_k = E^k(\widetilde{p}^k)$ and

$$\widehat{q}_k = \sum_{\kappa \neq k} E^\kappa(\widetilde{p}^k),$$

where $E^\kappa(\widetilde{p}^k) = (E^{1\kappa}(\widetilde{p}^k), \ldots, E^{I\kappa}(\widetilde{p}^k))$, and $\widetilde{p}^k = (\widetilde{p}_{1k}, \ldots, \widetilde{p}_{Ik}) > 0$ is a specific price vector announced by agent k. On the one hand, $\widetilde{q}_k$ is the desired excess demand vector of k at prices $\widetilde{p}^k$ and, as such, satisfies his budget constraint $\widetilde{p}^k \cdot \widetilde{q}_k = 0$ where, recall, the dot denotes inner product. On the other, $\widehat{q}_k$ is the vector presented to k by the markets at prices $\widetilde{p}_k$ and, therefore, $-\widehat{q}_k$ is the vector that k would have to accept if trade took place at $\widetilde{p}_k$. Clearly, if $\widetilde{q}_k = -\widehat{q}_k$, then the vector $\widetilde{p}_k$ announced by agent k is an equilibrium price vector.

Suppose $\widetilde{q}_k \neq -\widehat{q}_k$. Since each $E^\kappa(p)$ satisfies a budget constraint like (10.2-3) for all $p > 0$, it follows that

$$\widetilde{p}^k \cdot [-\widehat{q}_k] = -\sum_{\kappa \neq k} \widetilde{p}^k \cdot E^\kappa(\widetilde{p}^k) = 0.$$

Hence, although $-\widehat{q}_k$ might reach beyond the limits of agent k's initial endowment (*i.e.*, might require k to sell more than he has of particular goods), it nevertheless also satisfies his budget constraint. Were agent k's utility function defined at $\widehat{x}_k = -\widehat{q}_k + x_k^0$, then, it would be necessary that

$$u^k(\widetilde{x}_k) > u^k(\widehat{x}_k),$$

where $\widetilde{x}_k = \widetilde{q}_k + x_k^0$. Now the agent-price-adjustment mechanism essentially
requires that agent k raise his announced prices of those goods for which, at
$\widetilde{p}^k$, the market excess demands in the vector $\widetilde{q}_k + \widehat{q}_k$ are positive (quantities demanded are greater than quantities supplied), and lower his announced prices
for those goods such that market excess demands are negative (quantities demanded are less than quantities supplied). To the extent that these two kinds
of price changes call forth, respectively, (i) increases in supply where k is a
buyer and decreases in demand where k is a seller, and (ii) increases in demand where k is a seller and decreases in supply where k is a buyer, agent k,
as will be illustrated momentarily, has reason to hope that the components of
$\widehat{q}_k$ will be altered in such a manner as to raise his utility from $u^k(\widetilde{x}_k)$. In this
sense, the agent-price-adjustment rule is grounded in the individual's efforts
to increase his utility, and the "theory of price determination" associated with
it arises from the pursuit of self-interest in the same way as the individual's
decisions concerning quantities of goods to buy and sell.

Figure 10.3 illustrates, in a two-good case, why agent k has reason to
hope that the price adjustment described above might increase his utility. In
that diagram it is assumed that at his initially announced price vector (reflected
by the solid budget line through the initial endowment x_k^0), k's constrained
utility-maximizing position is at $\widetilde{x}_k$ on the indifference curve labeled 1. Suppose the quantity vector he would have to accept from the markets at these
prices is $\widehat{x}_k'$ on indifference curve 2. Then the market excess demand for good
i, or the difference $(\widetilde{x}_{ik} - \widehat{x}_{ik}')$ between the amount k desires and the amount
market i wants him to take at his initially announced prices, is positive when
$i = 1$ and negative when $i = 2$. Since agent k wishes to be a buyer of good 1
and a seller of good 2, and since, at $\widehat{x}_k'$, he would neither be buying the former
nor selling the latter, by raising his announced price for good 1 and lowering
that of good 2 (to achieve, say, the steeper, dashed budget line through x_k^0 in
Figure 10.3), he can hope that the markets will change what they want from
him to a point such as A (which could also lie on the other side of x_k^0 in the
diagram) where he would be buying (or at least selling less of) good 1, selling (or at least buying less of) good 2, and increasing his utility from $u^k(\widehat{x}_k')$.
However, even if the markets were to take him to a point like B, where he
would be selling less (or possibly even more) of good 1 but buying more of
good 2, his utility would still be higher than $u^k(\widehat{x}_k')$. Of course, A or B may
or may not be utility maximizing for k and, hence, may or may not represent

the equilibrium. And whether he can actually arrive at intermediate or equilibrium points like A or B depends on how the remaining market participants react to his new price announcement. But in any case, agent k will always proceed with the new price announcement because, since trade takes place only after equilibrium is reached, he knows he will wind up at a point that is at least as good as x_k^0 where he started. Similarly, if agent k were required, on the basis of his initial price announcement, to accept a vector of quantities on the other side of $\tilde{x}_k$, for example $\hat{x}_k''$ in Figure 10.3, he would, according to the agent-price-adjustment rule, lower his announced price of good 1 and raise his announced price of good 2 (to produce, for example, the flatter dashed budget

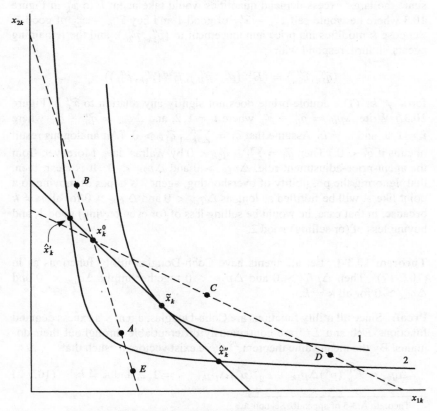

Figure 10.3 The agent-price-adjustment rule and person k.

line through x_k^0), hoping to obtain points such as C or D, which also increase his utility, this time from $u^k(\hat{x}_k'')$.

Actually, in the two-good case, it is not hard to show that when all utility functions are Cobb-Douglas, agent k's hopes for a market response that moves him from, say, $\hat{x}_k'$ in Figure 10.3 to a higher-utility point like A will always be fulfilled unless that mark is overshot by pushing him to a point such as E having lower utility than $u^k(\hat{x}_k')$. That is, points like B, where he would be buying more of the good he wants to sell, are ruled out. Let $(\hat{p}_{1k}, \hat{p}_{2k})$ be the initially announced price vector of agent k, and let

$$(\hat{q}_{1\kappa}, \hat{q}_{2\kappa}) = (E^{1\kappa}(\hat{p}_{1k}, \hat{p}_{2k}), E^{2\kappa}(\hat{p}_{1k}, \hat{p}_{2k}))$$

be agent κ's excess-demand quantities corresponding to it, for all $\kappa \neq k$. Assume the latter excess-demand quantities would take agent k to $\hat{x}_k'$ in Figure 10.3 where he would sell $x_{1k}^0 - \hat{x}_{1k}'$ of good 1 and buy $\hat{x}_{2k}' - x_{2k}^0$ of good 2. Suppose k modifies his price announcement to $(\hat{p}_{1k}'', \hat{p}_{2k}'')$, and the remaining agents, in turn, respond with

$$(\hat{q}_{1\kappa}'', \hat{q}_{2\kappa}'') = (E^{1\kappa}(\hat{p}_{1k}'', \hat{p}_{2k}''), E^{2\kappa}(\hat{p}_{1k}'', \hat{p}_{2k}'')),$$

for $\kappa \neq k$. (The double-prime does not signify any relation to $\hat{x}_k''$ in Figure 10.3.) Write $\Delta p_{ik} = \hat{p}_{ik}'' - \hat{p}_{ik}$ where $i = 1, 2$, and $\Delta q_{i\kappa} = \hat{q}_{i\kappa}'' - \hat{q}_{i\kappa}$ where $i = 1, 2$, and $\kappa \neq k$. Assume that $\hat{q}_1' = \sum_{k=1}^{K} \hat{q}_{1k} > 0$. (An analogous result obtains if $\hat{q}_1' < 0$.) Then $\hat{q}_2' = \sum_{k=1}^{K} \hat{q}_{2k} < 0$ by Walras' law. Moreover, from the agent-price-adjustment rule, $\Delta p_{1k} > 0$ and $\Delta p_{2k} < 0$. It is clear, then, that, ignoring the possibility of overshooting, agent k's hopes of moving to a point like A will be fulfilled as long as $\Delta q_{1\kappa} < 0$ and $\Delta q_{2\kappa} > 0$ for all $\kappa \neq k$ because, in that case, he would be selling less of (or even buying) good 1, and buying less of (or selling) good 2.

Theorem 10.3-1 Let all agents have Cobb-Douglas utility functions as in (10.2-17). Then $\Delta p_{1k} > 0$ and $\Delta p_{2k} < 0$ together imply $\Delta q_{1\kappa} < 0$ and $\Delta q_{2\kappa} > 0$ for all $\kappa \neq k$.

Proof: Since all utility functions are Cobb-Douglas, agent κ's excess demand functions $E^{1\kappa}$ and $E^{2\kappa}$ are continuously differentiable throughout their domains. By the mean value theorem,[29] there exist vectors p^k such that

$$\Delta q_{i\kappa} = E_1^{i\kappa}(p^k)\Delta p_{1k} + E_2^{i\kappa}(p^k)\Delta p_{2k}, \quad i = 1, 2, \text{ and } \kappa \neq k, \quad (10.3\text{-}2)$$

---

[29] Theorem A.3-5 of appendix Section A.3.

where

$$p^k = \psi(\widehat{p}_{1k}'', \widehat{p}_{2k}'') + [1 - \psi](\widehat{p}_{1k}', \widehat{p}_{2k}')$$

for some scalar ψ in the open interval (0,1), the subscripts on the $E^{i\kappa}$, recall, represent partial derivatives, and p^k and ψ are generally different for each i and κ. The conculsion of the theorem now follows by applying the inequalities (10.2-20), (10.2-21), $\Delta p_{1k} > 0$, and $\Delta p_{2k} < 0$ to (10.3-2).

Q.E.D.

Thus, in a two-good, Cobb-Douglas world, market reactions are always such that when the agent raises his announced price of a good, the residual excess demand forced upon him is reduced, and when he lowers it, the residual excess demand increases. That is, the market answer always moves him in a direction such that, if not too large, his utility rises. But that answer could still turn out to be substantial enough, even in the "right" direction, to leave him with a lower utility, such as at point E in Figure 10.3, than that associated with the initial market response. Therefore, although the agent-price-adjustment rule considered here cannot guarantee that the agent, through his price-announcement activity, is always able to call forth an immediate market reaction that will increase his utility, he is still able to proceed in the hope that he can.

It should also be noted that the proof of Theorem 10.3-1 does not carry over to exchange economies with more than two goods. For in that situation (10.3-2) becomes

$$\Delta q_{i\kappa} = \sum_{n=1}^{I} E_n^{i\kappa}(p^k)\Delta p_{nk}, \quad i = 1, \ldots, I, \text{ and } \kappa \neq k,$$

and, for at least one i and any values of the $E_n^{i\kappa}(p^k)$ consistent with (10.2-20) and (10.2-21), at least one product in the right-hand sum is positive and at least one other product is negative. Hence two vectors $(\Delta p_{1k}, \ldots, \Delta p_{Ik})$ can be found, each consistent with the agent-price-adjustment rule, but involving different magnitudes $|\Delta p_{nk}|$, such that one vector yields $\Delta q_{i\kappa} > 0$, and the other results in $\Delta q_{i\kappa} < 0$.[30] Therefore the sign of $\Delta q_{i\kappa}$ cannot be determined, as it is in the proof of Theorem 10.3-1, from the signs of the $E_n^{i\kappa}(p^k)$ and Δp_{nk} alone. Without further assumptions, then, the agent's success at calling forth an immediate market response that increases his utility by appropriately varying his

---

[30]   For example, to ensure that $\Delta q_{i\kappa} > 0$, make $|\Delta p_{nk}|$ relatively large when $E_n^{i\kappa}(p^k)\Delta p_{nk} > 0$ and relatively small when $E_n^{i\kappa}(p^k)\Delta p_{nk} < 0$.

price-vector announcements, though still possible and still reasonable to hope for, may be more difficult to achieve. An argument similar to that of Theorem 10.3-1 and the discussion surrounding it applies if the market response to k's initial price announcement lies elsewhere on the budget line connecting x_k^0 and $\widetilde{x}_k$ in Figure 10.3.

Obviously, Theorem 10.3-1 and the discussion following it may be extended to the more general situation in which, for each person, both pairs of goods (1,2) and (2,1) are gross substitutes and the partial derivatives $E_i^{ik}(p) < 0$ for all $p > 0$, $i = 1, 2$, and $k = 1, \ldots, K$. In that case, the inequalities of (10.2-20) and (10.2-21) needed in the proof of Theorem 10.3-1 are obtained by summing the parallel inequalities that arise with respect to the individual excess demand functions. But even though the fact remains that, for $n > 2$ or with still more general utility functions, the agent may not succeed in procuring an immediate response from the market that increases his utility, it is still clearly in his interest to continue to participate in the adjustment process as described here. For, as has been pointed out earlier, as long as a unique equilibrium exists that is globally stable, even if the agent appears to be losing ground at any particular juncture, eventually, when equilibrium is achieved, he will be no worse off than when he began. That is, his utility cannot be lower than $u^k(x_k^0)$. And it may be considerably higher.

To move to a concrete specification of agent-price adjustment rules in Walrasian models of exchange economies, let $p^k = (p_{1k}, \ldots, p_{Ik}) > 0$ vary over possible price announcements by agent k. The agent-price-adjustment story says that the change in announced price p^k varies directly with the difference between agent k's desired trades at p^k (previously denoted by $\widetilde{q}_k$) and those required in response to the desires of the remaining market participants at p^k (previously written $\widehat{q}_k$). The latter difference at the price vector $\widetilde{p}^k$ considered above is

$$\widetilde{q}_k - [-\widehat{q}_k] = \widetilde{\overline{q}},$$

or

$$E^k(\widetilde{p}^k) - \left[-\sum_{\kappa \neq k} E^\kappa(\widetilde{p}^k) \right] = E(\widetilde{p}^k),$$

where $\widetilde{\overline{q}}$ is the market-excess-demand vector at $\widetilde{p}^k$. In general, then, agent k changes p^k directly with the market-excess-demand function $E(p^k)$. Thus, letting θ_k be a known, nonzero constant for each k, one collection of price-adjustment rules that might accompany the agent-price-adjustment story is

$$\frac{dp^k}{d\tau} = \theta_k E(p^k), \quad k = 1, \ldots, K, \tag{10.3-3}$$

where, recall, τ denotes time. Observe that (10.3-3) is a system of equations that, for each k, is formally identical to, but has a different interpretation and significance than, (10.2-2). Observe also that, because, as suggested in previous discussion, agent k knows $E(p^k)$ from the responses of the remaining agents to his announcement of each p^k, he has sufficient information to change p^k in line with (10.3-3). Moreover, since it is based on market excess demand functions, the impact of Debreu's theorem impinges, with all of its force, on the analysis of the global stability of equilibria under (10.3-3).

It should be pointed out, however, that due, in part, to the formal equivalence of (10.3-3) and (10.2-2), the extra sufficient conditions at the level of the individual ensuring uniqueness and global stability in Theorems 10.2-9 and 10.2-15, including the special circumstances in which all utility functions take on the Cobb-Douglas form (and, if Theorem 10.2-9 is to be invoked, are identical), apply here as well. Under any of these sets of extra conditions, then, starting at a collection of K price vectors $p^k > 0$, where $k = 1, \ldots, K$, each different, say, from the unique, equilibrium price vector $\bar{p}$, the individual behaviors of the K agents will eventually lead everyone to $\bar{p}$. Equilibrium in this particular Walrasian exchange model with dynamic (10.3-3) is therefore unique and globally stable. And both (i) the additional conditions that ensure uniqueness and global stability, and (ii) the price adjustment mechanism in markets, derive, unlike the Walrasian tâtonnement of the previous section, from the properties of individual agents and their behaviors. Such a Walrasian model, then, fully meets the requirements of methodological individualism.

Of course, it would be better to have a story and associated price-adjustment rules for which the conditions on individual agents ensuring global stability of equilibria were expressible with greater generality than that of the above specifications. More general conditions yielding uniqueness of equilibria would also be desirable. But, as has already been indicated in the context of Section 10.2, the questions of whether there are such conditions relating to (10.3-3), and of whether there are alternative stories and adjustment rules which might further permit the manifestation of such conditions, have not yet been resolved. Regardless, it should be pointed out that, in so far as economic models, as noted in Section 10.1, are constructed as abstractions from and explanations of empirical occurrences, the special case of (not-necessarily-identical) Cobb-Douglas utility functions, highly restrictive though it is, is still adequate to cover all practical situations. For, as described in Section 10.1 and elsewhere, the purpose of the Walrasian construction is to explain, in part, the determination of observed vectors of prices and quantities that arise in the real economy. One way to do this is to interpret such prices and quantities as the unique and globally stable equilibrium prices and quantities in a suitable model. But by appropriately setting initial endowments and the parameters in agent utility functions, *any* such observed vectors arising in an exchange economy (even one having goods like coffee and cream that might be thought to be complements with respect to ordinary [not excess] market demand functions), can appear as an equilibrium of a Walrasian exchange model with only (not-necessarily-identical) Cobb-Douglas utility functions.[31] This is because, as pointed out by Exercise 10.2, given any vectors $x_k > 0$, for $k = 1, \ldots, K$, and $p > 0$, endowments and the parameters a_i^k can always be chosen to satisfy (10.2-18). Thus, even if more general uniqueness and global stability conditions turn out to be impossible to obtain, a Walrasian model (with a unique and globally stable equilibrium) always exists that is consistent with methodological individualism, and that is capable of explaining, at least for exchange economies, the determination of what actually has been seen. Therefore the question of whether more general uniqueness and global stability conditions can be found is irrelevant to the explanatory viability of the Walrasian exchange system.

EXERCISES

10.1 Show that the Cobb-Douglas utility function of (10.2-17) represents a homothetic preference ordering.

10.2 Let $\tilde{x}_k$ be an observed vector of person k's demand quantities at prices $\tilde{p} = (\tilde{p}_1, \ldots, \tilde{p}_I) > 0$. Take k's initial endowment to be any vector x_k^0 such that $\tilde{p} \cdot \tilde{x}_k = \tilde{p} \cdot x_k^0$ and set $\tilde{m}_k = \tilde{p} \cdot \tilde{x}_k$. Show that the α_i^k in (10.2-17) can always be selected so that (10.2-18) is satisfied by $\tilde{x}_k$, $\tilde{p}$, and $\tilde{m}_k$.

10.3 In a two-good, two-person, exchange model with initial endowments $x_1^0 = (x_{11}^0, x_{21}^0)$ and $x_2^0 = (x_{12}^0, x_{22}^0)$, let the utility functions of the two individuals be

$$u^1(x_{11}, x_{21}) = \min\left(ax_{11}, x_{21}\right),$$

$$u^2(x_{12}, x_{22}) = \min\left(bx_{12}, x_{22}\right),$$

---

[31] Remember that Cobb-Douglas functions force all goods to be gross substitutes.

where $a > 0$ and $b > 0$. Demonstrate that if $x_{21}^0 > ax_{11}^0$ and $x_{22}^0 > bx_{12}^0$ then, at the market level, the two goods are, at the same time, both gross substitutes and gross complements.

10.4 Let $\overline{p}$ in $\widehat{D} = \{p : p > 0 \text{ and } \sum_{i=1}^I (p_i)^2 = 1\}$ be an equilibrium price vector in the model of an exchange economy described in Section 10.2. Show that if

$$\sum_{i=1}^I \overline{p}_i E^i(p) > 0,$$

for all $p \neq \overline{p}$ in $\widehat{D}$, where E^i is the market excess demand function for good i, then the equilibrium $\overline{p}$ is unique in $\widehat{D}$. This is kind of a converse assertion to that of Theorem 10.2-10.

10.5 Consider a two-good, K-person exchange model with initial endowments $x_k^0 = (x_{1k}^0, x_{2k}^0)$ and individual utility functions of the Cobb-Douglas form (10.2-17). Normalize by setting $p_2 = 1$. Show that, for appropriate constants A and B, the market excess demand functions can be written in the form

$$q_1 = E^1(p) = \frac{A}{p_1} - B$$

and

$$q_2 = E^2(p) = Bp_1 - A,$$

and that the unique equilibrium price $\overline{p}_1 = A/B$.

Introduce the dynamic (10.2-2) with $\theta > 0$. Describe how p_1, q_1, and q_2 change over time when p_1 starts out (i) above A/B and (ii) below A/B.

REFERENCES

1. Arrow, K. J., "Samuelson Collected," *Journal of Political Economy* 75 (1967), pp. 730-737.

2. Bénassy, J.-P., "Nonclearing Markets: Microeconomic Concepts and Macroeconomic Applications," *Journal of Economic Literature* 31 (1993), pp. 732-761.

3. Blaug, M., "Kuhn vs. Lakatos, or Paradigms versus Research Programs in the History of Economics," *Method and Appraisal in Economics*, S. Latsis, ed. (Cambridge: Cambridge University Press, 1976), pp. 149-180.

4. Brodbeck, M., "Methodological Individualisms: Definition and Reduction," *Readings in the Philosophy of the Social Sciences*, M. Brodbeck, ed. (London: Macmillan, 1968), pp. 280-303.
5. Brown, D. J. and R. L. Matzkin, "Testable Restrictions on the Equilibrium Manifold," *Econometrica* 64 (1996), pp. 1249-1262.
6. Burtt, E. A., *The Methodological Foundations of Modern Physical Science*, 2nd ed. (London: Routledge and Kegan Paul, 1932).
7. Debreu, G., "Excess Demand Functions," *Journal of Mathematical Economics* 1 (1974), pp. 15-21.
8. Fisher, F. M., "Gross Substitutes and the Utility Function," *Journal of Economic Theory* 4 (1972), pp. 82-87.
9. ———, "On Price Adjustment without an Auctioneer," *Review of Economic Studies* 39 (1972), pp. 1-15.
10. Flaschel, P., "Dressing the Emperor in a New Dynamic Outfit," *Annals of Operations Research* 37 (1992), pp. 33-49.
11. Hahn, F., "Stability," *Handbook of Mathematical Economics*, v. 2, K. J. Arrow and M. D. Intriligator, eds (Amsterdam: North Holland, 1982), pp. 745-793.
12. ———, "Auctioneer," *The New Palgrave*, v. 1, J. Eatwell, M. Milgate, and P. Newman, eds. (London: Macmillan, 1987), pp. 136-138.
13. Hayek, F. A., "Individualism: True and False," *Individualism and Economic Order* (London: Routledge and Kegan Paul, 1949), pp. 1-32.
14. Hoover, K. D., *The New Classical Macroeconomics* (Oxford: Basil Blackwell, 1988).
15. Kirman, A., "The Intrinsic Limits of Modern Economic Theory: The Emperor Has No Clothes," *Economic Journal* 99 (Conference 1989), pp. 126-139.
16. Koopmans, T. C., *Three Essays on the State of Economic Science* (New York: McGraw-Hill, 1957).
17. Levins, R. and R. Lewontin, *The Dialectical Biologist* (Cambridge: Harvard University Press, 1985).
18. Mantel, R. R., "On the Characterization of Aggregate Excess Demand," *Journal of Economic Theory* 7 (1974), pp. 348-353.
19. Menger, C., *Principles of Economics*, J. Dingwall and B.F. Hoselitz, trans. (New York: New York University Press, 1981).
20. ———, *Investigations into the Method of the Social Sciences with Special Reference to Economics* (earlier published under the title, *Problems of Economics and Sociology*), F. J. Nock, trans. (New York: New York

University Press, 1985).

21. Samuelson, P. A., *Economics*, 11th ed. (New York: McGraw-Hill, 1980).

22. Schotter, A., *The Economic Theory of Social Institutions* (Cambridge: Cambridge University Press, 1981).

23. Sensat, J., "Methodological Individualism and Marxism," *Economics and Philosophy* 4 (1988), pp. 189-219.

24. Smale, S., "Exchange Processes with Price Adjustment," *Journal of Mathematical Economics* 3 (1976), pp. 211-226.

25. Sonnenschein, H., "Market Excess Demand Functions," *Econometrica* 40 (1972), pp. 549-563.

26. ——, "Do Walras' Identity and Continuity Characterize the Class of Community Excess Demand Functions?" *Journal of Economic Theory* 6 (1973), pp. 345-354.

27. Strodack, G. K., *The Philosophy of Epicurus* (Evanston: Northwestern University Press, 1963).

28. Strozier, R. M., *Epicurus and Hellenistic Philosophy* (Lanham: University Press of America, 1985).

29. Walker, D. A., "Review of *Equilibrium Analysis: Variations on Themes by Edgeworth and Walras*," *Journal of Economic Literature* 28 (1990), pp. 1720-1721.

30. Walras, L., *Elements of Pure Economics*, W. Jaffé, trans. (Homewood: Irwin, 1954).

31. Watkins, J. W. N., "Methodological Individualism and Social Tendencies," *Readings in the Philosophy of the Social Sciences*, M. Brodbeck, ed. (London: Macmillan, 1968), pp. 269-280.

Chapter 11

Imperfect Competition

The theory of the perfectly competitive firm and market presented in Chapters 5 and 6 was more or less fully worked out by the time of Marshall in the late 19th century and, by the mid 1920's, had gained wide acceptance as *the* explanation of the behavior of real-world industries that were not monopolies. (The theory of monopoly had been developed by Cournot [6] in 1838.) But at that juncture, Chamberlin [4] and Sraffa [15] reminded economists of the fact (known, of course, to Cournot — and implied here on pp. 185-187 above) that maximum profit under perfectly competitive conditions could not be secured at (interior) outputs with declining marginal costs. (Recall that, with cost curves of the Viner type, and with expansion paths that are rays from the origin, declining marginal costs signify falling average variable costs and, hence, increasing returns to scale.) Profit maximization can only occur uniquely where marginal cost is rising. Moreover, they suggested, there were many firms in the real world that were not monopolies and that actually produced with decreasing marginal costs. Thus economists really had no explanation of the behavior of this large class of firms since the theory of perfect competition could not be applied to them.

The resolution proposed by Chamberlin [5] and Robinson [13] in 1933 was to modify the assumptions of perfect competition by introducing monopoly-type demand curves facing the individual firm that were downward-sloping. Now to permit the demand curve the firm faces to slope downward, is to attribute market power to it (see Exercise 11.13). That is, unlike the situation under perfect competition, the firm is able to raise the price it charges for its output without losing all of its sales. Furthermore, the presence of downward-sloping demand curves also permits (interior) profit maximization to take place at points of falling marginal cost. Such reformulations of the theory of the perfectly competitive firm and market constitute, in part, the subject-matter of this chapter.

At the (isolated) market level, several varieties of competition, including that arising from the reformulation proposed by Chamberlin and Robinson, have been defined in the introduction to Chapter 6. These are as follows: A market is perfectly competitive if it is characterized by large numbers of small buyers and sellers, a standardized commodity, free entry and exit, and full information availability. It is monopolistically competitive if the market commodity varies across firms,[1] perfectly oligopolistic if sellers are large and their number small, and monopolistically oligopolistic if both of these properties appear simultaneously. With a single seller and entry of new firms blocked, the market is a monopoly. Only the notion of perfect competition has been applied to the economy as a whole (introduction to Chapter 7). Thus, recall, an economy is perfectly competitive if and only if all of its markets are perfectly competitive. For present purposes, a market is referred to as *imperfectly competitive* if at least one of the above characteristics necessary for perfect competition is violated. An economy is called *imperfectly competitive* whenever at least one of its markets is imperfectly competitive.

This chapter is concerned (mostly) with the long-run analysis of certain kinds of imperfectly competitive markets and economies. Although models of firm behavior under these conditions are standardized and well known, many of them rest on the implicit, if not explicit, assumption that other firms' reactions have no impact on the price and quantity decisions of the firm in question. Such an assumption is fine for perfectly competitive firms because, by their very nature, these firms are relatively immune to the activities of their competitors. In other words, because a perfectly competitive firm believes (incorrectly — as will be argued below) that it is able to sell as much output as it can produce and buy as much input as it needs at prevailing market prices, it always knows the demand curve it faces (a horizontal line at the level of the prevailing output price) and a straightforward computation permits it to choose its profit-maximizing position at these prices. Reactions to its choices by other firms, if they have any impact at all, change market

---

[1]   Actually, as noted earlier, subsequent discussion concerning the introduction of one or more monopolistically competitive industries into the economy-wide Walrasian model (Section 11.3) treats such commodity variation as illusory.

prices. The firm then adjusts to these changes by making new profit-maximizing decisions at the new prices.

But matters are not so clear-cut for many imperfectly competitive firms. (The exceptions are the monopolistically competitive firms who also maintain inaccurate beliefs about the demand functions facing them.) Their chief difficulty is to discover how much output they can sell at relevant market prices or, in other words, the demand curves or functions they face. Unlike perfect competitors, these firms set their output price and know they are unable to sell all they can produce. They also know that modifying their price alters sales and input usage and hence may cause input and output price changes that affect their competitors. This, in turn, can elicit reactions from competitors that affect them through further changes in input and output prices. Such conclusions apply within and across industries. In the latter case when, for example, two "competing" industries that are monopolies are considered, the reactions of one monopolist to the output-price changes of another arise from the possibility of interindustry substitution by buyers. Thus, in order to determine the demand functions they confront, imperfectly competitive firms must not only be aware of how consumers respond to price, but also how all other firms react as well. Unfortunately, it is highly unlikely that any firm in the real world is capable of collecting such detailed information.

One way out of this dilemma is to suppose that an imperfectly competitive firm is able to learn something about its sales at various prices by experimenting. Thus it could set its price at alternative levels, let the economy adjust, and, assuming that no parameters and functions change, observe its sales. Such an experiment would, in principle, provide the firm with enough information to compute the demand function it faces and its profit-maximizing price and output without knowing anything specific about other firms' reactions. Present discussion goes no further than postulating that, except under monopolistic competition, the imperfectly competitive firms considered here do base their price and output decisions on information gathered from these experiments. It does not delve into the structural and dynamic properties of the model which are necessary for experimentation to be relevant and fruitful.[2]

Actually, were a perfectly competitive firm to experiment in this way, it would be unlikely to confirm its belief that it could sell all the output it wishes without affecting the prevailing market price. This is due to the finiteness of

---

[2] The possibility that the carrying out of an experiment may, itself, so alter the industrial climate that the results of the experiment might be rendered useless is ignored.

the economy and the simple consequence that expansion of the firm's output necessarily increases market supply.[3] The same thing could be discovered by evaluating any derivative

$$\frac{\partial p_i}{\partial x_{i\ell}} \tag{11.0-1}$$

computed from the model of the general economy of Section 7.2. Regardless of the specification of production functions, one would not, in general, expect (11.0-1) to vanish. (A simple example is given in Exercise 11.1.) Even if (11.0-1) were "small" and "insignificant," it is likely that the total effect,

$$\frac{dp_i}{dx_{i\ell}} = \sum_{n=1}^{I} \frac{\partial p_i}{\partial x_n} \frac{dx_n}{dx_{i\ell}}, \tag{11.0-2}$$

is not.[4] Experimentation, then, would disillusion the firm and, assuming it continues to try to maximize profit, lead it to modify its behavior from the perfectly competitive norm. Thus the perfectly competitive market structure would break down. But the essence of perfect competition lies in the blind faith of firms that their beliefs are correct and there is no reason to experiment. Similar illusions are required to sustain monopolistic competition.

When thinking about the activity of an individual firm in the context of an entire economy, then, both the interaction of the firm with all other firms and the means by which the firm discovers the demand curve it faces have to be accounted for. The former is encapsulated in so-called "reaction functions" and determines, in part, the actual demand curve facing the firm. The latter is necessary if the firm is to be able to pursue the maximization of its profit. For the perfectly competitive firm, the reaction functions turn out to be implicit in the equations of Section 7.2, and the demand curve facing the firm emerges from the illusions under which it operates. In this case, the demand curve the firm thinks it confronts is a "subjective" demand curve that does not reflect the realities of the true or "objective" demand curve actually in force. For a monopolist or an oligopolist, the reaction functions have to be made explicit in order to define the (objective) demand function that the firm encounters

---

[3] A similar observation was made by Aumann [3]. Unlike that of the present chapter, Aumann's response was to think of perfect competition as having a nondenumerably infinite number of buyers and sellers. In such a context, the activities of any one participant are, indeed, negligible.

[4] In expression (11.0-2), the $\partial p_i / \partial x_n$, are partial derivatives of the ith inverse market demand relation with respect to the nth market quantity. The $dx_n / dx_{i\ell}$ reflect the output reactions of the firms in market n to the (small) change in output $x_{i\ell}$ of firm ℓ in industry i. These concepts are introduced formally and studied below.

and, because it cannot know the full extent of all of these reaction functions and because it has no illusions leading it astray, the firm has to experiment to discover what its demand curve really is.

The following discussion focuses on long-run models interpreted to reflect the behavior of several kinds of imperfectly competitive firms and industries in relation to the activity of the remaining firms in the economy. As suggested above, this necessarily requires explicit examination of reaction functions embodying the notion that firms react to the economic decisions of other firms. Only the comparative statics or timeless equilibrium equations are developed; accompanying dynamic adjustment processes are ignored. The analytic framework assumes fixed factor supplies as in Chapter 8 and is spelled out in Section 11.1. (Aggregation of firm production functions to industry production functions and the existence of a community utility function are not required.) Monopoly is taken up in Section 11.2, and monopolistic competition along with various forms of oligopoly are explored in Section 11.3. To simplify matters it is supposed that imperfectly competitive firms face imperfect competition in their output markets only. All firms purchase all inputs in perfectly competitive markets.

Rather than becoming involved with questions of existence and uniqueness of (long-run) equilibrium,[5] subsequent argument is based on the heuristic procedure of counting numbers of equations in relation to numbers of variables or unknowns. Systems of equations with the same number of independent equations as variables are called *determinate* and are assumed to have unique solutions. The prices and quantities in those solutions are all assumed to be positive. Systems with more independent equations than unknowns are *overdetermined*. They are internally inconsistent or contradictory in that it is impossible to find a vector of variable values that satisfy all equations simultaneously. With more unknowns than equations the system is *underdetermined* and usually has infinitely many solutions. Thus the central theme of this chapter is the study, under alternative forms and combinations of forms of competition, of determinate models (systems) whose solutions are assumed to exist uniquely and reflect long-run economic equilibrium.[6] Although considerable effort is devoted to examining the possibility of substituting certain equations for certain other equations, the property of determinateness is maintained throughout.

It should be noted that there is an alternative approach to imperfect

---

[5]   Readers interested in existence theorems should consult, for example, Arrow and Hahn [2, pp. 151-165] and FitzRoy [8].
[6]   The approach is similar to that of Pearce [10].

competition that is based on the theory of games.[7] This perspective, however, is ignored here because the intent of subsequent argument is to investigate the effects of inserting imperfectly competitive elements into the particular Walrasian model of Section 11.1 as it stands. The main conclusions suggested below are that, depending on the case, a single imperfectly competitive industry (defined in one of its traditional forms) can, with greater or less ease, be fitted into a model in which the remaining industries are perfectly competitive. But for all forms of imperfect competition, as the number of imperfectly competitive industries increases, the assumptions required to accommodate them become more and more untenable.[8] It is possible, however, to introduce, in a sensible way, several imperfectly competitive industries by modifying the forms that imperfect competition traditionally has taken. In the example briefly mentioned at the end of Section 11.2, a number of monopolies are included simultaneously, but the profit-maximizing condition that marginal cost equals marginal revenue is abandoned.

The material of this chapter is irrelevant for the particular grand view spelled out in Section 1.4.

11.1   THE SETTING

Part of the model of the economy employed here to analyze alternative forms of competition is taken, with the same notation, from Chapter 8. The relevant equations are summarized in short-run form first: Outputs or industries are indexed by $i = 1, \ldots, I$; factors or inputs by $j = 1, \ldots, J$. The number of firms in industry i is written L_i. Let $y_{i\ell j}$ be the quantity of input j used by firm ℓ in industry i, and set

$$y_{ij} = \sum_{\ell=1}^{L_i} y_{i\ell j}, \quad i = 1, \ldots, I, \ j = 1, \ldots, J.$$

The total amounts of output i supplied and input j demanded in the economy

---

[7]   See, for example, Shubik [14]. In game-theoretic analyses, firms calculate the "payoffs" they believe to be associated with each decision option under a variety of contingent reactions of their competitors. Of course, such calculations presume knowledge of the appropriate reaction functions. The theory of games is discussed briefly in Section 15.2.

[8]   By studying two concrete examples Roberts and Sonnenschein [12] have also concluded that there are problems with the way models incorporating traditional forms of imperfect competition fit together.

are, respectively,

$$x_i = \sum_{\ell=1}^{L_i} x_{i\ell}, \quad i = 1, \ldots, I, \tag{11.1-1}$$

and

$$\sum_{i=1}^{I} y_{ij} = \sum_{i=1}^{I} \sum_{\ell=1}^{L_i} y_{i\ell j}, \quad j = 1, \ldots, J, \tag{11.1-2}$$

where $x_{i\ell}$ denotes the output of firm ℓ in industry i. With $a_j > 0$ representing the fixed quantities of factor supplies available in the economy, the equations

$$\sum_{i=1}^{I} y_{ij} = a_j, \quad j = 1, \ldots, J, \tag{11.1-3}$$

assert that demand equals supply in all input markets.

The production function of firm ℓ in industry i (from the introduction to Chapter 8) is given by

$$x_{i\ell} = f^{i\ell}(y_{i\ell 1}, \ldots, y_{i\ell J}), \quad \begin{array}{l} \ell = 1, \ldots, L_i, \\ i = 1, \ldots, I, \end{array} \tag{11.1-4}$$

defined for every $(y_{i\ell 1}, \ldots, y_{i\ell J}) \geqslant 0$. All production functions are assumed to be nonnegative and continuous where defined. Continuous, second-order partial derivatives exist throughout the interiors of their respective input spaces. Between the ridge surfaces when those surfaces do not intersect, between the ridge surfaces up to a unique global maximum when they intersect at a single point or, if no ridge surfaces exist, for all $(y_{i\ell 1}, \ldots, y_{i\ell J}) > 0$, let marginal products be positive, isoquants be strictly convex, and bordered Hessian determinants be nonvanishing. Isoquants, where nonnegatively sloped and strictly convex, are not permitted to touch input space boundaries. And, of course

$$f^{i\ell}(0) = 0,$$

for every i and ℓ. Although not directly needed for present purposes, the transformation function or surface could now be secured as described in Chapter 8 by first aggregating (11.1-4) into industry production functions. Much of the argument of this chapter does not require the transformation surface to take on any particular shape. Hence, at this point, no further qualifications are imposed on the firm. Strictly concave, Viner, and constant returns to scale models are all possible. Where additional restrictions are necessary (to ensure, for example, that a particular firm is able to maximize profit or that an appropriate region of the transformation surface is strictly concave), either they are explicitly stated or are implicitly assumed to be in force.

Recall that $p = (p_1, \ldots, p_I)$, $r = (r_1, \ldots, r_J)$, $\pi_{i\ell}$, and $b_{i\ell}$ indicate, respectively, vectors of output prices, vectors of input prices, and the profit and fixed cost of firm $i\ell$. Aggregate income or expenditure is

$$M = \sum_{i=1}^{I} p_i x_i, \tag{11.1-5}$$

and the profit equations are

$$\pi_{i\ell} = p_i x_{i\ell} - \sum_{j=1}^{J} r_j y_{i\ell j} - b_{i\ell}, \quad \begin{matrix} \ell = 1, \ldots, L_i, \\ i = 1, \ldots, I. \end{matrix} \tag{11.1-6}$$

Summing (11.1-6) over i and ℓ and combining the result with (11.1-5) gives

$$M = \sum_{i=1}^{I} \sum_{\ell=1}^{L_i} (\pi_{i\ell} + b_{i\ell}) + \sum_{i=1}^{I} \sum_{\ell=1}^{L_i} \sum_{j=1}^{J} r_j y_{i\ell j},$$

which is the expression for aggregate income valued at factor cost. As usual, the $b_{i\ell}$ are taken to be predetermined parameters.

Market demand functions are written as

$$x_i = H^i(p_1, \ldots, p_I, M), \quad i = 1, \ldots, I. \tag{11.1-7}$$

Behind these demand functions are the fixed factor supplies $a = (a_{1k}, \ldots, a_{Jk})$ (where at least one $a_{jk} > 0$ for each k as j varies) and the usual individual utility functions with the continuity and differentiability, differential increasingness, strict quasi-concavity, and boundary properties of Section 2.3. Maximization subject to budget constraints yields demand functions for each consumer. The latter, in turn, are summed across persons to obtain, as described in Section 8.3, equations (11.1-7). It is not necessary to assume the extra conditions that ensure that a community utility function exists. Specification of the demand functions (11.1-7) is enough. Moreover, use of the same symbol x_i to denote market supply in (11.1-1) and market demand in (11.1-7) implicitly guarantees equilibrium in all output markets.

Since each firm is assumed to hire inputs so as to minimize cost,

$$\frac{f_j^{i\ell}}{f_J^{i\ell}} = \frac{r_j}{r_J}, \quad \begin{matrix} \ell = 1, \ldots, L_i, \quad i = 1, \ldots, I, \\ j = 1, \ldots, J-1, \end{matrix} \tag{11.1-8}$$

where functional arguments of the $f_j^{i\ell}$ have been dropped to simplify notation. According to the discussion of Section 8.2, any vector of outputs (together with appropriate price and input vectors) satisfying (11.1-1) – (11.1-8) necessarily lies on the transformation surface.

Because matters are simplified by treating all industries and goods symmetrically, it is convenient to employ a normalization somewhat different from those discussed in Chapter 7 and elsewhere. Thus set

$$M = \bar{M},   \qquad (11.1\text{-}9)$$

where $\bar{M}$ is an unspecified positive constant. Although this procedure fixes the nominal value of aggregate income, the value of aggregate income relative to market prices is still determined by the system.

The equations and variables described thus far are listed in Table 11.1. Since in any such model, Walras' law (7.2-20) always renders one equation redundant, inspection of the table reveals that to have the same number of independent equations as variables, an additional

$$\sum_{i=1}^{I} L_i$$

equations are needed.[9] The way the model is completed (that is, the kinds of extra equations that are added) depends on the forms of competition assumed in output markets. (The supposition of perfectly competitive input markets has already been introduced implicitly in equations (11.1-3) and (11.1-8)). But before considering alternatives, some additional concepts are needed.

The marginal cost functions of firms are defined as in Section 4.5 by

$$MC^{i\ell}(r, x_{i\ell}) = \frac{\partial \left(\sum\limits_{j=1}^{J} r_j y_{i\ell j} + b_{i\ell} \right)}{\partial x_{i\ell}}, \qquad (11.1\text{-}10)$$

where $\ell = 1, \ldots, L_i$, $i = 1, \ldots, I$, the right-hand derivative is evaluated along the expansion path, and the input price vector $r = (r_1, \ldots, r_J)$ is explicitly introduced here as a functional argument of $MC^{i\ell}$.

To define marginal revenue, the interaction of each firm with all others must be made explicit. More precisely, it is necessary to know how all firms in the economy react to the economic decisions of each one. For present purposes, these reactions can be expressed, following Cournot [6, pp. 80-81], in

---

[9]   The number $\sum_{i=1}^{I} L_i$ is the total number of firms in the model.

Table 11.1 Equations and variables in the model thus far

	Equations			Variables	
Reference number in text	Description	Number of this type	Number of this type	Description	Symbolic representation
(11.1-1)	definition of aggregate output quantities	I	I	aggregate outputs	x_i
(11.1-2)	definition of aggregate input quantities	J	J	aggregate inputs	$\sum\limits_{i=1}^{I} y_{ij}$
(11.1-3)	full employment of factors	J	J	input prices	r_i
(11.1-4)	production functions	$\sum\limits_{i=1}^{I} L_i$	$\sum\limits_{i=1}^{I} L_i$	individual firm output	$x_{i\ell}$
(11.1-5)	definition of aggregate income	1	1	aggregate income	M
(11.1-6)	definition of profits	$\sum\limits_{i=1}^{I} L_i$	$\sum\limits_{i=1}^{I} L_i$	individual firm profit	$\pi_{i\ell}$
(11.1-7)	market demands	I	I	output prices	p_i
(11.1-8)	cost minimization	$\sum\limits_{i=1}^{I} (J-1)L_i$	$\sum\limits_{i=1}^{I} JL_i$	individual firm inputs	$y_{i\ell j}$
(11.1-9)	normalization	1			

terms of output quantities alone. Thus let the output *reaction functions*

$$x_{\mu\sigma} = \zeta^{(\mu\sigma)(i\ell)}(x_{i\ell}), \quad (i,\ell) \neq (\mu,\sigma), \qquad (11.1\text{-}11)$$

describe the output reaction of firm σ in industry μ to the output of firm ℓ in industry i, where

$$\begin{aligned}
\mu, i &= 1, \ldots, I, \\
\sigma &= 1, \ldots, L_\mu, \\
\ell &= 1, \ldots, L_i.
\end{aligned}$$

In general, these functions are defined independently of the (implicit) transformation function or any constraints imposed by the fixed factor supplies. But, as indicated below, the model $(11.1\text{-}1)-(11.1\text{-}9)$ plus whatever additional equations are introduced to complete it sometimes provides enough information to determine the $\zeta^{(\mu\sigma)(i\ell)}$ and, in that case, the transformation function or fixed-factor-supplies typically constrain firm reactions. Regardless, without further specification of some sort, the form taken by output reaction functions remains unknown.

Set $\chi = (x_{11}, \ldots, x_{1L_1}, x_{21}, \ldots, x_{2L_2}, \ldots, x_{I1}, \ldots, x_{IL_I})$ and let H^{-1^i} denote the ith inverse demand function assumed to exist upon inversion of $(11.1\text{-}7)$ with respect to prices alone. That is,

$$p_i = H^{-1^i}(x_1, \ldots, x_I, M), \quad i = 1, \ldots, I. \qquad (11.1\text{-}12)$$

Using $(11.1\text{-}1)$, $(11.1\text{-}9)$, and $(11.1\text{-}12)$, the total revenue function $(5.1\text{-}1)$ of firm ℓ in industry i becomes

$$TR^{i\ell}(\chi) = x_{i\ell} H^{-1^i}\left(\sum_{\varepsilon=1}^{L_1} x_{1\varepsilon}, \ldots, \sum_{\varepsilon=1}^{L_I} x_{I\varepsilon}, \bar{M} \right). \qquad (11.1\text{-}13)$$

Totally differentiating $(11.1\text{-}13)$ with respect to $x_{i\ell}$ and recognizing the interaction possibilities among firms yields the marginal revenue function $(5.1\text{-}2)$ of firm $i\ell$:

$$MR^{i\ell}(\chi) = p_i + x_{i\ell} \sum_{\mu=1}^{I} \sum_{\sigma=1}^{L_\mu} \left(\frac{\partial p_i}{\partial x_{\mu\sigma}} \right) \left(\frac{dx_{\mu\sigma}}{dx_{i\ell}} \right), \qquad (11.1\text{-}14)$$

where, for all i, ℓ, μ, and σ,

$$\frac{\partial p_i}{\partial x_{\mu\sigma}} = \frac{\partial H^{-1^i}\left(\sum_{\varepsilon=1}^{L_1} x_{1\varepsilon}, \ldots, \sum_{\varepsilon=1}^{L_I} x_{I\varepsilon}, \bar{M}\right)}{\partial x_{\mu\sigma}},$$

and

$$\frac{dx_{\mu\sigma}}{dx_{i\ell}} = \frac{d\zeta^{(\mu\sigma)(i\ell)}(x_{i\ell})}{dx_{i\ell}}, \quad (i,\ell) \neq (\mu,\sigma).$$

Note that because $\zeta^{(\mu\sigma)(i\ell)}$ is not generally known by firm $i\ell$, neither is $dx_{\mu\sigma}/dx_{i\ell}$ nor $MR^{i\ell}(x)$.

It is useful to examine several ways of completing this model for a perfectly competitive economy. A perfectly competitive firm, recall, takes the price of its output as a parameter and behaves as if other firms are unaffected by its activity. It erroneously believes that the total derivatives of the reaction functions of all remaining firms in all industries with respect to its own output, along with the partial derivative of its output price also with respect to its own output, vanish identically. That the firm is deluding itself by maintaining such faith is irrelevant. Thus, although the true or *objective* marginal revenue function of firm $i\ell$ is given by (11.1-14), its *subjective* marginal revenue function (that is, the marginal revenue function it thinks it faces), $SMR^{i\ell}(\chi)$, reduces to

$$SMR^{i\ell}(\chi) = p_i,$$

where p_i, is independent of χ. When all firms cling to similar beliefs, as in the perfectly competitive economy,

$$SMR^{i\ell}(\chi) = p_i, \qquad \begin{array}{l} \ell = 1, \ldots, L_i, \\ i = 1, \ldots, I. \end{array} \tag{11.1-15}$$

Observe that the primary difference between the objective marginal revenue function of (11.1-14) and the subjective marginal revenue functions of (11.1-15) is that in the latter case, all interactions among firms, in particular between any firm and its competitors, are ignored.[10]

---

[10]   A similar distinction can be drawn between a firm's objective (inverse) demand function, obtained by substituting (11.1-1) and (11.1-9) into (11.1-12), and its subjective (inverse) demand function secured, like (11.1-15), as a constant p_i for all values of χ. Objective demand functions play a role in the analysis of all forms of imperfect competition discussed below. A subjective demand function for monopolistically competitive firms is introduced more formally in Section 11.3.

One way to complete the model so as to describe the short-run perfectly competitive economy, then, is to include the definitions of marginal cost (11.1-10), the definitions of subjective marginal revenue (11.1-15), and the apparently (from the perspective of each firm) profit-maximizing conditions

$$SMR^{i\ell}(\chi) = MC^{i\ell}(r, x_{i\ell}), \quad \begin{array}{l} \ell = 1, \ldots, L_i, \\ i = 1, \ldots, I. \end{array} \qquad (11.1\text{-}16)$$

To ensure that (11.1-16) indeed identifies a unique "maximum," it must among other things be the case that the partial derivative of $MC^{i\ell}$ with respect to $x_{i\ell}$ is positive where (11.1-16) holds (Section 5.1). To guarantee that the firm actually produces at the maximum requires the further assumption that the market price in (11.1-15) is above minimum average variable cost (recall the discussion preceding equation (5.1-8)). Now the admission of (11.1-10), (11.1-15), and (11.1-16) to the model adds

$$2 \sum_{i=1}^{I} L_i$$

variables (the marginal costs and subjective marginal revenues) and

$$3 \sum_{i=1}^{I} L_i$$

equations. The deficit of

$$\sum_{i=1}^{I} L_i$$

equations mentioned above has therefore been eliminated. Equations (11.1-1) – (11.1-10), (11.1-15), and (11.1-16) constitute a determinate model that, it is hypothesized, has a unique solution or equilibrium.

To obtain the perfectly competitive reaction functions (11.1-11) describing the output reaction of any firm $\mu\sigma$ to the output of firm $i\ell$ (that is, the $\zeta^{(\mu\sigma)(i\ell)}$ that sustain the illusions of the $\mu\sigma$ firms needed for the maintenance of perfect competition), combine (11.1-16), (11.1-15), (11.1-12), (11.1-9), and (11.1-1):

$$MC^{\mu\sigma}(r, x_{\mu\sigma}) = H^{-1^\mu}\left(\sum_{\varepsilon=1}^{L_1} x_{1\varepsilon}, \ldots, \sum_{\varepsilon=1}^{L_I} x_{I\varepsilon}, \bar{M} \right), \qquad (11.1\text{-}17)$$

where $(\mu, \sigma) \neq (i, \ell)$. Substitute also (11.1-1), (11.1-9), and (11.1-12) into the first-order profit-maximization conditions of firm $i\ell$ (recall equations (5.1-11)), namely,

$$r_j = p_i f_j^{i\ell}(y_{i\ell 1}, \ldots, y_{i\ell J}), \quad j = 1, \ldots, J,$$

to obtain

$$r_j = H^{-1^i}\left(\sum_{\varepsilon=1}^{L_1} x_{1\varepsilon}, \ldots, \sum_{\varepsilon=1}^{L_I} x_{I\varepsilon}, \bar{M}\right) f_j^{i\ell}(y_{i\ell 1}, \ldots, y_{i\ell J}), \quad (11.1\text{-}18)$$

for $j = 1, \ldots, J$. Now sometimes it may be possible, by manipulating (11.1-18) alone, to eliminate the $y_{i\ell 1}, \ldots, y_{i\ell J}$, and use the resulting equations to remove r from (11.1-17). In this case, (11.1-17) becomes a system of

$$\left[\sum_{i=1}^{I} L_i\right] - 1$$

equations in

$$\sum_{i=1}^{I} L_i$$

variables $x_{\mu\sigma}$ and $x_{i\ell}$. Thus there are enough equations relative to unknowns so that, when solutions exist, the $x_{\mu\sigma}$ can be expressed as functions of the single variable $x_{i\ell}$. Assuming enough solvability, then, the reaction functions $\zeta^{(\mu\sigma)(i\ell)}$ are secured. An example is given in Exercise 11.2.

Alternatively, to drop r from (11.1-17), it may be necessary to find an explicit expression for the transformation function and use that expression in conjunction with (11.1-18). However, the solutions of (11.1-17), when they exist, still provide the reaction functions $\zeta^{(\mu\sigma)(i\ell)}$. An illustration of this case appears in Exercise 11.3.

Of course, once the appropriate reaction functions are found, all objective marginal revenue functions $MR^{i\ell}$ can be computed from (11.1-14). But because, in general,

$$SMR^{i\ell}(\chi) \neq MR^{i\ell}(\chi), \quad \begin{array}{l} \ell = 1, \ldots, L_i, \\ i = 1, \ldots, I, \end{array}$$

equations (11.1-16) imply

$$MC^{i\ell}(r, x_{i\ell}) \neq MR^{i\ell}(\chi), \quad \begin{array}{l} \ell = 1, \ldots, L_i, \\ i = 1, \ldots, I. \end{array}$$

At equilibrium in the model, even though the perfectly competitive firm believes itself to be producing its profit-maximizing output, in objective terms this is not usually so. Because the objective first-order profit maximization conditions are not normally met, any one firm could increase its profit by appropriately changing production as long as all other firms continue to operate by equating subjective marginal revenue to marginal cost.

There are at least two ways to reset this model in a long-run context. In both instances set all fixed costs $b_{i\ell}$ at zero and assume that all firms within each industry are identical. These restrictions force certain modifications to be made in previous equations. Thus replace (11.1-1) and (11.1-2) by, respectively,

$$x_i = x_{i1}L_i, \quad i = 1, \ldots, I, \tag{11.1-1*}$$

and

$$\sum_{i=1}^{I} y_{ij} = \sum_{i=1}^{I} y_{i1j}L_i, \quad j = 1, \ldots, J; \tag{11.1-2*}$$

substitute

$$x_{i1} = f^{i1}(y_{i11}, \ldots, y_{i1J}), \quad i = 1, \ldots, I,$$

$$x_{i\ell} = x_{i1}, \qquad\qquad \begin{array}{l} \ell = 2, \ldots, L_i, \\ i = 1, \ldots, I, \end{array} \tag{11.1-4*}$$

for (11.1-4) and

$$\pi_{i1} = p_i x_{i1} - \sum_{j=1}^{J} r_j y_{i1j} - b_{i1}, \quad i = 1, \ldots, I,$$

$$\pi_{i\ell} = \pi_{i1}, \qquad\qquad \begin{array}{l} \ell = 2, \ldots, L_i, \\ i = 1, \ldots, I, \end{array} \tag{11.1-6*}$$

for (11.1-6); and modify (11.1-8) to

$$\frac{f_j^{i1}}{f_J^{i1}} = \frac{r_j}{r_J}, \quad i = 1, \ldots, I, \ j = 1, \ldots, J - 1,$$

$$y_{i\ell j} = y_{i1j}, \qquad \begin{array}{l} \ell = 2, \ldots, L_i, \ i = 1, \ldots, I, \\ j = 1, \ldots, J. \end{array} \tag{11.1-8*}$$

Equations (11.1-3), (11.1-5), (11.1-7), and (11.1-9) remain unchanged. Hence the number of equations and variables is the same as those counted in Table 11.1 except that (11.1-8*) contains

$$J \left[\sum_{i=1}^{I} L_i \right] - I$$

instead of

$$(J-1) \sum_{i=1}^{I} L_i$$

equations. It follows that the deficit of equations derived from Table 11.1 has been reduced from $\sum_{i=1}^{I} L_i$ to I.

Continuing to fill out the long-run model, (11.1-10) is rewritten as

$$MC^{i1}(r, x_{i1}) = \frac{\partial \left(\sum_{j=1}^{J} r_j y_{i1j} \right)}{\partial x_{i1}}, \quad i = 1, \ldots, I, \tag{11.1-10*}$$

$$MC^{i\ell}(r, x_{i\ell}) = MC^{i1}(r, x_{i1}), \quad \begin{array}{l} \ell = 2, \ldots, L_i, \\ i = 1, \ldots, I, \end{array}$$

and there are fewer independent reaction functions since

$$\zeta^{(\mu\sigma)(i\ell)}(x_{i\ell}) = \zeta^{(\mu1)(i1)}(x_{i1}),$$

for $\mu \neq i$. Moreover, using (11.1-1*), the inverse demand function (11.1-12) takes the form

$$p_i = H^{-1^i}(x_{11}L_1, \ldots, x_{I1}L_I, M), \quad i = 1, \ldots, I. \tag{11.1-12*}$$

so that (11.1-14) becomes

$$MR^{i1}(\chi) = p_i + x_{i1} \sum_{\mu=1}^{I} \left(\frac{\partial p_i}{\partial x_{\mu1}} L_\mu \right) \left(\frac{dx_{\mu1}}{dx_{i1}} \right), \tag{11.1-14*}$$

$$MR^{i\ell}(\chi) = MR^{i1}(\chi), \quad \ell = 2, \ldots, L_i,$$

where $i = 1, \ldots, I$, and, for convenience, the variables that could be omitted from the vector χ are not specified. In parallel fashion, the subjective marginal revenue functions (11.1-15) are revised to

$$SMR^{i1}(\chi) = p_i, \qquad\qquad i = 1, \ldots, I,$$

$$SMR^{i\ell}(\chi) = SMR^{i1}(\chi), \qquad \begin{aligned} \ell &= 2, \ldots, L_i, \\ i &= 1, \ldots, I. \end{aligned} \qquad (11.1\text{-}15^*)$$

Finally, having all firms identical within industries reduces the number of conditions needed for (apparent) profit maximization to I:

$$SMR^{i1}(\chi) = MC^{i1}(r, x_{i1}), \quad i = 1, \ldots, I. \qquad (11.1\text{-}16^*)$$

Thus the addition of (11.1-10*), (11.1-15*), and (11.1-16*) to the model now adds the

$$2 \sum_{i=1}^{I} L_i$$

marginal cost and subjective marginal revenue variables and

$$I + 2 \sum_{i=1}^{I} L_i$$

equations. Once again, the deficit (this time of I equations) has been made up. Moreover, the reaction functions of the perfectly competitive firms, $\zeta^{(\mu 1)(i1)}$ (x_{i1}) for $\mu \neq i$, which may sometimes be obtained from (11.1-17) and (11.1-18) are, when possible, derivable as before except that now (11.1-17) is an appropriately modified system of $I - 1$ equations in I variables.

With the $b_{i\ell} = 0$ and equations altered as indicated, the first long-run model (described the end of Section 7.2) is obtained by adding to the above

$$\pi_i = 0, \quad i = 1, \ldots, I, \qquad (11.1\text{-}19)$$

and taking $L_1, \ldots, L_I$ to be variables determined at long-run equilibrium rather than as parameters. These changes leave the system determinate. As pointed out earlier, this approach eliminates the strictly concave model from consideration for all firms.

The second approach to the long run is to add (11.1-19) as before, but keep the L_i as fixed parameters and assume instead that all production functions exhibit constant returns to scale. Of course, the $b_{i\ell}$ are kept at zero. (Such a perspective was also suggested at the end of Section 7.2.) This, too, is a determinate system. Furthermore, as implied near the end of Section 5.1, the assumptions of perfect competition, profit maximization at some positive output, and constant returns to scale ensure that for all $x_{i\ell} > 0$,

$$MC^{i1}(r, x_{i1}) = p_i, \quad i = 1, \ldots, I. \tag{11.1-20}$$

Hence adding the subjective marginal revenue variables and equations of (11.1-15*) yields the equality of marginal costs and subjective marginal revenues of (11.1-16*). Note that (11.1-20) does not imply

$$MR^{i1}(\chi) = MC^{i1}(r, x_{i1}), \tag{11.1-21}$$

for any i, because $MR^{i1}(\chi) \neq p_i$, according to (11.1-14*). Once again, at equilibrium each firm lives with the illusion that it is maximizing profit when, in fact, under the conditions described above, it can do better.[11] It should also be understood that in this approach, market equilibrium may be interpreted as being determined by the interaction of the (market) demand functions and the (implicit) transformation function. In that case, the output of an individual firm is found upon division of the relevant industry output by the number of firms that industry contains. (Recall that with constant returns to scale production functions, neither firm nor industry output can be secured through profit maximization alone.) Observe that here and in subsequent notation the "LR" part of the long-run cost function symbols $LRTC$, $LRAC$, and $LRMC$, employed in Sections 5.2 and 6.2, is dropped for purposes of notational simplification.

11.2 MONOPOLY

A convenient starting point for the present discussion of the possibility of introducing imperfectly competitive elements into the perfectly competitive Walrasian system is the long-run model consisting of equations $(11.1\text{-}1) - (11.1\text{-}9)$ and (11.1-19) using the equations with starred numbers where appropriate. As noted in the previous section, this is a determinate system. To adjust the model to the required context, assume that in all industries not singled out for special attention below, firms are identical and production is subject to constant returns to scale under perfectly competitive conditions. In those industries, then, the starred-numbered equations apply and, according to the discussion

---

[11] This conclusion, of course, is applicable to both approaches to long-run perfect competition — but only with respect to maximum profit. For in either case, were the firm, through experimentation, to give up its illusory belief in its subjective marginal revenue, and abandon (11.1-20) in favor of (11.1-21), the output it produces would change and its profit would surely rise. However, the latter increase would only be temporary since the entry of new firms would drive profit back to zero.

surrounding equation (11.1-20), firms in them necessarily produce where marginal cost equals price. For the firms on which subsequent analysis focuses, no modifications in the original equations of (11.1-1) – (11.1-9) and (11.1-19) are introduced (except as required by the starred equations employed for the perfectly competitive firms), and no extra restrictions on production functions are invoked for now. Of course, the markets in which these firms sell their outputs must exhibit "imperfections" if distance from perfect competition is to be maintained. Clearly equations (11.1-1) – (11.1-9) and (11.1-19) impose no profit-maximizing conditions on these latter firms. The issue of whether modifications could and should be introduced which would permit them to be thought of as profit maximizers still has to be resolved.

For concreteness, suppose industry 1 contains a single firm. Then $L_1 = 1$ and $x_1 = x_{11}$. This firm buys its inputs in perfectly competitive markets and sells its output as a monopolist.[12] (All other industries are perfectly competitive as indicated above.) Because monopoly profit tends to persist in the long run, the first zero-profit condition of (11.1-19), namely,

$$\pi_{11} = 0, \tag{11.2-1}$$

no longer seems appropriate. But dropping it deprives the model (11.1-1) – (11.1-9) and (11.1-19), adjusted as indicated above, of one of its equations.

To find a replacement, it is natural to turn to marginal revenue and marginal cost. From (11.1-14) and the assumption that all firms are identical within industries, the marginal revenue of firm 1,1 is

$$MR^{11}(\chi) = p_1 + x_{11} \sum_{\mu=1}^{I} \left(\frac{\partial p_1}{\partial x_{\mu 1}} L_\mu \right) \left(\frac{dx_{\mu 1}}{dx_{11}} \right), \tag{11.2-2}$$

where

$$\frac{\partial p_1}{\partial x_{\mu 1}} = \frac{\partial H^{-1^1}(x_{11}, x_{21} L_2, \ldots, x_{I1} L_I, \bar{M})}{\partial x_{\mu \sigma}},$$

and

$$\frac{dx_{\mu 1}}{dx_{11}} = \frac{d\zeta^{(\mu 1)(11)}(x_{11})}{dx_{11}}, \quad \mu \neq 1.$$

Thus MR^{11} cannot be determined until the reaction functions $\zeta^{(\mu 1)(11)}$ are

---

[12]   There are reasons why monopolies exist. For example, a firm may have unassailable patent rights, it may be the sole owner of a particular resource, or the technology of the industry may be such that one "large" firm is the most efficient means of producing the industry's output.

found. But it may be possible to secure the latter from the perfectly competitive sector as described in the discussion following equation (11.1-17). For in the present context, setting $\sigma = 1$ in (11.1-17) gives

$$MC^{\mu 1}(r, x_{\mu 1}) = H^{-1^\mu}(x_{11}, x_{21}L_2, \ldots, x_{I1}L_I, \bar{M}), \quad \mu = 2, \ldots, I.$$

With r eliminated, this defines a system of $I - 1$ independent equations in I unknowns. If these equations can be solved to express each $x_{\mu 1}$, where $\mu \neq 1$, as a function of x_{11}, then upon resolution, the result is the reaction functions $\zeta^{(\mu 1)(11)}$ with which to compute MR^{11}. Therefore (11.2-1) can be replaced by (11.2-2), the definition of MC^{11} from (11.1-10) with $b_{11} = 0$, and the first-order profit-maximization condition

$$MR^{11}(\chi) = MC^{11}(r, x_{11}). \tag{11.2-3}$$

As in Section 11.1, one must also assume that (where equation (11.2-3) holds) profit is nonnegative, and increasing x_{11} raises marginal cost faster than marginal revenue (see Exercise 11.4). With these two extra variables (that is, the monopolist's marginal revenue and marginal cost) and three extra equations, the model once again is determinate. It is assumed uniquely solvable. The standard analysis of monopoly behavior is relevant and will be considered shortly.

When reaction functions cannot be inferred from the perfectly competitive sector, independent specifications of them usually become necessary. Otherwise MR^{11} cannot be described. Alternatively, one might suppose that the interactive effects between the monopoly and all other firms offset each other, or

$$\sum_{\mu=2}^{I} \left(\frac{\partial p_1}{\partial x_{\mu 1}} L_\mu \right) \left(\frac{dx_{\mu 1}}{dx_{11}} \right) = 0, \tag{11.2-4}$$

so that the monopolist's marginal revenue reduces to

$$MR^{11}(\chi) = p_1 + x_{11} \frac{\partial p_1}{\partial x_{11}}. \tag{11.2-5}$$

In this case, then, knowledge of reaction functions is not needed to calculate MR^{11}. Clearly (11.2-4) is a highly specific restriction which cannot be expected to arise in many situations. It essentially says that the reactions of all perfectly competitive firms to changes in the monopolist's output exactly cancel each other out. But when valid, (11.2-4) also permits application of the standard analysis for understanding monopoly behavior (as already noted, this analysis is presented later on) even if the relevant reaction functions are unobtainable.

Returning to the more general framework in which (11.2-4) need not hold but in which reaction functions are still determined by the perfectly competitive sector, it is too much to expect the monopolist to know the reaction functions $\zeta^{(\mu 1)(11)}$ of all firms $\mu,1$ in the economy. Nor is he likely to know very much about the inverse demand relation

$$p_1 = H^{-1^1}(x_{11}, x_{21}L_2, \ldots, x_{I1}L_I, \bar{M}).$$

Thus the question of how the monopolist determines MR^{11} so that he can actually equate marginal cost and marginal revenue still needs to be answered. (Recall that the resolution of this problem under perfect competition [Section 11.1] was based on the distinction between subjective and objective [or true] marginal revenue. The former was determined by the firm's incorrect belief that its behavior had no repercussion anywhere in the economy. Hence the firm could say that its "marginal revenue" [actually, its subjective marginal revenue] was identical to market price. To determine its "profit-maximizing" output, it could then equate price, instead of its objective marginal revenue, to marginal cost.) Now, unlike the perfect competitor, the monopolist does not suffer from the delusion that his behavior has no impact on market prices and quantities. Moreover, he is always able to alter his output price, allow the economy to adjust, and observe his new sales. Such an experiment would permit the monopolist to formulate beliefs about the marginal revenue function facing him and thereby determine his subjective marginal revenue, *i.e.*, the marginal revenue he thinks he faces, $SMR^{11}(\chi)$. Under present assumptions, all other firms react to the monopolist's price change according to the reaction functions determined above. Therefore, as long as none of the model's given parameters or functions shift, the outcome of the experiment must be consistent with the objective marginal revenue function formulated in (11.2-2), that is,

$$SMR^{11}(\chi) = MR^{11}(\chi). \tag{11.2-6}$$

To follow the rule of (11.2-3), then, the monopolist need equate only subjective marginal revenue with marginal cost. Not only does he think he is maximizing his profit, but at equilibrium he actually succeeds in doing so.

The nature of the monopolist's experiment deserves a more detailed description. Begin by placing the economy at equilibrium on the transformation surface. To experiment, the monopolist alters his output price, waits for the economy to return to equilibrium, and notes his new output. In the interim, input prices, output prices other than the monopolist's price, and input and output quantities adjust. The ratio of the monopolist's increment in total revenue to the change in his output resulting from the experiment provides an approximation of his marginal revenue. The marginal revenue itself is the limit of this ratio as the change in price, and hence output, becomes small. Throughout the adjustment to the new equilibrium, all firms are assumed to be minimizing cost (equations (11.1-8) or (11.1-8*)) and exhausting input supplies (equations (11.1-3)). Hence the economy is on its transformation surface at all times. An experiment, therefore, can be regarded as a movement over the transformation surface generated by a small modification of the monopolist's price.

It is important to emphasize that the monopolist must experiment if he is to act rationally. There is simply no other way for him to obtain sufficient information about his marginal revenue so as to be able to maximize profit. Therefore, in order for the model to describe the actual long-run equilibrium or stationary state, the results of the monopolist's experiments must lead him to the same behavior as characterized by the model. This can only happen if (11.2-6) is satisfied. Furthermore, as long as equilibria are identified with observations in the real economy, the dynamic workings out of such experiments cannot be seen. The experimental process, then, plays much the same role here as the auctioneer story described earlier does in the context of Chapters 7-10. Although hidden from view, both still provide insight into the mechanism for achieving equilibrium.

An illustration of a two-output economy in which industry 1 is organized as a monopoly and industry 2 is perfectly competitive appears in Figure 11.1. (To enhance the distinction between industries, the representative firm in industry 2 is indicated by the symbol ℓ rather than 1.) Equilibrium occurs at δ where a community indifference curve w^H (assumed to exist for purposes of the diagram only) intersects but is not tangent to the transformation curve. The slope of the former is the negative of the price ratio, that of the latter is the negative of the ratio of marginal costs. These ratios cannot be the same because marginal cost equals price in one industry but not in the other. The competitive solution (recall Figure 8.3a) would be at, say, γ where a community indifference curve (not pictured) is tangent to the transformation curve. Exercise 11.5 provides a mathematical example.

With two monopolies, say, $L_1 = L_2 = 1$, $x_1 = x_{11}$, and $x_2 = x_{21}$, the system of equations needed to generate the reaction functions of the perfectly competitive firms is (11.1-17) altered along lines suggested previously and where $\mu = 3, \ldots, I$. As before, suppose r can be expressed as a function of the output of all firms. This leaves the modified (11.1-17) with only $I - 2$ equations but still I variables. Solving (under the assumption that solutions exist) gives $x_{\mu 1}$ as a function of both x_{11}, and x_{21}:

$$x_{\mu 1} = \xi^{\mu 1}(x_{11}, x_{21}), \quad \mu = 3, \ldots, I. \qquad (11.2\text{-}7)$$

Thus it is possible only to determine how the perfectly competitive firms react to both monopolists simultaneously. Without further hypotheses concerning the ways in which the monopolists interact in response to each other, there are not enough equations to specify the reaction functions $\zeta^{(\mu 1)(11)}$ and $\zeta^{(\mu 1)(21)}$ for any $\mu \neq 1, 2$. Hence $MR^{11}(\chi)$ and $MR^{21}(\chi)$ cannot be calculated.

One way to add further restrictions to the model so that reaction functions can be obtained is to assume that the monopolists do not react to each other at all. Thus consider a fixed vector $(\overline{x}_{11}, \overline{x}_{21})$ to be determined later and define

$$\zeta^{(21)(11)}(x_{11}) = \overline{x}_{21},$$

$$\zeta^{(11)(21)}(x_{21}) = \overline{x}_{11},$$
(11.2-8)

and

$$\zeta^{(\mu 1)(11)}(x_{11}) = \xi^{\mu 1}(x_{11}, \overline{x}_{21}),$$

$$\zeta^{(\mu 1)(21)}(x_{21}) = \xi^{\mu 1}(\overline{x}_{11}, x_{21}),$$
(11.2-9)

where the $\xi^{\mu 1}$ are obtained from (11.2-7) and $\mu = 3, \ldots, I$. Provided $(\overline{x}_{11}, \overline{x}_{21})$ remains fixed, all reaction functions $\zeta^{(\mu 1)(11)}$ and $\zeta^{(\mu 1)(21)}$, and hence $MR^{11}(\chi)$

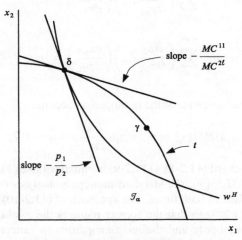

Figure 11.1 Fixed-factor-supply model with industry 1 a monopoly and industry 2 perfectly competitive

and $MR^{21}(\chi)$ are secured. Thus the relations

$$\pi_{11} = 0,$$

$$\pi_{12} = 0,$$

in the model (11.1-1) − (11.1-9) and (11.1-19) using equations with starred numbers in perfectly competitive industries can be replaced by

$$x_{\mu 1} = \overline{x}_{\mu 1}, \quad \mu = 1, 2,$$

$$MR^{\mu 1}(\chi) = MC^{\mu 1}(r, x_{\mu 1}), \quad \mu = 1, 2,$$

and the appropriate definitions of marginal cost (11.1-10) with $b_{11} = b_{21} = 0$ and marginal revenue (11.2-2). The deficit of two equations (which arises upon discarding the monopolists' zero-profit conditions) is made up by adding these eight equations and the six variables consisting of the marginal costs and marginal revenues of each monopolist, and $\overline{x}_{11}$ and $\overline{x}_{21}$. The fixed vector $(\overline{x}_{11}, \overline{x}_{21})$, therefore, is found as part of the equilibrium or solution (assumed to exist) of the system.

The alternative procedure, which avoids reaction functions (recall the single monopoly case and equation (11.2-4)) is to add the further constraints

$$\sum_{\mu=2}^{I} \left(\frac{\partial p_1}{\partial x_{\mu 1}} L_\mu \right) \left(\frac{dx_{\mu 1}}{dx_{11}} \right) = 0,$$

$$\sum_{\substack{\mu=1 \\ \mu \neq 2}}^{I} \left(\frac{\partial p_2}{\partial x_{\mu 1}} L_\mu \right) \left(\frac{dx_{\mu 1}}{dx_{21}} \right) = 0.$$

(11.2-10)

Then the marginal revenues of the monopolists become

$$MR^{\mu 1}(\chi) = p_\mu + x_{\mu 1} \frac{\partial p_\mu}{\partial x_{\mu 1}}, \quad \mu = 1, 2,$$

and, as with the use of (11.2-8) − (11.2-9) in equations like (11.2-2) to calculate $MR^{11}(\chi)$ and $MR^{21}(\chi)$, the standard monopoly analysis (discussed below) can now be applied to both firms. The approach of (11.2-10) differs from that of (11.2-8) − (11.2-9) in that the former requires the totality of interactions between each monopoly and the remaining firms to cancel themselves out, whereas the latter rests on an absence of reaction of each monopoly to the other.

When there are three or more monopolists, an argument similar to either of those described above could be employed to replace the appropriate zero-profit conditions in (11.1-19) with the corresponding first-order profit-maximization equalities

$$MR^{i\ell}(\chi) = MC^{i\ell}(r, x_{i\ell}).$$

Still, neither approach is entirely satisfactory as long as the number of monopolists is larger than one. For expanding the number of equations in (10.2-10) would seem to distance the analysis further and further from reality. And unease with respect to the alternative method arises for at least two reasons.

First, the assumption (that is, equations (11.2-8)) that monopoly outputs do not vary in reaction to modifications in other monopolists' prices, and hence outputs, even if all outputs already rest at equilibrium values, is improbable. It is usually true that each monopolist can experiment alone to determine his marginal revenue. (The case in which isolated experimentation is not possible arises momentarily.) For example, in the two-monopoly situation, let the fixed equilibrium outputs be $(\overline{x}_{11}, \overline{x}_{21})$. Firm 1,1 can experiment by changing its price p_1. With $\overline{x}_{21}$ frozen and the rest of the economy adjusting, 1,1 would calculate its marginal revenue and discover that its profit-maximizing position is back at $\overline{x}_{11}$ with the original price. Firm 2,2 can experiment similarly and would arrive at an analogous conclusion. Now, according to (11.2-8) and (11.2-9), both firms are not permitted to alter outputs simultaneously. (Although equations (11.2-7) allow such simultaneous variation in relation to the perfectly competitive sector by providing reactions of the perfectly competitive firms to each (x_{11}, x_{21}), these equations have already been shown to be insufficient for use in the model.) But when $x_{11}(= x_1)$ changes in response to the experimental modification in p_1, the value of

$$H^{-1^2}(x_{11}L_1, x_{21}, x_1L_3, \ldots, x_{I1}L_I, \bar{M})$$

varies. Consequently, so does the value of $MR^{21}(\chi)$ from (11.1-14). Moreover, to the extent that movements along the transformation surface (caused by the experimenting of firm 1,1) induce modifications in input prices (recall Section 8.2), the value of $MC^{21}(r, x_{21})$ also changes. Marginal cost, then, should equal marginal revenue at a different output. In other words, to be consistent with the maximization assumptions of the model, firm 2,2 must alter $\overline{x}_{21}$. Thus, on one hand, $\overline{x}_{21}$ has to remain fixed during 1,1's experiment; on the other hand, profit maximization says it cannot. The only way to avoid such an internal contradiction is to require that:

(11.2-11)   Either (i) $MR^{21}(\chi)$ is independent of x_{11}, and $x_{31}, \ldots, x_{I1}$, and $MC^{21}(r, x_{21})$ is independent of r, or (ii) insofar as influencing $\overline{x}_{21}$, is concerned, all changes in $x_{11}, x_{31}, \ldots, x_{I1}$ and r occurring from all experiments performed by firm 1,1 cancel each other out.

This requirement is stronger than that imposed in the second equation of (11.2-10). A similar condition is needed for firm 1,1. It is of course always possible that such independence might occasionally occur. But as a general hypothesis to maintain the internal consistency of the model, (11.2-11) leaves something to be desired. Furthermore, as the number of monopolies increases, the assumption that a restriction like (11.2-11) holds for each one of them becomes less and less plausible.

A second reason for uneasiness with the above replacement, for monopolies, of zero-profit conditions with marginal-revenue-equals-marginal-cost conditions is that logical deficiencies arise when all firms are monopolists. In this circumstance no equations from the perfectly competitive sector can be solved as a preliminary step in obtaining reaction functions because such a sector does not exist. Of course reaction functions would still be determined as in (11.2-8) by fixing all outputs at appropriate equilibrium values. But then isolated experimentation by firms to discover their marginal revenues and optimal behavior would no longer be possible. One firm could not change its price, and hence output, while the output of all others remained fixed without forcing the economy off of its transformation surface. As indicated earlier, the latter is prohibited by (11.1-3) and the appropriate equations from (11.1-8) and (11.1-8*). Thus the ability of firms to obtain the information they need to behave rationally (no firm, recall, can determine its marginal revenue without experimentation) breaks down.

One approach that avoids these difficulties has been suggested by Pearce [11]. To summarize it here, the idea is to go back to the model consisting of (11.1-1) – (11.1-9) and the zero-profit conditions (11.1-19), with constant returns to scale production functions and identical firms in perfectly competitive industries. Recall that, for the latter industries, the equations of (11.1-1) – (11.1-9) are replaced by those with starred numbers. The zero-profit condition in either monopoly or perfectly competitive cases can then be interpreted as follows: All revenues accruing to firms are divided among the factors of production. One of these factors is identified as a "controlling" factor, that is, as the decision-making element in every firm. The role of the controlling factor within firms is to minimize cost. Its rate of return in a firm is the price per unit quantity of the controlling factor employed in that firm. Because the market equalizes prices of the same marketable goods across the economy, the rate of return to the controlling factor is the same everywhere. Under certain assumptions, this means that even if profits vanish the controlling factor is still allocating its units so as to maximize its total return over all employments. Thus long-run equilibrium is determined by the efforts of the controlling factor to minimize cost within firms and maximize its aggregate return across them. Marginal revenue and profit maximization as described above become irrelevant and experimentation unnecessary.

Turning now to the standard analysis of isolated monopoly behavior, suppose as before that firm 1,1 is the monopolist while all other industries are perfectly competitive. The monopolist's production function, remember, is not required to exhibit constant returns to scale. The relationship between the price the monopolist charges and his sales is obtained by substituting (11.1-9) into the first inverse demand equation of (11.1-12*) so that

$$p_1 = H^{-1^1}(x_{11}, x_{21}L_2, \ldots, x_{I1}L_I, \bar{M}),$$

and then replacing the $x_{\mu 1}$ by the reaction functions $\zeta^{(\mu 1)(11)}$ for all $\mu \neq 1$. This results in the function

$$p_1 = \mathcal{H}(x_{11}), \tag{11.2-12}$$

where the usual superscript on $\mathcal{H}$ is dropped for convenience and $\bar{M}$ is subsumed in the functional symbol $\mathcal{H}$. Frequently $\mathcal{H}$ is referred to as the "demand function" facing the monopolist. His marginal revenue is the derivative of the total revenue function $x_{11}\mathcal{H}(x_{11})$:

$$MR(x_{11}) = \mathcal{H}(x_{11}) + x_{11}\frac{d\mathcal{H}(x_{11})}{dx_{11}}, \tag{11.2-13}$$

where MR has become a function of a single variable and its superscripts discarded. Of course (11.2-13) could also be obtained by substituting the same reaction functions into (11.2-2). When reaction functions are unspecified, marginal revenue can still be written as in (11.2-13) upon invoking either (11.2-4) — the assumption that cancels out interactions — or the partial-equilibrium requirement that all $x_{\mu 1}$ are fixed for $\mu \neq 1$, in which case the derivatives of the output reaction functions $d\zeta^{(\mu 1)(11)}/dx_{11} = 0$ for every $\mu \neq 1$ and, as a result, (11.2-4) is again satisfied.

Imposing the appropriate restrictions on the monopolist's production function and applying the results of Section 5.1 in the present format (Exercise

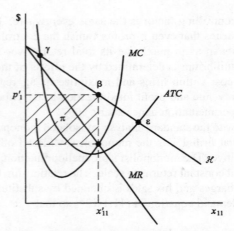

Figure 11.2 Profit maximization under monopoly

11.4), profit is maximized when output is produced so that[13]

$$MR(x_{11}) = MC(r, x_{11}), \tag{11.2-14}$$

where $r = (r_1, \ldots, r_J)$. (Here the superscripts are excluded from the MC notation.) The monopolist's output supply function is obtained by solving (11.2-14) for x_{11} as a function of r. An explicit representation of that solution appears in (11.2-18) below. The typical geometric picture associated with monopoly is drawn in Figure 11.2, where dollars are measured on the vertical axis and quantities of output appear on the horizontal. The long-run average total cost curve is of the Viner type, and the demand curve $\mathcal{H}$ is linear. Long-run marginal cost equals marginal revenue over the output x'_{11}, and the monopolist sets his price at p'_1. Monopoly profit — the shaded area — is positive and persists in the long run.

To obtain the monopolist's input demand functions it is convenient to follow the "alternative route" of Section 5.1 and think of profit as a function of inputs. Thus if $TR(x_{11})$ denotes the total revenue function,

$$TR(x_{11}) = x_{11}\mathcal{H}(x_{11}),$$

---

[13] Cournot [6, p. 57] achieved a similar result in 1838.

and if the production function is written

$$x_{11} = f(y_{11}),\qquad\qquad (11.2\text{-}15)$$

where $y_{11} = (y_{111}, \ldots, y_{11J})$ and the superscripts on f are deleted, then as in (5.1-10),

$$\pi(y_{11}) = TR(f(y_{11})) - r \cdot y_{11}.$$

(Recall there are no fixed costs in the long run.) Maximum profit occurs where the partial derivatives of π with respect to every y_{11j} are zero, or

$$[MR(f(y_{11}))]\,[f_j(y_{11})] = r_j, \quad j = 1, \ldots, J. \qquad (11.2\text{-}16)$$

Clearly (11.2-16) is the generalization of (5.1-11) to the case in which marginal revenue need not equal price. Provided the appropriate Jacobian is nonvanishing,[14] input demand functions

$$y_{11j} = g^j(r), \quad j = 1, \ldots, J, \qquad\qquad (11.2\text{-}17)$$

arise as the solution of (11.2-16). Substitution of (11.2-17) into the production function (11.2-15) yields the output supply function earlier derived from (11.2-4):

$$x_{11} = g^{J+1}(r). \qquad\qquad (11.2\text{-}18)$$

It is important to notice that neither the output supply function (11.2-18) nor the input demand functions (11.2-17) depend on output price. This reflects the fact that output price is chosen by the monopolist according to the demand function (11.2-12) after his profit-maximizing output has been determined. It follows that there can be no output supply curve in the usual sense of the term *i.e.*, that relates outputs supplied to output prices determined independently by the market. Once the demand function facing the monopolist is known and the input prices r are given by the perfectly competitive input markets, output supply is set. Changes in that supply can occur only through modifications in $\mathcal{H}$, f, and r.

It is also apparent (this point has come up earlier) that there are implicit restrictions on the demand function $\mathcal{H}$ in relation to input prices r and the production function f which ensure that profit is nonnegative at maximum output. Otherwise the monopolist would not produce at all in the long run. (See Exercise 11.7.) These conditions along with other properties of the g^j are left to the reader.

---

[14]   Apostol [1, p. 372]. See the discussion of the inverse function theorem of appendix Section A.4.

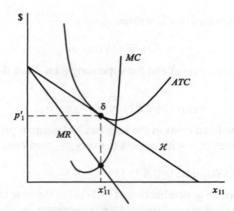

Figure 11.3 Profit maximization under
monopoly with zero profit

Of course, if the marginal-cost-equals-marginal-revenue condition (11.2-14) is discarded in favor of

$$\pi_{11} = 0,$$

then the monopoly solution would be at a point such as γ or ε in Figure 11.2 rather than at β. Hence the monopolist's demand and supply functions would be different from those discussed above. Moreover, if, as in Figure 11.2, there were more than one intersection of the demand curve, $\mathcal{H}$, and the (long-run) average total cost curve, ATC, then the solution would not be unique. The only way that the monopolist could simultaneously maximize profit (that is, equate marginal cost with marginal revenue) and have $\pi_{11} = 0$ is in the special case in which $\mathcal{H}$ happens to be tangent to ATC as in Figure 11.3. Long-run equilibrium in Figure 11.3 occurs at δ. Clearly the situation cannot be expected to arise in general.[15]

In constant-returns-to-scale cases, the long-run economic outcome of an industry organized as a monopoly may be compared with that of the identical industry structured perfectly competitively. Because the same technology is available to everyone, firms in both instances have identical production functions and hence the same horizontal, long-run average cost curve (recall Table 4.1 and equation (5.1-22)). The latter is coincident with the long-run mar-

---

[15]   Of course, if normal profit were included in long-run total cost (a possibility that has been mentioned earlier and will be taken up subsequently), then the long-run equilibrium position at δ in Figure 11.3 would arise more commonly.

ginal cost curve corresponding to it. Assume the perfectly competitive firms construct plants of optimal size for an output determined by dividing the aggregate output on the market by the number of firms in the industry. These firms, then, produce with plants of a much smaller size than that of an industry-wide monopolist. Moreover, the short-run average total cost curves associated with those plants are all tangent to the long-run average cost curve at the minimum points of the former (as in Exercise 5.11). When the industry is condensed into a monopoly, there is one (much larger) optimum plant (as determined by long-run profit maximization in relation to the market as a whole) whose short-run average total cost curve is also tangent to the same horizontal, long-run average cost curve at its minimum point. Now in the long run, the perfectly competitive outcome requires enough firms in the industry for zero profit and price equal to minimum long-run average cost,[16] whereas the monopoly solution, with marginal revenue equalling long-run marginal cost, has nonnegative profit and price greater than minimum long-run average cost. The market demand function is the same in either circumstance. Therefore long-run equilibrium price would have to be higher and long-run equilibrium output smaller under monopoly.

With respect to the economy as a whole, to make a similar comparison between the two competitive structures of a single industry requires examination of the effects on equilibrium in the complete, economy-wide model. With the two-industry world, a diagram such as Figure 11.1 would be relevant. In Figure 11.1, recall, γ indicates the perfectly competitive equilibrium and δ the equilibrium when one industry is organized as a monopoly. Along with the case of the isolated industry comparison above, industry production functions before and after the reorganization of the one industry into a monopoly are identical. Also w^H is an indifference curve of a community utility function assumed to exist only for purposes of the diagram. (Remember from Section 8.3 that the community utility function may or may not have anything to say about economic welfare.) Once γ and δ are known, the differences in market quantities of goods and the price ratio can be determined. (As the example of Exercise 11.5 shows, these differences cannot be predicted in advance of solving the relevant system of equations to obtain solution values. Unlike the previous isolated industry comparison, conversion of one industry into a monopoly is not always accompanied by a rise in that industry's price and a fall in its output.) If the community utility function were also a welfare function (Section 12.1), then it would follow that welfare is higher at γ where both industries are perfectly competitive.

---

[16]   Here, all points on the long-run average cost curve are minimum points.

444   IMPERFECT COMPETITION

11.3   OTHER FORMS OF IMPERFECT COMPETITION

The same method of introducing monopoly into the general model of Section 11.1 can be applied to other forms of imperfect competition as well. Of course, each competitive form has its own peculiarities.

Consider an economy with only one monopolistically competitive industry. Assume the remaining industries are all perfectly competitive. Now a firm in a monopolistically competitive industry is usually thought of as a "monopolist" producing its own distinct product.[17] Clearly, this notion has to be reinterpreted to fit the equations of (11.1-1) and (11.1-7) associated with that industry. It would not make sense to add up the heterogeneous outputs of each firm in calculating market quantity and then speak of only one price and one market demand function derived from utility maximization for the industry's product. The model of this chapter does not permit a commodity and its price to be, at the same time, many goods with many prices. But there is nothing wrong with supposing that the individual firm believes its product to be different from that of all competitors when in fact, and in the minds of consumers, it is not, and, under the assumptions of the previous section, employ the model consisting of (11.1-1) – (11.1-9) and (11.1-19) using the equations with starred numbers for perfectly competitive industries. Of course (11.1-19) has to be modified to account for more than one firm in the monopolistically competitive industry. (The number of firms in that industry is, for now, taken as a fixed parameter.) Long-run equilibrium therefore is determined. Even though firms within the monopolistically competitive industry need not be attempting to charge the same price as their competitors, at equilibrium they wind up doing so.

It should be pointed out that, apart from the unreality introduced by assuming that the products in a monopolistically competitive industry are actually homogeneous, there is the further problem that if firms believe their products to be distinct, they have a strong incentive to advertise and incur other marketing costs. But, of course, issues like these also have to be ignored to insert a monopolisitically competitive industry into the framework of the Walrasian system of Section 11.1.

Substitution of marginal revenue equals marginal cost for the zero-profit condition in one or more firms in the monopolistically competitive industry requires taking into account the fact that, in addition to their illusions about

---

[17]   The application of the phrase "monopolistic competition" in this situation is due to Chamberlin [5, p. 9]. Robinson took monopolistic competition to be a special case of what she referred to as "monopoly" [13, pp. 5,6].

product differentiation, firms also think (incorrectly) that their price and output decisions do not summon reactions by other firms within and outside of their industry. In this respect they are like perfect competitors. More precisely, firm ℓ in industry i (the monopolistically competitive industry) believes the actual demand function it faces to be

$$p_i = SD^{i\ell}(x_{i\ell}),$$

where $SD^{i\ell}$ is called the (inverse) *subjective demand function*[18] of firm $i\ell$. The way the firm arrives at a particular subjective demand function is not considered here. The subjective demand function is taken as given, much as the subjective marginal revenue of the perfectly competitive firm is assumed as a fact. Because of the firm's unshakable confidence in its subjective demand function, experimentation by the firm to discover its marginal revenue is unnecessary. But, again like the perfect competitor, actual experimentation would prove this confidence misplaced. Of course firm $i\ell$'s subjective marginal revenue function is the derivative of $x_{i\ell}SD^{i\ell}(x_{i\ell})$ or

$$SMR^{i\ell}(x_{i\ell}) = SD^{i\ell}(x_{i\ell}) + x_{i\ell}\frac{dSD^{i\ell}(x_{i\ell})}{dx_{i\ell}}, \qquad (11.3\text{-}1)$$

assuming $SD^{i\ell}$ to be differentiable. Thus the zero-profit condition of each monopolistically competitive firm can be replaced by adding first the marginal-cost and subjective-marginal-revenue variables and then the definitions of marginal cost (11.1-10) with $b_{i\ell} = 0$ and subjective marginal revenue (11.3-1), and the apparently profit-maximizing relations

$$SMR^{i\ell}(x_{i\ell}) = MC^{i\ell}(r, x_{i\ell}), \qquad \ell = 1,\ldots,L_i.$$

Once again the system is determinate.

   A diagrammatic representation of the behavior of firm $i\ell$ is given in Figure 11.4(a). It is similar to Figure 11.2 except for new labels on the demand and marginal revenue curves. At equilibrium, all firms sell their "differentiated" output at the same price. Also at equilibrium, firms are assumed to sell the output they expect to sell (namely, $x'_{i\ell}$ in Figure 11.4(a)) at the equilibrium price (p'_i in Figure 11.4(a)). Otherwise equilibrium could not exist. Note, however, that to suppose firms' beliefs about the relation between price and quantity are correct at equilibrium does not imply that the $SD^{i\ell}$ themselves are correct, but only that in Figue 11.4(a), say, $SD^{i\ell}$ goes through the point

---

[18]   Although not originating with him, the concept of subject demand curve (function) seems to have been first studied by Weintraub [17].

β in such a way that $SMR^{i\ell}$ intersects $MC^{i\ell}$ at $x'_{i\ell}$. In fact, the $SD^{i\ell}$ cannot be accurate reflections of the true demand functions facing firms $i\ell$ because, among other things, they do not take into account other firms' reaction functions.

Now as usual, the reactions of the perfectly competitive sector to the out-

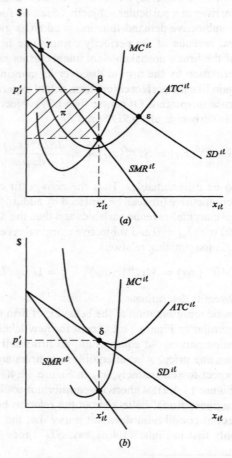

Figure 11.4 Profit maximization under monopolistic competition: (*a*) with positive profit; (*b*) with zero profit

puts of all monopolistically competitive firms simultaneously (equation (11.2-7) when there are two such firms) are found by solving an appropriate version of (11.1-17). Accordingly, to determine all reaction functions needed in calculating the objective (true) demand function $\mathcal{H}^{i\ell}$ facing any one firm (that is, equation (11.2-12)) requires further specification of those reaction functions of all other monopolistic firms in the industry. If this is not possible, the path suggested by (11.2-8) and (11.2-9) could be followed. Alternatively, assumptions like (11.2-10) could be invoked. In any of these cases, the objective marginal revenue, $MR^{i\ell}(\chi)$, is secured. Because, in general,

$$SMR^{i\ell}(x_{i\ell}) \neq MR^{i\ell}(\chi),$$

even though the firm thinks it is maximizing its profits, it could do better by casting aside its faith in its subjective demand function.

The expansion of monopolistic competition to more than one industry follows a similar pattern. And unlike monopoly situations which demand that firms experiment, the absence of experimentation in monopolistically competitive environments means that there is no logical limitation to supposing that every firm in the economy is a monopolistic competitor equating marginal cost with subjective marginal revenue. But there is a problem in throwing away even one of the zero-profit conditions that this approach requires. For monopolistically competitive industries have traditionally been defined so as to permit the long-run free entry of new firms or the expansion of existing firms when profits are positive. New firms, naturally, reduce market shares and hence profits of existing firms. Expansion of the market shares of existing firms has the same effect. Therefore, long-run equilibrium should be at δ in Figure 11.4(b) where profit vanishes,[19] not at β in Figure 11.4(a). Except in unusual circumstances, however, to obtain the equilibrium of Figure 11.4(b) necessitates inclusion in the model of both marginal-cost-equals-subjective-marginal-revenue and zero-profit conditions, and this plus (11.1-1) – (11.1-9) appropriately modified by using the relevant equations with starred numbers, overdetermines the system. (The numbers of firms in the monopolistically competitive industries are fixed parameters.) With the number of equations larger than the number of variables, there cannot, as a rule, exist a solution satisfying all equations simultaneously. Thus, to understand long-run monopolistic competition within the framework of the general model given here, either the zero-profit condition or the equality of marginal cost and revenue must be discarded. As a representation of isolated long-run firm behavior under monopolistic competition, then, Figure 11.4(b) is not ordinarily consistent with the model of (11.1-1) – (11.1-

---

[19]   An argument similar to that of n. 11 on p. 430 applies here.

9) and (11.1-19) modified as indicated above. Zero profit can be obtained by excluding marginal cost equals subjective marginal revenue (such an approach was suggested for the case of monopoly in the last section), but there is no way of knowing in general if the resulting long-run equilibrium lies at, say, γ or ε in Figure 11.4(a) or at δ in Figure 11.4(b).

The above problem can be avoided by taking the number of firms in monopolistically competitive industries, L_i, to be determined, along with the other variables, at long-run equilibrium, and by adding the assumption that all firms in such industries are identical. Thus, in effect, only one marginal-cost-equals-subjective-marginal-revenue condition and one zero-profit condition are tacked on to the appropriately modified $(11.1\text{-}1) - (11.1\text{-}9)$ for each monopolistically competitive industry and, with the corresponding L_i's changed from parameters to variables, the system becomes determinate. Long-run equilibrium for the monopolistically competitive firm must now arise at a point such as δ in Figure 11.4(b). However, not only does the identical-firm assumption ensure that all firms in a monopolistically competitive industry have the same production and cost functions, but it also requires that their subjective demand functions be the same — even though the product manufactured by each firm is believed (incorrectly) by that firm to be different from all other products in the industry. Hence this approach, too, is somewhat less than satisfying.

The analysis of oligopolistic markets, whether perfect (standardized output) or monopolistic (differentiated outputs), follows a similar pattern. For the same reason that firms in a monopolistically competitive industry cannot actually produce distinct goods and charge different prices, firms under monopolistic oligopoly also must, in reality, offer identical products and sell them at the same price. Hence as with monopolistic competition, monopolistic oligopoly has to be interpreted in terms of firms incorrectly believing that they each produce a different product. On the other hand, in both perfect and monopolistic oligopoly, firms know that their price and output decisions may affect all other firms in the economy. In this regard, they are more like the monopolist than the monopolistic and perfect competitor. As in the case of monopoly, the firm is able to discover its objective marginal revenue through experimentation (Section 11.2). Hence its objective and subjective marginal revenues are always the same.

From a mathematical point of view, no distinction is made here between modeling perfect and monopolistic oligopoly. Differences arise only in interpretation. Thus the demand function facing the monopolistically oligopolistic firm is wrongly thought by that firm to be the demand function for its unique product. Although the same firms, if perfectly oligopolistic, would not deceive themselves in this way, the equilibrium outcome is still the same. In the present framework, the illusions of monopolistic oligopoly have no impact.

To be concrete, suppose industry 1 is singled out as an oligopoly while all others are perfectly competitive. The assumption that all input markets are also perfectly competitive is continued. Matters are simplified by assuming that industry 1 has only two firms and thus may be referred to as a *duopoly*. As is the case with all forms of imperfect competition considered here, the long-run model (11.1-1) – (11.1-9) and (11.1-19) can be employed directly with separate zero-profit conditions for the duopolists and under the assumptions that the firms in each perfectly competitive industry are identical and have constant returns to scale production functions. Of course, the equations with starred numbers apply in the latter cases. The main issues to be considered are the effects and implications of replacing the zero-profit conditions for the two duopolists by the requirements that marginal costs and revenues be equal.

Assuming solutions exist and solving the relevant version of (11.1-17) for the perfectly competitive sector yields, as in (11.2-7), the reactions of that sector to the outputs of firms 1,1 and 1,2, that is, to x_{11} and x_{12}. Suppose these functions can be written as

$$x_{\mu 1} = \xi^{\mu 1}(x_{11} + x_{12}), \quad \mu = 1, \ldots, I. \tag{11.3-2}$$

Invoking the first inverse demand function of (11.1-12*), and then using (11.3-2), the inverse market demand function for good 1 reduces (as in equation (11.2-12)) to

$$p_1 = \mathcal{H}(x_{11} + x_{12}), \tag{11.3-3}$$

where $\bar{M}$ is once again subsumed in the functional symbol $\mathcal{H}$. If the reaction functions among the duopolists, namely,

$$x_{11} = \zeta^{(11)(12)}(x_{12}), \tag{11.3-4}$$

and

$$x_{12} = \zeta^{(12)(11)}(x_{11}), \tag{11.3-5}$$

were specified, then the demand functions facing each firm could be inferred upon substitution of (11.3-4) or (11.3-5) into (11.3-3). Moreover, these demand functions would be objective. Information about them can be obtained by experimentation provided firms experiment one at a time.

Now there are many different kinds of duopolistic (or oligopolistic) behavior. Each is defined by describing the exact nature of the reaction functions (11.3-4) and (11.3-5) and the way in which these reaction functions are used by the firms in maximizing profit. It is worth taking a look at several examples. Before doing so, however, note that the profit of each firm (that is, the difference between the firm's total revenue and total cost) can be expressed as a function of the outputs of both, or (subsuming r in appropriate functional symbols once again)

$$\pi^{1\ell}(x_{11}, x_{12}) = x_{1\ell}\mathcal{H}(x_{11} + x_{12}) - TC^{1\ell}(x_{1\ell}), \quad \ell = 1, 2. \qquad (11.3\text{-}6)$$

(In this notation, 1ℓ appears as a superscript on π rather than as a subscript because here π is thought of as a function instead of as a variable.) Hence in the absence of any relation between x_{11} and x_{12}, one firm can select its output so as to maximize its profit only when it knows the output of its competition. Assuming both firms behave in this way — that is, each observes the output of the other and then chooses its own according to the rule of profit maximization — x_{11} and x_{12} are determined by the equations

$$\frac{\partial \pi^{1\ell}(x_{11}, x_{12})}{\partial x_{1\ell}} = 0, \quad \ell = 1, 2. \qquad (11.3\text{-}7)$$

Clearly, each equation of (11.3-7) can be expressed as a statement of equality between marginal revenue and marginal cost.

The model of Cournot [6, pp. 79-84] takes (11.3-7), for $\ell = 1, 2$, to be precisely the reaction functions (11.3-4) and (11.3-5), respectively. Neither firm is assumed to know the reaction function of the other. Thus the zero-profit conditions for firms $1,1$ and $1,2$ in the system (11.1-1) – (11.1-9) and (11.1-19) using equations with starred numbers for perfectly competitive industries, can be replaced by (11.3-7) without giving up determinateness. It should be understood that firms do not have to believe that their competitors' output level is "permanently fixed" in order to satisfy the Cournot assumption. The only requirement is that each modifies its output according to (11.3-7) as the output of the other varies. The time-paths of outputs generated by these changes (from some given starting point) can be described by a system of dynamic equations not pursued here.[20] At long-run equilibrium (that is, at the solution of the determinate model described above) all change ceases and the system is at rest.

An alternative approach, associated with the name of von Stackelberg [16, pp. 194-195], is to think of one of the duopolists as a leader, say $1,1$, and the other, firm $1,2$, as a follower. The latter is assumed to obey her Cournot

---

[20]   See for example, Fisher [7].

reaction function

$$x_{12} = \zeta^{(12)(11)}(x_{11}), \tag{11.3-8}$$

obtained by solving (11.3-7) for $\ell = 2$. The leader, on the other hand, is hypothesized to have accurate knowledge of $\zeta^{(12)(11)}$, and to make use of it by choosing x_{11} so as to maximize

$$\pi^{11}\Big(x_{11}, \zeta^{(12)(11)}(x_{11})\Big).$$

Once again, (11.3-8) and the equation defining firm 1,1's reaction function, namely,

$$\frac{d\pi^{11}\Big(x_{11}, \zeta^{(12)(11)}(x_{11})\Big)}{dx_{11}} = 0,$$

can be substituted in place of the zero-profit conditions of firms 1,1 and 1,2.

The so-called *collusion* solution is based on the idea that the duopolists decide between themselves to act in unison in order to maximize their combined profit. That is, with

$$TR(x_{11} + x_{12}) = (x_{11} + x_{12})\mathcal{H}(x_{11} + x_{12})$$

from (11.3-3), x_{11} and x_{12} are selected so that

$$TR(x_{11} + x_{12}) - TC^{11}(x_{11}) - TC^{12}(x_{12})$$

achieves a maximum. At this maximum

$$MR(x_{11} + x_{12}) = MC^{1\ell}(x_{1\ell}), \quad \ell = 1, 2. \tag{11.3-9}$$

Hence the firms agree to produce up to the point at which their marginal costs are identical and equal to the market marginal revenue.

Note that all of the above efforts to eliminate zero-profit conditions in the general model (11.1-1) – (11.1-9) and (11.1-19) modified as indicated above, apply to a single oligopolistic (that is, duopolistic) industry. All remaining firms are assumed perfectly competitive. To be able to discard zero-profit conditions with more than one oligopoly, it would be necessary to specify, in addition to the output reactions of the firms within the oligopolistic industries to each other's output, the output reactions of firms in one oligopolistic industry to the outputs of firms in others. Alternatively, conditions such as (11.2-4) and (11.2-10), which ensure that all reactions coming in from outside the industry cancel each other out, could be assumed. The problems are similar to those discussed in the context of more than one monopoly in Section 11.2.

EXERCISES

11.1* Consider a model of a perfectly competitive economy with one factor, two outputs, and production functions

$$x_{i\ell} = f^{i\ell}(y_{i\ell}) = \sqrt{2L_i y_{i\ell}}, \quad \ell = 1, \dots, L_i, \quad i = 1, 2,$$

where $y_{i\ell}$ is the input used by firm $i\ell$. Assume for some scalar $a > 0$,

$$\sum_{i=1}^{2} \sum_{\ell=1}^{L_i} y_{i\ell} = a,$$

and normalize by setting $p_2 = 1$. Show that the derivative, say,

$$\frac{\partial p_1}{\partial x_{11}} \neq 0,$$

everywhere along the transformation curve. Hence the belief that the perfectly competitive firm cannot affect the market price of its output is incorrect — even at equilibrium.

11.2 Suppose a model of a perfectly competitive economy with two factors, two industries or outputs, and one firm in each industry, has production functions

$$f^i(y_{i1}, y_{i2}) = \sqrt{y_{i1} y_{i2}}, \quad i = 1, 2.$$

Let

$$y_{1j} + y_{2j} = a_j, \quad j = 1, 2,$$

where a_1 and a_2 are positive constants. Assume market demand functions for the two outputs are

$$x_i = \frac{M}{2p_i}, \quad i = 1, 2,$$

and normalize by setting $M = \bar{M} > 0$. Find the reaction functions indicating the reaction of each firm to the output of the other.

11.3 In a model of a perfectly competitive economy with two factors, three industries or outputs, and one firm in each industry, let the production functions be given by

$$f^1(y_{11}) = y_{11},$$

$$f^2(y_{22}) = \sqrt{y_{22}},$$

$$f^3(y_{31}, y_{32}) = \sqrt{y_{31}y_{32}}.$$

Suppose

$$y_{11} + y_{31} = a_1,$$

$$y_{22} + y_{32} = a_2,$$

for positive constants a_1 and a_2. Take market demand functions for the three outputs to be

$$x_i = \frac{\bar{M}}{3p_i}, \quad i = 1, 2, 3,$$

where $\bar{M} > 0$ is constant. Find the reaction function indicating the reaction of the firm in industry 1 to the output of the firm in industry 2.

11.4 With the scalar variable x representing an isolated monopolist's output, its profit function is

$$\pi(x) = TR(x) - TC(x).$$

Assume TR and TC are everywhere twice differentiable and state the first- and second-order necessary conditions for a particular value of x to maximize profit. (Recall the relevant discussion of Section 5.1.) Give sufficient conditions for an x to be a profit maximizer. Using the sufficient conditions show that imposition of a specific tax (Section 6.3) on the monopolist lowers his profit-maximizing output.

11.5 Consider a model of an economy with one consumer, two industries or outputs, one firm in each industry, and one input. Let the consumer's utility function be

$$u(x_1, x_2) = x_1 + \ln x_2,$$

and suppose firm production functions are

$$x_i = f^i(y_i) = y_i, \quad i = 1, 2,$$

where x_i varies over output quantities of good i, and y_i denotes the quantity of input used by industry (firm) i. (Note the violation of the boundary condition 2.3-4 for utility functions.) Denote the output prices by p_i, where $i = 1, 2$, and the input price by r. Take input supplies to be fixed:

$$y_1 + y_2 = a,$$

for some constant $a > 0$. Normalize by setting $M = \bar{M} > 0$. Assuming $a \geqslant 1$ and each firm to be perfectly competitive, find equilibrium values for x_1, y_1, x_2, y_2, p_1, p_2, r, π_1 and π_2. Discarding the long-run, zero-profit condition, find equilibrium values for these variables (i) when $a \geqslant 1$, firm 1 is a monopolist equating marginal cost with marginal revenue, and firm 2 is a perfect competitor; and (ii) when $a \leqslant 1$, firm 1 is a perfect competitor, and firm 2 is a monopolist equating marginal cost with marginal revenue. For $a > 1$, compare the perfectly competitive solution with the solution of case (i). For $a = 1$, compare all three solutions. Compute and compare the utility achieved by the consumer in the solutions of each of these last two comparisons.

11.6   Let an isolated monopolist's production function be

$$x = \sqrt{y_1 y_2},$$

where y_1 and y_2 are (scalar) inputs and x denotes her (scalar) output. Suppose the demand function (11.2-12) facing her is

$$p = \alpha x + 2\beta,$$

where p is the output price, $\alpha < 0$, $0 < (r_1 r_2)^{1/2} < \beta$, and r_1 and r_2 are respective input prices. Compute the monopolist's profit-maximizing output, output price, and inputs. (Note that due to the constant returns to scale, it is impossible to maximize profit uniquely when the same production function arises under perfectly competitive conditions. Recall the discussion at the end of Section 5.1.) Draw a picture of the total revenue, total cost, and profit curves and compare to Figure 5.5.

11.7   Draw a diagram similar to that of Figure 11.2 in which the monopolist's profit is negative. (In such a situation the monopolist would cease production.)

11.8   Show that the (isolated) monopolist never produces in the inelastic portion of his demand curve (as defined by the graph of equation (11.2-12)).

11.9   Imagine an isolated monopolist who sells his output in two separate markets that are sufficiently isolated so that someone else cannot buy the output in one market and sell it in the other. Let x_i and $MR^i(x_i)$ denote, respectively, the output sold and the marginal revenue of that output in market i, where $i = 1, 2$. Ignoring possible transportation costs, show that profit maximization by the monopolist requires

$$MR^1(x_1) = MR^2(x_2) = MC(x_1 + x_2),$$

at the maximum. Show also that the monopolist will charge different prices in these markets if and only if the elasticity of demand (at the profit-maximizing values of x_1 and x_2) is different in each market.

11.10 Consider an isolated monopolist who produces her output in two separate plants. Let x_i and $MC^i(x_i)$ denote, respectively, the output produced and the marginal cost of that output in plant i, where $i = 1, 2$. Ignoring possible transportation costs, show that at the maximum, profit maximization requires

$$MR(x_1 + x_2) = MC^1(x_1) = MC^2(x_2).$$

Compare this result to the collusion duopoly solution of Section 11.3. Note its symmetry to the corresponding equation of Exercise 11.9.

11.11* Suppose industry 1 is a duopoly in which the total costs of both firms are identically zero, and whose market demand function $\mathcal{H}$ is given by

$$p_1 = \mathcal{H}(x_{11} + x_{12}) = 50 - \tfrac{1}{2}\,(x_{11} + x_{12}).$$

Compute the Cournot reaction functions. Find and compare the values of p_1, x_{11}, x_{12}, $x_{11} + x_{12}$, and of individual and aggregate profits under perfectly competitive, Cournot, and Stackelberg assumptions. What would p_1, $x_{11}+x_{12}$, and aggregate profits be if the two firms combined to form a monopoly? Recompute all variable values supposing that the two firms collude by behaving as a single monopolist with each producing half of the monopoly output. What would you expect to happen to price, outputs, and profits under the Cournot assumptions as the number of firms increases? Prove your conjectures using the same demand function and assuming that the costs of all firms remain identically zero.

11.12 Assume firm 1,1 in the duopoly model of Section 11.3 always produces that output which would maintain the same market share θ, or in other words, satisfy the relation

$$\frac{x_{11}}{x_{11} + x_{12}} = \theta.$$

Take firm $1, 2$ to be the usual profit maximizer. What equations determine the values of x_{11}, x_{12}, and p_1 at long-run equilibrium?

11.13 Consider an isolated monopolist who faces the market demand function $x = \mathcal{H}(p)$, where the scalar variables x and p denote, respectively, market quantity and price. Let x^0 and p^0 be the profit-maximizing values of these variables. Suppose the monopolist's *market power*, ρ, is measured by[21]

$$\rho = \frac{p^0 - MC(x^0)}{p^0}.$$

Show that ρ is the reciprocal of the price-elasticity of demand at (p^0, x^0), that is,

$$\rho = -\frac{d\mathcal{H}^{-1}(x^0)}{dx}\left(\frac{x^0}{p^0}\right).$$

Determine an expression for the value of ρ in Exercise 11.6 and note that it is always positive.

Show also that, in general, the monopolist will never produce in the inelastic portion of the market demand curve he faces.

11.14 Imagine an isolated monopolistically competitive firm whose subjective demand function is

$$p = SD(x) = \frac{x - \beta\sigma}{\alpha},$$

where σ is a parameter representing the firm's perceived "share" of the market, $0 < x < \beta\sigma$, all sub- and superscripts have been dropped, $\alpha < 0$ and $\beta > 0$ are constants, and $0 < \sigma < 1$. Let the firm use one input, denoted by the scalar variable y, to produce output according to the constant-returns-to-scale production function

$$x = f(y) = y.$$

Show that $\partial p/\partial\sigma > 0$ and $\partial\pi/\partial\sigma > 0$ everywhere and, at the output that the firm believes to be profit-maximizing, $\partial x/\partial\sigma > 0$.

Repeat the above calculations for the subject demand function

$$p = SD(x) = \frac{(x - \beta)\sigma}{\alpha},$$

---

[21]   Lerner [9, p. 169].

with $0 < x < \beta$. Describe the differences in the way the graphs of the two sub-jective demand functions (*i.e.*, the subjective demand curves) shift in response to increases in market share σ.

REFERENCES

1. Apostol, T. M., *Mathematical Analysis*, 2nd ed. (Reading: Addison-Wesley, 1974).
2. Arrow, K. J. and F. H. Hahn, *General Competitive Analysis* (San Francisco: Holden-Day, 1971).
3. Aumann, R. J., "Markets with a Continuum of Traders," *Econometrica* 32 (1964), pp. 39-50.
4. Chamberlin, E. H., "The Theory of Monopolistic Competition," Ph. D. thesis, Harvard University, 1927.
5. ———, *The Theory of Monopolistic Competition*, 8th ed. (Cambridge: Harvard University Press, 1962).
6. Cournot, A., *Researches into the Mathematical Principles of the Theory of Wealth*, N. T. Bacon, trans. (New York: Kelley, 1960).
7. Fisher, F. M., "The Stability of the Cournot Oligopoly Solution: The Effects of Speeds of Adjustment and Increasing Marginal Costs," *Review of Economic Studies* 28 (1960-1961), pp. 125-135.
8. FitzRoy, F. R., "Monopolistic Equilibrium, Non-Convexity and Inverse Demand," *Journal of Economic Theory* 7 (1974), pp. 1-16.
9. Lerner, A. P., "The Concept of Monopoly and the Measurement of Monopoly Power," *Review of Economic Studies* 1 (1933-1934), pp. 157-175.
10. Pearce, I. F., "Monopolistic Competition and General Equilibrium," *Current Economic Problems*, J. M. Parkin and A. R. Nobay, eds. (Cambridge: Cambridge University Press, 1975), pp. 93-117.
11. ———, "Participation and Income Distribution," *The Economics of Co-Determination*, D. F. Heathfield, ed. (London: Macmillan, 1977), pp. 26-35.
12. Roberts, J. and H. Sonnenschein, "On the Foundations of the Theory of Monopolistic Competition," *Econometrica* 45 (1977), pp. 101-113.
13. Robinson, J., *The Economics of Imperfect Competition*, 2nd ed. (London: Macmillan, 1969).
14. Shubik, M., *Game Theory in the Social Sciences*, v.2., *A Game-Theoretic*

Approach to Political Economy (Cambridge: MIT Press, 1984).
15. Sraffa, P., "The Laws of Returns under Competitive Conditions," *Economic Journal* 36 (1926), pp. 535-550.
16. von Stackelberg, H., *The Theory of the Market Economy*, A. T. Peacock, trans. (New York: Oxford University Press, 1952).
17. Weintraub, S., "Monopoly Equilibrium and Anticipated Demand," *Journal of Political Economy* 50 (1942), pp. 427-434.

Chapter 12

Economic Welfare

The term "welfare" refers to a state of well-being, usually of an individual or a group in a particular circumstance. Generally, a broad variety of elements affect welfare. These may include such factors as freedom, self-esteem, spiritual and cultural needs, interpersonal relationships, and so on. Economic welfare, the subject of the present chapter, has to do with only one facet of general welfare, namely, that associated with the economic aspects of life.

To be more precise, suppose the noneconomic influences among all circumstances under consideration are, at least approximately, constant. In other words, across the relevant universe of circumstances, the only significant alterations occur in economic components. Modification in noneconomic areas, perhaps responding to variations in economic ones, are inconsequential. Such a universe may be called an *economically admissible* universe. The elements of an economically admissible universe are referred to as *economic circumstances*. Economic welfare, then, is general welfare arising from economic circumstances. Changes in economic welfare are generated solely by changes in economic circumstances.

To determine the economic welfare of a given economic circumstance, it is necessary to evaluate the desirability of that circumstance. Upon evaluation of several alternative circumstances in the universe, welfare comparisons become possible. If, in addition, each alternative can be generated by implementing a distinct government policy, then the welfare impact of these

459

policies can be ascertained.

It has already been suggested in Section 3.4 that, at the level of the individual, the phrase "economic circumstance" typically refers to a basket of commodities which might be consumed. The economic welfare of that circumstance is indicated by the utility assigned to it. This, of course, requires the introspective assumption that individuals do, in fact, think in terms of utility functions revealed, at least ordinally, in their demand behavior. Thus economic circumstances are described solely in terms of material goods and services, and their evaluation is expressed only with reference to the "pleasures" (Section 2.2) these goods and services provide. When there is more than one person, an economic circumstance is usually taken to be a distribution of commodities across individuals. Each is characterized, therefore, by a possibly different allocation of resources, and a different distribution of the rewards for economic activity. Welfare evaluations of them are couched in the language of a "welfare function," which embodies the notion of "social pleasure."

Such a view of economic welfare clearly falls in the tradition of what Samuelson [18, p. 225] refers to as the "Old Welfare Economics" of the nineteenth century, in which individual utilities (at that time taken to be cardinal) were combined (additively) to form "total social utility" so as to be able to evaluate economic distributions. By contrast, many economists of the twentieth century have concentrated exclusively on the relationship between equilibrium and Pareto optimality (defined in Section 12.2 below), scrupulously avoiding all welfare evaluations that require combinations or comparisons of utilities across individuals. Samuelson dates this switch in emphasis to the publication of Robbins' *An Essay on the Nature and Significance of Economic Science* in 1932. According to Samuelson [18, p. 226]:

> When Robbins sang out that the emperor had no clothes — that you could not prove or test by any empirical observations of objective science the normative validity of comparisons between different persons' utilities — suddenly all his generation of economists felt themselves to be naked in a cold world. Most of them had come into economics seeking the good. To learn in midlife that theirs was only the craft of a plumber, dentist or cost accountant was a sad shock.
>
> It was to salvage something from the ruins that the narrow new welfare economists worked toward the [free-from-interpersonal-comparisons] concept of [Pareto optimality].

Robbins' argument notwithstanding, it is obvious that interpersonal comparisons of utilities are made, and social welfare functions based on these comparisons are employed implicitly, if not explicitly, in real-life social decison-making every day. To ignore them in economic analysis is not to make them go away. The following discussion, then, takes the social welfare function and its attendant value judgments as given and explores the consequences that ensue.

With the individual having already been considered in some detail in Section 3.4, this chapter focuses, for the most part, on the analysis of group welfare. The basic model is essentially that of the fixed-factor-supply economy described in Chapter 8. The additional conditions of Section 8.3 ensuring the existence of a community utility function u^H are not assumed. Expanded conclusions applying to the more general world of variable factor supplies are not considered except for the simple illustration in Exercise 12.9. Also omitted is any examination of the dynamics of welfare and welfare changes over time.

The chapter begins with a discussion of the idea of a welfare function and the social ordering of economic circumstances it defines. Its relation to the Pareto ordering and Pareto optimality is considered next. This is followed by an examination of the connections between welfare maximization, Pareto optimality, and equilibrium under perfect competition. The last section is concerned with the use of areas under demand curves and differences among valuations of aggregate output as measures of welfare changes. Components of the particular grand view presented in Section 1.4 appear in Sections 12.2 and 12.3.

12.1   WELFARE FUNCTIONS

For democratic societies, welfare functions, which are here assumed to be given, are defined in a manner that supposes account has been taken of the desires of each of society's members. One way to do this (in the context of the fixed-factor-supply model of Chapter 8) is to begin with individuals' utility functions

$$\mu_k = u^k(x_k), \quad k = 1, \ldots, K, \tag{12.1-1}$$

where $x_k = (x_{1k}, \ldots, x_{Ik})$ for each k. (Recall that there are I commodities indexed by $i = 1, \ldots, I$, and K persons identified as $k = 1, \ldots, K$.) These functions are defined on the commodity spaces $X^k = \{x_k : x_k \geqslant 0\}$, respectively; have the properties of continuity and differentiability (2.3-1), differential increasingness (2.3-2), and strict quasi-concavity (2.3-3); and satisfy the boundary condition (2.3-4). The range of u^k is a subset of the extended real line. Denote it by the symbol $\mathcal{U}^k$, for each k, and write the Cartesian product

$$\mathcal{U} = \mathcal{U}^1 \times \cdots \times \mathcal{U}^K.$$

Elements of $\mathcal{U}$ are the vectors $\mu = (\mu_1, \ldots, \mu_K)$. One characterization of the notion of welfare function[1] is as a function W mapping $\mathcal{U}$ into the extended real line such that W is twice, continuously differentiable at all finite μ and differentially increasing, that is, the partial derivatives

$$W_k(\mu) > 0, \quad k = 1, \ldots, K, \tag{12.1-2}$$

again for all finite μ. Using ω to to represent elements of the range of W this welfare function is written

$$\omega = W(\mu), \tag{12.1-3}$$

and, emphasizing the nature of its domain of definition, it is called the *utility welfare function*.

By combining (12.1-3) and (12.1-1) it is easy to express ω as a function of what have earlier been referred to as economic circumstances. Economic circumstances consist of distributions of commodities among individuals and are summarized as vectors $x = (x_1, \ldots, x_K)$ contained in

$$X = X^1 \times \cdots \times X^K.$$

Letting $u = (u^1, \ldots, u^K)$, define the composition of W and u, that is, the *distribution welfare function*, as the function $W \circ u$ on X such that

$$W \circ u(x) = W(u^1(x_1), \ldots, u^K(x_K)).$$

It follows from the properties of W and u that $W \circ u$ is twice, continuously differentiable in the interior of X, and that its first-order partial derivatives

$$\frac{\partial W \circ u(x)}{\partial x_{ik}} = W_k(u^1(x_1), \ldots, u^K(x_K)) u_i^k(x_k), \quad \begin{array}{l} i = 1, \ldots, I, \\ k = 1, \ldots, K, \end{array}$$

are positive there. The latter assertion is the statement that $W \circ u$ is differentially increasing. Thus an alternative form for the utility welfare function (12.1-3) is the distribution welfare function

$$\omega = W \circ u(x), \tag{12.1-4}$$

which has X as its domain instead of $\mathcal{U}$.

---

[1] See Bergson [6].

It is understood in the previous definitions that ω ranges over a scale on which "social pleasure" is measured. In other words, each value of ω numerically represents the economic welfare or social desirability as measured on the social pleasure scale of a vector of individual pleasures μ or an economic circumstance x, as the case may be. The problems involved in obtaining social from individual pleasure scales and the interpersonal comparisons of utility they require have been discussed in Section 2.2. Suffice it here to recall that the social pleasure scale can be either ordinal or cardinal.

Observe that to specify the distribution welfare function $W \circ u$, the particular u^k employed, $k = 1, \ldots, K$, must be fixed. Substituting increasing or even linear transformations of them cannot be permitted because then economic welfare would turn on the choice of individual functions rather than on the economic circumstance involved. (A similar issue arose with respect to the determination of the social pleasure scale in Section 2.2.) An example is provided below in Exercise 12.1. But it should be emphasized that arbitrarily fixing individual utility functions imposes no real limitations on the nature of $W \circ u$. Such fixity is essential only to secure a basis from which the construction of $W \circ u$ can proceed. If one or more individual utility functions are altered subsequently by applying increasing transformations, then W could always be adjusted so that these alterations are "undone," leaving $W \circ u$ unchanged. Of course, the introspective hypothesis that the u^k employed furnish a legitimate way of measuring the individual pleasure provided by baskets of commodities (Section 3.4) clearly must be retained.

It is also true that any specification of the function W cannot help but include value judgments. This is because every W contains within it a valuation of the relative importance of the pleasure of each person in determining society's welfare. Whether all persons are to be treated equally or whether some are "more important" than others is a matter to be judged by society or the promulgators of a particular W. These value judgments, however, are distinct from those needed to obtain the social pleasure scale. For example, in a two-person situation, suppose the judgment is made that the social pleasure scale is the same as that of individual 1. In so far as defining the measure of social pleasure is concerned, person 2 does not count. On the other hand, even though it violates the differential increasingness of (12.1-2), for the sake of argument let the utility welfare function be

$$W(\mu_1, \mu_2) = \mu_2.$$

Then when it comes to allocating social pleasure (as measured on person 1's scale) the judgment is that person 1 does not count. Hence to each (μ_1, μ_2), the function W assigns a number μ_2. The definition of the social pleasure scale determines the meaning of that number in terms of an underlying space (Section 2.2). Even though μ_2 indicates a utility value for person 2 (measured on person 2's own scale of pleasure), here it also represents a value of economic welfare for society at large as measured on the scale adopted to record social pleasure, namely, person 1's scale of personal pleasure. Thus the conclusions arising from any analysis of group welfare rest on the value judgments appearing in both the welfare function and the scale on which social pleasure is measured. But in any case (the previous example is the only exception mentioned here), the differential increasingness of W and hence of $W \circ u$, is retained. Regardless of the weights assigned to individuals, then, more utility or goods is always better than less.

A further implication of the differential increasingness property of W also deserves mention. Thus let $x' = (x'_1, \ldots, x'_K)$ and $x'' = (x''_1, \ldots, x''_K)$ be in X. Now if $u^k(x'_k) > u^k(x''_k)$ for all k, then $W \circ u(x') > W \circ u(x'')$, and if $u^k(x'_k) = u^k(x''_k)$ where $k = 1, \ldots, K$, then $W \circ u(x') = W \circ u(x'')$. Translated into words these assertions mean that, in the former instance, if each person k prefers x'_k to x''_k, then x' is higher up in the "social" ordering defined by $W \circ u$ than is x''. In the latter case, if each person k is indifferent between x'_k and x''_k, then x' is indifferent to x'' at the social level as well. Discussion returns momentarily to the notion of social ordering.

Note first, however, that the community utility function u^H of Section 8.3 can also be thought of as a distribution welfare function. To express it in terms of the domain X requires replacement of its market-quantity functional arguments by sums of individual quantities. Thus

$$\omega = u^H\left(\sum_{k=1}^{K} x_{1k}, \ldots, \sum_{k=1}^{K} x_{Ik}\right), \tag{12.1-5}$$

is defined on X. But the determination of a function W so that (12.1-5) can be written as the composition (12.1-4) of W and the vector of individual utility functions u is not, in general, clear. There is one case, however, that is handled easily. Suppose all individual utility functions are identical and linearly homogeneous and market quantities always are divided equally among persons. (This is a particularization of the special case of identical and homothetic preferences discussed briefly at the end of Section 8.3.) Then

$$\sum_{k=1}^{K} x_{ik} = K x_{i1},$$

for each $i = 1, \ldots, I$. Letting[2]

$$W(\mu) = \sum_{k=1}^{K} \mu_k, \qquad (12.1\text{-}6)$$

these assumptions now imply that

$$W \circ u(x) = \sum_{k=1}^{K} u^k(x_k),$$

$$= K u^1(x_{11}, \ldots, x_{I1}),$$

$$= u^1(K x_{11}, \ldots, K x_{I1}),$$

$$= u^1\left(\sum_{k=1}^{K} x_{1k}, \ldots, \sum_{k=1}^{K} x_{Ik}\right).$$

Moreover, the argument of Section 8.3 indicates that under the above conditions u^H and u^1 are identical. Hence formulations (12.1-4) and (12.1-5) correspond.

An alternative approach to the definition of welfare functions is based on individual preference orderings. Let each person have a preference ordering over the economic circumstances or distributions $x = (x_1, \ldots, x_K)$ in X and denote it by $[\succsim]_k$ where $k = 1, \ldots, K$. These orderings are not the same as those (written here as $\succsim_k$ and discussed in Section 2.1) associated with the individual utility functions u^k because both $\succsim_k$ and u^k are defined only for commodity baskets x_k (that is, components of distributions x) in X^k. Use the symbol $[\succsim]_\omega$ to represent a possible social ordering of the elements of X. Thinking of $[\succsim]_\omega$ and the $[\succsim]_k$ as variables ranging over appropriately defined domains, the former can be conceived of as functionally dependent on the latter. This characterization of the welfare function is abbreviated symbolically as

$$[\succsim]_\omega = W^*([\succsim]_1, \ldots, [\succsim]_K), \qquad (12.1\text{-}7)$$

where W^* is said to be the *preference welfare function*. All orderings, both social and individual, are taken to be reflexive, transitive, and total. Each defines preference ($[\succ]_\omega$ or $[\succ]_k$) and indifference ($[\approx]_\omega$ or $[\approx]_k$) relations as in Section 2.1.

---

[2]   The additive form for W implicitly appears at least as far back as Bentham [5, p. 3].

There are two important distinctions between the approach of (12.1-7) and that of (12.1-3) or (12.1-4): First, the former is based on variable preference orderings, whereas the latter requires them to be fixed; and second, although the individuals' preference orderings employed by (12.1-7) represent (in part) the feelings of each person about the consumption of others, the individuals' preferences implicit in (12.1-3) or (12.1-4) do not. Each utility function u^k of (12.1-1) is associated with exactly one $\succsim_k$. Sometimes an individual's preferences over X can depend solely on her preferences over X^k, that is,

$$x' \, [\succsim]_k \, x'' \quad \text{if and only if} \quad x'_k \succsim_k x''_k, \qquad (12.1\text{-}8)$$

for all $x' = (x'_1, \ldots, x'_K)$ and $x'' = (x''_1, \ldots, x''_K)$ in X. In words, person k prefers economic circumstance x' to x'' when and only when she prefers her share of x' (that is, x'_k) to her share of x''. And she is indifferent between x' and x'' when and only when she is indifferent between her shares in them. Suppose for a moment that (12.1-8) holds for each k, and that W and $u = (u^1, \ldots, u^K)$ are given. Then (12.1-4) determines a unique social ordering $[\succsim]_\omega$ which can be identified with the $[\succsim]_k$ obtained through the u^k and (12.1-8). When (12.1-7) and (12.1-3) are "consistent" with each other, this provides a single "point" satisfying (12.1-7). Additional points cannot be secured from (12.1-4) without alternatives for W and u. On the other hand, to deduce a W and u from W^*, it is necessary to select a particular point or collection of orderings satisfying (12.1-7), infer the $\succsim_k$ from the $[\succsim]_k$ and (12.1-8), obtain utility representations $u = (u^1, \ldots, u^K)$ of all $\succsim_k$, and then define W so that $W \circ u$ represents the $[\succsim]_\omega$ that was selected. The latter will be achieved if W is chosen to represent an ordering $\succsim_\omega$ defined on $\mathcal{U}$ such that

$$\mu' \succsim_\omega \mu'' \quad \text{if and only if} \quad x' \, [\succsim]_\omega \, x'',$$

where $\mu' = (\mu'_1, \ldots, \mu'_K)$, $\mu'' = (\mu''_1, \ldots, \mu''_K)$, $\mu'_k = u^k(x'_k)$ and $\mu''_k = u^k(x''_k)$ for each k and, recall, $x' = (x'_1, \ldots, x'_K)$ and $x'' = (x''_1, \ldots, x''_K)$. Of course, the W and the u^k so obtained need not be differentially increasing unless, among other things, $\succsim_\omega$ and the $\succsim_k$ are increasing. Observe that although the issue of the measurement of social pleasure does not arise with (12.1-7), value judgments still are involved in the specification of W^*.

In practice, there are many ways of passing from individual preferences or utility to social preferences or welfare. Procedures can be based on tradition, established authority, convention, religious codes, and voting, to name but a few. Each determines a function W, $W \circ u$, or W^* with its own unique properties. In recent literature, the nature of welfare functions derived from individual preferences has been studied in particular depth with respect to W^*. Several general properties that W^*, however derived, can possess, are as follows: First of all, for any three distributions in X, W^* provides some reflexive, transitive, and total social ordering of them no matter how they are ordered by each individual. Second, in the absence of any other changes, suppose one distribution rises or remains still in the ordering of every individual. Then such a distribution does not fall in the social ordering $[\succsim]_\omega$. Third, the social ranking of the distributions in any subset of X is the same regardless of whether the subset is ordered under $[\succsim]_\omega$ independently by itself or in conjunction with one or more of the elements of X not contained in that subset. Thus, for example, the dropping of an element from $A \subseteq X$ does not change the ordering of the remaining elements of A. Fourth, W^* does not prevent the social ranking of any one distribution of X over another. (This condition would be violated if, say, it were always true that x' $[\succ]_\omega$ x'' for some x' and x'' in X, no matter what the preferences of individuals between x' and x'' were.) And fifth, the social ordering is not determined by the preferences of one person alone.

Although not done so here, all of the above properties can be stated with full mathematical rigor.[3] Now Arrow [3, p. 59] has shown (the result is sometimes referred to as *Arrow's impossibility theorem*) that as long as the number of distributions in X is greater than two, there cannot exist a preference welfare function W^* satisfying all five properties simultaneously. In other words, these properties, together with the definition of W^* requiring $[\succsim]_\omega$ and the $[\succsim]_k$ to be reflexive, transitive, and total, logically contradict each other. This need not be so when X contains only two distributions. To illustrate, define *majority rule* by requiring, for all x' and x'' in X, that x' $[\succsim]_\omega$ x'' if and only if the number of persons having x' $[\succsim]_k$ x'' is at least as large as the number having x'' $[\succsim]_k$ x'. Arrow [3, p. 48] has also demonstrated that majority rule does, in fact, characterize a preference welfare function satisfying the preceding five conditions when the number of distributions in X is reduced to two.

In order to see what can happen when the number of distributions increases beyond two, consider the case of majority rule and let $X = \{x', x'', x'''\}$. Suppose there are three persons whose preference relations ($[\succsim]_k$) are given by

$$x' \ [\succ]_1 \ x'', \quad x'' \ [\succ]_1 \ x''', \quad x' \ [\succ]_1 \ x''',$$

$$x'' \ [\succ]_2 \ x''', \quad x''' \ [\succ]_2 \ x', \quad x'' \ [\succ]_2 \ x',$$

$$x''' \ [\succ]_3 \ x', \quad x' \ [\succ]_3 \ x'', \quad x''' \ [\succ]_3 \ x'',$$

---

[3]   Arrow [3, Ch. 3].

Because $x'\ [\succ]_\omega\ x''$ means $x'\ [\succsim]_\omega\ x''$ and not $x''\ [\succsim]_\omega\ x'$, application of the definition of majority rule implies that $x'\ [\succ]_\omega\ x''$ if and only if more persons have $x'\ [\succ]_k\ x''$ than have $x''\ [\succ]_k\ x'$, Hence the social preference relation $([\succ]_\omega)$ is

$$x'\ [\succ]_\omega\ x'',\quad x''\ [\succ]_\omega\ x''',\quad x'''\ [\succ]_\omega\ x'.$$

But $[\succ]_\omega$ lacks transitivity, and so majority rule cannot yield a preference welfare function in this situation.

Arrow's impossibility theorem certainly does not mean that welfare functions such as W, $W \circ u$, or even W^* do not exist. But it clearly indicates the general impossibility of finding a W^* with all five properties listed above. Any particular W^* must therefore satisfy fewer, modified, or alternative conditions or must be defined differently from the characterization given here.

All modern societies have institutions whose purpose is to make social decisions. The ends motivating the making of such decisions are, of course, various. Social decisions may be undertaken, for example, in the interest of income or wealth redistribution, or with the desire to realize what might be considered to be higher levels of social equity. Involved also might be the achievement of certain perceived ethical standards requiring, say, increases in well-being for disadvantaged members of society. But regardless of the ends in view, administrators, legislators, and others, as previously suggested, regularly seem to employ, implicitly if not explicitly, welfare functions in the making of social decisions. Although these individuals are not always in complete agreement with either each other or the public at large over what the welfare function actually is or ought to be, decisions still have to be made. In the process of hammering them out, some sort of welfare function, with all of its attendant value judgments, emerges. This function therefore has a potentially significant impact on the distribution of commodities, and there is no reason why the economist should exorcise it from his analysis.

12.2   THE PARETO ORDERING

The fact that value judgments are required to move from individual to social preferences has been discussed in the previous section. But prior to their introduction, significant headway can still be made in the construction of social orderings by employing economic efficiency criteria. Because any useful welfare function must take both value judgments and efficiency into account, it is worth sorting out the role each plays in the identification of social with individual orderings. To do so, the idea of Pareto optimality is considered first.

That notion gives expression to efficiency as the impossibility of improving one person's position without hurting that of someone else.

Recall that in the fixed-factor-supply model, industry production functions (from equations (8.1-1)) are

$$x_i = f^i(y_i), \quad i = 1, \ldots, I, \tag{12.2-1}$$

where $y = (y_{i1}, \ldots, y_{iJ})$. The f^i satisfy the nonnegativity (8.1-2), differentiability (8.1-3), differential increasingness (8.1-4), and concavity (8.1-5) conditions of Section 8.1. Bordered Hessians are nonvanishing where defined and isoquants associated with positive outputs are not permitted to touch the boundaries of input spaces. In addition, each f^i is taken here to be strictly concave. Given a fixed, positive vector $a = (a_1, \ldots, a_J)$ of aggregate factor supplies, the graph of the transformation function

$$x_I = t(x_1, \ldots, x_{I-1}), \tag{12.2-2}$$

is the "interior boundary" of the production possibility set $\mathcal{T}_a$. As in Section 8.2, t is supposed continuous and differentiable (8.2-2), differentially decreasing (8.2-3), and strictly concave (8.2-4). (The last two properties, recall, actually follow from the differential increasingness and the strict concavity of production functions invoked above.) Hence, according to Theorem 8.1-12, there is a 1-1 correspondence between output vectors on the transformation surface and input vectors satisfying

$$\frac{f_j^i(y_i)}{f_{\hat{j}}^i(y_i)} = \frac{f_j^I(y_I)}{f_{\hat{j}}^I(y_I)}, \quad \begin{matrix} i = 1, \ldots, I-1, \\ j = 1, \ldots, J-1, \end{matrix} \tag{12.2-3}$$

and

$$\sum_{i=1}^{I} y_{ij} = a_j, \quad j = 1, \ldots, J. \tag{12.2-4}$$

Individual utility functions are those of (12.1-1), namely,

$$\mu_k = u^k(x_k), \quad k = 1, \ldots, K, \tag{12.2-5}$$

where $x_k = (x_{1k}, \ldots, x_{Ik})$ and the usual properties (2.3-1) – (2.3-4) are continued. For now utility can be measured either ordinally or cardinally. In the present notation $x = (x_1, \ldots, x_K)$ is an economic circumstance or distribution in X. Furthermore,

$$x_i = \sum_{k=1}^{K} x_{ik}, \quad i = 1, \ldots, I. \tag{12.2-6}$$

Thus x_i denotes a market quantity of good i obtained by summing across each person; whereas x_k represents a vector of goods for individual k. To each distribution $x = (x_1, \ldots, x_K)$ in X, then, there corresponds a unique vector of market quantities $(x_1, \ldots, x_I)$ obtained from (12.2-6). Conversely, each market vector $(x_1, \ldots, x_I)$ is associated with many distributions $(x_1, \ldots, x_K)$ that satisfy (12.2-6). The following discussion develops, under the assumptions listed above, a criterion for determining which market vectors and which distributions of them are more efficient than others.[4]

Consider a distribution $\overline{x} = (\overline{x}_1, \ldots, \overline{x}_K)$ in X with corresponding market vector $(\overline{x}_1, \ldots, \overline{x}_I) \neq 0$. Then $\overline{x}$ is called *Pareto optimal* (or *efficient*) *in consumption*[5] whenever there is no other distribution $x = (x_1, \ldots, x_K)$ in X such that

$$\sum_{k=1}^{K} x_{ik} = \overline{x}_i, \quad i = 1, \ldots, I,$$

$$u^k(x_k) \geqslant u^k(\overline{x}_k), \quad k = 1, \ldots, K,$$

and for at least one k,

$$u^k(x_k) > u^k(\overline{x}_k).$$

Hence, at (and only at) a consumption Pareto optimum, it is impossible to vary the distribution of commodities so as to increase the utility of one person without lowering that of someone else. Another equivalent way of saying the same thing is that $\overline{x}$ is Pareto optimal in consumption if and only if $\overline{x}_K$ uniquely

---

[4]   Although his purpose is somewhat different, a similar analysis of a special two-input, two-output, two person circumstance has been given by Bator [4].

[5]   As its name implies, the notion of consumption Pareto optimality (along with production Pareto optimality and general Pareto optimality as defined subsequently) is attributed to Pareto [14, Ch. 6 §33, App. §89], although Edgeworth [9, p. 27] employed it in the same consumption context some 25 years earlier. See n.5 on p. 256.

maximizes $u^K(x_K)$, say, subject to the constraints[6]

$$u^k(x_k) = \overline{\mu}_k, \quad k = 1, \ldots, K-1,$$

$$\sum_{k=1}^{K} x_{ik} = \overline{x}_i, \quad i = 1, \ldots, I, \tag{12.2-7}$$

where $\overline{\mu}_k = u^k(\overline{x}_k)$ for $k = 1, \ldots, K-1$.

The Lagrangian expression associated with the maximization approach to consumption Pareto optimality is

$$u^K(x_K) - \left\{ \sum_{k=1}^{K-1} \delta_k \left[\overline{\mu}_k - u^k(x_k) \right] \right\} - \sum_{i=1}^{I} \varepsilon_i \left[-\overline{x}_i + \sum_{k=1}^{K} x_{ik} \right], \tag{12.2-8}$$

where the δ_k and ε_i are multipliers. Ignoring the constraint qualification (A.3-17)[7] and equating to zero the derivatives of (12.2-8) with respect to every x_{ik} yields the first-order constrained maximization conditions in force at the interior consumption Pareto optimum $\overline{x}$. As in the discussion of utility maximization of Section 2.3, there are also necessary and (different) sufficient second-order conditions in terms of the derivatives of the u^k. However, the mathematics is rather complicated and not reproduced here.[8] To keep the present argument as simple as possible, second-order sufficiency problems are assumed away by supposing utility functions are shaped such that, except for distributions $x = (x_1, \ldots, x_K)$ having one or more $x_{ik} = 0$, all first-order conditions and only these are identified with unique maxima. The first-order conditions then become both necessary and sufficient for $\overline{x} > 0$ to maximize u^K subject to (12.2-7). This leads to the following proposition characterizing consumption Pareto optima:

Theorem 12.2-9   Under the above assumptions, $\overline{x} > 0$ is Pareto optimal in consumption if and only if

$$\frac{u_i^k(\overline{x}_k)}{u_I^k(\overline{x}_k)} = \frac{u_i^K(\overline{x}_K)}{u_I^K(\overline{x}_K)}, \quad \begin{array}{l} i = 1, \ldots, I-1, \\ k = 1, \ldots, K-1, \end{array} \tag{12.2-10}$$

---

[6]   That such a maximum always exists uniquely follows from an argument parallel to that establishing the unique existence of the constrained maximum of f^I on pp. 282-283 above.

[7]   As with the discussion in relation to the production contract set on pp. 286-287, subsequent argument proceeds only for the circumstance in which the Lagrangean first-order equations are valid — even when the constraint qualification (which is only a sufficient condition, recall, and not necessary) is not satisfied.

[8]   See, for example, Bliss [7, pp. 210-211] and Burger [8].

$$u^k(\overline{x}_k) = \overline{\mu}_k, \qquad k = 1, \ldots, K-1, \tag{12.2-11}$$

$$\sum_{k=1}^{K} \overline{x}_{ik} = \overline{x}_i, \qquad i = 1, \ldots, I, \tag{12.2-12}$$

where $\overline{x} = (\overline{x}_1, \ldots, \overline{x}_K)$, $\overline{x}_k = (\overline{x}_{1k}, \ldots, \overline{x}_{Ik})$ for each k, and $(\overline{x}_1, \ldots, \overline{x}_I)$ is the market vector corresponding to $\overline{x}$.

Proof: According to the previous paragraph, $\overline{x} > 0$ is Pareto optimal in consumption if and only if $\overline{x}$ satisfies constraints (12.2-7) and there exist vectors $(\delta_1, \ldots, \delta_{K-1}) > 0$ and $(\varepsilon_1, \ldots, \varepsilon_I) > 0$ such that

$$u_i^K(\overline{x}_K) - \varepsilon_i = 0, \quad i = 1, \ldots, I,$$

$$\delta_k u_i^k(\overline{x}_k) - \varepsilon_i = 0, \quad i = 1, \ldots, I, \quad k = 1, \ldots, K-1. \tag{12.2-13}$$

Equations (12.2-13) are obtained by setting the derivatives of (12.2-8) equal to zero. It remains to show that the two sets of equations (12.2-13) and (12.2-10) are equivalent. But this is easily done because (12.2-13) clearly implies (12.2-10), and given (12.2-10) and u^K, the multipliers required for (12.2-13) to hold are obtained from

$$\varepsilon_i = u_i^K(\overline{x}_K), \quad i = 1, \ldots, I,$$

and

$$\delta_k = \frac{u_i^K(\overline{x}_K)}{u_i^k(\overline{x}_k)}, \quad k = 1, \ldots, K-1,$$

for any i.

Q.E.D.

Analogously to the discussion of production in Section 8.1, the collection of all distributions in X satisfying both (12.2-10) and (12.2-12) is called the *(consumption) contract set* with respect to the market vector $(\overline{x}_1, \ldots, \overline{x}_I)$. As in the case of production, the contract set may be associated with one-dimensional curves in the commodity spaces of individual consumers.

The geometry of Theorem 12.2-9 is straightforward when there are two persons ($K = 2$) and two goods ($I = 2$). A consumption Edgeworth box similar to those of Figure 7.2 (but whose length and width now are determined by the market vector $(\overline{x}_1, \overline{x}_2)$ instead of by initial endowments) appears in Figure 12.1(a). Equations (12.2-10) assert that at an interior consumption optimum, the indifference curves of the two individuals have the same slope or, in other words, that their respective marginal rates of substitution are equal. This, in light of (12.2-11) and (12.2-12), implies a tangency at $\overline{x}$ as pictured in the diagram. (The auxiliary indifference curve in Figure 12.l(a) is for later use.) The collection of all such tangencies corresponds exactly to the set of all interior points (distributions) that are Pareto optimal in consumption, and describes the contract set which, in this case, is a curve. (Except for the fact that one is concerned with inputs and isoquants and the other has to do with consumption vectors and indifference curves, Figures 8.l(b) and 12.l(a), together with the mathematical equations describing them, are quite similar.) The boundary condition (2.3-4) on individual utility functions ensures that, apart from the distributions involving the two origins (which are also Pareto optimal in consumption), all consumption Pareto optimal points lie in the interior of the box. Hence the contract curve runs from one origin to the other without touching any boundaries.

In addition to Theorem 12.2-9, the three equivalent characterizations of Pareto optimality given above also can be visualized in Figure 12.1(a). Taking the last first, it is clear that with the market vector $(\overline{x}_1, \overline{x}_2) = (\overline{x}_{11} + \overline{x}_{12}, \overline{x}_{21} + \overline{x}_{22})$ given, $u^2(x_2)$ is maximized at $\overline{x}$ subject to the utility level of person 1 being held fixed at $\overline{\mu}_1$. Second, it is not possible to move from $\overline{x}$ without decreasing the utility of one individual (for example, from $\overline{x}$ to x' in Figure

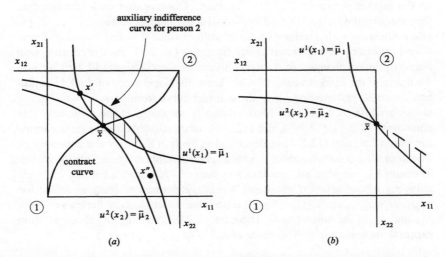

(a)   (b)

Figure 12.1 Pareto optimality in consumption: (a) in the interior of the Edgeworth box; (b) on the boundary of the Edgeworth box

12.l(a)) or both (for example, from $\overline{x}$ to x''). Certainly any gain accruing to, say, person 1 comes at the expense of person 2. Finally, there is no distribution in the box which is preferred to $\overline{x}$ by one individual and simultaneously either preferred or indifferent to $\overline{x}$ by the other. This cannot be said of x' in Figure 12.1(a) because a movement from x' to any distribution in the shaded region increases the utility of at least one person. In fact, for each distribution in the box and off the contract curve, there is a distribution on the contract curve providing more utility for each.

Dropping the boundary condition (2.3-4) on individual utility functions, and thus permitting indifference curves to run into the sides of their respective commodity spaces, opens the possibility of nonorigin, consumption Pareto optimal distributions lying on the boundaries of the Edgeworth box. An example appears at $\overline{x}$ in Figure 12.1(b). The dashed line to the right of the x_{22}-axis is intended to suggest the continuation of person 2's indifference curve if it were extended to include negative amounts of good 1. The shaded region would then correspond to that of Figure 12.1(a). Note that, as drawn, the two indifference curves are not tangent at $\overline{x}$, and so the first-order Lagrangian maximization conditions cannot hold there. However, tangencies would occur at consumption Pareto optimal distributions on the boundaries of the box provided the two indifference maps "fit together" properly. (This example reset in the context of production provides a basis for answering Exercise 8.3.)

Returning to the situation in which the boundary conditions are in force, let the market vector $(\overline{x}_1, \ldots, \overline{x}_I)$ be fixed. Observe that each consumption Pareto optimal distribution x identified with the market vector $(\overline{x}_1, \ldots, \overline{x}_I)$ is also associated with a unique vector of utility values $\mu = (\mu_1, \ldots, \mu_K)$ determined according to individual utility functions (12.2-5). As the consumption Pareto optimum changes, so does μ. This can be seen in Figure 12.1(a) because the fixing of the market vector $(\overline{x}_1, \overline{x}_2)$ keeps the dimensions of the Edgeworth box constant, and moving along the contract curve from person 1's origin, μ_1 is rising while μ_2 is falling. Mathematically speaking, in the same way that equations (12.2-1), (12.2-3), and (12.2-4), when solvable, delineate the transformation function (12.2-2) as described in Section 8.1, here the equations of Theorem 12.2-9, when solvable, characterize a relation among utility values. Theorem 12.2-9, after all, provides a system of IK equations in the IK variables x_{ik} whose solution, assuming it exists, expresses each x_{ik} as a function of $\mu_1, \ldots, \mu_{K-1}$ and $\overline{x}_1, \ldots, \overline{x}_I$. (It is now convenient to drop the bars over the x_{1k} and μ_k in the equations of Theorem 12.2-9.) Substituting those solution expressions having $k = K$ in place of $x_K = (x_{1K}, \ldots, x_{IK})$ in

$$u^K(x_K) = \mu_K,$$

produces a relation

$$\mu_K = \xi(\mu_1, \ldots, \mu_{K-1}, \overline{x}_1, \ldots, \overline{x}_I), \qquad (12.2\text{-}14)$$

usually referred to as the *utility possibility function*. Given $(\overline{x}_1, \ldots, \overline{x}_I)$, ξ describes the possible distributions of utility as the market vector $(\overline{x}_1, \ldots, \overline{x}_I)$ is allocated across individuals in alternative ways that are Pareto optimal in consumption. It is defined on an appropriate subset of the Cartesian product of the ranges of u^k for $k = 1, \ldots, K-1$, that is, on a subset of $\mathcal{U}^1 \times \cdots \times \mathcal{U}^{K-1}$. The graph of ξ, given $(\overline{x}_1, \ldots, \overline{x}_I)$, is said to be the *utility possibility frontier*. As in Theorem 8.1-12 there is 1–1 correspondence between distributions x in the contract set with respect to $(\overline{x}_1, \ldots, \overline{x}_I)$ and vectors $\mu = (\mu_1, \ldots, \mu_K)$ on the utility possibility frontier. But because individual utility functions are not unique and can vary up to linear or increasing transformations (a welfare function has not yet been defined, and so it is not yet necessary to fix the u^k), and because nothing has been assumed about the shapes of their graphs, the shape and location of the frontier is of no consequence: Different functions produce different frontiers for the same $(\overline{x}_1, \ldots, \overline{x}_I)$.

Still, ξ does have properties independent of the particular utility representations employed. For example, substitution of (12.2-5) and (12.2-6), with $x_i = \overline{x}_i$ for $i = 1, \ldots, I$, into (12.2-14) gives

$$u^K\left(\overline{x}_1 - \sum_{k=1}^{K-1} x_{1k}, \ldots, \overline{x}_I - \sum_{k=1}^{K-1} x_{Ik}\right) =$$

$$\xi\left(u^1(x_1), \ldots, u^{K-1}(x_{K-1}), \overline{x}_1, \ldots, \overline{x}_I\right).$$

Hence if ξ is continuously differentiable, then

$$\frac{u_i^K(x_K)}{u_i^k(x_k)} = -\xi_k(\mu_1, \ldots, \mu_{K-1}, \overline{x}_1, \ldots, \overline{x}_I), \qquad (12.2\text{-}15)$$

for $i = 1, \ldots, I$, and $k = 1, \ldots, K-1$, where $\mu_k = u^k(x_k)$ for each k, the $x_k = (x_{1k}, \ldots, x_{Ik})$ are related to the $\overline{x}_i$ by (12.2-6), and ξ_k denotes the partial derivative of ξ with respect to μ_k. Note that the derivation of (12.2-15) is parallel to that of a similar expression for the transformation function in (8.1-20). Furthermore, with respect to the two-dimensional case of Figure 12.1(a), it has already been suggested that the frontier must slope downward and to the right because traveling in one direction along the contract curve necessitates the utility level of one person rising and that of the other falling. An illustration is provided in Figure 12.2 for the case in which both $\mathcal{U}^1$ and $\mathcal{U}^2$

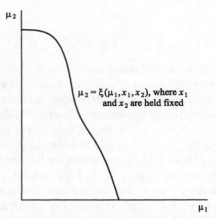

Figure 12.2 Utility possibility frontier

are the set of all nonnegative real numbers. More generally, (12.2-15) implies that except on the boundary of $\mathcal{U}^1 \times \cdots \mathcal{U}^{K-1}$, the ξ_k are everywhere negative because all u_i^k are assumed positive on the interiors of their respective domains. This conclusion does not depend on the particular utility representations in use because the signs of the u_i^k, though not their magnitudes, are the same for all representations.

As suggested by the foregoing, there is a parallel notion to consumption Pareto optimality with respect to production. Thus, given the fixed-factor-supply vector a, the distribution of factors $\overline{y} = (\overline{y}_1, \ldots, \overline{y}_I) \geqslant 0$ is said to be *Pareto optimal* (or *efficient*) *in production* provided that

$$\sum_{i=1}^{I} \overline{y}_{ij} = a_j, \quad j = 1, \ldots, J,$$

and there does not exist another vector $y = (y_1, \ldots, y_I) \geqslant 0$ such that

$$\sum_{i=1}^{I} y_{ij} = a_j, \quad j = 1, \ldots, J,$$

$$f^i(y_i) \geqslant f^i(\overline{y}_i), \quad i = 1, \ldots, I,$$

and for at least one i,

$$f^i(y_i) > f^i(\overline{y}_i).$$

At a production Pareto optimum, then, any redistribution of inputs among industries cannot raise the output of one without lowering the output of another. Clearly, the main difference between the definitions of production and consumption Pareto optima is that production functions and distributions of inputs across firms are substituted for, respectively, utility functions and distributions of outputs among individuals. Thus, production Pareto optima can be expressed in terms of maximization, and a statement of first-order maximization ratios analogous to that for consumption optima can be developed. The argument, however, has already been made in Section 8.1 and is contained in equations (12.2-1) – (12.2-4) above. Assuming away second-order-maximization-condition difficulties and ignoring the constraint qualification as before, the result parallel to Theorem 12.2-9 essentially restates (12.2-3), (12.2-1), and (12.2-4) as they stand and is as follows:

Theorem 12.2-16   Under the above assumptions, $\overline{y} > 0$ is Pareto optimal in production if and only if

$$\frac{f^i_j(\overline{y}_i)}{f^i_J(\overline{y}_i)} = \frac{f^I_j(\overline{y}_I)}{f^I_J(\overline{y}_I)}, \qquad \begin{matrix} i = 1, \ldots, I-1, \\ j = 1, \ldots, J-1, \end{matrix}$$

$$f^i(\overline{y}_i) = \overline{x}_i, \qquad i = 1, \ldots, I-1,$$

$$\sum_{i=1}^{I} \overline{y}_{ij} = a_j, \qquad j = 1, \ldots, J,$$

where $\overline{y} = (\overline{y}_1, \ldots, \overline{y}_I)$ and $\overline{y}_i = (\overline{y}_{i1}, \ldots, \overline{y}_{iJ})$ for each i.

Geometric analysis of production Pareto optimality in the two-industry, two-input case is similar to that of consumption Pareto optimality when there are two persons and two outputs. In particular, at a production Pareto optimum, two isoquants are tangent and the marginal rates of technical substitution from the industry production functions are equal.

Having come this far, the stage is now set for an examination of the general notion of Pareto optimality. Call a distribution x' in X *Pareto superior* to (or *more efficient* than) x'' in X whenever the associated market vectors

$(x'_1, \ldots, x'_I)$ and $(x''_1, \ldots, x''_I)$ lie in the production possibility set $\mathcal{T}_a$,

$$u^k(x'_k) \geqslant u^k(x''_k), \quad k = 1, \ldots, K,$$

and

$$u^k(x'_k) > u^k(x''_k),$$

for at least one k. To illustrate, as long as the market vector is in $\mathcal{T}_a$, any distribution in the shaded region of Figure 12.1(a) is Pareto superior to x', and for any distribution off the contract curve in that diagram, there exists a distribution on the contract curve which is Pareto superior to it. Now $\overline{x}$ in X is said to be *Pareto optimal* (or *efficient*) if the market vector associated with $\overline{x}$ is in $\mathcal{T}_a$ and there does not exist any other distribution in X with market vector in $\mathcal{T}_a$ which is Pareto superior to it. Clearly, if $\overline{x}$ is Pareto optimal, it is also Pareto optimal in consumption. Moreover, the differential increasingness of the u^k imply that the associated market vectors $(\overline{x}_1, \ldots, \overline{x}_I)$ of all Pareto optimal distributions $\overline{x}$ lie on the transformation surface and satisfy (12.2-2). Therefore, from Theorem 8.1-12, every Pareto optimal distribution $\overline{x}$ is identified with a unique input vector $\overline{y}$ corresponding to $(\overline{x}_1, \ldots, \overline{x}_I)$. Hence if $\overline{x}$ is Pareto optimal, then not only is it Pareto optimal in consumption, but its accompanying $\overline{y}$ is also Pareto optimal in production. The converse of this last assertion, of course, need not hold: $\overline{x}$ may be Pareto optimal in consumption and $\overline{y}$ in production, but $\overline{x}$ still need not be Pareto optimal. There may exist another distribution whose associated market vector lies elsewhere on the transformation surface and which is Pareto superior to $\overline{x}$

Evidently, $\overline{x}$ is Pareto optimal if and only if $\overline{x}$ uniquely maximizes $u^K(x_K)$ subject to

$$u^k(x_k) = \overline{\mu}_k, \quad k = 1, \ldots, K - 1,$$

$$\sum_{k=1}^{K} x_{Ik} = t\left(\sum_{k=1}^{K} x_{1k}, \ldots, \sum_{k=1}^{K} x_{I-1k}\right), \tag{12.2-17}$$

where $\overline{\mu}_k = u^k(\overline{x}^k)$ for $k = 1, \ldots, K-1$, and (12.2-6) has been used to eliminate the market variables $(x_1, \ldots, x_I)$ in the transformation function (12.2-2). Assuming away second-order problems and ignoring the constraint qualification once again so that first-order ratios exist and become both necessary and sufficient for interior maxima, a result encompassing both Theorems 12.2-9 and 12.2-16 is obtained. Its proof is left as Exercise 12.2.

Theorem 12.2-18 Under the above assumptions, $\overline{x} > 0$ is Pareto optimal if and only if

$$\frac{u_i^k(\overline{x}_k)}{u_I^k(\overline{x}_k)} = -t_i\left(\sum_{k=1}^{K}\overline{x}_{1k},\ldots,\sum_{k=1}^{K}\overline{x}_{I-1k}\right), \qquad \begin{array}{l} i=1,\ldots,I-1, \\ k=1,\ldots,K, \end{array}$$

$$u^k(\overline{x}_k) = \overline{\mu}_k, \qquad\qquad\qquad\qquad\qquad k=1,\ldots,K-1,$$

$$\sum_{k=1}^{K}\overline{x}_{Ik} = t\left(\sum_{k=1}^{K}\overline{x}_{1k},\ldots,\sum_{k=1}^{K}\overline{x}_{I-1k}\right),$$

$$\sum_{k=1}^{K}\overline{x}_{ik} = \overline{x}_i, \qquad\qquad\qquad\qquad\qquad i=1,\ldots,I,$$

$$\frac{f_j^i(\overline{y}_i)}{f_J^i(\overline{y}_i)} = \frac{f_j^I(\overline{y}_I)}{f_J^I(\overline{y}_I)}, \qquad\qquad\qquad\qquad \begin{array}{l} i=1,\ldots,I-1, \\ j=1,\ldots,J-1, \end{array}$$

$$f^i(\overline{y}_i) = \overline{x}_i, \qquad\qquad\qquad\qquad\qquad i=1,\ldots,I-1,$$

$$\sum_{i=1}^{I}\overline{y}_{ij} = a_j, \qquad\qquad\qquad\qquad\qquad j=1,\ldots,J,$$

where $\overline{y} = (\overline{y}_1,\ldots,\overline{y}_I) > 0$ is the unique input vector corresponding to $(\overline{x}_1,\ldots,\overline{x}_I)$ on the transformation surface.

It has already been remarked that Pareto optimality implies Pareto optimality in both consumption and production, but not conversely. The same conclusion arises from the observation that all equations of Theorems 12.2-9 and 12.2-16 appear either explicitly or implicitly in Theorem 12.2-18, but the first set of equations of Theorem 12.2-18 are not present and cannot be inferred from the equations of Theorem 12.2-9 and Theorem 12.2-16. The first set of equations of Theorem 12.2-18 represents the main difference, in terms of first-order ratios, between Pareto optimality and the combination of Pareto optimality in consumption and production. In the two-person, two-commodity context these equations state that at an optimum, the transformation curve and the indifference curve of each person have the same slope. (Thus the marginal rate of transformation is the same as the marginal rate of substitution of each individual.) But there is no actual tangency between these curves unless the distribution is such that one person receives all of the economy's output. In that case, an indifference curve of the person who is given everything is tangent to the transformation curve at the market vector $(\overline{x}_1,\overline{x}_2)$ and the person

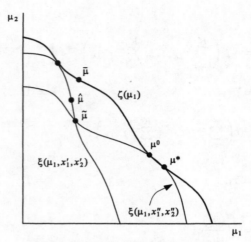

Figure 12.3 Grand utility possibility frontier

who does without winds up at $(0,0)$ where the slope of her indifference curve is not defined.

Recall that each $(\overline{x}_1, \ldots, \overline{x}_I)$ on the transformation surface is associated with a utility possibility function $\xi(\mu_1, \ldots, \mu_{K-1}, \overline{x}_1, \ldots, \overline{x}_I)$ and frontier that identify complete collections of consumption Pareto optimal distributions corresponding to that market vector. Hence with $(\overline{x}_1, \ldots, \overline{x}_I)$ moving across the transformation surface, the utility possibility function and frontier shift. (As shown at $\widetilde{\mu}$ in Figure 12.3, the various frontiers so obtained are likely to intersect.) Define the *grand utility possibility function*[9] ζ by

$$\zeta(\mu_1, \ldots, \mu_{K-1}) = \max \xi(\mu_1, \ldots, \mu_{K-1}, \overline{x}_1, \ldots, \overline{x}_I), \qquad (12.2\text{-}19)$$

where the maximum is taken over all $(\overline{x}_1, \ldots, \overline{x}_I)$ satisfying the transformation equation (12.2-2). That is to say, ζ associates to each vector $(\mu_1, \ldots, \mu_{K-1})$ the maximum value of μ_K attainable as $(\overline{x}_1, \ldots, \overline{x}_I)$ traverses the transformation surface and utility values $(\mu_1, \ldots, \mu_{K-1})$ are held constant. This means

$$\mu_K = \zeta(\mu_1, \ldots, \mu_{K-1})$$

if and only if the distribution $x = (x_1, \ldots, x_K)$ that produces utility values $\mu = (\mu_1, \ldots, \mu_K)$ also maximizes $u^K(x_K)$ subject to (12.2-17) with the bars

---

[9]   Samuelson [16, p. 244].

over the μ_k removed — that is, if and only if x is Pareto optimal. Note that (12.2-19) can also be obtained by solving $u^K(\overline{x}_K) = \mu_K$ plus all equations of Theorem 12.2-18 (with bars over the μ_k removed) for μ_K as a function of $(\mu_1, \ldots, \mu_{K-1})$.

The graph of the grand utility possibility function is called the *grand utility possibility frontier*. With enough differentiability, the grand frontier (ζ) can be thought of as the envelope of the collection of all utility possibility frontiers (ξ). An example is pictured in Figure 12.3 for the special circumstance in which μ_1 and μ_2 each range over the set of all nonnegative real numbers. Observe the similarity between (12.2-19) together with its illustration in Figure 12.3 and the definition of long-run average cost (5.2-2) with Figure 5.6(a). In general, there is no reason why the grand frontier could not be tangent to an ordinary frontier at more than one point (say, between μ^0 and μ^* in Figure 12.3). An instance in which the grand frontier coincides with an ordinary frontier everywhere appears in Exercise 12.8. It has already been pointed out that the distributions associated with points on any given utility possibility frontier are all consumption Pareto optima with respect to the same market vector on the transformation surface. (The corresponding input vector is Pareto optimal in production.) In Figure 12.3, then, assuming that there is only one ordinary frontier through each of $\widehat{\mu}$ and $\overline{\mu}$, the distributions connected with $\widehat{\mu}$ and $\overline{\mu}$ are both Pareto optimal in consumption but with respect to different market vectors. (Of course, the distribution corresponding to $\overline{\mu}$ is also Pareto optimal.) Because $\overline{\mu}$ provides more utility to each person than does $\widehat{\mu}$, the distribution associated with $\overline{\mu}$ is Pareto superior to that identified with $\widehat{\mu}$. In the simplified world of Figures 12.1, 12.2, and 12.3, all distributions linked to the same utility possibility frontier lie in the same Edgeworth box; those connected to different frontiers are in boxes of different dimensions. (Thus because two ordinary frontiers pass through $\widetilde{\mu}$ in Figure 12.3, there are two distributions, each in a distinct Edgeworth box, associated with it.) As long as no ordinary frontier has more than one point in common with the grand frontier (a condition that is violated in Figure 12.3 and in Exercise 12.8), each of the distributions corresponding to the grand frontier appear in separate boxes.

Along with ξ for fixed $(\overline{x}_1, \ldots, \overline{x}_I)$, the domain of definition of ζ is a subset of $\mathcal{U}^1 \times \cdots \times \mathcal{U}^{K-1}$. Again, because individual utility functions are not fixed and the shapes of their graphs are not specified, the shape and location of the grand frontier is meaningless. Each group of functions, one for each person, determines its own frontier. When ζ is continuously differentiable,

$$\frac{u_i^K(x_K)}{u_i^k(x_k)} = -\zeta_k(\mu_1, \ldots, \mu_{K-1}), \qquad \begin{array}{l} i = 1, \ldots, I, \\ k = 1, \ldots, K-1, \end{array} \qquad (12.2\text{-}20)$$

where ζ_k is the kth partial derivative of ζ, $\mu_k = u^k(x_k)$ for each k, and the distribution components x_k sum to the market quantities $\overline{x}_i$ as in (12.2-6). This can be proved either by using the same argument as that establishing (12.1-15) or by noting that, because it is an envelope, the grand frontier is tangent to an ordinary frontier at all $(\mu_1, \ldots, \mu_{K-1})$ for which it is defined. Hence at these points

$$\zeta_k(\mu_1, \ldots, \mu_{K-1}) = \xi_k(\mu_1, \ldots, \mu_{K-1}, \overline{x}_1, \ldots, \overline{x}_I),$$

for $k = 1, \ldots, K - 1$, so that (12.2-20) follows from (12.2-15). Thus, regardless of the utility representations employed, the ζ_k are negative everywhere for $k = 1, \ldots, K$, and the two-dimensional grand frontier must slope downward and to the right (Figure 12.3).

To summarize the argument thus far, think of a two-input, two-output (two-industry), two-consumer world. Let (μ'_1, μ'_2) be a point on the grand frontier. Then (μ'_1, μ'_2) is also on an ordinary frontier associated with some Pareto optimal distribution of outputs $x' = (x'_1, x'_2)$ between persons. At this distribution, two indifference curves (one for each individual) are tangent (equal marginal rates of substitution) in a consumption Edgeworth box whose dimensions are the total amounts of output 1 and output 2 distributed. Denote these latter totals by, respectively, $\overline{x}'_1$ and $\overline{x}'_2$ where subscripts here refer to goods rather than persons. Then $(\overline{x}'_1, \overline{x}'_2)$ lies on the transformation curve and, corresponding to it in a production Edgeworth box, is an input distribution (y'_1, y'_2) between industries at which two isoquants (one for each industry) are tangent (equal marginal rates of technical substitution). The dimensions of the second box are determined by the given quantities of factor supplies. Moreover, the marginal rate of transformation at $(\overline{x}'_1, \overline{x}'_2)$ is the same as the marginal rate of substitution for person 1 at x'_1 and the marginal rate of substitution for person 2 at x'_2.

Consider now the problem of constructing a social ordering $[\succsim]_\omega$, to be named the *Pareto ordering*, based on the notion of Pareto superiority. The natural thing to do is to define

$x' [\succ]_\omega x''$ if and only if x' is Pareto superior to x'',

$x' [\approx]_\omega x''$ if and only if $u^k(x'_k) = u^k(x''_k)$, for all k, and   (12.2-21)

$x' [\succsim]_\omega x''$ if and only if   either $x' [\succ]_\omega x''$ or $x' [\approx]_\omega x''$,

for all x' and x'' in X. Then $[\succ]_\omega$ is irreflexive and transitive, $[\approx]_\omega$ is reflexive, transitive and symmetric, and $[\succsim]_\omega$ is reflexive and transitive. Clearly the

Pareto optimal distributions are the "highest" in the Pareto ordering, and any distribution providing, say, smaller market quantities of each good or less utility to each person than a Pareto optimal distribution is lower down. But the Pareto ordering cannot be total. To illustrate, all x in X whose associated market quantity vectors lie outside of $\mathcal{T}_a$, are not ordered under $[\succ]_\omega$, and neither the Pareto optimal distributions nor the consumption Pareto optimal distributions relative to the same market vector can be compared. Although the definition of Pareto superiority can be extended to distributions with market vectors beyond $\mathcal{T}_a$ by increasing the vector a of fixed factor supplies, the latter difficulties (along with others) necessarily remain. Thus the Pareto ordering by itself does not determine if one of two such noncomparable distributions is socially preferred to the other. Nor is it able to identify which (if any) distributions are socially indifferent other than those already recognized as indifferent by all individuals according to $[\approx]_\omega$ in (12.2-21). Stated in the two-output, two-person context, some but not all pairs of distributions within the same Edgeworth box or even across boxes can be compared according to the Pareto superiority criterion. In particular, all consumption Pareto optimal pairs are noncomparable within the same box, although some can be compared across boxes. Generally speaking, all the Pareto ordering says is that when at least one person's level of utility rises and no one else's falls, society is better off. It is unable to make welfare statements about circumstances in which someone loses while another gains.

This is about as far as it is possible to go in generating a social ordering of distributions in X from individual orderings by using the concept of economic efficiency (for both production and consumption) embodied in the ideas of Pareto superiority and optimality. The Pareto ordering as described in (12.2-21) is different from the social ordering of (12.1-7) in that, with respect to the former, gaps exist in the comparability of numerous distributions. Employing the language of efficiency, more cannot be said of the Pareto ordering than the following two assertions: First, in the most efficient circumstances neither resources nor output is wasted because the production of one good cannot be increased except by lowering production of another, and the utility level of no individual can be raised without hurting someone else. Second, efficiency decreases across circumstances (distributions) as such waste increases. To transform the Pareto ordering into a total social ordering by adding comparisons among those distributions which are noncomparable under $[\succsim]_\omega$ in (12.2-21) requires value judgments.

As described in Section 12.1, value judgments can be introduced by specifying a welfare function. It is worth taking a moment to see what happens when this is done. Let W be the twice, continuously differentiable and differentially increasing utility welfare function of (12.1-3), and $W \circ u$ be the distribution welfare function of (12.1-4). Thus

$$\omega = W(\mu), \tag{12.2-22}$$

and

$$\omega = W \circ u(x), \tag{12.2-23}$$

where $\mu = (\mu_1, \ldots, \mu_K)$, μ is in $\mathcal{U} = \mathcal{U}^1 \times \cdots \times \mathcal{U}^K$, and $u = (u^1, \ldots, u^K)$. Recall (Section 12.1) that for (12.2-22) and (12.2-23) to make sense, all individual utility functions must now be assumed fixed. (Note that even with set utility functions, the shapes of the utility possibility frontiers are still not determined. This is because no assumptions are made about the shapes of the u^k: Indifference surfaces, not utility functions, are required to be strictly convex. If, for example, all u^k were strictly concave, then as with the transformation surface [Theorem 8.1-16], the utility possibility frontiers would be, too.)

Consider any x' and x'' in X whose associated market vectors $(x'_1, \ldots, x'_I)$ and $(x''_1, \ldots, x''_I)$ lie in $\mathcal{T}_a$. Then the definition of Pareto superiority and the differential increasingness of W imply that

$$W \circ u(x') > W \circ u(x''), \tag{12.2-24}$$

whenever $x' [\succ]_\omega x''$ under the Pareto ordering. Also, $x' [\approx]_\omega x''$ under the Pareto ordering leads to $W \circ u(x') = W \circ u(x'')$. Not only does the Pareto ordering remain intact in the social ordering $[\succsim]_\omega$ defined by $W \circ u$, but enough ordered pairs are added to it to yield a reflexive, transitive and total relation. These latter supplementary comparisons are based on the value judgments implicit in W. If x' and x'' were both Pareto optimal, conclusions like (12.2-24) could not be drawn from the differential increasingness of W because in moving from x' to x'', the utility level of at least one person goes up and that of at least one other goes down. In comparing such x' and x'', the only recourse would be to check the levels of ω assigned by $W \circ u$ to each. Differential increasingness does, however, provide the basis for a relationship between Pareto optima and distributions in X which maximize welfare:

Theorem 12.2-25 Let $\overline{x}$ be in X and have its associated market vector $(\overline{x}_1, \ldots, \overline{x}_I)$ in $\mathcal{T}_a$. If $\overline{x}$ maximizes $W \circ u(x)$ over the collection of all distributions in X whose associated market vectors $(x_1, \ldots, x_I)$ also lie in $\mathcal{T}_a$, then $\overline{x}$ is Pareto optimal.

The proof of Theorem 12.2-25 is relegated to Exercise 12.3. Application of Lagrange's theorem to the maximization (described in Theorem 12.2-25) of $W \circ u(x) = W\left(u^1(x_1), \ldots, u^K(x_K)\right)$ subject to the transformation function (12.2-2) with the x_i eliminated by (12.2-6) yields,[10] as long as the maximizing $\overline{x} > 0$,

$$\frac{u_i^K(\overline{x}_K)}{u_i^k(\overline{x}_k)} = \frac{W_k\left(u^1(\overline{x}_1), \ldots, u^K(\overline{x}_K)\right)}{W_K\left(u^1(\overline{x}_1), \ldots, u^K(\overline{x}_K)\right)}, \qquad (12.2\text{-}26)$$

and

$$\frac{u_i^k(\overline{x}_k)}{u_I^k(\overline{x}_k)} = -t_i\left(\sum_{k=1}^K \overline{x}_{1k}, \ldots, \sum_{k=1}^K \overline{x}_{I-1k}\right),$$

where $i = 1, \ldots, I$ and $k = 1, \ldots, K - 1$ in the first equation and $i = 1, \ldots, I - 1$ and $k = 1, \ldots, K$ in the second, W_k is the partial derivative of W with respect to k, for each k, and

$$\sum_{k=1}^K \overline{x}_{Ik} = t\left(\sum_{k=1}^K \overline{x}_{1k}, \ldots, \sum_{k=1}^K \overline{x}_{I-1k}\right).$$

Because $\overline{x}$ is Pareto optimal, the remaining first-order maximization and constraint conditions of Theorem 12.2-18 hold and all of the geometry of Figures 8.1, 12.1(a), and 12.3 apply in the two-input, two-output, two-person case.

But just as the notion of Pareto optimality goes beyond that of Pareto optimality in both consumption and production, completion of the Pareto ordering by including the value judgments contained in W adds something more — namely, equations (12.2-26) — to preceding results. On one hand, combining (12.2-26), (12.2-20), and the equations describing individual utility functions in (12.2-5) gives

$$\frac{W_k(\overline{\mu})}{W_K(\overline{\mu})} = -\zeta_k\left(\overline{\mu}_1, \ldots, \overline{\mu}_{K-1}\right), \quad k = 1, \ldots, K - 1,$$

where $\overline{\mu} = (\overline{\mu}_1, \ldots, \overline{\mu}_K)$ and $\overline{\mu}_k = u^k(\overline{x}_k)$ for each k. Thus, an "indifference surface" of W (defined analogously to those of utility functions in Section 2.3) is tangent to the grand utility possibility frontier at $\overline{\mu}$ in $\mathcal{U}$-space. Figure 12.4(a) provides a two-dimensional illustration in which the grand frontier is taken from Figure 12.3, the indifference curve is strictly convex, and the point

---

[10]   In this case, a maximum always exists by Theorem A.3-1, and the constraint qualification (A.3-17) is satisfied because the partial derivatives $t_i \neq 0$ where defined. Since the market vector associated with the welfare-maximizing distribution lies on the transformation surface, the transformation-function constraint can be treated as an equality.

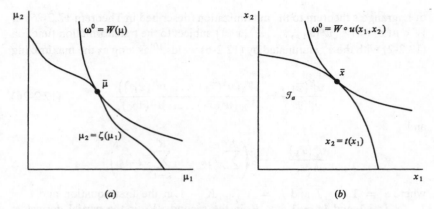

Figure 12.4 Welfare maximization: (a) W-indifference curve tangent to the grand utility possibility frontier; (b) $(W \circ u)$-indifference curve tangent to the transformation curve

of maximum welfare is unique. On the other hand, from (12.2-26) and (12.2-5),

$$\frac{\partial W \circ u(\overline{x})}{\partial x_{ik}} = W_k(\overline{\mu})\, u_i^k(\overline{x}_k)$$

$$(12.2\text{-}27)$$

$$= W_K(\overline{\mu})\, u_i^K(\overline{x}_K) = \frac{\partial W \circ u(\overline{x})}{\partial x_{iK}},$$

for $k = 1, \ldots, K-1$ and $i = 1, \ldots, I$. Loosely speaking, (12.2-27) asserts that at maximum welfare, commodities must be allocated across individuals so that the "additional" welfare obtained from the "last unit" of each is the same for all persons. Thus with (12.2-27) in force, it is possible to speak of the *marginal social value*, namely $\partial W \circ u(\overline{x})/\partial x_{ik}$, for any k, that good i secures for society.

For the special case in which it happens, as in the example immediately following (12.1-6), that

$$W \circ u(x) = W \circ u\left(\sum_{k=1}^{K} x_{1k}, \ldots, \sum_{k=1}^{K} x_{Ik}\right),$$

welfare reduces, by (12.2-6), to a function of market quantities

$$\omega = W \circ u(x_1, \ldots, x_I).$$

Along with everything else, welfare maximization now means that in $(x_1, \ldots,$ $x_I)$-space an indifference surface of $W \circ u$ is tangent, at the maximum, to the transformation surface (for an illustration, see Figure 12.4(b)). The reasoning is the same as that establishing a tangency between an indifference surface of u^H and the transformation surface at the beginning of Section 8.4. Details are left to the reader.

12.3   EQUILIBRIUM, OPTIMALITY AND WELFARE MAXIMIZATION

The idea that perfect competition achieves both Paretian efficiency and some form of welfare maximization pervades much of the history of economic thought. Certainly Adam Smith suggested as much with the assertion that in pursuing his own gain, the individual is led by an "invisible hand" to promote an end that he does not intend, and which is frequently in the interest of society [19, p. 423]. The modern interpretation of this proposition turns, to a considerable extent, on the relationship between equilibrium in a perfectly competitive environment (that is, competitive equilibrium) and Pareto optimality. It is explored here in terms of the fixed-factor-supply model of Chapter 8 without assuming the extra requirements of Section 8.3 introduced to guarantee the existence of a community utility function. Part of the model has already been restated in equations (12.2-1) – (12.2-6) of the previous section. The assumptions of that section are continued.

Let $(\overline{p}, \overline{r}, \overline{x}, \overline{y}) > 0$ be a competitive equilibrium in the fixed-factor-supply model, where $\overline{x} = (\overline{x}_1, \ldots, \overline{x}_K)$ is a distribution in X, the associated market vector $(\overline{x}_1, \ldots, \overline{x}_I)$ is in $\mathcal{T}_a$, and $\overline{p}$ and $\overline{r}$ denote, respectively, vectors of output and factor prices. (It is implicit here that, with respect to the fixed factor supplies $a_k = (a_{1k}, \ldots, a_{Jk})$ for $k = 1, \ldots, K$, at least one $a_{jk} > 0$ for each k as j varies, and for at least one j as k varies.) Then at $(\overline{p}, \overline{r})$ all consumers demand final goods so as to maximize utility subject to budget constraints, all firms hire factors and produce outputs so as to maximize profits, and supply equals demand in every market. This means on the consumer side (from equations (2.3-16), (2.3-17), and (8.3-4)), that

$$\frac{u_i^k(\overline{x}_k)}{u_I^k(\overline{x}_k)} = \frac{\overline{p}_i}{\overline{p}_I}, \quad \begin{matrix} i = 1, \ldots, I-1, \\ k = 1, \ldots, K, \end{matrix} \tag{12.3-1}$$

$$\overline{p} \cdot \overline{x}_k = \overline{m}_k, \quad k = 1, \ldots, K, \tag{12.3-2}$$

where

$$\overline{m}_k = \overline{r} \cdot a_k + \sum_{i=1}^{I} \sum_{\ell=1}^{L_i} \theta_{ki\ell} (\pi_{i\ell} + b_{i\ell}), \quad k = 1, \ldots, K,$$

and $\theta_{ki\ell}$ is the fraction of profit ($\pi_{i\ell}$) plus fixed cost ($b_{i\ell}$) of firm ℓ in industry i going to person k. (Although the present chapter does not disaggregate production functions below the industry level, industry production functions are still derived from firm production functions as described in the introduction to Chapter 8 or Exercise 8.1.) On the production side (from equations (5.1-5), (8.1-22), and (8.2-5)):

$$MC^i(\overline{x}_i) = \overline{p}_i, \quad i = 1, \ldots, I, \tag{12.3-3}$$

$$\frac{MC^i(\overline{x}_i)}{MC^I(\overline{x}_I)} = -t_i(\overline{x}_1, \ldots, \overline{x}_{I-1}), \quad i = 1, \ldots, I-1, \tag{12.3-4}$$

$$\frac{f_j^i(\overline{y}_i)}{f_J^i(\overline{y}_i)} = \frac{\overline{r}_j}{\overline{r}_J}, \quad \begin{array}{l} j = 1, \ldots, J-1, \\ i = 1, \ldots, I. \end{array} \tag{12.3-5}$$

Lastly, because supply equals demand in every market,

$$\sum_{k=1}^{K} \overline{x}_{ik} = \overline{x}_i, \quad i = 1, \ldots, I, \tag{12.3-6}$$

and

$$\sum_{i=1}^{I} \overline{y}_{ij} = a_j, \quad j = 1, \ldots, J. \tag{12.3-7}$$

Combining (12.3-1) with (12.3-2) – (12.3-7), and adding (from equations (12.2-1), (12.2-2), and (12.2-5)) the industry production function, transformation function, and utility function equations, namely,

$$\overline{x}_i = f^i(\overline{y}_i), \quad i = 1, \ldots, I, \tag{12.3-8}$$

$$\overline{x}_I = t(\overline{x}_1, \ldots, \overline{x}_{I-1}), \tag{12.3-9}$$

$$u^k(\overline{x}_k) = \overline{\mu}_k, \quad k = 1, \ldots, K, \tag{12.3-10}$$

where $\overline{\mu}_k$ is defined by (12.3-10), it is clear that all first-order ratio and constraint conditions of Theorem 12.2-18 are satisfied at $\overline{x}$. Under the hypotheses of that theorem, then, $\overline{x}$ is Pareto optimal. But the hypotheses of Theorem 12.2-18 are concerned partly with the satisfaction of second-order maximization conditions, which, although used in the preceding argument, can be avoided in proving the optimality of $\overline{x}$. In fact, the logic establishing that competitive equilibria are Pareto optimal need not rest on first-order maximization conditions either:

Theorem 12.3-11   Let $(\overline{p}, \overline{r}, \overline{x}, \overline{y}) > 0$ be a competitive equilibrium of the fixed-factor-supply model described above. Then $\overline{x}$ is Pareto optimal.

Proof: Suppose $\overline{x} = (\overline{x}_1, \ldots, \overline{x}_K)$ is not Pareto optimal. Then there exists a distinct $x' = (x'_1, \ldots, x'_K)$ in X whose associated market vector $(x'_1, \ldots, x'_I)$ lies in $\mathcal{T}_a$ such that

$$u^k(x'_k) \geqslant u^k(\overline{x}_k), \quad k = 1, \ldots, K,$$

and for at least one k,

$$u^k(x'_k) > u^k(\overline{x}_k).$$

But because $\overline{x}$ is a component of a competitive equilibrium, $\overline{x}_k$ maximizes $u^k(x_k)$ subject to

$$\overline{p} \cdot x_k \leqslant \overline{m}_k,$$

for each k, where $\overline{m}_k = \overline{p} \cdot \overline{x}_k$. Therefore, from the differential increasingness and strict quasi-concavity of the u^k, it follows that x'_k must lie on or above person k's budget hyperplane. Mathematically,

$$\overline{p} \cdot x'_k \geqslant \overline{m}_k, \quad k = 1, \ldots, K,$$

and for at least one k,

$$\overline{p} \cdot x'_k > \overline{m}_k.$$

Summing these inequalities over k and using (12.2-6),

$$\overline{p} \cdot \left(\sum_{k=1}^{K} x'_k \right) = \overline{p} \cdot (x'_1, \ldots, x'_I) > \bar{M}, \qquad (12.3\text{-}12)$$

where

$$\bar{M} = \sum_{k=1}^{K} \overline{m}_k. \qquad (12.3\text{-}13)$$

Again, because $(\overline{p}, \overline{r}, \overline{x}, \overline{y})$ is a competitive equilibrium, the argument of Section 8.2 shows that the market vector associated with $\overline{x}$, namely $(\overline{x}_1, \ldots, \overline{x}_I)$, maximizes

$$\overline{p} \cdot (x_1, \ldots, x_I)$$

over all $(x_1, \ldots, x_I)$ in $\mathcal{T}_a$. This, in conjunction with (12.3-2) and (12.3-13), implies

$$\overline{p} \cdot (x_1, \ldots, x_I) \leqslant \overline{M},$$

for all $(x_1, \ldots, x_I)$ in $\mathcal{T}_a$, including the market vector associated with x'. But that contradicts (12.3-12).

Q.E.D.

There is still more to the relationship between equilibrium and optimality. For let a vector of factor supplies, $a > 0$, be specified and suppose $\overline{x} > 0$ is a Pareto optimal distribution in X. Then the market vector $(\overline{x}_1, \ldots, \overline{x}_I)$ derived by summing the components of $\overline{x}$ over individuals, is associated with a unique input vector $\overline{y} > 0$ and, as indicated in Section 12.2, all first-order maximization equations and constraints characterizing Pareto optimality (Theorem 12.2-18) are satisfied at $(\overline{x}, \overline{y})$. Therefore (12.3-6) – (12.3-10) are met. (Although $u^K(\overline{x}_K) = \overline{\mu}_K$ and $\overline{x}_I = f^I(\overline{y}_I)$ are not stated as conclusions of Theorem 12.2-18, they are still available because they are part of the collection of equations that define the fixed-factor-supply model.) Now define the output price vector $\overline{p}$ according to (12.3-1) and

$$\overline{p}_I = 1,$$

and fix the input price vector $\overline{r}$ using (12.3-5) with

$$\overline{r}_J = f_J^I(\overline{y}_I),$$

from (8.2-12). At this point, the $b_{i\ell}$ and the aggregate factor supplies $a = (a_1, \ldots, a_J)$ may be taken as known parameters. But the a_{jk}, whose sums over k constitute the a_j, and the $\theta_{ki\ell}$ still have to be specified. These may be (nonuniquely) determined as follows: With the $\overline{m}_k$ and the $\overline{\pi}_{i\ell}$ secured from (12.3-2) and the definition of profit employing the $\overline{p}$ and $\overline{r}$ just described, summing the definitional equation for $\overline{m}_k$ following (12.3-2) over k yields

$$\sum_{k=1}^{K} \overline{m}_k - \sum_{i=1}^{I} \sum_{\ell=1}^{L_i} (\overline{\pi}_{i\ell} + b_{i\ell}) = \overline{r} \cdot a > 0.$$

Hence there exist fractions $\overline{\theta}_{ki\ell} \geqslant 0$ such that

$$\sum_{k=1}^{K} \overline{\theta}_{ki\ell} = 1$$

and

$$\overline{m}_k > \sum_{i=1}^{I} \sum_{\ell=1}^{L_i} \overline{\theta}_{ki\ell} \left(\overline{\pi}_{i\ell} + b_{i\ell} \right), \quad k = 1, \ldots, K.$$

Using these values of $\theta_{ki\ell}$, the relations

$$\overline{m}_k = \overline{r} \cdot a_k + \sum_{i=1}^{I} \sum_{\ell=1}^{L_i} \overline{\theta}_{ki\ell} \left(\overline{\pi}_{i\ell} + b_{i\ell} \right), \quad k = 1, \ldots, K,$$

$$\sum_{k=1}^{K} a_{jk} = a_j, \quad j = 1, \ldots, J,$$

can generally be viewed as a system of $J + K$ independent, linear equations in JK unknown individual factor supply variables a_{jk} where $a_k = (a_{1k}, \ldots, a_{Jk})$ is the factor supply vector for person k. Because

$$\overline{m}_k > \sum_{i=1}^{I} \sum_{\ell=1}^{L_i} \overline{\theta}_{ki\ell} \left(\overline{\pi}_{i\ell} + b_{i\ell} \right), \quad k = 1, \ldots, K,$$

this system always has a nondenumerable number of solutions with $a_k \geqslant 0$ and $a_k \neq (0, \ldots, 0)$ for each k. Let $\overline{a}_1, \ldots, \overline{a}_k$ denote one such solution. Clearly, under present assumptions $(\overline{p}, \overline{r}) > 0$, and at these prices supply equals demand in all markets. Moreover, the first-order conditions for utility maximization subject to the budget constraint (12.3-1) given the $\overline{\theta}_{ki\ell}$ and the individual factor supplies $\overline{a}_k$ hold for every individual, and the first-order conditions for cost minimization subject to the level of output (12.3-5) hold for every industry. Since $\overline{r}_J = f_J^I(\overline{y}_I)$ with $\overline{p}_I = 1$ implies $MC^I(\overline{x}_I) = \overline{p}_I = 1$ (recall p. 194 above), the remaining first-order profit maximization equations of (12.3-3) follow from the combination of (12.3-4) (a part of the defining structure of the fixed-factor-supply model), (12.3-1), and the first set of equations of Theorem 12.2-18. Taking the easy way out by assuming the appropriate second-order conditions are also in force, $(\overline{p}, \overline{r}, \overline{x}, \overline{y})$ is a competitive equilibrium. The argument is summarized by the proposition below.[11] Note its similarity to the

---

[11]   Theorem 12.3-14, like Theorem 12.3-11, can be proved without resort to the calculus. See

proof of Theorem 8.4-3.

Theorem 12.3-14 Let $\overline{x} > 0$ be a Pareto optimal distribution for some vector of factor supplies $a > 0$. Then under the above assumptions there exist nonnegative fractions $\overline{\theta}_{111}, \ldots, \overline{\theta}_{KIL_I}$ where $\sum_{k=1}^{K} \overline{\theta}_{ki\ell} = 1$ for all i and ℓ, nonnegative and nonzero individual factor supplies $\overline{a}_1, \ldots, \overline{a}_K$, and positive vectors $\overline{p}$, $\overline{r}$, and $\overline{y}$ such that $(\overline{p}, \overline{r}, \overline{x}, \overline{y})$ is a competitive equilibrium.

Theorem 12.3-11 and Theorem 12.3-14 establish important properties of perfect competition as modeled here. Restating Theorem 12.3-11, an equilibrium attained in a perfectly competitive structure is *nonwasteful*: Any modification in the distribution of outputs among persons from the equilibrium distribution, or any variation in the outputs themselves (by moving along the transformation surface), no matter how these latter changes are distributed, must either leave the utility levels of all individuals the same or lower the utility level of at least one person. Furthermore, according to Theorem 12.3-14 every perfectly competitive structure is also *unbiased*, that is, all positive Pareto optima are compatible with it. In other words, the institution of perfect competition itself does not favor one Pareto optimal distribution over another. Both equal distributions as well as distributions allocating almost all output to a single individual are possible equilibria. (In any particular case, the actual equilibrium achieved depends on the individual factor supplies and on the values of the $\theta_{ik\ell}$). It is in the senses of nonwastefulness and unbiasedness that perfect competition achieves Paretian efficiency.

In this connection, however, emphasis should also be placed on the fact that the achievement of a particular economy-wide Pareto optimal distribution as an equilibrium is vitally dependent on the initial distribution of resource endowments. The consumption opportunities an individual faces, and hence the basket of goods he buys and the share of total output he procures at equilibrium, are limited by the endowment he has available to sell and his "wealth" as indicated by the returns he receives from firms' profits and fixed costs. It is conceivable, therefore, that in the interest of certain perceptions of social justice, government policies might be designed to effect a redistribution of endowments with the object of achieving Pareto optimality at what might be thought to be a higher level of social welfare. The relation of competitive equilibrium to welfare maximization will be considered shortly.

Moreover, as a practical matter there are many reasons why the nonwastefulness and unbiasedness of perfect competition may break down. This

Koopmans [11, pp. 50-52].

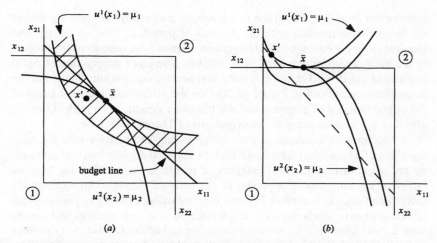

Figure 12.5 Breakdown of the nonwastefulness and unbiasedness of perfect competition: (*a*) equilibrium that is not optimal; (*b*) optimum that cannot be associated with an equilibrium

is because, in reality, the implicit and explicit assumptions upon which they rest can be breached in a variety of ways. Two illustrations of violations of explicit assumptions are provided in Figure 12.5. For both examples, production is assumed to occur at appropriate locations on the transformation surface. In Figure 12.5(a), utility functions are of the usual variety except for the violation of differential increasingness across the "flat" portion of the utility function of person 1: Over all points in the shaded region (including boundaries), the utility level of person 1 is constant. It is differentially increasing and strictly quasi-concave everywhere else. (The utility function of person 2 is differentially increasing and strictly quasi-concave throughout the box.) Although the utility-maximizing basket of commodities $\bar{x} = (\bar{x}_1, \bar{x}_2)$ is not unique for person 1, $\bar{x}$ is still a competitive equilibrium. However, x' is Pareto superior to $\bar{x}$, so $\bar{x}$ cannot be Pareto optimal.

On the other hand, $\bar{x}$ in Figure 12.5(b) is Pareto optimal but there does not exist a positive price vector so that $\bar{x}$ can also be identified as a competitive equilibrium.[12] Given budget lines like the dashed line in the diagram, the utility of person 1 is maximized in the usual way at x'. (It does not matter for person 1 that x' lies outside the box.) But the only budget line that can make $\bar{x}_1$ of

---

[12]   This example is due to Arrow [2, p. 528].

distribution $\overline{x} = (\overline{x}_1, \overline{x}_2)$ in the box a constrained utility-maximizing basket for her is that coincident with the x_{12}-axis of person 2. (Such a budget line requires $p_1 = 0$.) And with this budget line, person 2 maximizes utility subject to the budget constraint where x_2 is infinite. Therefore supply cannot equal demand in either market and $\overline{x}$ is not a competitive equilibrium. Note that the assumptions sacrificed in Figure 12.5(b) are the differential increasingness of the utility function of person 1 and the boundary condition on each. Observe also that $\overline{x}_{22} = 0$, contrary to the hypothesis of Theorem 12.3-14.

The implicit assumptions that can go wrong and thereby void the relationships of Theorems 12.3-11 and 12.3-14 between equilibrium and optimality are numerous. One broad category of problems arises when the level of utility or consumption of a person or the level of output of an industry affects that of another person or industry directly without having to pass through market channels. Such phenomena are referred to as *externalities* and are assumed away implicitly by writing production and utility functions in the form of (12.2-1) and (12.2-5). Thus, for example, externalities are present if a water-polluting industry (i) lowers the utility of downstream residents by forcing them to drink foul water or (ii) reduces the output of a downstream industry that requires clean water for production. In a third instance (iii), externalities arise when the utility level of one person is influenced by the consumption of his neighbor. In case (i) and case (iii), the respective utility function of the downstream resident and of the person with the neighbor (each designated as individual 1) are,

$$\mu_1 = u^1(x_1, f^i(y_i)),$$

$$\mu_1 = u^1(x_1, x_2), \qquad (12.3\text{-}15)$$

where f^i is the production function of the polluting industry and x_2 is the neighbor's consumption vector. Similarly, in case (ii), the production function of the downstream industry would have $f^i(y_i)$, in addition to the usual inputs, as one of its arguments.

To illustrate what can happen to previous argument when such externalities are introduced, consider the example of (12.3-15). Suppose all remaining persons have standard utility functions

$$\mu_k = u^k(x_k), \quad k = 2, \dots, K. \qquad (12.3\text{-}16)$$

Under perfect competition, of course, person 1 still chooses only his own consumption vector x_1 without regard for x_2. Hence maximization of u^1 subject to his budget constraint yields first-order ratio conditions for each value of x_2, or

$$\frac{p_i}{p_I} = \frac{u_i^1(x_1, x_2)}{u_I^1(x_1, x_2)}, \quad i = 1, \ldots, I-1,$$

where $u_i^1(x_1, x_2) = \partial u^1/\partial x_{i1}$ for $i = 1, \ldots, I$. There is no change in the first-order conditions for other individuals. Equilibrium under perfect competition, then, equates price ratios with marginal rates of substitution as before. It therefore ensures that (12.2-10) is satisfied, where u^1 contains the extra argument x_2. However, applying the definition of Pareto optimality with utility functions (12.3-15) and (12.3-16) gives first-order ratio conditions characterizing the Paretian optimum which are different from those of (12.2-10). (See, for example, Exercise 12.4.) Therefore, competitive equilibrium cannot be Pareto optimal.

A different kind of problem arises when a good is *public*, that is, when it has the property that if it is consumed by anyone at all, it is consumed by everyone in the same quantity. No one can be excluded from consuming the good once it is produced, and the pleasure one person receives from the good does not detract from that obtained by another. National defense and street lighting are two commodities that, broadly speaking at least, have this characteristic. In the first instance, the foreign policy and defense organization of a country tend to defend all citizens to the same extent; and in the second, once a street light is turned on, the street is lit for everyone. To convert a commodity, say good 1, into a public good in the fixed factor-supply model, observe that the above definition requires

$$x_{1k} = x_1, \quad k = 1, \ldots, K, \tag{12.3-17}$$

where x_1 varies over "market" quantities of good 1. Hence the utility functions (12.2-5) are written

$$\mu_k = u^k(x_1, x_{2k}, \ldots, x_{Ik}), \quad k = 1, \ldots, K, \tag{12.3-18}$$

and the transformation function of (12.2-17) becomes

$$\sum_{k=1}^{K} x_{Ik} = t\left(x_1, \sum_{k=1}^{K} x_{2k}, \ldots, \sum_{k=1}^{K} x_{I-1k}\right). \tag{12.3-19}$$

Combine (12.3-17) − (12.3-19) with the remaining equations of the fixed-factor-supply model, and let $\overline{x} = (\overline{x}_1, \ldots, \overline{x}_K)$ in X be Pareto optimal. Then application of Lagrange's theorem leads to[13]

$$\sum_{k=1}^{K} \frac{u_1^k(\overline{x}_k)}{u_I^k(\overline{x}_k)} = -t_1\left(\overline{x}_1, \sum_{k=1}^{K} \overline{x}_{2k}, \ldots, \sum_{k=1}^{K} \overline{x}_{I-1k}\right),$$

$$\frac{u_i^k(\overline{x}_k)}{u_I^k(\overline{x}_k)} = -t_i\left(\overline{x}_1, \sum_{k=1}^{K} \overline{x}_{2k}, \ldots, \sum_{k=1}^{K} \overline{x}_{I-1k}\right),$$

(12.3-20)

where $i = 2, \ldots, I - 1$ and $k = 1, \ldots, K$ in the second equation, and the first component of each $\overline{x}_k$ is the "market" quantity $\overline{x}_1$. (A two-person, two-commodity example can be found in Exercise 12.6.)

Public goods differ from ordinary commodities in that individuals are unable to choose the quantities of them they consume. In particular, there cannot be either individual or market demand functions indicating that certain quantities are demanded at specific prices. Hence it makes no sense to think of public goods as flowing through markets. Therefore the Walrasian system developed to this point necessarily excludes public goods and, were that system modified to include them, the nonwastefulness and unbiasedness theorems as previously formulated would not apply. In the latter case, although analysis of ordinary commodities would continue in terms of the usual utility and profit maximizations and the equating of market demand to market supply, determination of the production and consumption of public goods would have to proceed differently. Whether equilibrium in such a world turns out to be Pareto optimal depends on whether equations like (12.3-20) are satisfied.

Of course, to be able to set the level of production x_1 of the public good so that the equilibrium distribution x and associated market vector

$$\left(x_1, \sum_{k=1}^{K} x_{2k}, \ldots, \sum_{k=1}^{K} x_{Ik}\right)$$

satisfy (12.3-20) along with the other optimality and constraint conditions, requires knowledge of individual utility functions. Furthermore, without a way of paying for the public good, it could not be produced. Were each person willing to reveal his utility function truthfully, both difficulties could be resolved: The ratios of (12.3-20) could be computed, $\overline{x}_1$ and hence $\overline{x}$ determined, and everyone charged for the public good according to the utility each derives from it. But because the individual may be able to achieve the same level of consumption of the public good at lower personal cost, there is a strong incentive

---

[13] The first equation of (12.3-20) was originally derived by Samuelson [17, p. 387].

under such a scheme for him to understate the utility he would actually achieve and "ride free." The question of designing incentives to induce persons to reveal their true utility functions and thereby overcome what is known as this *free-rider* problem is not pursued here.[14]

Still further circumstances in which the above relationship between equilibrium and optimality can be destroyed (and which are ruled out implicitly by the hypotheses of Theorems 12.3-11 and 12.3-14) arise if marginal cost in an industry at equilibrium is unequal to output price. When this happens the derivation, from (12.3-1), (12.3-3), and (12.3-4), of the first group of Lagrangian equations characterizing Pareto optimality in Theorem 12.2-18 falls apart, and hence there is no longer any guarantee that equilibria are Pareto optimal. Several examples of output price deviating from marginal cost have already been presented. These include all of the forms of imperfect competition discussed in Chapter 11, and the imposition of a sales tax or subsidy on a perfectly competitive industry described in Section 6.3.

If, with respect to any particular market, one or more of the explicit and implicit assumptions ensuring a perfectly competitive outcome are not met and, as a consequence, that outcome is not achieved, then that market is said to have *failed*. Clearly, without any off-setting effects, the failure of only one market is enough to interfere with the attainment of nonwastefulness and unbiasedness of perfect competition in relation to the economy as a whole. The presence of market failure, then, provides a plausible justification for government intervention in the economy for the purpose of correcting that failure.

Returning to the situation in which all of the implicit and explicit assumptions are in force, the connection between equilibrium under perfect competition and Pareto optimality provides one way of linking competitive equilibria to constrained welfare maximization. Thus the following proposition is a trivial consequence of combining the unbiasedness of perfect competition (Theorem 12.3-14) with the relationship between constrained welfare maximization and Pareto optimality of Theorem 12.2-25.

Theorem 12.3-21   Under the assumptions of Theorem 12.3-14, let $a > 0$ be a given vector of factor supplies and let $\overline{x} > 0$ have its associated market vector $(\overline{x}_1, \ldots \overline{x}_I)$ in $\mathcal{T}_a$. Suppose W is a twice, continuously differentiable utility welfare function defined on $\mathcal{U}$. If $\overline{x}$ maximizes $W \circ u(x)$ over the collection of all distributions in X whose associated market vectors also lie in $\mathcal{T}_a$, then there exist nonnegative fractions $\overline{\theta}_{111}, \ldots, \overline{\theta}_{KIL_I}$ where $\sum_{k=1}^{K} \overline{\theta}_{ki\ell} = 1$ for all i and ℓ, nonnegative and nonzero individual factor supplies $\overline{a}_1, \ldots, \overline{a}_K$, and positive

---

[14]   Discussion of the problem can be found, for example, in Groves and Ledyard [10].

vectors $\overline{p}$, $\overline{r}$, and $\overline{y}$ such that $(\overline{p}, \overline{r}, \overline{x}, \overline{y})$ is a competitive equilibrium.

To obtain a kind of converse to Theorem 12.3-21, let $(\overline{p}, \overline{r}, \overline{x}, \overline{y}) > 0$ be a competitive equilibrium. Then from (12.3-15) and (3.4-2), utility maximization subject to the budget constraint by each person implies

$$u_i^k(\overline{x}_k) = \overline{\lambda}_k \overline{p}_i, \qquad \begin{matrix} i = 1, \ldots, I, \\ k = 1, \ldots, K, \end{matrix} \qquad (12.3\text{-}22)$$

where $\overline{\lambda}_k = v_m^k(\overline{p}, \overline{m}_k)$ is the marginal utility of income of person k at the equilibrium. Also, from (8.2-7), profit maximization by each firm gives

$$\overline{p}_i = -\overline{p}_I t_i\left(\sum_{k=1}^{K} \overline{x}_{1k}, \ldots, \sum_{k=1}^{K} \overline{x}_{I-1k}\right), \qquad i = 1, \ldots, I-1. \qquad (12.3\text{-}23)$$

Set $\varepsilon = \overline{p}_I$. Then combining (12.3-22) and (12.3-23) leads to

$$\frac{1}{\overline{\lambda}_k} u_I^k(\overline{x}_k) = \varepsilon, \qquad k = 1, \ldots, K,$$

$$\frac{1}{\overline{\lambda}_k} u_i^k(\overline{x}_k) = -\varepsilon t_i\left(\sum_{k=1}^{K} \overline{x}_{1k}, \ldots, \sum_{k=1}^{K} \overline{x}_{I-1k}\right), \qquad (12.3\text{-}24)$$

for $i = 1, \ldots, I-1$ and each k. Interpreting ε as a Lagrange multiplier, (12.3-24) provides the first-order maximization equations obtained from maximizing the distribution welfare function[15]

$$W \circ u(x) = \sum_{k=1}^{K} \frac{1}{\overline{\lambda}_k} u^k(x_k)$$

subject to

$$\sum_{k=1}^{K} x_{Ik} = t\left(\sum_{k=1}^{K} x_{1k}, \ldots, \sum_{k=1}^{K} x_{I-1k}\right).$$

Therefore, if individual utility functions are shaped so as to satisfy appropriate second-order maximization conditions, the sought-after "converse" to Theorem 12.3-21 has been proved:

---

[15]   Once again, the constraint qualification (A.3-17) is satisfied since the first-order partial derivatives of t are nonvanishing where defined.

Theorem 12.3-25   Under the above assumptions, if $(\overline{p}, \overline{r}, \overline{x}, \overline{y}) > 0$ is a competitive equilibrium, then there exists a utility welfare function, namely,

$$W(\mu) = \sum_{k=1}^{K} \frac{1}{\overline{\lambda}_k} \mu_k, \tag{12.3-26}$$

defined on $\mathcal{U}$, such that $\overline{x}$ uniquely maximizes $W \circ u(x)$ over the set of all distributions in X whose associated market vectors are contained in $\mathcal{T}_a$.

There is, of course, no reason why a society should have an additive, utility welfare function where individuals' utilities are weighted by the reciprocals of their marginal utilities of income as in (12.3-26). But in the event that it does, competitive equilibrium at $(\overline{p}, \overline{r}, \overline{x}, \overline{y})$ maximizes welfare subject to the transformation surface constraint.[16] Notice that for the special circumstance in which all marginal utilities of income diminish with rising income, the larger a person's income at $(\overline{p}, \overline{r}, \overline{x}, \overline{y})$, the greater the weight that her preferences have in (12.3-26). Returning to the general context without restrictions on marginal utilities of income, let i and $x_{ik'}$ for all k' different from some particular k be fixed. Then with $\omega = W \circ u(x)$ and x_i denoting market quantities of good i,

$$\left.\frac{\partial \omega}{\partial x_i}\right|_{x=\overline{x}} = \frac{\partial W \circ u(x)}{\partial x_{ik}} \left.\frac{\partial x_{ik}}{\partial x_i}\right|_{x=\overline{x}},$$

which, from (12.3-26), (12.2-5), and (12.2-6), is equal to

$$\frac{1}{\overline{\lambda}_k} u_i^k(\overline{x}_k).$$

Applying (12.3-22) now yields

$$\left.\frac{\partial \omega}{\partial x_i}\right|_{x=\overline{x}} = \overline{p}_i. \tag{12.3-27}$$

Clearly (12.3-27) remains in force for all $i = 1, \ldots, I$, and any fixed k can be used in its derivation. Employment of the welfare function of Theorem 12.3-25 in conjunction with (12.2-27) and the discussion following it therefore leads to the conclusion that, at equilibrium, the competitive price $\overline{p}_i$, represents the marginal social value of good i to society. Moreover, combining this and

---

[16]   It should be observed that if the economy were at an interior point of its production possibility set, competitive equilibrium would not prevail, and not all of the economy's resources would be fully employed. In that event, welfare would not be maximized regardless of the utility welfare function invoked.

(12.3-3), use of the same welfare function also ensures that at equilibrium the marginal social value of each produced good equals its marginal cost of production or that, again at equilibrium (and assuming everything is measured in comparable units), the spread between welfare and the sum of all total costs of production over all industries in the economy, which may be referred to as "net" welfare, is maximized. As indicated in the next section, this welfare function is convenient for other reasons as well.

12.4   THE MEASUREMENT OF WELFARE

In arriving at decisions that result in the movement from one distribution in X to another, society's governing decision-makers may wish to know the impact of their potential choices on economic welfare. Such information, however, is difficult to obtain from $W \circ u$ because neither W nor u normally is known with sufficient precision. Indeed, the typical state of affairs with respect to these functions is one of considerable ignorance. Thus it is natural to ask about alternative ways of recording welfare modifications in terms of readily available and observable facts. Subsequent discussion focuses on conditions under which values of aggregate output and areas under demand curves can serve as the basis for measures of changes in economic welfare. In most cases only equilibria are compared. For practical application, then, these equilibria have to be identified with the data that might be observed in the real economy before and after the change.

Let $(\overline{p}, \overline{r}, \overline{x}, \overline{y}) > 0$ be a competitive equilibrium for the fixed-factor-supply vector $\overline{a} > 0$, where $\overline{x}$ is the distribution $(\overline{x}_1, \ldots, \overline{x}_K)$ and the latter's associated market vector is $(\overline{x}_1, \ldots, \overline{x}_I)$. Without introducing any welfare functions at all, Pareto superiority can be linked to the relative values of associated market vectors (that is, aggregate output) as follows:

Theorem 12.4-1   For all x in X, if x is Pareto superior to $\overline{x}$, then

$$\overline{p} \cdot (x_1, \ldots, x_I) > \overline{p} \cdot (\overline{x}_1, \ldots, \overline{x}_I),$$

where $(x_1, \ldots, x_I)$ is the market vector associated with x.

Actually, Theorem 12.4-1 has already been established in the proof of Theorem 12.3-11. Relation (12.3-12) states the required inequality since, in that context, $\overline{M} = \overline{p} \cdot \overline{x}$. The contrapositive to Theorem 12.4-1 is worth listing as a separate result.

Corollary 12.4-2   For all $(x_1, \ldots, x_I) > 0$, if

$$\overline{p} \cdot (\overline{x}_1, \ldots, \overline{x}_I) \geqslant \overline{p} \cdot (x_1, \ldots, x_I),$$

then no distribution associated with $(x_1, \ldots, x_I)$ can be Pareto superior to $\overline{x}$.

Under additional conditions ensuring comparability with respect to the Pareto ordering, the inequality of Corollary 12.4-2 can also be used as an indicator of Pareto superiority.

Theorem 12.4-3   Let $(x_1, \ldots, x_I)$ be in $\mathcal{T}_{\overline{a}}$ so that

$$\overline{p} \cdot (\overline{x}_1, \ldots, \overline{x}_I) \geqslant \overline{p} \cdot (x_1, \ldots, x_I).$$

If $x = (x_1, \ldots, x_K)$ is any distribution associated with $(x_1, \ldots, x_I)$ such that $x \neq \overline{x}$ and

$$\overline{p} \cdot \overline{x}_k \geqslant \overline{p} \cdot x_k, \quad k = 1, \ldots, K,$$

then $\overline{x}$ is Pareto superior to x.

Proof: Since $(\overline{p}, \overline{r}, \overline{x}, \overline{y})$ is assumed to be a competitive equilibrium, since utility maximizing baskets $\overline{x}_k$ are unique (from the strict quasi-concavity of the u^k), and since

$$\overline{p} \cdot \overline{x}_k \geqslant \overline{p} \cdot x_k, \quad k = 1, \ldots, K,$$

with $x_k \neq \overline{x}_k$ for some k, it follows that

$$u^k(\overline{x}_k) \geqslant u^k(x_k), \quad k = 1, \ldots, K,$$

and for at least one k,

$$u^k(\overline{x}_k) > u^k(x_k).$$

Therefore $\overline{x}$ is Pareto superior to x.

$$\textbf{Q.E.D.}$$

In view of the fact that Pareto superiority implies greater welfare as described in conjunction with (12.2-24), Theorems 12.4-1 and 12.4-3 hint at a connection between welfare and the value of aggregate output. To move toward it, think of x as a component of the competitive equilibrium $(p, r, x, y) > 0$ given the fixed-factor-supply vector $a > 0$. (The distribution $\overline{x}$ already is a component of $(\bar{p}, \bar{r}, \bar{x}, \bar{y})$ given $\bar{a} > 0$.) Invoking (12.2-24), (12.2-6) and Theorem 12.4-1, if x is Pareto superior to $\bar{x}$, then both

$$\sum_{k=1}^{K}\sum_{i=1}^{I}\bar{p}_i x_{ik} - \sum_{k=1}^{K}\sum_{i=1}^{I}\bar{p}_i \bar{x}_{ik} > 0, \qquad (12.4\text{-}4)$$

and welfare is higher at x. Alternatively, if $\bar{x}$ is Pareto superior to x, and if

$$p \cdot (x_1, \ldots, x_I) = \bar{p}\,(\bar{x}_1, \ldots, \bar{x}_I), \qquad (12.4\text{-}5)$$

then further application of (12.2-24), (12.2-6), and Theorem 12.4-1 yields

$$\sum_{k=1}^{K}\sum_{i=1}^{I}p_i \bar{x}_{ik} - \sum_{k=1}^{K}\sum_{i=1}^{I}\bar{p}_i \bar{x}_{ik} > 0, \qquad (12.4\text{-}6)$$

with welfare higher at $\bar{x}$. In the converse direction, (12.4-4) with the inequality reversed and (12.2-24) imply greater welfare at $\bar{x}$ provided the remaining hypotheses of Theorem 12.4-3 are satisfied. And similarly, (12.4-6) with the inequality reversed, (12.4-5), and (12.2-24) ensure larger welfare at x, again under the extra assumptions ((12.4-5) guarantees that one of them is satisfied) necessary to be able to invoke Theorem 12.4-3.

Clearly the last two assertions permitting the inference of welfare comparisons from aggregate income data are the main interest here. But the extra requirements needed to employ Theorem 12.4-3 are highly restrictive. Of course, they have to be. To infer the Pareto superiority used in conjunction with (12.2-24), the value judgments inherent in W have to be neutralized and the aggregate income data must be forced to reflect certain efficiency variations only. However, it turns out that there are circumstances permitting retention of the full force of the value judgments behind W in which the left-hand sides of (12.4-4) and (12.4-6) can be used, under weaker conditions than those of Theorem 12.4-3, as approximations of welfare differences. But before developing the idea, a digression is necessary to express welfare as a function of prices and the distribution of income.

Let W and u be, respectively, the utility welfare function and the vector of individual utility functions of previous sections. Thus $W \circ u$ is twice, continuously differentiable and differentially increasing in the interior of X. Recall that at any competitive equilibrium, $(p, r, x, y) > 0$, indirect utility functions (3.4-1) are given by

$$\mu_k = v^k(p, m_k), \quad k = 1, \ldots, K,$$

where

$$v^k(p, m_k) = u^k(h^k(p, m_k)),$$

$x_k = h^k(p, m_k)$ are the demand functions of person k, and m_k is defined as in
(12.3-2) for each k. Hence at this competitive equilibrium, welfare can be expressed as a function of prices and the income distribution $m = (m_1, \ldots, m_K)$
according to

$$\omega = W \circ u(x) = W \circ v(p, m), \tag{12.4-7}$$

where $v = (v^1, \ldots, v^K)$,

$$x = h(p, m) = \left(h^1(p, m_1), \ldots, h^K(p, m_K)\right),$$

and $h = \left(h^1, \ldots, h^K\right)$. Let h be continuously differentiable throughout its domain. With the factor supplies $a = (a_1, \ldots, a_J)$ free to range over all positive
J-dimensional vectors, suppose that there exists a unique equilibrium distribution x in X for every $(p, m) > 0$, and each x in X is an equilibrium distribution associated with some $(p, m) > 0$ that is unique up to positive, scalar
multiples of (p, m). Then ω can be viewed equivalently either as a function
of x for all x in X, or as a function of (p, m) for all $(p, m) > 0$. Combining
this with earlier assumptions, $W \circ v$ is continuously differentiable everywhere.
Moreover, because W and the u^k are differentially increasing, and because the
$v_i^k(p, m_k) < 0$ for $k = 1, \ldots, K$ and $i = 1, \ldots, I$, and the $v_m^k(p, m_k) > 0$
where $k = 1, \ldots, K$ (recall Section 3.4),

$$\frac{\partial W \circ u(x)}{\partial x_{ik}} > 0,$$

$$\frac{\partial W \circ v(p, m)}{\partial p_i} < 0,$$

$$\frac{\partial W \circ v(p, m)}{\partial m_k} > 0,$$

for all i and k. Other things being equal, lowering prices or raising the income or consumption of any individual increases economic welfare. Similar
statements for incremental variations in x_{ik}, p_i, and m_k can be obtained upon
application of Theorem 3.4-7.

Consider the particular competitive equilibrium $(\overline{p}, \overline{r}, \overline{x}, \overline{y}) > 0$ for the
factor-supply vector fixed once again at $\overline{a}$, and restrict attention to the utility

welfare function of (12.3-26), namely,

$$W(\mu) = \sum_{k=1}^{K} \frac{1}{\overline{\lambda}_k} \mu_k, \qquad (12.4\text{-}8)$$

where

$$\overline{\lambda}_k = v_m^k(\overline{p}, \overline{m}_k), \quad k = 1, \dots, K.$$

Note that substitution of (12.4-8) into (12.4-7) gives

$$\omega = \sum_{k=1}^{K} \frac{1}{\overline{\lambda}_k} u^k(x_k) = \sum_{k=1}^{K} \frac{1}{\overline{\lambda}_k} v^k(p, m_k). \qquad (12.4\text{-}9)$$

From Theorem 12.3-25, the left-hand sum in (12.4-9) is maximized at $x = \overline{x}$ subject to market vectors lying in $\mathcal{T}_{\overline{a}}$. The right-hand sum is maximized at $(\overline{p}, \overline{m})$ subject to a parallel constraint.

Using (12.4-9), welfare differences arising between distinct equilibria $(p, r, x, y) > 0$ and $(\overline{p}, \overline{r}, \overline{x}, \overline{y}) > 0$ can be approximated according to Taylor's theorem.[17] On one hand,

$$W \circ u(x) - W \circ u(\overline{x}) \simeq \sum_{k=1}^{K} \sum_{i=1}^{I} \frac{1}{\overline{\lambda}_k} u_i^k(\overline{x}_k) (x_{ik} - \overline{x}_{ik}),$$

which, from the first-order Lagrangian maximization conditions $u_i^k(\overline{x}_k) = \overline{\lambda}_k \overline{p}_i$ for every i and k, collapses to

$$W \circ u(x) - W \circ u(\overline{x}) \simeq \left[\sum_{k=1}^{K} \sum_{i=1}^{I} \overline{p}_i x_{ik} \right] - \left[\sum_{k=1}^{K} \sum_{i=1}^{I} \overline{p}_i \overline{x}_{ik} \right]. \qquad (12.4\text{-}10)$$

The right-hand bracketed term is the value of aggregate output at equilibrium $(\overline{p}, \overline{r}, \overline{x}, \overline{y})$. The one on the left is the value of output x (from equilibrium (p, r, x, y)) at prices $\overline{p}$. Thus for x "sufficiently close" to, but still distinct from $\overline{x}$, welfare increments can be approximated by differences in the values of aggregate output. Observe that if the market vector associated with x is in $\mathcal{T}_{\overline{a}}$, then because $W \circ u$ is uniquely maximized at $\overline{x}$ with respect to all distributions whose associated market vectors lie in $\mathcal{T}_{\overline{a}}$ (Theorem 12.3-25),

$$W \circ u(x) - W \circ u(\overline{x}) < 0.$$

---

[17]   Apostol [1, pp. 361, 362]. Equation (A.3-7) in appendix section A.3 is all that is required here.

Moreover, as long as only the sign of $W \circ u(x) - W \circ u(\overline{x})$ is of interest, ordinality of the scale over which W ranges — that is, the scale on which social pleasure is measured — suffices. But when magnitudes of these differences are important, it becomes necessary to assume that the social pleasure scale is cardinal. (A similar assertion was made for the analysis of individual welfare in Section 3.4.)

On the other hand, returning to (12.4-9) with (p, m) distinct from all positive, scalar multiples of $(\overline{p}, \overline{m})$, application of Taylor's theorem once again yields,

$$W \circ v(p, m) - W \circ v(\overline{p}, \overline{m}) \simeq$$

$$\sum_{k=1}^{K} \left[\frac{1}{\overline{\lambda}_k} v_m^k(\overline{p}, \overline{m}_k)\,(m_k - \overline{m}_k) + \sum_{i=1}^{I} \frac{1}{\overline{\lambda}_k} v_i^k(\overline{p}, \overline{m}_k)\,(p_i - \overline{p}_i) \right].$$

Since v_i^k / v_m^k is the negative of person k's demand function for good i (Theorem 3.4-3), and because $\overline{\lambda}_k = v_m^k(\overline{p}, \overline{m}_k)$ from (3.4-2),

$$W \circ v(p, m) - W \circ v(\overline{p}, \overline{m}) \simeq$$

$$\left[\sum_{k=1}^{K} m_k \right] - \left[\sum_{k=1}^{K} \overline{m}_k \right] - \left[\sum_{k=1}^{K} \sum_{i=1}^{I} \overline{x}_{ik}\,(p_i - \overline{p}_i) \right].$$

When aggregate income is the same at both equilibria,[18] that is when

$$\sum_{k=1}^{K} m_k = \sum_{k=1}^{K} \overline{m}_k, \tag{12.4-11}$$

then

$$W \circ v(p, m) - W \circ v(\overline{p}, \overline{m}) \simeq \left[\sum_{k=1}^{K} \sum_{i=1}^{I} \overline{p}_i \overline{x}_{ik} \right] - \left[\sum_{k=1}^{K} \sum_{i=1}^{I} p_i \overline{x}_{ik} \right]. \tag{12.4-12}$$

Thus with $x = h(p, m)$ and $\overline{x} = h(\overline{p}, \overline{m})$, the same welfare increment of (12.4-10) also is approximated by the difference between the value of aggregate output at equilibrium $(\overline{p}, \overline{r}, \overline{x}, \overline{y})$ and the value of $\overline{x}$ at equilibrium prices p. For x close to $\overline{x}$, the right-hand sides of (12.4-10) and (12.4-12) have the

---

[18]   Actually, near equality would suffice for subsequent argument.

same sign, and therefore imply the identical sign for

$$W \circ u(x) - W \circ u(\overline{x}) = W \circ v(p, m) - W \circ v(\overline{p}, \overline{m}).$$

(Due to the continuity of the demand functions h, x is close to $\overline{x}$ if and only if (p, m) is close to $(\overline{p}, \overline{m})$, where $x = h(p, m)$ and $\overline{x} = h(\overline{p}, \overline{m})$.) Note that from the definition of individual budget constraints, (12.4-11) is the same as (12.4-5).

It should be pointed out that the ratio

$$\frac{\sum_{k=1}^{K} \sum_{i=1}^{I} p_i \overline{x}_{ik}}{\sum_{k=1}^{K} \sum_{i=1}^{I} \overline{p}_i \overline{x}_{ik}},$$

is called the *Laspeyre price index*, and the ratio

$$\frac{\sum_{k=1}^{K} \sum_{i=1}^{I} \overline{p}_i x_{ik}}{\sum_{k=1}^{K} \sum_{i=1}^{I} \overline{p}_i \overline{x}_{ik}},$$

is known as the *Laspeyre quantity index*. The former measures variation in the "cost of living" or "aggregate price" (as defined by the ratio of the two sums) between $(\overline{p}, \overline{r}, \overline{x}, \overline{y})$ and (p, r, x, y). In this measure the price of good i is weighted by the number of units of good i produced at $(\overline{p}, \overline{r}, \overline{x}, \overline{y})$. Similarly, the latter calibrates changes in "aggregate output" where weights are taken to be prices $\overline{p}_1, \ldots, \overline{p}_I$. Thus from Theorem 12.3-25 with x sufficiently close to $\overline{x}$ and the market vector associated with x in $\mathcal{T}_{\overline{a}}$, either

$$W \circ u(\overline{x}) > W \circ u(x)$$

and (in light of approximation (12.4-10)) the Laspeyre quantity index is less than one or, when aggregate income is the same at both equilibria,

$$W \circ v(\overline{p}, \overline{m}) > W \circ v(p, m)$$

and (invoking approximation (12.4-12)) the Laspeyre price index is greater than one. If the market vector associated with x is not in $\mathcal{T}_{\overline{a}}$ but x is still close to $\overline{x}$, then the Laspeyre quantity index is less than or greater than 1 according as

$$W \circ u(\overline{x}) \gtreqless W \circ u(x)$$

and, as long as the equal aggregate income requirement holds, the Laspeyre price index is larger or smaller than 1 as

$$W \circ v(\overline{p}, \overline{m}) \gtreqless W \circ v(p, m).$$

Thus the Laspeyre indices can be used as a basis for welfare comparisons. Recall that for the case of a single utility-maximizing individual, a result similar to those for $W \circ u$ (without the requirement that x be close to $\overline{x}$) appears as Exercise 3.12.

These ideas find simple illustration when there are two commodities. Two pairs of solid parallel lines appear in the market-quantity space of Figure 12.6. One line of each pair goes through the market vector labeled $\mathcal{M}(\overline{x})$, the other through $\mathcal{M}(x)$. Lines labeled $\overline{p}$ and p have slopes $-\overline{p}_1/\overline{p}_2$ and $-p_1/p_2$ respectively. It is clear from the geometry that

$$\overline{p}_1 \overline{x}_1 + \overline{p}_2 \overline{x}_2 > \overline{p}_1 x_1 + \overline{p}_2 x_2,$$

and

$$p_1 \overline{x}_1 + p_2 \overline{x}_2 > p_1 x_1 + p_2 x_2,$$

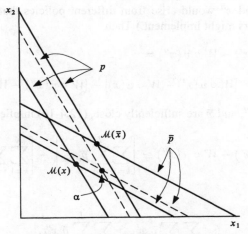

Figure 12.6 Comparison of welfare at $\overline{x}$ with welfare at x

where $\bar{x}_i = \sum_{k=1}^{K} \bar{x}_{ik}$ and $x_i = \sum_{k=1}^{K} x_{ik}$ for $i = 1, 2$. Hence if x is close enough to $\bar{x}$, welfare is higher at $\bar{x}$ by (12.4-10). If, in addition,

$$\bar{p}_1 \bar{x}_1 + \bar{p}_2 \bar{x}_2 = p_1 x_1 + p_2 x_2,$$

(for example, $x_1 = x_2 = 1$, $\bar{x}_1 = \bar{x}_2 = 2$, $\bar{p}_1 = \bar{p}_2 = p_2 = 1$, and $p_1 = 3$) then welfare is also higher at $\bar{x} = h(\bar{p}, \bar{m})$ according to (12.4-12). The fact that $\bar{x} > x$ in Figure 12.6 is irrelevant. The argument applies equally well to equilibria such that, say, $\bar{x}_1 > x_1$ and $\bar{x}_2 < x_2$, as long as the above equation and inequalities remain in force (e.g., were $\mathcal{M}(\bar{x})$ to be located at α in Figure 12.6).

The preceding discussion is based on the assumptions that $(\bar{p}, \bar{r}, \bar{x}, \bar{y})$ is a competitive equilibrium and that society's utility welfare function is additive where, as in (12.4-8), individuals' utilities are weighted by the reciprocals of their marginal utilities of income. Notice that because $W \circ u$ is maximized uniquely at $\bar{x}$ with respect to all distributions having associated market vectors in $\mathcal{T}_{\bar{a}}$ (Theorem 12.3-25), any movement from $\bar{x}$ that keeps the associated market vectors in $\mathcal{T}_{\bar{a}}$, must lower social welfare. In this situation, the only issue the above calculations resolve is, roughly, by how much welfare falls. (As remarked earlier, such magnitudes are meaningful only when the social pleasure scale is cardinal.)

These results, however, can be applied more generally by supposing that, although not at equilibrium $(\bar{p}, \bar{r}, \bar{x}, \bar{y})$, society's welfare function is still given by (12.4-8). To illustrate, consider two equilibria with distributions x' and x''. (Perhaps x' and x'' would arise from different policies that a government's decision-makers might implement.) Then

$$W \circ u(x') - W \circ u(x'') =$$

$$[W \circ u(x') - W \circ u(\bar{x})] - [W \circ u(x'') - W \circ u(\bar{x})].$$

Provided x', x'', and $\bar{x}$ are sufficiently close, (12.4-10) implies

$$W \circ u\left(x'\right) - W \circ u\left(x''\right) \simeq \left[\sum_{k=1}^{K} \sum_{i=1}^{I} \bar{p}_i x'_{ik}\right] - \left[\sum_{k=1}^{K} \sum_{i=1}^{I} \bar{p}_i x''_{ik}\right].$$

Therefore if

$$\sum_{k=1}^{K} \sum_{i=1}^{I} \bar{p}_i x'_{ik} > \sum_{k=1}^{K} \sum_{i=1}^{I} \bar{p}_i x''_{ik}, \qquad (12.4\text{-}13)$$

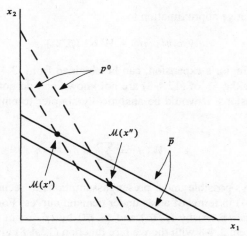

Figure 12.7 Welfare at x' and x'' compared relative to $\bar{p}$ and p^0

or, equivalently, if the Laspeyre quantity indices

$$\frac{\sum\limits_{k=1}^{K}\sum\limits_{i=1}^{I}\bar{p}_i x'_{ik}}{\sum\limits_{k=1}^{K}\sum\limits_{i=1}^{I}\bar{p}_i \bar{x}_{ik}} > \frac{\sum\limits_{k=1}^{K}\sum\limits_{i=1}^{I}\bar{p}_i x''_{ik}}{\sum\limits_{k=1}^{K}\sum\limits_{i=1}^{I}\bar{p}_i \bar{x}_{ik}},$$

then social welfare is greater at x'. Geometrically, in the two-dimensional market-quantity space of Figure 12.7, (12.4-13) means that the line through $\mathcal{M}(x')$ with slope $-\bar{p}_1/\bar{p}_2$ (labeled $\bar{p}$) lies farther from the origin than the parallel line (also labeled $\bar{p}$) through $\mathcal{M}(x'')$, where $\mathcal{M}(x)$ again denotes the market vector associated with x, for each x. As long as $\mathcal{M}(x') \not> \mathcal{M}(x'')$, the conclusion that welfare is larger at x' clearly depends on $\bar{p}$: The dashed lines in the diagram correspond to a price vector p^0 that reverses the inequality of (12.4-13) and implies greater welfare at x''. Hence the choice of $(\bar{p}, \bar{r}, \bar{x}, \bar{y})$ and, of course, the welfare function (12.4-8), is crucial. (Observe that if $\mathcal{M}(x') > \mathcal{M}(x'')$, then x' could be Pareto superior to x''. In such a case social welfare is always higher at x' regardless of $(\bar{p}, \bar{r}, \bar{x}, \bar{y})$ or the particular welfare function employed. Recall the argument involving (12.2-24).)

An alternative approximation to

$$W \circ v(p, m) - W \circ v(\overline{p}, \overline{m}),\tag{12.4-14}$$

also based on Taylor's expansion, can be obtained from (3.4-20). In this situation, because the $\overline{\lambda}_k$ of (12.4-8) are not known and do not drop out of the relevant expressions, it would be analytically simpler to employ the welfare function

$$W(\mu) = \sum_{k=1}^{K} \mu_k.$$

It is always possible under present assumptions to secure an exact measure of (12.4-14) in terms of areas under demand curves. For notational convenience replace (p, m) by $(\overline{p}, \overline{m})$ and $(\overline{p}, \overline{m})$ by $(\widehat{p}, \widehat{m})$ in (12.4-14). Now applying Theorem 3.4-8 with the welfare function (12.4-8) gives

$$W \circ v(\overline{p}, \overline{m}) - W \circ v(\widehat{p}, \widehat{m})$$

$$= \sum_{k=1}^{K} \frac{1}{\overline{\lambda}_k} \left\{ \int_{\widehat{m}_k}^{\overline{m}_k} v_m^k(\widehat{p}, m_k)\, dm_k \right.\tag{12.4-15}$$

$$\left. - \sum_{i=1}^{I} \int_{\widehat{p}_i}^{\overline{p}_i} v_m^k(p^i, \overline{m}_k)\, h^{ik}(p^i, \overline{m}_k)\, dp_i \right\},$$

where h^{ik} is the demand function of person k for good i and $p^i = (\widehat{p}_1, \ldots, \widehat{p}_{i-1}, p_i, \overline{p}_{i+1}, \ldots, \overline{p}_I)$, for every i and k. To simplify this result, suppose $\overline{m}_k = \widehat{m}_k$ for each k (a restriction that is stronger than equations (12.4-5) and (12.4-11)) and, along with (3.4-9), suppose also that

$$v_m^k(p, m_k) = \frac{1}{m_k}, \quad k = 1, \ldots, K,$$

for all $(p, m_k) > 0$. (Thus utility welfare function (12.4-8) reduces to weighting individuals' utilities by their incomes at $(\overline{p}, \overline{r}, \overline{x}, \overline{y})$ and, as pointed out in Section 3.4, all individual preferences orderings are homothetic.) Then (12.4-15) becomes

$$W \circ v(\overline{p}, \overline{m}) - W \circ v(\widehat{p}, \widehat{m}) = -\sum_{k=1}^{K} \sum_{i=1}^{I} \int_{\widehat{p}_i}^{\overline{p}_i} h^{ik}(p^i, \overline{m}_k)\, dp_i.\tag{12.4-16}$$

As in Section 3.4, the right-hand integrals represent areas under appropriate demand curves. Moving the summation over k beneath the integral sign, each integral is seen as the area under a market demand curve.

Equation (12.4-16) often serves as the basis for *cost-benefit analysis*.[19] Suppose a particular decision is under consideration by society's governing decision-makers which, if implemented, would have the effect of moving equilibrium from $(\widehat{p}, \widehat{m})$ to $(\overline{p}, \overline{m})$. Of course the total impact on economic welfare could be computed directly from (12.4-16). But in practice it is often convenient to split the welfare increment into "costs" and "benefits". These are estimated separately and then combined.

There are at least two ways of identifying costs and benefits in (12.4-16). First, call individual k a *gainer* or *loser* according as, respectively,

$$v^k(\overline{p}, \overline{m}) - v^k(\widehat{p}, \widehat{m}) \gtreqless 0.$$

Index individuals so that all gainers and persons whose utility remains constant range from $k = 1, \ldots, k^0$. Losers are numbered $k = k^0 + 1, \ldots, K$. The left-hand side of (12.4-16) can therefore be written as the difference between what the gainers gain (benefits) and the losers lose (costs):

$$W \circ v(\overline{p}, \overline{m}) - W \circ v(\widehat{p}, \widehat{m}) = \left\{ \sum_{k=1}^{k^0} \overline{m}_k [v^k(\overline{p}, \overline{m}) - v^k(\widehat{p}, \widehat{m})] \right\}$$

$$- \left\{ \sum_{k=k^0+1}^{K} \overline{m}_k [v^k(\widehat{p}, \widehat{m}) - v^k(\overline{p}, \overline{m})] \right\}.$$

Like (12.4-16), both bracketed terms are related to appropriate areas under demand curves,

The second approach divides the welfare increment with respect to commodities instead of individuals. It is easiest to think in the context of a two-good world in which, recall, the distributions in X associated with $(\overline{p}, \overline{m})$ and $(\widehat{p}, \widehat{m})$ are denoted, respectively, by $\overline{x}$ and $\widehat{x}$. Suppose the market vectors identified with $\overline{x}$ and $\widehat{x}$, namely $\mathcal{M}(\overline{x})$ and $\mathcal{M}(\widehat{x})$, lie on the same strictly concave transformation curve as shown in Figure 12.8. Then to move from $\overline{x}$ to $\widehat{x}$ (or, equivalently, from $(\overline{p}, \overline{m})$ to $(\widehat{p}, \widehat{m})$) requires the output of good 1 to increase and that of good 2 to fall. The equilibrium price ratio must also rise, that is, $\overline{p}_1/\overline{p}_2 < \widehat{p}_1/\widehat{p}_2$. It may be assumed without loss of generality that, in the

---

19   See, for example. Mishan [13].

present case,

$$\overline{p}_1 < \widehat{p}_1,$$

$$\overline{p}_2 > \widehat{p}_2.$$

Now from earlier discussion, welfare rises with an isolated increase in the market quantity x_1, or decline in p_2, and falls with an isolated decrease in the market quantity x_2 or rise in p_1. Hence (12.4-16) can be rewritten as the difference between these welfare increases (benefits) and decreases (costs) or,

$$W \circ v(\overline{p}, \overline{m}) - W \circ v(\widehat{p}, \widehat{m}) =$$

$$- \int_{\widehat{p}_1}^{\overline{p}_1} \left\{ \sum_{k=1}^{K} h^{1k}(p^1, \overline{m}_k) \right\} dp_1 - \int_{\widehat{p}_2}^{\overline{p}_2} \left\{ \sum_{k=1}^{K} h^{2k}(p^2, \overline{m}_k) \right\} dp_2.$$

(Note that, with the minus sign in front, the integral on the left is positive since $\widehat{p}_1 > \overline{p}_1$.) As before, both integrals represent areas under appropriate market demand curves.

In actual calculations it is difficult to reckon welfare changes by using the above cost-benefit formulas to relate them to areas under demand curves. This is because the complete collection of demand functions $\{h^{ik}(p, m_k) :$

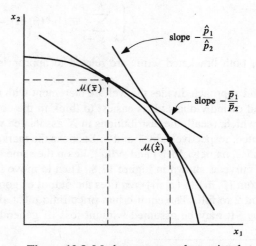

Figure 12.8 Market vectors and associated price ratios

$i = 1, \ldots, I$ and $k = 1, \ldots, K\}$ is never known with enough precision. At best, only parts of a few of the h^{ik} are ever available. And it is more commonly the case that no such demand information can be secured at all. Hence other ways have to be found to obtain the costs and benefits in specific cases. For example, consider a government attempting to decide whether to undertake a particular transportation project. The relevant welfare comparison is between $W \circ v(p', m')$ and $W \circ v(p'', m'')$ where, say, (p', m') is the equilibrium price-income vector before the project is undertaken and (p'', m'') is the equilibrium price-income vector afterward. The government should go ahead with the project if

$$W \circ v\left(p', m'\right) - W \circ v\left(p'', m''\right) < 0.$$

In splitting $W \circ v(p', m') - W \circ v(p'', m'')$ into costs and benefits, the former are often estimated as dollar costs. Benefits can be estimated in terms of cost-savings, time-savings, increased comfort and safety, etc.[20] Clearly, such an approach yields a very crude approximation of $W \circ v(p', m') - W \circ v(p'', m'')$ and implicitly, if not explicitly, may involve the computation of areas under demand curves.

EXERCISES

12.1 Consider a two-person, two-good world in which utility functions are given by

$$u^k(x_{1k}, x_{2k}) = x_{1k}x_{2k}, \quad k = 1, 2.$$

Specify the utility welfare function as $W(\mu_1, \mu_2) = \mu_1 + \mu_2$ on $\mathcal{U}$. Show that the economic circumstance $x = (1, 1, 1, 4)$ is socially preferable to $x = (1, 3, 1, 1)$. Now suppose that the utility function of person 2 is transformed either by taking the square root of all utility values or by dividing them in half, while that of person 1 remains unchanged. Demonstrate that in both cases $x = (1, 3, 1, 1)$ is now socially preferable to $x = (1, 1, 1, 4)$. Compare to Exercise 2.24.

12.2 Prove Theorem 12.2-18.

12.3 Prove Theorem 12.2-25.

---

[20] *Ibid.*

12.4 In a fixed-factor-supply economy, let there be two produced goods and two persons. Suppose utility functions are

$$\mu_1 = u^1(x_1, x_2),$$

$$\mu_2 = u^2(x_2),$$

where $x_k = (x_{1k}, x_{2k})$ for $k = 1, 2$. What are the first-order maximization ratios in force when $\overline{x} = (\overline{x}_1, \overline{x}_2) > 0$ is Pareto optimal? Is equilibrium under perfect competition Pareto optimal?

12.5 In the two-person, two-output situation of Exercise 12.4 with utility functions given by

$$\mu_1 = u^1(x_1, u^2(x_2)),$$

and

$$\mu_2 = u^2(x_2),$$

derive the first-order maximization ratios for $\overline{x} > 0$ to be Pareto optimal. Is equilibrium under perfect competition Pareto optimal?

12.6 Imagine a two-person, two-output, fixed-factor-supply economy in which the first commodity is a public good and the second is an ordinary good. Show that if $\overline{x} = (\overline{x}_1, \overline{x}_{21}, \overline{x}_1, \overline{x}_{22})$ in X is a Pareto optimal distribution, then

$$\frac{u_1^1(\overline{x}_1, \overline{x}_{21})}{u_2^1(\overline{x}_1, \overline{x}_{21})} + \frac{u_1^2(\overline{x}_1, \overline{x}_{22})}{u_2^2(\overline{x}_1, \overline{x}_{22})} = -t_1(\overline{x}_1),$$

where t_1 is the derivative of the transformation function

$$x_{21} + x_{22} = t(x_1).$$

12.7 Let there be a two-person economy with identical fixed utility functions and suppose all prices are also fixed. Then the indirect utility functions can be expressed as

$$\mu_k = v(m_k), \quad k = 1, 2,$$

where p is subsumed in the functional symbol v. Assume the second-order partial derivative v_{mm} is negative everywhere so that v is strictly concave and there is a 1–1 correspondence between values of the marginal utility of income

$v_m(m_k)$ and values of m_k. Let society's utility welfare function be

$$\omega = W(\mu) = \mu_1 + \mu_2,$$

defined on $\mathcal{U}$. Show that for any given level M of aggregate income, social pleasure (welfare) is maximized if and only if M is distributed equally among the two individuals.[21]

12.8 Suppose factor supplies are fixed in a two-person, two-output world. Let the transformation function be

$$x_2 = \alpha - x_1,$$

for $\alpha > 0$. Assume individual utility functions are

$$\mu_k = \sqrt{x_{1k} x_{2k}}, \quad k = 1, 2,$$

and recall

$$x_{i1} + x_{i2} = x_i, \quad i = 1, 2.$$

Find the grand utility possibility function. What happens to the grand function when the increasing transformation

$$\tau(\mu_1) = (\mu_1)^2$$

is applied to the utility function of person 1?

12.9 Robinson Crusoe is the sole inhabitant of an isolated island. Robinson's only scarce commodities are food and leisure, and his only variable (not fixed!) factor is his labor. At each "moment" there are Λ units of time to divide between leisure and labor (recall Section 3.3). As a consumer, Robinson has an ordinal utility function $u(x, y)$ expressing his preferences between quantities of food x and leisure y. As a firm, Robinson can transform his labor hours into food according to the production function $x = f(\Lambda - y)$. Assume u and f have appropriate properties and that the markets for food and labor are perfectly competitive. Define the notion of Pareto optimality in this economy. What is the first-order ratio condition in force at an interior Pareto optimum? Show that every positive competitive equilibrium is Pareto optimal.

---

[21] This result appears in Lerner [12, p. 28]. Earlier on, Pigou stated (under the assumption of diminishing marginal utility), "... any transference of income from a relatively rich man to a relatively poor man of similar temperament ... must increase the aggregate sum of satisfaction." [15, p. 89].

12.10* Consider an exchange economy with two persons and two goods. In spite of the fact that the usual properties (assumptions 2.3-1 – 2.3-4) required of utility functions are violated in various ways, let

$$u^1(x_{11}, x_{21}) = \min(x_{11}, x_{21}),$$

$$u^2(x_{12}, x_{22}) = \min(x_{12}, x_{22}),$$

be defined, respectively, for all $(x_{11}, x_{21}) \geqslant 0$ and $(x_{12}, x_{22}) \geqslant 0$. Suppose the total endowment (both individuals combined) of good 1 is one unit of good 1 and that of good 2 is two units of good 2. Draw, in an Edgeworth box diagram, the set of all Pareto optimal distributions. (In an exchange economy, the notions of Pareto optimality and consumption Pareto optimality coincide.) Which (if any) of these distributions, in association with an appropriate vector of prices, is also an equilibrium distribution?

12.11 Return to the exchange model of Exercise 7.8. Show that if a distribution x lies in the core (as defined in that exercise), then x is Pareto optimal in consumption.

REFERENCES

1. Apostol, T. M., *Mathematical Analysis*, 2nd ed. (Reading: Addison-Wesley, 1974).
2. Arrow, K. J., "An Extension of the Basic Theorems of Classical Welfare Economics," *Proceedings of the Second Berkeley Symposium on Mathematical Statistics and Probability*, J. Neyman, ed. (Berkeley: University of California Press, 1951), pp. 507-532.
3. ——, *Social Choice and Individual Values*, 2nd ed. (New York: Wiley, 1963).
4. Bator, F. M., "The Simple Analytics of Welfare Maximization," *American Economic Review*, 47 (1957), pp. 21-59.
5. Bentham, J., *An Introduction to the Principles of Morals and Legislation* (New York: Hafner, 1948).
6. Bergson (Burk), A., "A Reformulation of Certain Aspects of Welfare Economics", *Quarterly Journal of Economics* 52 (1938), pp. 310-334.
7. Bliss, G. A., *Lectures on the Calculus of Variations* (Chicago: University of Chicago Press, 1961).
8. Burger, E., "On Extrema with Side Conditions," *Econometrica* 23 (1955),

pp. 451, 452.

9. Edgeworth, F. Y., *Mathematical Psychics* (New York: Kelley 1967).

10. Groves, T. and J. Ledyard, "Optimal Allocation of Public Goods: A Solution to the 'Free Rider' Problem," *Econometrica* 45 (1977), pp. 783-809.

11. Koopmans, T. C., *Three Essays on the State of Economic Science* (New York: McGrawHill, 1957).

12. Lerner, A. P., *The Economics of Control* (New York: Macmillan, 1944).

13. Mishan, E. J., *Cost-Benefit Analysis*, revised ed. (London: Allen and Unwin, 1975).

14. Pareto, V., *Manuel d'économie politique*, trans. into French by A. Bonnet (Geneva: Droz, 1966). English translation from the French: *Manual of Political Economy*, A. S. Schwier, trans. (New York: Kelley, 1971).

15. Pigou, A. C., *The Economics of Welfare*, 4th ed. (London: Macmillan, 1952).

16. Samuelson, P. A., *Foundations of Economic Analysis* (Cambridge: Harvard University Press, 1947).

17. ——, "The Pure Theory of Public Expenditure", *Review of Economics and Statistics* 36 (1954), pp. 387-389.

18. ——, "Bergsonian Welfare Economics", *Economic Welfare and the Economics of Soviet Socialism*, S. Rosefielde, ed. (London: Cambridge University Press, 1981), pp. 223-266.

19. Smith, A., *An Inquiry into the Nature and Causes of the Wealth of Nations* (New York: Random House, 1937).

Chapter 13

Capital[1]

Capital is one of the most central and, at the same time, elusive elements of any economy. Identifying an appropriate characterization of it and, upon definition, determining its role in economic activity are issues over which economists have puzzled for a long time. Up to now examination of the difficulties involved has been postponed. This chapter and part of the next attempt to focus on them and explore the implications of introducing capital into the models developed in previous sections. One of the important consequences to emerge is the filling of the gap left in the argument of Section 5.2, which still exists because no explanation has yet been given as to why the perfectly competitive firm should produce a positive output at long-run equilibrium when the maximum profit it can earn is always zero. That section hinted at the possibility of using a particular notion of capital as a basis for formalizing the idea of normal profit which would, in turn, be included in the "cost" of operating the firm. Abnormal profit could then vanish without harm. Such is the resolution proposed below in the context of a slight, but insignificant, modification in the definition of perfect competition.

Two forms of capital need to be distinguished at the outset. *Physical*

---

[1] Parts of the following introduction and Sections 13.2 and 13.3 are taken, with modification and correction, from my "Capital and Walrasian Equilibrium", *Demand, Equilibrium and Trade*, A. Ingham and A. M. Ulph, eds. (London: Macmillan, 1984), pp. 123-148. Reprinted with permission.

capital, a stock (recall Section 1.1), consists of produced inputs which are employed in production and not exhausted completely by it "during" the instant (of continuous time) in question. The term *money capital*, on the other hand, refers to the stock of money borrowed from consumers by firms and used for the hiring of inputs that manufacture output and "work in progress". The inputs required to produce output and work in progress are not restricted to only physical capital but include natural resources and labor as well. The expenditure of money capital by firms is called *investment*. Investments are flows that normally provide returns in the future beyond repayment of the initial outlay of funds. Additions to the stocks of physical and money capital are also flows, with additions to the former a consequence of investments for that specific purpose.

One way to bring capital into the model of the firm developed in Chapters 4 and 5 is merely to identify certain inputs as physical capital and leave things at that. All previous discussion would then apply in its present form to the case in which both physical-capital and non-physical-capital inputs are employed by the firm. But apart from whatever weaknesses this might introduce into the argument itself (for example, physical capital would have to be treated as a flow rather than as a stock), such an approach is less than satisfying because it fails to explain how and why the presence of capital modifies the way in which economic activity is understood. In particular, it precludes analysis of issues like the impact of time and input durability on the production process, the role of money capital in determining the firm's choice of output and selection of inputs (and hence the optimal input mix) with which to produce that output, and the determination of the stock of money capital that accumulates in the economy along with the rate of return that that money capital commands. This kind of approach, therefore, is rejected here.

Recall that the theory of market behavior described in earlier chapters takes the perspective that the economic world consists of individuals and firms who make decisions to buy and sell baskets of inputs and outputs. These decisions are based on utility and profit maximization given prices and other parameters. Dynamic movement is defined (Chapters 9 and 10) with the specification of systematic price variation as time passes and the supposition that, at each instant, a separate maximization decision is made by every consumer and firm concerning quantities to be bought and sold only at that moment. An alternative view is that consumers and firms make maximizing decisions to buy and sell entire streams or flows of outputs and inputs instead of solitary baskets.[2] At each point in time, the firm, say, chooses not only its present production but also its production in all relevant future instants as

---

[2]   For example, Bliss [2].

well. Of course these selections may be permitted to be revised as time progresses. But regardless, such decisions are made for multiple as opposed to single time-frames.

To maintain consistency with previous development, subsequent discussion continues to build on the single-time-frame decision-making foundation. It recognizes the existence of a variety of physical capital inputs and makes no attempt to replace them with a single, unique input called "physical capital," quantities of which are employed by every firm. Its central focus is on the money capital required for production to be possible.[3] Firms need money capital because, even if decisions are made each instant, inputs must still be paid before sufficient revenue to cover their cost is received from the sale of the output in whose production they participated. In other words, money capital is necessary because production takes time.[4] Although disregarded until now, this fact along with its impact on the input and output decisions of the firm is not difficult to incorporate into the equilibrium equations of previous argument. The presence of physical capital also is easily handled in such a context.

It should be pointed out, however, that much of the economics literature on capital[5] has taken a different tack. Contrary to the present approach, consumers and firms sometimes are supposed to make decisions covering multiple instants of time simultaneously. At other times, one or more uniform or aggregate physical capital inputs are constructed from the disaggregated group of all physical capital inputs, and often the accumulation of these aggregate capital units (that is, economic growth) is explored in terms of both the single and multiple time-frame decision-making contexts. Of course, the latter investigation can lead to an examination of the changes in the stock of capital over time. Now when such aggregated capital units serve as part of the foundation of an analysis, the difficult question of how they are to be defined requires attention. Furthermore, if variations in their stock are to be studied, the phenomena of "capital reversals" (a rise in the "required" rate of return on capital that leads to greater employment of capital instead of less) and of "reswitching" (the same relative quantities of capital aggregates and labor are the most profitable at two or more rates of return so that as the rate of return changes, these relative quantities may move from a position of favor to being out of favor and then back in favor once again) have to be taken into account. Although such issues have generated considerable discussion and controversy

---

[3] See Lange [7, p. 173].
[4] Recognition of the importance of time in production dates at least to Menger [8, pp. 67-69].
[5] For example, Bliss [2], Burmeister and Dobel [4], and Harcourt [6].

elsewhere,[6] they are irrelevant here and are ignored. Even if the attempt were made to identify capital reversals and reswitching in the model of the isolated firm (with all inputs disaggregated) as presented below, these phenomena would easily be explained in terms of the usual microeconomic lexicon of shifting tangencies between isoquants and isocost surfaces.

The following discussion begins (Section 13.1) with a digression presenting the fundamental tools of compounding and discounting needed in later development. Then the notion of the money capital requirement is defined (Section 13.2) and incorporated into the long-run theory of the firm under perfect competition (Section 13.3). Sections 13.2 and 13.3 are part of the particular grand view mentioned in Section 1.4. For the most part, attention centers on the ongoing firm at long-run equilibrium. (Discussion of dynamic movement over time sometimes is employed in developing this equilibrium picture, but no attempt is made to present anything resembling a dynamic model. Thus, for example, although the existence of a process by which the firm starts up production and expands output is relevant for subsequent argument, the actual dynamic laws governing the process are not considered.) The economy-wide model is completed in Section 14.3 with the addition of consumers and the expansion to many firms and industries. As in Chapters 9 and 10, time is taken in its continuous form. For expository simplicity, however, examples are given with respect to discrete time. Moreover, the concept of "instant of time" hereafter is characterized specifically as an arbitrarily small time interval. The alternative possibility of thinking of an instant as the limit of a sequence of smaller and smaller intervals each contained in the one before it (recall Section 1.3) no longer is allowed. (The reason for requiring this particularization will become clear in Section 13.2.) The main ideas appearing below have already been worked out for discrete time by Gabor and Pearce [5] and Pearce [9]. Many are traceable to the so-called "Austrian" view of production and capital as exemplified by the work of Menger [8], von Böhm-Bawerk [3], and Wicksell [12].

It is worth noting at the outset that in order to simplify subsequent argument, three conditions (among others) are imposed in the specification of the model which, under more general circumstances, would be in force only at full, economy-wide equilibrium. (For the latter, see Section 14.3 below. Of course, all such assumptions are implicit there regardless of whether they are explicitly stated.) The conditions are first, that the required rate of return on the firm's money capital equals the actual rate of return on the same money capital; second, that residual profit as defined by the term B in equation

---

[6]   See especially Harcourt [6].

(13.2-13) below vanishes identically; and third, that the money capital requirement function employed by the firm in maximizing the rate of return on the money capital invested in it is actually its optimal money capital requirement function. These restrictions (they are explained in detail when introduced) serve to collapse what would otherwise be a very complicated structure into a somewhat more tractable framework.

13.1 INVESTMENTS AND RETURNS

Compounding and discounting are explained more easily if discrete time is considered first. For the moment, then, think of time in terms of nonoverlapping equal periods indexed by $\tau = 0, 1, \ldots$ As indicated above, an investment is an expenditure of money capital in anticipation of a future return. Let z denote a dollar sum invested at the start of period τ and ρ_τ the per-dollar rate of return per period during τ. Then at the start of period $\tau + 1$ (or the end of period τ), the *value* of the investment, written $\nu_{\tau+1}$, is

$$\nu_{\tau+1} = z\left(1 + \rho_\tau\right). \tag{13.1-1}$$

For example, when $\rho_\tau = 0.05$, every dollar invested at the beginning of τ returns the original dollar plus five cents at the end. Returning to the general case, if the entire amount $z(1 + \rho_\tau)$ is reinvested during period $\tau + 1$, then the value of the initial investment z at the onset of period $\tau + 2$ is

$$\nu_{\tau+2} = z\left(1 + \rho_\tau\right)\left(1 + \rho_{\tau+1}\right).$$

After $\beta - 1$ additional periods beyond τ, that is, at the commencement of period $\tau + \beta$, it is

$$\nu_{\tau+\beta} = z\left(1 + \rho_\tau\right) \cdots \left(1 + \rho_{\tau+\beta-1}\right). \tag{13.1-2}$$

The *overall* return on the initial investment z at this point in time is the value of the investment less the initial outlay, or

$$z\left(1 + \rho_\tau\right) \cdots \left(1 + \rho_{\tau+\beta-1}\right) - z. \tag{13.1-3}$$

Division of (13.1-3) by z yields the overall return *per dollar* on z for the β periods; differentiation with respect to z gives the (overall) *marginal* return. These turn out to be the same constant

$$\left(1 + \rho_\tau\right) \cdots \left(1 + \rho_{\tau+\beta-1}\right) - 1. \tag{13.1-4}$$

For the special case in which the per-period rate of return is independent of τ, that is,

$$\rho_\tau = \rho, \tag{13.1-5}$$

for all τ, the value of the investment after β periods in (13.1-2), which covers period τ plus the $\beta - 1$ periods following τ, reduces to

$$\nu_{\tau+\beta} = z\,(1+\rho)^\beta, \tag{13.1-6}$$

and (13.1-4) becomes

$$(1+\rho)^\beta - 1.$$

Another way of verbally describing $\nu_{\tau+\beta}$ in (13.1-6) is as the value of investment z *compounded* for β periods at a *rate of compounding* of ρ.

Equations (13.1-1) and (13.1-2) define a relationship between "present" and future values. Thus, according to (13.1-1),

$$\frac{\nu_{\tau+1}}{1+\rho_\tau}$$

at the start of period $\tau + 1$ is the equivalent of z at the start of period τ. This ratio is called the *present value* of $\nu_{\tau+1}$ at the start of period τ, and, in this latter context, ρ_τ is referred to as the *discount factor*. Note that the present value of $\nu_{\tau+1}$ at the start of period τ is the amount of money that, if invested at the start of period τ at a rate of return ρ_τ, would yield $\nu_{\tau+1}$ at the start of period $\tau + 1$. From (13.1-2), the present value of $\nu_{\tau+\beta}$ at the beginning of period τ is

$$\frac{\nu_{\tau+\beta}}{(1+\rho_\tau)\cdots(1+\rho_{\tau+\beta-1})},$$

and there are generally different discount factors for the different periods. In the constant per-period rate of return or single-discount factor case of (13.1-5), this last formula simplifies to

$$\frac{\nu_{\tau+\beta}}{(1+\rho)^\beta}. \tag{13.1-7}$$

It is worth illustrating these ideas in a concrete situation. Suppose the investment to be made consists of the purchase of a machine that performs without deterioration for β periods. At the end of the βth period, however, it has no economic usefulness left, and hence its value is zero. Assume that its scrap value is also zero. Suppose the per-period rate of return ρ on the machine is constant as in (13.1-5) and the purchase price of the machine is z. Then payment could be made either by giving up the sum z at the start of period τ (when the machine is introduced in production) or by making equal payments ν at the start of each of periods τ through $\tau + \beta - 1$. Usually ν is referred to as the *rental value* of the machine. It is determined as that number which equates the present value of the sequence or stream of rental payments to the machine's purchase price, or as the solution of

$$z = \nu + \frac{\nu}{1 + \rho} + \cdots + \frac{\nu}{(1 + \rho)^{\beta - 1}}.$$

Solving for ν yields

$$\nu = z \left[1 + \frac{1}{1 + \rho} + \cdots + \frac{1}{(1 + \rho)^{\beta - 1}} \right]^{-1}. \qquad (13.1\text{-}8)$$

Note that if all payments were made at the end of the payment period instead of at the beginning, then the above expression for the rental value of the machine would become

$$\nu = z \left[\frac{1}{1 + \rho} + \cdots + \frac{1}{(1 + \rho)^{\beta}} \right]^{-1}.$$

The transference of these notions into the continuous-time framework proceeds by considering a time interval (for example, ten years) and dividing it into β equal periods (ten one-year periods). Suppose the per-period (per-year in the example) rate of return, ρ, is constant. Then, according to (13.1-6), the value at the end of the interval (after ten years) of an investment z made at the start of the interval is

$$z \, (1 + \rho)^{\beta}.$$

Now suppose each of the β periods are split in half, and half of the per-period rate of return is paid at the end of every halved period. Then the value of the investment at the end of the interval becomes

$$z \left(1 + \frac{\rho}{2} \right)^{2\beta}.$$

In general, performing such a division with any integer γ would change the investment value at the end of the period to

$$z \left(1 + \frac{\rho}{\gamma} \right)^{\gamma\beta}.$$

As γ becomes larger, the subperiods grow smaller. The per-(sub)period rate of return declines and is applied over a shorter duration. In the limit, a continuous counterpart to (13.1-6) is obtained. For the continuous context, denote the value of investment z at the end of the interval initially divided into β periods by ν_β. (Clarity will be enhanced by keeping usage of the notation ν_β separate from that of $\nu_{\tau+\beta}$ introduced earlier. Only the former is employed below.) Thus,

$$\nu_\beta = \lim_{\gamma \to \infty} z \left(1 + \frac{\rho}{\gamma}\right)^{\gamma\beta}. \qquad (13.1\text{-}9)$$

To find the limit in (13.1-9) as γ becomes large, let $R = \gamma/\rho$. Then $\gamma = R\rho$ and $R \to \infty$ as and only as $\gamma \to \infty$. Substitution into (13.1-9) yields

$$\nu_\beta = \lim_{R \to \infty} z \left(1 + \frac{1}{R}\right)^{R\rho\beta}.$$

Employing the algebra of limits of sequences,[7]

$$\nu_\beta = z \left[\lim_{R \to \infty} \left(1 + \frac{1}{R}\right)^R\right]^{\rho\beta}$$

so that

$$\nu_\beta = ze^{\rho\beta}, \qquad (13.1\text{-}10)$$

where e is the base of the system of natural logarithms and ρ, in this continuous-time setting, becomes the rate of (continuous) compounding. Solving (13.1-10) for z yields the present value of ν_β at the start of the original time interval, or

$$\nu_\beta e^{-\rho\beta}. \qquad (13.1\text{-}11)$$

Observe that here the discount factor, in the language of continuous-time present value, is ρ, and (13.1-11) is the continuous-time analogue of (13.1-7). Also, recall that ρ is the constant per-period rate of return over the initial β periods.

In the example described earlier, where z is the purchase price of a machine whose life is β periods, denote the starting time of the first period by τ^0. Write the terminal time of the final period as $\tau^0 + \beta$. (To illustrate, if τ^0 is the year 1980 and the machine's life is ten years, then $\tau^0 + \beta = 1990$.) The rental value, ν, of the machine is, by definition, still constant but now paid out continuously (at each instant) across the closed interval from τ^0 to $\tau^0 + \beta$. Take τ^0 to be the "present," that is, set $\tau^0 = 0$, and consider any time τ between τ^0

---

[7]   See, for example, Rudin [10, pp. 49, 64].

and $\tau^0 + \beta$. Then the present value of the rent on the machine payable at time τ is, from (13.1-11),

$$\nu e^{-\rho\tau}.$$

The sum of the present values of all future rental payments (one at each instant of time) over the interval from τ^0 to $\tau^0 + \beta$ is given by the integral

$$\int_{\tau^0}^{\tau^0+\beta} \nu e^{-\rho\tau}d\tau = \int_0^\beta \nu e^{-\rho\tau}d\tau,$$

where ν, β, and ρ are all fixed parameters and $\tau^0 = 0$. Because ν is a constant equating the sum of present values of the stream of all future rental payments to the purchase price of the machine, and because

$$\int_0^\beta e^{-\rho\tau}d\tau = \frac{1}{\rho}\left[1 - e^{-\rho\beta}\right],$$

it follows that the rental value of the machine (that is, the continuous equivalent of equation (13.1-8)) can be expressed as

$$\nu = z\rho\left[1 - e^{-\rho\beta}\right]^{-1}. \tag{13.1-12}$$

Notice that the rental value does not depend on whether payments are made at the beginning or end of periods as it does when time is discrete.

Finally, it is worth pointing out that if z in equations (13.1-8) or (13.1-12) were interpreted as the magnitude of a specific money-capital investment at a particular date, and if, in parallel with the machine example above, ν were thought of as the per-period or instantaneous cash-flow return that that investment was expected to generate for β periods, then either equation would determine a value for ρ. These solution values which, in both cases, are referred to as the investment's *expected* or *internal* rate of return, may serve, in comparison with the cost of the money capital involved, as a decision criterion for proceeding with the investment. That is, for example, the investment would be undertaken whenever the former is greater than the latter.

13.2   MONEY CAPITAL REQUIREMENTS

To conceptualize the money capital requirement of the firm with some clarity and depth, it is necessary to expand the equilibrium framework of earlier chapters to include hypothetical nonequilibrium environments and think of production as a process that takes place over time. Although minor reinterpretation becomes necessary, such an enlargement does not vitiate previous argument. The next section returns to the equilibrium context and shows how the money capital requirement function developed here can be employed in the analysis of the firm of Chapters 4 and 5.

Begin with the obvious fact that production takes time because output whose manufacture is finished in the present was fashioned mostly from inputs hired in the past. More precisely, consider any firm and let $\overline{\tau}_j \geqslant 0$ denote the time elapsing between the introduction of a unit of input j into production (where $j = 1, \ldots, J$) and the instant at which the output in whose production this unit of input participated, is completed. The unfinished output during the period is called *work in progress*. For simplicity, suppose $\overline{\tau}_j$ is the same for all units of input j hired, and refer to it as the *maturity time* for input j.[8] By the phrase "a *batch* of input j" is meant a quantity of input j, all units of which are employed at the same time. A similar concept is defined for the firm's output.

To illustrate these ideas, consider a discrete-time world in which the production of bookcases takes three days. Ignoring for the moment the problem of how physical capital is obtained and abstracting from such things as the need for inventories of material inputs and for a building in which production takes place, suppose on day 1, labor is hired to cut wood with a saw. On day 2, labor is employed to put the bookcases together with a hammer and nails. And on day 3, labor is used to paint them. By the end of the third day, the production process is completed and the bookcases are ready to be sold. (The fixed input proportions implicit here are quite special and are not required in general.) In this example there are nine inputs (wood, saws, hammers, nails, paint, paint brushes, and three kinds of labor — one for each day), only three of which are needed at any stage (day) of the process. Clearly, all inputs employed on day 1 have maturity times of three days; those introduced on day 2 have maturity times of two days; and those hired on the last day have maturity times of a single day. Work in progress consists of sawn wood on day 1 and unpainted bookcases on day 2. Production, of course, can be continued through time by restarting the process every day. In that case the firm has units of all nine inputs employed and bookcases in progress at each stage of the production process on any given day. Discussion will return to this example later on.

An obvious consequence of the fact that production takes time is that it

---

[8]   The concept of maturity time is usually identified with the Austrian school: Similar notions appear in Menger [8, p. 157] and von Böhm-Bawerk [3, pp. 86-87]. The limitations imposed by employment of this concept are discussed by Baumol [1, pp. 417-419] and an alternative approach, which avoids it, is developed by Vickers [11].

would typically be necessary for the firm to pay for its inputs before receiving the revenue from the sale of the output to whose production those inputs contributed. In the bookcase example, day 1 inputs (wood, saws, and day 1 labor) would have to be paid on day 1 — two days before the bookcase is finished and at least three days before it is sold. Thus, in order to finance the production of the bookcase, the firm has to have funds available to cover these costs. In general, then, since it is money capital that provides the wherewithal for the firm to pay for inputs in advance of sales, money capital must be raised before production can begin.

Of the many ways in which inputs can differ from each other, one of the more important ones is with respect to their durability. Inputs that last longer than the unit of time identified for analytical purposes (here, the "instant") are called *durable*; those that do not are *nondurable*. (Durable inputs differ from physical capital in that the former do not always have to be previously produced. Land, for example, is a durable input that is not counted as physical capital. Because, according to its definition, physical capital consists only of durable commodities — as in the previous example, inventories are ignored throughout — the following discussion is able to account for the presence of physical capital by distinguishing between durable and nondurable inputs.) In the bookcase illustration, saws, hammers, and paint brushes would be thought of as durable inputs; whereas wood, nails, paint, and labor would be nondurable. From this point on, include durable inputs in the form of physical capital among those inputs counted by the index j. (Recall that, according to the notational rule adopted in Section 7.2, j has heretofore ranged only over nonproduced, though still possibly durable, factors.) Let α_j represent the *life* of input j in production, that is, the span of time between the moment a unit of j is introduced and the moment at which it wears out and must be replaced. Assume all units of each input j have the same fixed life and that their performance does not deteriorate as they wear out.[9] Two inputs, identical except for their productive lives, are considered distinct and identified with different values for j. Maintenance costs are ignored. The lives of nondurable and durable inputs are measured in different units: The former is expressed in terms of numbers of instants (that is, numbers of infinitesimal lengths of time) and assumed to be unity. Thus

$$\alpha_j = 1,$$

when j is nondurable. On the other hand, lives of durable inputs are scaled as

---

[9]   The question of the optimum production life of an input is not considered. See Vickers [11, p. 130].

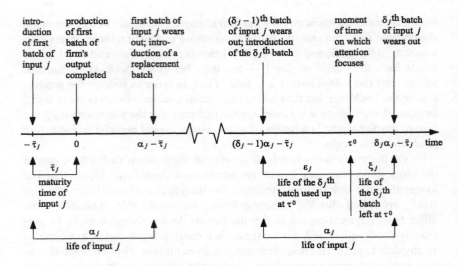

Figure 13.1 Employment of a durable input over time

numbers of periods of finite length such as years or months. In this case α_j can be any positive real number. These conventions are needed so that the usual relationship between prices and rental values described in equation (13.2-1) below can be applied to both durable and nondurable inputs. Observe that, as a result of imposing these conventions, the limit of α_j, for a durable j, as the life of the durable input declines is zero — not the life of a nondurable input.[10]

Without loss of generality, set the point in time at which the firm completes production of its first batch of output at $\tau = 0$. Suppose also that each time a batch of durable inputs wears out it is immediately replaced. A schematic picture of the employment of a durable input over time, say input j, appears in Figure 13.1.

Now number all inputs in such a way that nondurables are identified by the index j running from $j = 1, \ldots, \hat{j}$ for some $\hat{j}$ between 1 and J. The remaining inputs, $j = \hat{j} + 1, \ldots, J$, are durable. Let r_j denote the purchase price per unit of input j, for $j = 1, \ldots, \hat{j}$, and use the symbol r'_j for the purchase price when $j = \hat{j} + 1, \ldots, J$. (The money capital costs of carrying nondurable and durable inputs will be accounted for later.) If j is a durable

---

[10]   Note also that if the notion of "instant" were interpreted as the limit of a sequence of smaller and smaller intervals, then it would be necessary to set $\alpha_j = 0$ for nondurable j.

input, then either the firm pays out r'_j each time a unit of j is introduced in production, or it pays out (per unit of input) a rental value,[11] r^*_j, continuously throughout the unit's life α_j. From (13.1-12), this rental value is

$$r^*_j = r'_j \rho \left[1 - e^{-\rho \alpha_j} \right]^{-1}, \tag{13.2-1}$$

where ρ is a hypothetical rate of return (per unspecified period of time measured per instant of time) paid by the firm on the money capital it borrows to finance production. In other words, ρ is the hypothetical cost of money capital to the firm, or the hypothetical rate of return that the firm is contractually *required* to pay on borrowed funds by the lenders of those funds. The rate of return the firm *actually* pays is determined endogenously below.[12] For now, take the hypothetical ρ to be constant. By definition, r^*_j is constant over the life of the unit. A similar formula with $\alpha_j = 1$ is used to define "rental values" for nondurable inputs.[13]

Consider the calculation of input costs assuming the r_j and r'_j remain fixed across time. (Revenues resulting from the sale of output will be treated similarly later on.) Let j be a nondurable input. In the same instant, the firm both hires units of j and uses them up completely. Suppose a specific quantity or batch of this input, namely y_j where $1 \leqslant j \leqslant \widehat{j}$, is purchased through time. If τ^0 represents the length of time since the firm completed production of its first batch of output, then according to a previous convention, the initial units of input j were bought $\tau^0 + \overline{\tau}_j$ units of time ago (as in Figure 13.1 redrawn for a nondurable input). Moreover, at each moment of time, the firm is purchasing y_j units at a dollar amount of $r_j y_j$. But according to (13.1-10), an expenditure of $r_j y_j$ made at time τ (where $-\overline{\tau}_j \leqslant \tau \leqslant \tau^0$) has an accumulated "cost" to

---

[11]   The fact that the firm may pay rental values over inputs' lives rather than one-time purchase prices has nothing to do with whether the firm actually buys or only rents inputs. The two methods of payment merely represent different but equivalent price-accounting schemes. The convention introduced in Section 1.1 that physical capital is bought and not rented remains in force.

[12]   Since, as has already been indicated, the required rate of return will (as part of the contemplated conditions of full, economy-wide equilibrium) shortly be set equal to the actual rate of return, determination of the latter implies determination of the former.

[13]   The convention of setting nondurable input lives at unity ensures (from the relevant form of equation (13.2-1) and L'Hôpital's rule) that for these inputs, purchase prices equal rental values in the limit as $\rho \to 0$. The limiting case $\rho = 0$ arises in a world that does not need money capital (that is, a world in which all maturity times are zero and there are no durable inputs) and hence in which no rate of return is paid on it. Alternatively, if nondurable input lives were taken to be zero (see n. 10 on the previous page), then (13.2-1) would imply that their rental values would always be infinite.

the firm (or investment value) at time τ^0 of

$$r_j y_j e^{\rho(\tau^0 - \tau)}.$$

Hence the aggregate cost of (or investment value in) input j over the period from $-\overline{\tau}_j$ to τ^0 is given by the integral

$$\int_{-\overline{\tau}_j}^{\tau^0} r_j y_j e^{\rho(\tau^0 - \tau)} d\tau = r_j y_j \frac{e^{\rho(\tau^0 + \overline{\tau}_j)} - 1}{\rho}. \tag{13.2-2}$$

Summing over all nondurable inputs gives

$$\sum_{j=1}^{\widehat{j}} r_j y_j \frac{e^{\rho(\tau^0 + \overline{\tau}_j)} - 1}{\rho}. \tag{13.2-3}$$

Turning to durable inputs, consider the first batch, say y_j, of input j ever hired (with $\widehat{j} + 1 \leqslant j \leqslant J$). In order to maintain this quantity y_j in production from $-\overline{\tau}_j$ up to τ^0 (refer, again, to Figure 13.1), the firm must pay out $r'_j y_j$ for it δ_j times, where $\delta_j - 1$ is the number of whole lives of duration α_j in the span $\tau^0 + \overline{\tau}_j$. The accumulated cost at τ^0 of the first payment (again using equation (13.1-10)) is

$$r'_j y_j e^{\rho(\tau^0 + \overline{\tau}_j)}.$$

The cost of the remaining payments are, respectively,

$$r'_j y_j e^{\rho(\tau^0 + \overline{\tau}_j - \alpha_j)},$$

$$\vdots$$

$$r'_j y_j e^{\rho(\tau^0 + \overline{\tau}_j - [\delta_j - 1]\alpha_j)}.$$

Thus the aggregate cost of maintaining batches of input j equal to the first batch used in production can be shown to be (Exercise 13.2)[14]

$$\sum_{\sigma=0}^{\delta_j - 1} r'_j y_j e^{\rho(\tau^0 + \overline{\tau}_j - \sigma \alpha_j)} = r'_j y_j e^{\rho(\tau^0 + \overline{\tau}_j)} \frac{1 - e^{-\rho \delta_j \alpha_j}}{1 - e^{-\rho \alpha_j}}. \tag{13.2-4}$$

---

[14]   Note that in the limit as $\rho \to 0$, expression (13.2-2) reduces to $r_j y_j \left(\tau^0 + \overline{\tau}_j \right)$. Furthermore, shifting (13.2-4) back into the same nondurable context as (13.2-2) by setting $\alpha_j = 1$, $\delta_j = \tau^0 + \overline{\tau}_j$, removing the primes on the r_j's, and then letting ρ approach zero, leads to the same result. Thus when $\rho \to 0$, (13.2-2) arises as a special case of (13.2-4). See n. 13 on the previous page.

The right-hand side of (13.2-4) can be simplified somewhat upon replacing r'_j with the rental value r^*_j as described in (13.2-1). Thus the aggregate cost of maintaining, up to τ^0, a quantity y_j equal to the size of the first batch of input j employed in production becomes

$$\frac{1}{\rho}\left[r^*_j y_j e^{\rho(\tau^0+\overline{\tau}_j)} - r^*_j y_j e^{\rho(\tau^0+\overline{\tau}_j-\delta_j\alpha_j)}\right]. \tag{13.2-5}$$

Observe that with

$$\tau^0 + \overline{\tau}_j = (\delta_j - 1)\alpha_j + \varepsilon_j,$$

where ε_j represents the life used up at $\tau^0 + \overline{\tau}_j$ of the last batch of input j purchased, the negative of the parenthetical term in the right-hand exponent, written

$$\xi_j = -\left(\tau^0 + \overline{\tau}_j - \delta_j\alpha_j\right), \tag{13.2-6}$$

is the amount of life remaining in that batch (see Figure 13.1) or

$$\xi_j = \alpha_j - \varepsilon_j.$$

When $\xi_j = 0$, expressions (13.2-5) and the right-hand side of (13.2-2) are identical except that the former applies to durable inputs and employs rental values of inputs instead of input prices. Adding (13.2-5) over all durable inputs and invoking (13.2-6) yields

$$\sum_{j=\hat{j}+1}^{J} r^*_j y_j \frac{e^{\rho(\tau^0+\overline{\tau}_j)} - e^{-\rho\xi_j}}{\rho}. \tag{13.2-7}$$

The behavior of (13.2-5) as τ^0 varies is worth mentioning. Clearly the first term between the brackets increases exponentially with τ^0. The second term, abbreviated by the symbol

$$\omega_j = r^*_j y_j e^{\rho(\tau^0+\overline{\tau}_j-\delta_j\alpha_j)}, \tag{13.2-8}$$

is more interesting. The graph of ω_j, as τ^0 increases through time, has a discontinuity everywhere a batch y_j wears out because at that moment the value of δ_j increases by one. Using the same origin as before (Figure 13.1), these jumps occur when

$$\tau^0 = (\delta_j - 1)\alpha_j - \overline{\tau}_j,$$

for $\delta_j = 1, 2, \ldots$. In between jumps, the curve repeats itself over and over again. With each repeat the curve starts at the same value of ω_j and ends at the same value, although the starting and the ending values are different. The facts that, except for jump points, the first- and second-order derivatives of ω_j with respect to τ^0 exist and are both positive, are easily verified. Hence, where continuous (i.e., between the jumps), the graph of ω_j over time is upward sloping and strictly convex. Further details, as well as the combined movement in (13.2-5), are left to Exercise 13.3. Note that the cyclical pattern over time generated by any one durable input can be reinforced or muted when combined with that of others in (13.2-7).

Now suppose a potential firm (or its owners) is contemplating the possibility of starting up production. Its production function is known; the input and output prices and the cost of money capital (that is, the required rate of return) it will face are to be dictated by competitive market forces; and hence the output it will produce and the inputs it will hire can be determined (Section 13.3 below). The questions to be considered here are how much money capital will be needed to support that production, and what rate of return on the money capital invested will the firm actually be able to provide to its owners? Answers to these questions turn on certain financial aspects of the firm's operation. Part of the latter has already been discussed in terms of costs. Indeed, the firm's accumulated costs (or the accumulated value of investment in the firm) at future date τ^0 — accumulated at the required or contractual rate of return — are the sum of (13.2-3) and (13.2-7). Offsetting revenues still have to be examined.

In the continuous-time context a batch of output is sold at each instant of time. Assume there is no lag between the completion of production of output batches and the sale of them. Hence the flow of revenue to cover the costs totaled in (13.2-3) and (13.2-7) starts when sales begin at time $\tau = 0$. Supposing that the firm manages its funds optimally, revenues can be thought of as compounding from time 0 up to τ^0 at the actual rate of return determined at equilibrium. Assume further that the actual rate of return determined at equilibrium is the same as the required rate of return, ρ, previously employed in the calculation of accumulated costs. Such a condition would obtain at equilibrium anyway, and matters are simplified considerably by imposing it here. Taking output x and output price p to be invariant over time, the accumulated value of the flow of revenue up to τ^0 is therefore

$$\int_0^{\tau^0} pxe^{\rho(\tau^0-\tau)}d\tau = px\frac{e^{\rho\tau^0}-1}{\rho}. \qquad (13.2\text{-}9)$$

Remember that the previous calculation of accumulated costs is based on the supposition that, at each instant, the firm pays out the rate of return required by the suppliers of its money capital. These rate-of-return payments are included as part of accumulated costs. But in fact, the firm does not borrow money capital to cover any expenditure made out of the revenue it receives. Once the flow of revenue begins, then, the accumulated investment in the firm, which has hitherto been necessary in order to acquire factors of production, actually drops below accumulated cost. Moreover, borrowing is necessary only when revenue is insufficient to meet the cost of the inputs it has to buy plus the dollar obligations due on previous loans. Even if revenue exactly offsets input expenditure, the firm would still have to borrow to pay the required return on its money capital.[15]

Notice also that at any point in time τ^0, equilibrium demands that aggregate cost in (13.2-3) plus (13.2-7) be larger than aggregate revenue in (13.2-9). This is because durable and nondurable inputs have to be purchased and paid for before sales can begin. Were production to be subsequently reduced, part of the gap between these costs and revenues would be closed by hiring quantities of new inputs (durable and nondurable) that, in addition to completing current work in progress, would maintain a smaller amount of future work in progress. In the circumstance that production were to be eventually terminated and the firm go out of business, only sufficient quantities of inputs would be hired to complete existing work in progress. No new batches of output would be started. In that case, if it turned out that the durable inputs were entirely used up at the same time that all work in progress was finished, then the whole discrepancy between aggregate costs and revenues would have been made up. (An example is given in Section 13.3.) In general, the difference c obtained by subtracting (13.2-9) from the sum of (13.2-3) and (13.2-7) is called the *money capital requirement* of, or the money capital tied up in, the firm at τ^0. Thus

$$c = \left[\sum_{j=1}^{\widehat{j}} r_j y_j \frac{e^{\rho(\tau^0 + \overline{\tau}_j)} - 1}{\rho} \right.$$

$$\left. + \sum_{j=\widehat{j}+1}^{J} r_j^* y_j \frac{e^{\rho(\tau^0 + \overline{\tau}_j)} - e^{-\rho\xi_j}}{\rho} \right] - px \frac{e^{\rho\tau^0} - 1}{\rho}.$$

$$(13.2\text{-}10)$$

---

[15] It should be borne in mind that, as pointed out above, the present argument regarding the firm's operating costs and revenues envisages hypothetically the manner in which the firm accumulates money capital and builds production volume during the time preceding the achievement of its optimum operating position. The latter will be realized at partial equilibrium in the model of Section 13.3 and at full, economy-wide equilibrium in the model of Section 14.3.

Rewriting (13.2-10) gives

$$c = \frac{1}{\rho}\left[px - \sum_{j=1}^{\widehat{j}}\widehat{r}_j y_j - \sum_{j=\widehat{j}+1}^{J}\widehat{r}_j y_j e^{-\rho \xi_j}\right]$$

(13.2-11)

$$-\frac{e^{\rho \tau^0}}{\rho}\left[px - \sum_{j=1}^{J}\widehat{r}_j y_j e^{\rho \overline{\tau}_j}\right],$$

where

$$\widehat{r}_j = \begin{cases} r_j, & \text{if } j = 1, \ldots, \widehat{j}, \\ r_j^*, & \text{if } j = \widehat{j}+1, \ldots, J. \end{cases}$$

(13.2-12)

Because equation (13.2-10) or (13.2-11) determines the money capital necessary to sustain a pre-specified level of production at given input and output prices, the values of p, x, the $\widehat{r}_j$, and the y_j in these equations are all fixed independently of τ^0. Hence (13.2-11) is of the form

$$c = \frac{1}{\rho}\left(A - Be^{\rho \tau^0}\right),$$

(13.2-13)

where B remains constant with movement in τ^0 and A is bounded as τ^0 increases (recall that, although ξ_j modifies when τ^0 grows, $0 \leqslant \xi_j \leqslant \alpha_j$ for all τ^0 and all durable j). Consider, for a moment, the term B, which has been defined as

$$B = px - \sum_{j=1}^{J}\widehat{r}_j y_j e^{\rho \overline{\tau}_j}.$$

Observe that the right-hand sum in this equation represents the actual cost of inputs valued at the ends of their maturity times (based in the case of durables on rental values) or, in other words, the expenditure on inputs at the initial input dates plus the implicit return earned on that outlay during the maturity periods of the inputs. If all inputs were nondurable (so that rental values could be ignored), and if all maturity times were zero, then the expression $\sum_{j=1}^{J}\widehat{r}_j y_j e^{\rho \overline{\tau}_j}$ would reduce to the total of the products of purchase prices times quantities employed. In either case, B is the difference between total revenue and the total input cost outlay as just described. Henceforth B is referred to as *residual profit*.

Now except when $B = 0$, (13.2-13) implies that as τ^0 becomes large, c moves toward either plus or minus infinity. In other words, having determined all input and output prices and quantities and having set ρ, if

$$px > \sum_{j=1}^{J} \widehat{r}_j y_j e^{\rho \overline{\tau}_j},$$

then $B > 0$, and as time passes, sooner or later money capital would no longer be necessary to sustain production. Revenues would be large enough to pay off all debt and after that to accumulate in large amounts in the firm. Money capital raised to begin production would no longer be needed and would never be needed again, no matter how far into the future production continues. Alternatively, were the inequality reversed ($B < 0$), then more and more money capital would be required to sustain production, and the cost of carrying the firm's debt, ρc, would increase. Eventually

$$\rho c > px - \sum_{j=1}^{J} \widehat{r}_j y_j,$$

so that payments of the excess of ρc over current net revenue would have to be repeatedly financed by raising still more money capital. Clearly neither extreme is compatible with equilibrium. Hence, with the eventual end of describing equilibrium in mind, once again it is worth maintaining simplicity of argument by imposing enough restrictions to preclude these possibilities. Thus assume that B vanishes identically for all values of p, x, $\widehat{r}_1, \ldots, \widehat{r}_J$, and $y_1, \ldots, y_J$.

Of course, with $B = 0$, (13.2-11) implies

$$px = \sum_{j=1}^{J} \widehat{r}_j y_j e^{\rho \overline{\tau}_j}, \tag{13.2-14}$$

and

$$c = \frac{1}{\rho} \left(px - \sum_{j=1}^{\widehat{j}} \widehat{r}_j y_j - \sum_{j=\widehat{j}+1}^{J} \widehat{r}_j y_j e^{-\rho \xi_j} \right). \tag{13.2-15}$$

An interpretation of (13.2-14) as an assertion of zero residual profit has already been suggested. Turning to (13.2-15), the terms in the parentheses on the right-hand side of the equation together constitute the excess of the firm's current revenue over its true economic operating cost. The second term in the parentheses is the operating cost (per instant) of the nondurable inputs. As will be shown momentarily, the third term can be understood in terms of the periodic depreciation on the durable inputs or as the necessary contribution to a sinking fund that accumulates and becomes available to replace the durable inputs at the end of their economic lives. Upon multiplication by ρ, equation (13.2-15) therefore describes the net excess revenue on hand for payment as the dollar return to the suppliers of the firm's money capital. Another interpretation of the money capital requirement is obtained by substitution of (13.2-14) into (13.2-15), or

$$
\begin{aligned}
c &= \sum_{j=1}^{J} \widehat{r}_j y_j \frac{e^{\rho \overline{\tau}_j} - 1}{\rho} + \sum_{j=\widehat{j}+1}^{J} \widehat{r}_j y_j \frac{1 - e^{-\rho \xi_j}}{\rho} \\
&= \sum_{j=1}^{J} \int_{-\overline{\tau}_j}^{0} \widehat{r}_j y_j e^{\rho(0-\tau)} d\tau + \sum_{j=\widehat{j}+1}^{J} \int_{0}^{\xi_j} \widehat{r}_j y_j e^{\rho(0-\tau)} d\tau.
\end{aligned}
\tag{13.2-16}
$$

The left-hand sum after the second equality in equation (13.2-16) represents the aggregate investment needed to finance all expenditures on inputs up to the start of sales. It can also be viewed as the cost of work in progress or *working capital*. The right-hand sum is the total of the present values of rental obligations remaining due in the future on all durables in use at τ^0 up to the expiration of their lives. Alternatively, it is the residual cost, not yet recovered from revenue, of the durable goods purchased some time ago that are currently employed in production, or what may be referred to as *fixed capital*.

Thus money capital c tied up in the firm at any time $\tau^0 \geqslant 0$ consists of working capital plus fixed capital. Working capital would be necessary even if all inputs were nondurable because the firm would still have to pay for these inputs before it receives the revenue from the sale of the output they produce. Because durable inputs are purchased and not rented (n. 11 on p. 531), fixed capital would be necessary even if production were instantaneous (that is, all maturity times were zero) because revenue at each instant would still be insufficient to cover the cost of purchasing durable inputs. Clearly, if all inputs were nondurable and if all maturity times vanished, then money capital would not be required for the firm to produce.

Note further that since durable goods can be thought of as having already been paid for with borrowed funds, at any $\tau^0 \geqslant 0$ the firm's cash outflow from current receipts is the cost of nondurable inputs currently in use along with the return currently paid on the money capital previously borrowed. From (13.2-

15) and (13.2-12), this leaves

$$px - \sum_{j=1}^{\widehat{j}} \widehat{r}_j y_j - \rho c = \sum_{j=\widehat{j}+1}^{J} r_j^* y_j e^{-\rho \xi_j}$$

in the firm to set aside in a *sinking* fund that will provide the reserves for replacing the durable batches of inputs y_j ($j = \widehat{j} + 1, \ldots, J$) when they wear out.[16] (Replacement of work in progress as it moves through production to completion is automatically accomplished by the inputs in use at the moment in question.) Moreover, for any durable j, the per-unit quantity of funds so accumulated over the life of j exactly equals the purchase price of j, that is,

$$\int_0^{\alpha_j} r_j^* e^{-\rho \xi_j} d\xi_j = r_j', \quad j = \widehat{j} + 1, \ldots, J.$$

When durables wear out, then, the firm does not need to borrow additional money capital to replace them.

Clearly relations (13.2-14) and (13.2-15) form a system of two equations that are valid for all values of input and output prices and quantities. Hence they can be thought of as defining ρ and c as functions of p, x, the $\widehat{r}_j$ and the y_j. Once p and the $\widehat{r}_j$ are dictated by output and input markets, and once the firm sets x and the y_j in response to them, both the money capital needed to support production as well as the rate of return the firm is able to pay on it are determined.

Earlier discussion, however, has already pointed out that the money capital requirement defined in this way moves over time. Not only does it increase at least until sales begin, but it also is subject to the discontinuous cyclical variation discussed in conjunction with equation (13.2-8). Such behavior is reflected in (13.2-15). Unfortunately, the problems involved in integrating into the Walrasian vision of earlier chapters a money capital requirement that continually modifies with time are formidable indeed. To avoid these difficulties, the following abstracts from all cyclical fluctuations and assumes that the average money capital requirement (averaged, as indicated below, over the lives of the durable inputs) is a reasonable approximation of the actual money capital requirement.[17] Because the former turns out to be independent of time, it can be introduced into the Walrasian firm quite simply.

---

[16] It is assumed that the successive contributions to the sinking fund are invested at the required rate of return ρ. Recall that the latter has also been taken to equal the actual or equilibrium rate of return.

[17] A similar assumption is made by Gabor and Pearce [5, p. 549].

An expression for the average money capital requirement, denoted by the same symbol c, can be obtained from (13.2-15):

$$c = \frac{1}{\rho} \left(px - \sum_{j=1}^{\widehat{j}} \widehat{r}_j y_j - \sum_{j=\widehat{j}+1}^{J} \widehat{r}_j y_j \frac{\int_0^{\alpha_j} e^{-\rho \xi_j} d\xi_j}{\alpha_j} \right). \qquad (13.2\text{-}17)$$

Substitution from (13.2-12) and carrying out the integration in (13.2-17) using (13.2-1) gives

$$c = \frac{1}{\rho} \left(px - \sum_{j=1}^{\widehat{j}} r_j y_j - \sum_{j=\widehat{j}+1}^{J} \frac{r'_j}{\alpha_j} y_j \right). \qquad (13.2\text{-}18)$$

The bracketed term in (13.2-18) is net revenue, with durable inputs valued at their purchase price per unit of life. Letting

$$r_j = \frac{r'_j}{\alpha_j}, \quad j = \widehat{j} + 1, \ldots, J, \qquad (13.2\text{-}19)$$

relation (13.2-18) reduces to

$$c = \frac{1}{\rho} \left(px - \sum_{j=1}^{J} r_j y_j \right). \qquad (13.2\text{-}20)$$

Evidently, (13.2-20) is a simplified version of (13.2-15) with different pricing of durable inputs, and with c representing the average money capital requirement. Note that here the pricing of durables is the same as that of nondurables because $\alpha_j = 1$ for all nondurable inputs.[18] Equation (13.2-20), moreover, does not depend on time. The right-hand side of (13.2-20) is the capitalized value of the net revenue of the firm. In other words, (13.2-20) upon multiplication by ρ says that the return on the firm's average money capital requirement is the excess of total revenue over total operating cost of inputs in use.

Substitution of (13.2-14) into (13.2-18) provides a counterpart to (13.2-

---

[18] According to (13.2-1), the price per unit of life of a durable input is the same as its rental value in the limit as $\rho \to 0$. For nondurables, purchase prices equal rental values also when $\rho \to 0$ (recall n. 13 on p. 531). Hence all input prices in (13.2-20) can also be interpreted as "$\rho = 0$ rental values."

16) in terms of averages:

$$
c = \sum_{j=1}^{J} \widehat{r}_j y_j \frac{e^{\rho \overline{\tau}_j} - 1}{\rho} + \sum_{j=\widehat{j}+1}^{J} \left[\frac{r_j^* - \dfrac{r_j'}{\alpha_j}}{\rho} \right] y_j
$$

(13.2-21)

$$
= \sum_{j=1}^{J} \int_{-\overline{\tau}_j}^{0} \widehat{r}_j y_j e^{\rho(0-\tau)} d\tau + \sum_{j=\widehat{j}+1}^{J} \left[\frac{r_j^* - \dfrac{r_j'}{\alpha_j}}{\rho} \right] y_j.
$$

The interpretation of (13.2-21) is similar to that of (13.2-16) except that here the fixed capital term reduces to the sum of the products of y_j/ρ times the difference between rental values and purchase prices per unit of life. As one would expect, it can be shown that these differences are always positive, or

$$
r_j^* - \frac{r_j'}{\alpha_j} > 0, \quad j = \widehat{j} + 1, \dots, J.
$$

(See Exercise 13.6.) Furthermore, the average contribution to the firm's sinking fund for the replacement of worn out durables now is calculated from (13.2-20) as

$$
px - \sum_{j=1}^{\widehat{j}} r_j y_j - \rho c = \sum_{j=\widehat{j}+1}^{J} \frac{r_j'}{\alpha_j} y_j,
$$

(13.2-22)

and over the life of input j these funds per unit of j accumulate according to

$$
\int_{0}^{\alpha_j} \frac{r_j'}{\alpha_j} d\tau = r_j', \quad j = \widehat{j} + 1, \dots, J,
$$

(13.2-23)

so that upon wearing out, all durables can be replaced.

The money capital requirement as described in either (13.2-16) or (13.2-21) has a natural interpretation as the firm's cost of entering the industry because, in starting up production, durable inputs must be purchased and work in progress must be built up before finished output can be obtained and sales begin. In both of these circumstances this investment, *i.e.*, the money capital requirement, is also the *economic value* of the firm, or what the firm could be sold for.[19] But it is only in the case of formulation (13.2-21) (and its accompanying equation, (13.2-20)) that time drops out and that entry cost, average money capital required, economic value, and capitalized value of net revenue all amount to the same thing. The assumptions needed to achieve this result, of course, are restrictive and include (i) the equality of the actual rate of return on money capital and the required rate of return, (ii) the condition that residual profit or B in equation (13.2-13) is identically zero, and (iii) the supposition that the average money capital requirement can be used as an approximation of the actual money capital requirement.

However, it should be recalled that all perfectly competitive firms studied in previous sections have, according to the introduction to Chapter 6, been subject, among other things, to free entry. That is, in the context of those discussions, firms necessarily operate in the special environment in which there is no money capital requirement. As pointed out earlier, this situation would arise if all inputs were nondurable and all maturity times were zero. Nevertheless, the essence of perfect competition is not destroyed by permitting positive (but finite) money-capital entry costs, as long as there are no other barriers to entry. And such a modification of the definition of a perfectly competitive industry would still leave entry "free" in the sense that all outsiders would continue to have the same opportunity to enter the industry as before. But now, of course, the process of entry would demand that the requisite money capital be raised. Sections 13.3 and 14.3 recognize perfectly competitive markets in this modified light.

With these ideas in mind, introduce appropriate substitutions into the zero-residual-profit condition (13.2-14) so that the rental values of durable inputs appearing there are replaced by their corresponding prices per unit of life.[20] Assume that for all relevant vectors (p, r, x, y), the resulting equation determines a unique value for ρ, and define the *average money capital requirement function* by first solving that equation for ρ and then substituting the solution into (13.2-20). Write this function as

$$c = \Lambda(p, r, x, y),$$

where $r = (r_1, \ldots, r_J)$ and $y = (y_1, \ldots, y_J)$. It should be noted that although c started out as a decision variable of the firm in equation (13.2-10), it has now metamorphosed into a solution outcome of a system of equilibrium equations

---

[19] In general, when the firm is in a position other than equilibrium, its economic value could deviate from the actual amount of money capital invested in it. This may arise if, contrary to present assumptions, the firm's actual rate of return on money capital differed from the required rate.

[20] For an illustration in a slightly modified context, see equation (14.3-19) in the next chapter.

involving, in part, the zero-residual-profit condition (13.2-14). That is, the values that c is permitted to assume have been restricted from general answers to the question, "How much money capital does the firm need to support the production of output x with inputs y at prices p and r?" to only those values of c that both answer this question and are consistent with the constraining equilibrium conditions that have been imposed. Of course, the same thing happens, for example, to the output quantity variable when a model of a profit-maximizing firm is embedded in a general model of the entire economy. In that case, the output variable is transformed from a decision variable of the firm into an outcome variable of the entire system that is consistent with both profit maximization by the firm and, in part, the equality of demand and supply in the firm's output market.

The role played by the money capital requirement in determination of the firm's long-run output and input is considered next.

13.3   FIRM BEHAVIOR

Recall that the production function of previous chapters (namely, 4.1-1) relates current output to inputs currently in use. In earlier discussion "inputs currently in use" always meant the same thing as inputs purchased. But these notions necessarily become distinct when applied to durables because the latter are bought and paid for only when introduced in production. Thereafter they are used without having to purchase them again for the remainder of their lives. Furthermore, in the present context production cannot take place without money capital. As described in Section 13.2, money capital is needed because durable inputs have to be purchased before the firm has enough revenue to cover their costs, and because in the early moments when production first starts, inputs (both durable and nondurable) must be hired and paid for before any output is secured. Only after durable and nondurable inputs have been employed for a while and after work in progress has been built up within the firm does a stable relation exist between current inputs and current output. The fact that current output may have actually been produced, in part, by previously hired inputs (or that currently used inputs might contribute to the production of future output) is ignored in the production function but implicit in the money capital requirement.

To be more precise, the production function of the firm in question is written

$$x = f(y), \tag{13.3-1}$$

where $y = (y_1, \ldots, y_J)$ varies over current quantities of inputs in use and x reflects current output. Nondurable inputs y_j, where $j = 1, \ldots, \widehat{j}$, are purchased at their moment of use. Durable inputs y_j, where $j = \widehat{j} + 1, \ldots, J$, may have been purchased in the past. If so, the full purchase price was paid to the sellers of these inputs upon their initial employment. The only spending remaining from them is the return to be paid on the money capital tied up in them. A return also has to be paid on the money capital expended on past purchases of the nondurable inputs that took part in the production of output not yet completed and sold. Whatever portion of y that contributes to work in progress for future output, does not actually participate in the finishing of current output, but is counted as current input in use nonetheless. Of course, a return will have to be paid in the future on any money capital required to cover current expenditures on y. At each instant of time, then, current input in use completes and hence converts production begun earlier into current output according to (13.3-1). Note that during the period in which the firm is starting up production, that is, when it is expending money capital on inputs but does not yet have output to sell, $x = 0$ and (13.3-1) does not apply. Observe also that the derivatives of f, hereafter assumed to exist continuously, refer to the marginal products f_j of inputs with different maturity times and different lives or durabilities. For a durable input, f_j is calculated with respect to the stock of that input; whereas in the case of a nondurable input j it appears in terms of the flow of input j.

To account for money capital in the theory of the firm, let an average money capital requirement function

$$c = \Lambda(p, r, x, y), \tag{13.3-2}$$

defined for all relevant values of (p, r, x, y) be given which does not depend on time. Thus Λ specifies the necessary money capital tied up or invested in the firm on average so as to be able to sustain output x with input y, given prices p and r. A general method of computation of such a function (which requires that the prices of durable goods, r_j for $j = \widehat{j} + 1, \ldots, J$, be interpreted as prices per unit of durable-good life) has been provided in the previous section. Assume that Λ is continuously differentiable everywhere with respect to all of its arguments. Then under present assumptions with the zero-residual-profit condition (13.2-14) and equation (13.2-20) in force, that is with c the outcome variable of Section 13.2, the sign of the partial derivative Λ_j with respect to input j (not its price r_j) as well as the sign of that with respect to output Λ_x cannot be determined. This is because the first-order partial derivatives of (13.2-20) with respect to y_j and x each require the "addition" of two terms of opposite sign:

$$\frac{\partial c}{\partial y_j} = \frac{1}{\rho}\left(-r_j - c\frac{\partial \rho}{\partial y_j}\right) \quad \text{and} \quad \frac{\partial c}{\partial x} = \frac{1}{\rho}\left(p - c\frac{\partial \rho}{\partial x}\right),$$

where $\rho > 0$, $-r_j < 0$, $c > 0$, $p > 0$, and from implicit differentiation of (13.2-14),

$$\frac{\partial \rho}{\partial y_j} = \frac{-\widehat{r}_j e^{\rho \overline{\tau}_j}}{\displaystyle\sum_{n=1}^{J}(\widehat{r}_n y_n e^{\rho \overline{\tau}_n})\overline{\tau}_n} < 0,$$

and

$$\frac{\partial \rho}{\partial x} = \frac{p}{\displaystyle\sum_{j=1}^{J}(\widehat{r}_j y_j e^{\rho \overline{\tau}_j})\overline{\tau}_j} > 0.$$

However, absent the zero-residual-profit condition and returning c to its initial decision-variable status in Section 13.2, the signs of $\partial c/\partial y_j$ and $\partial c/\partial x$, still based on the average money capital requirement but amended to additionally depend on ρ, are, respectively, positive and negative (Exercise 13.7). In other words, and as is to be expected from the definition of the money capital requirement in Section 13.2, increasing input j in the averaged version of (13.2-10) with ρ and all other arguments of Λ held fixed (and $\tau^0 > 0$) necessarily increases input cost and enlarges that requirement; and similarly increasing x increases revenue and reduces it. Regardless, inputs with different maturity times and different durabilities are likely to be associated with different derivative functions Λ_j.

Up to here, the behavior of the long-run perfectly competitive firm has been postulated as arising from selections of x and y which maximize profit,

$$px - r \cdot y,$$

given fixed values for p and r (Section 5.2). With the introduction of a money capital requirement, however, it is more appropriate to take a slightly different perspective. For all relevant (p, r, x, y), define the function

$$\Phi(p, r, x, y) = \frac{px - r \cdot y}{\Lambda(p, r, x, y)}. \tag{13.3-3}$$

Then Φ indicates the actual rate of return the firm is able to pay on the average money capital required by it, or invested in it, for each (p, r, x, y) and, according to (13.2-20),

$$\rho = \Phi(p, r, x, y). \tag{13.3-4}$$

Recall that behind Λ, which is implicit in equation (13.3-4), are the assumptions that the actual and required rates of return on money capital (the latter designated by the symbol ρ) are equal, that residual profit or B in (13.2-13) vanishes identically, and that the average money capital requirement is used in place of the actual money capital requirement. To these restrictions add the further supposition that $\Lambda(p, r, x, y)$ gives the firm's "optimal" money capital required for each (p, r, x, y) — another condition, like the first two listed above, that holds at equilibrium.[21] The assumption of profit maximization can now be replaced as follows: Given its production and average money capital requirement functions, the firm takes p and r as parameters dictated by the markets and chooses x and y so as to maximize its rate of return Φ.[22] Indeed, the owners of the firm's money capital would probably not permit otherwise. If the firm did not provide its greatest attainable rate of return, then higher rates of return would be more likely to be available elsewhere and thus the firm would increase the risk of losing its money capital to these opportunities.

This view of firm behavior is clearly long run and partial equilibrium in character and parallels that of Section 5.2. Thus as p and r modulate, the maximizing values of x and y change. The average (optimal) money capital required to sustain output (that is, the value of Λ) and the actual rate of return earned by the firm on the money capital invested in it (the value of Φ) also modify. Moreover, hypothetical variation of p and r permit definition of the firm's input demand and output supply functions. It is further true that, depending on happenings elsewhere in the economy, the selection of x and y to maximize Φ, given p and r, may or may not lead to values of x and y which are consistent with economy-wide equilibrium. If not, the money capital invested in the firm may earn a larger or smaller rate of return than that obtainable elsewhere. Even from a partial equilibrium perspective, one might think that if, upon maximization, $\Phi(p, r, x, y)$ turns out to be smaller than the rate of return in some other industry, then rather than proceed with producing the Φ-maximizing output, the firm (or its owners) would attempt to liquidate its assets and divert all of its money capital toward the higher return. However,

---

[21]   This optimum is with respect to the structure of the firm's money capital obligations in terms of what is referred to as debt versus equity capital. See Vickers [11, Ch. 10].

[22]   If $\Lambda(p, r, x, y)$ were not assumed to give the firm's optimum money capital required for each (p, r, x, y), then the maximization of Φ would, in addition to (13.3-7), (13.2-11), and (13.3-14) below, result in still further first-order maximization conditions ensuring that the money capital required is, indeed, structured optimally (*Ibid.*, Ch. 10]).

such transfers of money capital to higher rates-of-return opportunities would likely occur only when the realizable value of the firm's assets in alternative uses is at least equal to the actual money capital invested in it. But regardless, the way money capital flows between firms is regulated by dynamic rules not specified here. And in any event, at economy-wide equilibrium all rates of return are equalized and the issue does not arise. Discussion will return to the point in Section 14.3.

To obtain the money capital necessary to finance the production of output, suppose the firm sells IOU's to consumers in an IOU market. (Consumer demand for IOU's is taken up in Section 14.3.) These IOU's pay a rate of return ρ at each subsequent instant of time in perpetuity.[23] IOU's are issued by the firm when it is starting up production or expanding output. Only at these times does it not have, on average, the funds to cover procurement of all of the inputs it needs (Section 13.2.). When output is contracting, old IOU's are repurchased. Funds for repurchasing are obtained by not replacing worn-out inputs (durable and nondurable) and hence making available the excess, when present, of current revenue over current input expense plus current return paid on the firm's money capital (recall equation (13.2-22)) for buying back previously sold IOU's. The total amount of money capital already invested in the firm, or the firm's debt D is the sum of the par values of all outstanding IOU's. For convenience, the price (par value) of IOU's is set at unity. Thus, corresponding to each vector (p, r), the firm's net supply function for IOU's is described by

$$\Lambda(p, r, x, y) - D,$$

where x and y are placed at appropriate Φ-maximum values. Note that in addition to quantities of money capital, c and D now represent quantities of IOU's as well.

These ideas can be illustrated in the special discrete-time, fixed-input-proportions world of the bookcase example of Section 13.2. Let p and r be given. Suppose one unit of day 1 labor cuts wood for one bookcase per day, one unit of day 2 labor assembles one bookcase per day, and one unit of day 3 labor paints one bookcase per day. Assume further that each unit of durable input (saws, hammers, and paint brushes) wears out and must be replaced after the second day of use. If the Φ-maximizing value of x is two bookcases per day, then the hiring schedule of inputs from the start of production through day

---

[23]   Of course, ρ is the rate of return required by the buyers of new IOU's, or what has earlier been referred to as the rate of return that firms are contractually required to pay on their money capital. Recall also that the actual rate of return that firms are able to pay at equilibrium has been assumed to equal this required rate.

Table 13.1 Hypothetical start-up schedule

	Units hired on			
Type of input	Day 1	Day 2	Day 3	Day 4
day 1 labor	2	2	2	2
saws*	2		2	
wood*	2	2	2	2
day 2 labor		2	2	2
hammers*		2		2
nails*		2	2	2
day 3 labor			2	2
paint brushes*			2	
paint*			2	2
units of output sold	0	0	0	2

*One unit of this input is enough to keep one unit of the labor using it busy for one day.

4 is as shown in Table 13.1. The first three days yield no output but require expenditure of money capital. At the end of day 3, two bookcases are available for sale on day 4. From day 4 on, two bookcases are finished and sold per day. Two saws and two paint brushes must be purchased on each odd-numbered day after day 1. (On day 1 only two saws are procured.) The firm has to buy two hammers on all even-numbered days. As long as $\Phi(p, r, x, y) > 0$, daily revenue from the sale of current output beyond day 3 is sufficient on average to cover the hiring of all current inputs needed to maintain current output at the rate of two bookcases per day, and also is sufficient to cover the cost (paid at rate $\Phi(p, r, x, y)$) of the money capital that sustains it. In particular, revenues on average are large enough each day to replace worn out durable inputs (saws, hammers, and paint brushes) without selling additional IOU's. (Refer again to equations (13.2-22) and (13.2-23).) The firm thus enters the IOU market as a

Table 13.2 Hypothetical liquidation schedule

Type of input	Units hired on			
	Day 1	Day 2	Day 3	Day 4
day 1 labor	2			
saws*				
wood*	2			
day 2 labor	2	2		
hammers*	2			
nails*	2	2		
day 3 labor	2	2	2	
paint brushes*		2		
paint*	2	2	2	
units of output sold	2	2	2	2

*One unit of this input is enough to keep one unit of the labor using it busy for one day.

seller on the first three days of production only. Were the maximizing rate of output to expand beyond two bookcases per day, the money capital necessary to support it might increase (recall the indeterminacy described on pp. 544-545) and, in that case, additional IOU's would have to be issued.

Suppose now that after a while the firm decided to liquidate its assets and go out of business. One orderly schedule for liquidation appears in Table 13.2. Output on day 1 is taken to be two bookcases, and inputs on that day are assumed to be identical to those of day 4 in Table 13.1. On day 2, the saws for day 1 labor have worn out and are not replaced. Those units of labor as well as the wood they would use also are not hired. The procedure continues according to Table 13.2 until liquidation. At the end of day 3 there is neither work in progress nor durable input left; but there are two bookcases still to be sold on day 4. Assuming prices have remained constant throughout, the excess of revenues over cost on the last three days is exactly sufficient to offset the money capital invested in the firm. It is on these days that the firm enters the IOU market to retire its debt.[24]

Although in presenting the above example, a complete dynamic cycle from the start to the termination of production has now been spelled out, primary interest here remains with the description of equilibrium. (Assuming no change in p and r, firm activity over its life in the example would not vary from day 4 in Table 13.1 through day 1 in Table 13.2 and would be consistent with equilibrium during that period.) In most of the following, then, dynamics are disregarded. At this point argument returns to the development of the equilibrium equations of the firm in general.

The conditions imposed on f so as to be able to maximize profit have been discussed in Chapters 4 and 5. To ensure that Φ has an appropriate maximum requires restrictions on both f and Λ. In earlier sections, considerable effort was expended on developing the requisites for profit maximization and the implications of them for the properties of the firm's input demand and output supply functions. This is not repeated here. Rather, attention is focused only on the derivation of firm behavior (that is, on the calculation of the firm's input demand and output supply functions) from unique maximization of the rate of return on the money capital invested in it. Without specification, sufficient properties are assumed on f and Λ so as to make all subsequent manipulations valid.

Before proceeding, however, note that the input demand functions so obtained render quantities demanded for use in production as dependent on p and r, where r_j for durable j represents price per unit of life. Also in the case of durables, demand for use is the demand for a stock and does not necessarily translate into actual purchases because the firm may already own what it demands. Thus the flow demand for durable input j is secured by subtracting the quantity of j in the firm's possession from the stock demand for that input. On the other hand, quantities of output supplied (from the firm's output supply function) derived from rate-of-return maximization are always flow quantities, regardless of the durability of the good produced.

Two ways of inferring the firm's input demand and output supply functions were employed in the context of profit maximization under perfectly competitive conditions in Chapters 4 and 5. One required first the construction of the firm's expansion path from cost minimization, second the derivation of

---

[24]   It should be noted, however, that if the reason for the liquidation of its assets reflects a decline in the firm's income-generating ability, then its economic value and, therefore, the market value of its previously issued IOU's will have diminished. In that event, the holders of those IOU's would realize a capital loss on their investment.

a cost function that described the firm's cost of producing each level of output, and finally the maximization of the firm's profit as a function of that output. The other was a one-step process based on the direct maximization of profit as a function of input. Parallel lines of argument are available in the present setting.

Let p and r be given. In place of (unique) cost minimization, inputs y can be chosen so as to uniquely maximize $\Phi(p, r, x, y)$, subject to $x = f(y)$, where x is a fixed parameter identifying a given isoquant. The functions relating such y to parameter values p, r, and x are defined similarly to those of (4.4-3):

$$y = g^*(p, r, x).\qquad(13.3\text{-}5)$$

Observe that, unlike (4.4-3), p appears as an argument of g^*. In the setting of Section 4.4, Φ reduces to $px - r \cdot y$, and maximization of this modified Φ subject to $x = f(y)$ where x is fixed, is equivalent to minimization of $r \cdot y$ subject to $x = f(y)$. Thus the parameter p drops out of (4.4-3). But the presence of Λ in (13.3-3) precludes such a simplification.

According to the theorem of Lagrange, maximization of Φ in (13.3-3) subject to $x = f(y)$ results in the first-order conditions[25]

$$r_j + \Phi\Lambda_j = \Lambda\eta f_j, \quad j = 1, \ldots, J, \qquad(13.3\text{-}6)$$

in force at the maximum, where functional arguments have been deleted to simplify notation, η is an undetermined multiplier, and Λ_j denotes the partial derivative of Λ with respect to the jth input. Dividing the last equation into those remaining,

$$\frac{r_j + \Phi\Lambda_j}{r_J + \Phi\Lambda_J} = \frac{f_j}{f_J}, \quad j = 1, \ldots, J - 1, \qquad(13.3\text{-}7)$$

In words, inputs are combined so that ratios of marginal products equal ratios of input costs, the latter including an appropriate adjustment (positive or negative depending on the sign of Λ_j) that reflects, at the margin, the cost of the money capital required to carry the input. Because (13.3-6) only holds at the maximum, this adjustment, namely $\Phi\Lambda_j$ for input j, must also be computed at the maximum. As the maximum varies in response to changes in p, r, and x, so will $\Phi\Lambda_j$. Thus the optimal input mix defined by (13.3-7) depends, in part, on the rate of return ρ in the guise of Φ and on the rates at which the (average, optimal) money capital requirement varies with modifications in inputs. It

---

[25] The constraint qualification (A.3-17) is met as long as $f_j(y) > 0$ at maximizing values of y, for all j.

follows that a change in the rate of return on money capital may induce substitution of factors within the firm in order to economize on those factors whose (marginal) money-capital carrying costs have gone up or become less negative. Equations (13.3-7) with $x = f(y)$ also assert a tangency between cost hyperplanes (which take into account these money capital expenses) and isoquants. As in Section 4.4, the collection of all input baskets y satisfying (13.3-7), given p and r, define an expansion path. An equivalent characterization of the expansion path is obtained by fixing p and r in (13.3-5).

Analogously to (4.5-1), the long-run total cost of any output x, given p and r, is found from

$$TC(x) = r \cdot g^*(p, r, x), \qquad (13.3-8)$$

where p and r are subsumed in the symbol TC and the "LR" part of the "$LRTC$" symbolism of Section 5.2 has been dropped. Average and marginal costs are defined as in Section 4.5. Substitution of (13.3-5) into (13.3-2) and (13.3-3) expresses the average money capital requirement and rate of return as functions Λ^* and Φ^*, respectively, which are independent of y:

$$\Lambda^*(p, r, x) = \Lambda(p, r, x, g^*(p, r, x)),$$
$$\qquad (13.3-9)$$
$$\Phi^*(p, r, x) = \Phi(p, r, x, g^*(p, r, x)).$$

Using (13.3-8) and (13.3-9) in (13.3-3), the rate of return on money capital invested in the firm can be written as

$$\frac{px - TC(x)}{\Lambda^*(p, r, x)}. \qquad (13.3-10)$$

If x is chosen so as to uniquely maximize this rate of return, then x is secured so that the derivative of (13.3-10) with respect to x vanishes. It follows that at the maximizing output,

$$p = MC + \Phi^* \Lambda_x^*, \qquad (13.3-11)$$

where functional arguments have again been eliminated and MC and Λ_x^* represent, respectively, the marginal cost of x given p and r, and the partial derivative of Λ^* with respect to x. Thus price equals marginal cost plus the appropriate marginal money-capital-carrying cost adjustment again computed at the maximum. As in Section 5.1, equation (13.3-11) can be solved to obtain output supplied by the firm as a function of p and r. Substitution into (13.3-5) then yields the firm's input demand functions.

To deduce the same functions by the second method, eliminate x in (13.3-3) with (13.3-1). The rate of return on money capital invested in the firm becomes

$$\frac{pf(y) - r \cdot y}{\bar{\Lambda}(p, r, y)}, \tag{13.3-12}$$

where

$$\bar{\Lambda}(p, r, y) = \Lambda(p, r, f(y), y), \tag{13.3-13}$$

at appropriate (p, r, y). Equating the partial derivatives of (13.3-12), with respect to the y_j, to zero leaves

$$pf_j = r_j + \bar{\Phi}\bar{\Lambda}_j, \quad j = 1, \ldots, J, \tag{13.3-14}$$

holding at the unique maximum. (Here, $\bar{\Phi}(p, r, y) = \Phi(p, r, f(y), y)$ and $\bar{\Lambda}_j$ is the partial derivative of $\bar{\Lambda}$ with respect to y_j). Input demand functions can now be obtained by solving (13.3-14) for y as a function of (p, r). The output supply function is found by substituting these solutions into the production function (13.3-1). Because

$$\bar{\Lambda}_j(p, r, y) = \Lambda_j(p, r, f(y), y), \quad j = 1, \ldots, J,$$

division of the first $J - 1$ equations of (13.3-14) by the last gives (13.3-7).

In the present context normal profit for the firm (originally defined in Section 5.2) can be interpreted as the minimum return on money capital necessary to induce the suppliers of that capital (that is, the holders of the firm's IOU's) to keep it invested in the firm. Letting $\bar{\rho}$ represent the maximum rate of return available over all other firms in the economy, the lowest return the owners of the firm's money capital need accept, and hence normal profit, is $\bar{\rho}\Lambda$. The return associated with the maximization of (13.3-3), however, is $\Phi\Lambda$, evaluated at the appropriate maximum. Hence abnormal profit (also defined in Section 5.2) is described by

$$\pi = \Phi\Lambda - \bar{\rho}\Lambda. \tag{13.3-15}$$

(Note the same symbol, π, formerly used to denote profit, represents abnormal profit here. With appropriate interpretation of earlier cost functions as described in Section 5.2, the two notions of profit are identical.) As long as $\pi > 0$, the rate of return on money capital invested in the firm is greater than the maximum rate of return available elsewhere. Thus new money capital enters the industry through the IOU market. This new money capital either expands existing firms or creates new ones. The resulting additional output produced lowers output price and abnormal profit. (Recall the argument of Section 6.2.) The flow of money capital into the industry continues until, at long-run equilibrium,

$$\pi = 0, \tag{13.3-16}$$

or

$$\Phi(p, r, x, y) = \overline{p}.$$

(As in Section 5.2, equation (13.3-16) eliminates output price as an argument of the firm's output supply and input demand functions.) Similarly, if $\pi < 0$ money capital leaves the industry. Existing firms either contract or disappear. Thus, in terms of the resource categories land, labor, money capital, and enterprise of Section 1.1, there is no return to enterprise in the long run. The model really includes enterprise as a part of the category "money capital" whose general return is $\rho\Lambda + \pi$, and whose long-run equilibrium return is $\overline{\rho}\Lambda$. The fact that π vanishes in the long run does not discourage the firm from producing its equilibrium output. In answer to the question raised in Section 5.2, the firm produces when $\pi = 0$ because (under a concept of perfect competition that permits positive entry costs) the owners of the firm's money capital are being adequately compensated.

Money capital flowing into an industry can come from increased saving on the part of consumers (Section 14.3 in the next chapter), from other industries as they contract (contracting firms repurchase IOU's from consumers who use the funds so obtained to buy new IOU's from expanding firms), or from a combination of both. The rules determining how this inflow is divided between existing firms and the creation of new ones are not considered here. Similarly, as capital leaves an industry it can either reduce consumer saving or expand another industry. Provided that such capital does not depart faster than permitted by the wearing out of relevant inputs (recall Table 13.2 and the bookcase example), or if it does, as long as expendable inputs (and, if necessary, work in progress) are purchased by expanding industries at appropriately discounted prices, all IOU's repurchased in contracting industries can be paid off at par value and no capital losses from holding IOU's are incurred. Note, however, that this presumes dynamic adjustment rules that (as in a tâtonnement dynamic) permit the lowering of output before π becomes negative. For once $\pi < 0$ actually is experienced, capital losses are likely to be absorbed by the holders of the firm's IOU's.

Geometrically, there are at least two ways to picture the firm in long-run equilibrium with Viner-type cost curves. Either normal profit can be included in the average and marginal cost curves so that equilibrium occurs where market price $\overline{p}$ is the same as the minimum value of average total cost including the money capital cost per unit of output produced (Figure 13.2(a)), or it can be excluded as shown in Figure 13.2(b). In the latter case, the rectangle whose vertices are marked a, b, c, and $\bar{p}$ represents normal profit at $\bar{x}$ as indicated by $\bar{\rho}\Lambda^*$ in the diagram (see Exercise 3.8). Abnormal profit is zero in both cases. (These diagrams should be compared with the left-hand picture of firm long-run equilibrium in Figure 6.2. Recall, however, that the cost curves in the left-hand part of Figure 6.2 are appropriate short-run curves, whereas all cost curves in Figure 13.2 are long-run curves).

Market output supply and input demand functions are secured by summing individual functions across firms and, in the case of the latter, across industries (Section 6.1). Parallel to Section 6.2, the equality of supply and demand in, say, the industry output market, and the long-run equilibrium condition that abnormal profit in each firm vanish, are not necessarily consistent with each other unless the latter is used to locate values for p and x while the former determines the number of firms in the industry.

Finally, to pursue a remark at the end of the previous section, it is now abundantly clear that in insisting on "free" entry, the definition of a perfectly competitive market given in the introduction to Chapter 6 is unnecessarily restrictive. Recall that for entry to be free, in addition to the general absence of obstructions, all money capital requirements must vanish. But as suggested earlier, there is no reason why the notion of perfect competition cannot be generalized to include the possibility of positive entry cost in the form of a money capital requirement provided there are still no further barriers to entry. Any

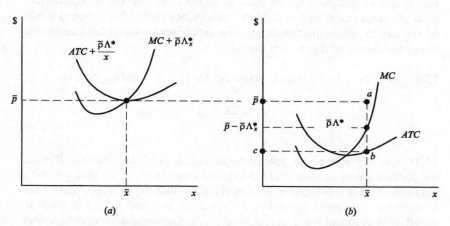

Figure 13.2 The firm in long-run equilibrium: (a) normal profit included in average and marginal costs; (b) normal profit excluded from average and marginal costs

firm may enter as long as it first sells IOU's to raise the necessary money capital. Clearly, all ideas underlying the traditional concept of perfect competition are preserved in this generalization.

EXERCISES

13.1 Consider two investments, one returning \$50 immediately and \$371 after one year, and the other providing \$150 now and \$266 a year later. What rate of return would make these investments equivalent today?

13.2 Verify equation (13.2-4).

13.3 As τ^0 varies, what are the values of ω_j in (13.2-8) at jump-points (discontinuities)? Discuss the behavior of (13.2-5) over time.

13.4 Assume a constant rate of return over time. What is the total present value of an investment that pays back a constant dollar sum at each instant for all subsequent time?

13.5 Consider a perfectly competitive firm, not yet in existence, which would use one nondurable input (y) to produce its output (x) according to the production function $x = f(y) = 2y$. Let the maturity time of the input be $\frac{1}{2}$ year. Suppose the firm knows before it enters the industry that it would be able to sell its output and purchase its input at \$1 per unit, and that its equilibrium level of output would be $x = 2$. How much money capital (on average) would be required to sustain this output and what rate of return would the firm be able to pay for the use of this money capital?

13.6* Let j be a durable input. Show that for all $p > 0$ and $\alpha_j > 0$,

$$r_j^* - \frac{r_j'}{\alpha_j} > 0.$$

13.7* Let $\Lambda(p, r, x, y)$ be defined by averaging (13.2-10) over the lives of the durable inputs instead of (13.2-15), and suppose $\tau^0 > 0$. Take ρ to be a parameter that is subsumed in the functional symbol $\Lambda(p, r, x, y)$. Show that, in this case, the partial derivatives $\Lambda_j(p, r, x, y) > 0$ and $\Lambda_x(p, r, x, y) < 0$, for all (p, r, x, y) and $j = 1, \ldots, J$, where Λ_j is the partial derivative of Λ with respect to y_j, and Λ_x is that with respect to x.

13.8 Given Figure 13.2(a), prove algebraically that, in Figure 13.2(b),

$$\overline{p} - \overline{p}\Lambda_x^*(\overline{x}) = MC(\overline{x}),$$

and that the area of the rectangle with vertices a, b, c, and $\overline{p}$ is normal profit $\overline{p}\Lambda^*(\overline{x})$. (Observe that in this notation, $\overline{p}$ and $\overline{r}$ have been subsumed in the functional symbols MC, Λ^*, and Λ_x^*.)

REFERENCES

1. Baumol, W. J., *Economic Theory and Operations Analysis* 2nd ed. (Engelwood Cliffs: Prentice-Hall, 1965).
2. Bliss, C. J., *Capital Theory and the Distribution of Income* (Amsterdam: North-Holland, 1975).
3. von Böhm-Bawerk, E., *Capital and Interest*, v. 2: *Positive Theory of Capital*. G. D. Huncke and H. F. Stennholz, trans. (South Holland: Libertarian Press, 1959).
4. Burmeister, E. and A. R. Dobel, *Mathematical Theories of Economic Growth* (New York: Macmillan, 1970).
5. Gabor, A. and I. F. Pearce, "The Place of Money Capital in the Theory of Production," *Quarterly Journal of Economics* 72 (1958), pp. 537-557.
6. Harcourt, G. C., *Some Cambridge Controversies in the Theory of Capital* (Cambridge: Cambridge University Press, 1972).
7. Lange, O., "The Place of Interest in the Theory of Production," *Review of Economic Studies* 3 (1935-36), pp. 159-192.
8. Menger, C., *Principles of Economics*, J. Dingwall and B. F. Hoselitz, trans. (Glencoe: Free Press, 1950).
9. Pearce, I. F., "A Theory of Money Capital, General Equilibrium and Income Distribution," *The Measurement of Capital: Theory and Practice*, K. D. Patterson and K. Schott, eds. (London: Macmillan, 1979), pp. 25-64.
10. Rudin, W., *Principles of Mathematical Analysis*, 3rd ed. (New York: McGraw-Hill, 1976).
11. Vickers, D., *The Theory of the Firm: Production, Capital and Finance* (New York: McGraw-Hill, 1968).
12. Wicksell, K., *Lectures on Political Economy*, v. 1, E. Classen, trans. (New York: Kelley, 1967).

Chapter 14

The Grand View[1]

It is now time to draw together loose threads and summarize the Walrasian theory of market behavior. In so doing an attempt will be made to provide, in part, a panorama of the theoretical landscape developed in earlier chapters. Naturally, to achieve such a picture in the large requires a broad brush, which hides many details. The models without capital are informally considered in this way first. Then a more limited and more detailed notion of governmental economic activity is discussed briefly before capital is reintroduced and the formal model of the firm developed in the previous section is reset in the context of a model of the entire economy. The particular grand view (with or without capital) outlined in Section 1.4 is a special case of that (with or without capital) described here.

14.1 WITHOUT CAPITAL

The Walrasian theory of market behavior consists of a collection of concepts, assumptions, arguments, propositions, and models, all of which derive their theoretical force and significance from each other. The concepts include such

---

[1] Parts of Sections 14.1 and 14.3 are taken, with modification and correction, from my "Capital and Walrasian Equilibrium," *Demand, Equilibrium and Trade*, A. Ingham and A. M. Ulph, eds. (London: Macmillan, 1984), pp. 123-148. Reprinted with permission.

things as preferences, production functions, prices, initial endowments, and Pareto optimal distributions. Differentiability, strict concavity, identical firms within industries, and rationality (or maximization) are examples of assumptions that are imposed in various settings. The arguments of the Walrasian theory encompass the construction of revealed preferences from preference orderings, the derivation of input demand and output supply functions of the (perfectly competitive) firm, the proof of existence of economy-wide equilibrium, the demonstration of nonwastefulness and unbiasedness of perfect competition, and so on. Three illustrations of its propositions are

i) under certain conditions, decreasing returns to scale and linear expansion paths imply rising average variable costs;

ii) under certain other conditions, a community utility function exists which, when maximized subject to an aggregate budget constraint, yields the same market demand functions obtained by summing individual consumer demand functions themselves derived from constrained, individual utility maximization; and

iii) Walras' law (which also obtains only under specific conditions).

The models of the Walrasian theory are numerous too, ranging from something as small as the Cobb-Douglas production function model of production in the firm, through more full-blown models of the firm (such as the strictly concave model, the Viner model, and the constant returns to scale model) and of the consumer (for example, the classical and revealed preference models of demand behavior), to models of industries (the short-run perfectly competitive model and the monopoly model are examples) and models of the entire economy (including perfectly competitive models with or without capital and with or without fixed-factor supplies). All of the above elements are intimately linked to each other and draw their theoretical meaning and importance from these interrelationships. Taken together they form the conceptual basis of the Walrasian vision of the microeconomy.

It is possible to ascribe one or more of a variety of purposes to the Walrasian theory of market behavior. First, the Walrasian theory can be said to explain observed facts, that is, to provide an understanding of the economic world that is seen. Of course this statement is not intended to be interpreted literally. The Walrasian vision is, by its very nature, an abstraction from reality. Its intent is to describe only an idealized world. Hence it cannot provide explanations and understandings of everything that is seen, and those explanations and understandings that it does provide are necessarily only approximations of what actually goes on. Second, the Walrasian theory can be taken to be a body of analysis whose purpose is to examine the theoretical coherence of an economy in which all individuals (consumers and firms) are motivated by their own self-interest. In this regard, it furnishes various conditions under which "coherence" (unique and globally stable solutions), as opposed to "chaos" (the absence of such solutions) obtains. In so doing it makes precise the limits of microeconomic theorizing. Third, the Walrasian theory can be viewed as a source of models and propositions for analyzing real-world issues. In other words, it allows for the development of particular hypotheses which can be empirically tested against reality. To the extent that observations turn out to be consistent with these hypotheses or their projections, the models from which the hypotheses are derived yield ways of understanding what is observed. Fourth, the Walrasian theory provides standards or norms for evaluating behavior. For example, by watching a given consumer or a particular market, it is possible to determine if the consumer's behavior is "rational" (that is, consistent with the postulate of utility maximization in Chapter 2) or if the market is perfectly competitive. Last, the Walrasian theory supplies a context in which evaluations of economic outcomes, such as distributions of final commodities, and of economic policies, such as the imposition of a sales tax, can be made.

Regardless of the view one takes concerning which of the above purposes the Walrasian theory of market behavior sets out to fulfill, the theory accomplishes its purpose or purposes through the thought-forms set out in previous chapters. The following summarizes the main themes of this construction on the assumption that capital (money or physical) is not employed by the firm. In that respect the analysis recapitulated below may be understood as an initial approximation to the fuller explanation of economic outcomes to be summarized in Section 14.3. Clearly there are many contexts within which such an overview can be set. For example, the long-run or short-run perspective may be taken, factor supplies may be fixed or variable, and differentiability of functions may or may not be assumed. All approaches, however, have certain elements in common. These shared features are emphasized below. The accompanying equations are not repeated.

From the Walrasian vantage point, the economic world is a collection of consumers and firms, each making decisions relevant for a single isolated instant at every moment of time. (Although time is taken to be continuous, a similar conceptualization would result if it were thought of as discrete.) These decisions interact simultaneously through markets. Markets, in turn, are guided according to certain rules of price adjustment, which beget dynamic behavior across time as consumers and firms react to the changing market prices dictated by the rules. Ideally, although this has not been true of depictions of the

Walrasian system in the past, the price-adjustment rules should reflect directly the actions of individual market participants.

The institutional structure of markets is taken to be perfectly competitive. Thus within any one market there are "large" numbers of "small" buyers and sellers, the market's commodity is standardized, entry into and exit from the market is free, and the same information is available to all of the market's participants. In part, these traits may be taken to imply that firms and consumers perceive prices as elements over which they have no control, and sometimes that all firms in any given market are identical.

To model this economy, consumer decisions are assumed to be based on preferences expressed in utility functions. Given market prices, the baskets of final commodities and factors that consumers want to buy and sell are selected by maximizing utility subject to budget constraints. Utility functions must be supposed to possess sufficient properties so that such constrained maximization can be carried out. As consumers face alternative hypothetical price vectors, repeated maximization generates consumption demand and factor supply functions (Sections 2.3 and 3.3). All properties assumed of utility functions are reflected as restrictions imposed on these derived functions (Sections 2.3 and 2.4).

Firms, on the other hand, are confronted by technology in the form of production functions. Subject also to given market prices, they hire inputs and produce outputs (in the models) so as to maximize profit. The profit, with respect to which this maximization is accomplished, may be thought of as dependent solely on either inputs or output. In both cases, input demand and output supply functions are secured as the prices of inputs and output vary (in theory) and the maximization is repeated (Chapters 4 and 5). Once again it is necessary to require production functions to exhibit properties sufficient to ensure that profit maximization can be accomplished, and these properties force input demand and output supply functions to take on corresponding characteristics.

Combining the relevant demand functions of all buyers in any market gives the market's demand function, and combining the relevant supply functions of all sellers in any market gives the market's supply function. Equilibrium in a model of a market (at a positive price) arises when market demand equals market supply. In a short-run model this determines an equilibrium market price and a market quantity (Section 6.1). In a long-run model it determines a market quantity and the number of firms in the market (industry) because price already is equated to the minimum long-run average total cost of the representative firm (Section 6.2).

Markets, of course, do not operate in isolation. Changes in one bring about changes in others. Walras' law (equation (7.2-20)) implies that in a model with, say, N markets, if any $N - 1$ of them are in equilibrium together, then so is the Nth. In general, equilibrium in a Walrasian model of an economy occurs when all consumers are buying final outputs and selling factors so as to maximize utility subject to budget constraints, all firms are hiring inputs and producing outputs that maximize profits, and supply equals demand in all markets. Such an equilibrium is described in Section 7.2. Under the same conditions required to ensure that utility and profit maximization are possible, this equilibrium always exists (Theorem 9.2-23). Additional hypotheses are needed to guarantee its uniqueness (Section 9.4) and global stability (Sections 9.3, 10.2, and 10.3).

At Walrasian equilibrium (that is, at a unique equilibrium in a Walrasian model of the economy), it is not permissible to speak of things like demand and supply curves and movements along them. Walrasian equilibrium, after all, yields only a collection of numerical values, one for each variable. At such an equilibrium, demand and supply quantities in any particular market are interdependent, and neither changes in response to alterations in that market's price alone.[2] Indeed, the market price cannot vary by itself in the first place. The only way to have a price and its associated quantity change is if they modify, together with all other prices and quantities, as the "fixed" parameters and functions of the model modulate. It is in the context of partial equilibrium, where certain endogenous variables in addition to the parameters are held constant, that it becomes possible to identify demand and supply curves. Here one can legitimately arrive at the assertion that the quantity demanded and the quantity supplied in a market each depend on the market price as the market price varies hypothetically. In the same setting one can also say that the market equilibrium price depends on the interaction of market demand and market supply. But at Walrasian equilibrium, the only meaningful statement in this regard is that all equilibrium prices and all equilibrium quantities are determined simultaneously as the solution of all equations of the model.

Walrasian equilibrium also has important welfare and efficiency characteristics. Although established only for the special case of fixed-factor supplies in Chapter 12, they apply in general. Thus equilibrium is Pareto optimal (nonwasteful) in that equilibrium outputs can be neither feasibly enlarged nor redistributed among consumers so as to increase the utility of one person without lowering that of someone else (Theorem 12.3-11). Likewise, the equilibrium

---

[2]   The multi-market interdependence envisaged here neglects, as indicated earlier, the possibility of different market-clearing velocities.

output of any firm cannot be expanded except by reducing production in another (also Theorem 12.3-11). Equilibrium, moreover, is unbiased in the sense that it is compatible with all Pareto optimal distributions; that is, each such distribution can appear as an equilibrium (Theorem 12.3-14). Finally, the distribution of outputs associated with any equilibrium maximizes social welfare for some suitably chosen welfare function constructed from individual preferences (Theorem 12.3-25). This function may or may not be society's actual welfare function.

In the absence of shifts in functions or parameter values, and with an economy-wide equilibrium in place in a particular model, all equilibrium values are maintained as constants over time. One way to discuss behavior in models out of equilibrium is to assume something about the price-adjustment rules mentioned above, that is, about how prices modify under all nonequilibrium contingencies. Having as yet no theory to determine them, assumptions about rules of price adjustment are arbitrary and different specifications produce different results. But once the rules are settled on, the conditions under which all markets eventually find their equilibria (that is, the conditions under which the economy-wide equilibrium is globally stable) can be explored (Sections 9.3, 10.2, and 10.3). The nature of these conditions depends, in part, on whether the dynamic is a tâtonnement so that trading is precluded before equilibrium is achieved (the circumstance studied in this volume), or whether trade takes place as part of the process of establishing equilibrium. Furthermore, starting at an initial out-of-equilibrium price vector, the adjustment rules determine market prices in the model at every instant thereafter. Hence individual consumer and firm behavior at each out-of-equilibrium moment can be inferred from the appropriate individual demand and supply functions.

Observations of the real economy can be interpreted as reflecting or approximating equilibria achieved in this kind of model. That is, any vector of quantities and prices actually sighted can be explained as the outcome of interactions between consumers, firms, and markets which may, in an imaginary experiment, have begun out of equilibrium, but which ended up at equilibrium with exactly or approximately the same quantities and prices as those seen in reality. Subsequent observations of the identical world exhibiting different prices and quantities would be conceived of similarly, with the understanding that alterations in the underlying parameter values or changed utility and (or) production functions were responsible for the modified results. Identification of actual data with equilibria relegates all dynamic movement out of equilibrium to the unseeable universe of the hypothetical. On this view, descriptions of price-adjustment rules or mechanisms, although an aid in comprehending the real economy, are necessarily fictions. Reality cannot be recognized apart from the theoretical equilibrium toward which it tends. Of course, alternative interpretations of data permitting observation of a moving economy not at equilibrium also are possible. These might associate what is seen with non-equilibrium time-paths, thus rendering the adjustment mechanism observable but hiding the equilibrium itself from view.

A special case of the above that is studied extensively in this book is identified by adding the extra assumption that all factor supplies are fixed at given amounts. In such a context, the economy's transformation surface can be defined (Section 8.1). Its properties depend on those of firm or industry production functions. The same market output supplies of final goods and demands for factors described earlier can often be viewed equivalently as arising from the maximization of the value of the economy's output subject to the transformation function (Section 8.2). Furthermore, under certain extra conditions conditions, there turns out to be a 1–1 correspondence between input and output price ratios (Theorem 8.2-11). On the other hand, imposition of further assumptions on consumer demand permits the construction of a community utility function (Section 8.3) and the expression of equilibrium in terms of the maximization of this function subject to the transformation function (Section 8.4). The community utility function does not necessarily reflect social welfare.

It is in the fixed-factor-supply framework that the previously stated welfare and efficiency assertions were proved (Chapter 12). It is in the same framework that the difficulties arising from the introduction of alternative forms of imperfect competition also were explored (Chapter 11). And it is in this framework that government participation in the economy is examined briefly in Section 14.2 and the model with capital (begun in Chapter 13) is completed in Section 14.3.

The significance of the Walrasian theory of market behavior arises in the intellectual and social usefulness of the purposes of the theory as outlined above. But there is more to it than that. For the Walrasian theory has a power all its own, which has transcended its stated purposes and allowed it to become a central paradigm in modern microeconomic thought. Its power stems not only from its success at achieving what it sets out to do, but also, in part, from its ability to solve the coherence problem in sufficient generality to suggest that even though the Walrasian vision is an abstraction, a crude approximation of economic reality, there is still some form of coherence in economic life. Moreover, the outcome of this coherence can be evaluated and ethical judgements made about it. In the context of the theory, these outcomes are the equilibria (the solutions) that depend on initial endowments and other parameters. Although the theory itself makes efficiency judgments about them in establishing their Pareto optimality, ethical evaluations are left for expression in terms of a general, but unspecified, welfare function. Thus the options open to society through the choice of parameter values are clearly and precisely characterized. It is this image of a well-defined collection of outcomes among which society may choose, all consistent with the self-interest-motivated behavior that reflects the strong current of individualism present in Western thought and culture, that has made the Walrasian vision so popular and so appealing.

Apart from the appeal of the vision itself, another source of the power of the Walrasian theory of market behavior lies in its role as a metaphor in a field that is heavily dependent on metaphors as a basis for analysis. Metaphors in economics serve both as instruments of thought and as devices for communicating meaning.[3] Their force rests in their ability to transfer the sense of one person's insight to another. They are figures of communication in which one thing — say thing A — is taken to represent to a different thing — call it thing B — by speaking of A "as if" it were B. Thus a market operates as if it equated demand to supply, a consumer behaves as if he maximized utility subject to his budget constraint, and the economy functions as if it were a Walrasian system. Such metaphors are incisive because they permit the analyst to focus her thoughts in a concrete and precise way on variables and relations that, by current professional standards, seem important. The model so obtained constitutes an "ideal type" or mental construction that isolates what are thought to be the "fundamental" elements of reality for study by themselves in the absence of the "secondary" and less important features also thought to be present. Hence the investigator can gain an understanding of the ideal system functioning alone as a "first step" in her exploration of the economic world.

But the Walrasian theory of market behavior has its limitations too. These mostly lie in the distance from reality that the Walrasian abstraction requires. They arise in the nature of the theory's assumptions and methods of analysis and the resulting exclusion of certain phenomena that are known to exist in economic reality. To illustrate, although the economist is unable to penetrate the mind of the consumer,[4] is it reasonable to suppose that individual preferences are transitive and total? Alternatively, labor markets do not always appear to clear in reality; they do, however, clear in the Walrasian vision. It is not surprising, then, that economists have already spent and continue to spend considerable energy on trying to reduce such limitations by altering the as-

---

3   McCloskey [2].
4   Recall the discussion on p. 7.

sumptions and methods of analysis of the theory and generating new models and new propositions. A few of these efforts are described in the next chapter. Certainly, the more limitations that are eliminated, the greater the power and attractiveness of the Walrasian theory.

14.2   GOVERNMENT AND THE ECONOMY

Throughout this book there have been suggestions that government interacts with and influences the economy. Although sometimes more implicit than explicit, these suggestions have appeared most notably in the discussions of welfare in Section 3.4 and Chapter 12, and in the partial-equilibrium analysis of the imposition of sales and profits taxes on isolated perfectly competitive industries in Section 6.3. Moreover, the previous section has indicated that one plausible aim of the Walrasian theory of market behavior is to delineate and analyze government policy options. (The ability of the Walrasian theory to do so was also identified as a source of its appeal.) Of course, to obtain specific policy recommendations requires the inclusion of a distinct policy-making unit in the models of the Walrasian theory so that the government becomes a partner in the simultaneous determination of equilibrium. Like any consumer or any firm, the government would be assumed to make its policy decisions according to certain prespecified criteria and against certain given parameters. These decisions would affect the flows of goods and payments through markets and thereby interact with all nongovernment decisions in the attainment of equilibrium. The present section briefly explores such an arrangement.

There are many ways for governments to participate in the economy. They can enter markets as buyers or sellers. They can tax and subsidize. They can provide incentives to alter the behavior of consumers and firms. They can regulate economic activity by imposing rules. And they can hire inputs to produce outputs as do ordinary firms. The motives behind governmental economic participation are different from those driving persons and firms. Rather than pursuing their own self interest, governments presumably operate for the "good" of society. The statement of what is good for society can, in part, be expressed in terms of a welfare function as in Chapter 12, but it can also involve noneconomic elements such as the "preservation of freedom" and "national security."[5]

---

[5]   Another possibility arises when, contrary to the assumptions imposed here, the real economy appears to "equilibrate" at less than full employment levels of factor resources, or is subject to pressures that appear to propel it beyond those full employment levels. In such circumstances, governments may adopt policies designed to, respectively, supplement or reduce market de-

The introduction of government economic activity into the Walrasian theory of market behavior is not easy. The entire complex of effects of both the government on the economy and the economy on the government have to be accounted for. Old relations need modification; new variables, functions, and equations must be added. Some idea of what is involved has already been suggested in the very limited partial-equilibrium discussion of Section 6.3. General theories and models of governmental interaction with the economy, however, are far too intricate to develop here.[6] Present purposes are served by restricting attention to a few basic ideas as illustrated in two highly simplified examples, the first of which embeds, in a very elementary manner, the specific tax of Section 6.3 in a model of the entire perfectly competitive economy. Capital continues to be ignored (until the next section). These examples can also be seen as particularizations of the grand view described in the previous section.

Consider a two-final-good, one-factor economy in which the quantity supplied of the factor is fixed at the scalar value a. Let there be only one person and suppose he is the one who supplies all units of a. Denote the factor price by r. Assume this person's preferences are represented by the utility function[7]

$$u(x_1, x_2) = x_1 x_2, \tag{14.2-1}$$

defined for all $(x_1, x_2) \geqslant 0$, where x_1 indicates quantities of final good 1 and x_2 indicates quantities of final good 2. Note that u possesses the usual properties required of utility functions to enable their constrained maximization (Section 2.3).

Suppose that final good 1 is produced by a single firm according to the production function

$$x_1 = f^1(y_1) = y_1, \tag{14.2-2}$$

where y_1 varies over (scalar) quantities of the factor employed by the firm. Final good 2, on the other hand, is produced and supplied solely by the government. Like all firms, government production is subject to technological constraints (that is, a production function) limiting the output obtainable from

---

mands.
[6] See, for example, Diamond and Mirrlees [1].
[7] Strictly speaking, the parameter a ought to appear somewhere in the utility function (Section 8.3). But with δ an arbitrary function such that $\delta(a) > 0$, it is clear that $u(x_1, x_2) = \delta(a) x_1 x_2$, say, represents this person's preferences if and only if (14.2-1) does also. In this restricted sense, (14.2-1) implicitly takes a into account.

any given input. Let this be

$$x_2 = f^2(y_2) = y_2, \qquad (14.2\text{-}3)$$

where y_2 represents amounts of the factor used by the government.

Assume the government decides on its own how much of final good 2 to supply (subject, of course, to the constraint $y_2 \leqslant a$). The individual has no choice but to accept this amount. There are thus two markets in the economy, one for final good 1 and one for the factor. These markets are thought of as perfectly competitive in the usual sense that the participants in both markets take market prices to be parameters over which they have no control. The price of final good 1 is written p_1; there is no market price for final good 2.

In order to produce final good 2, the government must buy units of the factor at the factor's market price r. Suppose it raises revenue by imposing a specific tax on the production of final good 1. Let τ symbolize the dollar amount of the tax per unit of final good 1. If the government balances its budget, then

$$\tau x_1 = r y_2. \qquad (14.2\text{-}4)$$

Once the government decides on x_2, the value of y_2 is determined by (14.2-3). Hence, given r, the tax τ depends on how much the firm supplying final good 1 produces.

As in Section 6.3, the profit of the firm producing final good 1 is given by

$$\pi_1 = (p_1 - \tau)\, x_1 - r y_1, \qquad (14.2\text{-}5)$$

where fixed cost is taken to be zero. Assuming the firm hires input and produces output so as to maximize profit, and assuming that at the maximum $\pi_1 = 0$, equations (14.2-2) and (14.2-5) imply

$$p_1 - \tau = r. \qquad (14.2\text{-}6)$$

Note that although profit maximization is not required to obtain (14.2-6) (equation (14.2-6) follows directly from the requirement that $\pi_1 = 0$ at $x_1 > 0$ and equations (14.2-2) and (14.2-5)), it is certainly consistent with this equation.

Because the consumer is allowed to choose only how much of final good 1 he purchases, and because the first-order partial derivative of his utility function with respect to that good is everywhere positive, utility maximization subject to the budget constraint requires him to spend all of his income on final good 1. Supposing that the consumer has no income beyond what he earns from the sale of the factor, his demand function must be

$$x_1 = h^1(p_1, ra) = \frac{ra}{p_1}, \tag{14.2-7}$$

for all $(p, ra) > 0$. As indicated earlier, the consumer supplies a units of the factor for every value of $r > 0$.

Equilibrium in the market for final good 1 means that x_1 supplied by the firm must be identical to x_1 demanded by the individual. This has already been accounted for by using the same symbol x_1 to denote both quantities demanded and supplied in equations (14.2-2), (14.2-4), and (14.2-7). For the factor market to be in equilibrium, it is necessary that

$$y_1 + y_2 = a. \tag{14.2-8}$$

Adding the normalization

$$r = 1, \tag{14.2-9}$$

equations (14.2-2) – (14.2-4), (14.2-6) – (14.2-9) constitute a system of seven equations in the seven variables x_1, x_2, y_1, y_2, p_1, r, and τ. But Walras' law applies even here so that not all equations are independent. (Thus from equations (14.2-2) and (14.2-6),

$$(p_1 - \tau) x_1 = ry_1. \tag{14.2-10}$$

Summing equations (14.2-10) and (14.2-4) and substituting equation (14.2-7) into the result gives equation (14.2-8).) Hence x_2 must be set by the government before the equilibrium values of the remaining variables can be found.

Upon solving this system it is easily verified that,

$$x_1 = y_1 = \frac{1}{1+\tau},$$

$$x_2 = y_2 = \frac{a\tau}{1+\tau},$$

and

$$p_1 = 1 + \tau.$$

Therefore an increase in the tax shifts factor resources from the privately produced good to the government produced good and raises the market price of the privately produced good. The equilibrium value of τ, along with everything else, still depends on the value of x_2 chosen by the government.

Suppose now that the government were to determine x_2 so as to maximize social welfare subject to the transformation curve, where social welfare was to be based on the preferences of its constituents (Section 12.1). In the present context, a natural choice for the welfare function would be the individual's utility function of (14.2-1). Thus, noting that the equation of the economy's transformation curve is

$$x_1 + x_2 = a, \qquad\qquad (14.2\text{-}11)$$

maximization of (14.2-1) subject to (14.2-11) gives

$$x_1 = x_2. \qquad\qquad (14.2\text{-}12)$$

Adding (14.2-12) to (14.2-2) – (14.2-4) and (14.2-6) – (14.2-9) determines equilibrium values for all variables:

$$\tau = 1,$$

$$x_1 = x_2 = y_1 = y_2 = \frac{a}{2},$$

$$p_1 = 2.$$

These values are clearly Pareto optimal and correspond to the competitive solution that would arise if final good 2 were produced by a profit-maximizing, perfectly competitive firm.

An alternative way for the government to secure the revenue needed to produce final good 2 in the above example is with an income tax. Let τ, where $0 \leqslant \tau \leqslant 1$, be the tax rate. Then the tax paid by the individual is $\tau r a$, and his after tax income is $(1 - \tau)r a$. Now the second illustration of government participation in the economy provided here is obtained from the first by replacing the balanced budget, profit maximization, and demand relations — that is, equations (14.2-4), (14.2-6), and (14.2-7) — with, respectively,

$$\tau r a = r y_2, \qquad\qquad (14.2\text{-}13)$$

$$p_1 = r, \qquad\qquad (14.2\text{-}14)$$

and

$$x_1 = \frac{(1 - \tau)\, r a}{p_1}. \qquad\qquad (14.2\text{-}15)$$

Solving (14.2-2), (14.2-3), (14.2-8), (14.2-9), and (14.2-13) – (14.2-15) yields

$$x_1 = y_1 = a - \tau a,$$

$$x_2 = y_2 = \tau a,$$

and

$$p_1 = 1.$$

As before, increasing τ lowers x_1 and raises x_2. But this time p_1 remains constant. To determine x_2 by maximizing society's welfare function (14.2-1) subject to the transformation function (14.2-11), requires that (14.2-12) be added to the system. The equilibrium values are therefore

$$x_1 = x_2 = y_1 = y_2 = \frac{a}{2},$$

$$\tau = \frac{1}{2},$$

and

$$p_1 = 1.$$

Once again the result is Pareto optimal and corresponds to the competitive solution. Note that the only difference in equilibrium values between these two examples arises with regard to τ and p_1. In both cases the allocation of input and the production of outputs are identical.

The fact that the solution in each of these examples is Pareto optimal is due, in part, to the simplistic structures of the models. In general, Pareto optimality at equilibrium obtains in the presence of a sales tax only when

   i) the tax is expressed as a percentage of the selling price or total revenue (that is, the tax is an ad valorem tax) and

   ii) the same tax is imposed in every input and output market so that after-tax price ratios are unaffected.

Otherwise, the distortions that arise between the price the buyers of a good pay and the price the sellers of the same good receive are enough to ensure that, as described on p. 497 above, the first-order ratio conditions characterizing Pareto optimality no longer hold at equilibrium. In the first of the above examples, even though there is no market for output 2, the quantity of good 2 the government produces and supplies, along with that produced and supplied by the firm in the market for good 1 is determined by welfare maximization.

Hence the levy of a τ-dollar-per-unit-of-output sales tax (that is, a specific tax) in the latter market cannot interfere sufficiently to destroy Pareto optimality. Similarly, the introduction of an income tax into a previously tax-free economy creates a discrepancy between the prices firms pay for factors and the income consumers secure from the sale of the same factors, and generally results in non-Pareto-optimal equilibria. But with factor supplies fixed in the second of the above examples, these distortions are unable to modify the equilibrium factor quantities and therefore have no effect on the Pareto optimality of the equilibrium.

14.3   WITH CAPITAL

As indicated in Chapter 13, the introduction of capital into the Walrasian vision adds new dimensions and new avenues of thought to the Walrasian landscape. The particular dimensions introduced in the present work include the effect of time and durability on production, the influence of capital on firms' least-cost-input combinations and on their optimum outputs, and the determination of the economy's stock of money capital and the equilibrium rate of return paid on that money capital. (The last two determinations do not take place at the level of the individual firm and were not discussed in Chapter 13. They are, however, addressed below.) Although the presence of these new analytical dimensions does not alter the purposes of the Walrasian theory of market behavior as outlined in Section 14.1, it nevertheless broadens the relevance and applicability of the theory in accomplishing those purposes. Hence it serves to enhance the theory's appeal as well. Note that because present argument has been and continues to be focused mostly on the description of Walrasian models at equilibrium, and because equilibrium over time requires, by its very definition, that variable values do not change as time passes, surprise should not accompany the observation that, even though time figures into the calculation of firms' money capital requirements and the rates of return they are able to pay on the money capital invested in them, all significant reference to time disappears in the equations that characterize equilibrium. Discussion now centers on the formal description of a grand equilibrium, one that includes determination of the economy's stock of money capital along with the equilibrium rate of return paid on that money capital.

Place the grand view of Section 14.1 in a long-run setting and introduce capital as described in Section 13.3. The latter section sets out the theory of the perfectly competitive firm (perfect competition, that is, which allows positive money-capital entry cost but no other barriers to entry) in relation to the money capital required for production. Recall that money capital is needed because the production of output has to begin and both durable and nondurable inputs have to be purchased before all cost-covering revenues from the sale of the output produced are received. Although no distinction between durable and nondurable inputs is made in the firm's production function (except, of course, that the former is a stock and the latter a flow), this difference becomes important in the computation of its money capital requirement (Section 13.2).

The long-run equilibrium equations of the Walrasian model with capital included are exhibited momentarily.[8] Once again, the argument takes advantage of the convenience of assuming that factor supplies are fixed. Unlike in Chapter 8, however, here the intermediate goods comprising physical capital are not precluded: To obtain physical capital, firms are permitted to purchase the output of other firms. Although the transformation surface with respect to final outputs sold to consumers could still be defined, it is not necessary to do so. (Of course this transformation surface is implicit in subsequent development.) Assume that all durable inputs and only durable inputs are produced inputs, thus eliminating the distinction in Chapter 13 between durable inputs and physical capital. Generalization to the case in which factor supplies vary, and nondurable intermediate goods and durable nonproduced goods are present parallels that of Section 7.2 and is left to the reader. Discussion begins with a restatement in the full-economy context of the long-run equilibrium equations of the firm (from Section 13.3) and is preceded by a notational reminder.

Let there be I industries indexed by i, and suppose industry i is composed of L_i firms. Firms within industries are labeled as ℓ so that $\ell = 1, \ldots, L_i$, for each i. As before, inputs run from $j = 1, \ldots, J$. Retaining the convention introduced in Section 13.2, inputs are split into nondurables $j = 1, \ldots, \widehat{j}$ and durables $j = \widehat{j} + 1, \ldots, J$. To keep notation as simple as possible, let each durable input be produced by a separate industry and identify the durable-goods-producing industries by the signatures $i = \widehat{i} + 1, \ldots, I$, where $\widehat{i} = I - (J - \widehat{j})$. Thus industries producing nondurable commodities are indexed as $i = 1, \ldots, \widehat{i}$. The number of durable commodities is the same whether counted as $j = \widehat{j} + 1, \ldots, J$ or $i = \widehat{i} + 1, \ldots, I$.

Write $x_{i\ell}$ for quantities of current output of firm ℓ in industry i. Let $y_{i\ell j}$ vary over quantities of current nondurable input j employed by firm ℓ in industry i. Similarly, durable input quantities appear as $y'_{i\ell j}$. (Use of the prime on durable input variables is intended to enhance the visual distinction between them as stocks and nondurable input variables as flows. Of course input j is still durable as long as $j > \widehat{j}$, and nondurable otherwise. Thus different j's ap-

---

8   A similar model can be found in Pearce [4].

pear in the symbolisms $y_{i\ell j}$ and $y'_{i\ell j}$.) It has already been pointed out in Section 6.2 that descriptions of long-run equilibrium in a perfectly competitive industry usually result in an overdetermined system of equations unless the number of firms in that industry is taken to be variable. The latter is accomplished easily by making use of the assumption that all firms within industries are identical. When this is done, it is necessary to specify only a single production function in each industry, say,

$$x_{i1} = f^{i1}(y_{i11}, \ldots, y_{i1\widehat{j}}, y'_{i1\widehat{j}+1}, \ldots, y'_{i1J}), \quad i = 1, \ldots, I. \quad (14.3\text{-}1)$$

Equation (14.3-1) is intended to reflect the same production function as (13.3-1) in Section 13.3. Frequently, the y'_{i1j} are referred to as "circular" inputs. Determination of input demand and output supply functions for firm 1 yields input demand and output supply functions for all firms in industry i because they are the same. Firm $i1$ is taken to be the representative firm of industry i.

With c_{i1} representing average money capital needed by firm $i1$, the average (optimal) money capital requirement functions are

$$c_{i1} = \bar{\Lambda}^{i1}(p_i, r, y_{i1}), \quad i = 1, \ldots, I, \quad (14.3\text{-}2)$$

where p_i is the purchase price of output i, $r = (r_1, \ldots, r_J)$ is a vector of input prices, $y_{i1} = (y_{i11}, \ldots, y'_{i1J})$ is a vector of input quantities, and $\bar{\Lambda}^{i1}$ is defined by (13.3-13). As described at the end of Section 13.2, the prices of durable inputs are reckoned as prices per unit of durable-good life. Let ρ_{i1} denote the required rate-of-return variable and $\bar{\Phi}^{i1}$ indicate the actual rate-of-return function for firm $i1$. (The use of the bar in $\bar{\Phi}^{i1}$ is the same as that over Φ following equations (13.3-14).) Then according to (13.3-3) and (13.3-4) which, recall, contain the assumption that the required rate of return on $\bar{\Lambda}^{i1}$ equals the actual rate of return on $\bar{\Lambda}^{i1}$ for every (p_i, r, y_{i1}),

$$\rho_{i1}\bar{\Lambda}^{i1}(p_i, r, y_{i1}) = p_i f^{i1}(y_{i1}) - r \cdot y_{i1}, \quad i = 1, \ldots, I. \quad (14.3\text{-}3)$$

Note that $p_i = \alpha_j r_j$ for durable i and j such that industry i produces durable input j, where α_j is the life of durable j. Furthermore, (14.3-3) is essentially the identity (13.2-20) for the money capital requirement variable c_{i1}. From (13.3-14), selection of inputs and output to maximize $\bar{\Phi}^{i1}$ given input and output prices leads to

$$p_i f_j^{i1}(y_{i1}) = r_j + \rho_{i1}\bar{\Lambda}_j^{i1}(p_i, r, y_{i1}), \quad \begin{array}{l} j = 1, \ldots, J, \\ i = 1, \ldots, I. \end{array} \quad (14.3\text{-}4)$$

Sufficient conditions on the f^{i1} and the $\bar{\Lambda}^{i1}$ ensuring the validity of (14.3-4) are assumed. As pointed out in Section 13.3, each subset of J equations in (14.3-4), obtained with i fixed and $j = 1, \ldots, J$, can often be solved to give input demand y_{i1j} as a function of p_i and r. Output supply x_{i1} as a function of the same variables then is derived from (14.3-1). For present purposes, however, it is not necessary to secure these functions explicitly. Their implicit expression in (14.3-4) and (14.3-1) is enough.

Recall further that to secure the money capital necessary to support production, firms supply IOU's on the IOU market when they require more money capital than their existing debt. Summing over all firms and industries, the aggregate amount of IOU's supplied is

$$\sum_{i=1}^{I} L_i(c_{i1} - D_{i1}),$$

where D_{i1} is the outstanding debt previously accumulated by firm $i1$. The market price of IOU's is taken to be unity.[9] Suppose these IOU's are acquired only by consumers as a form of saving.

IOU's are purchased in an IOU market in which both previously issued IOU's are bought and sold, and in which new issues are marketed. It is trading in the IOU market that, by determining the relative price of IOU's, effectively establishes the required rate of return on new issues. When full, economy-wide equilibrium conditions prevail, that required rate of return will, as previously indicated, equal the actual rate of return that firms earn on the money capital invested in them. Clearly, then, the market for IOU's and the market for money capital are one and the same.

Consumers (indexed by $k = 1, \ldots, K$) purchase final goods and IOU's using the income they generate both from past lending (that is, previous acquisitions of IOU's) and from current sales of factors they possess. No income is received from the expenditures made by firms' to cover their fixed costs (the $b_{i\ell}$ of Section 7.2) because, in the long run, all fixed costs vanish. Let x_{ik} range over quantities of nondurable good i consumed by person k. Individuals are not permitted to buy durable goods for consumption. Suppose all nondurable inputs are supplied by consumers in fixed nonnegative quantities a_{jk}, where

---

[9]   This is, in effect, a normalization. In the IOU market, the market price of existing IOU's is the actual dollar return per IOU divided by the required rate of return. The issue price of new IOU's is the required dollar return per IOU (the dollar return contractually stated on the IOU) also divided by the required rate of return or, because IOU's are issued in \$1 denominations, unity. Because it has been assumed (Section 13.2) that the actual rate of return equals the requred rate of return, the market price of IOU's must be identical to the issue price of IOU's and hence must also be unity.

$j = 1, \ldots, \widehat{j}$, $k = 1, \ldots, K$, at least one $a_{jk} > 0$ for each k, and at least one $a_{jk} > 0$ for each j. Individuals do not supply durable inputs. Finally, designate θ_k to be the fraction of $\rho_{i1}c_{i1}$, going to person k as a consequence of her previous expenditure on the IOU's of firm $i1$. In the distribution of the firm's earnings envisaged here, person k, who supplies θ_k of the firm's money capital, receives θ_k of the actual dollar return $\bar{\bar{\Phi}}^{i1}(p_i, r, y_{i1}) \bar{\Lambda}^{i1}(p_i, r, y_{i1})$ paid by the firm for each (p_i, r, y_{i1}). (Recall equation (13.3-3) and the definition of $\bar{\bar{\Phi}}$ subsequent to equations (13.3-14).) But because $\rho_{i1} = \bar{\bar{\Phi}}^{i1}(p_i, r, y_{i1})$ according to (14.3-3), ρ_{i1} can be used in place of $\bar{\bar{\Phi}}^{i1}(p_i, r, y_{i1})$. From this, and in light of (14.3-2), the income accruing to person k out of the earnings of firm $i1$ reduces to $\theta_k\rho_{i1}c_{i1}$. It is convenient to suppose that each consumer receives the same fraction of the return paid out by each firm in the economy. The θ_k are such that

$$\sum_{k=1}^{K} \theta_k = 1, \tag{14.3-5}$$

and

$$0 \leqslant \theta_k \leqslant 1,$$

for every k. (In Section 7.2, these variables — written there as $\theta_{ki\ell}$ — were taken as fixed parameters. Here they are endogenously determined at long-run equilibrium.) Using these conventions and notation, consumers' incomes are defined by

$$m_k = \widetilde{r} \cdot a_k + \theta_k \sum_{i=1}^{I} L_i \rho_{i1} c_{i1}, \quad k = 1, \ldots, K, \tag{14.3-6}$$

where $a_k = (a_{1k}, \ldots, a_{\widehat{j}k})$, and $\widetilde{r} = (r_1, \ldots, r_{\widehat{j}})$.

Write s_k for quantities of IOU's purchased by consumer k out of current income. When old IOU's are sold, s_k is negative. Let S_k denote the present quantity of IOU's held by person k which have been accumulated as the result of saving decisions made by her in the past, that is,

$$S_k = \theta_k \sum_{i=1}^{I} L_i c_{i1}, \quad k = 1, \ldots, K, \tag{14.3-7}$$

Clearly, $S_k \geqslant 0$ for each k. Moreover, budget constraints now arise as in (8.3-3):

$$p \cdot x_k + s_k = m_k, \quad k = 1, \ldots, K, \tag{14.3-8}$$

where $x_k = (x_{1k}, \ldots, x_{\widehat{i}k})$ and $p = (p_1, \ldots, p_{\widehat{i}})$.

Because nondurable inputs supplied by consumers are taken to be fixed, individual utility functions can be written in the form of Section 8.3, namely,

$$\mu_k = u^k(x_k, s_k), \quad k = 1, \ldots, K.$$

Note that s_k represents current saving (or dissaving) for person k. Thus consumers are supposed to save just for the pleasure of saving. They ignore whatever risks, uncertainty, and changes in future consumption are involved.[10] Maximization of utility subject to the savings constraints $s_k \geqslant -S_k$ for all k (which prevent consumers from going into debt) and the budget constraints (14.3-8), begets the individual demand functions

$$x_{ik} = h^{ik}(p, m_k), \quad i = 1, \ldots, \widehat{i}, \tag{14.3-9}$$

$$s_k = h^{\widehat{i}+1k}(p, m_k), \tag{14.3-10}$$

for $k = 1, \ldots, K$. (In this notation, the superscript $\widehat{i} + 1$ does not refer to the $\widehat{i} + 1^{\text{st}}$ industry. Rather, it is used here to identify the demand function for savings of person k.) Adequate restrictions are imposed on utility functions to ensure that all demand functions are defined and possess appropriate properties. Both the restrictions and the properties must be modified slightly from those of Chapter 2 or 3 because individuals now are permitted to "purchase" positive, negative, and zero amounts of saving. (See Exercise 3.15.)

Long-run equilibrium in nondurable input markets requires that quantities demanded by firms equal those supplied by consumers, or

$$\sum_{i=1}^{I} L_i y_{i1j} = \sum_{k=1}^{K} a_{jk}, \quad j = 1, \ldots, \widehat{j}. \tag{14.3-11}$$

In nondurable output markets the roles of firms and consumers are reversed so that at equilibrium,

$$L_i x_{i1} = \sum_{k=1}^{K} x_{ik}, \quad i = 1, \ldots, \widehat{i}. \tag{14.3-12}$$

Firms are both buyers and sellers in durable goods markets; consumers are not participants. Thus one might think that, at long-run equilibrium in a durable

---

[10] Because the present model describes an equilibrium state in which both time and uncertainty have been exorcised, there are no interesting questions about saving and the rate of interest that cannot be answered by treating saving as an argument of utility functions and by interpreting the "rate of interest" as coincident with the rate of return on money capital.

good market, the quantity demanded by firms for use in production would equal the quantity supplied by the firms producing the durable good, where both quantities demanded and supplied are determined by the rate-of-return-maximization equation (14.3-4). But this cannot be so because, as described in Chapter 13, such a quantity demanded is actually a demand for an (economy-wide) aggregate stock of the durable good, whereas such a quantity supplied is merely a flow of the good currently produced. Hence it is necessary to look elsewhere for "market" equilibrium conditions for durable goods.

One way to obtain appropriate equilibrium conditions is to recognize that at long-run equilibrium, the capital stock of durables can be neither increasing nor decreasing. The only demand for durables is the demand to replace worn out durable units. The funds for replacement accumulate in the firm as described in equations (13.2-22) and (13.2-23). For each durable good, then, equilibrium requires that at every instant the funds for replacement generated at that instant exactly offset the revenue at the same instant that the production and sale of the durable goods creates.[11] Therefore the long-run equilibrium conditions in durable goods markets are

$$\sum_{n=1}^{I} L_n r_j y'_{n1j} = L_i p_i x_{i1}, \tag{14.3-13}$$

where $i = j = \widehat{i} + 1, \ldots, I$ or $i = j = \widehat{j} + 1, \ldots, J$, and the index i has been changed to n in the left-hand summation to avoid confusion. (A prime does not appear on x_{i1} because no notational distinction in terms of primes was made in equation (14.3-1) to distinguish the output of firms producing durables from that of firms producing nondurables. Unlike the case of inputs, in which durable inputs are stocks and nondurable inputs are flows, both durable and nondurable outputs are flows.) Observe that in any particular equation of (14.3-13), the i and j reflect the same durable good. Hence division of that equation by $\alpha_j r_j = p_i$ (where, recall, α_j is the life of j), gives

$$\frac{\sum_{n=1}^{I} L_n y'_{n1j}}{\alpha_j} = L_i x_{i1}.$$

---

[11]   Actually, since at equilibrium firms buy durable inputs only when old units wear out, there may be a gap between the moment the production of a unit of a durable good is completed and the moment it is sold. In such a case, additional money capital would be required by the durable-good-producing firm to sustain it over that interval. But in what follows, this complication is ignored.

This provides an alternative expression of the long-run equilibrium condition in market i (or j). It says that, at equilibrium, the total stock of the durable, as input j, per unit of life (that is, replacement demand) is identical to the current production of the durable as output i (that is, replacement supply).

At long-run equilibrium it is also necessary that the rate of return on money capital be the same for all firms in the economy. Otherwise, money capital would flow through the IOU market (via consumers) from firms with lower rates of return to those with higher rates of return (Section 13.3). Hence

$$\rho_{i1} = \rho_{11}, \quad i = 2, \ldots, I. \tag{14.3-14}$$

Evidently, then, the required rates of return on money capital borrowed by firms, which have already been taken to be identical to the respective actual rates of return on money capital paid by them, are all equal to the equilibrium or market-clearing rate of return on IOU's. In that sense, the market-clearing rate of return on IOU's defines the opportunity cost, with respect to alternative uses, of employing money capital. Moreover, long-run equilibrium in the IOU market dictates that

$$\sum_{k=1}^{K} s_k = \sum_{i=1}^{I} L_i(c_{i1} - D_{i1}). \tag{14.3-15}$$

There are, however, still further restrictions that must be met at long-run equilibrium. To begin with, as long as individuals purchase IOU's from firms out of current income, or sell IOU's back to them, money capital is moving between consumers and firms. Hence industries and outputs are expanding or, respectively, contracting. To preclude such activity the equilibrium condition

$$\sum_{k=1}^{K} s_k = 0 \tag{14.3-16}$$

has to be introduced.

In addition to the aggregate quantity of IOU's demanded, the debts D_{i1} of firms and the quantities S_k of IOU's previously accumulated by consumers need to be restrained if long-run equilibrium is to be fully described. Consider the S_k first: If S_k is growing for some k, that is if $s_k > 0$ for that k, then even with (14.3-16) in force, which would imply a transfer of IOU's among consumers, the income of k and hence her share of consumption is expanding over time. Because redistributions of goods and savings among consumers do not take place at long-run equilibrium, it is necessary to require that

$$s_k = 0, \quad k = 1, \ldots, K - 1. \tag{14.3-17}$$

Clearly, (14.3-17) in conjunction with (14.3-16) implies zero saving for person K as well: $s_K = 0$.

Similarly, with D_{i1} changing for some i, the output of industry i would modulate as time passes (Section 13.2).[12] Such variation of $L_i x_{i1}$ must also be excluded at long-run equilibrium. The appropriate way to do so here is to insert the equations

$$D_{i1} = c_{i1}, \quad i = 1, \ldots, I - 1. \tag{14.3-18}$$

Once again, combining (14.3-16), (14.3-15), and (14.3-18) yields $D_{I1} = c_{I1}$, so that the same equilibrium conditions expressed in (14.3-18) also apply to industry I.

The last equation to be added is the zero-residual-profit condition (13.2-14) involving the rate of return variable ρ_{11}. (Although there is one such equation for each firm, in light of equilibrium conditions (14.3-14), it is necessary to include the identity for only a single firm.) To express (13.2-14) in the appropriate context, first substitute in (13.2-12), then (13.2-1), and finally (13.2-19). Adding subscripts where appropriate, this gives

$$p_1 x_{11} = \sum_{j=1}^{\widehat{j}} r_j y_{11j} e^{\rho_{11} \overline{\tau}_j} + \sum_{j=\widehat{j}+1}^{J} \alpha_j r_j y_{11j}' \frac{\rho_{11} e^{\rho_{11} \overline{\tau}_j}}{1 - e^{-\rho_{11} \alpha_j}}, \tag{14.3-19}$$

where the maturity times $\overline{\tau}_j$ (for $j = 1, \ldots, J$) and the durable input lives α_j (for $j = \widehat{j} + 1, \ldots, J$) are fixed parameters.

The model describing long-run, Walrasian (competitive) equilibrium with capital included therefore consists of equations (14.3-1) − (14.3-7) and (14.3-9) − (14.3-19). It is summarized in Table 14.1. A brief glance at the table indicates that the number of equations exceeds the number of variables by one. But Walras' law applies so that not all equations can be independent.[13] Hence the number of variables and independent equations are the same. The system is determinate. Assuming unique solvability given parameters $\overline{\tau}_1, \ldots, \overline{\tau}_J$,

---

[12]   Here (14.3-16) implies that debt is being transfered among firms through sales of IOU's to, and repurchases of IOU's from consumers..

[13]   To prove Walras' law, sum budget constraints (14.3-8) (which are implicit in demand functions (14.3-9) and (14.3-10)) over k, substitute in (14.3-6) and then (14.3-2) and (14.3-3), and use (14.3-5) together with equilibrium conditions (14.3-11) − (14.3-13). This will result in equation (14.3-16).

Table 14.1 Equations and variables in the model

Equations			Variables		
Reference number in text	Description	Number of this type	Number of this type	Description	Symbolic representation
(14.3-1)	production functions	I	I	output quantities	x_{i1}
(14.3-2)	money capital requirement functions	I	I	money capital requirements	c_{i1}
(14.3-3)	money capital requirement identities	I	I	numbers of firms in industries	L_i
(14.3-4)	rate-of-return maximization	IJ	IJ	input quantities	y_{i1j}, y'_{i1j}
(14.3-5)	full distribution of the returns to money capital invested	1			
(14.3-6)	definition of consumer incomes	K	K	consumer incomes	m_i
(14.3-7)	definition of past savings	K	K	previously accumulated IOUs held by consumers	S_k
(14.3-9) (14.3-10)	consumer demand functions	$(\hat{i}+1)K$	$(\hat{i}+1)K$	consumer demand quantities	x_{ik}, s_{ik}
(14.3-11)	nondurable input markets equilibrium	j	j	nondurable input prices	r_j

Table 14.1 (continued) Equations and variables in the model

Equations			Variables		
Reference number in text	Description	Number of this type	Number of this type	Description	Symbolic representation
(14.3-12)	nondurable output markets equilibrium	$\hat{i}$	$\hat{i}$	nondurable output prices	p_i
(14.3-13)	durable good markets equilibrium	$J - \hat{j} = I - \hat{i}$	$J - \hat{j} = I - \hat{i}$	durable good prices	$\alpha_j r_j = p_i$
(14.3-14)	rate-of-return equilibrium	$I - 1$	I	firm rates of return	ρ_{i1}
(14.3-15)	IOU market equilibrium	1			
(14.3-16)	zero aggregate savings equilibrium	1			
(14.3-17)	no change in individual stocks of IOUs	$K - 1$	K	fractions of returns on money capital going to consumers	θ_k
(14.3-18)	no change in stocks of firm debt	$I - 1$	I	firm debt previously accumulated	D_{i1}
(14.3-19)	zero residual profit	1			

$\alpha_{\hat{j}+1}, \ldots, \alpha_J$, and fixed-factor supplies $a_{11}, \ldots, a_{JK}$, Walrasian equilibrium exists and is unique.[14] It is also Pareto optimal in a sense appropriately modified to suit present circumstances. Note that a normalization has already been incorporated in the model by setting the price of IOU's at unity.

Notice that summing (14.3-7) over k yields, in view of (14.3-5),

$$\sum_{k=1}^{K} S_k = \sum_{i=1}^{I} L_i c_{i1}, \qquad (14.3\text{-}20)$$

It follows, according to Section 13.2, that aggregate past saving is the sum of aggregate working capital (or aggregate past investment in work in progress) plus aggregate fixed capital (or aggregate past investment in durable inputs). Furthermore, substitution in (14.3-20) of (14.3-18) and the implied condition $D_{I1} = c_{I1}$ gives

$$\sum_{k=1}^{K} S_k = \sum_{i=1}^{I} L_i D_{i1}.$$

Of course, the left-hand sum in the above expression is the total of all outstanding IOU's previously purchased by consumers, whereas the right-hand sum is the total of all outstanding firm debt.

Combining equations (14.3-14) and (14.3-6) – (14.3-8), summing over k, and invoking (14.3-16),

$$\sum_{k=1}^{K} p \cdot x_k = \sum_{k=1}^{K} \widetilde{r} \cdot a_k + \rho_{11} \sum_{k=1}^{K} S_k. \qquad (14.3\text{-}21)$$

Thus the value of output sold to consumers is identical to aggregate income received from the sale of factors and the returns on previously purchased IOU's. Relation (14.3-21) also reflects the fact that no "new" saving takes place by individuals at long-run equilibrium. Now define aggregate (current) *investment expenditure* as the sum of the left-hand side of (14.3-13):

$$\sum_{i=1}^{I} \sum_{j=\hat{j}+1}^{J} L_i r_j y'_{i1j}, \qquad (14.3\text{-}22)$$

where the index n in (14.3-13) has been changed back to i. Then investment evidently occurs at long-run equilibrium, but only that which is necessary to re-

---

[14]   Conditions ensuring existence and uniqueness of equilibrium could be expressed in terms of the functions of the model as in Chapters 8 and 9.

place worn out durable inputs.[15] "New" investment is not present. As indicated by equation (13.2-22), replacement investment expenditure at equilibrium is financed within the firm by using the fund for durable good replacement which will have accumulated from the excess of revenue over nondurable-input-plus-debt cost. No further transactions in the IOU market are required (equation (13.2-23)). The retention of this excess by firms (as opposed to returning it to consumers) can be thought of as a second form of saving. Therefore, adding (14.3-22) as investment expenditure to the left-hand side of (14.3-21), and (14.3-22) as retained earnings to the right-hand side of (14.3-21), the national income accounting assertion that consumption plus "gross" investment equals national income is obtained. In the national income accounting parlance, there is neither "net" saving nor "net" investment at long-run equilibrium. Gross saving and investment, however, are positive (and equal) and exist only to replace worn out durables. Such an equilibrium, which in the absence of parameter or function modification reproduces itself over time, is what the classical economists would have called the "stationary state."[16]

Observe that to set out the course of this Walrasian system over time, there are two kinds of dynamics to consider. On one hand, price dynamics operate in markets to determine equilibrium prices according to adjustment rules such as those described in Sections 9.3, 10.2, and 10.3. On the other hand, non-market equilibrium conditions, such as, for example, equation (14.3-16), are supported by their own separate dynamics. Thus rules of adjustment that may equalize all rates of return ρ_{i1}, that may equate the demand for and supply of IOU's, that may drive aggregate (net) saving out of current income to zero, and that may lead to nonchanging stocks of firm debt and individual IOU's, must also be taken into account. Specification of the differential equations that would describe these dynamic adjustments is not pursued here.[17] Note, however, that contingent on parameter values and functional particularizations,

---

[15]   Implicit in the equations $\alpha_j r_j = p_i$, where i and j represent the same durable good, is the assumption that the replacement prices of durable inputs always equal their original purchase prices. If price differences were permitted between the acquisition and replacement dates of durable inputs (as a result, for example, of a general price inflation), then the funds accumulating in firms to replace worn out durable inputs may not be sufficient to cover actual replacement costs, and hence the physical capital in the economy might not be able to be maintained intact. In the (timeless) equilibrium described above, however, all such possibilities are assumed away.

[16]   See, for example, Mill [3, pp. 752-757].

[17]   In this regard, it should be borne in mind that, for example, any change in the money capital market's required rate of return (implying alteration in the relative market value of existing IOU's) would generate modifications in firms' money capital needs. The latter, in turn, would force adjustments in firms' decisions regarding the employment of factors and the production of output. Such interactions between the money capital and goods markets presumably would be accounted for in the differential equations that describe the dynamics of those markets. Of

such a system could generate stable, cyclical, or explosive behavior relative to equilibrium — although, for explanatory purposes, global stability is usually required.

It is clear that the system with capital described above provides a model of the perfectly competitive economy where the notion of perfect competition is generalized to permit positive money-capital entry cost. This model reflects the Walrasian single-time-frame decision-making perspective, and is consistent with the convention of identifying equilibria in the model with observations of economic reality. It is also consistent with other interpretations as well. Moreover, the model without capital but with fixed-factor supplies described in Section 14.1 can be regarded as a special case. And the discussion in that section of the purposes, power, limitations, and appeal of the Walrasian theory of market behavior applies here as well.

REFERENCES

1. Diamond, P. A. and J. A. Mirrlees, "Optimal Taxation and Public Production: I and II, *American Economic Review* 61(1971), pp. 8-27, 261-278.
2. McCloskey, D. N., "The Rhetoric of Economics," *Journal of Economic Literature* 21 (1983), pp. 481-517.
3. Mill, J. S., *Principles of Political Economy with Some of Their Applications to Social Philosophy*, V. W. Bladen and J. M. Robson, eds. (Toronto: University of Toronto Press, 1965).
4. Pearce, I. F., "A Theory of Money Capital, General Equilibrium and Income Distribution," *The Measurement of Capital: Theory and Practice*, K. D. Patterson and D. Schott, eds. (London: Macmillan, 1979), pp. 25-64.

course, any additional non-market interactions, where relevant, would also have to be incorporated in the specification of these and other differential equations.

Chapter 15

Some Alternative Assumptions and Methods of Analysis

The Walrasian theory of market behavior is a truly remarkable intellectual achievement. Its principal conclusion — that an economy motivated only by self-interest, in which all relevant information is transmitted by price signals, is capable in principle of bringing about a coherent allocation of economic resources superior to many alternative allocations — is both surprising and significant. This nonobvious result is powerful enough to have gained acceptance among large numbers of people, many of whom are not serious students of economics, and to have, as a result, deeply influenced Western thought and culture. The Walrasian theory itself is internally consistent and cohesive, extensive in coverage, sophisticated in argument, and its implications are, by and large, well worked out. It is the basis for the dominant paradigm in which today's economists think and communicate about the microeconomy as a whole. Surely it must stand as one of the important and elegant creations of the human mind.

But, like most theories (and as pointed out at the end of Section 14.1), the Walrasian theory of market behavior has its weaknesses.[1] The purpose of

---

[1]   A discussion of some of the strengths and weaknesses of microeconomic theory in general may be found in Katzner [12]

this concluding chapter is to outline briefly several charges or complaints that have been brought against it, and some of the theoretical modifications they have inspired. Because over the decades most flaws in internal reasoning are likely to have been eliminated, the possibility of logical inconsistency within the theory itself, given its assumption content, is not considered. Instead, subsequent discussion focuses on two broad categories of complaints, namely, those directed against the methods of analysis employed and those attacking the specific assumptions invoked. No effort to be comprehensive is made; only a few examples of each are provided.

Before proceeding, however, it is worth noting that the Walrasian theory of market behavior has applicability beyond that to the usual market economy. Lange [16] has shown that it can also be used as a guide by the planners or Central Planning Board of a socialist economy. His argument (ignoring capital) runs as follows:[2]

Consider, for example, a world in which consumers are free to choose quantities of commodities they wish to buy and labor time they wish to sell. Let there be perfectly competitive markets for all consumer goods and labor, but no markets at all for factors other than labor. Nonlabor factors are owned and supplied by the state. Prices of consumer goods and labor are determined by the interaction of demand and supply as in a market economy; those for nonlabor factors exist only in the form of accounting prices at levels set by the Central Planning Board. To avoid unnecessary complications, assume that there are no intermediate goods and that factor supplies are fixed.

Let utility and production functions have properties as described in earlier chapters and assume all firms within industries are identical. Suppose consumer behavior is determined by the maximization of utility subject to budget constraints. Firm behavior results from two rules imposed by the Central Planning Board. These are to produce the output that equates marginal cost to price and to employ quantities of inputs that minimize the cost of producing that output. The Central Planning Board expands the number of firms in industries whose firms are producing at output levels larger than those associated with minimum long-run average cost (cost curves are assumed to be Viner curves as in Figure 4.12) and reduces the number of firms in industries whose firms are producing at output levels below those corresponding to minimum long-run average cost. Firms sell their output to, and buy their labor from, consumers in markets. Nonlabor factors are obtained at the accounting prices from the state in amounts consistent with the above rules. All revenues from the sale of nonlabor factors accrue to the Central Planning Board. These are then returned to consumers according to

---

2   Lange [16, pp. 72-83].

certain predetermined guidelines for distribution.

As indicated above, the prices of consumer goods and labor are determined in their respective markets. All accounting prices of nonlabor factors are set by the Central Planning Board. When shortages of nonlabor factors occur, the Central Planning Board raises the accounting prices of them. Similarly their prices are lowered in the face of surpluses. No price changes are required when there are neither shortages nor surpluses. In that case, if there were markets for these factors, they would be in equilibrium. Thus the Central Planning Board is able to achieve a long-run "competitive equilibrium" in this socialist economy with a distribution of income generated by the guidelines for the distribution of nonlabor-factor revenue. The equilibrium is efficient in the sense of Pareto optimality and maximizes the welfare function (12.3-26) of Theorem 12.3-25. In fact, it is the same equilibrium that would arise if the economy were perfectly competitive throughout and initial endowments were consistent with the determination of the appropriate distribution of income.

15.1   METHODS OF ANALYSIS

Two weaknesses of the analytical methods described in Chapter 1 and employed by the Walrasian theory of market behavior are considered here. One is concerned with the identification of concepts and the other with the role of time and the often related notion of uncertainty. Each is discussed in turn.

In certain cases, the human mind is perfectly capable of sharply delineating the boundaries of an idea. The result is what Georgescu-Roegen has called an *arithmomorphic* concept.[3] Arithmomorphic concepts have the property that they can be clearly distinguished and separated from all other arithmomorphic concepts. They are distinctly discrete; there is no overlap between them and their opposites. The velocity of a moving object is an arithmomorphic concept, as is the temperature of a pot of water and the length of a train.

On the other hand, there are concepts whose boundaries human powers seem unable to define clearly and precisely. Exact characterizations are either arbitrary in that they do not conform to standard notions, or, at least in analytical contexts, extraordinarily difficult to employ. Where, for example, does one quality of experience leave off and another begin? Democracy and non-democracy are two different ideas, each with a variety of shades of meaning and, what is more important, with certain shades of democracy overlapping

---

[3]   Georgescu-Roegen [3, pp. 43-45].

certain shades of nondemocracy. Concepts such as these can be referred to as *dialectical*.[4] Dialectical notions are distinct, though not, as their arithmomorphic counterparts, discretely so. Each is surrounded by its own penumbra of meanings. Any dialectical concept is distinguishable from all others (including its opposite), because no two penumbras can be identical. Nevertheless (and this is impossible with arithmomorphic concepts), a country can be both a democracy and a nondemocracy at the same time.

Now the structure of analysis based on arithmomorphic concepts is well known. Discretely distinct (often "operational" or quantifiable) notions are defined, assumptions pertaining to them made, and propositions derived by appeal to the rules of Aristotelian logic. Reasoning is checked and rechecked, and hypotheses and propositions frequently are subjected to empirical tests. But Aristotelian logic, and hence the entire procedure, cannot be applied to dialectical concepts because the fundamental requirement that a thing cannot be both A and not A simultaneously and in the same respect may be violated.[5] It is still possible, however, to make assumptions about, and to reason with, dialectical ideas, as the following passage due to Bertrand Russell shows:[6]

> Not only are we aware of particular yellows, but if we have seen a sufficient number of yellows and have sufficient intelligence, we are aware of the universal yellow; this universal is the subject in such judgements as "yellow differs from blue" or "yellow resembles blue less than green does." And the universal yellow is the predicate in such judgments as "this is yellow"....

Dialectical reasoning can be checked in two ways.[7] The first is by use of the ancient Socratic method: systematic questioning of all aspects of the argument. The second is by working through arithmomorphic similes. For dialectical reasoning can often be likened to various arithmomorphic arguments, although none of these test arguments is ever capable of replacing the original in its entirety. Clearly, error uncovered by either the Socratic method or the employment of Aristotelian logic in an arithmomorphic simile casts doubt on the original dialectical reasoning. But although it may provide a certain comfort and satisfaction, a lack of detection of error does not imply correctness.

The Walrasian vision of market behavior fits into this scheme as an arith-

---

4   *Ibid.*, pp. 45-47.
5   *Ibid.*, p. 46.
6   Russell [24, p. 212].
7   Georgescu-Roegen [3, p. 337].

momorphic simile of an underlying dialectical reality.[8] Certainly all of the concepts and variables employed in the Walrasian description are discrete. None overlaps its opposite. But the ideas from which many of them derive are clearly dialectical. In actuality there is not just one unique price, but an entire penumbra of prices at which any commodity is sold. Moreover, because of the great variety of forms in which a given commodity can be produced, the boundaries of the ending of one commodity and the beginning of another may be difficult to specify. Thus "commodity" and "price" are dialectical concepts and the problem of determining in the real world what "goods" are sold in what "markets" and at what "prices" is not easily resolved. The Walrasian vision abstracts from these notions to obtain a collection of discrete markets and, for each market, a discrete commodity with a unique price. It therefore stands as an arithmomorphic simile.

Other examples of such abstractions appearing in the Walrasian theory of market behavior are the preferences of any individual, the technology underlying the production function of any firm, the form of competition in any market, and the ideas of change and time. Consider, for a moment, the last. As far as human capacity to sense Nature is concerned, there is no such thing as an "instant of time." Time is, rather, a series of imprecise and overlapping durations in which the future becomes the present and then slips into the past.[9] It is obviously a dialectical notion. The idea of distinct instants of time (or discretely distinct time periods) all lined up one after the other is an arithmomorphic abstraction — regardless of whether an instant is defined to be an arbitrarily small interval or the limit of a sequence of intervals each contained in the one before it. Either conception permits identification of the linear continuum as the standard reference for keeping track of the movement of time. The use of simultaneous differential equations to describe change (Chapters 9 and 10) depends on it. Of course, such equations may themselves be abstractions comprising part or all of an arithmomorphic simile.

Because the Walrasian theory of market behavior is an arithmomorphic simile, it is somewhat removed from real economic life.[10] As argued above, it is properly seen as a part of a more general dialectical vision of economic

---

[8]   *Ibid.*, p. 332. See also Katzner [9].
[9]   *Ibid.*, pp. 69-72.
[10]   *Ibid.*, p. 79. Although not specified with as much precision, Marshall arrived at a similar conclusion: "The theory of stable equilibrium ... helps indeed to give definiteness to our ideas; and in its elementary stages it does not diverge from the actual facts of life, so far as to prevent its giving a fairly trustworthy picture of the chief methods of action of the strongest and most persistent group of economic forces. But when pushed to its more remote and intricate logical consequences, it slips away from the conditions of real life." [18, p. 461].

actuality. Unfortunately, economists have done little to clarify this dialectical vision. But criticism of the Walrasian theory because it deals with discrete instead of overlapping notions misses the mark. Being an arithmomorphic simile it necessarily is concerned with arithmomorphic entities. The more appropriate complaint is that the dialectical base from which it comes has been ignored. And to account for the latter would require further analysis based on appropriate additions to the methodological approach employed.

The second issue concerning analytical methods to be aired here rests, in part, on a distinction between two interpretations of arithmomorphic time. In the Walrasian theory, change in time occurs according to certain prescribed rules (Chapters 9 and 10). The rules themselves remain fixed as time passes. The only role that time plays is to order events by indicating those events that come before or after other events. Thus given appropriate functions, parameter values, and an initial vector of variable values, the system generates specific behavior for all time starting at the initial vector. When or how often the system is started does not matter. In every case it reproduces the same time-path over again as long as the given functions, parameters, and initial values are unaltered. The internal clock time with respect to which such a system, itself independent of time, determines behavior is sometimes called *logical* time.

It has been argued, however, that time in economics is *historical*, not logical.[11] That is, in addition to ordering events, time distinguishes between past, present, and possible future events. And each of these categories of events has its own special qualities that can only be addressed by altering the method of analysis employed. The latter qualities imply, in part, that every instant of time is unique and beyond recapture. The behavior occurring at that instant can neither be known in advance nor recreated in quite the same way. For example, consumers and firms arrive at moments of decisions with their own peculiar pasts and find themselves in an environment that cannot arise again. Because their personal histories as well as the decision-making environments are different at all other instants, the decision problems they face at these points are never repeated identically. Thus, in general, to account for historical time, the structure of the system generating behavior at each moment of time has to itself depend on time.[12] In particular, objective functions such as utility and profit functions, along with the behavioral relations derived from them, are not time-invariant. Each vector of variable values along a time-path, then, must be

---

[11]   See, for example, Vickers [28, pp. 24-28], Bausor [1], [2], and Katzner [11, Ch. 1].

[12]   However, it should be noted as a special case that even if the system's structure were unchanging over time, meaning would still attach to the examination of the system's behavior across historical time if the potential impact of unforeseen changes in variable and parameter values and the external environment were recognized.

determined by a different system relevant for that moment alone.

The Walrasian theory of market behavior may be thought to approximate events across historical time, but only in a highly imperfect way. When identifying equilibria (stationary time-paths) with observations in the real world, it is clear that if sightings vary from one instance to the next, then something must have changed. The only possible candidates in a Walrasian model for such change are the given functions and parameter values, which generally modify across historical time. However, the nature of these changes and the way they are brought about through time have not yet been spelled out by economists very systematically in the single decision-making time-frame, Walrasian context. Still, the comparative-statics assertions of previous chapters (which involve, recall, the comparisons of alternative equilibrium values) are valid as long as the assumptions they entail remain intact. Thus in the appropriate partial-equilibrium setting, if the supply curve of a particular market were to stay put from one set of observations to the next, then it would be possible to discern a movement along this curve if market price and quantity had, say, gone up. One could then state that the rise in price was due to an increased demand. In many instances, however, neither curve remains fixed and no such conclusion can be drawn. On the other hand, if observations are permitted to correspond to points in the model off the equilibrium path, and hence an effort is made to explain historical data directly with nonstationary dynamic time-paths generated by the model in logical time, the problem of the influence of time on the model itself remains.

Two additional aspects of the presence of historical time have far-reaching implications. First, consumer and firm decisions made at one moment of time come to fruition and have their full impact at future dates. Second, in so far as human affairs are concerned, the future (including the decision outcome and its effects) is both unknown and unknowable. It is not possible for an individual to comprehend today what he and the world will be like tomorrow.[13] Such ignorance of the future leads to uncertainty in the making of decisions. For example, a consumer may know his preferences at the time he purchases a basket of goods. But if he actually intends to consume those goods later, he cannot know that his preferences might not modify by then. Similarly, consumers and firms cannot be certain about future prices or the future environment (*e.g.*, hot or cold, friendly or hostile) in which they are to use their purchases or, respectively, sell their products. The standard approach to including these kinds of uncertainties (as well as others that have little relation to historical time) in the Walrasian theory is to define (perhaps subjective) probability distributions for

---

[13] Of course, he can always make intelligent guesses. But knowledge itself is unavailable.

the relevant uncertain variables and to use such things as "expected utilities," "expected profits," and "expected prices" in place of the utilities, profits, and prices employed in the context of certainty. As a rule, the model that emerges is quite parallel to that of Section 7.2. Moreover, the introduction of probabilistic uncertainty in this manner has permitted the analysis, in a Walrasian framework, of a whole host of questions that cannot be raised in an environment of certainty. These include issues relating to portfolio selection and asset pricing, differences in information available to different consumers and firms, contracting for present and future delivery of goods, and the incompleteness of markets. Such matters, however, are beyond the scope of present discussion.[14]

Nevertheless, there is still a serious problem with the use of probabilities in these conventional analyses. Difficulty arises because the fact of historical time renders probabilities, like all human-related elements pertaining to the future, unknowable. There simply is not enough information about possible future occurrences available in the present to formulate probabilities of subsequent events — even subjectively.[15] From this perspective, then, and based on what has been said previously, it would seem that to handle historical time, ignorance of the future, and the accompanying (nonprobabilistic) uncertainty properly, would necessitate considerable modification in the Walrasian system along with the methods of analysis it utilizes. One approach that abandons large parts of that system and replaces them with alternative structures, and that substitutes a notion called "potential surprise" for probability,[16] has been provided by Katzner [11].

The above considerations have some bearing on the applicability of the Walrasian theory of market behavior to problems of prediction. A typical prediction procedure might be as follows: Let observations of actuality be interpreted as globally stable equilibria in a Walrasian model with an unchanging functional structure, and suppose the position of the real world at some future instant, τ^*, is to be predicted. Based on past data, all functions are estimated or otherwise determined. Guesses or estimates of all parameters at τ^* also are made. Then, assuming that the model itself, the functional estimates, and the future values of the parameters are "correct," the equilibrium values at τ^* can be computed. These serve as predictions of what is expected to occur in reality at τ^*.

Prediction of this sort can produce (and has produced) reasonable results during periods of time in which the real world is not changing very rapidly

---

14 Examinations of many of them may be found in Mas-Collel, Whinston, and Green [19].
15 See, for example, Shackle [26, Ch. 7] and Katzner [11, Sect. 2.4].
16 Potential surprise carries no knowledge-of-the-future requirement as does probability.

or significantly. If the model is "accurate," then differences between the past and the near future often are not large enough to interrupt significantly the fulfillment of such predictions. Use of today's model and functions tomorrow is a tolerable approximation of actuality even as tomorrow unfolds in historical time. But when change occurs too quickly or to too large an extent, the entire procedure breaks down. Large change can render the model inappropriate. Quick change may mean that estimated functions cannot be re-estimated fast enough to have much relevance for future instants. Moreover, to predict successfully in a modulating world, current models may have to account for the novelty or newness generated by current change.[17] Now there are novelties that emerge as fresh variations within existing forms, and some of them are discoverable by deductions from available information. These, of course, are predictable as described above. But other novelties remaining within existing forms cannot be known until they are seen. There are no reasonable grounds emerging from past experience on which any advance statement regarding either what they might be or the timing of their possible future appearance can be made. A third possibility is that new and different forms may emerge from an old and repeatedly observed base. Thus the kind of society a given group of people will mold cannot be determined in advance, even though considerable information of what other groups have done is available. Clearly prediction, as set out here, of the second and third types of newness is hopeless. To the extent that such newness arises, current models must be modified appropriately after the fact if they are to be relevant for future instants. And the more rapidly change takes place, the more likely it is that these elements will interfere with subsequent prediction. Thus the facts of historical time and the uncertainty it generates become more important as the speed and extent of change rises and the ability to predict erodes.

15.2   ASSUMPTIONS

There are many ways to attack the specific assumptions of the Walrasian theory of market behavior.[18] Some complaints are quite inconsequential. For example, unease with the assumption of identical firms in each industry is easily relieved by doing away with it. In most cases very little is changed except for the necessary and obvious complications that have to be added to the relevant equations (recall, for example, the introduction to Chapter 8 and Exercise 8.1). Similarly, differentiability of utility functions can be discarded, as intimated in

---

17   Georgescu-Roegen [3, pp. 116, 117].
18   One fairly long list is given by Kornai [15, p. 29].

Section 3.2. At the opposite extreme, the use of preferences and technology as a basis for maximization by consumers and firms, or even the postulate that some form of maximization guides human behavior, might be rejected. These tenets are so fundamental to the Walrasian theory that objections to them are not easily overcome by introducing minor theoretical modifications. In between lie a variety of charges that have inspired proposals for relatively simple revision so as to make the theory more acceptable and appealing. The following discussion presents a sampling of suggested alterations both in between and at the latter extreme.

Consider first the fact that there is another independent theory of demand, having nothing to do with the maximization of utility, which seeks to explain consumer behavior.[19] This theory, located in the marketing literature, is interdisciplinary in nature and focuses on personalities, attitudes, cultural influences, social class, and so on. Although the link between an individual's personality and the number and kinds of commodities he buys has not yet been firmly established, exploration of this area continues. Attitudes, on the other hand, do seem to influence behavior. The more favorable an attitude toward any given product brand, the more likely it appears that the brand will be purchased. Attitudes, in turn, may depend on such things as the way information is presented to and processed by the individual; on his beliefs, emotions, and readiness to react toward the given objects or ideas; on his underlying needs; and on the extent to which the given objects or ideas are central in relation to his values. Cultural and social influences also matter. Patterns of consumption vary across groups defined by ethnic origin, age, sex, education and income level, geographic location and climate, marital status, family size, and social class membership.

Unlike the Walrasian approach to demand of Chapters 2 and 3, marketing theory often is concerned more with an individual's or group's selection of brands of goods rather than with the choice of quantities of goods independently of brand. Indeed, one of its main purposes is to provide a basis for determining how firms might successfully advertise and sell their products. Its presence, however, still raises some interesting questions. Can the theory of utility maximization be reformulated to accommodate choices among brands? What is the relationship between personality, attitudes, and cultural and social factors on one hand, and the individual's utility and demand functions on the other? How does advertising affect the latter through the former? There is clearly a great wealth of ideas and information in marketing theory that could potentially enrich Walrasian theory if the two could be brought together in the

---

[19]   The material of this paragraph is taken from Robertson [23]. See also Katzner [10].

right way.

The foregoing suggests that the Walrasian theory of market behavior might be accused of taking too constricted a view. But the narrowness extends further still. It is manifest in the avoidance of any effort to include such elements as, say, the effects on production of interpersonal relations among workers within the firm, or the impact of political, social, and cultural pressures in the determination (along with demand and supply) of certain market prices and (or) quantities. Perhaps part of the reason these components have been ignored in the past is that many of the variables representing them appear to be incapable of numerical calibration. Economists may therefore have felt that their inclusion could have led to indeterminacy, fuzziness, and error. But it has recently been demonstrated[20] that formal, mathematical models analogous to those of the Walrasian theory can be constructed even in the absence of measurement. Thus exactness and quantification are not synonymous, and a lack of numerical scales is no barrier to the conduct of scientific inquiry. These methods, moreover, are relevant for the understanding of market phenomena.

It ought to be possible, then, to go some distance in accommodating those critics who, for example, believe that power and conflict have a role to play in determining certain market prices.[21] Models explaining, say, how public utility rates are set by examining the internal political process in the regulatory agencies responsible for them could focus on the personalities involved and the political, social, and cultural pressures under which they operate, as well as on the relevant economic factors. These might be integrated with, or simply replace, the traditional market analysis where relevant. A similar approach could be taken for labor markets whose price is determined as the outcome of collective bargaining between union and management. In either case the Marxian notion of class struggle might also prove useful.

To illustrate analysis with nonquantifiable variables and the theoretical consequences it may entail, consider an application to the theory of the firm.[22] Think of the firm as having an internal, pyramidal job structure such that the typical worker has a supervisor immediately above her and one or more subordinates below. Each worker is capable of performing a variety of "acts" in her job, and the collection of all acts performed — one for each worker — in conjunction with the amount of time worked determines the firm's output. An act, then, is a complete description for the carrying out of the worker's job. It is not necessarily quantifiable. In choosing an act to pursue in her job, the

---

[20]   Katzner [8], [13].
[21]   For example, Hollis and Nell [5, p. 3].
[22]   Katzner [9] and Gintis and Katzner [4].

worker is constrained according to rules issued by those above her, and she, in turn, issues rules that constrain those, if any, below. Although the firm would prefer to see workers select acts that enhance profitability, actual choices are assumed to be made by the maximization of individual utility subject to these constraints, where utility is taken to depend not only on acts and constraining rules issued for subordinates, but also on income; on goals and premises emanating from supervisors' leadership; on value orientations arising from acts chosen by co-workers; and on the information received and transmitted to others by all persons in the firm. There is, however, an incentive structure that rewards with larger incomes those acts that make greater contributions to the firm's profit.

A set of acts and constraining rules for all persons in the firm is called "Pareto optimal" if no feasible reorganization of them can make one individual better off (and no one else worse off) without lowering the firm's output (or, depending on the perspective, profit). It turns out that under a variety of different collections of conditions on utility functions and on incentive and other structures, the firm achieves a Pareto optimal state. But the sets of conditions ensuring Pareto optimality are restrictive and work in rather unconventional ways. This is because the property of Pareto optimality usually arises in a typical Walrasian context in which all relevant forces at play are restrained sufficiently by markets and competition to bring about the result. The presence of factors such as premises, value orientations, and information transmissions, which avoid such constraints, tends to render the attainment of Pareto optimality dependent on social as well as economic phenomena. Thus the question of Pareto optimality among acts and rules within the firm is very different from the standard issues of Pareto optimality in production and Pareto optimality beyond the firm in a model of the perfectly competitive economy.

In a less formal manner, Leibenstein [17] also contends that behavior in the best interests of workers will not necessarily be in the best interest of the firm. Consequently, inefficiencies having nothing to do with the allocation of resources across firms (Leibenstein calls them "X-inefficiencies") may arise. His approach implies that firms neither minimize cost nor maximize profit.

Now it is commonplace among economists to question the assumption that consumers and firms behave rationally in the sense of maximizing utility and profit. Apart from Leibenstein's, one of the more serious challenges has been raised by Simon [27]. Simon argues that to be rational, as described in the Walrasian theory, it is necessary to have complete knowledge of the consequences that follow from all possible alternatives. For only then can the true maximizing choice be determined. But because in most situations the number of options is so great and the information needed to evaluate them so vast, such rationality is beyond the capacity of human achievement.[23] Faced with this difficulty, the next best thing for consumers and firms is to do as well as they can by pursuing a course of action that seems satisfactory or good enough. Thus the rationality assumed in the Walrasian theory of market behavior needs to be modified by introducing limits or bounds.

One application of the "good enough" idea in the theory of demand is as follows:[24] Let prices and income determine a budget set and place the consumer at a point x^0 within it. Suppose the consumer knows his preferences only imperfectly and locally near x^0, but well enough to discern in which directions from x^0, if any, he would like to move small distances. These movements would procure baskets that are preferred to x^0. Some directions may be preferred to others because they would secure more preferred baskets. The consumer might not want to depart in any direction from certain baskets called "best" points. (That is, from a best point there is no direction in which a small movement would provide a basket that is preferred. Thus, if x^0 were such a basket, the consumer would stay there.) In addition to being only "locally" defined, these preferences need not be transitive. Now let the consumer travel a small distance in his most preferred direction (if one exists) to a new point x' still in the budget set. Assume preferences are known locally at x' and continue the process, always requiring movement in the most preferred direction until the consumer no longer wishes to move.[25] In spite of the fact that the consumer might not know in advance where the best point in the budget set is, under certain conditions (weaker than those ensuring the existence of a continuous utility function and hence of a utility-maximizing basket) the procedure described here would eventually take him there. The consumer's demand function would identify with each vector of prices and income the associated best point obtained. Thus a rationality assumption based on continual passage in the most preferred directions permits a characterization of demand. The definition of these functions does not require that the consumer be able to compare and evaluate all pairs of points in every budget set. Although the approach has not yet been pushed far enough to actually replace utility maximization in the Walrasian theory of market behavior, it has been established (parallel to Theorems 12.3-11 and 12.3-14) that (local) equilibria and (local) Pareto optima correspond in models of exchange economies where consumers are assumed

---

[23] Simon [27, pp. 79-84].
[24] Katzner [6, Sec. 6.4], [7].
[25] Throughout this process the consumer's preferences are presumed to remain unchanged, and his movements are understood to be hypothetical in the sense that no actual market transactions are effected until full, economy-wide equilibrium is achieved.

to operate in this way.

A proposal for revising the theory of the firm to meet Simon's objections has been suggested by Winter [30]. In his argument, the firms of an industry are thought of as making output or price decisions by the routine application of simple rules such as the setting of price by a constant percentage mark-up from unit cost. All firms continually search (some more passively, perhaps, than others) for improved decision rules and, if a better one happens to be found, it is adopted by at least one firm. But usually, as long as existing rules appear to be performing well, they are retained. When performance deteriorates, the search for new rules intensifies. Winter also supposes that firms with profits in excess of normal profit expand, and those with profits below the normal level contract. Finally, he shows that there is at least one particularization of his model in which the industry is likely to settle eventually at a (profit-maximizing) competitive equilibrium.

Apart from weakening the postulate of rationality or maximization, attention might also be given to the possibility of discarding it entirely and substituting something quite different in its place. One reason for doing so lies in the fact that in certain cultures, maximization does not seem to be an appropriate representation of the driving force behind human behavior. The argument for substitution in these cases has been made by Katzner [14] and, although the importance of culture in determining both individual economic behavior and the economist's understanding of it has been implied more or less explicitly at various junctures in Section 1.2, the possiblilty of that substitution will not be pursued further here.

For those who are still uneasy even with modified versions of the theories of individual firm and consumer behavior, there is an approach to modeling the full microeconomy that avoids them entirely. Identified with so-called "classical economic theory" and the names of Leontief and Sraffa, it takes market demand as given and focuses on interindustry interactions. The equations describing the equilibrium or stationary path are as follows:[26]

Let x_{in} vary over quantities of output of industry i used in production by industry n, where $i, n = 1, \ldots, I$. Suppose d_i represents the portion of industry i's output that goes to satisfy consumer demand. Then the total output of industry i, namely x_i, is given by

$$x_i = d_i + \sum_{n=1}^{I} x_{in}, \quad i = 1, \ldots, I. \tag{15.2-1}$$

---

[26] See Pasinetti [22, Ch. 5].

Define the *coefficient of production*, ξ_{in}, for industry i with respect to industry n by

$$\xi_{in} = \frac{x_{in}}{x_i}, \quad i, n = 1, \dots, I, \tag{15.2-2}$$

and specify s_i, the *rate of surplus* in industry i, by

$$s_i = \frac{d_i}{x_i - d_i}, \quad i = 1, \dots, I.$$

Then (15.2-1) can be rewritten as

$$(1 + s_i) \sum_{n=1}^{I} \xi_{in} x_i = x_i, \quad i = 1, \dots, I. \tag{15.2-3}$$

Assume that all coefficients of production are known parameters. Assume further that, at equilibrium, all rates of surplus are the same, or

$$s_i = s, \quad i = 1, \dots, I.$$

Thus (15.2-3) reduces to

$$(1 + s) \sum_{n=1}^{I} \xi_{in} x_i = x_i, \quad i = 1, \dots, I. \tag{15.2-4}$$

Lastly, suppose s is given independently of (15.2-4).[27] Then (15.2-4) is a system of I equations in the I unknowns $x_1, \dots, x_I$, which, with appropriate restrictions imposed on the ξ_{in} can be resolved to secure unique values for the x_i. These can properly be regarded as market equilibrium quantities. The x_{in} are then obtained from (15.2-2).

Write y_i for the labor employed in industry i and ξ_i for the production coefficient

$$\xi_i = \frac{y_i}{x_i}, \quad i = 1, \dots, I. \tag{15.2-5}$$

As before, the ξ_i are taken as known constants. Denote the price of good i by p_i, where $i = 1, \dots, I$, and the price (wage) of labor by the scalar variable r. Suppose that at equilibrium all industries enjoy the same rate of profit ρ, where ρ is defined with respect to nonlabor cost. Thus dollar profit in industry n is

---

[27]   *Ibid.*, p. 97.

given by

$$\rho \sum_{i=1}^{I} p_i x_{in}, \quad n = 1, \ldots, I.$$

Moreover, the statement that for industry n, revenues equal total cost plus profit appears as

$$ry_n + (1 + \rho) \sum_{i=1}^{I} p_i x_{in} = p_n x_n, \quad n = 1, \ldots, I. \tag{15.2-6}$$

Upon division by x_n and employment of (15.2-2) and (15.2-5), relation (15.2-6) becomes

$$r\xi_n + (1 + \rho) \sum_{i=1}^{I} p_i \xi_{in} = p_n, \quad n = 1, \ldots, I. \tag{15.2-7}$$

Taking the coefficients of production to be fixed and ρ to be determined independently, (15.2-7) constitutes a system[28] of I equations in the $I + 1$ unknowns $p_1, \ldots, p_I, r$. This system is usually solved by adding a normalization, say

$$r = 1, \tag{15.2-8}$$

and assuming sufficient conditions on the coefficients of production so that $p_1, \ldots, p_I$ can be found as unique solutions. These values can be viewed as market equilibrium prices.

Thus, with one exception not to be specified here,[29] market equilibrium prices and quantities are each determined by independent systems of equations. Issues concerning the behavior of consumers and firms, such as the plausibility of utility and profit maximization, are irrelevant. The two sets of conditions imposed on production coefficients ensuring the unique solvability of first (15.2-4) and then (15.2-7) with (15.2-8) are not incompatible and can hold simultaneously. With both sets of conditions in force, equilibrium in the model exists and is unique. Like equilibrium in the Walrasian theory of market behavior, this equilibrium is identified with what is observed in reality. The two approaches therefore provide separate interpretations of the same seen phenomena. But only the Walrasian theory demonstrates in a formal model

---

[28] *Ibid.*, pp. 73, 74.
[29] *Ibid.*, p. 117.

that the pursuit of self-interest in an economic environment does not necessarily lead the world to chaos and confusion. And only the Walrasian theory provides an explanation of how consumers determine the goods they buy and factors they supply, and how firms decide on the outputs they produce and the inputs they use to produce those outputs.

Another vision of the way the economy operates, alternative but related to that provided by the Walrasian system, and one that explicitly incorporates probabilistic uncertainty within its structure, is based on the theory of games. Consumers and firms become players and the type of game invoked determines the vision that emerges. Although each player does not know in advance the exact moves the others will make, he does know the collection of all possible moves. Against this uncertainty, and rather than merely choosing quantities to buy and sell in response to given prices, each consumer and firm is thought of more generally as choosing a *strategy* or a complete plan for playing the game that describes what will be done to counter each possible move of the other players. Thus the rationality assumption of Walrasian theory is reformulated and extended to include reaction rules on behalf of each player in a wider class of situations. These rules become a part of the reconstructed vision describing the nature of the individual and firm, and are usually taken to be exogenous to the outcome of the game. A vector of strategies, one chosen by each player, is a *solution* of the game. Each solution corresponds to one play of the game. Every solution results in a payoff to each player that can be represented in terms of the utility or profit accruing to that player. A *Nash equilibrium* is a solution in which no player can, by changing his chosen strategy, increase his payoff as long as all other players hold fixed to theirs.[30] Games can permit cooperation among players or exclude it. They can be structured so that all players move simultaneously or that players move in sequence. In the latter case, of course, players moving later know what players moving earlier have done. Games can also be structured to have one or many plays.

With respect to the Walrasian model of exchange if, in the definition of Nash equilibrium, the phrase "all other players hold fixed to theirs" were interpreted to mean that the other players remain on unchanging indifference surfaces, and the phrase "no player can ... increase his payoff" were understood as each player maximizing his utility over the remaining possibilities, then the Nash equilibrium would be equivalent to a Pareto optimum. It is also clear that the Cournot duopoly model of Section 11.3 and Exercise 11.11 can be formulated in terms of a game. In the latter case, the players are two firms,

---

[30]   Nash [21, p. 49]. This is not the same thing as the Nash two-person bargaining equilibrium of Exercise 7.9.

each strategy of each firm is the output-production response of that firm to the output produced by the other firm as determined by the reaction functions (11.3-7), and the payoffs are the respective profits received. The Nash equilibrium is the simultaneous solution of the equations of (11.3-7) — the same outcome earlier identified as the Cournot solution.

There is little doubt that the theory of games has provided useful and important insights into the analyses of behavior (such as in the cases of oligopoly, bargaining, search, *etc.*) where the number of players is small and the impact of the decisions of each on the others is significant.[31] But under conditions of economy-wide perfect competition, where there are large numbers of players, each behaving, in part, as if his presence (or absence) is of no consequence to the markets in which he participates, the contributions of game theory to date have not been especially noteworthy. It is true that general equilibrium in a Walrasian model can be viewed as a Nash equilibrium. But little other than this statement, which many regard as not particularly significant, is gained by doing so. However, there is still the matter of the core.

Imagine a model of an exchange economy in which consumers or agents, in an exploratory process, make, cancel, and remake tentative arrangements to trade with each other out of their initial endowments. When all agents have arrived at arrangements providing each with the most utility they are able to achieve, the trades are carried out. This can be thought of as a game in which individuals do *not* respond to given market prices, and in which various subgroups of agents called *coalitions* can seek to do better by trading only among themselves. As in Exercise 7.8, an allocation of commodities, call it A, is in the core of this model if (before the consummation of trades) there is no coalition that can increase the utility of each of its members beyond that attained in A by trading with their initial endowments. It turns out that while the competitive equilibrium allocation of commodities (assuming it exists) for any initial endowment is in the core, there are other non-competitive-equilibrium allocations in the core as well. However, as the number of agents increases through a process of replication in which each added agent is identical with respect to his preferences and initial endowment to one of the original agents, the core shrinks to the competitive equilibrium allocation (recall Exercise 7.8). The game lying behind the core, then, although it provides a second game-theoretic way of viewing exchange behavior in the microeconomy, does not, like the game framework behind Nash equilibria, yield much new insight into the workings of competitive economies at large.

---

[31]   It has also been employed to explain how the markets taken as given by the Walrasian system developed over a long period of time (e.g., Schotter [25]).

15.3   CONCLUSION

The central achievement of the Walrasian theory of market behavior is the con-struction of a coherent arithmomorphic simile of dialectical economic reality. The significance, power, and appeal of this particular simile has been discussed in Section 14.1. Moreover, demonstrating the existence of one simile clearly opens up the possibility of finding others. Each such simile would establish a vision of the same dialectical reality in terms of its own thought system based on its own assumptions and its own methods of analysis. Several alternative ways to proceed have been suggested in Sections 15.1 and 15.2. Models to re-place those of the consumer, the firm, and even the economy have been cited, along with a method of analysis resting on the use of historical rather than logical time. With the aforementioned exceptions of the classical model of Leontief and Sraffa (drawn from Pasinetti [22, Ch. 5] above) and the historical-time structure developed by Katzner [11], however, these possibilities can, at present, be regarded as only fragments of theories of market behavior, none having been developed to the point where it provides a complete and coherent arithmomorphic simile of the dialectical microeconomy. There is, therefore, considerable room for further work in this regard.

It should be emphasized that the need for complete and coherent arith-momorphic similes that incorporate historical time into the theoretical land-scape is especially important. Although the future can never be foretold in any completely systematic way, the exclusion of historical time from the Wal-rasian vision unnecessarily clouds and obscures the statements that are made about coming prospects. Thus predictions of the results of implementing cer-tain policies, for example, have to be couched in the language of "other things being equal" and are necessarily independent of the unique historical moment at which they are developed. But once historical time is included as an integral part of the analytical framework, a more clear, precise, and accurate meaning can be given to discussions of potential future outcomes.

Other directions in which the discipline of microeconomic theory might logically proceed from the Walrasian foundation include the following: First, investigations might be made of the significance of still further variations in the assumption content of the Walrasian theory, at the same time as analyses employing those alternative assumptions remain within the logical framework of the Walrasian construction. As described in Section 15.2, these efforts al-ready have produced interesting and important results, and there is no reason to suppose that all potential for further achievement has been exhausted. Second, the same thing can be said about explorations of additional possible methods of analysis. Third, the well-established tradition in economics of employing part or all of the Walrasian structure in the examination of applied questions and in the analysis of various policies to achieve welfare objectives[32] could be continued. Although hardly touched upon in this book, issues arising in such a context have always been fertile ground for researchers armed with the Walrasian vision and Walrasian analytical techniques.

Another avenue that economists have pursued with considerable vigor in the past is the use of the Walrasian theory of market behavior as the source of building blocks with which aggregative or macroeconomic models and theories are erected.[33] Howver, inquiries along this line have revealed that there are a number of serious analytical difficulties in interpreting the Walrasian vision as a foundation for macroeconomic analysis. In addition to the well-known aggregation problem, the clearing of markets at the micro level might not be reflected in a macro analogue because macro-analysis often admits the possibility that not all income generated in the economy is respent on the economy's output. As a result, there might exist economic resources, most notably labor, that go unemployed. In other words, not all macro markets clear at levels that guarantee that the macro-labor market itself clears at its full-employment level. Thus, macroeconomic analysis deals with phenomena that can be "incompatible" with the Walrasian vision of the market economy. One way to explain this lack of confluence and suggest, in light of previous discussion, a corrective approach, is to view the problem as arising from the omission in the (micro-) Walrasian theory of three elements, referred to earlier, that are central to any understanding of macroeconomic phenomena, namely, historical time, nonprobabilistic uncertainty, and a realistic notion of money based on them that permits consideration of the problems arising from variations in the demand for money, its purchasing power, and its circulation. Nevertheless, the integrity of the Walrasian theory of market behavior is preserved by the consistency in the logical implications of its assumptions and analytical methods, and by the cohesiveness of the vision it presents of the economic reality that inspires it. The theory points, in the manner exhibited at length in previous chapters, to the possibility (under the conditions it envisages) of economic coherence rather than chaos, and the potential economic benefits that might, as a result, ensue from that coherence.

The Walrasian theory of market behavior is, of course, only one of many scholarly contributions that the discipline of economics can make to the understanding of economic society and the achievement of economic objectives.

---

[32]   See, for example, Mishan [20].
[33]   Theorem 8.4-6 and the comment following it suggest how the Walrasian system has been used in this way. Also, recall previous discussion on pp. 271 and 380 and, for further exploration, see Weintraub [29].

Perspectives employing different methodologies (as suggested above) and even epistemologies are possible. Indeed, given the endless creative energy of the human mind, the potential is unlimited. All the same, the Walrasian theory of market behavior stands not only as an imposing intellectual structure in its own right, but also, in the hands of skilled and judicious practitioners, as a potentially significant advance in the march toward social betterment.

REFERENCES

1. Bausor, R., "Time and the Structure of Economic Analysis," *Journal of Post Keynesian Economics* 5, no. 2 (Winter, 1982-83), pp. 163-179.
2. ——, "Time and Equilibrium," *The Reconstruction of Economic Theory*, P. Mirowski, ed. (Boston: Kluwer Nijhoff, 1986), Ch. 4.
3. Georgescu-Roegen, N., *The Entropy Law and the Economic Process* (Cambridge: Harvard University Press, 1971).
4. Gintis, H. and D. W. Katzner, "Profits, Optimality and the Social Division of Labor in the Firm," *Sociological Economics*, L. Lêvy-Garboua, ed. (London: Sage, 1979), pp. 269-297. Reprinted as Ch. 11 in D. W. Katzner, *Analysis without Measurement* (Cambridge: Cambridge University Press, 1983).
5. Hollis, M. and E. J. Nell, *Rational Economic Man* (London: Cambridge University Press, 1975).
6. Katzner, D. W., *Static Demand Theory* (New York: Macmillan, 1970).
7. ——,"Demand and Exchange Analysis in the Absence of Integrability Conditions," *Preferences Utility and Demand*, J. S. Chipman, *et al.*, eds. (New York: Harcourt, Brace & Jovanovich, 1971), pp. 254-270.
8. ——, *Analysis without Measurement* (Cambridge: Cambridge University Press, 1983).
9. ——, "The Role of Formalism in Economic Thought, with Illustration Drawn from the Analysis of Social Interaction in the Firm," *The Reconstruction of Economic Theory*, P. Mirowski, ed. (Boston: Kluwer Nijhoff, 1986), Ch. 5. Reprinted as Ch. 6 in D. W. Katzner, *Unmeasured Information and the Methodology of Social Scientific Inquiry* (Boston: Kluwer, 2001).
10. ——, "Attitudes, Rationality and Consumer Demand," *Essays in Honour of Sidney Weintraub*, J. A. Kregel, ed. (London: Macmillan, 1989), pp. 133-153. Repringed as Ch. 12 in D. W. Katzner, *Unmeasured Information and the Methodology of Social Scientific Inquiry* (Boston: Kluwer, 2001).

11. ——, *Time, Ignorance, and Uncertainty in Economic Models* (Ann Arbor: University of Michigan Press, 1998).
12. ——, "The Significance, Success, and Failure of Microeconomic Theory," *Journal of Post Keynesian Economics* 24, no. 1 (Fall, 2001), pp. 41-58.
13. ——, *Unmeasured Information and the Methodology of Social Scientific Inquiry* (Boston: Kluwer, 2001).
14. ——, *Culture and Economic Explanation* (unpublished manuscript, 2005).
15. Kornai, J., *Anti-Equilibrium* (Amsterdam: North-Holland, 1971).
16. Lange, O., "On the, Economic Theory of Socialism," *On the Economic Theory of Socialism*, O. Lange and F. M. Taylor, with B. E. Lippincott, ed. (Minneapolis: University of Minnesota Press, 1938),pp. 55-143.
17. Leibenstein, H., *Beyond Economic Man* (Cambridge: Harvard University Press, 1976).
18. Marshall, A., *Principles of Economics*, 8th ed. (New York: Macmillan, 1948).
19. Mas-Colell, A., M. D. Whinston, and J. R. Green, *Microeconomic Theory* (Oxford: Oxford University Pess, 1995).
20. Mishan, E. J., *Cost-Benefit Analysis*, revised ed. (London: Allen and Unwin, 1975).
21. Nash, J. F., Jr., "Equilibrium Points in n-Person Games," *Proceedings of the National Accademy of Science USA* 36 (1950), pp. 48-49.
22. Pasinetti, L., *Lectures on the Theory of Production* (New York: Columbia University Press, 1977).
23. Robertson, T. S., *Consumer Behavior* (Glenview, Ill: Scott, Foresman, 1970).
24. Russell, B., "Knowledge by Acquaintance and Knowledge by Description," *Mysticism and Logic and other Essays* (London: George Allen and Unwin, 1959), pp. 209-232.
25. Schotter, A., *The Economic Theory of Social Institutions* (Cambridge: Cambridge University Press, 1981).
26. Shackle, G. L. S., *Decision, Order and Time in Human Affairs*, 2nd ed. (Cambridge: Cambridge University Press, 1969).
27. Simon, H. A., *Administrative Behavior*, 2nd ed. (New York, Macmillan, 1957).
28. Vickers, D., *Financial Markets in the Capitalist Process* (Philadelphia: University of Pennsylvania Press, 1978).
29. Weintraub, E. R., *Microfoundations: The Compatibility of Microeconomics and Macroeconomics* (Cambridge: Cambridge University Press, 1979).

30. Winter, S. G., "Satisficing, Selection, and the Innovating Remnant," *Quarterly Journal of Economics* 85 (1971), pp. 237-261.

Appendix A

Mathematical Notes

The purpose of this appendix is to list, in a more or less self-contained way, various mathematical ideas employed in the text. Most often, concepts are defined very briefly with little or no discussion. Only a few are illustrated. Propositions are stated without proof. In two instances, the importance of each hypothesis in obtaining its associated propositional conclusion is emphasized. The notation employed below is not related to that of the text.

A.1   SETS

A *set* is a collection S of well-defined elements. In what follows the elements of S always are taken to be points in a Euclidean space, that is, vectors of real numbers. Call X a *subset* of S, and write $X \subseteq S$, if every element of X is also an element of S. When $X \subseteq S$ and $S \neq X$, then X is said to be a *proper* subset of S. The set with no elements, or the *empty* set, is denoted by ϕ.

Let X and Y be subsets of another set S. Define

$$X \cup Y = \{x : x \text{ is in } X \text{ or } Y\},$$

$$X \cap Y = \{x : x \text{ is in both } X \text{ and } Y\},$$

$$Y^c = \{x : x \text{ is in } S \text{ but not in } Y\},$$

and

$$X - Y = X \cap Y^c.$$

The symbol $\cup$ is referred to as *union*, $\cap$ is called *intersection*, and Y^c is said to be the *complement* of Y in S. In addition, $X - Y$ is the *difference* between X and Y. These ideas are illustrated for two dimensions by Figures A.1(a)-(c), where S is represented as a rectangle and X and Y as disks. The complement of Y is the shaded area in Figure A.1(a), and $X \cup Y$ is shaded in Figure A.1(b). The cross-hatched region in Figure A.1(c) is $X \cap Y$ and the remaining shaded part of that picture is $X - Y$. The *Cartesian product* of X and Y is the set

$$X \times Y = \{(x, y) : x \text{ is in } X \text{ and } y \text{ is in } Y\}.$$

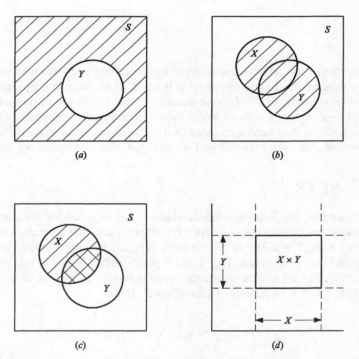

Figure A.1 Operations with sets: (*a*) complement; (*b*) union; (*c*) intersection and difference; (*d*) Cartesian product

A two-dimensional example is given in Figure A.1(d).

Let $x = (x_1, \ldots, x_n)$ and $y = (y_1, \ldots, y_n)$ be vectors of real numbers. The (*Euclidean*) *distance* between x and y is given by

$$|x - y| = \left[\sum_{i=1}^{n} (x_i - y_i)^2\right]^{1/2}.$$

For the special case in which $y = 0$, the symbol $|x|$ denotes the "length" of the vector x.

A *neighborhood* of radius $r > 0$ about a point x is the collection of points y such that $|x - y| < r$.

A point x is a *limit point* of a set S provided that every neighborhood of x contains a point of S distinct from x. Note that neighborhoods of limit points of S can include points not in S.

A set S is *closed* if every limit point of S is also an element of S. Loosely speaking, a closed set contains its "boundary."

A point x is an *interior* point of a set S if there exists a neighborhood of x wholly contained in S. The *interior* of S is the set of all interior points of S. Thus, for example, if $S = \{x : x \geqslant 0\}$ then the interior of S is $\{x : x > 0\}$.

A set S is *open* whenever every point of S is an interior point of S. An open set, then, does not contain any points on its boundary. Moreover, S is open if and only if its complement S^c is closed. A set S is *open relative to* another set X provided that $S \cap X$ is open. The relevant notion of neighborhood to employ in determining the openness of S relative to X is

$$\{y : |x - y| < r \text{ and } y \text{ is in } X\},$$

for appropriate radii $r > 0$, and x in S.

Consider, for a moment, the special case in which the elements of S are real numbers (scalars). The *absolute value* of x in S is the distance, as indicated above, between x and the origin. Thus the absolute value of x is written $|x|$. But in this circumstance it is also true that

$$|x| = \begin{cases} x, & \text{if } x \geqslant 0, \\ -x, & \text{if } x < 0. \end{cases}$$

A real number y is a *lower bound* of S if $y \leqslant x$, for all x in S. It is an *upper bound* of S provided that $x \leqslant y$, for all x in S. Moreover, the largest of all of the lower bounds of S is called the *greatest* lower bound of S, and the smallest of all of the upper bounds of S is the *least* upper bound of S.

When S is the real line and a and b are real numbers in S with $a \leqslant b$, the *closed interval* between a and b is the set $[a, b] = \{x : a \leqslant x \leqslant b\}$. Similarly, the *open interval* between a and b is $(a, b) = \{x : a < x < b\}$. There are two *half-open* (or *half-closed*) intervals, namely, $[a, b) = \{x : a \leqslant x < b\}$ and $(a, b] = \{x : a < x \leqslant b\}$. In the notation $[a, b]$, (a, b), $[a, b)$, and $(a, b]$, a square bracket on the left, say, signifies that the left-hand endpoint a is included in the interval, whereas a rounded bracket indicates that it is not. A similar principle applies to the right-hand bracket.

Returning to the general situation in which the elements of S can be vectors of any dimension, the set S is *bounded* if there is a real number $b > 0$ such that $|y| < b$ for all y in S. (Clearly, for the previous special case in which S is a set of real numbers, S is bounded if and only if S has both a lower bound and an upper bound.)

A set S is *compact* when it is closed and bounded.

Two sets A and B having the property that $A \cap B = \phi$ are called *disjoint*.

Two sets S and X are *separated* if there exist two disjoint, open sets A and B such that $S \subseteq A$ and $X \subseteq B$.

A set S is *connected* whenever it cannot be written as the union of two separated sets.

Let x and y be two vectors. The *line segment connecting* x and y is given by $\{\theta x + (1 - \theta)y : 0 \leqslant \theta \leqslant 1\}$.

A set S is *convex* provided that for any x and y in S, the line segment connecting x and y lies entirely within S. The sets S (taken to be either open or closed) in Figures A.2(a) and (b) are convex. Figure A.2(c) illustrates a set that is not convex.

A.2 RELATIONS

Let S be a set. A *relation* (that is, a *binary relation*) ρ on S is a collection of ordered pairs: $\rho \subseteq S \times S$. The notation $x \rho y$ means (x, y) is in ρ. The *complement* of ρ, written $\overline{\rho}$, is defined by:

$$\overline{\rho} = \{(x, y) : x \text{ and } y \text{ are in } S \text{ and } (x, y) \text{ is not in } \rho\},$$

or

$$\overline{\rho} = S \times S - \rho.$$

A relation can exhibit one or more of a variety of properties. As examples, ρ may be

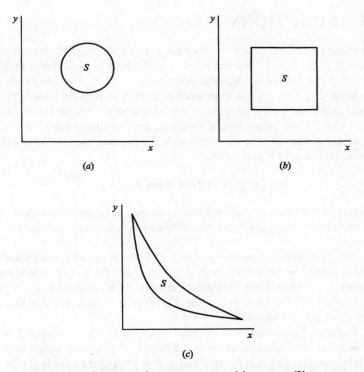

Figure A.2 Convex and nonconvex sets: (*a*) convex; (*b*) convex; (*c*) nonconvex

1. *Reflexive*: $x \rho x$, for all x in S.

2. *Irreflexive*: $x \overline{\rho} x$, for all x in S.

3. *Symmetric*: $x \rho y$ implies $y \rho x$, for all x and y in S.

4. *Asymmetric*: $x \rho y$ implies $y \overline{\rho} x$, for all x and y in S.

5. *Transitive*: $x \rho y$ and $y \rho z$ implies $x \rho z$, for all x, y, and z in S.

6. *Total*: Either $x \rho y$ or $y \rho x$, for all distinct x and y in S.

A relation is called an *equivalence* relation when it is reflexive, symmetric, and transitive.

A.3   FUNCTIONS

A *function* from a set X into another set Y is a collection of ordered pairs f such that $f \subseteq X \times Y$ and for every x in X there is a unique y in Y with (x, y) in f. In the usual functional notation, $y = f(x)$. (Because only one y is associated to each x, f is sometimes described as *single valued*. Functions defined in the same way but without this uniqueness property are *multivalued* or *set valued*. Only single-valued functions are considered here.) When $X = Y$, f is also a relation. The set over which f is defined, namely X, is called its *domain*. Its *range* is Y and its *image* is

$$\{ y : (x, y) \text{ is in } f \text{ for some } x \text{ in } X \} \subseteq Y.$$

Elements of the range of f are referred to as *images* or *function values*. Terms such as "map," "mapping," and "transformation" are often synonymous with function.

Let f be a function mapping X into Y. If the image of f is identical to Y, then f is said to be *onto*. Moreover, f is *one to one* (or 1–1) provided distinct elements of X correspond to distinct elements of Y; that is, $f(x') = f(x'')$ implies $x' = x''$, for all x' and x'' in X. When f is both 1–1 and onto, it is called a 1–1 *correspondence*.

Suppose f is a one-to-one function of X into Y. The *inverse* of f, written f^{-1}, is a function whose domain is the image of f, whose image is X, and which has the property that for all x and y, $x = f^{-1}(y)$ if and only if $y = f(x)$. Clearly $x = f^{-1}(f(x))$, for all x in X.

Let f be a real-valued function defined on a collection X of real numbers or vectors. Then f is called *continuous* at x in X if for every $\varepsilon > 0$ there is a $\delta > 0$ such that

$$|f(y) - f(x)| < \varepsilon,$$

for all points y of X with $|y - x| < \delta$. Equivalently, suppose x is a limit point of X. Then f is continuous at x if and only if[1]

$$\lim_{y \to x} f(y) = f(x).$$

Two propositions concerning continuous functions are of interest. The first asserts that a continuous function defined on a compact set always attains a maximum and a minimum on that set.

---

[1]   Rudin [11, p. 86].

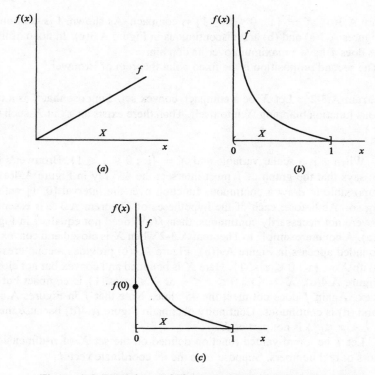

Figure A.3 Breakdown of Theorem A.3-1: (a) X is not bounded;
(b) X is not closed; (c) f is discontinuous

Theorem A.3-1[2] Let f be continuous on a compact set X. Then there exists
an x' and an x'' in X such that $f(x) \leqslant f(x')$ and $f(x) \geqslant f(x'')$, for all x in X.

Note that the maximum and minimum obtained in Theorem A.3-1 need
not be unique: Any constant function defined on X has a maximum and a
minimum at every x in X.

Each of the hypotheses of Theorem A.3-1 is essential. If f were not
continuous, or if X were not closed or not bounded (and hence not compact), a
maximum, say, need not exist. The possibilities are illustrated by the diagrams
of Figure A.3. In Figure A.3(a), X is the closed, unbounded set $\{x : x \geqslant 0\}$.
In Figure A.3(b), X is bounded but not closed: $X = \{x : 0 < x \leqslant 1\}$. In

---

2 Rudin [11, p. 89].

Figure A.3(c), $X = \{x : 0 \le x \le 1\}$ is compact. As shown, f is continuous in Figures A.3(a) and (b) and discontinuous in Figure A.3(c). In none of these cases does f have a maximum over its domain.

The second proposition is the fixed point theorem of Brouwer.

Theorem A.3-2[3]   Let X be a compact, convex set. Suppose that f is a continuous function mapping X into itself. Then there exists an x^0 in X such that $f(x^0) = x^0$.

When x is a scalar variable and $X = \{x : 0 \le x \le 1\}$, Brouwer's theorem says that the graph of f must intersect the 45° ray in Figure A.4(a). It is impossible to draw a continuous function over the interval [0, 1] without doing so. As before, each of the hypotheses of Theorem A.3-2 is essential. If f were not necessarily continuous, then $f(x^0)$ need not equal x^0 in Figure A.4(a). A counterexample to Theorem A.3-2 when X is closed and convex but unbounded appears in Figure A.4(b). Figure A.4(c) provides a counterexample with $X = \{x : 0 \le x < 1\}$. Here X is bounded and convex but not closed. In Figure A.4(d), $X = \{x : 0 \le x \le \frac{1}{2}$ or $\frac{3}{4} \le x \le 1\}$ is compact but not convex. Again f does not meet the 45° line. Note that f in Figures A.4(b), (c) and (d) is continuous. Continuity obtains in Figure A.4(d) because the set $\{x : \frac{1}{2} < x < \frac{3}{4}\}$ is not part of X.

Let f be a real-valued function defined on the set X of n-dimensional vectors of real numbers. Suppose u^i is the ith coordinate vector

$$u^i = (0, \ldots, 0, 1, 0, \ldots, 0),$$

where the 1 appears as the ith component of u^i and the remaining $n-1$ components are zero. Provided it exists, the *first-order partial derivative* with respect to x_i of f at an interior x in X, written $f_i(x)$, is given by

$$f_i(x) = \lim_{\lambda \to 0} \frac{f(x + \lambda u^i) - f(x)}{\lambda}.$$

(When x is a scalar, replace u^i in this expression by the number 1 to obtain the derivative, $f'(x)$, of f at x. In that case, the second-order derivative, $f''(x)$, at x is the derivative of $f'(x)$ at x.) Now let $\zeta = (\zeta_1, \ldots, \zeta_n)$ be any vector whose distance from the origin $|\zeta| = 1$. Then substitution of ζ in place of u^i in the above limit yields (as long as the limit exists) the directional derivative, $f_\zeta(x)$, at x in the direction defined by moving from the origin through

---

[3]   Dunford and Schwartz [6, p. 456].

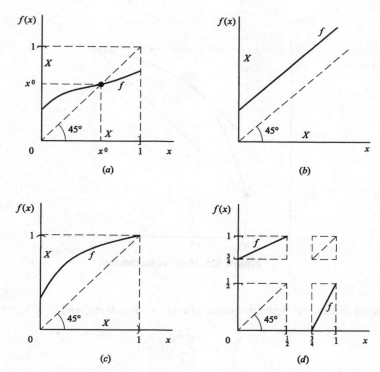

Figure A.4 Brouwer's theorem and when it breaks down: (*a*) theorem holds with x^0 as the fixed point; (*b*) theorem does not hold when X is not bounded; (*c*) theorem does not hold when X is not closed; (*d*) theorem does not hold when X is not convex

ζ. The *second-order partial derivative* with respect to x_i and x_j of f at x, denoted by $f_{ij}(x)$, is the first-order partial derivative with respect to x_j of $f_i(x)$. Higher-order derivatives are defined similarly and denoted by adding appropriate subscripts. To say that f is *continuously differentiable* (or *twice, continuously differentiable*) at x means that all first-order (or first- and second-order) partial derivatives exist and are continuous at x. The following result is well known:

Theorem A.3-3[4]   If f is continuously differentiable at an interior point x,

---

[4]   Rudin [11, pp. 218, 235-236].

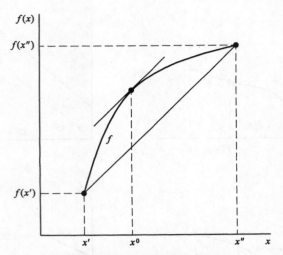

Figure A.5 Mean value theorem

then the directional derivative exists at x in any direction ζ and

$$f_\zeta(x) = \sum_{i=1}^n \zeta_i f_i(x) \, .$$

Moreover, if f is twice, continuously differentiable at x, then

$$f_{ij}(x) = f_{ji}(x) \, , \quad i, j = 1, \dots, n.$$

Consider a continuously differentiable function f of a scalar variable x defined on the open interval $\{x : x' < x < x''\}$ as shown in Figure A.5. Geometrically it is obvious that at some x^0 between x' and x'' there is a line tangent to the graph of f whose slope is the same as that of the chord connecting the points $(x', f(x'))$ and $(x'', f(x''))$. In other words, there is an x^0 such that

$$\frac{f(x'') - f(x')}{x'' - x'} = f'(x^0) \, .$$

The formal statement of this assertion is the mean value theorem:

Theorem A.3-4[5] Let f be continuously differentiable on an open interval X.

---

[5] Apostol [1, p. 110].

Then for any x' and x'' in X, there exists an x^0 in X such that

$$x^0 = \theta x' + [1 - \theta] x'',$$

where $0 < \theta < 1$, and

$$f(x'') - f(x') = (x'' - x') f'(x^0).$$

For functions of n variables defined on an n-dimensional domain X the mean value theorem is generalized as follows:

Theorem A.3-5[6]   Let f be continuously differentiable on an open, convex set X. Then for any n-dimensional vectors x' and x'' in X, there exists an n-dimensional vector x^0 in X such that

$$x^0 = \theta x' + [1 - \theta] x'',$$

where $0 < \theta < 1$, and

$$f(x'') - f(x') = \sum_{i=1}^{n} (x_i'' - x_i') f_i(x^0).$$

Another useful result for continuously differentiable functions is that differences in function values at, say, x' and x'' in X can be approximated by an expression involving the derivatives of the function at x' or x''. For functions of a single variable, Figure A.6 illustrates the fact that the closer x'' is to x', the smaller the difference between the slope of f at x' and the slope of the straight line through $(x', f(x'))$ and $(x'', f(x''))$. This approximation is written

$$f'(x') \simeq \frac{f(x'') - f(x')}{x'' - x'},$$

for x'' close to x'. Alternatively, the related approximation

$$f(x'') - f(x') \simeq (x'' - x') f'(x'), \qquad (A.3\text{-}6)$$

can also be seen in Figure A.6. The generalization of (A.3-6) to functions of n variables is[7]

$$f(x'') - f(x') \simeq \sum_{i=1}^{n} (x_i'' - x_i') f_i(x'), \qquad (A.3\text{-}7)$$

---

[6]   Apostol [1, p. 355].
[7]   Apostol [1, p. 348].

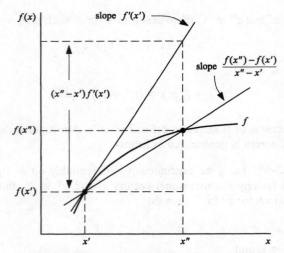

Figure A.6 Approximation of a derivative

for x'' close to x'.

The approximation in (A.3-7) is the special case of that of Taylor's theorem in which only first-order derivatives are employed. The Taylor approximation using first- and second-order derivatives is, for x'' close to x',

$$f(x'') - f(x') \simeq \sum_{i=1}^{n} (x_i'' - x_i') f_i(x')$$

$$+ \frac{1}{2} \sum_{i=1}^{n} \sum_{j=1}^{n} (x_i'' - x_i') (x_j'' - x_j') f_{ij}(x'). \tag{A.3-8}$$

It is not necessary to consider approximations involving higher-order derivatives here.[8]

Let k be a real number. A function f defined on $X = \{x : x > 0\}$ is *homogeneous of degree k* whenever $f(\alpha x) = \alpha^k f(x)$, for all x in X and $\alpha > 0$. The next result is known as *Euler's theorem*.

Theorem A.3-9 Let f be continuously differentiable on $X = \{x : x > 0\}$. Then f is homogeneous of degree k on X if and only if the partial derivatives

---

8   A discussion of the latter may be found in Apostol [1, pp. 241-244, 361-362].

$f_i(x)$, for $i = 1, \ldots, n$, are homogeneous of degree $k - 1$ and

$$kf(x) = \sum_{i=1}^{n} x_i f_i(x),$$

for all x in X.

Theorem 4.2-21 is a special case of Theorem A.3-9. The proof of the latter is similar to that of the former (p. 142).

Consider a real-valued function f on a convex set X of real numbers or vectors. Now f is *concave* on X provided that

$$f\left(\theta x' + [1 - \theta] x''\right) \geqslant \theta f\left(x'\right) + [1 - \theta] f\left(x''\right),$$

for all x' and x'' in X, and any θ where $0 \leqslant \theta \leqslant 1$. An example for the case in which x is a scalar is pictured in Figure A.7. The function f is *convex* on X whenever

$$f\left(\theta x' + [1 - \theta] x''\right) \leqslant \theta f\left(x'\right) + [1 - \theta] f\left(x''\right),$$

for all x' and x'' in X, and any θ where $0 \leqslant \theta \leqslant 1$. Note that f is convex if and only if $-f$ is concave. The notions of *strictly concave* and *strictly convex* functions are obtained from the definitions of concave and convex functions,

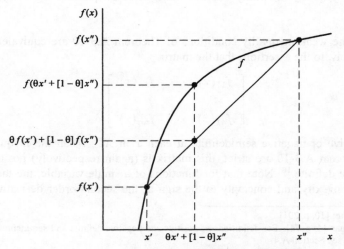

Figure A.7 Strictly concave function

respectively, by replacing the weak inequality with a strong inequality wherever it occurs and requiring that x' and x'' be restricted to the interior of X. The properties of convexity and concavity can be expressed in terms of partial derivatives:

Theorem A.3-10[9] Let f be twice, continuously differentiable on an open, convex set X. Then f is convex if and only if the determinants

$$f_{11}(x) \geqslant 0, \qquad \begin{vmatrix} f_{11}(x) & f_{12}(x) \\ f_{21}(x) & f_{22}(x) \end{vmatrix} \geqslant 0,$$

$$\begin{vmatrix} f_{11}(x) & f_{12}(x) & f_{13}(x) \\ f_{21}(x) & f_{22}(x) & f_{23}(x) \\ f_{31}(x) & f_{32}(x) & f_{33}(x) \end{vmatrix} \geqslant 0, \ldots,$$

for every x in X. If these inequalities are strict on X, then f is strictly convex. Also, f is concave if and only if

$$f_{11}(x) \leqslant 0, \qquad \begin{vmatrix} f_{11}(x) & f_{12}(x) \\ f_{21}(x) & f_{22}(x) \end{vmatrix} \geqslant 0,$$

$$\begin{vmatrix} f_{11}(x) & f_{12}(x) & f_{13}(x) \\ f_{21}(x) & f_{22}(x) & f_{23}(x) \\ f_{31}(x) & f_{32}(x) & f_{33}(x) \end{vmatrix} \leqslant 0, \ldots,$$

at each x, and f is strictly concave when these inequalities are everywhere strict.

The weak inequality conditions of Theorem A.3-10 are equivalent, respectively, to the assertions that the matrix

$$\begin{bmatrix} f_{11}(x) & \cdots & f_{1n}(x) \\ \vdots & & \vdots \\ f_{n1}(x) & \cdots & f_{nn}(x) \end{bmatrix}$$

is positive or negative semidefinite at each x in X. When the inequalities of Theorem A.3-10 are strict, this matrix is (again respectively) positive or negative definite.[10] Note that for functions of a single variable, the theorem links convexity and concavity to the sign of the second-order derivative f''.

---

[9]   Katzner [10, p. 201].
[10]   Bellman [4, p. 74]. For definitions of positive and negative definite and semidefinite matrices, see Section A.4.

Thus if $f''(x) < 0$ for all x, say, then f is strictly concave. The converse assertion cannot hold because the function given by $f(x) = -x^4$, is strictly concave but $f''(0) = 0$. Hence the inequalities of Theorem A.3-10 in their strict form are sufficient (as stated by the theorem) but not necessary for f to be strictly convex or concave.

The function f on X is *linear* if there are constants $\alpha_1, \ldots, \alpha_n$ and β such that[11]

$$f(x) = \beta + \sum_{i=1}^{n} \alpha_i x_i.$$

Functions are linear if and only if they are both concave and convex. (A partial proof is provided by Exercise 2.6.) When f is linear, all second-order derivatives and all determinants of Theorem A.3-10 vanish. Furthermore, let the zero vector be in X. Then f is linear with $f(0) = 0$ if and only if f is additive and homogeneous of degree 1 with respect to X, that is,

$$f(x' + x'') = f(x') + f(x''),$$

and

$$f(\gamma x') = \gamma f(x'),$$

for all x' and x'' in X and all real γ such that $\gamma x'$ is in X. (The difference between the second condition here and homogeneity of the first degree defined above is that in the present case there is no requirement that $x' > 0$.) To establish the proposition, note that if f is linear with $f(0) = \beta = 0$, then additivity and homogeneity obviously follow. Conversely, let x be in X. Then

$$x = \sum_{i=1}^{n} x_i u^i,$$

where u^i is the ith coordinate vector introduced earlier. Hence from additivity and homogeneity,

$$f(x) = f\left(\sum_{i=1}^{I} x_i u^i\right) = \sum_{i=1}^{I} x_i f(u^i).$$

A function f defined on a convex set X is *quasi-concave* provided that

---

[11]   Sometimes the word "linear" is reserved only for the case in which $\beta = 0$. In that language, f is called *affine* when $\beta > 0$.

for all x' and x'' in X, if $f(x') = f(x'')$ then

$$f\big(\theta x' + [1 - \theta]\, x''\big) \geqslant f(x''),$$

for every θ such that $0 \leqslant \theta \leqslant 1$. It is called *quasi-convex* when the inequality is reversed. With strict inequalities and x' and x'' in the interior of X, f would be, respectively, *strictly quasi-concave* and *strictly quasi-convex*. Quasi-concavity means that lower function values cannot appear along line segments in X connecting any two points with equal function values. Hence any function of a scalar variable whose derivative is positive everywhere or negative everywhere is vacuously strictly quasi-concave (and also strictly quasi-convex) since two points with equal function values cannot exist. Clearly (Exercise 2.7), functions of n variables that are concave (or convex) are also quasi-concave (or quasi-convex). That the converse assertions cannot be true is seen from the example

$$f(x_1, x_2) = (x_1 x_2)^2, \tag{A.3-11}$$

on $X = \{(x_1, x_2) : (x_1, x_2) \geqslant 0\}$. This function is neither convex nor concave, but it is strictly quasi-concave. Its geometry is explored momentarily. The differential implications of quasi-concavity are that the determinants

$$\begin{vmatrix} 0 & f_1(x) & f_2(x) \\ f_1(x) & f_{11}(x) & f_{12}(x) \\ f_2(x) & f_{21}(x) & f_{22}(x) \end{vmatrix} \geqslant 0,$$

$$\begin{vmatrix} 0 & f_1(x) & f_2(x) & f_3(x) \\ f_1(x) & f_{11}(x) & f_{12}(x) & f_{13}(x) \\ f_2(x) & f_{21}(x) & f_{22}(x) & f_{23}(x) \\ f_3(x) & f_{31}(x) & f_{22}(x) & f_{33}(x) \end{vmatrix} \leqslant 0,$$

$$\vdots$$

assuming these derivatives exist.[12] Because (analogously with concave and convex functions) f is quasi-concave if and only if $-f$ is quasi-convex, the corresponding inequalities for quasi-convex functions are:

$$\begin{vmatrix} 0 & f_1(x) & f_2(x) \\ f_1(x) & f_{11}(x) & f_{12}(x) \\ f_2(x) & f_{21}(x) & f_{22}(x) \end{vmatrix} \leqslant 0,$$

---

[12]   Arrow and Enthoven [2, p. 797].

$$\begin{vmatrix} 0 & f_1(x) & f_2(x) & f_3(x) \\ f_1(x) & f_{11}(x) & f_{12}(x) & f_{13}(x) \\ f_2(x) & f_{21}(x) & f_{22}(x) & f_{23}(x) \\ f_3(x) & f_{31}(x) & f_{22}(x) & f_{33}(x) \end{vmatrix} \leqslant 0,$$

To illustrate these ideas, consider the function

$$f(x_1, x_2) = - (x_1)^2 - (x_2)^2,$$

defined on the Euclidean plane. In three-dimensional space, f describes an upsidedown bowl with its unique maximum and maximum function value at the origin. The *level contours* (often identified as indifference curves or isoquants in the text) of f, namely,

$$\{(x_1, x_2) : f(x_1, x_2) = \gamma\},$$

where $\gamma \leqslant 0$, are concentric circles about the origin. One of these appears in Figure A.8. Now f is both strictly concave and strictly quasi-concave. Regardless of where a chord is drawn connecting two points on the level contour, the function values $f(x^0)$ at points x^0 on the chord in the interior of the circle are higher than at the end-points of the chord on the contour. It matters

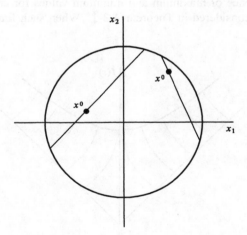

Figure A.8 Level contour of $f(x_1, x_2) = -(x_1)^2 - (x_2)^2$

not, insofar as the quasi-concavity is concerned, that tangents to the contour at some points slope upward and at others slope downward. Nor does it matter that the contour has a concave shape above the x_1-axis and a convex shape below it. The determinantal conditions on the partial derivatives of f imposed by the concavity and quasi-concavity are satisfied.

Alternatively, the function

$$f(x_1, x_2) = (x_1)^2 + (x_2)^2,$$

is strictly convex and strictly quasi-convex. Its level contours are identical to those in the previous example, but here function values $f(x^0)$ over chords in the interior of the circle (Figure A.8) are lower than at chord end-points on the contour. The graph of f is a right-side up bowl with minimum value zero at the origin. Also, the signs of the appropriate determinants have changed as required by previously stated results.

Return now to the function described in (A.3-11). The portion of its three dimensional graph up to some level ℓ is shown in Figure A.9. Over every straight line in the interior of its domain such that either x_1 or x_2 is fixed, and over every ray into that interior from the origin, f is strictly convex. But f cannot be strictly convex or even convex in general because the function values it associates to all points (except end-points) on the straight-line segment between any $x' > 0$ and $x'' > 0$ with $f(x') = f(x'')$ are larger than $f(x')$; that is, f is strictly quasi-concave.

The existence of maximum and minimum values for continuous functions has been considered in Theorem A.3-1. When such functions are con-

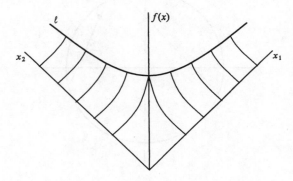

Figure A.9 Graph of $f(x_1, x_2) = (x_1 x_2)^2$
up to level ℓ

tinuously differentiable, rules for locating those values and distinguishing between them can be specified.[13] The necessary conditions for maximum and minimum values when x is a scalar are considered first.

Theorem A.3-12 Let f be twice, continuously differentiable at the scalar value x^0 in an open set X. If $f(x^0) \geqslant f(x)$ for all x in X, then $f'(x^0) = 0$ and $f''(x^0) \leqslant 0$. Alternatively, if $f(x^0) \leqslant f(x)$ for all x in X, then $f'(x^0) = 0$ and $f''(x^0) \geqslant 0$.

With regard to Theorem A.3-12, even if the maximizing x^0, say, were unique, as pointed out on p. 65 above, it still does not follow that $f''(x^0) < 0$: The function $f(x) = -x^4$ has a unique maximum at $x = 0$, but $f''(0) = 0$. The next result presents sufficient conditions for unique maximum and minimum values over an open set X.

Theorem A.3-13 Let f be twice, continuously differentiable on an open set of scalar values X. If $f'(x^0) = 0$ for x^0 in X, and if $f''(x) < 0$ for all x in X, then $f(x^0) > f(x)$ for all $x \neq x^0$ in X. Moreover, if $f'(x^0) = 0$ for x^0 in X, and if $f''(x) > 0$ for all x in X, then $f(x^0) < f(x)$ for all $x \neq x^0$ in X.

The generalizations of Theorems A.3-12 and A.3-13 to the situations in which x is the vector $(x_1, \ldots, x_n)$ are stated for maxima only.

Theorem A.3-14 Let f be twice, continuously differentiable at the vector value x^0 in an open set X. If $f(x^0) \geqslant f(x)$ for all x in X, then $f_i(x^0) = 0$ for $i = 1, \ldots, n$, and for all permutations of the components of x,

$$f_{11}(x^0) \leqslant 0, \qquad \begin{vmatrix} f_{11}(x^0) & f_{12}(x^0) \\ f_{21}(x^0) & f_{22}(x^0) \end{vmatrix} \geqslant 0,$$

$$\begin{vmatrix} f_{11}(x^0) & f_{12}(x^0) & f_{13}(x^0) \\ f_{21}(x^0) & f_{22}(x^0) & f_{23}(x^0) \\ f_{31}(x^0) & f_{32}(x^0) & f_{33}(x^0) \end{vmatrix} \leqslant 0, \ldots.$$

Theorem A.3-15 Let f be twice, continuously differentiable on an open set of vectors X. If $f_i(x^0) = 0$ for $i = 1, \ldots, n$ and x^0 in X and if, for all x in X

---

[13]   Rules similar to those described in the next four theorems are established, for example, by Apostol [1, pp. 109, 362, 376-379].

and all permutations of the components of x,

$$f_{11}(x) < 0, \quad \begin{vmatrix} f_{11}(x) & f_{12}(x) \\ f_{21}(x) & f_{22}(x) \end{vmatrix} > 0,$$

$$\begin{vmatrix} f_{11}(x) & f_{12}(x) & f_{13}(x) \\ f_{21}(x) & f_{22}(x) & f_{23}(x) \\ f_{31}(x) & f_{32}(x) & f_{33}(x) \end{vmatrix} < 0, \dots,$$

then $f(x^0) > f(x)$ for all $x \neq x^0$ in X.

The theorem of Lagrange establishing the validity of his "multiplier" method for locating maximum and minimum values subject to constraints is also stated with respect to vectors $x = (x_1, \dots, x_n)$:

Theorem A.3-16[14] Let f and $g = (g^1, \dots, g^m)$ be continuously differentiable functions defined on an open set of vectors X, where $m < n$. Write $T = \{x : g(x) = 0\}$ and suppose there is an x^0 in X and a neighborhood $N \subseteq X$ of x^0 such that either

  i) $f(x^0) \geqslant f(x)$ for all x in $T \cap N$, or

  ii) $f(x^0) \leqslant f(x)$ for all x in $T \cap N$.

If

$$\begin{vmatrix} g_1^1(x^0) & \cdots & g_m^1(x^0) \\ \vdots & & \vdots \\ g_1^m(x^0) & \cdots & g_m^m(x^0) \end{vmatrix} \neq 0 \qquad\qquad (A.3\text{-}17)$$

then there exist real numbers $\lambda_1, \dots, \lambda_m$ such that

$$f_i(x^0) + \sum_{j=1}^m \lambda_j g_i^j(x^0) = 0, \quad i = 1, \dots, n.$$

Inequality (A.3-17) is often referred to as the *constraint qualification*. It implies that, in a neighborhood of the constrained maximum, the first m constraints are independent of each other and can be solved to express x_{m+1}, $\dots, x_n$ as functions of $x_1, \dots, x_m$ (see the discussion of the implicit function theorem in the next section). Since Theorem A.3-16 demands that $m < n$, by employing different combinations of partial derivatives of the g^j's, more than

---

[14]   Apostol [1, p. 381].

one determinant could potentially satisfy (A.3-17). It is not necessary, however, that all such determinants be nonvanishing at the point in question. The only requirement is that there be at least one. (See, for example, the discussion in the answer to Exercise 8.4.)

Observe also that the conditions of Theorem A.3-16, including the constraint qualification, are sufficient for the validity of Lagrange's method, but not necessary. To illustrate, the unique maximum of the function $f(x_1, x_2) = -(x_1)^2 - (x_2)^2$ occurs, as indicated earlier, at the origin. Were this function to be maximized subject to the constraint $g(x_1, x_2) = (x_2)^2 - (x_1)^3 = 0$, then since the graph of g passes though the origin, the constrained maximum must also appear at $(x_1, x_2) = (0, 0)$. But both partial derivatives $g_1(0, 0) = 0$ and $g_2(0, 0) = 0$ in violation of (A.3-17). Nevertheless, applying the Lagrange method to this constrained maximization problem yields the correct solution $(x_1, x_2) = (0, 0)$.

A.4 SYSTEMS OF EQUATIONS

Consider the system of linear equations

$$a_{11}x_1 + \cdots + a_{1n}x_n = b_1,$$
$$\vdots \qquad\qquad\qquad \text{(A.4-1)}$$
$$a_{n1}x_1 + \cdots + a_{nn}x_n = b_n,$$

where the a_{ij} and b_i are fixed, real numbers and the x_i are real (scalar) variables. In matrix notation (A.4-1) becomes $Ax = b$, where A is the n by n (square) matrix of coefficients

$$A = \begin{bmatrix} a_{11} & \cdots & a_{1n} \\ \vdots & & \vdots \\ a_{n1} & \cdots & a_{nn} \end{bmatrix},$$

and x and b are the column vectors

$$x = \begin{bmatrix} x_1 \\ \vdots \\ x_n \end{bmatrix}, \qquad b = \begin{bmatrix} b_1 \\ \vdots \\ b_n \end{bmatrix}.$$

The transpose of, say, x is the row vector $x' = (x_1, \ldots, x_n)$.

Square matrices can possess numerous properties. Thus, A is called *sym-*

metric when

$$a_{ij} = a_{ji},$$

for $i, j = 1, \ldots, n$. A symmetric matrix A is said to be *negative definite* if $y'Ay < 0$, for all row vectors $y' = (y_1, \ldots, y_n) \neq 0$. It is *positive definite* when $y'Ay > 0$, for all $y' \neq 0$. Replacing the strong inequalities by their weak counterparts and permitting y' to be the zero vector (in addition to all others), A becomes, respectively, *negative semidefinite* and *positive semidefinite*.[15] (From here on, the use of the prime to indicate the transpose of a vector is dropped. Unless otherwise stated, all vectors are row vectors.) An n by n matrix A has an *inverse* whenever there exists another n by n matrix A^{-1} such that $AA^{-1} = A^{-1}A = \mathcal{I}$, where $\mathcal{I}$ is the n by n *identity* matrix

$$\mathcal{I} = \begin{bmatrix} 1 & 0 & \cdots & 0 \\ 0 & 1 & \cdots & 0 \\ \vdots & \vdots & \ddots & \vdots \\ 0 & 0 & \cdots & 1 \end{bmatrix},$$

and A^{-1} is called the inverse of A. Provided A^{-1} exists, A is, respectively, symmetric, negative and positive definite if and only if A^{-1} is also.[16] Lastly, A is *nonsingular* as long as its determinant $|A| \neq 0$. Note that A has an inverse if and only if it is nonsingular.[17] The property of nonsingularity also arises in the following proposition, known as *Cramer's rule*.

Theorem A.4-2[18]   If the determinant $|A| \neq 0$, then there is a unique solution

---

[15]   It is common practice to define, as is done here, positive and negative definiteness and semidefiniteness with respect to matrices that are already taken to be symmetric (*e.g.*, Bellman [4, p. 40]). This is because definite and semidefinite matrices are often considered in relation to the quadratic forms they generate and, for an arbitrary matrix A, both A and the symmetric matrix $(A + A')/2$, where A' is the transpose of A, define the same quadratic form. However, although all definite and semidefinite matrices appearing in this book are also symmetric, there is no reason to require symmetry in so far as the definitions themselves are concerned. Indeed, Gale's example cited in n. 13 on p. 98 employs a negative definite matrix that is not symmetric.

[16]   The assertion follows for positive definiteness because all the characteristic roots of a positive definite matrix A are (necessarily and sufficiently) positive (Bellman [4, p. 54]), and also the reciprocals of the characteristic roots of A^{-1} (Bellman [4, p. 90]). A parallel argument applies to the case of negative definiteness. For symmetry, see Bellman [4, p. 91].

[17]   Bellman [4, p. 90].

[18]   Birkhoff and MacLane [5, p. 306].

of (A.4-1), and it is given by

$$x_i = \frac{\begin{vmatrix} a_{11} & \cdots & a_{1i-1} & b_1 & a_{1i+1} & \cdots & a_{1n} \\ \vdots & & \vdots & \vdots & \vdots & & \vdots \\ a_{n1} & \cdots & a_{ni-1} & b_n & a_{ni+1} & \cdots & a_{nn} \end{vmatrix}}{|A|},$$

for $i = 1, \ldots, n$.

To illustrate, set $n = 2$. Then (A.4-1) consists of two linear equations in two variables, x_1 and x_2. Each equation describes a line in the x_1-x_2 plane. The condition $|A| \neq 0$ says that these lines are neither coincident nor parallel. Hence they must intersect and the solution identifies the coordinates of their intersection.

More generally, systems of functional equations in explicit form are written as

$$y_1 = f^1(x_1, \ldots, x_n),$$
$$\vdots \qquad\qquad\qquad (A.4\text{-}3)$$
$$y_m = f^m(x_1, \ldots, x_n),$$

or

$$y = f(x),$$

where $f = (f^1, \ldots, f^m)$, $x = (x_1, \ldots, x_n)$ and $y = (y_1, \ldots, y_m)$ are vectors of real numbers, and the f^i are functions defined on X. Suppose the set X is open, and take f to be continuously differentiable everywhere. When $m = n$, the *Jacobian* of (A.4-3) is the determinant

$$\begin{vmatrix} f_1^1(x) & \cdots & f_n^1(x) \\ \vdots & & \vdots \\ f_1^n(x) & \cdots & f_n^n(x) \end{vmatrix},$$

where f_j^i is the partial derivative of f^i with respect to x_j. (Actually, the term "Jacobian" can also refer to the associated matrix of partial derivatives of f.) For the special case of (A.4-1) in which $b_1, \ldots, b_n$ replaces $y_1, \ldots, y_m$, the Jacobian is $|A|$. If the Jacobian of (A.4-3) is nonvanishing at x^0 in X and if $y^0 = f(x^0)$, then the inverse function theorem[19] guarantees the existence of an inverse function g defined in a neighborhood of y^0 such that $x = g(y)$. In particular, it is possible to solve (A.4-3) for x^0 knowing y^0. Moreover, g is

---

[19]   For a precise statement of the theorem see Apostol [1, p. 372].

continuously differentiable in a neighborhood of y^0, and its Jacobian at y^0 is the inverse of that of f at x^0. Note also that these inverse-function-theorem conditions are only sufficient. The Jacobian may still equal zero at an x^0 even when an inverse exists around y^0, where $y^0 = f(x^0)$. This happens with the function $y = f(x) = x^3$, defined for all real (scalar) x. In spite of the fact that the Jacobian

$$\frac{df(x)}{dx} = 3x^2$$

vanishes at $x = 0$, the inverse $x = g(y) = y^{1/3}$, although not differentiable at $y = 0$, clearly exists in a neighborhood of $y^0 = f(0) = 0$.

Systems of equations with continuously differentiable, implicit functions, namely,

$$f^1(x_1, \ldots, x_n, y_1, \ldots, y_m) = 0,$$
$$\vdots \qquad\qquad (A.4\text{-}4)$$
$$f^n(x_1, \ldots, x_n, y_1, \ldots, y_m) = 0,$$

or

$$f(x, y) = 0,$$

defined on $X \times Y$, have $(n+m)!/n!m!$ possible $n \times n$ Jacobians. When only partial derivatives with respect to $x_1, \ldots, x_n$ are involved, the same Jacobian as in (A.4-3) arises. In that circumstance, sufficient conditions ensuring the existence of a continuously differentiable, explicit function $x = g(y)$ defined in a neighborhood of y^0 in Y are provided by the implicit function theorem.[20] Chief among these are the existence of an x^0 in X such that

$$f(x^0, y^0) = 0, \qquad\qquad (A.4\text{-}5)$$

and at (x^0, y^0) the Jacobian of (A.4-4) is nonzero. Evidently (A.4-5) means that to apply the implicit function theorem there must already exist a solution of (A.4-4) for x^0 given y^0.

Consider the differentiable function $f(x, y, t) = 0$, where x and y are real, scalar variables and t is a parameter. Then f defines a family of curves in the x-y plane as t varies. An *envelope* of this family is a curve such that

    i) each curve of the family is tangent to the envelope curve at some point, and

    ii) at each point on the envelope curve, a curve of the family is tangent to the envelope curve.

---

20   Apostol [1, p. 374].

Points on the envelope often satisfy the system of equations

$$f(x, y, t) = 0,$$

$$f_t(x, y, t) = 0,$$

(A.4-6)

where x and y each depend on t and f_t is the partial derivative of f with respect to t. The equation of the envelope itself may sometimes be found by using (A.4-6) to eliminate t and express y as a function of x. Alternatively, the parametric expression of the envelope, namely,

$$x = g^1(t),$$

$$y = g^2(t),$$

is obtained by eliminating x from one equation of (A.4-6) and y from the other.[21]

A.5   DIFFERENTIAL EQUATIONS

Let X be an open, connected collection of vectors $x = (x_1, \ldots, x_n)$ of real numbers and set $T = \{t : 0 \leqslant t < \infty\}$, where t is a scalar frequently thought of as time. Consider the differential equation

$$\frac{dx}{dt} = f(x, t),$$

(A.5-1)

for some real-valued function $f = (f^1, \ldots, f^n)$ defined on $X \times T$. Thus (A.5-1) implicitly describes a relation between x and t by postulating that the rate of change of x over time at moment t depends both on t and on the value of x at t. To "solve" (A.5-1) means to find this implicit relation. Definitions of such notions as solution or path of (A.5-1), equilibrium point and path, locally and globally stable paths, and stability of (A.5-1) have been given in the text (Section 9.1) and are not repeated here.

A special case of (A.5-1) is the *nonhomogeneous* linear equation

$$\frac{dx}{dt} = Ax + b,$$

(A.5-2)

where A is an n by n matrix and b is an n-dimensional column vector of constants. One solution of (A.5-2) is obtained by setting $x = c$ for some

---

[21]   Wilson [12, pp. 135, 136].

vector of as-yet-to-be-determined constants $c = (c_1, \ldots, c_n)$. (It is sometimes convenient to write column vectors, like c, in row-vector form.) This results in

$$Ac + b = 0, \tag{A.5-3}$$

which can now be solved to produce c by Cramer's rule, provided the determinant $|A| \neq 0$. If $|A| = 0$, an alternative method must be used to find a c satisfying (A.5-3). In either case, c is an equilibrium point of (A.5-2). Note that when $|A| \neq 0$, the equilibrium point is unique.

To find the general solution of (A.5-2), consider first the *homogeneous* equation

$$\frac{dx}{dt} = Ax. \tag{A.5-4}$$

Substituting

$$x = ke^{\lambda t}, \tag{A.5-5}$$

into (A.5-4), with constants λ (a scalar) and $k = (k_1, \ldots, k_n)$ still to be determined, gives

$$\lambda k e^{\lambda t} = Ak e^{\lambda t},$$

or, denoting the identity matrix by $\mathcal{I}$,

$$(A - \lambda \mathcal{I})\, k = 0. \tag{A.5-6}$$

Thus, if (A.5-5) is to be a solution of (A.5-4), λ and k must satisfy (A.5-6). For the latter to occur when $k \neq 0$, λ has to be a root of the polynomial equation $|A - \lambda \mathcal{I}| = 0$. In general there are n such roots, $\lambda_1, \ldots, \lambda_n$. Corresponding to each root λ_i, a value for the vector k, namely k^i, is secured as a solution of

$$(A - \lambda_i \mathcal{I})\, k = 0.$$

This yields n solutions of (A.5-4) as follows:

$$x = k^i e^{\lambda_i t},$$

for $i = 1, \ldots, n$.

If all roots λ_i are distinct, then the general solution of (A.5-2) is

$$x = c + \sum_{i=1}^{n} \phi_i k^i e^{\lambda_i t}, \tag{A.5-7}$$

where the λ_i, k^i and c are found as indicated above, and the ϕ_i are arbitrary scalar constants.[22] Imposing the initial condition, say, $x = x^0$ when $t = 0$, on (A.5-7) leads to

$$x^0 - c = \sum_{i=1}^{n} \phi_i k^i. \tag{A.5-8}$$

Because the n by n matrix made up of rows $k^1, \ldots, k^n$ is nonsingular,[23] (A.5-8) can be solved so as to express the ϕ_i in terms of the elements of $x^0 - c$ and the k^i. Therefore the ϕ_i can be eliminated from (A.5-7) and the general solution written as a function of the starting point x^0 and t. When all roots are not distinct, more intricate formulae are required.[24]

Suppose now that all roots λ_i are distinct, negative real numbers. Then taking the limit of the right-hand term in (A.5-7),

$$\lim_{t \to \infty} \sum_{i=1}^{n} \phi_i k^i e^{\lambda_i t} = 0, \tag{A.5-9}$$

and hence all paths (A.5-7) converge to the equilibrium path defined by c. Not only are all equilibria locally stable, but the equation (A.5-2) itself is stable. Moreover, if c were a unique solution of (A.5-3), then the equilibrium path would be globally stable. When the limits in (A.5-9) are infinite, all nonequilibrium paths (A.5-7) diverge from each equilibrium path.

With complex and possibly nondistinct roots, a necessary and sufficient condition for (A.5-2) to stable is that the real parts of all roots be negative.[25] In addition, necessary and sufficient conditions ensuring negative real parts of all roots are provided by theorems of Liapunov and Routh-Hurwitz.[26] These latter results are not stated here.

Another special case of (A.5-l), more general than the linear equation of (A.5-2), is

$$\frac{dx}{dt} = g(x), \tag{A.5-10}$$

where g, defined on X, is independent of t. Sufficient conditions for the existence of a globally stable equilibrium path are derived from the so-called direct (or second) method of Liapunov. This is of interest because it yields

---

[22]   Hurewicz [9, Ch. 3].
[23]   Bellman [3, p. 17].
[24]   See Bellman [3, p. 24] and Hurewicz [9, Ch. 3].
[25]   Bellman [3, p. 25].
[26]   See Gantmacher [7, pp. 185-195].

stability information about a large class of equations that are not necessarily linear without requiring explicit knowledge of their solutions.

A *Liapunov* function with respect to $\overline{x}$ in X is a real-valued, continuous function V defined on X such that:

i) V is continuously differentiable on $X - \{\overline{x}\}$.

ii) $V(\overline{x}) = 0$, and $V(x) > 0$ for all x in X distinct from $\overline{x}$.

iii) For all x in X with $x \neq \overline{x}$,

$$\frac{dV(x)}{dt} = \sum_{i=1}^{n} \frac{\partial V(x)}{\partial x_i} \frac{dx_i}{dt} < 0.$$

The following theorem indicates that one way to infer global stability of an equilibrium path of (A.5- 10) is to produce a Liapunov function.

Theorem A.5-11[27]   Let $\overline{x}$ in X be an equilibrium point of (A.5-10). If a Liapunov function with respect to $\overline{x}$ exists, then the equilibrium path defined by $\overline{x}$ is globally stable.

REFERENCES

1. Apostol, T. M., *Mathematical Analysis*, 2nd ed. (Reading: Addison-Wesley, 1974).
2. Arrow, K. J. and A. C. Enthoven, "Quasi-Concave Programming," *Econometrica* 29 (1961), pp. 779-800.
3. Bellman, R., *Stability Theory of Differential Equations* (New York: McGraw-Hill, 1953).
4. ——, *Introduction to Matrix Analysis* (New York: McGraw-Hill, 1960).
5. Birkhoff, G. and S. MacLane, *A Survey of Modern Algebra*, revised ed. (New York: Macmillan, 1953).
6. Dunford, N. and J. T. Schwartz, *Linear Operators*, Part I: *General Theory* (New York: Interscience, 1964).
7. Gantmacher, F. R., *The Theory of Matrices*, v. 2 (New York: Chelsea, 1959).
8. Hirsch, M. and S. Smale, *Differential Equations, Dynamical Systems, and Linear Algebra* (New York: Academic Press, 1974).

---

27   Hirsch and Smale [8, p. 193].

9. Hurewicz, W., *Lectures on Ordinary Differential Equations* (New York: Wiley and Technology Press of Massachusetts Institute of Technology, 1958).

10. Katzner, D. W., *Static Demand Theory* (New York: Macmillan, 1970).

11. Rudin, W., *Principles of Mathematical Analysis*, 3rd ed. (New York: McGraw-Hill, 1976).

12. Wilson, E. B., *Advanced Calculus* (New York: Dover, 1958).

Appendix B

Hints, Partial Answers, and Answers for Selected Exercises

1.1 $(x,p) = (0,0)$, $\quad (x,p) = (1,1)$, $\quad (x,p) = (2,2)$.

2.3 For all x' and x'' in X, define the preference ordering $\succsim$ by

$$x' \succsim x'' \quad \text{if and only if} \quad u(x') \geqslant u(x'').$$

2.4 If $u(x)$ is a continuous representation of $\succsim$ and μ^0 is in the range of u,

$$\tau(\mu) = \begin{cases} \mu, & \text{if } \mu \leqslant \mu^0, \\[2mm] 2\mu, & \text{if } \mu > \mu^0, \end{cases}$$

then $\tau(u(x))$ is a representation of $\succsim$ that is not continuous.

2.6 Fix distinct scalars x' and x'' in X. If f defined on X is both concave and convex, then for any θ between 0 and 1,

$$f(x) = \theta f(x') + [1 - \theta] f(x''),$$

where

$$x = \theta x' + [1 - \theta] x''.$$

From the second equality,

$$\theta = \frac{x - x''}{x' - x''}, \qquad 1 - \theta = \frac{x' - x}{x' - x''}.$$

Hence, substituting these values for θ into the first equality,

$$f(x) = ax + b,$$

where a and b are the constants

$$a = \frac{f(x') - f(x'')}{x' - x''},$$

and

$$b = \frac{x'f(x'') - x''f(x')}{x' - x''}.$$

Therefore f is linear.

2.8 The preference ordering $\succsim$ is linear if and only if for any x' and x'' in X, $x' \approx x''$ implies

$$\alpha x' + \beta x \approx \alpha x'' + \beta x,$$

for any x in X and any real $\alpha \geqslant 0$ and $\beta \geqslant 0$.

2.9 Write $\mu^i = u(x^i)$ for $i = 1, 2, 3, 4$. Then the problem is to prove that the statement

$$\mu^1 - \mu^2 \geqslant \mu^3 - \mu^4 \quad \text{if and only if} \quad \tau(\mu^1) - \tau(\mu^2) \geqslant \tau(\mu^3) - \tau(\mu^4),$$

for all $\mu^1, \ldots, \mu^4$ in the range of u, is equivalent to the linearity of τ. Clearly, if τ is linear then the if-and-only-if statement follows.

Conversely, assume the if-and-only-if statement. Then an equality version of the if-and-only-if statement is implied, namely,

$$\mu^1 - \mu^2 = \mu^3 - \mu^4 \quad \text{if and only if} \quad \tau(\mu^1) - \tau(\mu^2) = \tau(\mu^3) - \tau(\mu^4),$$

for all $\mu^1, \ldots, \mu^4$ in the range of u. Without loss of generality, assume $\mu = 0$ is in the range of u and set $\tau(0) = 0$. The linearity of τ is shown once it is demonstrated that for all μ' and μ'' in the range of u,

$$\tau(\mu' + \mu'') = \tau(\mu') + \tau(\mu''),$$

and

$$\tau(\alpha\mu') = \alpha\tau(\mu'),$$

for all real α such that $\alpha\mu'$ is in the range of u. (See appendix Section A.3.) The first equation asserts that τ is additive; the second, that τ is linearly homogeneous.

Let μ' and μ'' in the range of u be given. Then first with $\mu^1 = (\mu' + \mu'')$, $\mu^2 = \mu'$, $\mu^3 = \mu''$ and $\mu^4 = 0$, and second with $\mu^1 = (\mu' - \mu'')$, $\mu^2 = \mu'$, $\mu^3 = 0$ and $\mu^4 = \mu''$, the equality version of the if-and-only-if statement ensures that

$$\tau(\mu' \pm \mu'') = \tau(\mu') \pm \tau(\mu'').$$

In particular, this proves additivity. Moreover, letting $\mu' = 0$,

$$\tau(-\mu'') = -\tau(\mu'').$$

Now, if α is any integer such that $\alpha\mu'$ and $(1/\alpha)\,\mu'$ are in the range of u, then repeated use of additivity implies

$$\tau(\alpha\mu') = \tau(\Sigma\mu') = \alpha\tau(\mu'),$$

and

$$\tau(\mu') = \tau\left(\Sigma\frac{1}{\alpha}\mu'\right) = \alpha\tau\left(\frac{1}{\alpha}\mu'\right),$$

where there are α terms in each sum. From the second equation,

$$\tau\left(\frac{1}{\alpha}\mu'\right) = \frac{1}{\alpha}\tau(\mu').$$

A similar argument applies to any rational α such that $\alpha\mu'$ is in the range of u. Thus, for such α, $\tau(\alpha\mu') = \alpha\tau(\mu')$. It remains to show that the same equality holds for all appropriate real α.

Thus let α be any real number such that $\alpha\mu'$ is in the range of u. Consider any rational sequence $\{\alpha^\varsigma\}$ converging to α, where $\alpha^\varsigma\mu'$ is in the range of u for each integer ς. Then,

$$\tau(\alpha\mu') = \tau\left(\left[\lim_{\varsigma\to\infty} a^\varsigma\right]\mu'\right)$$

$$= \lim_{\varsigma\to\infty} \tau(a^\varsigma\mu')$$

$$= \lim_{\varsigma\to\infty} a^\varsigma\tau(\mu')$$

$$= \alpha\tau(\mu').$$

Therefore τ is linearly homogeneous.

2.11 Differentiating $w_1 = -u_1/u_2$ with respect to x_1 (and remembering that $x_2 = w(x_1, \mu)$ where μ is constant) gives

$$w_{11} = -\frac{1}{(u_2)^2} \left[u_2 u_{11} - u_1 u_{21} + (u_2 u_{12} - u_1 u_{22}) w_1 \right].$$

Now substitute for w_1 and factor out $-1/u_2$.

2.12 Because, under (2.3-1) – (2.3-4), utility functions need not be continuous on the boundary of X. Consider, for example,

$$u(x_1, x_2) = \ln x_1 + \ln x_2.$$

2.14 $\mathcal{D} = \{(x_1, x_2) : x_1 \neq x_2\}, \qquad \Omega = \{(p_1, p_2, m) : p_1 \neq p_2\}.$

2.15 The demand function for good 1 in case (a) is

$$h^1(p, m) = \begin{cases} 0, & \text{if } p_1/p_2 > \alpha/\beta, \\[2mm] \left\{ x_1 : 0 \leqslant x_1 \leqslant \dfrac{m}{p_1} \right\}, & \text{if } p_1/p_2 = \alpha/\beta, \\[2mm] \dfrac{m}{p_1}, & \text{if } p_1/p_2 < \alpha/\beta. \end{cases}$$

In case (b) it is

$$h^1(p, m) = \frac{\beta m}{\beta p_1 + \alpha p_2}.$$

For case (c), h^1 is the same as in case (a) except that $\{x_1 : 0 \leqslant x_1 \leqslant m/p_1\}$ is replaced by $\{0, m/p_1\}$. In case (d), since the utility function reduces to $u(x_1, x_2) = \alpha x_1 + \beta x_2$, the demand function h^1 is identical to that of case (a).

2.16 The demand functions are

$$h^1(p, m) = \frac{2p_2 - m}{p_1} + 2,$$

$$h^2(p, m) = 2\frac{m - p_1}{p_2} - 2,$$

defined for all $(p, m) > 0$ such that

$$2p_2 + 2p_1 - m > 0,$$

$$m - p_1 - p_2 > 0.$$

From the second inequality $m - p_1 > 0$, so $h_2^2 < 0$ on this domain. (Good 2 is superior because $h_m^2 > 0$.) The plane $2p_2 = m$ separates points in the domain at which good 1 is Giffen ($m > 2p_2$) from those at which it is not ($m < 2p_2$).

2.17 The demand function for good 1 is

$$h^1(p, m) = \frac{m}{2p_1}.$$

The compensated demand function for good 1 is

$$h^{*1}(p, \mu) = \sqrt{\frac{\mu p_2}{p_1}}.$$

2.19 For any $(p, m) > 0$,

$$p_1 s^{11}(p, m) + p_2 s^{12}(p, m) = p_1(h_1^1 + h^1 h_m^1) + p_2(h_2^1 + h^2 h_m^1)$$

$$= p_1 h_1^1 + p_2 h_2^1 + m h_m^1$$

$$= 0,$$

by Euler's theorem (Theorem A.3-9 in appendix Section A.3). A similar argument shows $p_1 s^{21} + p_2 s^{22} = 0$. Hence the columns of S are linearly dependent and $|S|$ vanishes everywhere.

2.20 Differentiate the budget constraint with respect to m.

2.21 The first equality follows from Euler's theorem (Theorem A.3-9 in appendix Section A.3) and the last two are obtained by differentiation of the budget constraint.

2.22 Set $y' = (1, 0, \ldots, 0)$ in the definition of negative definiteness given in appendix Section A.4 as applied to $S(p, m)$.

2.25 For each value of μ, the μ-indifference curve is a $\frac{1}{4}$-circle of radius μ whose center lies at (μ, μ). The $\frac{1}{4}$-circle ends at $(\mu, 0)$ on the x_1-axis and at

$(0, \mu)$ on the x_2-axis where it is "tangent," respectively to those axes. Thus, for all $(p, m) > 0$, a tangency between an indifference curve and a budget line that defines the constrained utility-maximizing basket occurs at a vector interior to X. The only way a utility-maximizing basket could lie on the x_1-axis or x_2-axis is if $p_1 = 0$ or $p_2 = 0$, respectively. But $h(p, m)$ is defined only for $(p, m) > 0$.

2.26 To verify (c), show that, in general, $s^{12}(p, m) \neq s^{21}(p, m)$.

2.27 The "horizontal" distance between any two indifference curves is constant along those curves. That is, as x_2 changes, the difference between the x_1-values associated with x_2 on any two curves remains the same. The demand functions are

$$h^1(p, m) = \frac{m - p_1}{p_1},$$

$$h^2(p, m) = \frac{p_1}{p_2},$$

which are nonnegative on the domain $\{(p_1, p_2, m) : 0 < p_1 \leqslant m, p_2 > 0, m > 0\}$.

2.28 The first-order Lagrangean maximization equations include

$$\frac{u_1(x)}{u_2(x)} = \frac{p_1}{p_2},$$

$$\sum_{i=1}^{4} p_i x_i = m.$$

In view of the weak separability, these may be written as

$$\frac{\psi_1(x_1, x_2)}{\psi_2(x_1, x_2)} = \frac{p_1}{p_2},$$

$$p_1 x_1 + p_2 x_2 = \widehat{m},$$

where $\widehat{m} = m - p_3 x_3 + p_4 x_4$. Solving now yields

$$x_1 = \widehat{h}^1(p_1, p_2, \widehat{m}),$$

$$x_2 = \widehat{h}^2(p_1, p_2, \widehat{m}),$$

for appropriate functions $\widehat{h}^1$ and $\widehat{h}^2$.

3.1 From Exercise 2.19, $p_1 s^{11}(p, m) + p_2 s^{12}(p, m) = 0$. Because $p > 0$ and $s^{11}(p, m) < 0$ everywhere, $s^{12}(p, m) > 0$ everywhere.

3.2 $u(x_1, x_2) = x_1 x_2$.

3.5 $x^0 = h(p, m)$ and $x' = h(\alpha p, \alpha m)$ where $x^0 \neq x'$ and $\alpha > 0$, then $x^0 \widetilde{R} x'$ and $x' \widetilde{R} x^0$, contradicting the weak axiom of revealed preference.

3.7 From Theorem 3.4-3,

$$h^n = \frac{v_n}{v_i} h^i,$$

for all i and n. Hence

$$m = \sum_{n=1}^{I} p_n h^n = \frac{h^i}{v_i} \sum_{n=1}^{I} p_n v^n.$$

3.9 $v(p, m) = \ln m - \dfrac{1}{2} \ln 4 p_1 p_2$, $v_m(p, m) = \dfrac{1}{m}$.

3.11 No. It is inconsistent with the weak axiom of revealed preference.

3.12 $\mathcal{L} \leqslant 1$ implies $x' \widetilde{R} x''$.

3.13 For any i and $\theta > 0$,

$$v_m(\theta p, \theta m) = \frac{u_i(h(\theta p, \theta m))}{\theta p_i} = \theta^{-1} \frac{u_i(h(p, m))}{p_i} = \theta^{-1} v_m(p, m).$$

3.14 With $u(x_1, x_2) = u^1(x_1) + u^2(x_2)$, write

$$u_i^i(x_i) = \frac{du^i(x_i)}{dx_i} \quad \text{and} \quad u_{ii}^i(x_i) = \frac{d^2 u^i(x_i)}{(dx_i)^2},$$

for $i = 1, 2$. Then, from the first-order constrained maximization conditions,

$$u_i^i(h^i(p, m)) = \lambda p_i = \frac{p_i}{m}, \quad i = 1, 2.$$

Differentiation with respect to p_n, where $n \neq i$, now yields $u_{ii}^i h_n^i = 0$. Because $u_{ii}^i < 0$ by assumption,

$$h_n^i = 0, \quad i \neq n.$$

Therefore differentiation of the budget constraint $p_1 h^1 + p_2 h^2 = m$ with respect to, say p_1 leaves $p_1 h_1^1 + h^1 = 0$, whence

$$-h_1^1 \frac{p_1}{h^1} = 1.$$

3.15 Because the change from commodity space X to commodity space $\bar{X}$ can be viewed as a translation of the coordinate axes which shifts $(0,0)$ to $(0, -x_2^0)$, the only substantive alteration occurs in the positivity requirement of Figure 3.1. The new positivity property is:

$$h^1(p, m) > 0,$$

$$h^2(p, m) > -x_2^0,$$

for all $p > 0$ and $m > -p_2 x_2^0$.

3.17 Let $(p', m') > 0$ and $(p'', m'') > 0$ be such that $v(p', m') = v(p'', m'')$. It is necessary to show that for all θ where $0 \leq \theta \leq 1$,

$$v(\theta p' + [1 - \theta]p'', \theta m' + [1 - \theta]m'') \leq v(p', m').$$

Clearly if $\theta = 0$ or $\theta = 1$, then the latter inequality holds trivially as an equality.

Otherwise, consider any θ such that $0 < \theta < 1$ and suppose, for that θ, the required inequality were violated. Then there would exist an $\bar{x} > 0$ for which

$$(\theta p' + [1 - \theta]p'') \cdot \bar{x} = \theta m' + [1 - \theta]m'',$$

and

$$u(\bar{x}) > u(x') = u(x''),$$

where $\bar{x} = h(\theta p' + [1 - \theta]p'', \theta m' + [1 - \theta]m'')$, $x' = h(p', m')$, and $x'' = h(p'', m'')$. Since x' and x'' are utility maximizing baskets over their respective budget sets, this would mean that

$$p' \cdot \bar{x} > m',$$

$$p'' \cdot \bar{x} > m''.$$

Multiplying the first of these inequalities by θ and the second by $1 - \theta$, and then adding gives

$$(\theta p' + [1 - \theta]p'') \cdot \overline{x} > \theta m' + [1 - \theta]m'',$$

contrary to the original choice of $\overline{x}$. Therefore the required inequality must be satisfied.

3.18 First, since h^* is homogeneous of degree zero in p for each μ, the definition of e given in the exercise implies that e is homogeneous of degree one in p for each μ. Second, the derivatives e_μ and e_i (for all i) are positive on Υ because, using the properties of those derivatives stated in the exercise, both $h^*(p, \mu)$ and η (which depends on p and μ) are positive on Υ. Finally, the relationship between v and e may be stated as follows: For all $p > 0$,

$$v(p, e(p, \mu)) = \mu,$$

$$e(p, v(p, m)) = m,$$

where $v(p, m) = \mu$ and $e(p, \mu) = m$.

4.4 If f is homogeneous of degree one, then the partial derivatives f_1 and f_2 are homogeneous of degree zero. Now apply the equation of the general version of Euler's theorem (Theorem A.3-9 of appendix Section A.3) to f_1 and f_2.

4.6 By direct calculation,

$$\frac{f_1}{f_2} = \frac{\beta_1}{\beta_2} \frac{y_2}{y_1},$$

$$\frac{d(f_1/f_2)}{dy_1} = -\frac{\beta_1}{\beta_2} \frac{y_2}{(y_1)^2},$$

and

$$\frac{d(y_2/y_1)}{dy_1} = -\frac{y_2}{(y_1)^2}.$$

Now use (4.3-6).

4.7 Consider an isoquant $x^0 = f(y_1, y_2)$ where $x^0 > 0$. Because $0 < \sigma < 1$,

$$x^0 = \frac{Ay_1y_2}{[\alpha (y_2)^\rho + (1-\alpha)(y_1)^\rho]^{1/\rho}}.$$

Solving for y_2 gives

$$y_2 = \left[\frac{(1-\alpha)(x^0)^\rho}{A^\rho - \dfrac{(x^0)^\rho \alpha}{(y_1)^\rho}} \right]^{1/\rho}.$$

Hence

$$\lim_{y_1 \to \infty} \left[\frac{(1-\alpha)(x^0)^\rho}{A^\rho - \dfrac{(x^0)^\rho \alpha}{(y_1)^\rho}} \right]^{1/\rho} = \frac{x^0}{A}(1-\alpha)^{1/\rho},$$

so this isoquant is asymptotic to the line

$$\frac{x^0}{A}(1-\alpha)^{1/\rho}.$$

4.8 Homothetic production functions can be written in the form $\tau \circ f(y) = \tau(f(y))$, where the derivative $\tau'(x) > 0$ everywhere and f is homogeneous of some degree k. Since the partial derivatives of f are homogeneous of degree $k - 1$ (by Euler's theorem — Theorem A.3-9 of appendix Section A.3), those of $\tau \circ f$ may be expressed as

$$(\tau \circ f)_j(\alpha y) = \tau'(f(\alpha y))f_j(\alpha y),$$

$$= \tau'(f(\alpha y))\alpha^{k-1}f_j(y),$$

for $j = 1, \ldots, J$, all y in the interior of Y, and all $\alpha > 0$. Hence

$$\frac{(\tau \circ f)_j(\alpha y)}{(\tau \circ f)_J(\alpha y)} = \frac{f_j(y)}{f_J(y)} = \frac{(\tau \circ f)_j(y)}{(\tau \circ f)_J(y)},$$

where $j = 1, \ldots, J - 1$, so that the marginal rates of technical substitution generated by $\tau \circ f$ are constant along rays from the origin into the interior of Y.

4.9 For each $x > 0$,

$$
g^{*1}(r, x) = \begin{cases}
0, & \text{if } \dfrac{r_1}{r_2} \geqslant \dfrac{3}{2}, \\[2.5ex]
\{y_1 : 0 \leqslant y_1 \leqslant 2x\}, & \text{if } \dfrac{r_1}{r_2} = \dfrac{3}{2}, \\[2.5ex]
2x, & \text{if } \dfrac{3}{2} \geqslant \dfrac{r_1}{r_2} \geqslant \dfrac{1}{2}, \\[2.5ex]
\{y_1 : 2x \leqslant y_1 \leqslant 6x\}, & \text{if } \dfrac{r_1}{r_2} = \dfrac{1}{2}, \\[2.5ex]
6x, & \text{if } \dfrac{1}{2} \geqslant \dfrac{r_1}{r_2} > 0.
\end{cases}
$$

An analogous expression is obtained for $g^{*2}(r, x)$.

4.11 The expansion path in Y is

$$
y_2 = \frac{r_1}{r_2} \frac{\beta_2}{\beta_1} y_1.
$$

Hence

$$
g^{*1}(r, x) = \left[\frac{x}{B} \left(\frac{r_2 \beta_1}{r_1 \beta_2} \right)^{\beta_2} \right]^{1/(\beta_1 + \beta_2)},
$$

$$
g^{*2}(r, x) = \left[\frac{x}{B} \left(\frac{r_1 \beta_2}{r_2 \beta_1} \right)^{\beta_1} \right]^{1/(\beta_1 + \beta_2)},
$$

and

$$
TC(x) = Ax^{1/(\beta_1 + \beta_2)} + b,
$$

where

$$
A = (\beta_1 + \beta_2) \left[\frac{1}{B} \left(\frac{r_1}{\beta_1} \right)^{\beta_1} \left(\frac{r_2}{\beta_2} \right)^{\beta_2} \right]^{1/(\beta_1 + \beta_2)}
$$

and b is the firm's fixed cost.

4.13 The production function is $f(y_1, y_2) = (y_1 y_2)^{1/8}$.

4.14 As in the proof of Theorem 4.2-27,

$$\frac{dAP^1(y_1^0)}{dy_1} = -\frac{y_2^0}{(y_1^0)^2} MP^2(y_2^0).$$

4.15 According to Table 4.1, if f is homogeneous of degree one, then

$$\frac{dAVC(x)}{dx} = 0,$$

for all x in Γ. Hence $AVC(x)$ is independent of x. But as described in Section 4.5, $AVC(x)$ still depends on r. Thus set $\xi(r) = AVC(x)$.

4.16 If $f(y_1, y_2) = (y_1 y_2)^{1/2}$, then $TC(r, x) = 2x \, (r_1 r_2)^{1/2}$. This is concave in r but not strictly so. Actually, any example satisfying (4.1-2) $-$ (4.1-5) will do. For, in the proof of Theorem 4.5-4, if $r' = \alpha r''$ for some scalar $\alpha > 0$, then the cost-minimizing baskets of inputs associated with r', r'', and $\theta r' + [1 - \theta] \, r''$, namely y', y'', and $\overline{y}$, respectively, are all the same. Hence

$$TC(\theta r' + [1 - \theta] \, r'', x) = (\theta r' + [1 - \theta] \, r'') \cdot \overline{y}$$

$$= \theta r' \cdot y' + [1 - \theta] \, r'' \cdot y''$$

$$= \theta TC(r', x) + [1 - \theta] \, TC(r'', x).$$

No strict inequality is possible here.

4.17 The elasticity of $\zeta(y)$ with respect to the marginal rate of technical substitution along an isoquant is

$$\frac{f_1(y) \, / f_2(y)}{\zeta(y)} \frac{d\zeta(y)}{d(f_1(y) \, / f_2(y))}.$$

Substitution of $y_1 f_1 / y_2 f_2$ for $\zeta(y)$ and application of the implicit function theorem gives

$$\frac{1}{y_1/y_2} \frac{d\left(\dfrac{f_1(y) \, / f_2(y)}{y_2/y_1} \right)}{dy_1} \Bigg/ \left(\frac{d(f_1(y) \, / f_2(y))}{dy_1} \right).$$

Differentiation of the numerator using the quotient rule and employing (4.3-6) now yields $1 - \sigma(y)$.

4.19 Use the inequalities of (4.2-16) and (4.2-14) or (4.2-15). If f is homogeneous of degree κ, where $0 < \kappa < 1$, then, by Theorem A.3-9 of appendix Section A.3,

$$\sum_{j=1}^{J} y_j f_j(y) = \kappa f(y) < f(y),$$

for all $y > 0$. Now apply Theorem 4.5-9.

4.20 Pick any input, say the first, and let $\gamma_j = y_j^0/y_1^0$ be fixed parameters for $j = 2, \ldots, J$. Then along the ray $\{\alpha y^0 : \alpha \geqslant 0\}$, inputs vary according to $y_j = \gamma_j y_1$, for $j = 2, \ldots, J$. Hence, from the constant returns to scale,

$$x = f(y_1, \gamma_2 y_1, \ldots, \gamma_J y_1) = y_1 \Theta,$$

where $\Theta = f(1, \gamma_2, \ldots, \gamma_J)$ is also fixed. Differentiating with respect to τ gives

$$\frac{dx}{d\tau} = \frac{dy_1}{d\tau} \Theta,$$

which, upon division by $x = y_1 \Theta$ from above, results in

$$\frac{dx/d\tau}{x} = \frac{dy_1/d\tau}{y_1}.$$

A similar argument holds for each $j = 2, \ldots, J$.

4.21 Differentiate (4.5-1) and $x = f(g^*(r, x))$ with respect to r_j and combine the results.

4.22 The maximum output that can be produced is $x = 25$ and the unique basket of inputs producing it is $y = (4, 3)$. Each isoquant is a circle with center $y = (4, 3)$ and radius $\sqrt{25 - x}$, where x is the output associated with the isoquant and $0 \leq x \leq 25$.

The lower ridge line is given by the equation $y_1 = 4$ and the upper ridge line by $y_2 = 3$. The equation of the expansion path is

$$y_2 = \frac{r_2}{r_1} y_1 - 4 \frac{r_2}{r_1} + 3.$$

When $r_1 = r_2$, the equation of the expansion path reduces to $y_2 = y_1 - 1$. Substituting $x = 23$ and $y_2 = y_1 - 1$ into the equation defining the production function gives

$$(y_1)^2 - 8y_1 + 15 = 0,$$

whose left-hand side can be factored into

$$(y_1 - 3)(y_1 - 5) = 0.$$

From this and the equation of the expansion path it follows that there are two input baskets, namely $(3, 2)$ and $(5, 4)$, each of which is associated with a tangency between an isocost line whose slope is -1 and the given isoquant. But $(5, 4)$ lies beyond the unique output-maximizing basket and therefore maximizes the cost of producing output $x = 23$. It follows that $(3, 2)$ must be the cost minimizing basket.

4.23 Use Theorem 4.2-27 to calculate the lower ridge line from TP^2.

5.1 To avoid confusion in notation define the functions

$$\phi(y) = \pi(y) = pf(y) - r \cdot y - b,$$

$$\psi(x) = \pi(x) = px - r \cdot g^*(r, x) - b.$$

Then clearly $\phi(y) = \psi(f(y))$. Differentiating with respect to y_j gives

$$\phi_j(y) = \psi'(f(y)) f_j(y), \quad j = 1, \ldots J,$$

where ϕ_j indicates the partial derivative of ϕ with respect to y_j, and ψ' denotes the derivative of ψ with respect to the scalar x. Now ϕ and ψ can have maxima only where $f_j > 0$ for each j. Hence $\phi_j(y^0) = 0$ for each j if and only if $\psi'(x^0) = 0$ where $x^0 = f(y^0)$. Thus critical points of ϕ correspond to critical points of ψ. Because ϕ_j and ψ' must also have the same signs where $f_j > 0$, maxima of ϕ must correspond to maxima of ψ.

5.3 The output supply function (5.1-8) for $r > 0$ and $p \geqslant \tilde{p} > 0$, is the solution of $MC(x) = p$. Because $MC(x)$ is continuously differentiable, the solution of $MC(x) = p$ is too. The input demand functions of (5.1-9) for $r > 0$ and $p \geqslant \tilde{p} > 0$ are continuously differentiable because both g^* and g^{J+1} are continuously differentiable.

5.7 Proofs can be based on either Theorem 4.5-9 or on Equation (5.1-7).

5.8

$$g^3(r,p) = \left(\frac{\beta_1 + \beta_2}{A} p\right)^{(\beta_1+\beta_2)/(1-\beta_1-\beta_2)},$$

$$g^2(r,p) = \left(\frac{1}{B}\right)^{1/(\beta_1+\beta_2)} \left(\frac{r_1\beta_2}{r_2\beta_1}\right)^{\beta_1/(\beta_1+\beta_2)} \left(\frac{\beta_1 + \beta_2}{A} p\right)^{1/(1-\beta_1-\beta_2)},$$

$$g^1(r,p) = \left(\frac{1}{B}\right)^{1/(\beta_1+\beta_2)} \left(\frac{r_2\beta_1}{r_1\beta_2}\right)^{\beta_2/(\beta_1+\beta_2)} \left(\frac{\beta_1 + \beta_2}{A} p\right)^{1/(1-\beta_1-\beta_2)},$$

where A is defined in the answer to Exercise 4.11. The last two functions can be written as

$$g^2(r,p) = \left[Bp\left(\frac{\beta_1}{r_1}\right)^{\beta_1}\left(\frac{\beta_2}{r_2}\right)^{1-\beta_1}\right]^{1/(1-\beta_1-\beta_2)},$$

$$g^1(r,p) = \left[Bp\left(\frac{\beta_1}{r_1}\right)^{1-\beta_2}\left(\frac{\beta_2}{r_2}\right)^{\beta_2}\right]^{1/(1-\beta_1-\beta_2)},$$

which are also derivable directly from appropriate equations of the form of (5.1-11).

5.9

$$g^1(r,p) = g^2(r,p) = \left[\frac{p}{2(r_1+r_2)}\right]^2,$$

$$g^3(r,p) = \frac{p}{2(r_1+r_2)},$$

for all $(r,p) > 0$.

5.10 On the one hand, to obtain long-run total cost by setting $b = 0$ in the argument of Section 5.1 means that the function $LRTC(x)$ is derived by minimizing

$$\sum_{j=1}^{J} r_j y_j$$

over all $(y_1, \ldots, y_J)$ subject to $f(y_1, \ldots, y_J) = x$. On the other hand, if short-run average (or, equivalently, total) cost is to be minimized over all vectors defining associated plants that the firm might construct, then using (5.2-1), the function $LRTC(x)$ is obtained from minimizing

$$\sum_{j=1}^{\delta} r_j g^{*j}(r_1, \ldots, r_\delta, x, y_{\delta+1}, \ldots, y_J) + \sum_{j=\delta+1}^{J} r_j y_j$$

over all $(y_{\delta+1}, \ldots, y_J)$ subject to

$$f(g^{*1}(r_1, \ldots, r_\delta, x, y_{\delta+1}, \ldots, y_J), \ldots,$$

$$g^{*\delta}(r_1, \ldots, r_\delta, x, y_{\delta+1}, \ldots, y_J), y_{\delta+1}, \ldots, y_J) = x.$$

Because x is the same in either case, and because, at the minimizing $(y_{\delta+1}, \ldots, y_J)$, the two y_j's are the same with

$$y_j = g^{*j}(r_1, \ldots, r_\delta, x, y_{\delta+1}, \ldots, y_J),$$

for $j = 1, \ldots, \delta$, these two minimizations amount to the same thing.

5.11   The short-run average total cost functions are

$$ATC(x) = \frac{r_1 x}{y_2^0} + \frac{r_2 y_2^0}{x}.$$

For each value of x, $ATC(x)$ is minimized with respect to y_2^0 when

$$y_2^0 = x\sqrt{\frac{r_1}{r_2}}.$$

Substitution of this value back into $ATC(x)$ gives

$$LRAC(x) = 2\sqrt{r_1 r_2},$$

which is the same as the average total cost function derived through equation (4.5-1) using the long-run production function and setting $b = 0$. Differentiation of $ATC(x)$ with respect to x and equating the result to zero gives the minimizing value

$$x = y_2^0 \sqrt{\frac{r_2}{r_1}}$$

of each short-run average total cost function. To the left of this value, the graph of $ATC(x)$ is downward sloping; to the right it slopes upward. At the minimum,

$$ATC(x) = 2\sqrt{r_1 r_2}.$$

5.13

$$\frac{\partial p}{\partial r_1} = \frac{\left(r_1 \dfrac{\partial y_1}{\partial r_1} + y_1 + r_2 \dfrac{\partial y_2}{\partial r_1}\right) f - (r_1 y_1 + r_2 y_2)\left(f_1 \dfrac{\partial y_1}{\partial r_1} + f_2 \dfrac{\partial y_2}{\partial r_1}\right)}{(f)^2}.$$

Using (5.2-12) to eliminate f_1 and f_2, and noting that $r_1 y_1 + r_2 y_2 = pf$ this reduces to

$$\frac{\partial p}{\partial r_1} = \frac{y_1}{f(y)}.$$

5.14 Because

i) $x > \ln(1 + x)$, for all $x > 0$,

ii) $x = \ln(1 + x)$, for $x = 0$, and

iii) $x - \ln(1 + x)$ declines continuously to zero as $x \to 0$ and is unbounded as $x \to +\infty$.

it follows that $f(0) = 0$ and $f(y) > 0$ for $y > 0$. Applying the technique for implicit differentiation of the production function yields the first-order derivative

$$f'(y) = \frac{1+x}{x} > 1,$$

for $y > 0$. Because the second derivative

$$f''(y) = -\frac{1}{x^2}\frac{dx}{dy} = -\frac{x+1}{x^3} < 0,$$

for all $y > 0$, f is strictly concave.

Now

$$TC(x) = r\left[x - \ln\left(1 + x\right)\right] - b,$$

and so

$$MC(x) = r\frac{x}{1+x} > 0,$$

and

$$\frac{dMC(x)}{dx} = r\frac{1}{(1+x)^2} > 0,$$

for $x > 0$. Clearly $MC(x) < r$ for each $x > 0$. Finally, the input demand and output supply functions are, respectively,

$$g^2(r,p) = \frac{p}{r-p},$$

and

$$g^1(r,p) = \frac{p}{r-p} - \ln\frac{r}{r-p},$$

each on the domain for which $r > 0$ and $0 < p < r$.

5.16 If $f(y)$ is strictly concave on Y then for any y' and y'' in Y and any θ, where $0 < \theta < 1$,

$$\pi(\theta y' + [1-\theta]y'') = pf(\theta y' + [1-\theta]y'') - r \cdot (\theta y' + [1-\theta]y'') - b$$

$$> p\{\theta f(y') + [1-\theta]f(y'')\} - \theta r \cdot y' - [1-\theta]r \cdot y''$$

$$- \{\theta b + [1-\theta]b\}$$

$$= \theta\pi(y') + [1-\theta]\pi(y'').$$

The strict convexity of $TC(x)$ follows from Theorem 5.1-6, and the strict concavity of $\pi(x)$ follows from Theorem 5.1-6 and the fact that

$$\frac{d\pi^2(x)}{dx^2} = -\frac{dMC(x)}{dx},$$

on Γ.

5.17

$$\frac{r_2}{p} = \left[B(\beta_1)^{\beta_1}(1-\beta_1)^{1-\beta_1}\right]^{1/(1-\beta_1)}\left(\frac{r_1}{p}\right)^{-\beta_1/(1-\beta_1)}.$$

5.18

$$TC(r, x) = \frac{r_1 r_2}{r_1 + r_2}(x)^2 + b,$$

$$g^1(r, p) = \left(\frac{p}{2r_1}\right)^2,$$

$$g^2(r, p) = \left(\frac{p}{2r_2}\right)^2,$$

$$g^3(r, p) = \frac{r_1 + r_2}{r_1 r_2}\left(\frac{p}{2}\right).$$

5.19

$$TC(r, x) = \frac{r_1}{a_1}(x - c) + b.$$

The profit-maximizing output is $x = 2c$.

5.20 With $r_1 = 1$ and $r_2 = 4$, the firm's expansion path is

$$y_2 = \tfrac{1}{4}y_1.$$

Since, along this path, $MC(r, x) = 4$ and $p = 10$, the firm's profit over that path is maximized where $y_1 = 5$ and $y_2 = 5/4$. At that maximum, $\pi = 15$.

However, with $y_1 = 5$, profit as a function of y_2 is

$$\pi(y_2) = 10\sqrt{5y_2} - 4y_2 - 5,$$

which is maximized with respect to y_2 where $y_2 = 125/16 < 20$. Hence the maximum profit the firm is able to secure occurs where $y_1 = 5$ and $y_2 = 125/16$. Using this latter basket of inputs, $x = 25/4$ and $\pi = 26.25$. Clearly the input basket $(5, 125/16)$ does not lie on the firm's expansion path.

5.21 Write the firm's profit as

$$\pi = p_1 x_1 + p_2 x_2 - r_1 y_1 - r_2 y_2,$$

and choose (x_1, x_2, y_1, y_2) so as to maximize π subject to $f(x_1, x_2, y_1, y_2) = 0$.

6.1 Market equilibrium values are

$$p_1 = \left[\frac{(r_1 + r_2)\, mK}{L_1} \right]^{1/2},$$

$$x_1 = \frac{1}{2} \left[\frac{mKL_1}{r_1 + r_2} \right]^{1/2}.$$

6.2 $p_1 = 4, \quad x_1 = 100, \quad L_1 = 50.$

6.5 Before taxation, $p_1 \cong 2.4$ and $x_1 \cong 21$. After imposition of the specific tax, $p_1 = 3$ and $x_1 \cong 17$. After imposition of the ad valorem tax, $p_1 \cong 3.2$ and $x_1 \cong 16$.

7.1 $p_1/p_2 = 1, \quad x_{11} = x_{21} = 2, \quad x_{12} = x_{22} = 3.$

7.3 $p_1 = p_2 = \frac{1}{2}$. The equilibrium price ratio and equilibrium quantities are the same as those of Exercise 7.1.

7.4 The equation of the offer curve of person 1 is

$$2x_{11}x_{21} = 3x_{11} + x_{21}.$$

The equation of the offer curve of person 2 is

$$2x_{12}x_{22} = 2x_{12} + 4x_{22}.$$

Expressed in terms of the coordinates of person 1, the offer curve of person 2 is

$$2x_{11}x_{21} = 8x_{11} + 6x_{21} - 20.$$

7.5 With $x_{01}^0 = 4$ and $x_{02}^0 = 6$, equilibrium money prices are $p_1 = p_2 = 1$, and equilibrium quantities are the same as in Exercise 7.1.

7.8 (a) The minimum utility that person 1 has to accept is $u^1(1, 3) = 3$ and his indifference curve through basket $(1, 3)$ is $x_{11}x_{21} = 3$. The minimum utility that person 2 has to accept is $u^2(4, 2) = 8$ and his indifference curve through basket $(4, 2)$ is $x_{11}x_{21} = 8$.

    Maximizing person 1's utility subject to the constraints $u^2(x_{12}, x_{22}) = \mu^0$, $x_{11} + x_{12} = 5$, and $x_{21} + x_{22} = 5$ leads to the equation $x_{11}x_{22} = x_{12}x_{21}$.

Expressing the latter equation in the coordinate system of person 1 (by combining it with the constraints $x_{11} + x_{12} = 5$ and $x_{21} + x_{22} = 5$) gives $x_{11} = x_{21}$. In the coordinate system of person 2 that equation is $x_{12} = x_{22}$.

Person 1's indifference curve through $(1, 3)$ intersects the graph of $x_{11} = x_{21}$ at $x_{11} = x_{21} = \sqrt{3}$. This leaves person 2 with $x_{12} = x_{22} = 5 - \sqrt{3}$. Person 2's indifference curve through $(4, 2)$ intersects the graph of $x_{12} = x_{22}$ at $x_{12} = x_{22} = 2\sqrt{2}$. This leaves person 1 with $x_{11} = x_{21} = 5 - 2\sqrt{2}$. Therefore the core of the exchange model is $\{(x_{11}, x_{21}, x_{12}, x_{22}) : x_{11} = x_{21}, x_{12} = x_{22}, \sqrt{3} \leqslant x_{11} \leqslant 5 - 2\sqrt{2}, \text{ and } 2\sqrt{2} \leqslant x_{12} \leqslant 5 - \sqrt{3}\}$ and the equilibrium distribution (from the answer to Exercise 7.1) $x_{11} = x_{21} = 2$, $x_{12} = x_{22} = 3$ is in the core.

(b) In this case, $u^1(1, 2) = u^1(2, 1) = 2$ for both 1_A and 1_B. Now the midpoint of the straight line segment connecting these two baskets is $\frac{1}{2}(1, 2) + \frac{1}{2}(2, 1) = \left(\frac{3}{2}, \frac{3}{2}\right)$ and

$$u^1\left(\frac{3}{2}, \frac{3}{2}\right) = 2\frac{1}{4} > u^1(1, 2) = u^1(2, 1).$$

This means that 1_A and 1_B prefer $\left(\frac{3}{2}, \frac{3}{2}\right)$ to both $(1, 2)$ and $(2, 1)$. Moreover, since the combined quantities of goods are the same as their combined initial endowments, namely $(3, 3)$, by trading among themselves, each can achieve $\left(\frac{3}{2}, \frac{3}{2}\right)$. Therefore the distribution $(1, 2, 2, 1, x_{12_A}, x_{22_A}, x_{12_B}, x_{22_B})$ cannot be in the core regardless of the values that are assigned to $x_{12_A}, x_{22_A}, x_{12_B}$, and x_{22_B}.

(c) Here $u^1(3, 1) = 3$ for 1_A and the midpoint on the straight line segment connecting this baskets and $(2, 4)$ is $(2.5, 2.5)$. Furthermore, $u^2(2, 1) = 2$ for 2_A and the midpoint on the straight line segment connecting this baskets and $(3, 4)$ is also $(2.5, 2.5)$. Since, for each i, $u^i(2.5, 2.5) = 6.25$ is larger than $u^1(3, 1)$ and $u^2(2, 1)$, person 1_A prefers $(2.5, 2.5)$ to $(3, 1)$ and person 2_A prefers $(2.5, 2.5)$ to $(2, 1)$. And since the combined quantities of goods remains the same as their combined initial endowments, namely $(5, 5)$, both 1_A and 2_A can achieve $(2.5, 2.5)$ by trading among themselves. Hence the redistribution $(3, 1, 2, 4, 2, 1, 3, 4)$ is not in the core.

(d) This follows from the equal treatment result previously stated in the exercise and a maximization argument similar to that of the answer to Exercise 7.8(a).

(e) At the redistribution $(1.8, 1.8, 1.8, 1.8, 3.2, 3.2, 3.2, 3.2)$, $u^1(1.8, 1.8) = 3.24$ and $u^2(3.2, 3.2) = 10.24$. Obtain the requisite "nearby" baskets as follows: From the linear combination $\frac{1}{2}(1, 3) + \frac{1}{2}(1.8, 1.8) = (1.4, 2.4)$ subtract .02 from good 1 for persons 1_A and 1_B, and give what was taken from these individuals to person 2_A. The resulting allocation among 1_A, 1_B, and 2_A is:

$$(x_{11_A}, x_{21_A}) = (x_{11_B}, x_{21_B}) = (1.38, 2.4)$$

and

$$(x_{12_A}, x_{22_A}) = (3.24, 3.2).$$

This allocation uses up $(6, 8)$, which is the combined initial endowments for these three persons. But since

$$u^1(1.38, 2.4) = 3.312 > u^1(1.8, 1.8)$$

for both 1_A and 1_B, and

$$u^2(3.24, 3.2) = 10.368 > u^2(3.2, 3.2)$$

for 2_A, these persons all prefer their portion of the new allocation to what they receive in $(1.8,1.8,1.8,1.8,3.2,3.2,3.2,3.2)$. But the new allocation for the three persons requires the same quantities of goods as their combined initial endowments. Therefore $(1.8,1.8,1.8,1.8,3.2,3.2,3.2,3.2)$ cannot be contained in the core.

7.9 Using the utility functions and initial endowments of Exercise 7.1, the product to be maximized is

$$z = (x_{11}x_{21} - 3)(x_{12}x_{22} - 8).$$

From the equations $x_{i1} + x_{i2} = x_{i1}^0 + x_{i2}^0$, for $i = 1, 2$, and the given initial endowments,

$$x_{12} = 5 - x_{11} \quad \text{and} \quad x_{22} = 5 - x_{21}.$$

Substituting these into the product to be maximized leads to

$$z = 14x_{11}x_{21} - 5(x_{11})^2x_{21} - 5x_{11}(x_{21})^2 + (x_{11}x_{21})^2 + 15(x_{11} + x_{21}) - 51.$$

Differentiating and equating the derivatives to zero gives the first-order maximization equations

$$\frac{\partial z}{\partial x_{11}} = 14x_{21} - 10x_{11}x_{21} - 5(x_{21})^2 + 2x_{11}(x_{21})^2 + 15 = 0,$$

$$\frac{\partial z}{\partial x_{21}} = 14x_{11} - 5(x_{11})^2 - 10x_{11}x_{21} + 2(x_{11})^2x_{21} + 15 = 0.$$

If the solution of these equations, *i.e.*, the Nash equilibrium, is to be in the core, then from the answer to Exercise 7.8(a), $x_{11} = x_{21} = a$ and $x_{12} = x_{22} = b$, for appropriate values a and b. Substitution of the former into either of the first-order maximization equations yields the polynomial equation

$$2a^3 - 15a^2 + 14a + 15 = 0.$$

Since the competitive equilibrium distribution has (from the answer to Exercise 7.1) $a = 2$ and $b = 3$, and since $a = 2$ does not satisfy this equation, the Nash equilibrium cannot be the competitive equilibrium.

To demonstrate that the Nash equilibrium exists and is in the core, it is only necessary to show that a solution of the polynomial equation, call it $\bar{a}$, exists and satisfies, from the answer to Exercise 7.8(a), the inequality

$$\sqrt{3} \leqslant a \leqslant 5 - 2\sqrt{2}.$$

Once this is established, set $\bar{b} = 5 - \bar{a}$. The Nash equilibrium is $\bar{x} = (\bar{a}, \bar{a}, \bar{b}, \bar{b})$. Now the existence of the requisite $\bar{a}$ can be verified by exhibiting two distinct values a' and a'', both satisfying the above inequality, and such that, evaluated at, a', say, the left-hand side of the polynomial equation is positive, while at a'' it is negative. Then, since the left-hand side is continuous, there would have to exist an $\bar{a}$ between a' and a'' that satisfies both the inequality and the polynomial equation. The following values of a' and a'' accomplish what is required:

 i) At $a' = 1.75$ ($> \sqrt{3} = 1.73$), the left-hand side of the polynomial equation is $4.28 > 0$.

 ii) At $a'' = 2$ ($< 5 - 2\sqrt{2} = 2.17$), the left-hand side of the polynomial equation is $-1 < 0$.

8.1 Out of all the $y_{i\ell j}$ choose one variable from each constraint j and, using the x-notation of (A.3-17), label it x_j for $j = 1, \dots, J$. Write $x = (x_1, \dots, x_J, \dots)$, where the order of the $y_{i\ell j}$ following x_J in the vector x is arbitrary. Employing the g-notation of (A.3-17), represent the system of constraints as

$$g^j(x) = \sum_{\ell=1}^{L_i} y_{i\ell j} - y_{ij}, \quad j = 1, \dots, J.$$

Then the constraint-qualification matrix of interest is

$$\begin{bmatrix} \dfrac{\partial g^1}{\partial x_1} & \cdots & \dfrac{\partial g^1}{\partial x_J} \\ \vdots & & \vdots \\ \dfrac{\partial g^J}{\partial x_1} & \cdots & \dfrac{\partial g^J}{\partial x_J} \end{bmatrix},$$

which is the identity matrix whose determinant is unity. Therefore the constraint qualification is satisfied.

Now maximizing

$$x_i = \sum_{\ell=1}^{L_i} f^{i\ell}(y_{i\ell 1}, \ldots, y_{i\ell J}),$$

subject to the J constraints

$$\sum_{\ell=1}^{L_i} y_{i\ell j} = y_{ij}, \quad j = 1, \ldots, J,$$

yields the $JL_i - J$ equations

$$f_j^{i\ell} = f_j^{i1}, \quad j = 1, \ldots, J, \ \ell = 2, \ldots, L_i.$$

The last two sets of equations constitute a system of JL_i equations, which can be solved to express each $y_{i\ell j}$ as a function of all y_{ij}. Substitution of these solutions into the first equation above gives the industry production function.

8.2 The equation

$$y_{11} y_{22} = y_{12} y_{21},$$

together with the input constraints

$$y_{11} + y_{21} = a_1,$$

$$y_{12} + y_{22} = a_2,$$

define the contract set. The implied curve in the coordinate system of industry 1 representing that industry's behavior is

$$y_{12} = \frac{a_2}{a_1} y_{11},$$

where a_1 and a_2 are, respectively, the fixed supplies of factors 1 and 2. The transformation curve is

$$x_2 = \sqrt{a_1 a_2} - x_1.$$

8.4 Each row of the matrix of the constraint qualification is made up of the partial derivatives of the four constraints with respect to one of the six input variables. There are 15 different 4×4 matrices that can be constructed from different combinations of such rows. Only three of these have a vanishing determinant; the remainder do not. The constraint qualification is satisfied since it is only necessary for one of the determinants to be different from zero.

If a_1 and a_2 are, respectively, the fixed supplies of factors 1 and 2, then the curve identified with the contract set in the coordinate system of industry 1 is

$$y_{12} = \frac{a_2}{a_1} y_{11}.$$

8.6 With minor modification, the argument in the first paragraph of the answer to Exercise 8.4 that the constraint qualification is satisfied applies here. The curve identified with the contract set is the line determined by the intersection of the planes $y_{12} = (a_2/a_1)\, y_{11}$ and $y_{13} = (a_3/a_1)\, y_{11}$, where a_1, a_2, and a_3 are, respectively, the fixed supplies of factors 1, 2, and 3. The equation of the transformation curve is

$$(x_1)^{4/3} + (x_2)^{4/3} = (a_1 a_2 a_3)^{1/3}.$$

8.7 The supply function for industry 1 is

$$\widehat{G}^1(p) = \begin{cases} 0, & \text{if } p_1 < p_2, \\[2mm] \left\{x : 0 \leqslant x_1 \leqslant \sqrt{a_1 a_2}\right\}, & \text{if } p_1 = p_2, \\[2mm] \sqrt{a_1 a_2}, & \text{if } p_1 > p_2. \end{cases}$$

8.8 The curve identified with the contract set in terms of the input variables of industry 1 is

$$y_{12} = \frac{4 a_2 y_{11}}{a_1 + 3 y_{11}},$$

where a_1 and a_2 are, respectively, the fixed supplies of factors 1 and 2. That the transformation curve is not linear now follows from Theorem 8.1-15.

8.9 The equation of the transformation curve is

$$x_2 = a - \tfrac{1}{2}\left(x_1\right)^2.$$

The output supply and input demand functions in industry 1 are, respectively,

$$\widehat{G}^{12}(p) = \begin{cases} \dfrac{p_1}{p_2}, & \text{if } \sqrt{2a} \geqslant \dfrac{p_1}{p_2} > 0, \\[2ex] \sqrt{2a}, & \text{if } \dfrac{p_1}{p_2} > \sqrt{2a}, \end{cases}$$

$$\widehat{G}^{11}(p) = \begin{cases} \dfrac{1}{2}\left(\dfrac{p_1}{p_2}\right)^2, & \text{if } \sqrt{2a} \geqslant \dfrac{p_1}{p_2} > 0, \\[2ex] a, & \text{if } \dfrac{p_1}{p_2} > \sqrt{2a}. \end{cases}$$

Those in industry 2 are

$$\widehat{G}^{22}(p) = \widehat{G}^{21}(p) = \begin{cases} a - \dfrac{1}{2}\left(\dfrac{p_1}{p_2}\right)^2, & \text{if } \sqrt{2a} \geqslant \dfrac{p_1}{p_2} > 0, \\[2ex] 0, & \text{if } \dfrac{p_1}{p_2} > \sqrt{2a}. \end{cases}$$

8.10 Let A and B be matrices whose representative elements are, respectively, a_{ij} and b_{ij}. Denote the matrix of elements $a_{ij} + b_{ij}$ by $A + B$. Then for any column vector y,

$$y'(A + B)\,y = y'Ay + y'By,$$

where y' is the transpose of y.

8.11 When both factors are fully employed, $x_1 = 240$ and $x_2 = 60$. The range of price ratios consistent with the full employment of both factors is $1/3 \leqslant p_1/p_2 \leqslant 4/5$. When factor 1 is not fully utilized, $p_1/p_2 = 1/3$ and $r_2/p_2 = 1/6$. When factor 2 is not fully utilized, $p_1/p_2 = 4/5$ and $r_1/p_2 = 1/5$.

8.12 The community utility function is

$$u^H(x_1, x_2) = x_1 x_2.$$

At long-run equilibrium, $p_1 = p_2 = 1$, $x_1 = x_2 = \frac{1}{2}(a_1 a_2)^{1/2}$, $y_{ij} = \frac{1}{2}a_j$ for $i = 1, 2$ and $j = 1, 2$, $r_1 = \frac{1}{2}(a_2/a_1)^{1/2}$, $r_2 = \frac{1}{2}(a_1/a_2)^{1/2}$, $x_{11} = x_{21} = (5/24)(a_1 a_2)^{1/2}$, and $x_{12} = x_{22} = (7/24)(a_1 a_2)^{1/2}$.

8.13 The community utility function is

$$
u^H(x) = \begin{cases} 3x_1 x_2, & \text{if } x_1 \geqslant 3x_2 \text{ or } 3x_1 \leqslant x_2, \\ \dfrac{9}{16}(x_1 + x_2)^2, & \text{if } x_1 < 3x_2 \text{ and } 3x_1 > x_2. \end{cases}
$$

At short-run equilibrium, $p_1 = p_2 = 1$, $x_1 = x_2 = 5$, $y_1 = y_2 = 12\frac{1}{2}$, the input price is $1/5$, and $x_{11} = x_{21} = x_{12} = x_{22} = 5/2$.

8.14 Homotheticity implies all expansion paths are rays from origins into input spaces. Hence if the contract curve and any expansion path have two interior points in common, then they must coincide.

8.15 Note first the assumptions of differentiability "as needed" and of sufficient properties to ensure a 1–1 correspondence between input and output prices permit p_2/p_1 to be thought of as the differentiable function of the single variable r_2/r_1 required in (ii) and also permit each z_i to be thought of as the differentiable function of the same single variable in (i). Note further that the results of Exercise 5.15, appropriately modified to apply here, are

(iii) $\qquad r_1 = p_i \dfrac{dv^i(z_i)}{dz_i}$,

(iv) $\qquad r_2 = p_i \left[v^i(z_i) - z_i \dfrac{dv^i(z_i)}{dz_i} \right]$,

for $i = 1, 2$.

To prove (i), divide (iii) into (iv) so that

$$
\frac{r_2}{r_1} = \frac{v^i(z_i)}{\dfrac{dv^i(z_i)}{dz_i}} - z_i.
$$

Upon differentiating with respect to z_i and simplifying,

(v) $$\frac{d\left(\dfrac{r_2}{r_1}\right)}{dz_i} = -\frac{v^i(z_i)\dfrac{d^2 v^i(z_i)}{(dz_i)^2}}{\left[\dfrac{dv^i(z_i)}{dz_i}\right]^2}, \quad i = 1, 2.$$

According to the inverse function theorem (see appendix Section A.4), $dz_i/d(r_2/r_1)$ is the reciprocal of $d(r_2/r_1)/dz_1$ in (v). Result (i) now follows from the assumptions made on v^i and its derivatives.

To prove (ii), divide one equation of (iii) into the other:

(vi) $$\frac{p_2}{p_1} = \frac{\dfrac{dv^1(z_1)}{dz_1}}{\dfrac{dv^2(z_2)}{dz_2}}.$$

Differentiation with respect to r_1/r_2 and elimination of $dz_i/d(r_2/r_1)$ by substitution from the reciprocal of (v) yields

$$\frac{d\left(\dfrac{p_2}{p_1}\right)}{d\left(\dfrac{r_2}{r_1}\right)} = \frac{\dfrac{dv^1(z_1)}{dz_1}}{v^2(z_2)} - \frac{\left[\dfrac{dv^1(z_1)}{dz_1}\right]^2}{v^1(z_1)\dfrac{dv^2(z_2)}{dz_2}}.$$

Dividing this equation by (vi), and using the fact, obtained by combining (iii) and (iv), that

$$\frac{\dfrac{dv^i(z_i)}{dz_i}}{v^i(z_i)} = \frac{1}{z_i + \dfrac{r_2}{r_1}}, \quad i = 1, 2,$$

gives

$$\frac{p_1}{p_2}\frac{d(p_2/p_1)}{d(r_2/r_1)} = \frac{1}{z_2 + (r_2/r_1)} - \frac{1}{z_1 + (r_2/r_1)}.$$

Result (ii) follows immediately.

8.16 If the transformation surface is linear, then as in the proof of Theorem 8.1-15, any point on it can be written in the form

$$\left(f^1(\gamma_1 a_1, \ldots, \gamma_1 a_J), \ldots, f^I(\gamma_I a_1, \ldots, \gamma_I a_J)\right),$$

for suitable $(\gamma_1, \ldots, \gamma_I)$. Hence the input proportions

$$\frac{y_{ij}}{y_{iJ}} = \frac{a_j}{a_J}, \quad i = 1, \ldots I, \ j = 1, \ldots, J-1,$$

are fixed over the transformation surface and identical for all firms.
  Conversely, if

$$\frac{y_{ij}}{y_{iJ}} = \psi_j, \quad i = 1, \ldots, I, \ j = 1, \ldots, J-1,$$

for some constants $\psi_1, \ldots, \psi_J$, then in the input space of each industry i, the curve identified with the contract set and defined by

$$y_{ij} = \psi_j y_{iJ}, \quad j = 1, \ldots, J-1,$$

is linear. By Theorem 8.1-15, the transformation surface is linear.

8.18 Since the price of circulating money is set at unity, the normalization employed in the proof of Theorem 8.4-3, namely $\bar{p}_I = 1$, has to be discarded. Hence it also becomes necessary to replace the equation $\bar{r}_J = f_J^I(\bar{y}_I)$ with

$$\frac{\bar{r}_J}{\bar{p}_I} = f_J^I(\bar{y}_I).$$

However, this, together with the input price ratios $\bar{r}_j/\bar{r}_J$ (obtained in Theorem 8.4-3 from the marginal rates of technical substitution) determine all ratios of the form

$$\frac{\bar{r}_j}{\bar{p}_I}, \quad j = 1, \ldots, J.$$

Therefore, instead of $\bar{p}_I = 1$, the price $\bar{p}_I$ may be defined as the right-hand side of the following equation derived from (8.4-7):

$$\bar{p}_I = \frac{\displaystyle\sum_{k=1}^{K} x_{0k}^0}{\delta \left[\displaystyle\sum_{n=I+1}^{I+J} \frac{\bar{r}_n}{\bar{p}_I} z_n^0 \right]},$$

where δ and the x_{0k}^0 and z_n^0 are given parameters as described at the end of Section 8.4. The remainder of the argument is similar to Theorem 8.4-3.

9.4 The market excess price function is

$$\Xi(x) = \frac{(\gamma - \alpha)\,x - \gamma\beta + \alpha\delta}{\alpha\gamma}.$$

Equilibrium occurs when $\omega = 0$ and

$$x = \frac{\beta\gamma - \alpha\delta}{\gamma - \alpha},$$

which is identical to equilibrium in the two-good example of Section 9.3. Stability requires

$$\frac{\gamma - \alpha}{\alpha\gamma}\theta < 0,$$

and if $\theta > 0$ this reduces to $1/\alpha < 1/\gamma$. Therefore, as in the two-good example of Section 9.3 with $\theta > 0$, Figure 9.3(a) depicts a stable situation and Figure 9.3(d) an unstable one. But the results for the other two diagrams are reversed: Figure 9.3(b) now exhibits instability, and Figure 9.3(c) displays stability.

9.5 First, because $\mathcal{E}^{(I+J)}$ is continuously differentiable, so is V. Second, $V\big(\bar{P}^{(I+J)}\big) = 0$ and, for all $P^{(I+J)} \neq \bar{P}^{(I+J)}$, it is clear that $V\big(P^{(I+J)}\big) > 0$. Third, for $P^{(I+J)} \neq \bar{P}^{(I+J)}$,

$$\frac{dV\big(P^{(I+J)}\big)}{d\tau} = 2\mathcal{E}^{(I+J)}\big(P^{(I+J)}\big)\,\mathcal{B}\big(P^{(I+J)}\big)\,\frac{dP^{(I+J)}}{d\tau}$$

$$= 2\mathcal{E}^{(I+J)}\big(P^{(I+J)}\big)\,\mathcal{B}\big(P^{(I+J)}\big)\,\mathcal{B}^{-1}\big(\mathcal{E}^{(I+J)}\big(P^{(I+J)}\big)\big)$$

$$\big[\theta\mathcal{E}^{(I+J)}\big(P^{(I+J)}\big)\big]$$

$$= 2\sum_{n=1}^{I+J-1}\theta\left[\mathcal{E}^{n}\big(P^{(I+J)}\big)\right]^{2}$$

$$< 0,$$

because $\theta < 0$. The result now follows from Theorem A.5-11.

9.6 Show that both goods are gross substitutes everywhere and apply Theorem 9.4-2.

9.7 With this definition it need no longer be true that each $\Upsilon^{n}(P) > 0$ on

D. Hence Φ would not necessarily map D into itself, and Brouwer's theorem could not be applied.

9.8 The differential equation is

$$\frac{dQ}{d\tau} = (\alpha - \gamma)(B + Q)^{1-\theta},$$

with solution

$$v^Q(Q^0, \tau) = \left[(\alpha - \gamma)\theta\tau + (B + Q^0)^\theta\right]^{1/\theta} - B.$$

Starting the solution at equilibrium in the economic — that is, at $Q^0 = 0$ — gives

$$v^Q(0, \tau) = \left[(\alpha - \gamma)\theta\tau + B^\theta\right]^{1/\theta} - B,$$

which cannot be an equilibrium path because it varies with τ.

9.9 The differential equation is

$$\frac{dQ}{d\tau} = (\alpha - \gamma - \tau)Q,$$

with solution

$$v^Q(Q^0, \tau) = Q^0 e^{(\alpha - \gamma)\tau - (1/2)\tau^2}.$$

At equilibrium in the economic, that is, at $Q^0 = 0$,

$$v^Q(0, \tau) = 0,$$

for all τ. Because

$$\lim_{\tau \to \infty} (\alpha - \gamma)\tau - \tfrac{1}{2}\tau^2 = -\infty,$$

it follows that for any Q^0,

$$\lim_{\tau \to \infty} v^Q(Q^0, \tau) = 0.$$

9.10 Use Exercise 5.16.

10.1 Prove by direct calculation that if $u^k(x'_k) = u^k(x''_k)$ for $x'_k > 0$ and $x''_k > 0$, then $u^k(\gamma x'_k) = u^k(\gamma x''_k)$ for all $\gamma > 0$.

10.2 Choose $\alpha_i^k = \widetilde{p}_i \widetilde{x}_{ik}/(\widetilde{p} \cdot \widetilde{x}_k)$. Then $0 < \alpha_i^k < 1$, $\sum_{i=1}^{I} \alpha_i^k = 1$, and $\widetilde{x}_{ik} = \alpha_i^k [\widetilde{m}_k/\widetilde{p}_i]$, for all $i = 1, \ldots, I$, and $k = 1, \ldots, K$.

10.3 For example,

$$E^{11}(p) = \frac{p_1 x_{11}^0 + p_2 x_{21}^0}{p_1 + ap_2} - x_{11}^0.$$

Differentiating with respect to p_2,

$$E_2^{11}(p) = \frac{p_1(x_{21}^0 - ax_{11}^0)}{(p_1 + ap_2)^2},$$

which is positive when $x_{21}^0 > ax_{11}^0$. Similarly, $E_1^{21}(p) < 0$, $E_2^{12}(p) > 0$, and $E_1^{22}(p) < 0$. Now sum across the two persons.

10.4 Let $p \neq \overline{p}$ be in $\widehat{D}$. If p were an equilibrium price vector, then $E^i(p) = 0$ for $i = 1, \ldots, I$. But then

$$\sum_{i=1}^{I} \overline{p}_i E^i(p) = 0,$$

contrary to the requirement that $\sum_{i=1}^{I} \overline{p}_i E^i(p) > 0$.

10.5 In this case, $A = \sum_{k=1}^{K} \alpha_1^k x_{2k}^0$ and $B = \sum_{k=1}^{K} \alpha_2^k x_{1k}^0$. If the initial value $p_1 > A/B$, then $E^1(p) < 0$. Hence $dp_1/d\tau < 0$ and p_1 declines. From the market excess demand functions, q_1 rises and q_2 falls. These conclusions are reversed when the initial value $p_1 < A/B$.

11.1

$$\frac{\partial p_1}{\partial x_{11}} = \frac{2aL_2}{L_1 (x_{21})^3} > 0,$$

everywhere on the transformation curve.

11.2 Because there is only one firm in each industry the symbols σ and ℓ can be dropped from (11.1-11). The reaction functions are

$$\zeta^{(\mu)(i)}(x_i) = x_i,$$

for $i, \mu = 1, 2$ and $i \neq \mu$.

11.3 Because there is only one firm in each industry, the symbols σ and ℓ can be dropped from (11.1-11). The reaction function is

$$\zeta^{(1)(2)}(x_2) = \frac{2a_1a_2 - 2a_1(x_2)^2}{2a_2 - (x_2)^2}.$$

11.4 Let τ denote the specific tax per unit of output. Differentiate the equation $MR(x) = MC(x) + \tau$ with respect to τ and solve for $dx/d\tau$.

11.5 The solutions are as follows:

Case	$x_1 = y_1$	p_1	π_1	$x_2 = y_2$	p_2	π_2	r
perfect competition everywhere $(a \geq 1)$	$a-1$	$\dfrac{\overline{M}}{a}$	0	1	$\dfrac{\overline{M}}{a}$	0	$\dfrac{\overline{M}}{a}$
case (i) $(a \geq 1)$	$\dfrac{a-1}{2}$	$\dfrac{2\overline{M}}{a+1}$	$\overline{M}\left(\dfrac{a-1}{a+1}\right)^2$	$\dfrac{a+1}{2}$	$\dfrac{4\overline{M}}{(a+1)^2}$	0	$\dfrac{4\overline{M}}{(a+1)^2}$
case (ii) $(a \leq 1)$	0	$\overline{M}$	0	a	$\dfrac{\overline{M}}{a}$	$M(1-a)$	$\overline{M}$

Note that in case (i), $\pi_1 > 0$ unless $a = 1$, and in case (ii), $\pi_2 > 0$ also unless $a = 1$. Comparing with the perfectly competitive solution when $a > 1$, in case (i) x_1, y_1, p_2, and r are smaller, π_2 is the same, and p_1, x_2, y_2 and π_1 are larger. When $a = 1$, the three solutions are identical.

11.6 At maximum profit,

$$x = \frac{\sqrt{r_1 r_2} - \beta}{\alpha}$$

and

$$p = \sqrt{r_1 r_2} + \beta.$$

11.9 The first part follows by differentiating

$$\pi(x_1, x_2) = TR^1(x_1) + TR^2(x_2) - TC(x_1 + x_2),$$

with respect to x_1 and x_2, where $TR^i(x)$ is the total revenue from market i, for $i = 1, 2$. The second part is obtained by applying equation (1.5-5) to the equality $MR^1(x_1) = MR^2(x_2)$.

11.11 The reaction function of firm 1,1 given the output of firm 1, 2 is

$$\zeta^{(11)(12)}(x_{12}) = 50 - \tfrac{1}{2}x_{12}.$$

Letting π_{11} and π_{12} denote, respectively, the profits of firms 1,1 and 1, 2, the solutions are as follows:

Type of solution	p_1	x_{11}	x_{12}	$x_{11}+x_{12}$	π_{11}	π_{12}	$\pi_{11}+\pi_{12}$
perfectly competitive	0	indeterminate		100	0	0	0
Cournot	16.7	33.3	33.3	66.6	556.1	556.1	1112.2
Stackelberg with firm 1,1 as leader	12.5	50	25	75	625	312.5	937.5
collusion	25	25	25	50	625	625	1250
monopoly	25	—	—	50	—	—	1250

As the number of firms increases to ∞, a competitive solution is approached: Individual firm output and profit along with the market price all decline to 0, while the market quantity supplied rises to 100.

11.12 Differentiate the profit function of firm 1, 2, namely,

$$x_{12}\mathcal{H}\left(\frac{x_{12}}{1-\theta}\right) - TC^{12}(x_{12}),$$

with respect to x_{12}, and equate the result to zero. Solve to obtain the equilibrium value of x_{12}. The equilibrium value of x_{11} is then secured from the market share equation given in the exercise. Lastly, the equilibrium value of p_1 is found by substituting these values for x_{11} and x_{12} into the demand equation

$$p = \mathcal{H}(x_{11} + x_{12}).$$

11.13 Since the monopolist is isolated, the reaction functions of other firms are irrelevant. In the notation of the present exercise, (11.2-5) becomes

$$MR(x) = p + x\frac{d\mathcal{H}^{-1}(x)}{dx}.$$

Using this expression, the profit-maximizing condition $MR(x) = MC(x)$, and the definition of ρ, all evaluated at (p^0, x^0), gives the desired result.

In Exercise 11.6,

$$\rho = \frac{\beta - \sqrt{r_1 r_2}}{\beta + \sqrt{r_1 r_2}}.$$

Since, in that exercise, $\beta > \sqrt{r_1 r_2}$, it follows that $\rho > 0$.

11.14 In the first instance, the firm believes $x = \frac{1}{2}[\alpha r + \beta\sigma]$ to be profit maximizing, where r is the input price. Hence the derivatives $\partial x/\partial\sigma = \beta/2$, $\partial\pi/\partial\sigma = -\beta x/\alpha$, and $\partial p/\partial\sigma = -\beta/\alpha$ are all positive since $\beta > 0$ and $\alpha < 0$. As σ increases, the subjective demand curve shifts out, each subsequent curve parallel to the one before.

In the second instance, the firm believes

$$x = \frac{1}{2}\left[\frac{\alpha r}{\sigma} + \beta\right]$$

to be profit maximizing so that

$$\partial x/\partial\sigma = -\frac{\alpha r}{2\sigma^2}, \quad \partial\pi/\partial\sigma = \frac{x}{\alpha}[x - \beta], \quad\text{and}\quad \partial p/\partial\sigma = \frac{x - \beta}{\alpha}.$$

These derivatives are all positive since $\alpha < 0$, $r > 0$, $\sigma > 0$, $\beta > 0$, and $0 < x < \beta$. Here the subjective demand curve rotates in a clockwise fashion through the point $(x, p) = (\beta, 0)$ as σ increases.

12.2 Setting the partial derivatives of the Lagrangian expression

$$u^K(x_K) - \left\{\sum_{k=1}^{K-1}\delta_k\left[\bar{\mu}_k - u^k(x_k)\right]\right\}$$

$$-\delta_K\left\{t\left(\sum_{k=1}^{K}x_{1k}, \ldots, \sum_{k=1}^{K}x_{I-1k}\right) - \sum_{k=1}^{K}x_{Ik}\right\}$$

equal to zero gives

$$u_i^K(\overline{x}_K) - \delta_K t_i\left(\sum_{k=1}^K \overline{x}_{1k}, \ldots, \sum_{k=1}^K \overline{x}_{I-1k}\right) = 0, \quad i = 1, \ldots, I-1,$$

$$u_I^K(\overline{x}_K) + \delta_K = 0,$$

$$\delta_k u_i^k(\overline{x}_k) - \delta_K t_i\left(\sum_{k=1}^K \overline{x}_{1k}, \ldots, \sum_{k=1}^K \overline{x}_{I-1k}\right) = 0, \quad \begin{array}{l} i = 1, \ldots, I-1, \\ k = 1, \ldots, K-1, \end{array}$$

$$\delta_k u_I^k(\overline{x}_k) + \delta_K = 0, \quad k = 1, \ldots, K.$$

Argument now proceeds as in the proof of Theorem 12.2-9. The last four groups of equations are obtained as in Theorem 12.2-16 and from definition (12.2-6).

12.3 If $\overline{x} = (\overline{x}_1, \ldots, \overline{x}_K)$ were not Pareto optimal, then there would exist an $x = (x_1, \ldots, x_K)$ Pareto superior to it. This would mean

$$u^k(x_k) \geqslant u^k(\overline{x}_k), \quad k = 1, \ldots, K,$$

and for at least one k,

$$u^k(x_k) > u^k(\overline{x}_k).$$

But then the differential increasingness of W would imply

$$W \circ u(x) > W \circ u(\overline{x}),$$

contrary to the maximality of $\overline{x}$.

12.4 At a Pareto optimal $\overline{x} = (\overline{x}_1, \overline{x}_2) > 0$,

$$\frac{u_1^1(\overline{x})}{u_2^1(\overline{x})} = -t'(\overline{x}_{11} + \overline{x}_{12}),$$

$$\frac{u_1^2(\overline{x}_2)}{u_2^2(\overline{x}_2)} + \frac{u_3^1(\overline{x})\,u_2^2(\overline{x}_2) - u_4^1(\overline{x})\,u_1^2(\overline{x}_2)}{u_2^1(\overline{x})\,u_2^2(\overline{x}_2)} = -t'(\overline{x}_{11} + \overline{x}_{12}),$$

where t' is the derivative of the transformation function $x_{21} + x_{22} = t(x_{11}$

$+ x_{12}$) and

$$u_3^1(x) = \frac{\partial u^1(x)}{\partial x_{12}},$$

$$u_4^1(x) = \frac{\partial u^1(x)}{\partial x_{22}}.$$

The first pair of equalities imply

$$\frac{u_1^2(\overline{x}_2)}{u_2^2(\overline{x}_2)} = \frac{u_3^1(\overline{x}) - u_1^1(\overline{x})}{u_4^1(\overline{x}) - u_2^1(\overline{x})}.$$

Equilibrium under perfect competition is not Pareto optimal.

12.5 If $\overline{x} > 0$ is Pareto optimal, then

$$\frac{u_1^1\left(\overline{x}_1, u^2\left(\overline{x}_2\right)\right)}{u_2^1\left(\overline{x}_1, u^2\left(\overline{x}_2\right)\right)} = -t'(\overline{x}_{11} + \overline{x}_{12}),$$

$$\frac{u_1^2(\overline{x}_2)}{u_2^2(\overline{x}_2)} = -t'(\overline{x}_{11} + \overline{x}_{12}),$$

where t' is the derivative of the transformation function $x_{21} + x_{22} = t(x_{11} + x_{12})$. In this case, equilibrium under perfect competition is still Pareto optimal.

12.6 The Lagrangian expression is

$$u^2(x_1, x_{22}) - \delta_1\left[\overline{\mu}_1 - u^1(x_1, x_{21})\right] - \delta_2\left[t(x_1) - x_{21} - x_{22}\right].$$

12.7 Let M be given. If $(\overline{m}_1, \overline{m}_2)$ maximizes $v(m_1) + v(m_2)$ subject to $m_1 + m_2 = M$, then $v_m(\overline{m}_1) = v_m(\overline{m}_2)$. Because there is a 1–1 correspondence between values for $v_m(m_k)$ and values of m_k, it follows that $\overline{m}_1 = \overline{m}_2$. The sufficient second-order condition for a constrained maximum, namely,

$$\begin{vmatrix} 0 & v_m(m_1) & v_m(m_2) \\ v_m(m_1) & v_{mm}(m_1) & 0 \\ v_m(m_2) & 0 & v_{mm}(m_2) \end{vmatrix} > 0,$$

is satisfied everywhere because, by assumption, $v_{mm}(m_k) < 0$ for all $m_k > 0$.

12.8 As in Exercise 8.2 (with x_{ik} replacing y_{ij} and x_i replacing a_j), the utility possibility function given (x_1, x_2) is

$$\mu_2 = \sqrt{x_1 x_2} - \mu_1.$$

Substitution from the transformation function yields

$$\mu_2 = \sqrt{\alpha x_1 - (x_1)^2} - \mu_1.$$

Because the utility possibility frontiers are all parallel straight lines, the grand frontier is the ordinary frontier for which $(\alpha x_1 - (x_1)^2)^{1/2}$ is maximal with respect to x_1. Since $(\alpha x_1 - (x_1)^2)^{1/2}$ is maximized when $x_1 = \alpha/2$, the grand function is

$$\mu_2 = \frac{\alpha}{2} - \mu_1.$$

A similar argument shows that if the increasing transformation $\tau(\mu_1) = (\mu_1)^2$ is applied to the utility function of person 1, then the grand function becomes

$$\mu_2 = \frac{\alpha}{2} - \sqrt{\mu_1}.$$

This is strictly convex rather than linear.

12.9 The first-order ratio condition satisfied at an interior Pareto optimum is

$$\frac{u_y(x, y)}{u_x(x, y)} = f'(\Lambda - y),$$

where

$$u_x(x, y) = \frac{\partial u(x, y)}{\partial x},$$

$$u_y(x, y) = \frac{\partial u(x, y)}{\partial y},$$

and f' is the derivative of f with respect to $\Lambda - y$.

12.10 The collection of all (consumption) Pareto optimal distributions is

$$\{(x_{11}, x_{21}, x_{12}, x_{22}) : 0 \leqslant x_{11} \leqslant 1, \ x_{11} \leqslant x_{21} \leqslant x_{11} + 1,$$

$$x_{11} + x_{12} = 1, \text{ and } x_{21} + x_{22} = 2\}.$$

For none of these distributions x does there exist a price vector p such that (p, x) is a competitive equilibrium.

13.1 $\rho = 0.05$.

13.2 Let

$$A = 1 + e^{-\rho\alpha_j} + e^{-2\rho\alpha_j} + \cdots + e^{-(\delta_j-1)\rho\alpha_j}.$$

Then

$$e^{-\rho\alpha_j} A = e^{-\rho\alpha_j} + e^{-2\rho\alpha_j} + \cdots + e^{-\delta_j\rho\alpha_j}.$$

Upon subtraction of the second from the first,

$$A - e^{-\rho\alpha_j} A = 1 - e^{-\rho\delta_j\alpha_j}.$$

Hence

$$A = \frac{1 - e^{-\rho\delta_j\alpha_j}}{1 - e^{-\rho\alpha_j}}.$$

13.3 Let τ^0 vary over the interval whose left-hand endpoint is

$$\tau^0 = (\delta_j - 1)\,\alpha_j - \overline{\tau}_j,$$

and whose right-hand endpoint is

$$\tau^0 = \delta_j a_j - \overline{\tau}_j.$$

Evaluating (13.2-8) at the left-hand endpoint gives

$$\omega_j = r_j^* y_j e^{-\rho\alpha_j}.$$

At the right-hand endpoint, δ_j in (13.2-8) increases to $\delta_j + 1$. Hence the value of ω_j, there is also

$$\omega_j = r_j^* y_j e^{-\rho\alpha_j}.$$

However, the limiting value of ω_j as τ^0 moves across the interval to the right-hand endpoint is found by substitution of $\tau^0 = \delta_j\alpha_j - \overline{\tau}_j$ into (13.2-8) as written. Thus

$$\lim_{\tau^0 \to (\delta_j a_j - \overline{\tau}_j)} \omega_j = r_j^* y_j.$$

13.4 As in the computation of (13.1-12), an investment lasting β periods which pays back ν dollars at each instant of time has a total present value of

$$\frac{\nu}{\rho}\left[1 - e^{-\rho\beta}\right],$$

where ρ is the rate of return. Now let $\beta \to \infty$.

13.5

$$\rho = 2 \ln 2,$$

$$c = \frac{1}{2 \ln 2}.$$

13.6 For any real scalar variable z,

$$e^z = 1 + z + \frac{z^2}{2!} + \frac{z^3}{3!} + \cdots.$$

Hence

$$ze^z = z + z^2 + \frac{z^3}{2!} + \frac{z^4}{3!} + \cdots,$$

and

$$e^z - 1 = z + \frac{z^2}{2!} + \frac{z^3}{3!} + \frac{z^4}{4!} + \cdots.$$

By comparing terms,

$$ze^z > e^z - 1,$$

or

$$z > 1 - e^{-z}.$$

Setting $z = \rho\alpha_j$, where $\rho > 0$ and $\alpha_j > 0$, gives

$$\frac{\rho}{1 - e^{-\rho\alpha_j}} - \frac{1}{a_j} > 0.$$

Therefore from (13.2-1)

$$r_j^* - \frac{r_j'}{\alpha_j} = r_j' \left[\frac{\rho}{1 - e^{-\rho\alpha_j}} - \frac{1}{\alpha_j} \right] > 0.$$

13.7 To determine the average money capital requirement based on (13.2-10), it is only necessary to replace $e^{-\rho\xi_j}$ in (13.2-10) by

$$\frac{1}{\alpha_j} \int_0^{\alpha_j} e^{-\rho\xi_j} d\xi_j = \frac{1 - e^{-\rho\alpha_j}}{\rho\alpha_j}.$$

Then differentiating the result partially with respect to y_j gives

$$\frac{\partial c}{\partial y_j} = r_j \frac{e^{\rho(\tau^0 + \bar{\tau}_j)} - 1}{\rho} > 0, \quad j = 1, \ldots, \hat{j}.$$

For $j = \hat{j} + 1, \ldots, J$, partial differentiation combined with (13.2-1) yields

$$\frac{\partial c}{\partial y_j} = \frac{r_j'}{\rho} \left[\frac{\rho e^{\rho(\tau^0 + \bar{\tau}_j)}}{1 - e^{-\rho \alpha_j}} - \frac{1}{\alpha_j} \right].$$

Because e to any positive power is larger than unity,

$$\frac{\partial c}{\partial y_j} > \frac{r_j'}{\rho} \left[\frac{\rho}{1 - e^{-\rho \alpha_j}} - \frac{1}{\alpha_j} \right], \quad j = \hat{j} + 1, \ldots, J.$$

Now according to the next-to-last inequality in the argument of the answer to Exercise 13.6, the bracketed term is positive. Since, in the present context, $\Lambda_j(p, r, x, y) = \partial c / \partial y_j$, it follows that $\Lambda_j(p, r, x, y) > 0$ for $j = 1, \ldots, J$.
    Similarly,

$$\Lambda_x(p, r, x, y) = \frac{\partial c}{\partial x} = -p \frac{e^{\rho \tau^0} - 1}{\rho} < 0.$$

13.8 According to Figure 13.2(a), $\bar{p} = MC(\bar{x}) + \bar{p} \Lambda_x^*(\bar{x})$. Hence, since both diagrams reflect the same position of the firm, $\bar{p} - \bar{p} \Lambda_x^*(\bar{x}) = MC(\bar{x})$ in Figure 13.2(b).
    Also $\bar{p} = ATC(\bar{x}) + \bar{p} \Lambda^*(\bar{x}) / \bar{x}$ in Figure 13.2(a). It follows from this that the length of the line segment connecting a to b in Figure 13.2(b), which is $\bar{p} - ATC(\bar{x})$, becomes

$$\bar{p} - ATC(\bar{x}) = \frac{\bar{p} \Lambda^*(\bar{x})}{\bar{x}}.$$

Multiplying this latter expression by the length $\bar{x}$ of the line segment connecting b to c, gives the area of the desired rectangle $\bar{p} \Lambda^*(\bar{x})$.

Index